Also by Alan Blyth

WAGNER'S RING: AN INTRODUCTION

Edited by Alan Blyth

OPERA ON RECORD
REMEMBERING BRITTEN
OPERA ON RECORD 2

Opera on Record 3

Edited by Alan Blyth
Discographies compiled by
Malcolm Walker

HUTCHINSON
London Melbourne Sydney Auckland Johannesburg

Hutchinson & Co. (Publishers) Ltd
An imprint of the Hutchinson Publishing Group
17–21 Conway Street, London W1P 6JD

Hutchinson Publishing Group (Australia) Pty Ltd
PO Box 496, 16–22 Church Street, Hawthorne, Melbourne,
Victoria 3122
PO Box 151, Broadway, New South Wales 2007

Hutchinson Group (NZ) Ltd
32–34 View Road, PO Box 40–086, Glenfield, Auckland 10

Hutchinson Group (SA) Pty Ltd
PO Box 337, Bergvlei 2012, South Africa

First published 1984
Text © Hutchinson & Co. (Publishers) Ltd 1984
Introduction © Alan Blyth 1984
Set in Times by Input Typesetting Ltd, London

Printed and bound in Great Britain by Anchor Brendon Ltd,
Tiptree, Essex
ISBN 0 09 158620 8

Contents

Introduction

ALAN BLYTH

After two volumes, *Opera on Record 3* hardly needs any introduction: the format has been firmly established, and there are few innovations this time. The choice of works has not quite dictated itself, and I suppose there are operas, *Martha* perhaps or *Ernani,* that might equally have claimed our attention, but by and large I have chosen those that are interesting operas in themselves or have a long recorded history. I was also determined to bring our discussions well into the current century by including Gershwin, Weill and the still-active Tippett. The inclusion of Verdi's *Requiem* is wholly my responsibility, and may be regarded as an editor's licence at the end of a long and arduous stint, for this will definitely be the final volume of *Opera on Record.* There may be scope in the future to revise Volume 1, a considerable undertaking, but one necessitated by the march of time.

As regards the presentation of items and numbers, the approach is as before. As far as possible in the text, the numbers for items have been given in brackets according to the following principle. The number is that of the original 78rpm records, where applicable. After a semicolon there is the most recent LP reissue, or that which is considered most readily accessible. With the help of Eric Hughes of the National Sound Archive and of John Hughes, I hope that this information is as up-to-date and accurate as possible at the time of going to press. Reissues of 78rpm records continue unabated. Besides those from the larger companies, most importantly EMI/Electrola with their huge archives (Continental issues beginning with a 1C, 2C etc. prefix, according to country of origin), the smaller companies have continued to work unceasingly on reissues. The chief among them are the Austrian firm of Preiser, with its Lebendige Vergangenheit (LV prefix) and Court Opera (CO) series, Rubini Records (GV) masterminded by Syd Gray, and Charles Haynes's Pearl catalogue (GEMM). Then there are the American or Canadian firms Rococo, Club 99 and OASI, whose records are available intermittently from specialist dealers in Britain. Only where 78s have not been reissued from any of these sources have older, deleted numbers been resorted to. Some numbers of 'private' and 'off-the-air' issues emanating from live performances have now been included in the discographies, but their distribution is inevitably haphazard. As regards the big companies only the numbers of their records are given: the rest of the information is readily available in the *Gramophone* catalogue or those of its Continental and American equivalents.

As regards 78rpm numbering, this is the same as in *Opera on Record* 1 and 2. All those numbers without prefixes are those of the acoustic Gramophone and Typewriter (G&T), Gramophone Company, Monarch, Amour, Grammophon etc. labels. Where titles were reissued on double-sided DB (twelve-inch) or DA (ten-inch) series, these numbers have been preferred. Other early labels have been shortened thus: Fono. for Fonotipia; Od. for Odeon; Poly. for Polydor; Parlo. for Parlophone/Parlophon; Col. for Columbia; and H&D for Pathé 'hill-and-dale' records, made by the vertical cut process. HMV prefixes are: DB, DA, D, E, C, B; Columbia prefixes are L, LX, DX. Columbia ten-inch DBs have 'Col.' before them to indicate they are not HMV DBs. Discs originally issued by Victor in the USA but later issued in Britain are given their British numbering. Most points of doubt in the electrical era of 78s can usually be clarified by reference to the still-invaluable *World Encyclopedia of Recorded Music* by Clough and Cuming (original volume with three supplements). More details of numbers and items can be found in the eleven volumes of *Voices of the Past*, though most are at present out of print. It remains to thank my contributors once again for their hours and hours of fruitful labour, and for the knowledge and wise opinions dispensed therefrom, enlightening and useful, I hope, to those who read their words; Malcolm Walker for again providing so much exhaustive detail in his discographies. Record collectors without whose assistance this volume would have been impossible to compile include John Hughes, Edward and Peter Lack, Vivian Liff, George Stuart, Arthur Carton, Christopher Norton-Welsh and Brian Gould. The help and advice given by Derek Lewis, BBC Record Librarian has, as always, been invaluable. Charles Clark and Valerie Hudson, as editors, have been a constant source of encouragement.

THE DISCOGRAPHIES

The policy adopted in the discographies in regard to issuing companies plus record and cassette numbers has been to quote both the UK and US information citing the most up-to-date or, in the case of deleted recordings, the most recent details. Where a recording was not released in either of these two countries we have quoted the relevant country in question.

SYMBOLS USED

* denotes 78 rpm disc(s); Ⓜ mono; ④ cassette; © electronically reprocessed stereo.
  Country of origin is indicated only where otherwise unclear. For complete information on country of origin, see list of record companies and labels.

The Operas of Haydn

PETER BRANSCOMBE

Despite numerous performances of Haydn's operas since the Second World War, often in the framework of festivals, it has been left to the gramophone companies to give the public at large the chance to gain familiarity with at least a representative selection of these works. Haydn's operas have on the whole had a bad press. In his lifetime a few of them were quite widely successful, but the majority were confined to the theatre for which they were written. As Haydn wrote at the end of 1787, in reply to an invitation to compose an opera for Prague: 'You ask for an *opera buffa* from me – very willingly, if you desire to possess some vocal composition of mine for your own use. But if it is to be performed in the theatre in Prague, I cannot oblige on this occasion, because all my operas are too closely bound up with our personnel (at Esterháza in Hungary), and would furthermore never produce the effect [elsewhere] which I devised according to local conditions.' Of course, this attitude accords with standard eighteenth-century practice, whereby works were normally devised with an eye to a particular perform- ance by particular artists. In itself this did not limit the effectiveness of a work to the house for which it was written, as the example of Mozart makes clear; but it did provide an obstacle which it took more determination to overcome than Haydn evidently had. He prepared operas by many of his contemporaries for production at Prince Esterházy's theatre, often writing additional numbers for them, but his attitude towards the reverse procedure is suggested by the quotation above. After Haydn's death his operas were largely forgotten, and most early twentieth-century attempts to revive them were hampered by the attitudes of their arrangers, who lacked confidence in the stageworthiness of the works they were preparing for performance.

Opera was no occasional occupation for Haydn; during the twenty-two years from the first of the Italian operas written for Eisenstadt shortly after he entered the employment of the Esterházy family, until *Armida* (1784), the last of his operas for the splendid new theatre at Esterháza, he composed around twenty Italian operas and German puppet operettas. *Armida* was followed only by the opera on Orpheus and Eurydice intended for London in 1791; but it is very likely that stage works played a large part in his activities before he was appointed assistant *Kapellmeister* by Prince Paul

Anton in 1761. From his Viennese 'prentice years we have definite knowledge
only of the (lost) score to Kurz-Bernardon's *Der krumme Teufel* of 1752; but
Robert Haas has persuasively argued that some of the German comedy arias
from the mid-1750s (published in *Denkmäler der Tonkunst in Österreich*,
volumes 64 and 131) are probably by Haydn. Further, he may well have
composed other (since lost) scores for *Singspiele* which were given at Vienna's
German theatre during the years between his leaving the St Stephan's
Cathedral choir around 1748, and his appointment to the Morzin family in
1759.

Acide, the one-act *festa teatrale* of 1762, does not survive in its entirety;
the earliest complete Haydn opera we do have, one that awaits its first
'official' recording, is the nimble, even vivid little *Intermezzo in musica* of
1766, *La canterina*. Keen collectors will have noticed that this work – which
lasts about forty-five minutes in all – has been made available on a record,
coupled with the *Applausus* Cantata and several songs and arias, in a two-
disc 'private' set. The performance took place in New York on 29 December
1967, with Alexander Schneider conducting, Murray Perahia providing the
harpsichord continuo, and four good singers.

There are problems over casting *La canterina* – not with Gasparina, the
singer of the title, who is a soprano, nor with Don Pelagio, an elderly *maestro
di capella*, one of her admirers (tenor). It is the other two roles which provide
the difficulty: Apollonia, Gasparina's pretended mother, was originally taken
by Leopold Dichtler, one of the finest tenors at Haydn's disposal, who
presumably sang the part falsetto (it was originally notated in the soprano
clef); and Don Ettore, a rich merchant's son, and the other admirer of
Gasparina, was taken by Dichtler's wife Barbara, as a breeches part. The
three sopranos in the New York recording have rather similar voices –
Patricia Brooks, fiery if not absolutely accurate in the heroine's superb mock-
heroic C minor aria, Benita Valente as Apollonia, and Mary Burgess as Don
Ettore (neither has an aria, both make much of the lively recitatives, which
swing adeptly between *secco* and *accompagnato*). Jon Humphrey, in the part
of the *maestro di capella*, is strained by the As in his first aria, but later
favours the occasional unwritten high note; he is firm if not supple, or subtle.
The two act-finales – quartets – are fine pieces, and go well. Despite the
variable recording quality, and a few hefty winter coughs, this is a performance worth looking out for, until a good studio recording appears.

Lo speziale, which followed two years after *La canterina*, has probably
been the most frequently performed, and is certainly the most often recorded,
of all Haydn's stage works. Like its predecessor it too has only four roles
(two sopranos, and two tenors); but it is quite a lot bigger and has a pleasing
libretto, based on Goldoni. For years this witty, stylish opera was known
only in the corrupt German version of Robert Hirschfeld, which dates from
the 1890s, *Der Apotheker*; and as we shall see, its shadow lies over several
of the abridged recordings. *Lo speziale* was the work with which, under
Haydn's direction, the new theatre at Esterháza was opened in late

September 1768. Again Barbara Dichtler had a breeches role – that of Volpino, the unsuccessful young admirer of Grilletta, the apothecary Sempronio's ward. Both Sempronio and Mengone, the apothecary's assistant who wins the girl, are tenors. Though there are long and not very exciting recitatives and, as usual in Haydn, ensembles are virtually confined to act-conclusions, there is abundant variety, skill and beauty in the mainly long arias. Of these the best known are Mengone's second, with vigorous and graphic demonstration of the efficacy of his cure for constipation ('NB', writes Haydn in the score); and Volpino's mock-Turkish aria in the last act. The second finale is especially enjoyable, with plaintive, nasal-toned oboes setting off the two pretended notaries. It is a great pity that a large chunk of the third act is lost, for this makes stage performance difficult.

The earliest recording of *Lo speziale* was made in 1950 on the Magic-Tone label. Performed in an American English version by William Kaye, and with a small body of strings (no winds) under Fritz Kramer, it is extremely amateurish in musical and sound quality. Piano is prominent in arias, and at times takes over entirely what should be accompanied recitative. The score is heavily cut, in places rewritten; and the impetus is at times allowed to drop dangerously. Gordon Meyers as a baritone Sempronio is wooden in phrasing, but he sings decently; there is no distinction here.

The 1958 Salzburg Mozarteum recording under Rolf Maedel is distinctly preferable. It is sung in Italian, and if the overture and some of the recitatives have been deleted, and some of the numbers abridged, at least all the lyrical numbers are there. Erich zur Eck is a nimble Mengone, and Wladimir Smid-Kowar a sound, sprightly Sempronio, even though he is a baritone. It is good to have Volpino sung at the correct pitch – Eva Brinck is at her best early on; later she overdoes the vocal disguises as false notary and Turk. Elisabeth Schönauer is a disappointingly querulous Grilletta. The principal drawback to this performance is that it was made just before the Complete Edition score was published in 1959.

The Cetra recording, made in 1960, cannot escape criticism on that count: the version used is a travesty of the score. Ferdinando Guarnieri directs a droopy, turgid performance, much cut, with curious tempi, and with some numbers so altered and emended as to take on a *pasticcio* character. The orchestra is rough, usually ready, but overworked – there is no keyboard continuo in the recitatives, merely heavy string chording, with much *pizzicato*. Of the singers, Edith Martelli makes a matronly, and in the arias shrill-voiced, Grilletta; Otello Borgonovo does what he can with the here denuded role of Sempronio; and Florindo Andreolli and Carlo Franzini show nice touches though too little contrast as the young suitors.

In 1967 Amadeo brought out a recording which is quite as far from Haydn's opera as was the 1950 American recording. Erich Schwarzbauer conducts the Mozart-Sängerknaben of Vienna, and a chamber orchestra from the Wiener Symphoniker, in the sort of perversion of the work that readers may have experienced in concerts given by the Vienna Boys' Choir. Done in

German – or rather, Austrian – as *Der Apotheker*, it includes at least part of almost all the lyrical numbers, but they are often heavily cut, musically simplified, and naive dialogue replaces the recitatives. Of the anonymous choristers, the Sempronio and Volpino are the best. The recording is shallow, with odd changes of perspective and banal staging. Strictly for the parents and friends of the performers (but how would it strike them, a decade and a half on?).

It is a relief to progress from this dispiriting batch of abridged recordings to the complete performance on two Hungaroton discs made in 1978 by Hungarian forces under György Lehel. Judged by the highest standards, perhaps, both recording and performance leave something to be desired, but there is nothing negligible about the achievement of Lehel and his cast of lively young singers. The orchestra is the Ferenc Liszt Chamber Orchestra, the normal 'house' ensemble for the Hungaroton Haydn series. It is a small, alert body, lacking perhaps the degree of polish and tonal beauty with which we are spoiled in western Europe – but its timbre and general approach arguably come closer to the sound Haydn had in mind. The singing is sprightly, thoroughly enjoyable, even if the casting is not always appropriate: Attila Fülöp is neat, secure over more than two octaves, but he hardly suggests the crusty absurdity of Sempronio. And Veronika Kincses in the *travesti* role of Volpino sounds altogether too light-toned; she sings with spirit, but slightly overplays her hand in the comedy of the mock notary and in the 'Turkish' aria. The other two parts are filled by Magda Kalmár, whose Grilletta is pure-voiced and touching (she sings the later, adagio version of 'Caro Volpino', and provides the best singing in the set in the process), and István Rozsos, the Mengone, who shows a bright little tenor in numbers (especially the recitatives) which call for clarity of enunciation, but he is baffled by the *fioriture* in virtually all the numbers in which he appears. The recitatives are crisp and rapid, but devoid of most appoggiaturas.

Next in order of composition of Haydn's operas comes *Le pescatrici* (1769) which, despite stage productions in the last two decades, still waits for its first recording. In contrast, the following work, *L'infedeltà delusa* (1773), has been the most fortunate of all Haydn's operas in the studio: in 1969 Anton de Almeida recorded it for Chant du Monde, in 1976 Frigyes Sándor included it as part of the Hungaroton series, and in summer 1980 Antal Dorati added it to his magnificent Philips series of the operas.

Almeida, a fine Haydn stylist, deserves the credit for being the first person to record one of Haydn's Italian operatic comedies complete. This venture, made with the Orchestra of the Haydn Foundation, Rome, has never been properly appreciated in Britain as the set has not been issued here. Even in these days of unexpected affluence which allow us two other complete recordings of the work, the Almeida version is well worth looking out for. The *Burletta per musica* itself is accommodated comfortably on five sides, leaving the sixth available for the longer concert versions of the overture and the two big arias for Vespina in Act 2 which Haydn himself shortened. Right from the start of the overture, Almeida's feeling for crisp phrasing and lucid textures is apparent; the balance is excellent, with the important wind parts admirably clear and fresh, and with lively harpsichord thoroughbass. There is nothing obsessive about this liveliness, certainly no feeling of superficiality in a score that must be allowed to unfold at its own leisurely pace. The complicated but by no means absurd story concerns the attempts of a poor but resourceful brother and sister (Nanni and Vespina) to improve their lot through advantageous marriages into wealthy land-owning families; Filippo, the father of Nanni's intended, Sandrina, proposes that Nencio (Vespina's intended) should marry his daughter. It takes all of Vespina's wit and cunning to frustrate that plan and, with Nanni's help, bring about the desired pairings. As usual with Haydn, arias predominate – apart from the two finales and a duet for brother and sister in the first act, the only ensemble is the wonderful quintet which opens the opera and, in some of its pairings, introduces the personal problems to come. Thereafter one cannot suppress regrets that easily the biggest ensemble of the opera is already in the past, with the regular series of dry recitatives and (usually exit) arias to be leavened only by one fine but brief duet, and two fairly conventional and brief finales. A further curiosity – but one that spices rather than weakens the work – is, as László Somfai has pointed out, that the first arias of four of the five characters are in moods that we later recognize as being untypical of their real natures.

Easily the largest role is Vespina, with four arias and a hand in all the concerted numbers. Emilia Ravaglia sings it delightfully; more, she creates a character out of the various separate arias and recitatives – her vocal disguises as an old crone, German serving-man (with a lovely macaronic aria), Marquess, and finally as notary, are models of wit, decorum and vocal art; as herself in her first and last arias, she sings with sweetness and grace. Elisabeth Speiser, the Sandrina, is suitably fiery in her first aria, neat if pale in the second. There is perhaps too little contrast between the tenors. Umberto Grilli as Nencio, the unfavoured suitor of Sandrina, sings his big and taxing serenade loudly, uningratiatingly; he is altogether happier in his other, and striking, aria, with its fascinating string sonorities and its laughter. As Filippo, the touchy father looking for a good match for his daughter, Giorgio Grimaldi is acceptable but again unyielding, tonally unvaried. Nanni, the bass part, is well taken by Robert El Hage; so warmly rounded is his tone, so easy his delivery in the fiery F minor aria early in the opera, that one regrets the smallness of the role. The recitatives are decently sung, with appoggiaturas, and with string bass as well as harpsichord accompaniment. They are on the whole well paced, if on the slow side – the last recitative scene of Act 1 is tame and dull, but by contrast the first in Act 2 is especially felicitous, with the haze of orchestral strings each time Vespina (now as old crone) speaks in proverbs.

When the Hungaroton set of *L'infedeltà delusa* was issued in Britain in 1977 it was, inevitably, reviewed in isolation, since the Chant du Monde recording had not appeared here. It is an attractive set, combining the experience of the elderly conductor Sándor with the youthful enthusiasm of the singers. However, progress is leisurely – the cuts that Haydn himself made are not followed here, and the recitatives last a very long time, so ponderously are they taken. I certainly do not look for a specious jocularity, speed for speed's sake, but do wish Sándor had kept things moving at a brisker conversational pace. Of the singers, none is outstanding, each is reliable or rather more than reliable. However, the extent to which Magda Kalmár is encouraged, or allowed, to go in Vespina's vocal disguises seems to me counter-productive; as herself she is altogether more ingratiating. Attila Fülöp manages to make Nencio's serenade more elegant than does his opposite number in the Almeida set, surely in no small measure thanks to Sándor's markedly more sprightly tempo. István Rozsos is more at home as the elderly peasant Filippo than as Mengone in *Lo speziale*, making much of his bold C major aria early in Act 2. József Gregor is a reliable Nanni, and Júlia Pászthy, though thin-voiced, reedy above the stave, is a pleasing Sandrina. The performance includes as overture to Act 2 a striking C major prestissimo which Robbins Landon includes in the Philharmonia score; it comes from a Berlin MS.

The third complete recording of *L'infedeltà delusa* is Antal Dorati's, issued by Philips in celebration of the conductor's seventy-fifth birthday, just a few months before the start of rejoicings in honour of the 250th birthday of the composer whom he has served so assiduously and well. Rumour has it – may it be proved false even before these words appear in print! – that this, the seventh Haydn opera in the Dorati series, is to be the last. There is nothing valedictory about the sparkling if occasionally over-emphatic performance of a light, substantial and entirely delightful score. Edith Mathis is a resourceful and vocally accomplished Vespina, Barbara Hendricks charming if at times rather thin-toned as Sandrina. Of the men, Claes H. Ahnsjö and Aldo Baldin as Nencio and Filippo respectively are excellent in the tenor roles, though not always readily enough told apart; and Michael Devlin is strong and warm-toned in the solitary bass part. The recitatives have been somewhat cut. The sixth side of the set contains four numbers which Haydn wrote for other operas: Devlin sings the reasonably familiar aria for Neptune written for the 1773 revival of Haydn's own (largely lost) *Acide,* Ahnsjö and Baldin sing the superb arias which Haydn wrote for his Esterháza productions of Traetta's *Ifigenia in Tauride* (1786) and Sarti's *I finti eredi* (1788), and the three men join in the delectable trio from the pasticcio *La Circe* (1789). It may sound perverse to suggest that even those who already have one of the other versions of *L'infedeltà delusa* need the Philips set (which is unfussily produced and excellently recorded), not least for the sake of its sixth side.

With *L'incontro improvviso* (1775), Haydn moved into the fashionable world of oriental elopement opera – his text is a remodelling of that set by Gluck (*La rencontre imprévue*) in 1763, and has obvious affinities with (and interesting differences from) Mozart's *Die Entführung aus dem Serail* (1781–2). New for Haydn also was the chance – the need – to balance the worlds of *buffa* and *seria*. Hitherto his stage works had been either in the comic vein (the early German *Singspiele*, and the Italian operas already discussed) or entirely serious (*Acide*). In *L'incontro improvviso* the serious action, with Rezia – Prince Ali's wife, and the Sultan's slave – taking the dominant role in the escape, is only loosely linked to the comic action, in which the morally weak Calender teaches beggars' ways to Osmin, Ali's greedy servant. The unexpectedly early return of the Sultan (who appears only in recitative at the close) threatens disaster, but he proves magnanimous and lets his various foreign visitors depart in peace.

Haydn's score is masterly, and it is surprising that this work (with clever libretto by Fribert, the first Ali, after the French of Dancourt) has not been seen more often on the stage or heard in gramophone recordings. There are typical touches of 'Turkish' scoring, some impressive accompanied recitatives, a meltingly beautiful trio (with cor anglais parts) for the three ladies of the cast, two love duets and one comic duet, and a wide variety of arias and songs. Progress is slow and predictable, perhaps, and some of the numbers (not the ensembles) are inclined to outstay their welcome from the dramatic viewpoint.

With some years of mutual experience behind them by the time they recorded this work, Dorati, the Lausanne Chamber Orchestra and the Philips team had reached a superb standard; the freshness and vitality of the performance is in doubt only in one or two slower-moving recitative scenes. The solo singing is wonderfully assured. Linda Zoghby as Rezia sings with such ravishing tone and fluency that one readily overlooks her casual diction and uncertainty of intonation in her first aria. Della Jones and, especially, Margaret Marshall provide nicely contrasted timbres and great delicacy, brio and charm as the heroine's companions. Of the men, Claes H. Ahnsjö, one of the stalwarts of the Philips Haydn series, sings with fine style and spirit, if without special tonal beauty. Domenico Trimarchi and Benjamin Luxon enjoy themselves as comic servant and Dervish (Calender), with hardly more than a touch of exaggeration and much full-blooded and often subtle singing.

Conveniently, the two surviving German *Singspiele* may be considered together without our departing far, if at all, from the chronological sequence observed in this chapter. *Philemon und Baucis* was first performed in Prince Esterházy's puppet theatre on 2 September 1773 in the presence of the Empress Maria Theresa, preceded by a partly burlesque mythological prelude *Der Götterrath* (which, though its text survives complete, cannot be performed owing to the loss of all the music except a tiny ritornello and the overture, which consists of what we know as the first two movements of Symphony No. 50). *Philemon und Baucis* was revived in a slightly altered form in or around 1776, for human actors rather than puppets; and it is the score of this version which survives complete.

It was recorded in Vienna by Vox in 1953 and, despite the age of the disc, it would be worth reissuing unless plans are in hand to provide a superior modern alternative. Two well-filled sides contain the whole score (and a lot of dialogue), though the second of the ballets, with music from Gluck's *Paride ed Elena*, is not included. The sound quality is good for the period; only in the opening and closing choral numbers is it constricted and shallow. The production includes footsteps, the closing of doors, etc., and the spoken verse is strongly declaimed (if hardly in perspective with the singing voices). The Vienna Symphony Orchestra sounds a bit thin, with the wind instruments backward, but Meinhard von Zallinger directs a firm yet sensitive account of the work. The music, descriptive rather than dramatic, is unfailingly pleasing – though it is surely an elementary miscalculation on Haydn's part that between the urgent D minor opening chorus, and the finale in contrasting tempi, there is a string of five slow numbers (all in the adagio and andante region). The only true contrast is provided by the inclusion of what is better known as Flaminia's 'Se la mia stella' from Act 2 of *Il mondo della luna*. It is normally assumed that the borrowing was from the Italian work – but if that is the case, then the second version of *Philemon* must date from after *Il mondo della luna*, which was written mainly or entirely in 1777.

Of the singers, Erich Majkut makes a firm, musicianly impression as old Philemon; his two arias which open the action convey a tender, controlled melancholy. Susana Naidič suggests Baucis's age more by her wobble than by subtler means. Waldemar Kmentt as the couple's resurrected son, Aret, sings his superb G minor aria raptly if too extrovertly. Elisabeth Roon as Narcissa, his bride, produces a neat trill and ringing high C in her aria. An enjoyable performance; more than that, for some years it provided the only chance to hear any of Haydn's German-language stage music.

One of the major musicological events of the sixties was the rediscovery in Yale University Music Library of a manuscript score of Haydn's German puppet opera variously entitled *Das abgebrannte Haus* and *Die Feuersbrunst*. This work, identified, edited and supplied with spoken texts by the indefatigable Robbins Landon, was staged at University College London in February 1966, and a recording from one of the performances, in an English version by Norman Platt, was issued in June 1968 by Rare Recorded Editions. The piece probably dates from 1775–8, the only period when Haydn had the clarinets available in his orchestra which the score calls for. It is a Hanswurst comedy of the type that was at its most popular in the 1740s and 1750s, though affection for these broad dialect plays-with-music lingered on in the provinces even more than in Vienna. The score contains no fewer than twenty-one arias, though there are three duets in Act 2, and both acts end with a chorus. There is charming and often witty music; the numbers are mainly short and lively. Nothing is more delightful than the series of arias in which Hanswurst, disguised successively as soldier, gentleman, milliner and old beggarwoman, lays siege to his estranged girlfriend, Colombina, eventually winning her back to sweet reason and his own unaffected, resourceful self.

The recording as it emerges from the live performance has the disadvantages of stage and audience noise and musical slips; it also conveys the atmosphere of what was clearly an enjoyable evening in the theatre. George Badacsonyi's orchestra is variable, but at its best the playing is decent. What cannot be denied is that much of the singing is barely adequate, and some of it less than that. Richard Virdin as the porter, Steckel, and Terry Jenkins as the fop, Leander, give neat character portrayals, and Howard Bentley as Hanswurst, though lacking the force of personality and the vocal agility which the part requires, puts several of his songs across neatly. What can be achieved in these unpretentious numbers is demonstrated on a Preiser disc (Preiser SPR 3170) by Julius Patzak in Odoardo's 'Nicht fressen, nicht saufen' – an unforgettable voice, still full of charm and pointful musicianship at the end of his career – and by Elfriede Ott in Colombina's winsome little 'Jetzt bin ich, was ich war'.

If it is disappointing that the second recording of *Die Feuersbrunst* is also taken from a live performance (at the Stadttheater Berndorf in June 1979; it was issued three years later on the Pan label), its faults and virtues are rather different from those of the London production. The disadvantages include the cuts (seven complete numbers are missing, among them a couple of gems, and parts of others have been discarded), the frantically busy production (stage bustle and bangings, but also excessive weeping and laughter) and some musical shortcomings. The cast is mainly adequate, and Michael Roider as Leander and Peter Weber as Odoardo are better than that. Christian Boesch fails to enhance his reputation – or at times even to live up to it. His Hanswurst clearly delighted the audience, and some of his music is charmingly put across, yet part of his success comes at the cost of Haydn's note-values and melodic line; his is a lively but undisciplined assumption. Erwin Ortner conducts decently, and there is some good playing from the orchestra. But he should have insisted on repose and dignity at least in the pensive numbers. The recorded quality is low, with incipient distortion and indifferent balance. I wish it had been possible to record the score in the studio, without an audience – for *Die Feuersbrunst* is a better piece than either set suggests.

Haydn's next opera, *Il mondo della luna,* was performed in celebration of an Esterházy family wedding in August 1777. Since its performances at the Holland Festival in 1959 it has had several productions and has proved a charming and reasonably hardy work. Back in the early thirties it was given a new lease of life (with hindsight we can see it was more a kiss of death) by the German edition with text by W. M. Treichtlinger and music arranged by Mark Lothar. A sparkling performance of this version was doubtless a lively theatrical experience, but Lothar plundered numbers from other Haydn works, and the unfortunate nature of his efforts can be felt in the abridged recording of 1956, with the Munich Chamber Opera under Johannes Weissenbach on Lyrichord. The label calls it '*Il mondo della luna/The man in the moon*', but it is actually sung in German. The recitatives are heavy handed, with added orchestral accompaniment (a harpsichord was apparently not available at the start of the sessions); false accentuation abounds, and there isn't an appoggiatura in sight. A tasteless scene-setting chorus (based on the finale of *Orlando Paladino*) after the overture gives an indication of what is to come; it reappears after the 'Vorspiel'. The singing is undistinguished, though Walter Hagner as the duped Buonafede does create a semblance of character, even if the style is unsubtle.

It is doubly refreshing to turn to Dorati's 1977 recording. Here one can appreciate to the full a delightful score which, whether in the Robbins Landon edition (Bärenreiter), or that of Günter Thomas (Henle, which contains the numerous revisions of individual numbers), is likely to prove one of the cornerstones of the Haydn renaissance during the last quarter of the century. *Il mondo della luna* may contain few concerted numbers – apart from the three act-finales there are only two duets and three quite short numbers for small chorus with one or two soloists – but so skilfully does Haydn integrate the brief ballets and instrumental intermezzi, so careful is he not to let individual arias outstay their welcome, that no one's attention wanders. The plot, with triple wedding imminent at the end, and only the gullible old father discomfited, offers the opportunity (which is avidly seized) to write music depicting lunar travel and beautiful moonscapes.

The performance rises to the challenge, with a wealth of strong yet delicate detail from the Lausanne Chamber Orchestra, aided by a real nightingale and cuckoo for the extended scene on the moon (a splendidly spacious acoustic, here). In a lovely performance the palms go to the women: Arleen Augér brilliant, relaxed and charming in Flaminia's music, Edith Mathis nicely contrasted as her more playful sister, and Frederica von Stade warm, spirited and neat in her role as the sisters' servant, Lisetta. Lucia Valentini Terrani, midway between the sexes in her trousers role (Haydn originally began to write it for tenor voice), neither quite suggests masculinity, nor entirely avoids a feminine flutter. Of the men, Domenico Trimarchi by purely musical means breathes life into the easily duped old star-gazer; he sings his varied numbers with relish, savouring the inflections and pointing the phrases neatly. Luigi Alva as the scheming lover and bogus astronomer is as stylish and vocally pleasing as usual, and Anthony Rolfe Johnson is equally good as resourceful servant, lover, and Emperor of the Moon. This set makes an ideal introduction to Haydn as an opera composer.

La vera costanza, written around 1778–9 and revised in 1785 after most of the original material had been destroyed in the theatre fire of 1779, contains much notable music; yet the plot is so confusing, and in one respect so gratuitously unpleasant, that the opera has had few revivals apart from the Dorati recording of 1977. Nothing much can be done with the story, which concerns the ambitious Baroness Irene's plan to marry off advantageously her nephew, Count Errico, who is secretly married to the fishergirl Rosina (her trials provide the unpleasantness referred to). In this performance the recitatives and some sung numbers have been shortened. There is no unanimity in the treatment of vocal graces, nor are the recitatives kept moving rapidly enough. The numerous fine arias are well sung. Ahnsjö is his usual dependable self in the Count's part, relishing his Act 1 aria (in which the high C-horn parts are surprisingly taken by trumpets), and in Act 2 helping make the Anfossi aria, which Haydn was evidently content to borrow, an experience as enjoyable as it is unusual. Jessye Norman is a fiery, musicianly Rosina, entirely deserving her aristocratic lover's attentions. Trimarchi, as her brother, and Wladimiro Ganzarolli as the man the Baroness intends to fob her off with, give much pleasure in the two comic roles; and Helen Donath's assumption of Lisetta, the Baroness's maid, is a delight. Kari Lövaas is suitably imperious as the Baroness, and Rolfe Johnson gives an elegant performance as the colourless Marquis who finally marries her. The big finales to Acts 1 and 2 are impressive ensembles judged by any standards other than those of Mozart, which are hard to avoid invoking, though of course Mozart in 1778–9 had all his major operas still to write. Dorati sees to it that the ensembles are well paced, and they are vividly sung, too. Act 3, as so often in Haydn's operas, is a distinct anticlimax, but the work as a whole contains a wealth of marvellous music and the performance is without a single weakness.

1779 was a very busy year for Haydn as opera composer and director. Its last fruit was *L'isola disabitata*, a short, serious opera in two parts and employing only four singers. The slow-moving and undramatic libretto (Haydn's only operatic meeting with his former downstairs neighbour, Metastasio) is of little disadvantage in a recording, especially since the composer responded with consistent inspiration to the predicament of two sisters ship-wrecked alone on a desert island. There is no *secco* at all; instead, the fate of the sisters is depicted in lengthy and superbly sustained *accompagnati*, often with almost melodrama-like ritornellos of striking beauty and psychological penetration. The scoring is only for strings with flute, oboes, bassoon, horns and timpani; but there is no sense of impoverishment, thanks to the variety and eloquence of the orchestral writing, as well as the rewarding vocal parts. This is a notable milestone in Dorati's pilgrimage through Haydn's operas with the Lausanne Chamber Orchestra. The role of the younger sister, Silvia – too young to remember the time before the shipwreck – is sung with great sensibility and style by Linda Zoghby. The elder sister, Costanza, who believes herself abandoned (though in fact pirates carried off her husband shortly after the shipwreck), is taken by Norma Lerer; her warm, expressive voice is mainly employed in ringing the changes on grief and heartbreak. Of the men, Gernando (Costanza's husband) is reliably sung by Luigi Alva, though on this occasion without the easy flexibility in runs that is ideally required; his companion Enrico (Pylades to Gernando's Orestes, as it were) is strongly, rather gruffly sung by Renato Bruson. But the impact of the whole far exceeds the individual beauties – which include a large-scale closing quartet, with a wealth of solo instrumental writing.

The next opera in chronological order, *La fedeltà premiata* (1780), is probably the most widely known of the entire series nowadays, thanks to the gramophone and also to public performances – in Britain we think particularly of the Glyndebourne production of 1979 and 1980, even though the work might have made a stronger and more convincing impression had it been given 'straight', according to Haydn's letter and spirit, rather than half-apologetically, half-defiantly as something at once more and less than Haydn intended. Assuredly Haydn himself employed irony – in the part of Count Perrucchetto there are good examples – and indeed it would not have been easy, even in pre-Mozartian Esterháza, to take the story seriously: an amazingly complicated imbroglio with various couplings between lovers who are prepared, or not prepared, to die as the sacrifice that Diana annually exacts from the people of Cumae.

There are two excellent complete recordings of this opera. The one conducted by Dorati was made in 1975 and issued a year later; the other, conducted by Sándor, was made in 1977 and issued here in the following year. It was with *La fedeltà premiata* that Philips and the European Broadcasting Union began their exploratory, indeed revelatory progress through Haydn's Italian operas: a series which from the beginning set new standards for enthusiastic and scholarly performance, under a proven Haydn conductor, with casts carefully chosen from among the finest stylists of the day, and straightforward studio production, with spacious sound-quality and no gimcrackery. The cast in the Dorati performance is very strong; there are particularly fine assumptions from Ileana Cotrubas and Luigi Alva as the secondary (and light-hearted) pair of lovers, Nerina and Lindoro, and from Frederica von Stade (Amoranta) and Alan Titus (Perrucchetto) as the more flirtatious and ridiculous pair. The two serious, indeed near-tragic lovers are taken by Valentini Terrani (Celia) and Tonny Landy (Fileno) with commitment and style, though the mezzo's voluptuous voice is a shade unwieldy at times, and the tenor, for all his forthrightness, lacks something in charm. Maurizio Mazzieri as Melibeo, the lustful priest, is heavy and hectoring, though he is nicely within the part and savours the recitatives. A slight disappointment is the inconsistent attitude towards appoggiaturas and cadenzas in arias; the cuts, especially in the recitatives, are not likely to worry many people, though Alva would surely have given pleasure in Lindoro's aria at the start of Act 2 if allowed to sing it.

The Hungaroton performance lacks the international stars that adorn the Philips set, but it emerges from any comparison with honour, and at times with the greater distinction. Sándor goes for absolute completeness, which means not only that he declines to follow the cuts which Haydn himself made, but gives us the recitatives in full, too (maintaining impetus even on dull pages), with appoggiaturas and with flourishes in the arias. One arguable miscalculation is to prefer the solo bassoon to horn at the largo in Celia's 'Deh soccorri' – a revision which, as Robbins Landon has argued, was surely imposed on Haydn by the departure of his champion horn-player rather than by inclination. It is less easy to distinguish among the women in Sándor's performance than in Dorati's, partially because his Celia (Júlia Pászthy) is a true soprano, opting for the high versions of two arias, whereas Philips use a mezzo. Miss Pászthy is the best of the women in the set, with clear, fresh tone and much delicacy. Mária Zempléni as Nerina is neat and charming, and much the same is true of Veronika Kincses as Amaranta – who should, however, come across as a more positive, fiery character. The men are very good: Attila Fülöp is a musical Fileno, especially impressive in the second aria, and István Rozsos's Lindoro, with neat articulation, is a nicely contrasted second tenor. Gábor Vághelyi blusters splendidly as the cowardly Perrucchetto, though his tone is often woolly – singing alongside József Gregor, the admirable Melibeo, should have been an object-lesson to him. Gregor sings with crispness and focus, and manages to suggest a seedy yet endearing charm, whilst remaining a dangerous adversary. One or two aural effects are exaggerated, but apart from some congestion in the final chorus, the recording is pleasantly uncluttered and open-textured. The orchestral playing is first-rate, with the important string bass-line delightfully crisp yet sonorous. A less exciting account than Dorati's, perhaps, but overall its sense of balance, its completeness and its measured elegance make it one of the very best Haydn opera recordings there have yet been.

In 1782 Haydn wrote his last semi-serious opera, *Orlando Paladino*. In German translation it enjoyed considerable success in the composer's life-time, but it has taken the gramophone – and the Philips/Dorati flair – to give it a renewed lease of life in our own day. *Orlando Paladino*'s complicated plot turns on the infatuation of the mad Roland (George Shirley) for the otherwise-engaged Angelica (Arleen Augér). Her lover is the Don Ottavio-like Medoro (Claes H. Ahnsjö), gentle and ineffectual, though Rodomonte (Benjamin Luxon) introduces complications by wishing to press his service on her as well as by seeking battle with Roland. Alcina (Gwendolyn Kille-brew) by her magic brings about a happy ending – she requests Charon (Maurizio Mazzieri) to cure Roland with Lethe water; the union of Roland's squire Pasquale (Domenico Trimarchi) and the shepherdess Eurilla (Elly Ameling) rounds off the comic action. Beautiful arias, interspersed with noble *accompagnati* as well as *secco* recitatives, rare vocal ensembles, and grand finales, bear witness to Haydn's involvement. He is served proudly by the singers – Augér at her most delicate and sweet-toned, though also imperious in coloratura; Killebrew making a grand impact with ringing tone and precise focus in her first aria, and just as impressive whenever she is called upon; and Ameling her usual reliable, charming self in her small part. The men are as distinguished: Ahnsjö and Shirley showing the two sides of the tenor coin, Luxon raging ingratiatingly as the King of Barbary, Mazzieri sonorous in Charon's one scene, and Trimarchi exhibiting his dramatic and comic flair and accurate, clean phrasing as the comic servant. Pasquale is indeed the plum part, looking back to the Hanswurst and Bernardon comedy of Haydn's young years, and forward towards Leporello. As always in these Philips sets – and one must risk wearying the reader with repetition – high praise must go to Dorati with his excellent little Lausanne orchestra, for vivid yet relaxed music-making, and to Erik Smith and the Philips recording team for unfailingly clean, natural sound.

The last of Haydn's operas for Esterháza was *Armida* (1783), a wholly serious work and in that theatre the most successful of all. As so often, we are indebted to Dorati for the chance to get to know a remarkable score. There is little to the plot beyond the attempts of Armida (Jessye Norman) to ensnare and then hold Rinaldo (Claes H. Ahnsjö). Two Christian generals (Robin Leggate and Anthony Rolfe Johnson) try to win back Rinaldo to his duty, whilst on the heathen side Armida's uncle, King Idreno (Samuel Ramey) and the Egyptian Princess Zelmira (Norma Burrowes) complete the line-up. Despite the attractive arias which come their way, Miss Burrowes and Messrs Leggate, Rolfe Johnson and Ramey have little share in the drama and can only stand and sing – which they do with great skill and persuasiveness. The drama is within the minds, and between the persons, of Armida and Rinaldo. The finest scene of all – and how seldom one can say that of a Haydn opera! – comes in the last act, when Rinaldo is confronted by the apparition of Armida from a myrtle tree; here the orchestral writing is of the highest excellence (no chance of mistaking the ritornellos here for passages from a symphony!), and the vocal writing, in accompanied recitatives and arias, is apt, lean and powerful. The principals sing with superb assurance, eloquence and beauty here. Ahnsjö had earlier sounded overtaxed in his martial aria; in the great last-act confrontation his fine legato line and pliant phrasing make him an entirely worthy antagonist to Miss Norman. She is in superb voice, alternately melting the heart with her pleas, and chilling the spine with her threats of vengeance. Another ideal gramophone opera.

Haydn's last opera, *L'anima del filosofo* or, as he also and more helpfully called it, *Orfeo ed Euridice,* was written in 1791 for a vain operatic endeavour during Haydn's first stay in London. It had to wait until 1951 for its stage première (at the Florentine Maggio Musicale, with Maria Callas as Eurydice); but by then it had become the first Haydn opera to be recorded complete: by the Haydn Society, in Vienna in 1950. None of Haydn's other stage works demonstrates quite as forcefully the splendours and the miseries of which he was capable in opera – a demonstration made at a slow pace through two acts which take us roughly up to the Calzabigi/Gluck starting point, and then with stunning succinctness in the finale to the fourth and last act: a wretchedly feeble chorus of bacchantes leads into a wonderfully vivid storm chorus. In the final few minutes we plumb the depths and scale the heights of Haydn's operatic achievement.

The 1950 recording shows its age, not surprisingly. It nevertheless has still to be replaced, or even equalled, thirty years later. Despite Hans Swarowsky's evident affection and admiration for the score, he cannot persuade us that it is a very dramatic work. He does procure good, keen playing from the Vienna State Opera Orchestra, and fine, sonorous attack from the Opera Chorus – in a work with more than a dozen choral numbers this is a vital issue; and it is hardly Swarowsky's fault that the bacchantes sound chaste and decorous. Of the soloists, Herbert Handt is a sensitive and stylish Orpheus; he shows much more awareness of appoggiaturas and graces than was usual at this time, and he is lithe and clean in the often taxing divisions. As Eurydice, Judith Hellwig flatters in her opening *accompagnato* only to disappoint as soon as she is faced with the coloratura of her first aria, 'Filomena abbandonata'. This sets the pattern: warm, pure vocal quality for Eurydice's slow-moving and especially her lower-lying music, technical shortcomings as soon as she is faced with rapid divisions and ornaments. Hedda Heusser sings the aria of the Genius with some skill, but without the easy brilliance, or the penetration in recitative, that the part needs. Alfred Poell is a dry, not entirely comfortable Creon; and the young Walter Berry hardly makes much impact in the tiny part of Pluto.

A 'private' recording is available of the 1967 festival production of *L'anima del filosofo*. The production was seen at the Vienna Festival in June before it came to Edinburgh in August. The recording originates in the performance in the Theater an der Wien on 21 May 1967. The stars are Joan Sutherland, Nicolai Gedda and Spiro Malas; Sutherland also misappropriates the aria of the Genius, thereby robbing the light but unfailingly neat-voiced Mary O'Brien of her one big moment. Richard Bonynge directs the Vienna Symphony Orchestra and Vienna Academy Chamber Choir – this last providing one of the most impressive features of the performance. My memories of the Edinburgh production (at which the Scottish National Orchestra and Scottish Opera Chorus took over) are happier than my experience of the recording. Frankly, so harsh are the cuts (few numbers are given complete) that the work itself suffers sadly. The performance was clearly to the liking of the Viennese, who applaud enthusiastically, but listening to it at home, with the Henle score in the Complete Edition (not available until 1974), one has different reactions. It is easier to overlook the odd mishap in a stage performance (bad ensemble in one or two numbers, clumsy phrasing, sour notes from the singers) than it is the dogged tramp through the recitatives, the variation in pulse between jerkiness and languor, above all the remarkable elaboration of the vocal line. Even the basic melody of Eurydice's first aria is disfigured in this way; and the big duet takes on an almost Donizettian colour. I enjoyed most Malas's Creon; he provides the crisp, straightforward projection appropriate to the music of his three arias. Gedda produces some beautiful singing, but he bursts into his first aria with more brio than delicacy, and he is strained by the low notes (Haydn was writing for Giacomo Davide, who had a wide range). Sutherland is in variable voice; she too is strained by her low notes (she often avoids them), and her phrasing is limp at times, but the coloratura is deftly managed, and her diction is pleasingly incisive. Let us hope that a really good recording of this interesting score will soon come our way.

The final section of this conspectus of Haydn the opera composer considers those records I have been able to hear that contain arias he wrote for interpolation into the operas of his contemporaries, mainly of course for the Esterháza opera house, as well as a few excerpts from his own stage works. It is to be hoped that Philips, or some other company with Haydn's and our interests at heart, will one day put out a set containing all the *Einlagearien* – not so much for the sake of completeness, but because all the examples I have heard have turned out to be strikingly beautiful, original numbers. Indeed, in the not-so-distant past, when we had to rely on a few isolated numbers to get any aural impression of Haydn's work for the opera house, I was sufficiently excited by the arias I came across to think that he was a finer opera composer than turns out to be the case. Hear a few Haydn arias, and you are likely to think that the deft touches of characterization they contain, as well as the superb craftsmanship, melodic delights and unexpected phrase-lengths and harmonic surprises, are the work of a major opera composer. Alas, there is in the complete works all too little of the incisiveness, strong contrasts and above all dramatic insight which can shape a whole act; without these, no opera is going to hold the stage easily.

An early LP of Haydn arias was issued by Nixa in the mid-fifties: Gertrud Hopf accompanied by Zallinger and the Vienna Symphony Orchestra (HLP 2045). It contains the German *Cantilena pro Adventu,* the *Scena di Berenice,* the Petrarch setting 'Sole e pensoso', and – important in the present context – two of Haydn's invariably interesting *Einlagearien:* Erisena's 'Chi vive amante' for Bianchi's *Alessandro nell'Indie* (1787), and 'Son pietosa', Lindora's aria for *La Circe.* The former is a dignified *andante*, which requires steadier, neater singing than it gets from Miss Hopf. She is more at home in 'Son pietosa' – if rather solemn in the *andante,* she is lively in the quicker closing section, though lacking the charm it ideally calls for.

For years the most valuable single record from the operas was the ten-inch Qualiton HLPMK 1532 with excerpts from seven works. Leaving aside the overture to *Orlando Paladino* and the little dance-sequence from Act 2 of *Il mondo della luna* – for the boxy acoustic and shallow sound of the Hungarian State Concert Orchestra under György Lehel are hardly beguiling – we have six arias and a duet, three of them real rarities. Judit Sándor sings Gasperina's half-parodistic, half-serious C minor aria from *La canterina* neatly if without the prima donna qualities it really needs; Mária Gyurkovics sings Lesbina's cavatina 'Voglio amar' from *Le pescatrici* rather shrilly, with fragile tone, so that we are grateful mainly to have anything from this quite often staged but unrecorded opera on disc; and Sylvia Geszty and Margit László are melodious and sweet-voiced in the chorus of *amorini* (here taken as a duet) from *Orfeo.* In the more readily duplicated numbers, György Melis is very good in Buonafede's first-act cavatina from *Il mondo* (done without the little intermezzi which separate the three strophes), and in Perrucchetto's 'Coll'amoroso foco' from *La fedeltà premiata*; in Vespina's mixed-language drinking song from *L'infedeltà delusa* Mária Gyurkovics effaces thoughts of the *Pescatrici* number as she relishes the spirit and wit of the music. For this skilfully chosen programme, Jenö Vécsey deserves the thanks of all Haydn lovers.

Another valuable disc from Hungary is the 45rpm offering (Qualiton LPM 1561) of two insertion-numbers tucked into the supplementary volume (which contains the score of the then recently discovered 'Scena di Pedrillo', written in 1789 for the pasticcio *La Circe*) to *Haydn als Opernkapellmeister*, the magisterial documentation by Denes Bartha and László Somfai (Budapest, 1960). József Réti sings the scena neatly, lightly, though without appoggiaturas; and the second side has space for the warm, charming little cavatina 'Quando la rosa', written in 1779 for Anfossi's *La Matilde ritrovata,* and palely sung by Judit Sándor.

Time was when the German Columbia record (STC 91104) of works by Werner and Haydn for the Esterházys contained the only excerpt from Haydn's stage works that could readily be had (it was later obtainable in HMV's Baroque Library on HQS 1071). It contains, alongside instrumental music and the great Te Deum, a spirited account by Theo Altmeyer of Mengone's aperient aria 'Per quel che ha mal di stomaco' – a splendid number with, as it were, a sting in the tail.

Jakob Stämpfli, that dignified Swiss bass whom we know primarily as a cantata and oratorio singer, includes two Haydn arias in a record of vocal and orchestral music made by the Wiener Barockensemble under Theodor Guschlbauer on the American Musical Heritage Society label (MHS 768). Stämpfli finds an appropriately tender quality for the charming aria 'Un cor si tenero', which Haydn wrote for Bianchi's *Il disertore* in 1787, and he sings 'Tergi i vezzosi rai' from *Acide* with warm tone though little awareness of dramatic characterization. This is one of the surviving numbers from Haydn's earliest known Italian opera (1762), in the revised setting of 1773; it is a virile allegro, spacious and resplendent.

Dietrich Fischer-Dieskau included four Haydn arias in his 1971 Decca recital 'Haydn and Mozart Discoveries', on which he is accompanied by the Vienna Haydn Orchestra under Reinhard Peters (JB 100). Among them are the two arias sung by Stämpfli. Fischer-Dieskau is far more dramatic in the *Acide* aria, though less comfortable in runs; in the number from *Il disertore,* which he and Peters take distinctly fast both for the music and for the andantino marking, Fischer-Dieskau is alternately heavy, or else mock-light, in his approach. He is happier in 'Spann deine langen Ohren' ('So che una bestia sei' in the original Italian) from *List und Liebe* – one of the numerous German names for *La vera costanza*. It is a cheerful patter song, neatly sung – though with a few moments of frayed ensemble. I enjoyed most the aria 'Dice benissimo', written in 1780 for Salieri's *La scuola de gelosi* – a lovely E flat Andante, with nice horn parts; here the singer is entirely at ease in a number which deserves to be better known.

For the lover Haydn's operatic music, the most welcome of all recital discs is that recorded in 1982 for Erato (NUM 75038) by Teresa Berganza with the Scottish Chamber Orchestra under Raymond Leppard. It includes 'Chi vive amante' from Bianchi's *Alessandro nell'Indie* and 'Son pietosa' from the pasticcio *La Circe*, both of which, along with the Advent cantilena 'Ein' Magd, ein' Dienerin', figure in the undistinguished old recital record by Gertrud Hopf. Otherwise this is virgin territory: 'La moglie quando è buona' from Cimarosa's *Giannina e Bernardone* (1790), a charming two-tempo number which is zestfully done, full of fun and wit; 'Ah, crudel' from Gazzaniga's *La vendemmia* (1780), the fine Andante of which is by Gazzaniga, the merry and then graver Presto by Haydn; 'Miseri noi! Misera patria!', a substantial scena in four sections which may have been intended for interpolation into late Esterháza opera; 'Sono Alcina' from Gazzaniga's *L'isola di Alcina* (1786), a slow, tender number with cello *obbligato* and pretty wind writing which some will recognize as a reworking of (or the orignal for?) one of the lyra concertos written for the King of Naples; and 'Il meglio mio carattere' from Cimarosa's *L'impresario in angustie* (1790), another number in contrasting slow and fast tempi, though less striking than most in this well-chosen programme. The orchestral textures tend towards the glutinous, but Berganza gives much pleasure, especially when she can display her strong, creamy lower register; in some fast sections she is under strain, and there is at times insufficient tenderness and sense of characterization. This is nevertheless an invaluable record, mellowly and faithfully recorded.

Finally, I mention two arias not otherwise recorded which are available in an interesting 'private' issue (which includes, as well as *La canterina*, discussed earlier, the *Applausus* cantata). Benita Valente is the singer of the arias, which were recorded at a New York concert in December 1967 under Alexander Schneider. The numbers are 'D'una sposa meschinella', probably written in 1777 for Paisiello's *La frascatana*; and 'Infelice, sventurata', written for Cimarosa's *I due suppositi conti* a dozen years later. In both numbers Miss Valente sings the slow opening section dully, with shallow tone, but in the faster sections she displays charm and real agility; both pieces are well worth hearing, and the former in particular, with its lovely oboe obbligato, would be a strong candidate for inclusion in any recital record. 'Infelice, sventurata' would really suit an altogether bigger voice, though Benita Valente makes a fine attempt at it.

ARMIDA

A Armida; *R* Rinaldo; *Z* Zelmira; *I* Idreno; *U* Ubaldo; *C* Clotarco

1979 Norman *A*; Ahnsjö *R*; Burrowes   Dorati
    Z; Ramey *I*; Leggate *U*; Rolfe   Philips 6769 021
    Johnson *C* / Lausanne CO /

LA FEDELTÀ PREMIATA

C Celia; F Fileno; A Amaranta; P Perrucchetto; N Nerina; L Lindoro; M Melibeo; D Diana

1975 Valentini Terrani C; Landy F; Von Stade A; Titus P; Alva L; Cotrubas N; Mazzieri M; Lövaas D / Suisse Romande Radio Chorus, Lausanne CO / Dorati Philips 6707 028

1977 Pászthy C; Fülöp F; Kincses A; Vághelyi P; Zempléni N; Rozsos L; Gregor M; Tokody D / Ferenc Liszt Academy Chamber Choir, Ferenc Liszt CO / Sándor Hungaroton SLPX 11854–7

DIE FEUERSBRUNST

(live performance – Stadttheater Berndorf)
H Hanswurst; S Steckel; O Odoardo; C Columbine; L Leander; G Ghost

1979 Boesch H; Suttheimer S; Weber O; Fuchs C; Roider L; Wildhaber G / Lower Austrian Chamber

Orchestra and Arnold Schoenberg Choir conducted by Erwin Ortner. PAN 0120 342 (2 records)

L' INCONTRO IMPROVVISO

R Rezia; A Ali; O Osmin; B Balkis; D Dardane; C Calender

1980 Zoghby R; Ahnsjö A; Trimarchi O; Marshall B; D. Jones D;

Luxon C / Lausanne CO / Dorati Philips 6769 040

L' INFEDELTÀ DELUSA

V Vespina; S Sandrina; N Nencio; F Filippo; Na Nanni

1969 Ravaglia V; Speiser S; Grilli N; Grimaldi F; El Hage Na / Haydn Foundation Orch., Rome / Almeida Chant du Monde LDX78447–9 Musical Heritage Society (US) MHS1262–4
1976 Kalmár V; Pászthy S; Fülöp N;

Rozsos F; Gregor Na / Ferenc Liszt CO / Sándor Hungaroton SLPX 11832–4
1980 Mathis V; Hendricks S; Ahnsjö N; Baldin F; Devlin Na / Lausanne CO / Dorati Philips 6769 061 ④ 7654 061

L' ISOLA DISABITATA

C Costanza; S Silvia; G Gernando; E Enrico

1978 Lerer C; Zoghby S; Alva G; Bruson E / Lausanne CO / Dorati

Philips 6700 119

IL MONDO DELLA LUNA

B Buonafede; *E* Ecclitico: *C* Clarissa; *Lis* Lisetta; *Ern* Ernesto; *F* Flaminia *F*;
Cec Cecco

1956 (abridged – in German: ed. M.
    Lothar)
    Hagner *B*; Schwert *E*; F.
    Schneider *C*; Münch *Lis*: Gassner
    Ern; Lindner *Cec* / Munich
    Chamber Opera Orch. /
    Weissenbach
    Period ⓜ SPL 703

Lyrichord ⓒ LLST 7120
1977 Trimarchi *B*; Alva *E*; Mathis *C*;
    von Stade *Lis*; Valentini Terrani
    Ern; Augér *F*; Rolfe Johnson *Cec*
    / Suisse Romande choirs,
    Lausanne CO / Dorati
    Philips 6769 003

ORFEO ED EURIDICE

O Orpheus; *E* Eurydice; *C* Creon; *G* Genio; *P* Pluto

1950 Handt *O*; Hellwig *E*; Poell *C*;
    Heusser *G*; Berry *P* / Vienna
    State Opera Chorus and Orch. /

Swarowsky
Haydn Society ⓜ HLP 2029
Vox (US) ⓜ OPBX 193

ORLANDO PALADINO

A Angelica; *E* Eurilla; *Al* Alcina; *O* Orlando; *M* Medoro; *R* Rodomonte;
P Pasquale; *C* Caronte; *L* Licone

1976 Augér *A*; Ameling *E*; Killebrew
    Al; Shirley *O*; Ahnsjö *M*; Luxon
    R; Trimarchi *P*; Mazzieri *C*;

Carelli *L* / Lausanne CO / Dorati
Philips 6707 029

PHILEMON UND BAUCIS

J Jupiter; *M* Mercury; *P* Philemon; *B* Baucis; *A* Aret; *N* Narcissa

1953 Steinbock *J*; Davy *M*; Majkut
    P;Naidic *B*; Kmentt *A*; Roon *N* /
    Vienna State Opera Chorus,

Vienna SO / von Zallinger
Vox ⓜ DL 770

LO SPEZIALE

S Sempronio; *M* Mengone; *G* Grilletta; *V* Volpino

1950 (abridged – in English)
    Chelsi; Meyers; K. Davis; Wolf /
    orch. / F. Kramer
    Magic-Tone ⓜ 1007
1958 (abridged – in German)
    Smid-Kowar *S*; zur Eck *M*;
    Schönauer *G*; Brinck *V* / Salzburg
    Mozarteum Orch. / Maedel
    Philips 835021 AY
    Epic BC 1105

1960 (abridged)
    Borgonovo *S*; Franzini *M*;
    Martelli *G*; Andreolli *V* / I
    Commedianti in Musica della
    Cetra, Compagnia del Teatro
    Musicale di Villa Olmo / F.
    Guarnieri
    Cetra ⓜ LPC 55024
1967 (abridged – in German)
    Vienna Mozart Boys' Choir /

Schwarzbauer
Amadeo AVRS6318
1978 Fülöp *S*; Rozsos *M*; Kalmár *G*;

Kincses *V* / Ferenc Liszt CO / Lehel
Hungaroton SLPX 11926–7

LA VERA COSTANZA

R Rosina; *L* Lisetta; *CE* Count Errico; *VV* Villotto Villano; *M* Masino; *BI* Baroness
Irene; *ME* Marquis Ernesto

1977 Norman *R*; Donath *L*; Ahnsjö   Lausanne CO / Dorati
     CE; Ganzarolli *VV*; Trimarchi *M*;   Philips 6703 077
     Lövaas *BI*; Rolfe Johnson *ME* /

Médée

LIONEL SALTER

Médée, Cherubini's seventeenth opera, was Schubert's favourite stage work: Brahms called it a composition 'which we musicians regard as the summit of dramatic music'. Beethoven wrote to Cherubini that he 'honoured and loved' him as 'the contemporary whom I most respect' and that he valued his stage works above all others; Weber, Spohr, Mendelssohn and Schumann were other composers who expressed their admiration. *Médée* is indeed a remarkable work, especially when one remembers that it was written a mere six years after *Die Zauberflöte* and preceded *Fidelio* by eight years. Anyone familiar with the extent of the Paris public's appreciation of serious musical stage pieces (as evidenced by its reactions to operas like *Guillaume Tell* or *Les Troyens*) will, however, not be surprised that *Médée*, which follows the strictest tradition of classical drama, was not successful at its première and was not revived in France, though it had an enthusiastic following in German-speaking countries: what may not be generally realized is that it still remains unrecorded.

That statement calls for some expansion, in view of the lists at the end of this chapter. At first presented at the Théâtre Feydeau on 13 March 1797, *Médée* had spoken dialogue; and Cherubini planned the work with great skill so as to use this to maximum effect. Medea makes her first entry – where she appears in order to appeal to Jason – in speech, which serves to heighten the later tensions of the drama and the contrast with her agonized accompanied recitative preceding the opera's finale; and there is a particularly telling scene in Act 2, where Jason's wedding ceremony takes place musically in the background while Medea, at the front of the stage, utters savage imprecations to her attendant, Neris. In this *opéra-comique* form the work was translated into German for productions in Berlin in 1801 and Vienna (for which Cherubini made some cuts) two years later.

London showed an interest in it in 1815, but the composer discouraged plans for a production, writing that the character of the music was 'too severe for English tastes', and another half-century was to elapse before it was played in London – in Italian, with the dialogue replaced by recitatives by Arditi. Meanwhile, however, Schubert's friend Franz Lachner, musical director at Munich, had also composed accompanied recitatives for the production (in German) at Frankfurt in 1855: the first Italian performances in 1909, in Milan, were based on this version, and it is this which was published by Ricordi (though the score makes no mention of Lachner) and is always performed nowadays. *Médée* has not only been changed from a French to an Italian opera, in style as well as language, and its character and dramatic pace thereby fundamentally altered, but Lachner's additions also involved removing over 400 bars of Cherubini's original. Defenders of the current version point to the public's antipathy to spoken dialogue in opera (though *Die Zauberflöte* and *Fidelio* seem to survive that handicap), to the inability of many singers to deliver spoken lines well (which would seem to argue a case for greater diversity in training), and to the musicality and power of Lachner's recitatives. Undeniable as is this last, it is particularly strange that, at a time when 'authenticity' has been elevated to a fashionable shibboleth, a musical hybrid incorporating additions made more than half a century later by another hand should be preferred to the composer's original. (A directly opposite view is taken, for example, of Mozart's version of *Messiah,* though there the 'improver' was a genius.)

The nearest we have come on records to Cherubini's *Médée* is the single disc of extracts with Rita Gorr in the title role, though practically all even of the numbers included are heavily cut. The distinguished nineteenth-century critic Henry Chorley well summed up the requirements of the central figure, who from her first entry is not off the scene for a single moment, and on whom the entire action centres (there are no sub-plots, and the rest of the cast are two-dimensional characters who come to life only when illuminated by the blaze of her dominating personality): Medea, he wrote, needs 'a voice like a clarion and a frame of adamant and gold [as well as] grandeur of expression ere the creation of the composer can be rightly filled up'. For all the beauty and firmness of tone Gorr produces in the lower part of her voice, the clarity of her enunciation and her obvious intelligence, she is miscast as Medea, the tessitura of whose part lies too high for a mezzo-soprano; and above the stave the strain is often apparent in shrill or ill-supported notes. She is at her best in the feigned pathos of her Act 2 duet 'Chers enfants', though there her Jason, Guy Chauvet, sings without much sensitivity – even if not with the raucous harshness he brings to his one solo aria, 'Eloigné pour jamais', which he plainly does not understand is an expression of loving devotion to his new bride, Dirce. Her one contribution, 'Hymen, viens dissiper', starts freshly and with true intonation, but by the taxing coloratura at the end she is tired and inexact. The most wholly successful piece of casting is that of René Bianco as a formidable Creon – that is, if one does not count the choice of Georges Prêtre as conductor. He gives quite the most exciting account available of the overture, which he takes faster than usual but to which he imparts a dramatic urgency, and the Paris Opéra orchestra responds with enthusiasm. He does, however, take the *Largo* opening of Medea's Act 3 aria 'Du trouble affreux' (which Gorr ends with an unofficial high B flat) four-in-a-bar instead of *alla breve*. The recorded sound throughout is bright, though a little shallow.

Without exception, all other recordings are of the Italian-version Cherub-ini-Lachner *Medea* (in which, with a commendable regard for the niceties of classical mythology, Dirce more accurately becomes Glauce). In recent years the name indelibly associated with the work is, of course, that of Callas, for whom it was revived at the 1953 Maggio Musicale in Florence (the first Italian performances since 1909), and who created a sensation by the ferocity of her portrayal of the deserted Medea, who in crazed vengefulness for her rejection murders her husband's new bride and kills her own children. No fewer than five recordings by her in the opera are extant – all but one taken in theatres, and mostly so technically inadequate (ranging from the amateurish to the excruciating) that it is hard to believe that they could ever have been authorized. They run from one at La Scala, a week after her thirtieth birthday, to that in the same theatre eight years later almost to the day, and overall reveal a melancholy decline in her vocal powers in so short a space of time.

Yet the 1953 performance, given in the same year as her first assumption of the role in Florence, is dazzling to those whose knowledge of Callas is confined to her later recordings. Not only is there the freshness of attack that might be expected from an artist who had thrown herself heart and soul into a challenging but rewarding new part, but the security and quality of tone are striking, the numerous high notes free and brilliant (including a top C she adds at the end of Act 2), and the dramatic intensity is searing. This is especially so in Act 3, where she becomes an avenging Fury incarnate: the savagery with which she repulses her children is exceeded only by the hideous exultation with which she hears that Glauce has accepted her deadly gift (both these passages are pure Lachner). In the first act her opening recitative is remarkable for its emotional range, and her aria 'Dei tuoi figli' has a pathos that amply justifies the storm of applause which greets it.

Callas was fortunate on this occasion to have had as conductor Leonard Bernstein, who at short notice had replaced the indisposed Victor de Sabata, and who at the age of thirty-five was making his professional operatic debut. His involvement in the drama, the nuances he draws from the orchestra, his perceptive underlining of significant orchestral detail, make this one of the most illuminating of all readings; and though one or two of his tempi are arguable (in Act 2 the Medea-Creon scene too changeable, Neris's aria too slow), in general his speeds are most convincing. He is almost the only conductor not to make the perverse mistake, in the first Medea-Jason duet, of counteracting Cherubini's slackening of the tension and rhythmic thrust as the antagonists recall the past ('O fatal vello d'or') by *increasing* the pace. The main charge to be brought against Bernstein, however, is his wholesale mutilation of the score – death by a thousand cuts, indeed: the last line of Medea's 'Dei tuoi figli' is hacked off, and Glauce's aria is mangled by tearing out the middle and lopping off the coloratura at the end; yet he plays in full the long introduction with a bassoon solo to Neris's aria (abbreviated in the Ricordi score), which Fedora Barbieri sings most sympathetically. Gino Penno is a likable Jason, lyrical in his Romance, and Giuseppe Modesti is an acceptable Creon; but in Act 3 the prompter (merely annoyingly audible in Act 2) becomes practically a full member of the cast – despite which, or perhaps because of which, both Medea and Neris forget their words and Jason fails to come in for one entry. Yet with all these mishaps and truly appalling distortion of the chorus throughout (suggesting a miniature tape-recorder smuggled into a chorus member's shoe) this is a performance of gripping excitement.

It might reasonably have been expected that the September 1957 recording under studio conditions (originally made by Mercury for Ricordi, but reissued on Columbia, EMI, Everest and Deutsche Grammophon) would at least be acoustically satisfactory; but the results reflect little credit on the technical team. The orchestra sounds thin and dry (and its playing is rough compared with the standard it attained under Bernstein), the chorus is absurdly distant, particularly in the wedding scene, and its words are inaudible (the cries of horror at Glauce's death thus being rendered quite ineffective), and balance is sometimes faulty, both in vocal ensembles and as between singers and orchestra (the flute obbligato to Glauce's aria, for example, is much too faint).

Artistically too this set is uneven. After a classically conceived overture, the veteran Serafin (then aged seventy-nine) sets a lumbering pace for the opening scene which completely decharacterizes the happy eagerness ('nostra allegrezza') of Glauce's attendants; and in general his direction is lacking in momentum. His cuts are extensive, if less barbarous than Bernstein's. Callas, who by then had slimmed down considerably and at the time was suffering from near-exhaustion, is not in good voice, her upper register sounding screamy and strained. Yet her ability to convey Medea's changing moods is still masterly – in one scene alone her indignation with Jason, which gives way to tenderness at the recollection of their first meeting, her tearful pleading at 'Torna a me' at the end of her aria, and her excess of fury in the succeeding duet; or in Act 2 the hardening of tone as she implores the gods after her touching plea to Creon, her diabolical triumph as she realizes that she can strike at her faithless husband through his children, and the artfulness of her wheedling until she obtains custody of them for a day. She has a virile Jason in Mirto Picchi, though in his Act 1 Romance a quick vibrato in the voice is noticeable; but outstanding among the supporting cast is Miriam Pirazzini, whose singing of the aria in which Neris swears devotion to Medea is touchingly beautiful. Renata Scotto unfortunately is tentative in her one aria, especially in the latter half; and Modesti's voice is drier than in the 1953 recording.

If Callas was off form in that recording, her performance in Dallas a year later, as heard in a 'private' recording taken on November 6, is positively electrifying, cutting through the general muddy overload-distortion like forked lightning. It could indeed be claimed that Act 3 represents her at the peak of her form as a dramatic actress. John Ardoin, in his book *The Callas Legacy,* makes it plain that the vitriol which pours from her was due to her having received, only a few hours before the performance, a telegram from Rudolf Bing dismissing her from the Metropolitan for violation of contract; and in both her stage and her real-life situations she demonstrates that Hell indeed has no fury like a woman scorned. The rush of adrenalin is responsible for renewing her firmness on the role's high notes (whose number she augments by an extra C at the end of Act 2 and a B flat at the end of 'Del fiero duol'), as well as for restricting, though intensifying, her emotional palette: little tenderness emerges from this recording, and though her various appeals can be heart-rending (particularly that to Creon in Act 2), they are more overwrought and anguished than melting. Not until the last act – in which she lives up to Verdi's desideratum for Lady Macbeth ('the voice of a she-devil') in her 'La uccida!' and her blood-curdling line to Jason 'Sospettar non puoi dove andrà la vendetta!' – is there any real softening of the timbre, as at her momentary weakening, 'Son vinta già' (written by Lachner), and her cry, like that of a wounded animal, 'O figli miei, io v'amo tanto'.

The high tension of the performance results, in Act 1, in everyone singing *ff,* so that the prompter (certainly heard by us) cannot get through to prevent a couple of memory fluffs. The Dallas audience, too, is noisy, coughing and talking through the purely orchestral sections and repeatedly interrupting them to applaud Callas's entrances. Rescigno's conducting has drive, if not much finesse, and his cuts are less damaging than in the previous versions. The supporting cast is unusually strong. Nicola Zaccaria is a weighty and authoritative Creon, and Jon Vickers phrases well and makes his recitatives meaningful, though in his solo aria he is more intent on projecting his fine voice than in soothing Glauce: Elizabeth Carron gives that part more character than most of her rivals, conveying terror of Medea but joyous enthusiasm in her invocation of Love, and it is a pity that in the middle of her aria she wanders far away from the microphone and that her final *fioriture* are cut. Finally, Teresa Berganza (in her US debut) adds distinction to Neris, whose aria she shapes with firm tone and some admirable soft singing.

The Covent Garden performance of the following year was basically the Dallas production transplanted to London, with the two minor female roles reallocated. The recording is cloudy, levels are erratic, and the prompter is even more intrusive; and when the thunder effects in the storm that opens Act 3 overwhelm the orchestra, which has been tame in the overture, indifferent in the C minor introduction to Act 2, and faulty elsewhere (a woodwind mistake before 'O fatal vello d'or' calling forth a shocked expostulation from the conductor), one almost suspects that the wrath of Cherubini's spirit has been aroused. The chief target for such a protest would undoubtedly be Nicola Rescigno, whose direction throughout is so sluggish as to drain the work of vitality. From the dispirited introduction to Act 1, devoid of all happiness, to Medea's interminably long-spun-out indecision in' Act 3, where her voice is obviously tiring, there is an extraordinary lack of forward drive. This devalues both Joan Carlyle's sweet-toned performance of Glauce's aria (again shorn of its ending) and Fiorenza Cossotto's sensitive singing of Neris's – though she makes a false entry on her last 'Infelice!' before the pause. Zaccaria repeats his splendid representation of Creon, and Vickers produces a fine 'classical' legato line for his Romance. As for Callas herself, she is sadly lacklustre after the excitement of the Dallas recording. There are, of course, flashes: 'Dei tuoi figli' is well sung, she skilfully conveys the secrecy of her joy at discovering Jason's weakness (his love for his children) and her glee that she has gulled him; and her invocation to the 'inferni Dei' at the start of Act 3 and her supercharged 'Oh fosca Erinni' reek of evil. But elsewhere she reflects Rescigno's limpness: she mixes up her words near the start of Act 3, entirely misses one of her interventions in the wedding scene, and ill-advisedly adds a disastrously shaky high C at the end of Act 2.

Three advantages are to be heard in Callas's performance of 11 December 1961 in La Scala: a tolerable technical quality in this 'private' recording; a reasonably discreet prompter; and a good, full-throated chorus. Unfortunately, these are outweighed by the disadvantages. Thomas Schippers's extensive cuts, which include taking tucks wherever possible in every orchestral ritornello or interlude, further change the proportions of Cherubini to Lachner; and his inadequate control is shown not only by many wildly vacillating speeds (from which the Act 2 Medea-Jason duet suffers most) and much lagging (Jason's solo aria, Medea's 'Ebben! tutto mi manca' and the start of the Act 3 finale) but by the precarious ensemble between stage and pit. The opening chorus (which omits the initial solos by the two hand-maidens), the wedding march and the final chorus are all uncomfortably ragged; the start of the duet 'Nemici senza cor' is untidy; and there is a conspicuous disagreement between Schippers and the bright-voiced, youthful-sounding Ivana Tosini over the speed of Glauce's aria, in which he forces the pace.

In Act 1 Callas is clearly below par, dragging her recitatives, unstable rhythmically in 'Dei tuoi figli', and generally far less menacing than in her previous recordings: she fails to dominate the scene, and in fact is vocally upstaged by Vickers, in excellent form, and by Nicolai Ghiaurov as a dark-toned, resonant Creon. Giulietta Simionato earns the ovation she receives for Neris's aria, in which she employs her rich, vibrant voice most affectingly. Callas, whose top notes have been strident and disconcertingly unsteady, comes to life at the wedding chorus (which seemingly goads her to fury), and in the last act she recovers something of her old self, though the 'break' of register up from her chest voice is very obvious.

Medea had been first heard in the United States in 1955, when it was given in New York in concert form with Eileen Farrell in the title role: three years later it was staged, again with her, in San Francisco; and it was at that time that she recorded a single disc of extracts from the opera. Vocally she is superbly assured, with rock-steady, precisely placed high notes, a lovely quality and a firm, warm low register, and her enunciation is an object-lesson to all singers; and partnered as she is by an admirably lyrical André Turp as Jason, it is a pity that they did not record the whole opera – but with a better orchestra than this (heard on its own here in the Act 3 prelude) and a less pedestrian conductor. Arnold Gamson (of the New York City Opera) at least does not commit the usual error of speeding up at 'O fatal vello d'or' (though its effect would have been greater had it been *piano*, as marked), but he takes Medea's Act 2 'Date almen' much too languidly, ignoring its *allegro* indication, barely moves at 'Ebben! tutto mi manca', is absurdly slow and flaccid in 'Figli miei', and does not observe the *alla breve* pulse of 'Del fiero duol'. His cuts are slightly different from those encountered elsewhere, but it was not a good idea to retain Creon's lines (sung somewhat syllabically by Ezio Flagello) in ensembles in the absence of the other voices. Farrell starts Act 3 surprisingly mildly for an invocation to the infernal gods; and though she brings more vehemence and fury to later passages, and the 'Nemici senza cor' duet has fire, one gains the impression that she is at her best when expressing pathos: her 'Dei tuoi figli' is quite excellent, perhaps the best performance on disc. She misses a point by projecting 'Finzione! . . . Ch'io menta!' full voice and not 'aside': she takes the final bars of 'Date almen' up an octave, and like Callas ends 'Del fiero duol' with a high B flat. While not equalling Callas's searing passion, hers is nevertheless a splendidly sung performance.

If ever it may have been thought that Magda Olivero was taking a risk by making her US debut in Dallas in a role for which Callas (twenty years her junior at the time of singing) had been feted, the evidence of an unofficial recording on 4 November 1967 makes it clear that she had nothing whatever to fear by the comparison. Dramatically this is a commanding performance, encompassing the full gamut of emotional intensity from poignancy to hell-cat savagery, and making use of every shade of colour; and technically she is in far better voice than her predecessor, her high notes secure and cleanly poised without loss of quality. (If there has to be an interpolated high C at the end of Act 2, this is the way it should be sung.) Among many outstanding moments are her anguished pleas, mingled with indignation, to Creon; the glint of triumph in her voice at 'Non ha dei figli?'; the softly floated aside of 'Ch'io menta!' leading to the lachrymose appeal of 'Figli miei'; a passionate 'Del fiero duol'; the harshness of her resolve at 'implacabile Dea'; and a spine-chilling final exit line. The only disappointment is her 'Dei tuoi figli', which has a flawed start. That this remarkable and intelligent artist should never have recorded the role commercially is a great loss.

She has a worthy Jason in Bruno Prevedi, and their second-act duet is a high spot of the performance: his clean-cut, ringing tone makes the character convincing as a wronged hero, and it is the more regrettable that his solo aria should be marred by some flattening. The single microphone which appears to have been used on this occasion is placed beside the woodwind: this gives rise to innumerable problems of balance, and voices upstage become all but inaudible, as in the opening scene; in Neris's aria, most tenderly sung by Biancamaria Casoni, she becomes as it were the obbligato to the foreground bassoon solo. Zaccaria once again makes a dignified Creon, but Graziella Sciutti is over-parted as Glauce, indulging in too many *portamenti*, tonally lightweight and conspicuously lacking in *sostenuto*. Rescigno's unreliable instinct for tempi is, as in Callas's Covent Garden performance, a constant handicap: in the overture he unconvincingly and needlessly drops down to an unrelated slower tempo at the eleventh bar of the second subject on each appearance; he makes a violent *accelerando* in the middle of Glauce's aria; he produces no impetus in 'Pronube Dive' or Neris's aria; in Act 3 he changes both a *moderato* and an *andante molto sostenuto* to *adagissimo*; he rushes his singers unmercifully in 'Nemici senza cor' and lags behind Olivero in 'Del fiero duol'.

The Decca recording's chief claim on our attention is that it gives far more of the score than any previous version: there are only five small cuts (of 140 bars in all) instead of the dozens normally imposed, and with the exception of a high B flat at the end of 'Del fiero duol' no liberties are taken with the text. In theory this should have given a truer representation of the work than usual; but expectations are dashed. This is what is sometimes politely called a full-blooded reading, or less politely an unconsidered bash-through. Except for Cossotto, who invests Neris's aria with a loving compassion despite being hurried by the conductor, none of the singers seem to have thought about verbal nuance or characterization at all, but simply 'stand and deliver' without any real involvement in the action.

To a large extent this must be blamed on the prosaic direction of Lamberto Gardelli, who appears to have renounced finesse, flexibility and imagination for the duration: the general reluctance to play or sing *piano* is particularly striking. The opera begins inauspiciously with a tremulous soprano handmaiden, coarsely accompanied by the orchestra, and a far from steady Pilar Lorengar, who sounds ill at ease as Glauce (vocally, not from terror of the 'grim sorceress'). Justino Diaz is stiff and heavy, Prevedi manly but too uniformly forthright. Gwyneth Jones (at about the same age as Callas in her first recording) produces some superb ringing tones and thrilling individual phrases, but hers is a monochrome reading, relying on a generalized menace, and in places (such as 'Re degli Dei! Giove immortal!') she is almost perfunctory. Firm as is her singing, as an interpretation it needed much more mature thought and insight, and her last act conveys little of the conflicting torments in Medea's mind.

Mention may be made here of a 'private' recording of parts of a performance in Treviso during the 1972 season, in which the role of Medea is taken by Orianna Santunione. Besides revealing an impressively powerful voice, an alert intelligence, a solid technique and a vigorous temperament, she invests every word with meaning, employing the widest possible spectrum of colour and of dynamics. There is blazing fury in her 'Nemici senza cor', subtlety in her asides, gentleness in her 'Figli miei', volatile changes of mood in her final scene: her one fault is a slight tendency to sharpen on occasion. She has a competent Jason in Giorgio Casellato-Lamberti (except that he goes badly astray at 'Ancor potrai gioir') and a regal Creon in Paolo Washington. With only a small orchestra at his command, Rescigno shows more vitality than in his major-league recordings of the opera.

Gardelli's recording for Hungaroton is as full as his Decca version – in fact more so, since he includes the long original introduction to Neris's 'Solo un pianto' – but, more importantly, he here shows the sensitivity and the light and shade that were so sadly lacking before: it is scarcely credible that this is the same conductor. He has at his disposal an excellent orchestra and chorus, whose quality is immediately apparent in the opening scene, which for once captures the right kind of light-heartedness and has the benefit of two youthful-sounding handmaidens and an altogether charming Glauce. Magda Kalmár's steady line, pure intonation and reliable coloratura make hers easily the best performance of 'Amore, vieni a me', though her consonants needed to be stronger. Jason's aria is attractively sung by Veriano Luchetti, whose authentic lyric Italian timbre sets him somewhat apart from the otherwise all-Hungarian cast. They not only occasionally produce doubtful Italian vowels (and Kolos Kováts's 'kvesta' for 'questa' jars badly), but often give the impression of not fully understanding the significance of all the words they are singing. This certainly applies to Kováts, who makes a soft-focus and woolly Creon, and to the Neris of Klara Takács, whose alternate shrillness and plumminess may be partly attributable to poor microphone placing.

Even Sylvia Sass arouses momentary suspicions by one extraordinary piece of bad phrasing: 'Il mio segreto tu (*breath*) saprai tra poco'. Her assumption of the title role is uneven: some of her *affettuoso* and *mezza voce* passages are lovely, and in vindictive vein hers is a powerful Medea – but overall her performance is one of exaggerated extremes. It is difficult for any artist to avoid 'hamming up' so melodramatic a part, but Sass goes over the top several times; and while her 'Dei tuoi figli' has pathos (as, even more, has her 'Date almen') the cries of 'Crudel!' that punctuate it are out of proportion, and the final 'Pietà!' is bellowed. Her top notes, too, vary between the richly sonorous and the shrill. One suspects that she might have given a more integrated performance with a few more years' experience.

Only three arias appear in isolated recordings, and of those only one in French. On Véga Polaris L 80 007 Guy Chauvet sings 'Eloigné pour jamais' a great deal more mellifluously than on the 'highlights' record mentioned at the start of this chapter. Here he brings to this aria unexceptionable intonation and firm-toned *sostenuto* phrasing but the minimum of nuance – good singing as such, but little sense of character, though he is helped by the slight *accelerando* introduced halfway through by the conductor, Jésus Etcheverry. Medea's Act 1 'Dei tuoi figli' and Neris's Act 2 'Solo un pianto' are also available separately – both, needless to say, in the Italian version. (The loss from Cherubini's original that this entails may be appreciated if I say that without the four cuts imposed in each number, both would be exactly half as long again.) Callas's 1955 'Dei tuoi figli' (SLS 5057) is studio-bound, and languidly conducted by Serafin: Medea's reproaches of 'Crudel!' carry little conviction. Gwyneth Jones, recording the aria in Vienna with Argeo Quadri (Decca 6.35 463DX) two years before she undertook the complete opera, shows a beautiful tone but little involvement with the words, which in any case are barely intelligible. As for Grace Bumbry (1C 063 02055), the bad rhythmic mistake she makes in bar 14 suggests that she had not seen or heard the music before: this 'take' should certainly never have been issued. Quite apart from this, the aria is mostly sung at a uniformly loud level which ignores the significance of the words. Whereas Cossotto was hustled along in 'Solo un pianto' by Gardelli in the Decca complete recording, in her 1960 performance of the aria (Ricordi OCL 16091) Gavazzeni dawdles, making cohesion harder for her to achieve; but she spins a smooth line, and the relative lack of temperament is not entirely her fault. She is positively animated, however, by the side of Alexandrina Milcheva-Nonova (Harmonia Mundi HMU 263), in whose recording the bassoon is replaced by a cello. Though the voice itself is warm, albeit with a marked vibrato, both recitative and aria are delivered in a bland fashion without any commitment to the dramatic context. Teresa Berganza (SDD 193) also includes the introductory recitative and gives a beautifully expressive reading in which one could perhaps have wished only for a less unsuitably jaunty accompaniment and more precise intonation from the solo bassoon.

MÉDÉE

M Medea; *G* Glauce; *J* Jason; *N* Neris; *C* Creon
All recordings sung in Italian unless otherwise stated

1953 (live performance – Teatro alla Scala, Milan)
Callas *M*; Nache *G*; Penno *J*; Barbieri *N*; Modesti *C* / La Scala Chorus and Orch. / Bernstein
Cetra ⓜ LO 36 (3)

1957 Callas *M*; Scotto *G*; Picchi *J*; Pirazzini *N*; Modesti *C* / La Scala Chorus and Orch. / Serafin
Orizzonte AOCL 316001 (3)
Everest S437 (3)

1959 (live performance – Royal Opera House, Covent Garden)
Callas *M*; Carlyle *G*; Vickers *J*; Cossotto *N*; Zaccaria *C* / Royal Opera House Chorus and Orch. / Rescigno
Foyer ⓜ FO 1001 (3)

1967 (live performance – Dallas State Fair Music Hall)
Olivero *M*; Sciutti *G*; Prevedi *J*; Casoni *N*; Zaccaria *C* / Dallas Civic Opera Chorus and Orch. / escigno
Ricordi/CLS ⓜ AMDRL 32817

1968 Jones *M*; Lorengar *G*; Prevedi *J*; Cossotto *N*; Diaz *C* / Santa Cecilia Academy Chorus and Orch. / Gardelli
Decca SET 376–8
London OSA 1389

1977 Sass *M*; Kalmár *G*; Luchetti *J*; Takács *N*; Kováts *C* / Hungarian Radio and TV Chorus, Budapest SO / Gardelli
Hungaroton SLPX 11904–6

1958 (excerpts)
Farrell *M*; Turp *J*; Flagello *C* / Columbia SO / Gamson
Philips ⓜ ABL 3253

CBS (US) ⓜ Y-32358
1962 (excerpts – in French)
Gorr *M*; Esposito *G*; Chauvet *J*;

Bianco *C* / Paris Opéra Chorus
and Orch. / Prêtre
Columbia SAX 2482

Guillaume Tell

RICHARD OSBORNE

There was a time when *Guillaume Tell,* finest and most influential of early nineteenth-century grand operas, was regularly heard. On 10 February 1868 – a month or two prematurely archivists tell us – the artists of the Paris Opéra presented Rossini with a laurel wreath 'To Rossini, in memory of the 500th performance, 1829–68'. To succeeding generations, though, it has remained an enigma. Accounted 'seminal' by reference books, it is rarely performed save for its overture whose representative moments, the cellos' romantic colloquy or the pastoral cor anglais solo, are often sacrificed by conductors as they hasten to the famous equestrian *stretto.*

That *Guillaume Tell* points the way forward to the later nineteenth-century Italian and French traditions is indisputable. Though a composer like Meyerbeer was content merely to seize the ground plan, the blueprint on which he was able to raise his own musical emporia, monstrous halls filled with shoddy produce, it is arguable that *Tell* equally well paved the way for the great political dramas of the Verdi years – *Nabucco, Don Carlos*, and *Simon Boccanegra* – as well as Verdi's own great drama of paternity, *Rigoletto*. What Rossini's shrewder heirs inherited from *Guillaume Tell* was a new musical plasticity and power; a reorientation and humanization of the near-defunct baroque and neo-classical styles. Inspired by Schiller's magnificent play, Rossini takes heroic opera out of the fabled world of high romance and brings it into the mainstream of contemporary thought and feeling.

To his own taste, classical and conservative and as much at home with Handel's dramas of national liberation as Verdi's, he probably went too far. Written by a composer who feared civil insurrection, what he called 'the spirit of the barricades', *Guillaume Tell* is in many respects the first great opera of the *risorgimento,* a piece instinct with the revolutionary urge. This is a paradox to which, in performance, there is no easy resolution. Like the vision of Janus, the work, politically and stylistically, defies easy assimilation.

Where the work most happily and successfully arbitrates between the classical and romantic styles is in its highly developed sense of the suggestive beauty of landscape. From the cellos and cor anglais in the overture, through the folksongs and dances of the Swiss peoples, to the glorious end in which liberation and sunrise are blended with a mastery which the composer of

Das Rheingold and the author of *Zarathustra* must have wondered at, the score's tonal colourings are richly and sensitively handled. In the single soft drum-roll which punctuates Mathilde's cavatina – her dusk vigil by Lake Lucerne beneath the towering mountains of the Rütli plateau – we have one of the supremely affecting gestures of early nineteenth-century instrumental writing. Indeed, just as Verdi shows himself to be possessed of a sense of humour long before *Falstaff*, so Rossini, ever the man of sensibility, had long been a student of the picturesque, as pages in *Otello* and *La donna del lago* clearly reveal.

In later years Rossini was inclined moodily to write off the score's romantic elements – 'Music of a melancholy tint, peasants, mountains, and miseries'; but if the work caused him problems in later years their origin was not in mountains or miseries but in the tenor role of Arnold. It is a problem which is with us still.

In love with Mathilde, scion of the hated house of Habsburg, but committed to the Swiss cause by dint of his beloved father's murder by the tyrant Gessler, Arnold is the most highly individualized character in the drama. He is also confronted with one of the most fearsome roles in the tenor's repertory. By James Joyce's reckoning, his friend O'Sullivan ('incomparably the greatest voice I have ever heard, beside which Chaliapin is Braggadochio and McCormack insignificant': a judgement peculiar to Joyce) was faced in the role of Arnold with 456 Gs, 93 A flats, 54 B flats, 15 Bs, 19 Cs, and two C sharps. It is a formidable list. Even if it is remotely accurate, and assuming that the *ottocento* tenor took the 456 Gs on the chest, the modern tenor, to whom falsetto is anathema and head tone an implausible substitute, is still left with 183 fearsome ascents in the course of the role. Though the role, written at a turning-point in the history of the tenor voice, produced a new breed of iron-chested tenors, Rossini himself was never happy with the tribe he had unwittingly fathered. Speaking of the first of the breed, Gilbert-Louis Duprez, Rossini observed: 'That tone [the high C taken in the chest] rarely falls agreeably on the ear. Nourrit [the first Arnold] sang it in head voice, and that's how it should be sung.'

The role has destroyed a number of men. Adolphe Nourrit, one of the most gifted singers of his generation, a man who, under Rossini's influence, had helped effect a rapprochement between the Italian *bel canto* school and the declamatory style of the Opéra, was obliged to abandon 'Asile héréditaire' and its cabaletta after the third performance. Duprez's emergence in 1837 put paid both to Nourrit (who committed suicide in Naples in 1839) and to Rossini's faith in the vocal tradition for which *Tell* had been originally conceived. Since the time of Duprez *Tell* has been ruinously dogged by the dangers it holds for tenors. In his autobiography, *My Own Story*,* Luciano Pavarotti, Decca's Arnold on the newest complete recording, writes:

I once turned down an offer to sing Rossini's *William Tell,* though I was

* Sidgwick & Jackson, London, 1981

frantic to make my debut at La Scala. The role would have ruined my voice. I finished recording *William Tell* for London [Decca] not long ago, but we made the recording over two years [eleven months according to the Decca booklet] and my voice is stronger after eighteen years of singing. I still would not want to attempt *William Tell* on the stage.

With that salutary observation in mind we may now turn to the opera on record.

The first complete recording, complete in spirit if not in fact, cannot be much commended, though it promises well at the outset. It was made by Cetra in Turin in 1952. Its strengths are a dark-browed Tell, Giuseppe Taddei, imposing and implacable in the face of the tyrant Gessler; a Mathilde, Rosanna Carteri, who though frail and and frightened none the less cradles her cavatina affectionately; and a conductor, Mario Rossi, who vigorously pursues the score's ardent, revolutionary aspect, encouraging the assembled peasants, townsfolk, and confederate Swiss to a proper pitch of political disenchantment and a will to civil strife. There is also a powerful portrait of Melchthal, Arnold's father, by Plinio Clabassi. The recording, though, is coarse, blurring the opera's fine peroration; and there are weaknesses else-where in the cast. Fernando Corena is a muddle-voiced Gessler, Graziella Sciutti a shrill Jemmy and, worst of all, Mario Filippeschi is a scarifying Arnold. This is the set's effective undoing, for although Filippeschi begins plausibly, his duet with Mathilde and his Act 4 *scena* reveal him as progressi-vely inept: ill-tuned, lachrymose, and brutal. The performance is in Italian.

The 1973 HMV recording is sung in the original French; it is also genuinely complete. The Tell is Gabriel Bacquier, the Arnold Nicolai Gedda, Riccardo Muti's Arnold for the important Florence revival of 1972, the Mathilde, Montserrat Caballé, whose involvement in the recording of four roles in a single summer (Mathilde, Norma, Liù, and Giovanna d'Arco) drew sharp comment about 'assembly line' opera from Andrew Porter in *Opera on Record*. Some claim to find the set pallid. Primed for a first essay in romantic grand opera, they find a final essay in classical heroic opera, a performance conducted with sweetness, sensibility, and classical decorum by Lamberto Gardelli.

Bacquier's Tell is an essentially sympathetic figure, as much a father as a rabid patriot; an approach which would have sorted well with Rossini's own private predilections. 'I will tell you,' observed Rossini to Wagner in the famous conversation of 1860, 'that the sentiment that moved me most during my life was the love I had for my mother and father, which they repaid at usurious rates . . . It was there, I think, that I found the note that I needed for the scene of the apple in *Guillaume Tell*.' 'Quel fardeau que la vie!' sings Tell in the first scene, and Bacquier's Tell suggests, indeed, a Hamlet-like circumspection – 'Who would fardels bear / To grunt and sweat under a weary life . . . ?'. Later, he sings a poignant 'Sois immobile', always retaining the line's poise, the aria's essentially classical curve.

The classical restraint extends to some of the opera's critical moments, the start of the trio, for instance, the moment at which Arnold learns of his father's death at the hands of Gessler. Musically, it is a scene of untrammelled eloquence and Gedda allows it to register in its own terms. The duet with Tell in Act 1 is tolerably done; in 'Asil héreditaire' Gedda strikes the right note of heroic regret. Best of all are the scenes with Mathilde; 'Doux aveu' is especially fine. Throughout Gedda's performance there is a not unwelcome tendency to sketch high notes quietly in, head tone rather than the bludgeoning 'Ut de poitrine'. Some will put the approach down to technical incapacity, but it accords with the precedent of the Nourrit style.

However many recordings Caballé was engaged in at the time, she is ideally cast as the aristocratic Mathilde. The cavatina is especially affecting after a recitative which, it must be admitted, might be more purposefully shaped. The recording being complete, Caballé also has her Act 3 scene, finely done. There are no obvious weaknesses among the *comprimario* roles; Jocelyne Taillon sings Hedwige in exemplary French and Gwynne Howell, in one of his first major recordings, is an imposing Melchthal. Overall, the set has a pleasingly homogeneous feel, for which much of the credit must go to the conductor, Lamberto Gardelli. In the overture he stresses tone-painting more than pace. Occasionally he is too patient. Thus, though the reading has its own cumulative power, in the gathering of the Swiss vassals in Act 1 there is little of the score's revolutionary ardour, the danger that Rossi and Chailly so vividly articulate. On the other hand, the opera's end, which so magically arbitrates between Beethoven's brightening into thanksgiving in the *Pastoral* symphony and the close of *Das Rheingold* is handled with tact by the excellent HMV engineers and great imaginative inwardness by Gardelli himself.

The Decca recording, published in 1980, is a lavish and imposing affair built round the considerable person of Luciano Pavarotti. Italianate in origin, it is an Italian *Tell, Guglielmo Tell* rather than the elegant, sweet-sounding French version which Rossini originally composed. It is a red-blooded reading (roaring trombones in the overture) which cuts its way through Rossini's score in broad and purposeful swathes. As the set's prime mover, Pavarotti is something of a mixed blessing. Cast as the set's protagonist, he inevitably and wittingly invites comparison with the finest interpreters of the role on record. Certainly the voice is full of splendour, now trumpet-toned, now honey-sweet; yet it is often carelessly used. 'O muto asil', to take the most substantial scene first, is, comparatively speaking, a disappointment. Pavarotti's habit of making everything above the stave shine like fully polished and presented high Cs robs the singing of its subtler shades and half-lights. Older collectors will listen in vain for the suggestively soft placing of the high G in the third bar which was so compelling a feature of Tamagno's reading of the role. Worse, for this is not a detail but a structural fact, the great central *crescendo,* 'egli non m'ode più', is poorly prepared for and hastily phrased by both singer and conductor, dissipating a climax which now in no way organically flowers. The cabaletta, by contrast, is superb. In the great instigatory Act 1 duet between Tell and Arnold it is Chailly's fiery and purposeful conducting, conducting which would serve well middle-period Verdi, which gives point and dramatic coherence to Pavarotti's virile and generous (though in the pitching and pointing of descents occasionally casual) reading.

As much of the set's success is directly attributable to the fervent conducting of Chailly, it is odd how often in slower numbers he seems to misjudge the music's pace. There is, throughout, a tendency towards romantically protracted slowness in moments of introspection. In the great Act 2 duet between Arnold and Mathilde, the lyrical central section is taken at quaver = 60, ten beats slower than Gardelli and twenty beats slower than the score's metronome. And though Pavarotti is more expressive than Gedda at this point, and vastly superior to Filippeschi, the somnambulistic pulse militates against the score's dramatic sense. Mathilde, ever alert to the all-encircling danger, is no love-sick crooner (nor does Mirella Freni characterize her as such). This, and the wonderfully blazing cabaletta, suggests that Chailly, with all the characteristic waywardness of youth, prefers something a good deal more boldly drawn than Rossini has perhaps given us.

In the big tableaux the approach works well. The opening drags; but later there is no danger of the opera's civil and military panoply bogging down. Backed by a strong cast of *comprimarii* (Gessler and a wayward-sounding fisherman the only failures, Richard Van Allan, Della Jones, Elizabeth Connell and John Tomlinson all substantial successes), Chailly makes set pieces and dramatic transitions especially exciting. The Act 1 rescue is thrilling, Sherrill Milnes, the powerful saturnine Tell, at his blackest; and the act's end is a gramophonic epic, compelling to the ear alone thanks to the exceptionally bold playing and recording.

When Nicolai Ghiaurov joins Milnes and Pavarotti for the great trio in Act 2, we have another clear highpoint in the recording, made the more memorable by Pavarotti's compassionate rendering of Arnold's harrowing response to the news of his father's death. The sheer tonal thrust of the performance of the trio will test the tolerance both of machines' and collectors' nerves. To some ears the reading will smack of that very spirit of the barricades that Rossini so disliked; some will prefer the finely modulated HMV performance at this point; just as later, in the apple shooting, there is much to be said for Bacquier's way with 'Sois immobile': an intimate act of assurance beside public oration, the volcanic manner of Milnes, who continues (compare his recital on SER 5584) to treat the cadential phrase as a cue for a set-piece cadenza of disruptive force. As a foil to so much male aggression, Freni is a sensitive heroine. In the absence of some contemporary Muzio, Callas, or Tebaldi she serves admirably, less inclined to lose her way in recitative than Caballé on HMV, particularly thrilling in her Act 3 scene with Arnold, one of the set's highlights, and only occasionally yielding to Caballé in accuracy of detail or brilliance of tone.

On points of detail, Decca fit the opera onto four generously filled records as against HMV's five; they do not add, as HMV do, the putative Act 3 aria for Jemmy and they curiously banish the pas de six from Act 1 to a private cul-de-sac on side eight. As to a final choice, this must rest with personal predilections. Rossini, I fancy, would have preferred the French text and the general poise of the Gardelli reading, for all that Bacquier and Gedda are less than wholly heroic at times. The natural restraint of the HMV version yields a certain rare beauty at several key points. But no artist has a pre-emptive right over how his work should be performed, especially a work as stylistically ambiguous as this. And so, though cultivated Rossinians will probably continue to prefer the Gardelli, it is to Chailly that the unconverted should turn. His Verdian approach is arguably anachronistic but the perform-ance as a whole is as theatrically compelling an account of this seminal work as we are likely to hear on record for many a long year.

The highlights conducted by Marcel Couraud, with Jean Borthayre as Tell, Tony Poncet as Arnold and Irène Jaumillot as Mathilde can be largely discounted. The playing is rousing but the singing is sour. The EMI Electrola disc suffers from hectic, insensitive playing by the Orchestre du Théâtre National de l'Opéra under Alain Lombard and a woolly Tell, Ernest Blanc. As Gedda is heard to better effect in the complete HMV set, the record's interest is effectively confined to Andrea Guiot's Mathilde. She is an inter-esting artist; the voice has presence and a certain fresh charm. If the cavatina is less than wholly affecting it is again the conducting that is to blame, the drums rolling like harbingers of some revolutionary gibbet scene. To judge by these two French highlights records, France once again needs to reform its musical style. Crude declamation and insensitivity to *bel canto* values seem as rife now as they were at the time of Rossini's reforms in the late 1820s.

Neither Tell nor Arnold has a formal entrance aria. The opera's protagonist is the libertarian ideal, its context the mountains and mountain communities of beleaguered Switzerland. Tell and Arnold appear, as it were, *in media res*, figures in a landscape, the one mourning Helvetia's fate, the other a father's demise and an illicit love. Rossini grants Arnold no more than an impassioned recitative before the drama of love and paternity is subsumed into the larger theme of a nation's fate, the demands of a formal cavatina, mere subjective utterance, set aside in favour of a duet in which personal ambitions are subject to the discipline of human debate. The necessary poise is sensed by Gedda, Bacquier and Gardelli in the HMV recording. For many interpreters, though, the fact of ideals powerfully opposed, Verdian *scontro* some time before the thing itself, is the irresistible, simplifying element. The Decca team clearly feels this, and Taddei and Filippeschi are at their boldest here on the Cetra set. It is also evident on earlier 78rpm recordings. With Benvenuto Franci as Tell and Carlo Sabajno the lively conductor, Aureliano Pertile is pressured into conjuring up a 'dramatic' reading which sounds oddly dishevelled (DB 1480; LV 46). By contrast, Leo Slezak and Leopold Demuth sound genuinely stirring on a 1907 Hofoper record recorded in Vienna in

German (VA 57; LV 46). On the second side there is the opera's end, sounding, in German, even more like the final pages of *Das Rheingold*.

With recordings by Slezak and Demuth, Hermann Jadlowker and Eduard Habich (Poly 70524), Jacques Urlus and Walter Soomer (2–44231; GV 67), Robert Hutt and Heinrich Schlusnus (Gramm. 72748; LV 187), it is clear that, at the the turn of the century, the role of Arnold had been strangely transmogrified. In the wake of Duprez and Tamberlik it had become the preserve of the German *Heldentenor*. Given the coloratura potential of a singer like Jadlowker the effect is not necessarily unpleasing. Urlus's record is especially fine, cherishable for its tact and memorable for the clarity, the ease of vocal emission. Finest of all the confrontatory accounts of this stirring Act 1 meeting, though, is Giovanni Martinelli's (DK 129; Cantilena 6239). Here a fierce martial splendour is matched with a certain sensuous ease that at once heightens and humanizes the debate. The Tell in this memorable exchange is Marcel Journet.

Act 2 of *Guillaume Tell* includes Mathilde's cavatina, her duet with Arnold, and the great trio. Francis Toye wrote of it: 'It can scarcely be mere coincidence that this act, which is by far the best in the libretto and moreover the most closely related to Schiller's original, inspired Rossini to compose music, not only splendid in itself but exceptionally true to the psychology of the action. In short, once again we see of what this man was capable when his imagination really caught fire.'

It would be pleasant to be able to distinguish between the French and the Italian schools in Mathilde's 'Sombre forêt'; alas, 'Selva opaca' is more the rule than the exception. The finest French version is probably Caballé's on the complete set. Here are fine-spun tone, subtle placements, and authentic vowels. Joan Hammond's French (HLM 7042) is plausible, in spite of her disclaimer on the record's sleeve. In this, a Philharmonia recording made with Stanford Robinson, and in a 78rpm version with the Philharmonia Orchestra and Vilem Tausky (DB 21549), there is beauty touched with fear, wonder not entirely vitiated by the occasionally nasal intonation. Strangely, Hammond must be preferred to Eidé Norena (Parlo. RO 20177; EX 2901693) whose version, potentially bewitching, is cut to a single verse and over-elaborated at the cadenza.

Italian versions are heard from Frances Alda (DA 123; Club 99.45), Maria Callas (ASD 3984), Giannina Arangi-Lombardi (GQX 10281; LV 267), Toti Dal Monte (DB 831; LV 246), Claudio Muzio (Pathé 54025; OASI 564), Lina Pagliughi (LPC 50032), Rosa Ponselle (Am Col 68058D; GVC 9), and Renata Tebaldi (SDD 287). Riches indeed. Sadly, neither Pagliughi nor Ponselle is to be heard at her best, the one frail, the other dimly recorded, cut, and, like Norena, unstylishly elaborate in the cadenza. Nor does Dal Monte's consciously *bel canto* version stir the affections deeply. In the recordings by Alda and Arangi-Lombardi (the latter finely floated, virginal, sympathetic) the drum rolls are unceremoniously removed. Tebaldi's version, though by no means free from passing flaws in intonation, is the most aristocratic of the postwar versions. Callas's, frayed, memorable in spite of itself, is the most vividly alive to the *dilemma* of Mathilde. It is Claudia Muzio, though, who has most compelled the attention of this collector. That the version is cut is irrelevant; the performance, glowingly sung, has about it a certain romantic exaltation. In the dark voice and in the singer's bearing, there is both a royalty (here truly is a Habsburg princess) and a symbiotic kinship with the dark, glowering landscapes that hedge her in. It is, in short, a distillation of the imaginative world that is *Guillaume Tell*.

The duet between Mathilde and Arnold, alpha beta in an act that is more or less persistently alpha minus, has been poorly served by the gramophone. On the complete sets, Filippeschi appals, Gedda lacks romantic fervour, and Pavarotti is hamstrung by Chailly's dolorous tempi. Elsewhere the duet has been scarcely better served. A piano-accompanied version by Dezsö Aranyi and Margarete Siems (44273; Rococo 5379) is perhaps worth hearing but not collecting; Leo Slezak, with Grete Forst, is hypnotically beautiful, but are a dozen honeyed repetitions of 'Seligkeit', lovingly crooned, quite what this duet, in substance, is?

Three recordings of the great trio need to be noted. In French there is a version (Pathé 2501; Club 99.58) in which Agustarello Affre is joined by Henri Albers and Hippolyte Belhomme. There is a fine ringing quality in Affre's voice, but the characterization tends towards the statuesque; the sense of personal trauma is rarely uppermost. The Arnold of Léon Escalaïs (Fono. 39196; OASI 597) has a brilliant and heroic quality, dimmed only by the recording and some vagaries of pitch. 'Stupenda, estesa, vibrante e robusta' is how Fonotipia, his issuing company, put it. The record, and its sequel which continues the scene (Fono. 39342; ORX 506 – again with Antonio Magini-Coletti and Oreste Luppi) has a wind-tunnel surface. Finer and better recorded is the version in which Martinelli is joined by Giuseppe de Luca and José Mardones. Recorded in 1923, this version (DK 120; Cantilena 6239) is again exceptional.

The most recorded of all the arias from *Guillaume Tell* is 'Sois immobile', Tell's address to his son before the apple-shooting. Sweet-sounding, humane, elegantly and economically shaped, it is a piece which baritones have been happy to record. The aria was characterized by Wagner during his conversation with Rossini in Paris in 1860. Melody, proposed Wagner, must be free, independent, unfettered. 'As for that sort of melody, Maestro, you have stereotyped a sublime specimen in the scene of *Guillaume Tell*, "Sois immobile", where the very free song, accentuating each word and sustained by the breathing strokes of the violoncellos, reaches the highest summits of lyric expression.' Rossini's retort – 'So I made the music of the future without knowing' – and Wagner's unctuous reply – 'There, Maestro, you made music for all time, and that is best' – should not obscure from notice Rossini's earlier aside in which Wagner's unfolding theory is ironically characterized in the phrase *mélodie de combat*. In short, is 'Sois immobile' a *mélodie de combat*, Tell wrestling in phrases of declamatory beauty with a traumatic situation, or is it, as Julian Budden suggests in a perceptive analysis (*The Operas of Verdi*, Volume 1), a passionate plea sublimated into formalized lyric utterance, an essentially classical piece in which emotion, 'like a frieze' in the cello's melody, exists within a preordained lyric structure? Great baritones have offered both approaches, though they ignore the latter view at their peril.

The aria has perhaps been best served by three singers, Arthur Endrèze (Pathé X 90060), Giuseppe de Luca (66133; LV 173), and Giuseppe Taddei (LPC 55006); though Tito Gobbi's 1955 version (RLS 738) is deeply affecting, compellingly understated with a lovely tactile legato. Endrèze, a protégé of Reynaldo Hahn, is both eloquent and affecting. Though the voice is not of the richest, it is well used to distil many aspects of Tell's personality: tenderness, fear, and a certain majesty. One is moved by Tell's predicament in this version (which is sung in French), touched by his *politesse du coeur*. Taddei is compassionate but not lachrymose. The voice is in superb shape; there is much memorable legato singing; and the aria's classical pedigree is persistently respected. De Luca prefaces the aria with some recitative. Though more down-to-earth than some interpreters, he has the necessary fineness of spirit; and the vocal bearing is generally admirable.

Rival versions tend to fall into a number of broad categories, strongly influenced by language and nationality. Endrèze apart, the French versions are strangely mixed. Jean Noté (Od. 33185) and Henri Albers (Pathé 3518; GV 23) give mellow, sympathetic readings but others are undistinguished: Etienne Billot (Od. 188676; CBS 78313), Maurice Renaud (G&T 32079; RS 304 – the great baritone not at his best) and, in execrable French, Tom Krause (SXL 6327). Turning to the German school, the unobtrusive beauty of Leopold Demuth's 1903 version (2–42582; CO 303), a vocal exercise conducted largely independently of the encircling drama, is followed by the less evenly sung version of Karl Scheidemantel (3–42821; Discophilia DIS 251) and Joseph Schwarz (042508; LV 86), solemn and hieratic, more father confessor than father, before being transformed into the vaulted calm and strangely sentimentalized characterization of Dietrich Fischer-Dieskau (SLPM 138700), sung in Italian but very much of the German school. The Italian school yields declamatory performances in the high-Victorian manner by Battistini (DB 189; Cantilena 6210) and Nicola Rossi-Lemeni (3C 053–03249); *verismo* performances by Giuseppe Valdengo (SUA 10617), Francesco Maria Bonini (in many ways fluent, sensitive, and true on Fonotipia 59069) and Sherrill Milnes (SER 5584); long-drawn performances by Alessandro Sved (DB 5366; LV 33) and Paolo Silveri (DX 1585), hushed and imaginative in spite of a tendency to drag the pulse; unexceptionable performances by Gobbi (an alternative version on HQS 1436721), Benvenuto Franci (DB 1393; LV 171) and, the Gobbi style without the healing legato, Gino Bechi (DB 11322).

With 'Asile héreditaire', Arnold's aria of reminiscence with its fierce *Trovatore*-like cabaletta, we enter cowboy country. Happily, there are at least four distinguished French versions to see us through, as well as the celebrated Tamagno and Martinelli recordings. Of the French versions, Georges Thill (LFX 110) is the most easeful in timbre and aristocratic in line; André d'Arkor gives a finely coloured account (RFX 22; 2C 061–10672); René Verdière (Od. 188041; CBS 78313) is at once stylish and heroic; and Louis Orliac, though unduly impassioned for some tastes, shows a fine mastery of the text (ORX 132). The most assiduous collectors may also care to track down versions by Charles Fontaine (Pathé 59077), generally pleasing in spite of a swift pace, Grégoire (Polydor 52295), Ken Neate (heard to best effect on Le Chant du Monde LDXA 8170) and César Vezzani, a juicy-toned French *spinto* tenor, whose version (P816; Rococo 5234) has virility if nothing else.

With the Germans generally implausible in this music – the curious may care to hunt down Jadlowker (Poly. 72667; Rococo 5336) and Rudolf Gerlach-Rusnak (EG 2886; LV 71) or the Bulgarian Todor Mazarov (Preiser PR 9945) – we are left with 'O muto asil' and the Italians. Here several versions can be discounted. Escalaïs (39427; OASI 597) sings with deadened tone and climaxes which seem jumpy, inorganic; Francesco Merli is merely stentorian (GQ7145; 3C 053-1766); Mario Gilion (Fono. 39655; GV 96) is heavy-handed; and Giacomo Lauri-Volpi (LPC 55067), a famous Arnold in his day ('Bravo O'Sullivan – Merde pour Lauri-Volpi!' was James Joyce's insistent cry) was recorded too late in his career for us to hear him at his best. Alfredo Kraus (Carillon CAL 13) sings the Act 1 fisherman's air and 'O muto asil', gently, caressingly until the cadenza which strains badly. None the less, he is worth sampling as is Francesco Signorini (052230; GV 69) whose version has linear sweep and considerable tonal beauty.

The Italian versions are dominated, though, by Tamagno and Martinelli. Tamagno's versions (the 1903 sessions yielded the aria and cabaletta, 52682 and 52683, reissued on GEMM 208/9) are memorable for the softly placed G in the third bar and for the fine matching of the lyric and heroic styles. In the 1905 recording (052103; GEMM 208/9) we are aware of some technical constraints (a final high C is avoided) but the spaciousness of the reading is deeply satisfying. Martinelli (DB 339; Cantilena 6239) takes the music more swiftly than Tamagno. At times there is some sense of the singer straining for effect, but there is so much that is purely intoxicating, not least the rise through 'egli non m'ode più' and the climax's sovereign release, that criticism is effectively silenced.

No contemporary tenor equals Martinelli in mingled brilliance and intensity; though we should be grateful for Pavarotti's 1971 account of the scene (SXL 6498). The high tessitura singing would be accounted remarkable in any age. Where the complete recording seems portentous, strenuous, heavy-handed, the 1971 account is altogether finer-grained with cleaner more translucent tone. There is in this earlier version a sweetness, a tenderness, a fidelity to the essentially lyric character of Pavarotti's voice and style which compels attention; and Nicola Rescigno is a more sensitive accompanist than

Chailly. The twelve-second unwritten high C at the cabaletta's conclusion (by 1979 Pavarotti had cut its length by half) will not please the purist. 'Like the squawk of a capon whose throat is being cut' was Rossini's judgement on Duprez's high C. He would have probably said much the same thing about Pavarotti's, whilst at the same time showing appreciation of earlier sensitivity and restraint in the aria itself.

GUILLAUME TELL

M Mathilde; *J* Jemmy; *E* Edwige; *GT* Guillaume Tell; *A* Arnold; *G* Gessler; *Gu* Gualtier; *Mel* Melchthal

1952 (in Italian)
    Carteri *M*; Sciutti *J*; Pace *E*;
    Taddei *GT*; Filippeschi *A*; Corena
    G; Tozzi *Gu*; Clabassi *Mel* /
    Italian Radio Chorus and Orch.,
    Turin / Rossi Cetra ⓒ LPS 3232
    Turnabout ⓜ THS 65099–101
1973 Caballé *M*; Mesplé *J*; Taillon *E*;
    Bacquier *GT*; Gedda *A*; Hendriks
    G; Kováts *Gu*; Howell *Mel* /
    Ambrosian Opera Chorus, RPO
    / Gardelli EMI SLS 970
    Angel SELX 3793
1978–9 (in Italian)
    Freni *M*; D. Jones *J*; Connell
    E; Milnes *GT*; Pavarotti *A*;
    Mazzoli *G*; Ghiaurov *Gu*;

Tomlinson *Mel* / Ambrosian
Opera Chorus, National PO /
Chailly
Decca D219D4 ④ K219K44
London OSA 1446
1961 (excerpts)
    Jaumillot *M*; Kotthoff *J*; Mühl *E*;
    Poncet *A*; Borthayre *GT*; Van
    Haasteren *G*; *Gu* / Karlsruhe
    Opera Chorus and Orch. /
    Couraud
    Philips SGL 5650
1970 (excerpts)
    Guiot *M*; Gedda *A*; Blanc *GT* /
    Paris Opéra Orch. / Lombard
    EMI 2C 061 10899
    Seraphim S 60181

Donizetti's Tudor Queens

RICHARD FAIRMAN

In terms of survival, Donizetti's three Tudor operas have been as luckless as their wretched heroines. *Anna Bolena* was the most successful in its day, though even that was grudgingly received when it first came to London. The other two fared worse: neither *Maria Stuarda*, troubled by censorship problems, nor *Roberto Devereux* won itself a lasting foothold in the repertory. All three had faded from the stage by the 1880s. From then on, though *Lucia di Lammermoor* and *Don Pasquale* continued to play to appreciative audiences, the Tudor queens waited in the wings and were destined to stay there until the Donizetti revival of the 1950s. As a result these are works with no aural history. If anyone wants to know how singers at the turn of the century might have sounded in these operas he can only guess, for such records do not exist. Instead we have recent complete recordings of each work – a good deal more than could have been foreseen thirty years ago – and must be content with them. None of them makes any claim to authenticity as some Baroque reconstructions do. What we have here are modern productions in every way, aimed at audiences with different ideas about singing and acting styles. The performances all belong to what may be termed the 'post-Callas' era.

ANNA BOLENA

Anna Bolena had its first performance at the Teatro Carcano in Milan on 26 December 1830. Hailed as 'a triumphant success' even by Donizetti himself, it was to establish him in the front rank of Italian composers and spread his fame to both London and Paris. In all these cities the cast was headed by two of the greatest singers of the day, Giuditta Pasta and Giovanni Battista Rubini. The role of Anna Bolena had been specially tailored for Pasta, the great tragedian. On stage she was said to be majestic and restrained – one turn of her beautiful head or glance of her eye was enough to reveal a passion. Her style of singing was 'chaste and expressive', 'never disfigured by meretricious ornament'. (Writers from Chorley to Stendhal commend her very sparing use of embellishments.) As one biographer remarked, 'The crowning excellence of her art was its grand simplicity.' In Donizetti's first masterpiece it is precisely that 'grand simplicity' that confers distinction. This is a long opera, if performed complete. It has a conscious dignity of scale and execution: the recitative is rich in invention, the ensembles have strength of purpose and the style as a whole mines new reserves of musical character. *Anna Bolena* proclaims its composer's burgeoning authority at every turn. The work was given regular performances until the latter part of the nineteenth century and received more respectful treatment than most operas of its period.

The first modern revival of the opera took place in Bergamo in 1956, but it was the La Scala production a year later which restored *Anna Bolena* to her former glory. The opera was revived for Maria Callas in the title role, and it scored a triumph, both for her and the Donizetti revival. It is no coincidence that a live recording of this event marks the beginning of the Tudor trilogy on record. Callas gave only twelve performances of *Anna Bolena* – seven in this opening series, five in its revival the next year – but one would hardly realize it. Her portrayal is a totality, embracing intimate knowledge of the role. So often does she recall accounts of Pasta in the way she performs that the old tradition seems to be alive again. When Chorley saw Pasta in *Anna Bolena,* he said that her singing of the single word 'Sorgi' was enough to rouse a whole audience to enthusiasm. So it is with Callas here. It is impossible to forget her Olympian fury at 'Tu . . . mia rivale', or the grand resignation of her 'Va, infelice'. Just the words 'Coppia iniqua' can send a shudder down the spine.

Almost alone of latter-day artists, she has the power to grasp the emotional crux of every line and put it across. Like her predecessor, Callas is also economical in means. There is no place here for melodrama or dazzling ornamentation, the easy effects of those who have followed her. It is rather an instinctive feel for the music that shapes her performance. No detail is false to the overall conception; in drama and vocal colour she is wholly consistent, always weighty in timbre, rich in sovereign authority. When the conductor Rescigno asked her after a concert why she had shaped a phrase of this role in a certain way, Callas remarked simply, 'Because she is a queen.' Donizetti's Anna Bolena has been reborn. In the autumn of 1958 she made a commercial recording of the final scene (ASD 3801). This is a most accomplished piece of singing. Her command of the *bel canto* line is supreme and in the rising turns of 'Al dolce guidami' the covered tone is so expressive as to suggest some uncanny distant voice singing from the depths of Anna's soul. It recalls, perhaps inevitably, one of Chorley's descriptions of Pasta: 'There were a breadth, an expressiveness in her roulades, which imparted to every passage a significance totally beyond the reach of lighter, more spontaneous singers . . . The greatest grace of all, depth and reality of expression was possessed by this remarkable artist.' It is not enough for other singers to take up forgotten *bel canto* works just for the sake of novelty. These operas do have dramatic power; they will respond to serious study and devotion. Callas has established a tradition for others to follow.

She was fortunate in her colleagues at La Scala. Giulietta Simionato offers a forthright, strongly sung Jane Seymour; she is quite at ease in the high tessitura of the role. (The vocal range implies a soprano, but in recordings the part has been taken exclusively by mezzos and it is remarkable how successful they have been with it.) Gianni Raimondi is a capable Percy, not much more. Nicola Rossi-Lemeni sings well enough as Henry VIII, but has no imagination. The role looks interesting on the page, yet here it singularly fails to come to life. Under the trenchant, cumulative conducting of Gianandrea Gavazzeni the score builds up urgency and compulsion, reaching white heat at some climaxes. Only Serafin, in his short extract with Callas (see above), has the edge on this. Both maestros have an intuitive way with the music. They remind us that there is a world of freedom to be had in the *bel canto* style, known only to those who are inheritors of the grand tradition. The music sounds so much better for it – a far cry from the brash, circus-like tonic and dominant beaten out by some operatic ringmasters who have come after them.

Gavazzeni is also the conductor in another 'private' recording with Leyla Gencer in the title role. In general, this is a less compelling performance. Gencer is an impressive Anna Bolena, very much in the Callas tradition even down to details of phrasing. (Gavazzeni presumably coached them both.) The attack is true and the voice has brilliance and weight; but Gencer lacks the full vocal quality of her rival, and also her depth and memorability.

The Callas/La Scala performance is more than an introduction to the work; it is essential listening for anyone who wants to explore the uncharted emotional depths of Donizetti's score. But there is still a lot more of the opera to be heard. Gavazzeni's cuts in Milan were extreme. The overture has gone; so have Smeton's cavatina and the whole of the tenor's second-act scene, including the aria 'Vivi tu'. Smaller cuts remove a large proportion of the score. The arguments are obvious – the work is long; its score is weak in parts; the audience has only come to see the soprano, or the tenor, or whomever – but they are not sufficient. Too much of this music is indispensable. Indeed, Smeton's 'Ah, parea' and Percy's 'Vivi tu', sung by Rubini, were two items that were always picked out by critics for special merit. Henry VIII's music, savaged by Gavazzeni, is also too good to lose. He is no stock bass character, but a striking individual, imposing and thunderous, aweful in his power. (It is a measure of Donizetti's depth of composition that the King's domination is built up solely through the recitatives and ensembles; the role – a novel feature – has no aria.)

Commercial recordings have wisely rejected cuts as a self-defeating solution. Two have been issued so far, both of them admirably complete in text: Silvio Varviso's Decca set has a few minor cuts; Julius Rudel's HMV recording is complete to the letter, giving us every note of the Ricordi vocal score. Here is the whole grand design, the 'musical epic' noted by Giuseppe Mazzini after the première. Only when the opera is given in its entirety is it possible to appreciate the full scale and scope of Donizetti's imagination, the work's very backbone of grandeur. The mere presence of an overture is revealing: Donizetti often only supplied overtures for foreign theatres, notably Paris, where performance standards and audience expectations were higher than in Italy. But in *Anna Bolena* the overture is there, summoning our fullest attention, right from the start. In opening smaller cuts the complete recordings also reveal a strange paradox: Donizetti often constructs a scene by setting answering verses or sections for two soloists; take one away – as Gavazzeni does, for example, when he removes Henry's verse in the first act Henry VIII/Jane Seymour duet – and the audience is left at sea, unable to sense any structure or plan. We are simply tossed from one wave of new ideas to the next. The opera, perversely, seems longer. In the theatre, however, the old ideas still prevail. The only other live recording (Previtali 1975) keeps the overture, but discards just as much elsewhere as Gavazzeni did in Milan.

The expanded sections of the work do not always bring out the best in Varviso's set. Janet Coster's Smeton brings full, rich tone, but not much boyish spirit to 'Ah, parea'. John Alexander is no more than sturdy and reliable as Percy. But the recording should not be rejected, because the other three principals all give interesting, well-projected performances. In particular, Nicolai Ghiaurov is by far the best Henry VIII, the only bass with a first-rate voice in good condition and the vocal presence to match the role. The part was always strongly cast (Filippo Galli in Milan; Luigi Lablache in Paris and London) and it provides vocal writing of novel character, including coloratura scales and arpeggios which Ghiaurov accomplishes with ease. His handling of the slower *bel canto* line is also masterly and eloquent. Marilyn Horne's Jane Seymour is also well versed in the vocal arts of the period. Her coloratura is exact (she adds impressive decorations to the second-act *scena*); her singing in the lyrical passages is even and fluent, moving between notes without the explosive consonants that disrupt the vocal lines of her rivals. Unlike them, she does not make points by power alone, and hers is the most varied, many-sided Jane Seymour to be heard.

In the title role Elena Suliotis gives the set its most controversial element. On an earlier recital disc (SXL 6306) she gave a performance of Anna Bolena's final scene which comes closest of all to matching the achievement of Callas. For a singer in her early twenties it is a remarkable demonstration of gifts: the voice is glorious, rich in musical and dramatic overtones, and she displays a wholly mature grasp of the scene's dramatic temperature. Unfortunately by the time of the complete set her control has begun to slip. Intonation and phrasing go awry and the instrument, still often lustrous, is held on a looser rein. She has become a heroine of extremes: gusts of passion at one moment, lyric sensibility the next. To some extent Varviso's direction mirrors her wide-ranging, but flawed conception. His conducting never sounds idiomatic, but its restless examination of tempi and orchestral colour illuminates many concealed beauties in the score.

Julius Rudel in the HMV set takes a very different road. His manner is strict and rhythmically exact, securing a performance which has a sure feel for the way this music lays the basis for drama. We feel a stronger sense of direction than with Varviso in every scene. Rudel's cast is less magnificent in vocal quality, less diverse in vocal talents. The Anna Bolena is Beverly Sills, who is neither a Callas nor a Suliotis in voice, nor – one suspects – a Pasta. (All were commended on their grandeur of utterance.) It is a voice we shall come to know well in this chapter: shallow in tone and liable to a wobble under pressure, but at ease on high and fluent in coloratura. She is no canary; if anything, the opposite is true, and Sills is the most consciously dramatic Anna Bolena, always pushing her voice to greater limits for extra stress and excitement. Many lines are raised by an octave to give her more power. So much of what she does is commendable – the vitality of the text, the quick response to drama – that one wishes the final product were more impressive. But ultimately the role's dignity eludes her and we miss the 'profound sensibility' that has been noted in Pasta and the best that have followed her.

Shirley Verrett as Jane Seymour sounds more like a queen and might well have been considered for the title role. Hers is an impassioned performance. The way she attacks words (not in itself always a welcome feature) announces an authoritative figure, strong in profile. The top of the voice, so crucial to this role, sounds splendid, whether at *piano* or *forte*; the middle register, often hoarse or husky, does not. A further recording of 'Per questa fiamma' (SB 6790) confirms her striding attack. Stuart Burrows is the most musical Percy on any set and phrases with exemplary feeling. Yet one imagines that the original tenor's portrayal was rather different. When Rubini approached an aria like 'Vivi tu', he is said to have left hesitation and coldness behind him and poured forth 'fervour', 'passion' and 'consummate vocal art'. Burrows's Percy is never cold or hesitant; but he is not passionate either. His singing is respectful in the modern way. Paul Plishka is a dull Henry VIII.

One final performance demands attention, a 'private' live recording with Renata Scotto (Dallas 1975). This is an important set because Scotto is – remarkably – the only Italian prima donna of note to be heard in any of these three operas. (What would Donizetti have said of that?) She proclaims her nationality from the opening bars. The voice sounds Italian, clean and clear in tone, rarely varying in colour. Here too is the kick on the consonants, the bite in the vowels, the authentic rhythm of the speech that marks out the native Italian. All the recitative – and there is much of it in this score – comes alive. Nobody else delivers the tremendous line 'Giudici! . . . ad Anna!' with such verbal immediacy. (Only Callas has the grandiloquence for it.) Scotto's Anna Bolena is medium in scale, compact in power, generating forward drive from the words and their Italianate rhythms. Her individual seal is stamped upon the opera. More than any other, she has stayed apart from the influence of Callas; her singing is free from the older singer's colours, mannerisms and inflexions. But then Scotto's way too has its limitations. Her Anna Bolena is rarely moving. Even the final scene, often agonizingly slow, palpably unhinged by madness, fails to touch us as it should. Artifice and calculation reign here; and spontaneity, that crucial part of *bel canto* art, has been banished. One unexpected point: Scotto is the only singer of note who does not add appoggiaturas to grace the music. Her Jane Seymour, Tatiana Troyanos, is at the opposite pole, rich in tone but sometimes lacking in verbal nuance. The Percy and Henry VIII are both ordinary. Fernando Previtali conducts: his version has all the intense excitement of the La Scala performance, but also most of its cuts.

A few separate recordings exist from the opera. The full scene between Jane Seymour and Henry VIII starting at 'Fama! Si: l'avrete' is given by Fiorenza Cossotto and Ivo Vinco (LMR 5019) as a single, lengthy extract, notable for the mezzo's radiant tone, clear words and fine legato line. Montserrat Caballé (SER 5598) sings the first half of the final scene. The tone is luminous, but there is an over-burdening wealth of interpretative ideas, ever less effective as their number increases. Likewise, her duet recording of 'Dio che mi veda' with Verrett (SER 5590) has all the trappings of drama to little disciplined result. The same section of the finale is included on a recital disc by Maria Chiara (SXL 6548) with much beauty of voice, but there are no trills – a necessity in this piece – and the singer concentrates on notes rather than phrases. 'Private' souvenirs also remain of Virginia Zeani and Milla Andrew in the final scene. Neither is of great interest. Artists of English National Opera with Ava June in the title role offer 'Cielo, a miei lunghi spasimi' to piano accompaniment (ENO 1001); and there is a 'private' excerpt of part of the Jane Seymour/Henry VIII duet from Eiddwen Harrhy and John Tomlinson.

MARIA STUARDA

Of the three operas *Maria Stuarda* still causes the most controversy, albeit now for musicological reasons. The text exists in several different versions.*
Originally planned for a première at the Teatro San Carlo in Naples in 1834, the work was forbidden on the personal order of the King at the last moment and hastily rewritten by the desperate composer to a new story entitled *Buondelmonte*. From Donizetti's own description we learn of the dispiriting result, which involved a tenor in the lead role and the final prayer becoming a 'fine, full conspiracy'. Undeterred, however, he pressed for a production of *Maria Stuarda* in Milan and made the offer more attractive by revising the score: a newly composed overture was added and the title role was specially adapted for its new prima donna, Maria Malibran. Some numbers from the opera, published at the time by Ricordi, also suggest other minor changes, including a different version of the tenor's first-act cabaletta 'Se

---

* For a more detailed discussion of this complex problem see the *Donizetti Society Journal,* issue No. 3.

fida tanto'. This version of the work had its première at La Scala, Milan on 30 December 1835. Unfortunately the autograph scores of both versions have been lost. Recent recordings, forced to rely on secondary material, have usually chosen to give the opera as it is known from the edition published by Gérard in Paris (c.1855). It is argued that this version is the closest to Donizetti's Naples original – it is headed 'Riduzione per canto e pianoforte dell'autore' – and for that reason it has gained a wide currency. Two recordings, however, introduce material from the 1835 Milan version; most, regardless of text, have cuts or transpositions. A letter of 1837 suggests that Donizetti would have been less outraged at this than modern critics:

> [The duet for] Mary and Leicester before the first finale – cut it, because it is intrusive and does not stand well . . . Cut also the duet for Leicester and Elizabeth; if the latter is not a strong performer, let it be reduced to recitative. This is my opinion; for other things I recommend myself to you, either to leave in or to cut out whatever you believe better or worse.

Such alterations were often made to suit individuals. When the composer was not present, the singers took the matter into their own hands: rewriting of florid passages and transpositions were usual, and some artists would arrive with *arie di baule* (arias in their trunks) to insert into an opera, regardless of whether they were appropriate or not. In revising the role of Maria Stuarda for Malibran, Donizetti had to adapt it for a mezzo and a virtuoso. The results are fascinating. Not only is the coloratura more dazzling, but the vocal writing also makes great play at both extremes of the singer's compass. Countess Merlin tells us in her memoirs that Malibran's range descended 'to F and E flat below the lower C and reached C and D in alt'. No wonder present-day Mary Stuarts prefer to stay with Gérard. Only Sutherland, of the singers in the complete sets, chooses to include some of the variants made in Milan.

The pieces of the Milan edition published by Ricordi suggest that Malibran did not use transpositions in this opera, though we know that she did so elsewhere. If mezzos today want to follow her lead and take on Donizetti's soprano roles, it is ungenerous of us to complain. They are carrying on tradition, not breaking it. Two singers in the recordings under discussion do so: Huguette Tourangeau as Queen Elizabeth in the Decca set keeps mostly to the original keys, but rearranges the vocal line and cadenzas; Janet Baker in the title role of the HMV set retains the original vocal part but transposes down, either by a tone or semitone. (When Bellini transposed 'Qui la voce' in *I Puritani* for Malibran, he lowered it by a minor third.) By nineteenth-century standards these are minor alterations.

Even in its revised version *Maria Stuarda* failed to win a success. The story goes that Malibran was ill on the opening night and sang only to collect her fee of 3000 francs. After a mere handful of performances the censors intervened again and from then on the first act was given alone, followed by two acts of Rossini's *Otello* to make up an evening. It seems that the strong language and audacious portrayal of royalty and religion in the libretto were felt as acutely in Milan as they had been in Naples. A few other theatres, including Florence and Venice, mounted the opera with their own emendations. But by this time *Maria Stuarda* had won itself a reputation as a work that not even Malibran could rescue. For almost a hundred years it remained unperformed, the 'vil bastarda' of the Tudor trilogy.

After such misfortune the work deserves a sympathetic hearing. Its score may not be uniform in quality, but it does have the power to stir emotion. *Maria Stuarda* is a work of compassion and never more so than in the portrayal of its heroine, who is drawn in lines of limpid tenderness. Donizetti has worked with skill here, focusing attention on Mary Stuart in ever more penetrating detail. Her confession scene with Talbot – though not great music – goes to the heart. The high point of the drama is the famous, unhistorical meeting of the two queens, carried off with such brilliance by the composer and his librettist, Bardari. (It was not an original idea; many operas were written on this subject and a *Maria Stuarda* by Coccia, including a similar confrontation scene, had already been mounted for none other than Giuditta Pasta.) Rival sopranos today may no longer regard this as an excuse for a scrap on stage, as Ronzi and Del Serre did at one of the last rehearsals in Naples in 1834, but the scene still guarantees dramatic excitement, as the numerous live recordings show. History's judgement has turned upside down. The opera now attracts more attention than its Tudor counterparts.

Maria Stuarda made a typically unfortunate return to the stage when it had its first modern revival at Bergamo in 1958. A 'private' recording shows that the text was heavily truncated and what remains gets shabby treatment. Cabalettas and cadential passages are cut throughout the score; even Mary's entrance aria is reduced by half. The set has more importance as history than as art. Dina Soresi is a musically polite Mary Stuart with barely the spirit for the role. More positive characterization comes from Renata Heredia Capnist as Queen Elizabeth; but neither she, Nicola Tagger as Leicester nor Antonio Zerbini as Talbot is more than adequate. At best the singing is free from the choppy phrasing and aspiration which have marred some other performances. Olivero de Fabritiis leads an inert account which belies its live origins. The Gérard edition is used, but its orchestration demands attention. The full score in general use, unexpectedly weighty in orchestration, is believed to have handed down a corrupt version of Donizetti's original, revised to suit the tastes of a later generation. But this Bergamo performance has revised that revision yet again, probably to avoid copyright restrictions, and the composer's intentions recede still further from view.

A similar text is found in the 'private' recordings with Montserrat Caballé in the title role. These include performances from New York (American Opera Society at Carnegie Hall cond. Cillario 6 December 1967), Milan (La Scala cond. Cillario 13 April 1971) and Paris (Salle Pleyel cond. Santi 26 March 1974). The Gérard edition is used; and so is the doubly corrupt orchestration of the Bergamo performances. In the French recording especially, Caballé excels in the tender, lyrical passages which are such a feature of the part. Generous and balmy, her golden voice basks in the long cantilena of her opening aria (transposed down to C) and proves not immobile in the cabaletta. She decorates very little but has no need for more, because she finds all the expressive material she needs in the essential notes that Donizetti provides. This is, in general, a passive heroine, though the confrontation scene excites her to excess. Faced with a performance as melodramatic as this, we can believe stories of Malibran tearing up her handkerchief and gloves at this point in compulsive rage. Caballé is clumsy in her few moments of dramatic awareness. But her glowing, de luxe vocalism has – almost accidentally, one feels – hit upon a basic truth of the role: her Mary Stuart exudes warmth and sympathy. In New York she is paired with Shirley Verrett, a scalding Elizabeth who sings with the full efficiency of tone and attack missed by other interpreters; and in Paris José Carreras is an ardent Leicester. None of the other singers rises above the routine. Carlo Felice Cillario in New York is a less exciting conductor than his counterpart in Paris, Nello Santi. Both indulge their prima donna's penchant for slow tempi and make the usual cuts.

The text of the ABC/HMV commercial recording marks a great advance. It offers as complete a version as possible, made from a combination of sources. The Gérard edition is preserved complete (no cuts) and is supplemented for good measure by the additional overture composed for Milan in 1835. (This is, sadly, a weak piece, unconvincingly episodic in structure. The main point of interest is an unusual link with the opera in its quotation of the cabaletta 'Nella pace del mesto riposo'.) The 1865 orchestration is played without further revisions. In the title role, Beverly Sills gives us the best of her three Tudor queens. There is less need for grandeur here, and the role adapts well to her resources.

The first aria is representative of strengths and weaknesses: Sills phrases fluently and with feeling – but, in contrast, Caballé has a wealth of tone, a finer eloquence; and Janet Baker will bring to it more haunting, nostalgic colours. Each stays in the memory as a more special performer. The final scene has the same limitations. Sills is vivid and wins real sympathy, but she fails to stir the underlying feelings of hurt and injustice. The drama does not cut deep, as it should. One is, at least, unlikely to forget her decorations. She is extravagant with ornaments throughout, starting from her first line where the word 'gioir' becomes a vast cadenza over one-and-a-half octaves. The aria 'Di un cor che more' is almost unrecognizable. (At this point a modern composer would sue.) Many critics have chided her, but a precedent is close to hand. This is just the kind of embellishment that Malibran loved. In *Il matrimonio segreto* she is said to have taken the word 'insolente' and turned it into a brilliant cadenza from high C to the bottom of her voice.

The other soloists on the HMV set lack a dominating presence. Eileen Farrell's Elizabeth has traces of a former grandeur, but her singing is insufficiently firm and has little of the specific perception needed to bring the part to life. Stuart Burrows is a very English-sounding Leicester and Louis Quilico an adequate Talbot. Aldo Ceccato's direction is sluggardly, but idiomatic. At best it senses the mood of the work and moves without undue fuss to match its atmosphere.

Nothing could be more different than the Decca set which followed it. Here are glorious voices in their prime, stars full of temperament, and a conductor eager to impress us with his fast tempi and overt theatricality. At times the result comes close to being a boisterous vocal jamboree. The text is the most complex so far. In short, we have another amalgam of versions: the 1835 overture is not included; nor are the minor variants believed to have been made for Milan; but this is the only recording which does make use of the major changes introduced for Malibran at that time. The rewritten parts occur in Mary Stuart's opening and closing scenes. (The version that we are given here presents the two verses of the cabaletta 'Nella pace nel mesto riposo' in different keys, the first in B flat, the second in D flat, an extraordinary effect.) The 1835 orchestration is used. In addition, there are cuts; modifications have been made for the mezzo Huguette Tourangeau as Queen Elizabeth; and the leading singers decorate their parts. Mary Stuart's vocal line cannot be taken to represent exactly what Malibran was given to sing. This performing version is true to the spirit rather than the letter of the score.

Joan Sutherland in the title role excels in just that brilliant and exuberant writing that we know Malibran liked best. Her singing is remarkable for its agility and fullness of tone, outstanding not only in the cabalettas but also in the precise delivery of those small trills and turns which decorate the slower melodies. The role is characterized in a general way. But there is no individuality, and those 'tender strokes of art which pierce instantly to the heart', such as made Malibran so memorable, are missing. The role of Elizabeth has been skilfully arranged so as not to take Huguette Tourangeau often above a G, but the way every climax is lowered down into her chest register – even ending one duet lower than her tenor – begins to sound like exhibitionism. Her singing is idiosyncratic in its managing of tone and words. Luciano Pavarotti is a first-rate Leicester, ardent and full-throated in manner. Here is some of the Latin excitement that we might wish for in tenors elsewhere. Roger Soyer is an imposing Talbot. All the cast are at the top of their vocal form.

HMV's live recording of a production by English National Opera gives the opera in English translation. In the early 1970s, when the production was new, it was possible to admire Janet Baker's performance in the title role as a vocal display. By 1982, the year of the recording, it is rather the careful husbanding of resources that commands respect. The voice sounds hard pressed and is managed with obvious strain around the top of the stave; the tone can jar and there is often a wobble. Yet what remains is more than a shadow of the original. Here, for the first time, we seem to 'live' the role and sense the full impact of Donizetti's score.

One advantage, of course, is unique: Baker is the only important Mary Stuart who is singing in her native language, but then it is typical of her that the fact should register with such boldness. It is not simply that the words are clear – often, in fact, they are not; the vowels are too heavily covered – but that she projects them with such a powerful charge of emotion. 'Heaven rejects me' is a cry of bitter finality; 'Ah, what torture' speaks of suffering to the core. Nothing she does is casual or complacent. One senses that she is always exploring her voice for expressive effect and the performance ranges widely over colours and inflexions. In the confrontation duet there is painful humiliation; in the confession scene deep religious devotion. All aspects of the character are here. Where Caballé and Sutherland remain fairly anonymous figures, Baker has become quite recognizably the Mary Stuart of tradition. Hers is the only performance to touch tragedy in its final moments.

The set as a whole does not provide exalted singing, as do the best of its rivals. It does, however, have an impressive Elizabeth in Rosalind Plowright, a singer who works on a grand scale, filling the auditorium with sound and leaving doubts only when her huge voice takes time to open out on high notes. The phrasing that results can sound gusty. David Rendall as Leicester has some exciting moments but is not always consistent in tone. Decent support comes from Alan Opie as Cecil and John Tomlinson, notable for his clear diction, as Talbot. Charles Mackerras's direction is the best that can be heard, urgent and concentrated, but also quick in appreciating the changing moods of the score. This is a 'live' performance in every sense. The text is the Gérard edition – despite the presence of the only mezzo Mary Stuart – and has the usual cuts in cadential passages. A few extra bars are added at the end to give Mary time to leave the stage. One small point: when Mary Stuart rounds on Queen Elizabeth with the single word 'No!' in the confrontation scene, Janet Baker leaves the written note (a low E) and substitutes a higher, dramatic exclamation. (Though a mezzo, she lacks strength in the lower register.) She did not do so at earlier performances. Sutherland takes the E up an octave; some just shout it to make an effect.

This HMV recording widens our perception of the opera. It also throws up an interesting precedent. When the Spanish Malibran came to sing *La Sonnambula* in London in 1833, she did so in English – 'that language of parrots', as Bellini remarked – and so moved the composer with her singing of the words 'Ah, embrace me' that he called out in admiration from his box. (One longs to know how she stayed afloat in the rest; the translation she had was enough to scupper a native English speaker.) It is a salutary reminder of the power these operas should wield. This is the real *bel canto*, alive in its words, demanding spontaneous approval. In the recordings of *Maria Stuarda* the art is only spasmodically in evidence. Baker has it; so, in a less original way, does Sills. But the others in the title role do not: they make the most of the insults in the confrontation scene, then lapse into the kind of vague enunciation that would be appropriate for any operatic situation. Artists in lesser roles (notably Verrett and Pavarotti) often make more effect. Donizetti is the loser: his music seems drained of strength and variety, the empty sort of rum-ti-tum that his detractors accuse him of writing.

Other recordings add little to our knowledge. There are few excerpts: one 'private' issue offers the overture performed by the Philomusica Orchestra under Alun Francis, Elizabeth's aria from Eiddwen Harrhy and Mary Stuart's entrance aria from Yvonne Kenny. (The last is the Milan edition arranged for Malibran, but now – unlike what we hear in Bonynge's set – the two verses of the cabaletta are both in the key of B flat.) Another record has Franco Tagliavini in a reasonable account of the tenor's aria. This may come from another 'private' recording made at the Florence Festival of 1967, where he sang opposite Leyla Gencer and Shirley Verrett. (The issue is difficult to obtain.) In the future we may well get a more accurate account of the 1835 Milan version of the score than we have had so far. But, for all the different editions and the extra sparkle written into the Milan version for Malibran, the choice of text ultimately makes little difference. *Maria Stuarda* is much the same opera, whichever version is used. It is the performer of the title role who dictates its success or failure.

ROBERTO DEVEREUX

Roberto Devereux is the least well represented of the three Tudor operas on record. The work had its première in Naples on 29 October 1837, its cast led by Giuseppina Ronzi de Begnis as Queen Elizabeth, the singer who was to have taken the title role in the Naples première of *Maria Stuarda*. She received handsome compensation. The Elizabeth of *Roberto Devereux* is a formidable portrait, setting the singer high on a pedestal of awesome power and regality. (Ronzi, fresh from her queenly brawl in *Maria Stuarda*, must have loved it.) In vocal terms she is Donizetti's Norma: there are the same torrents of anger, the same biting declamations in the chest register and raging downward scales as in Bellini's masterpiece. In the final scene Donizetti also aspires to a comparable nobility of stature. (This last is despite Cammarano's melodramatic text.) It is no surprise to find that the role was soon taken by Giulia Grisi, a noted Norma in her day.

The overbearing presence of Queen Elizabeth gives this opera as a whole its special character; but, for all that, *Roberto Devereux* is more than a one-woman show. The other major roles, notably the baritone Nottingham, are developed at length and the work also has the capacity – even if fitfully displayed – to build up a powerful charge of dramatic tension. It is not enough for a performance to have a soprano and nothing else. We need a fully capable company, ready to deliver the work as viable theatre. In Naples, the première of the opera was a success and Donizetti himself supervised four further productions. One of these was the Paris première of the work at the Théâtre-Italien in 1838, for which he wrote three new pieces: an overture; a new cabaletta for the first act duet between Elizabeth and Robert; and a new tenor aria in Act 3. (The tenor was Rubini.) The opera continued to have revivals until the 1870s. As with *Maria Stuarda*, there are problems regarding the text. The original manuscript is believed to have been lost during the Second World War and the current score is one compiled and orchestrated by Mario Parenti. It has been the basis for all the recordings. The original Ricordi vocal score, undated, reveals a number of discrepancies: in particular, there is no overture and the first-act duet between Elizabeth and Robert is different, but the third-act tenor aria (last of the Paris amendments) is the same. In either version the opera has a lot of good music and is well worth its revival.

The first important modern production of *Roberto Devereux* was in Naples, its home town, in 1964. The performances did not get good reviews at the time, but a 'private' recording of one of them now tells a slightly different story. The opera was given almost complete (only a few minor cuts) and was well cast. Leyla Gencer is a regal Queen Elizabeth; she really commands the role. Her voice, especially at the beginning of the evening, lacks ease and a sure centre, but by the *Norma*-like trio she has built up an imposing presence. The shadow of Callas is with us, as always. Glottal stops, covered tones and flashes of a growling chest register pay homage to her influence. Ruggero Bondino is a workaday Roberto Devereux; Anna Maria Rota a dramatic Sara. The most valuable contribution, especially in retrospect, comes from the Nottingham of Piero Cappuccilli, whose firmness of tone and sure handling of the drama have yet to be equalled. The part is a rewarding one, spanning *bel canto* lyricism and dramatic brilliance – a showpiece for the artistry of a Battistini. (The opera was in his repertory, but he recorded nothing from it.) Mario Rossi in Naples leads his forces with a fine sense of theatre. The singers are well balanced; the text is spoken with just sense and proportion. In short, the opera 'works' and this remains one of its most convincing performances.

Any singer who takes on the role of Queen Elizabeth needs a formidable range of virtues. As well as the usual demands of *bel canto*, this part calls for commanding power in the finales, unusual stamina and a truly majestic vocal presence for the extraordinary *maestoso* cabaletta which is the crown of the work. If Nottingham is to be a Battistini, then Queen Elizabeth must be a Lilli Lehmann or a Callas and nothing less. In recent years the most successful exponent has been Montserrat Caballé. Her interpretation can be heard from various sources: there is a single commercial extract of the final aria 'Vivi ingrato' (SB 6647); and complete 'private' recordings exist from New York (American Opera Society cond. Cillario 1965) and Aix-en-Provence (with José Carreras cond. Rudel 2 August 1977). The separate 'Vivi ingrato' has no cabaletta or chorus backing, but it does give us Caballé at her best. The pacing in the recitative may sometimes seem hasty and some of her mannerisms are careless, but there is in her broad musical span an amplitude of voice and phrasing that sets her among the most considerable of present-day sopranos. On stage her vocal capabilities are hardly diminished. She rearranges some of the awkward coloratura to suit her, but

contemporary sopranos would certainly have done the same. The main difference in these live performances is that her desire to be dramatic has introduced unwelcome features – aspiration, melodramatic enunciation and
extremes of volume – which compromise her eloquence. All this hard work
betrays dramatic insecurity. The role is not hers by divine right. In general,
she is poorly supported by her accompanying casts.

The performances of Beverly Sills in the role are also well documented.
She plays Queen Elizabeth in the only commercial set of the opera and there
are, in addition, a separate extract of 'Vivi ingrato' (ASD 2578) and a
complete 'private' recording of a live performance given at New York City
Opera (1970). The live recording is the most interesting. Heard in the ambience of a theatre, Sills's vocal powers are easier to establish: the voice sounds
small and the fast vibrato is unappealing, but the sheer precision of the
singing cannot be denied. The coloratura is absolutely accurate; the ornaments are well chosen. The role is also vividly exploited, but at crucial
climaxes she shouts out in a vulgar way to make an effect. This last failing
is symptomatic of a larger problem: Sills's portrayal is simply too small in
scale and, try as she may, she is unable to rise to tragic heights. Her Elizabeth
is a fiery, dominating woman – but she is not a Tudor queen. The commercial
set confirms her characteristics.

Among the supporting cast in New York is the young Placido Domingo
as Roberto Devereux. He brings to the part full, warm tone and great variety
of expression. Tenor singing of this strength would be welcome in all the
sets. Louis Quilico's Nottingham is clumsy, a sign of the difficulty present-
day baritones, reared on Verdi and the *verismo* repertory, have in making
a role like this interesting. The great advantage of the performance is the
company spirit, led by the conductor Julius Rudel. His direction has the
ability to mark rhythms with point and purpose, finding meaning in all that
is small without losing direction in the overall design. The HMV commercial
set is not on the same level of achievement. Neither Robert Ilosfalvy as
Roberto Devereux nor Peter Glossop as Nottingham offers much of distinction: the former is wanting in musical grace; the latter is gruff in tone
and four-square in phrasing. Charles Mackerras conducts the score with
musicianship, but not enough life. Rossi's set, rough and unsubtle, is better;
the opera thrills and with it imprints itself on the memory.

With its quotations from 'God save the Queen' and busy contrapuntal
writing, the overture makes an attractive extract. There is a performance by
the LSO under Richard Bonynge (SXL 6235), notable for the high quality
of its orchestral playing and its rumbustious delivery. Vocal excerpts are
again few. A 'private' recording exists of Janet Price, Graham Clark and
Christian du Plessis in anonymous readings of the second and third act finales
under Alun Francis. On commercial records, the first act duet between Sara
and Roberto Devereux is sung by Katia Ricciarelli, a sympathetic and
soprano Sara, and José Carreras (9500 750). Two singers surpass their rivals
on the commercial set: Renato Bruson, who sings Nottingham's aria and

cabaletta (GRV 9) with a fine legato and resonant tone; and Raina Kabaiv-anska in the whole of the final scene (RL 31555), giving a good, professional performance. Now that Callas has 'opened the door' to these operas, as Caballé has put it, may there be more sopranos who take them on. There is plenty of opportunity for advancement.

ANNA BOLENA

E Enrico; *AB* Anna Bolena; *G* Giovanna Seymour; *RP* Riccardo Percy; *R* Rochefort; *S* Smeton; *H* Hervey

1957 (live performance – Teatro alla Scala, Milan) Rossi-Lemeni *E*; Callas *AB*; Simionato *G*; Raimondi *RP*; Clabassi *R*; Carturan *S*; Rumbo *H* / La Scala Chorus and Orch. / Gavazzeni Cetra ⓜ LO 53(2)

1959 (broadcast performance) Clabassi *E*; Gencer *AB*; Simionato *G*; Bertocci *RP*; Maionica *R*; Rota *S*; Carlin *H* / Italian Radio Chorus and Orch. / Gavazzeni Melodram ⓜ MEL 081 Replica ⓜ RPL 2407–9

1970 Ghiaurov *E*; Suliotis *AB*; Horne *G*; Alexander *RP*; Dean *R*; Coster *S*; De Palma *H* / Vienna State Opera Chorus, Vienna Opera Orch. / Varviso Decca SET 446–9 London OSA 1436

1972 Plishka *E*; Sills *AB*; Verrett *G*; Burrows *RP*; Lloyd *R*; Kern *S*; Tear *H* / John Alldis Choir, London SO / Rudel HMV SLS 878 (4) MCA ATS 20015

1975 (live performance – Dallas Civic Opera) Flagello *E*; Scotto *AB*; Troyanos *G*; Grilli *RP* / Dallas Civic Opera Chorus and Orch. / Previtali HRE HRE 348 (3)

MARIA STUARDA

MS Maria Stuarda; *E* Elisabetta; *L* Leicester; *T* Talbot; *A* Anna; *C* Cecil

1958 (live performance – Teatro Donizetti, Bergamo) Soresi *MS*; Capnist *E*; Tagger *L*; Zerbini *T*; Zannini *A*; Jori *C* / Teatro Donizetti Chorus and Orch., Bergamo / De Fabritiis EJS ⓜ EJS 174

1967 (live performance – Florence Festival) Gencer *MS*; Verrett *E*; Tagliavini *L*; Ferrin *T*; Di Stasio *A*; Fioravanti *C* / Florence Festival Chorus and Orch. / Molinari-Pradelli Opera Viva ⓜ JLT7

1967 (live performance – Carnegie Hall, New York) Caballé *MS*; Verrett *E*; Gimenez *L*; Bottcher *T*; Kieffer *A*; Baker *C* / Chorus and Orch. / Cillario

MRF 13 S

1971 (live performance – Teatro alla Scala, Milan) Caballé *MS*; Verrett *E*; Garaventa *L*; Washington *T*; Fioravanti *C* / La Scala Chorus and Orch. / Cillario Morgan 7101 (3)

1971 Sills *MS*; Farrell *E*; Burrows *L*; Quilico *T*; Kern *A*; Du Plessis *C* / John Alldis Choir, London PO / Ceccato HMV SLS 848 MCA ATS 20010

1974 (live performance – Salle Pleyel, Paris) Caballé *MS*; Vilma *E*; Carreras / Chomsand Orch. / Santi HRE HRE 296

1974–5 Sutherland *MS*; Tourangeau *E*;

Pavarotti *L*; Soyer *T*; Elkins *A*;
Morris *C* / Teatro Communale
Chorus and Orch., Bologna /
Bonynge
Decca D2D3 ④ K2A33
London OSA 13117

1983 Baker *MS*; Plowright *E*; Rendall
L; Tomlinson *T*; Opie *C*; Bostock
A / English National Opera
Chorus and Orch. / Mackerras
HMV SLS 5277

ROBERTO DEVEREUX

E Elisabetita; *N* Nottingham; *S* Sara; *R* Roberto

1964 (live performance) Gencer *E*;
Cappuccilli *N*; Rota *S*; Bondino *R*
/ San Carlo Opera Chorus and
Orch., Naples / Rossi
EJS ⑩ EJS 307 (2)

1965 (concert performance – Carnegie
Hall, New York) Caballé *E*;
Alberti *N*; Chookasian *S*; Oncina
R / American Opera Society
Chorus and Orch. / Cillario
⑩ MRF 823

1969 Sills *E*; Glossop *N*; Wolff *S*;
Ilosfalvy *R* / Ambrosian Opera
Chorus, RPO / Mackerras

HMV SLS 787 (3)
MCA ATS 20003

1970 (live performance – New York
City Opera) Sills *E*; Quilico *N*;
Marsee *S*; Domingo *R* / New York
City Opera Chorus and Orch. /
Rudel
HRE HRE 374 (3)

1977 (live performance – Aix-en-
Provence Festival) Caballé *E*;
Sardinero *N*; Marsee *S*; Carreras
R / Aix-en-Provence Festival
Chorus and Orch. / Rudel
HRE HRE 231 (3)

Lucrezia Borgia and La Favorite

MAX LOPPERT

Even a convinced Donizettian could not quite foresee how rewarding and enjoyable the discharging of this assignment would prove to be. That both operas require to be numbered among the most durable of Donizetti can be demonstrated in the tenacity with which, even in the long period when most of his works were banished from popular and critical favour, they maintained a hold on the repertory (*La Favorite*, because of its mezzo-soprano heroine, has been kept in circulation this century, particularly in Italy, by leading singers from Stignani to Cossotto eager to take advantage of opportunities all too rarely offered to their vocal type). Listening on records, repeatedly and in bulk, represents another kind of test of a work's staying power. Both passed it triumphantly.

The fact is that, as the enthusiasts of the Donizetti Society are always insisting, in the finest of his works there is more to the composer than purveyor of surefire operatic entertainment. Both these operas are certainly that: the boldly assorted colour contrasts of *Lucrezia Borgia* can be relied upon to make an irresistible effect in the theatre, while the grander and more spacious vein of *La Favorite* (befitting a work composed for the Opéra of Meyerbeer's heyday) needs only a similarly elevated style of performance too seldom granted it to make its mark as a powerful and eloquent music-drama. Yet repeated exposure to the operas underlines the innovative imagination Donizetti brought to both tasks; devices we may be used to thinking of as Verdian turn out to be wittingly exploited by his predecessor (*Rigoletto* and *Trovatore* are repeatedly 'heard' in *Lucrezia Borgia*, and *Forza* and *Don Carlos* in *La Favorite*). Repeated exposure underlines, no less, those passages in which, by contrast with the most striking inventions of the operas, Donizetti's inspiration shows signs of flagging, or of settling for a vigorously conventional mode of expression rather than the circumvention or even contradiction thereof for which both works are notable. 'In the tragic genre,' Julian Budden concludes in his Donizetti entry for the *New Grove Dictionary*, '[he] was both more and less than a great composer: more in that he summed up within himself a whole epoch: less in that no single one of his tragic operas makes the impact that one expects of an unqualified masterpiece. All are subject to relapses into routine craftsmanship. . . . [They] survive through the grace and spontaneity of their melodies, their formal poise, their effortless dramatic pace and above all the romantic vitality that underlines their veneer of artificiality.'

LUCREZIA BORGIA

1833 was a year of exceptional activity even for so prolific a composer as Donizetti. It saw four premières: *Il furioso all'isola di San Domingo* (in Rome), *Parisina* (Florence), *Torquato Tasso* (Rome again) and, the culmination of the year in all senses, *Lucrezia Borgia* (Milan). In differing degree all four are works of special interest, of features both 'advanced' and dramatically astute; only the last-listed can be deemed a complete and rounded success – and even it temporarily weakens, in the cabaletta of the Duke's aria, into formula unrelieved by some touch of novelty. Romani's libretto, though in an *Avvertimento* he complained of the difficulty of compressing the Hugo play into a form apt for the lyric stage, is an elegant piece of work – witty, succinct, its every scene strongly shaped and motivated. Donizetti not only responded to, but capitalized upon, its strengths: few of his operas manifest such immediacy in capturing a particular atmosphere, such economy in delineating character and situation. People who love the Sparafucile scenes of *Rigoletto,* or the twinkle spread by Oscar amid the prevailing gloom of *Ballo,* are hardly likely to remain indifferent to the music of Gennaro's companions, with the travesty contralto part of Orsini the highest 'male' voice, or to the serio-comic scenes for the ducal henchmen, glinting with understated irony. Against this assembly of rich, dark sounds, Lucrezia's soprano stands out in relief. While the instrumental introduction to her 'Com'è bello' threads a delicate tapestry of moonlit sounds, or while the tolling of a distant bell strikes a chill into the carousing of the already poisoned companions, we recognize that, no less than Bellini, Donizetti was a poet of Romanticism.

Lucrezia Borgia sets a feast of wonderfully varied and contrasted scenes; it is an opera that could afford a sensitive and musicianly record producer splendid opportunities. So far, it has not done so. The two complete modern recordings, whatever good qualities they may possess, give off the feeling – or rather, the non-feeling – of the studio.

As Lucrezia, in the now legendary 1965 series of New York concert performances, Montserrat Caballé leapt to operatic stardom. No more than a couple of years intervened between these and the Rome-made RCA recording; the conductor, Perlea, was common to both ventures. Yet the contrast between her two Lucrezias is startling. That can be confidently stated because of the existence of a 'private' recording made at the second New York concert (and quite widely circulated thereafter). There, the opera is even more savagely cut than it usually is. (I long to, but have yet to hear *Lucrezia Borgia* complete; the point often made, that Donizetti's forms, with their integral repeats, are weakened, not strengthened, by snipping, is always most cogently argued by those performances that *do* present complete numbers.) Perlea seems less limp in New York than later in Rome – where at least he has the advantage of the excellent RCA orchestra and wholly idiomatic-sounding chorus and *comprimarii;* yet even at his best he gains only a fitful command over the paragraphs and even the sentences of the music. But the New York performance, we speedily sense, is an occasion; and Caballé rises to it magnificently. Where later in the studio reading she often gives the listener cause to complain of an all-purpose expressivity, a wistful, dreamy manner that takes insufficient account of situation and mood, on the 'private' records her Lucrezia is a flashing, lustrous, fascinating creature, full of temperamental and tonal variety. In both performances, the florid singing alternates between the most marvellous lightness and fine-spun precision, and a kind of fluent sketchiness (trills are never the real thing). A mid-ground between the two Lucrezias, the vivid and the droopy, is explored in the Caballé recital version (SB 6647) of 'Com'è bello'.

I prefer the youthful-sounding Orsini, Jane Berbié, and the Alfonso, Kostas Paskalis, of the concert performance, the former not always accurate in intonation or indeed style but more than promising, the latter a brave, bold voice and personality rather roughly communicated. RCA's Orsini, Shirley Verrett, lacks the proper spark, and lines in middle and low registers tend to be scoopily, not steadily, struck; more important, she lacks the proper weight of timbre. Ezio Flagello's Duke, securely deploying a substantial bass-baritone, is very dull. The line 'Vin de' Borgia è desso' he delivers as unemphatically as though the liquid in question were Ribena. The New York Gennaro is Alain Vanzo, fresh and melting, even if a touch of sentimentality intrudes upon his creditable attempts at an Italianate manner. In the studio recording Alfredo Kraus stirs things to life with his every appearance, every utterance: the voice sounds frank, forward, and unfailingly stylish, alert equally to conversational exchange, to limpid cantilena, and to boyish good humour (his pealing-off of the triplets in the 'friendship duet' with Orsini remains an unstaled pleasure). He is the undoubted star of the RCA set, even if it was obviously planned around its prima donna, who is granted not only the cabaletta, 'Si voli il primo a cogliere', to the first aria (Donizetti wrote it for a later revival), but also the showy finale, 'Era desso il figlio mio', which, as is well known, was produced for the first Lucrezia, Méric-Lalande, against the composer's wishes (and was later replaced with a beautiful G major death scene for Gennaro). Since in the 1833 finale Caballé at last finds her best form, Méric-Lalande's 'case' is stated for her more cogently than it deserves to be.

After her first venture in the role (Vancouver, 1972), Joan Sutherland made the role of the Borgia one of the mainstays of the later part of her career. Except in its lowest octave, now dry and chary of dramatic declamation, the voice of the mature Sutherland must be reckoned in healthier state than was evidently Méric-Lalande's at the time of her 'creation'. (The vocal writing, carefully adapting tessitura and florid figuration so as not to overtax the singer until her final scene, is another example of Donizetti's combination of practicality and purpose: in purely vocal characterization Lucrezia is like no other Donizetti female role.) The enjoyment of the Decca set derives in principal part from hearing the large, golden instrument cope serenely with the more strenuous vocal demands. It is a considerable portion of enjoyment; but it does not tamper with my conviction that Sutherland hardly begins to compass the role. Words are partly the problem: often they are inaudible, and when clear are mostly quite inexpressive (Sutherland's Italian is barbarous). More important, pathetic or tender emotion encourages not a tightly bound legato but (notably in 'Com'è bello') the singer's familiar brand of 'mooning and mooching' (an Andrew Porter description) that lays a wholly undesirable weight of languor on the drama. Sutherland's Lucrezia emerges, much like her Lucy, her Mary Stuart, her Norma, as a generalized *bel canto* personage. This not a negligible contribution; it is certainly a sufficient one for the army of Sutherland admirers. Whether it can be considered sufficient for one of Donizetti's most interesting characters seems to me highly doubtful.

If Sutherland is the focal point of the Decca recording, the conducting of Bonynge is its weakest feature. From the prelude to the closing bars he evinces lively ideas about the music, but, all too frequently, an incomplete technical control over their fulfilment – untidy instrumental strands abound, bursts of ill-judged speed momentarily threaten disaster (and this even with so practised a band of sight-readers as the National Philharmonic), the 'bottom' of the instrumental sound is ill defined in a way that has nothing to do with the recorded sound. While Marilyn Horne – the other piece of star casting – lavishes on Orsini much of her wonted dash and prodigious virtuosity, the tone is now too puffed-up, too portentous, to suggest the young blade (the recording catches an unfortunate quantity of breathy intake in her vocal admixture). Gennaro's naive, mooncalfish side is well drawn by Aragall, generally heard to be in good form – that is, until we compare his singing with that on another 'private' issue, taken from a 1966 Naples production (and notable otherwise only for the now-wispy, now-curdled heroine of Leyla Gencer, whose immense following in Italy constituted one of the continuing mysteries of opera-going in that country in the 1960s and 1970s). The tenor's natural flow of clear, pleasing tone here shows up the somewhat reedy and not always well-tuned sound of a decade later, but on the Decca set he makes much of the additional aria, 'T'amo qual dama' (composed for the Gennaro of the Russian tenor Ivanoff). Bonynge's Act 2 is in fact plumped out with alternatives – both endings are given, Gennaro's death followed (via a most unconvincing modulation) by Lucrezia's finale, a practice that works more acceptably on record than it did at Covent Garden in 1980. While the gritty overlay to Wixell's baritone may not actually hinder the impersonation of an unscrupulous aristocrat, it hardly allows a display of suave *bel canto* manners. Among the non-Italian *comprimarii* Piero di Palma's Vitelozzo shines out like a lighthouse beacon; these vary from the just tolerable to the painfully unidiomatic (Graeme Ewer's Rustighello, Richard Van Allan's Gubetta). A pity: the opera's passages of conspiracy and camaraderie are among its most potent strengths.

Few sections offer themselves for extraction as solos – a mark of Donizetti's concern to bind numbers into a flowering dramatic progress. In the opera, 'Com'è bello' stands as a completely realized dramatic entity, and is most beautiful: it comprises a delicate orchestral prelude (with motifs to be picked up at later points in the opera); a long recitative for Lucrezia followed by whispered conversation with her spy, Gubetta; and then the two verses of the *romanza,* separated by side-stage murmurings from the Duke and *his* spy, unseen onlookers as Lucrezia beholds her sleeping son. Most solo versions offer no more than the verses (in earlier years only one), and perhaps the preceding recitative. One account of the piece, more poetically than any other I know, sets the scene – despite the absence of secondary singers, and despite the demonstrably frail condition of the soprano in question. Callas (ASD 3984) included it on her last 'official' recital record; even at this late stage of her career, when every note requires 'negotiation', when hollow, desperate sounds accompany every rise above the stave, she manages to explore, in the lingering, legato shaping of the semiquaver tracery, a vein of expression, a range of timbres, unknown to other recorded Lucrezias. The whole role might have been tackled marvellously well even with these reduced means; the record inspires a powerful regret for Callas's failure to do so.

From this to the bright-toned, rather piercing, but very healthy utterance of Giannina Arangi-Lombardi (GQX 10703; GV 582) is a leap. Her semiquavers are not truly centred, and a slow downward chromatic scale becomes a swoop; but the trill is real, and so is the authority, the *grandezza,* of a type of Italian dramatic soprano unknown today. Of Celestina Boninsegna (Pathé 60036; RLS 7706) the same must be said – and perhaps the dark glow of the tone responds more appropriately to the atmosphere of the nocturnal scene. Against this must be set a certain squareness in the phrasing – triplet quavers and semiquavers are rushed, not savoured. Teresa Arkel's account (with piano, aria only: G&T 053062), with added top notes in the second verse and a tendency to whizz thoughtlessly through the florid writing, is a disconcerting mixture of beauty and triviality. Maria de Macchi (with piano: IRCC 3150; Rococo 5364) squalls unpleasantly, and implants, to unhappy effect, a kind of *verismo* emotionalism on the music. Back in our own day, Silvana Bocchino (Cetra LPL 69002) sounds like a promising, imperfectly finished student; and Gencer, in a studio reading (Cetra LPL 69001) taken some years after the Naples performance, is on characteristic form: touches of dignity and haunting coloration there may be, but the voice is mostly in a cloud, and 'real' notes are in real shortage.

Also from the prologue, tenors have not infrequently extracted 'Di pescatore ignobile', a simple larghetto enclosed as an 'inset' within the scene for Lucrezia and Gennaro. It is difficult to persuade the listener that this uncomplicated piece of narrative can sustain interest when removed from context. Both Bonci (with piano: Fono. 39673; CO 343)) and Anselmi (with piano: Fono. 62273; CO 359) wholly succeed, in their different ways, in supplying such a persuasion – Bonci by his endlessly graceful and 'timeless' deployment of phrases (though the tone is not intrinsically beautiful, and a final interpolated B flat makes a raw sound), Anselmi because the same caressing style is allied to a timbre I find marvellously warm and romantic. I like the manly style, at once vibrant and sensitive, of Carlo Albani, who remembers that he is telling a story (Victor 74098; Club 99.113); less the lachrymose Francesco Marconi – 'era mia madre' incites a risible outburst of filial sobbing (052200; Rococo 22); less still, though a voice of heroic size is disclosed, the strenuous Francesco Vignas (with piano: Fono. 39854; GV 86); and not at all the very ordinary Augusto Dianni (down a minor third: Arena 13168), the tremulous Edoardo Garbin (Fono. 92033), or, more recently, the homemade *bel canto* of Benvenuto Finelli (with piano: GV 6).

'Vieni la mia vendetta' (Act 1), a broad and rather noble melodic span at odds with its verbal content, followed by a trumpery cabaletta, is the Duke's big solo. In both passages, Chaliapin is magnificent: the voice caught in all its black splendour, the phrases taut with dramatic tension expertly controlled – like Battistini, he makes one aware that it is perfectly possible to be alertly rhythmic at a slow tempo. The intrusive w-sound breaking up semiquaver flourishes fails to damage the total effect. Chaliapin also lends weight to the conviction that the later appropriation of the role by baritones has done it a disservice (DB 403; GEMM 170). In the same music Francesco Navarrini, a veteran singer at the time of recording, shows his age, and also a sizeable residue of interpretative distinction (Fono. 62027; GV 14). José Mardones, not of the front rank interpretatively (something rather lifeless in his enunciation), discloses a bass of suave and melancholy beauty (Am. Col.; Club 99.85).

Orsini's Brindisi, the most familiar number from the opera, also loses something by being withdrawn from its dramatic surroundings: how 'operatically' thrilling the confrontation of light-hearted C major six-eight bounce and melodramatically darkening shadows. As a 'party piece' for vocally dapper contraltos it has been subjected to a whole armoury of interpolated ornaments, cadenzas, divisions, and long-held notes extra high and extra low. Few singers undertake all this and communicate delicious high spirits in the manner of the great Schumann-Heink (in German: 043068; GV 514): the tone bubbles with mirth, miraculously pure, steady, and ample at the same time, bearing the trills and flourishes on a tide of merriment. This is a glorious and lovable record. Schumann-Heink with piano (Am. Col. 1379; Odyssey Y35067) is perhaps a degree less infectious, though one long F at the top of the stave proclaims with even more imperturbable eloquence the quality and 'school' of the voice. By comparison, Sigrid Onegin spreads a pallor of – not exactly gloom, but something akin to determined sobriety. The variants may peal out, the trills may be even longer and the tone quite as ample and pure, yet every trace of a smile has been effaced, and so the virtuosity comes to seem externalized, even a little excrescent (Vic. 1367; LV 7). Two versions (Col. 7317; GEMM 168, and 2–033010; HLM 7025) affirm the extraordinary agility, in a voice of such depth and size, of Clara Butt. To my ears, in this music, she is really rather awful, slamming home the low notes – very low indeed: both versions are transposed down at least a semitone and probably a minor third – with the obduracy of a gale force warning. Sophie Braslau's strong contralto is spoiled by squeezed attack, though her *tenuti* are beautiful (DA 141; OASI 514); Marianne Brandt (in German, with piano: Pathé 1926) sketches the lines roughly and loosely, making small amends with an impressively sustained trill. Guerrina Fabbri (with piano: 53322) is strong, and rough. Marilyn Horne, taking part in one of the Sutherland/Bonynge 'Art of Bel Canto' collections (SET 269) reissued on GRV 8, boasts the luxury of an accompanying chorus; she seems much smoother, much less spirited, than on the Decca set, and the sprinkling of high notes tossed into the second verse (including a dodgy final top C) is uncertainly achieved.

Four sopranos have extrapolated 'M'odi, ah m'odi', Lucrezia's Bellinian cantabile, from the final scene. Apart from her strong top Bs and an unfettered C sharp, the fluttery Charlotte von Seebök (with piano, in German – Pathé 38222; RLS 743) has little of interest to offer; Elena Teodorini (with piano – 53299; RLS 7706) makes an approximate and squeaky effect; Ines de Frate (53552; RLS 7706), in her fifties, discloses a still bright, well-informed instrument and an expansive manner, though one or two mannerisms begin to nag on a second or third hearing. As companion-piece to her 'Com'è bello', Arangi-Lombardi, taking the music at a true *largo*, is richly and generously emotional, investing the repetitions of 'bevi, cedi' with imperious urgency; as in the earlier solo I hear a slight but disconcerting squeal in the tone, and find the completion of downward runs a little too sketchy for comfort (GQX 1073; GV 582). Gennaro's G-major death scene, written for Moriani (he was the *tenore della bella morte*, here and in *Lucia*), is done, with its preceding page, by Bice Mililotti and Marconi, who shapes the long rising *larghetto* phrases with some elegance, until he declines into sobs in the final bars (054190; Rococo R 22). Still on the subject of later additions to the tenor's music, let me briefly note a version, with piano, of the Ivanoff aria by John Brecknock (ENO 1001): nice intentions, clouded tone, and a careful, lifeless traversal of the notes.

LA FAVORITE

The history of Donizetti's second opera for the Paris Opéra, first given there in December 1840, is complicated. It needs to be briefly recounted here,* in

---

* For a much longer and more detailed discussion of *La Favorite* and its transformation into *La favorita*, see Andrew Porter's review of the 1978 Metropolitan Opera production (*New Yorker*, 13 March 1978, pp 113–118).

explanation of just how and why the opera encountered on the Italian-language records that form the bulk of its discography differs in significant detail from the work Donizetti wrote (and which may be discovered not only in the French vocal scores and librettos in existence but also in a number of original-language recordings).

The project of *La Favorite* was initiated and undertaken in haste after the theatre for which Donizetti had written his most recent opera, *L'Ange de Nisida*, was forced by bankruptcy to close down. From that opera (completed but not performed), from the unfinished *Adelaide* of 1834, and from the begun-but-never-to-be-completed *Duc d'Albe* he drew the music for a new opera, its text an adaptation overseen by Scribe of the *Ange de Nisida* libretto by Royer and Vaëz. New music was also composed, notably the ballet, the solos for Alphonse, king of Castille (baritone), and Léonore's 'Fernand, imite la clémence' in the Act 4 finale. That the opera is in some senses a compendium of ideas first conceived in other contexts and hurriedly redeployed might lead one to expect unevenness and inconsistency. In fact, *La Favorite* is one of Donizetti's most consistent operas, 'welded together with such skill' (according to Julian Budden) 'that the listener is unaware of any incongruity'. Lapses in quality, of a kind found in the rum-ti-tum cabaletta to Alphonse's aria, 'Léonore, viens', and in *stretta* sections of the large-scale Meyerbeerian finales, appear no more nor less worthy of comment than those noted in operas made of wholly 'original' Donizettian material. Like Gluck, whose mature operas are all compilations in this sense, Donizetti was an intensely practised and practical man of the theatre. When he reassembled earlier musical ideas, he knew what he was about.

A *grand opéra* in four acts, *La Favorite* proposes and explores, earnestly and with dignity, a clear and consistent subject: the struggle, in the young novice Fernand (tenor), between sacred and profane love, between duty to his religious vows and the passion he conceives for an unknown woman, revealed (though to him only later) as Léonore de Gusmann, mistress of the King (mezzo-soprano). Historical locations and personages are aptly invoked; the church, as represented by the monk Balthazar (bass), Superior of St James of Compostela, and the throne are in conflict, and Fernand, who leaves the monastery to seek wordly fame, is unwittingly placed at its centre. At its best, this is a noble and serious work. The musical forms are large in scale, the orchestration shows a new richness, and the vocal writing is severely simplified, achieving in the solos and duets a spacious 'Verdian' cantilena in which decorative figuration has been suppressed. ('Forbidden are the usual cadenzas. What joy! joy! joy!', the composer had written to Mayr about the earlier reworking of *Poliuto* as *Les Martyrs*.) Donizetti, who might, for the most important theatre in Europe, have attained only an empty grandeur of style, rose higher than the particular occasion, as the opera's final act so beautifully demonstrates. From here to the Verdi of *Forza* and *Don Carlos* is but a small step.

In the Italian translation, in which the work gained and has kept its widest

audience, clarity and consistency are hopelessly traduced. The exigencies of
Italian censorship on the 1840s, concerned particularly with the inclusion of
religious matters and historical figures in opera, caused Balthazar to become,
in an early Italian translation, the father of both Fernand and Alphonse's
queen. By 1860, a revival for La Scala could return the first scene of Act 1
and Act 4 to its monastic setting; yet to this there was still attached the
central alteration of Balthazar's identity, with drastic consequences. Several
crucial nonsenses are perpetrated in the 1860 version: among them, that
Balthazar should be both monk and father of royal offspring; that Fernand
should be both the King's brother-in-law and the 'montanaro abbietto'
disdained by courtiers in the third act; and, most incredible, that Fernand,
connected by his sister's marriage to the affairs of Alphonse's court, should
somehow have remained in ignorance of the existence of the King's mistress
and of her identity. This 1860 version became, by means of the Ricordi
publication, the standard text of La favorita – 'a patchwork', Andrew Porter
has described it, 'of what the Catholic censorship did in the 1840s, the partial,
ineffective repair job of 1860, and the inertia of singers, conductors, and
managements content for more than a century to pick up and perpetuate the
nearest available score instead of discovering what the composer wrote. The
result is an insult to Donizetti'. It becomes a hard but necessary task, when
listening particularly to the Italian-language complete recordings of the
opera, to learn to accept the exchange of the original narrative sense for
nonsense – hard not least because, simply as a rendering of Royer, Vaëz,
and Scribe in translation, the Italian of the Ricordi score is so clumsy,
verbose, and inept.* The standard Italian score also differs in musical particu-
lars from the original: to take the most striking example, the very end is
vulgarly abbreviated. All this failed to spoil my own pleasure in exploring
the *Favorite*/*favorita* treasure trove on records, which is vast – the existence
of several French items testifying, incidentally, to the long popularity, ended
only in our century, of the opera in that country. But is it not long past time
that, on records quite as much as in the theatre, the slur on the work was
finally removed? – in Italy by the commissioning of a new and sensible Italian
translation, and internationally by the re-emergence of the work in its original
language.

   The sheer abundance of the opera on records forces me to deal summarily
with less worthy samples of it. These include the abridged set of ten 78rpm
sides, featuring the bleaty tenor of Cristy Solari and the gusty mezzo-soprano
of Giuseppina Zinetti; and, from the 1950s, a set of mediocre Italian highlights (in which the tenor Dino Formichini at least attempts to master a kind
of vocal style) and the wretched first side of a Monarch LP (the second
devoted to *Norma*), with Maria Mandalari, Antonio Manca-Serra, and Pier

---

* See Ralph Leavis, '*La Favorite* and *La favorita* – one opera, two librettos', in the second
Donizetti Society Journal, issue no. 2 (1975), which undertakes a close comparison, with musical
examples, of the French and Italian texts, and examines the crude fit of the latter to Donizetti's
vocal lines.

Miranda Ferraro, whose Act 4 aria is just about the most awful of my experience. Indeed, in most of the *Favorite/favorita* recordings from a period quite early on in this century, style is the problem: for neither the highly emotional *verismo* mannerisms that overtook Italian singing nor the hefty, utilitarian vocalization later deemed fit (not, of course, by Callas) for the interpretation of all Italian operas alike, proved well adapted to lines that presuppose refinements, delicacies and eloquence in the handling of every detail and the shaping of every phrase. That much of the opera's native qualities contrive often to come through, despite stylistic vicissitude, is a sign of their strength.

In the most recent studio recording – made in Bologna in 1974, only released in Britain four years later – proper style is at least a fleeting consideration. If we compare, say, the Fernands of Gianni Poggi and even the gifted Gianni Raimondi with Luciano Pavarotti's hero, we must at once note the more fluent, graceful manner of the last-named. He is not really to be compared, in either of the well-known tenor arias, with their most honeyed and loving exponents; and he tends to make unpleasantly explosive bursts of the famous top notes – the opera, of course, affords him a C and a C sharp, to which, in *marziale* aria 'Oui, ta voix m'inspire'/'Si, che un tu solo accento' that closes Act 1 (included by Bonynge, almost always cut elsewhere), the tenor throws in a couple more. But the role of Fernand, unlike more recent, heavier acquisitions to his repertory, lies well on his voice; and if no great subtlety informs the characterization, we are not made to feel, as in these 'Pavarotti Superstar' days we so often are, that this is a special guest appearance, rather than a real performance. The improvement of 'Ange si pur'/'Spirto gentil' here on an earlier recital version (SXL 6658) is marked: the earlier is clear, unspecific, and decently provincial, with a soup-ladle of emotion thrown over the middle section.

For Pavarotti an otherwise flawed set is worth hearing – flawed above all by the spread condition and uncertain tuning of Cossotto's higher notes, and to me the adamantine tone quality of the lower, enforced by gusty breathing, is deeply unsympathetic; in a much earlier recital version of 'O mon Fernand'/'O mio Fernando' plus cabaletta (Philips AL 3443) she shows a more poised, a gentler way with the role. Gabriel Bacquier strives admirably but unequally after the requirements of *bel canto* (would the voice have sounded less rusty in his native tongue?); in the small but delightful role of Inès (the confidant) Ileana Cotrubas is tremulous. Nicolai Ghiaurov's Balthazar self-consciously parades a big, beautiful bass, sitting portentously on the notes in what seems at times almost a Padre Guardiano parody. The orchestral and choral contribution is middling-to-feeble, slips and stumbles appearing even more readily than on the same conductor's *Lucrezia Borgia*, which shares with this Donizetti opera his infirm control of pace and movement. The edition bears out Bonynge's consultation of the original score, and internal repeats are regularly supplied as on no other recording; but

Pavarotti is permitted the cheap shortened ending. The dispensable ballet music occupies most of side three.

Provincial is the word for the earlier Decca set, conducted with an experienced hand prone to limpness by Alberto Erede, which shows Gianni Poggi, if not quite the blaring brute remembered, nevertheless fairly disastrous, and Giulietta Simionato's heroine imaginative in too few of her phrases (she does the little pre-wedding scene touchingly). The splendid baritone of Ettore Bastianini deals out sledgehammer blows to Alphonse's music – in the intimate duet in thirds and sixths with Léonore, it is almost laughable to hear her line assumed to be a kind of obbligato accompaniment to his. Jerome Hines's Balthazar is a routine, big-voiced bass. By contrast, Cetra's issue from the first part of the same decade communicates a much more enjoyable, if not exactly 'correct', sense of Italian tradition. The voluptuous Fedora Barbieri and the attractively alert, not very suave Gianni Raimondi sound like adults, and their romance gains commensurately. The contra-bassoonish Giulio Neri brings a touch of Fafner to Balthazar; Carlo Tagliabue's Alphonse is worn and juddery. I warm to the orchestral playing, also to the insinuating way the conductor, Angelo Questa, unfolds the third-act episode for Don Gaspard and the courtiers, a little gem of a scene. In both these recordings 'house' cuts are the order of the day. A live example of the same tradition – if it can be dignified with the name – is given on the Cetra Live Opera album of a 1950 Mexico City performance, dimly recorded and attended by all the usual drawbacks of claque-inspired cheers, loud prompter's contributions etc; the value comes from hearing a younger Simionato in fresh and greatly appealing form and from Di Stefano, still at the top of his youthful bent even if in the romantic warmth of style vocal coarsenings can already be detected (Cetra LO2–3).

The single set to present Donizetti in the original language is an issue of the highest interest. A complete opera recording in 1912 was obviously an immense undertaking, yet Pathé's does in fact constitute one of the fuller representations of *Favorite/favorita* on record, supplying (for instance) whole texts of the Act 1 tenor aria and tenor-bass duet, and at least one verse of Fernand's *marziale*. Cuts seem to come thicker and faster towards the end, as if to fit the opera somehow into its allotted schedule of discs, yet what goes missing *in toto* is certainly no greater than in the average Italian 'house performance'. One is unlikely, in any case, to turn hither for the last word in Donizettian orchestral or choral achievement – in these departments the reading proves distinctly chancy in parts, though the conductor Ruhlmann manages to keep his head even through the hairiest passages of dissolving ensemble. (A slightly more serious problem for the modern listener to the Bourg LP reprint concerns its pitch: the original, recorded at speeds varying between 80 and 100rpm, has apparently been transcribed so as to present certain sections a semitone or so below the norm established by others.)

The value of the original, and even more its republication, lies in its Frenchness. It is a 'real' performance we hear, with a cast, not perhaps 'front-line Paris 1912', but such as might have been engaged for an Opéra *Favorite* of the time; and after the wordy inexactitude of the Italian text and the stylistic aberrations to which elsewhere it is prey, the clean cut of the French singing lines is nothing less than a revelation. Henri Albers, perhaps the most notable name of the cast, is also its most distinguished member, an Alphonse with a warmth of tone and an elegance of line to approach (if not to rival) Maurice Renaud. The mezzo, Ketty Lapeyrette (a Paris singer with a long and honourable career whose other milestones include the creation of the title role in Roussel's *Padmâvatî*), is a strong, passionate performer, with weight and firm attack at her disposal at both ends of Léonore's wide compass – not perhaps the most affecting exponent of the role, but a grandly mettlesome one; and the tenor, Robert Lassalle (son of the more famous baritone), makes up in ardour for what he lacks in vocal skill and tonal finish.

The Véga disc of French excerpts makes an effect of a similar but less definite kind. It offers three principals (no Balthazar); of these only Simone Couderc is at all worthy of comment – 'O mon Fernand', complete with both verses of its cabaletta and the long linking cadenza as given in the French vocal score, calls on a 'personal', characterful manner of utterance that offsets patches of suspect intonation. The 1975 New York concert performance, of which a 'private' set is in circulation, could not, as originally intended, be given in the original language because of inaccessible performing material. It, too, is worth seeking out. Verrett (who finds her form fairly late in the evening) and Kraus (as ever a polished, but now a studied, unspontaneous artist) are loudly and endlessly cheered – it was evidently very much that sort of occasion. I derive greatest pleasure from the Alphonse of Pablo Elvira, whose very even, focused baritone touches the vein of elegant melancholy in 'Léonor, viens'/'Vien Leonora'; and from the truly 'vocal' conducting of Eve Queler, at one with the singers' impulses in the old way, yet never losing the shape of each passage.

Each of the opera's principals – and, in the enchanting female-chorus numbers of Act 1, even the *comprimaria* Inès – is given a solo chance to shine. For Balthazar these are not extensive. He thunders out powerful warnings of excommunication in the long, complicated Act 2 finale; a sample (in French) of Marcel Journet's grave, perfectly weighted restraint in the 'Anathème de Balthazar' demonstrates that, as so often in Donizetti, such passages appear from stock only when routinely handled (034076; GV 562). Otherwise, the bass music is the least 'extractable'. In the duet (truncated) from Act 1 we find Albert Vaguet's lightly lyrical Fernand opposite the forceful Marius Chambon (in French – Pathé 0204; Rococo 5347) – both singers took these roles at the Opéra around the turn of the century. Bonci, long-phrased and expansive, is not well matched to the unimpressive bass of Oreste Luppi (Fono. 37169); and Pinza's magnificence and imperturbable authority are even less happily answered by Roberto d'Alessio (DA 566; HLM 1435561). From the final act, Balthazar's beautiful C major prayer with chorus makes an effect out of all proportion to its length in Pinza's two majestic versions, the earlier (1924 – DA 708; HLM 1435561) even more awe-inspiring than the later (1930: DB 1750; LV 27). Journet chooses to sing the same passage in Italian, and imparts thereto almost the 'roll' of Pinza, if not the glorious vibrancy and humanity (74273; GV 562). Tancredi Pasero, less magisterially solemn than either of these, is also very fine (Col. D 18072; LV 261). I have not heard the records of the great Russian bass Lev Sibiriakov in this music.

Fernand has the largest number (three) of arias, and two of these comprise the music from the opera, along with Léonore's aria, most often recorded. Let me list all the versions, in addition to those already mentioned, that I have heard; no doubt several names are missing (all performances in Italian unless otherwise specified):

Un ange, une femme inconnue/Una vergine, un angiol di Dio (Act 1)

Giuseppe Anselmi (with piano: Fono. 62318; BC 213)
Alessandro Bonci
  i) (with piano: Fono. 39111; CO 343)
  ii) (with orch.: Col. D 8084)
Franco Bonisolli (Acanta DC 21.723)
Léon Campagnola (in French: Disque U 4)
Antonio Cortis (DA 757; OASI 531)
Fernando de Lucia (with piano: 52081; RS 305)
Benvenuto Finelli (with piano: GV 6)
Miguel Fleta (DB 1053; LV 96)
Aristodemo Giorgini (2–52565; Rococo 5339)
Léon Lafitte (in French with piano: G&T 32100)
Giacomo Lauri-Volpi
  i) (Fono. 152018; Scala 830)
  ii) (GV 500)
René Maison (in French Od. 123564; CBS 76691)
John O'Sullivan (Col. D 4941; Club 99.6)
Aureliano Pertile (DA 1183; LV 46)
Alfred Piccaver (Od. LXX 76958)
Tito Schipa (DA 1016; LV 185)
Anatoly Solovyanenko (Melodiya SM 02607/8)
David Stockman (in Swedish: Swedish Gramm. 188; GV 17)
César Vezzani (in French: DA 4863)
Miguel Villabella (in French: Pathé PGT 6)

Ange si pur/Spirto gentil (Act 4)

Agustarello Affre (French: Od. 36732; Club 99.90)
Mikhail Alexandrovich (in Russian: D3268/9; Club. 99.105)
Giuseppe Anselmi (Fono. 62319)
Alessandro Bonci (with piano: Fono. 39338; CO 343)
Dino Borgioli (D16379; GV 538)
Michel Cadiou (in French: Versailles STDX 8025)
Enrico Caruso (DB 129; RL 12766)
Eugene Conley (LXT 2514)
Florencio Constantino (2–52403)
Franco Corelli (ASD 529)
Giulio Crimi (Vocalion A-0226)
Carlo Dani (Fono. 39969; GV 81)
Tudor Davies (in English: E 264)
Nino Ederle (Parlo. E 11276; OASI 629)
Tanos Ferendinos (DX 1546)
Miguel Fleta (DB 986; LV 96)
Nicolai Gedda (33CX 1130)
Rudolf Gerlach-Rusnak (in German: EG 2911; LV 71)
Beniamino Gigli (2–052141; GEMM 202)
Aristodemo Giorgini (052106; Rococo 5339)
Giacomo Lauri-Volpi
  i) (Fono. 74910)
  ii) (GV 500)
Hipolito Lazaro (RG 16120; GV 506)
Enzo de Muro Lomanto (Col. D 18079)
René Maison (in French: Od. 123564)
Giovanni Malipiero (Parlo. DPX 24; OASI 607)

John McCormack (Od. 84230; GEMM 155)
Costa Milona (Parlo. P 1631; SYO 2)
Barry Morell (LSC 3221)
Heddle Nash (in English: C 3409)
Aureliano Pertile (HMV DB 1480; LV 46)
Alfred Piccaver (Od. 99935; LV 26)
Gianni Poggi (LX 1364)
Gianni Raimondi (Philips AL 3442)

Emile Scaremberg (in French, with piano: Fono. 39359; Rococo R 18)
Dmitri Smirnov (052296; R 33)
Anatoly Solovyanenko (Melodiya SM O2607/8)
Josef Traxel (1C 147–30 774/75)
César Vezzani (in French: DA 4863; FALP 50037)
Evan Williams (in English: 02860)

In these two arias Donizetti's evocation of Italianate melodic sweetness within the context of an elevated French formal structure is at its most affecting. Both pieces are of inordinate difficulty, calling for a tenor of supple movement from chest to head registers, from soft dynamics to loud, calling above all for sustained legato in both cantabile and declamatory phrasing. In 'Un ange, une femme' (its second, differently orchestrated verse all too often cut), the coda rises in a gentle scale to a C sharp above the stave (not always included); in the reprise of 'Ange si pur' the climax takes in a top C. For top-note tenors these *acuti* have offered particularly ill guidance: the notes, and the music, are 'about' something quite different.

Accounts of the first-act *cavatine* that can be dismissed without much ado include those by the aged Lauri-Volpi (ii) in the list – how *could* he allow himself to be remembered by this or by the later 'Spirto gentil'?; the thick, graceless O'Sullivan, Fleta in carpet-chewing mood, Benvenuto Finelli's peculiar hybrid of supposed *bel canto* and English cathedral-chorister tenorisms, and the soft-timbred, sleepy Giorgini. Léon Lafitte, singing in French, with a second verse but no top C sharp, is ordinary. Solovyanenko, recorded in the early 1960s, discloses a dark, vibrant, large-scaled instrument, like that of a Russian Corelli – and noisily emotional after the same model. (This holds even truer for his 'Spirto gentil'.) David Stockman cuts square phrases; the effect of the Swedish language and of his blond tone is to summon up a (not unappealing) picture of Lohengrin arriving at Compostela. Singing both verses, Bonisolli makes an effort at style, only to abandon it at crucial points, such as on reaching the C sharps (he throws in a second at the end). Pertile (down a semitone) demonstrates the graphic quality of his art, 'illustrating' the emotions, leaving nothing to the power of melody – as in 'Spirto gentil' (also down a semitone) his vein of expression proves at once thrilling and almost comical.

On another level we find Piccaver, much less uncommunicative than in his Act 4 aria, tonally even more attractive and the younger Lauri-Volpi, a singer so appealing, free and ardent that lachrymose touches and moments of overloaded vibrato seem of minor importance while the spell of the voice lasts. Schipa – a voice not intrinsically beautiful, an artist of even greater individuality – is here less than the stylist he is so often proclaimed to be: semiquavers are flecked with aspirates (he goes up only to A at the end).

Reaction to an undeniably great stylist, de Lucia (down a tone, low ending), must be personal. For me, in this at least, the tone is ungrateful. The romantic, smoky, firm tone – each note distinct and glowing – of Cortis gives especial pleasure even in those phrases carrying a suggestion of jerkiness. The batch of French tenors, a species almost unknown today, gives no less pleasure – Maison, ringing and large-scaled but throaty, perhaps least so. He sings both verses, as do the impassioned, not very lyrical Vezzani, whose top notes (the highest a B) glare, and the astringent, penetrative Villabella, French by adoption, admirable in dignity and manly directness. Campagnola uses effortfully a voice of very good quality (one verse only). But the unhurriedly expressive style, touched with *portamento* and grace notes never carelessly undertaken, by which the music is most poetically revealed is undertaken by Italians – Bonci, who with piano spins out the voice with even greater caress (low endings); and – my favourite of all – Anselmi, exquisite in every note, even in those notes allowed fractionally to sharpen (low ending).

The fourth-act arias of Ederle, Crimi (down a tone), Cadiou, Lazaro (with the 'temperament' of a pettish infant), the clumsy Morell, the colourless Constantino (who sings the longest cadenza of all) and d'Alcaide (down a tone), the Gigli-epigones Poggi (a decade or so before the Decca set), Milona, de Muro Lomanto, Ferendinos, and Dani (who attempts a *diminuendo* on his top C), also Conley (though I like the touch of muscularity in his timbre) and Giorgini (down a tone) – all can be speedily dispatched. All fail an invaluable demisemiquaver test: all sing 'sogni mie-he-he-i' and 'mentita spe-he-he-me' (or in the case of Cadiou, the original-French equivalents). So does Corelli, who lathers the line with scoops, slides, and 'emotion' – and yet I find it impossible not to succumb to the intensity and glamour of the voice. Another glamorous voice, Piccaver's, sounds at its most indolent – he can hardly bring himself to utter the words. Fleta (down a tone) makes a soft and very beautiful start; then the pressure turns on and the wobbles take over. Gianni Raimondi, recorded after the Cetra set, begins hardly less attractively, but soon mars the impression, if less comprehensively so than Fleta. Maison is too strenuous, even, at times, rather bleaty. In German, and in the back-of-the-throat placing of Gerlach-Rusnak, Donizetti takes on an alien, not altogether unpleasing sentimentality; there is a lovely *dim.* into the reprise. The elegantly finished Nash version seems to me of an impossible stuffiness; Evan Williams is matt and stiff-upper-lip, and Tudor Davies (down a semitone) sturdy and solid but hardly intimate. (Does it need the ear of a foreigner not to wince at the kind of English enunciation that turns a line into 'leeving mee heerr everr to pine'?)

Altogether more successful attempts, by transalpine voices, to accommodate themselves to the style of the music are made by the young Gedda, technically of exceptional ease and proficiency, tasteful, pure and uninvolving; and, more interestingly if with less smooth accomplishment, by Josef Traxel – he does not fully achieve the 'bending' of a Germanic instrument to the shape of the lines, but a sympathetic, musicianly personality emerges from the enterprise. It could be said that Borgioli's precious, disembodied lyricism represents something no more essentially Italianate than these; that troubles me less than the apparent absence of spontaneity in his impulses. Further north I find Smirnov (down a semitone), though slow and poetic in the authentic Imperial Russian manner, a touch less haunting than expected; the *mezza voce* of the reprise is elegant, yet finespun phrases give way, on occasion, to something a little laboured. Also, a trace of self-consciousness affects his attack – something wholly missing in Malipiero's performance, obviously that of a less well-groomed singer, but conveying a sense of character, of contained passion, that urge tolerance of vocalism not continuously smooth. Lauri-Volpi's first 'Spirto gentil', like his Act 1 aria, shows a wonderful voice not quite nobly used. Of Gigli (did he really take it a semitone down?) the same, only more so, must be said: details careless and even coarse, a maudlin cadenza at the close, a voice so beautifully liquid as to compel delight in its every movement. Comparison with McCormack is interesting. Where Gigli risks looseness, of spirit if not of sound, the honeyed line of the senior singer stays marvellously firm, with a *dolce* start that is the image of unforced suavity. Yet it is, strangely, Gigli who remains in the memory. My own Italian tenor peak (and for these purposes it is fair to count McCormack among the Italians) is conquered by Caruso and Bonci: the uninhibited emotionalism of the former held in check by the rapt flow of gorgeous tone, the latter so limpid – with one word, 'gentil', he conjures up the mood – and so cherishing of detail as temporarily to render all other tenors crude and insensitive. The top C begins hard and grittily, then softens; into the final *messa di voce* everything fine in Bonci's art is concentrated. Again, alongside Bonci, there is Anselmi, chivalrous, warm-toned, spinning out the reprise in a velvety *mezza voce* that is the answer to Bonci's moments of *bel canto* illumination.

In this personal pantheon I would also find places for three others. Vezzani uncovers an insight into the *cavatine* unlike any other: a first paragraph forward-moving, electric, that bursts into what can only be called violence at the close, in a fearfully spreading top C followed by a bitter, explosive coda. It is not 'right', and in description must sound monstrous; but it is unforgettable. By a tenor of a previous decade, Scaremberg, the classically moulded French style is demonstrated: his performance, at once candid and passionate, dramatic and pure, argues a 'case' for the original language that no insinuation of little sobs into the coda can weaken. Something looked for in Smirnov, plangent Russian sweetness, comes out in a less heralded, younger tenor, Alexandrovich (now, according to report, an *émigré* in his seventies). The voice may not be absolutely first-rate quality, yet the reflective eloquence is; he throws away the little demisemiquaver turns with the artistry of one who understands their point. A tiny crack opens in the C; it hardly matters.

While still with Fernand, let me briefly mention his duets with Léonore.

A section from Act 1 – the C major *moderato* 'Toi ma seule amie' (rendered with particular imprecision in the Italian as 'Fia vero? lasciarti!') – couples the listless Giorgini with Ester Lavin de Casas on a 78rpm side equalled for dullness only by its reverse side, an extract from the last-act *Duo et final* beginning with 'Fernand, imite la clémence' ('Pietoso al par del Nume') (054196–7; ORL 223). Moving towards the climax of the same scene, we find three French duos, each commencing at a different point, each able, in the reconciliatory outburst 'Viens, viens, je cède éperdu', to stretch the triplets into unmechanical, indeed radiant expression. Lucien Muratore and Marcelle Demougeot, heard through a terribly cramped, 'bottled' recording, are the least classical (G&T 314461; Rococo 5317). Agustarello Affre, thrillingly bold, like a French Tamagno, and the distinctive, curdled Mathilde Comes might be thought slightly ill-matched (Pathé P1502; Club 99.59). (Affre recorded several other excerpts; I have not located them.) Partners in the 1899 Opéra revival, Albert Alvarez, heroic and impassioned, and the magnificently full-voiced Marie Delna offer the shortest, most intensely rewarding excerpt (IRCC 88; Club 99.55). After these three, the playing-to-the-gallery rhetoric and mindless freedom over note values of Gigli and Elvira Casazza seem particularly blatant (in Italian – DB 269; RLS 729).

Though relatively short – he appears only in the middle two acts – the baritone role of Alphonse XI is one of the most rounded in Donizetti's serious operas, hinting, in music of suavely lyrical simplicity shot with a vein of melancholy, at an elegant, aristocratic, and intentionally ambiguous characterization. The opening scene of Act 2 comprises, in full, a mini-*scena*; in extract, only a snatch of the opening recitative is likely to be supplied, and the written-to-formula F major cabaletta, low point of the entire score, is often but not always appended (in those few performances where its two verses and middle section *are* heard in full, the whole immediately seems less shallow). The *larghetto*, 'Léonore, viens'/'Vien, Leonora', in a poignant, flute-tinted A minor, demands the long, expansive phrasing and aristocratic savouring of detail not granted it by the sadly aged Giuseppe Valdengo and Alexander Svéd (amid the judders of whose singing one may note a moment or two of distinction), the slack and sentimental Francesco d'Andrade, the unexpectedly disappointing Emilio de Gogorza (white voice and dully moulded line), or, in his single appearance on records (in French: Rococo 5347), the great but here old and woefully unsteady Faure, who offers a bizarre truncation of aria and cabaletta. The art of the Donizetti baritone is uncertainly preserved in our own era by Giuseppe Taddei, intelligent as ever but cloudy and inexact; he livens up in the cabaletta (Preiser PR 9832). In his younger compatriot, Renato Bruson, one recognizes, by contrast, a modern version of the *baritono nobile* capable at least of sustaining and controlling a Donizettian line, even if at either end of the compass limitations become apparent (Decca GRV 9). Ivan Petrov's fine, strong voice pokes stiffly at the music (Remington R-199–93). Uneven impressions are left by Paolo Silveri, the focus of whose lean baritone slips as pitch rises (Col. DB 2428), and by Umberto Urbano, forceful but gritty (G&T 72949; LV 35). Michael Scott's controversial qualification (in *The Record of Singing**) of Giuseppe de Luca's *bel canto* mastery makes sense in this music – for, although the line is unwavering, and wonderfully clear, the phrases are left plain, not shaped or caressed (52423; R 24). Titta Ruffo's magnificent voice bursts out unstylishly (with piano: Pathé 4024). The 'real thing' I find exemplified in the almost overpowering vocal magnetism and richness of Riccardo Stracciari (Fono. 92428; GV 501) – overpowering in tonal allure, never overpowering indeed notably restrained, in expression – and by Battistini, whose very first operatic role Alphonse was (Rome, 1878). By 1913 (2–52848; Perennial 3002), the relative weakness of low notes is being clearly advertised, and a touch of breathlessness intrudes; but the sculpted phrasing, the endlessly imaginative nuances of dynamic variation, the subtle colourings and verbal pointings are nothing short of fabulous. The 1921 recording does not disguise further decline, yet the first phrase is, if anything, even more poetically uttered (DB 148; Perennial 3002).

If Battistini may be said to head the 'Italian school', then Maurice Renaud must be offered the same place of honour in the French, which here numbers (among its adherents) Etienne Billot (thin-toned but clear, with a good trill – Col. 188678; CBS 76691), the ill-tuned, unwinning Julien Lafont (Odeon 188569; CBS 76691), and the warmer and better controlled Louis Lestelly (Gram. 03233; Rubini RS 304). I find Renaud's record (032095; GV 52) of inexhaustible fascination, amazing in his command of dramatic tension at a slow tempo, enthralling in a disciplined, unhurried command of ornamental detail, imbued with a potent nobility of character that even Battistini fails to convey. Random juxtaposition can bring with it unhappy and even cruel contrasts. I wonder whether Sherrill Milnes, who bravely chose to sing the piece in full (two verses of the cabaletta) and in French, might have sounded more than competently colourless in company less exalted then Renaud's. The reading is well studied up to a point (the French is passable, though no one in the studio appears to have noticed the nonsense, at one stage, of 'viens' for 'rien'); beyond that point, it seems, is where the acquisition of stylistic command really begins. A top B flat affords a coarsely show-off end (SXL 6609).

'Pour tant d'amour'/'A tanto amor' (Act 3), Alphonse's second solo, inter-polates comments from Léonore and Fernand (not supplied, obviously, in extract form). Let me not repeat my praise of Renaud (032092; GV 52), Battistini (two versions – 1907, DB 228; GV 98; 1923, DB 736; Perennial 3002), or Stracciari (Fono. 92429; GV 501). Previous comment applies a second time to Silveri, Urbano, and Lafont. Reputations not fully upheld by their records of the piece include those of Antonio Magini-Coletti, Mario Sammarco, Mariano Stabile, John Forsell (in Swedish), and Arthur Endrèze (in French). Caught in his pre-*Otello* baritone days, Renato Zanelli displays

* Duckworth, London, 1973.

a soft-centred, over-accented approach – especially if Stracciari has preceded
him on the turntable – but the tone is warm, even melting (Vic. A 23401;
RLS 743). Every note of Mario Ancona's reading (Vic. 88063; Rococo 5213)
is touched with enormous quiet distinction; I regret not tracking down his
'Vien, Leonora'. In the Alphonse-Léonore duet of Act 2 – it lies low for her
and high for him, and the temptation has to be resisted by the baritone of
unchivalrously drowning his partner out – Battistini (in 1902) and de Luca
have chosen to pair themselves with minor singers, respectively Cartonini
(with piano – 54034; Rubini GV 99) and Ceresoli (54021; R 24). The result
is not, as it should be, harmonious concord, so much as the display of a fine
baritone voice with a sort of human accompaniment. It is a joy to hear the
equivalently weighted artistry of Margarethe Matzenauer and Pasquale
Amato in partnership: in the chains of thirds and sixths, two large, sensuous
voices tune into each other, wrap around one another, with rare precision
(DK 101). Marie Charbonnel and François Mezy cannot achieve quite this
degree of harmonious closeness in the same passages; otherwise their version,
taken slowly and steadily, each French word eloquently but never emphatically touched, is of high distinction (Odéon 111206–7). I have not heard
Eugenia Burzio and Taurino Parvis (Pathé 86445).

And so to Léonore herself, one of the earliest female roles of nineteenth-
century opera to portray a complex emotional predicament, the depth and
roundness of whose vocal characterization may be said to emerge directly
from Donizetti's responsiveness to the possibilities of the *falcon* voice (mezzo-
soprano or dramatic soprano: the term resists classification as did Rosine
Stoltz, the first Léonore, Cornélie Falcon herself, the first Valentine, or
Gueymard, the first Eboli). These three roles – mature women, troubled and
full-hearted – show ties of kinship; and Léonore in her monastery death
scene we can confidently proclaim an important ancestress of Verdi's second
Leonora.

The centre point of the role, as it is of the opera, is found in the spacious,
simply phrased C-major *air*, preceded by recitative, accompanied by a delicate harp obbligato, and followed by a cabaletta whose energy aptly describes
the character's access of more urgent emotion (this, of course, is even more
effective for being given, as it seldom is, in full). The following table gives
the performances of it that I have heard, in Italian unless otherwise indicated:

O mon Fernand/O mio Fernando
(Act 3)

Nadia Afeyan (Balkanton BOA 572)
Rosette Anday (ES 729; LV 15)
Marian Anderson (Belvox 504; GEMM
  193)
Phyllis Archibald (aria only: Vocalion K
  – 05245)

Agnes Baltsa (ASD 4279)
Fedora Barbieri (DB 11323; 3C 061
  17014M)
Karin Branzell (Brunswick 50158;
  Rococo 5214)
Eugenia Burzio (aria only Pathé 86427;
  Club 99.87/8)
Clara Butt (Col 317; GEMM 168)
Mme Charles Cahier (Sarah Jane

Walker) (in French; 1RCC 162; SJG
012)
Marie Charbonnel (in French, aria only:
Od. XAR 615)
Viorica Cortez (Electrecord ECE 0713)
Fiorica Cristoforeanu (Parlo. R 2169;
Club 99.38)
Marie Delna (in French, aria only: Pathé
0134)
Oralia Dominguez (SLPM 136025)
Frozier-Marrot (in French, aria only:
Pathé X 517)
Rita Gorr (ASDF 857)
Nina Isakova (Melodiya 33S 04631/2
329)
Félia Litvinne (in French, aria only: Od.
56220; Rococo R 38)
Eugenia Mantelli (aria only, with piano:

Zono 12591; Club 99.79)
Nan Merriman (Vic. 11–9793)
Irene Minghini-Cattaneo (DB 1441; LV
66)
Elena Obraztsova (Melodiya M33931)
Sigrid Onegin (DB 1292; LV 7)
Armida Parsi-Pettinella (Fono.
92054–55; CO 372)
Ruža Pospiš-Baldani (Jugoton LPY-V-
647)
Risë Stevens (Am. Col. 71440D; Y
31738)
Ebe Stignani
i) (LX 1106; 3C 153–17659)
ii) (aria only – Parlo. E 11344; LV
237)
Shirley Verrett (LSC 3045; SB 6979)

Four of the five original-language performances take pride of place: for they
embody a peculiarly French vocal art, that combination of *pudeur* and passion
poured into a line of ravishingly unemphatic smoothness; and to that art
Léonore's music seems peculiarly well suited. Litvinne's 'O mon Fernand' is
famous. More than any of her records that I have heard, except for the
equally famous 'Pleurez mes yeux', it captures the grandeur of her singing,
also an intimacy evoked in the careful, loving definition and binding of each
note (in the seven-note scale running downwards on 'Ah!', which links the
middle section to the melodic reprise, and which provides a moment of
exquisite 'breathing' in each of these four performances, she is supreme).
Quite as grandly beautiful, yet quite differently so, is the contained richness,
the disciplined amplitude of Delna, pressing each note close to the next,
expanding the tempo where the markings require it in a way that discovers
an extraordinary depth of feeling. If Charbonnel seems a singer of less
remarkable vocal substance, and her intonation is suspect once or twice, a
touch of astringency, of forwardness, in the timbre is fascinating. A similar
proviso, concerning insecure intonation, holds good for the Frozier-Marrot
version, and also similar praise for the fascinating colour, at once rich and
clear, of the timbre; this is the kind of French mezzo voice of which today's
operatic scene is particularly bereft, and particularly in need. All four singers
stick absolutely to the letter of the score; the traditional additions of Italian
mezzo-sopranos (e.g. G for F on the second 'dis*degno*') are stylistically
correct, but it is only the exceptional singer who draws expressive intensity
from them. The fifth account in French, by Mme Cahier *née* Sarah Jane
Walker, the American-born De Reszke pupil who sang much under Mahler,
is dispiritingly rough and unequal in register alignment, with strong notes
sticking out.

None of the others is entirely without merit; I pass over, as acceptable
rather than specially eventful, Cortez (singing in Italian on a self-proclaimed

recital of French airs!), Pospiš-Baldani, the very English-sounding Archibald (down a semitone), the swoopy Anday, even – though the fine quality of the voices comes across – Branzell and Risë Stevens, singing from far outside the role. The colourful Romanian, Cristoforeanu, is evidently well within it, but mistakes Léonore for Carmen. Mantelli is strangely lightweight, even trivial. Clara Butt (down, it seems, a semitone), sewing together snippets of aria and cabaletta, lacks any and every kind of sensuousness, for all the deep glory of the low notes (she trills brilliantly). Merriman and Anderson, two beautiful American voices, warm, rounded, dignified, suggest demure, lady-like Léonores; Anderson's simplicity and directness, though, are so potent that one enjoys her record as one would the best sort of concert performance. By contrast, two East Europeans, Afeyan and the Russian Isakova, both sound like full-blooded creatures of the theatre. The first is continuously squally; the second, squally under pressure, makes one admire her breadth of phrase, her slightly 'old-fashioned' largeness of temperament. She sings, incidentally, the whole of the cabaletta, all the cadenzas as written, and even the low ending of the Ricordi vocal score. Let me note, also in passing, the splendidly unhurried control of her conductor, Boris Khaikin. Obraztsova, recorded (again with Khaikin) at a stage in her career slightly prior to her vogue in the West, proves a more patrician kind of singer than the one we now generally hear; except when loud and high, indeed, she seems almost *too* restrained, communicating either inhibition or else an incomplete mastery of style. (Alone among all these singers, she closes with the leap of a minor ninth given in the French vocal score.) Among modern mezzos Agnes Baltsa reveals, as well as a shining, colourful mezzo, a real aptitude for the music and the role; as yet, though, she hardly begins to *interpret* either (a big top B at the close of the coda is impressive, not ideally stylish). I hear in the low phrases of the Mexican Oralia Dominguez an almost unrivalled fullness among non-French singers, a sumptuousness that is also graced by poignancy; higher up, the timbre goes edgy. So does Gorr's, the metal of whose voice might have been tamed by the original language. Shirley Verrett, on her 'Pauline Viardot portrait' recital record, makes likewise the curious (and un-Viardot-like) choice of singing in Italian; she gently moulds the start of the aria, with a smoothness elsewhere somewhat sacrificed to an unevenness of vocal scale (much less so, however, than in the Queler concert performance). Sigrid Onegin's text is the same patchwork as Butt's, and quite as dislikable. Magisterially pure and unflustered as the singing undeniably is, I cannot accustom myself to its distanced, disembodied personality. Matzenauer, who in one verse of the cabaletta (plus cadenza) and coda sticks to the letter of the score, is no less magisterial than Onegin, and a good deal warmer besides; I find her magnificent, masterly in *portamento,* rich in feeling, a singer on the grandest scale.

A line of leading Italian mezzo-sopranos this century kept the role in the repertory at a time when Donizetti operas other than *Lucia* and perhaps *Elisir* and *Pasquale* were being derided and placed in cold storage. I have not heard Gianna Pederzini. Irene Minghini-Cattaneo, vibrant, thrilling in emotional sweep, sets a standard not easily equalled. And, indeed, it is not by Stignani (i), with its less than complete command of cantilena, while even in (ii) moments of roughness mar the attack; on both versions the downward run is botched. The classic largeness of the personality, the special beauty of the voice, come through. Barbieri, very youthful in sound – the recording was made in 1949, before the Cetra set – already composes the familiar features of the mature artist: voluptuous low phrases, vehemence and even wildness above, an unmistakable urgency in the delivery. My own happiest introduction has been to the record of a much earlier Italian, Parsi-Pettinella, who combines sensuousness, evenness, and excitement, in tones picturesque and darkly glowing: a wonderful singer. Burzio is a soprano in mezzo territory – which matters much less than the hysterical dramatization of feelings, and with it the rending in pieces of the line. She was a powerful artist, and the listener – this listener, at least – is not left entirely unmoved; but her style constitutes a total misapprehension of the piece.

I have heard three singers in solos extracted from the last act. The recitative-arioso 'Fernand, Fernand', Léonore's entrance into the chapel, needs a more penetrating appreciation of its complex of suffering emotions than Fanny Anitua (in Italian) can find, though soft notes are of lovely texture, light and full (D5501; RLS 743). The same holds true, except that the strong, impressively knit tone suggests an even more unlikely robustness, for 'Fernand, imite la clémence' as sung in her native tongue by the Swedish mezzo Sigrid Schillander (7C 153–35354 M). Burzio here (Club 99.87/88D), as earlier in her aria, goes over the top in a way that prompts a smile – and also the slightest lump in the throat.

Ideal casts? For *Lucrezia Borgia,* my imagination assembles Callas, Anselmi or Kraus, a Berbié schooled to merriment, lightness, and technical high finish by Schumann-Heink (it jibs over the actual stage presence of the latter because of an inability to picture her in Orsini's breeches), Chaliapin. For *Favorite* in the original – which is what I desire to hear most – Litvinne or Delna, Affre or Alvarez (with Vezzani every so often to stir things up – what luxury!), Renaud, Journet; and – with the proviso of their willingness to learn a new, and meaningful, Italian translation – Parsi-Pettinella or Matzenauer, Anselmi or Bonci, Battistini or Stracciari, Pinza. A 'singers' conductor' – Queler, Khaikin, Serafin, Gui, Bellezza (the latter three heard, but for reasons of space not praised, on more than one excerpt) – presides, firmly but spaciously, over both operas. And there are absolutely no cuts!

LUCREZIA BORGIA

LB Lucrezia Borgia; *G* Gennaro; *MO* Maffio Orsini; *A* Alfonso; *R* Rustighello;
Gu Gubetta; *As* Astolfo

1965 (Live performance – Carnegie
Hall, New York) Caballé *LB*;
Vanzo *G*; Berbié *MO*; Paskalis *A*;
Lampi *R*; Fazah *Gu*; Voketaitis
As / Chorus and Orch. of
American Opera Society / Perlea
Private C204

1966 (Live performance – San Carlo,
Naples) Gencer *LB*; Aragall *G*;
Rota *MO*; Petri *A*; Ricciardi *R*;
Frati *Gu*; Savoldi *As* / San Carlo
Opera Chorus and Orch. / Franci

1966 Caballé *LB*; Kraus *G*; Verrett
MO; Flagello *A*; Baratti *R*;

Brunetti *Gu*; El Hage *As* / RCA
Italiana Chorus and Orch. /
Perlea
RCA (UK) SER 5553–5
(US) LSC 6176

1978 Sutherland *LB*; Aragall *G*; Horne
MO; Wixell *A*; Ewer *R*; Van
Allan *Gu*; Zaccaria *As* / London
Opera Voices, National PO /
Bonynge
Decca D93D3 ④ K93K32
London OSA 13129 ④ OSA
5–13129

LA FAVORITE

L Léonore; *F* Fernand; *A* Alphonse; *B* Balthazar; *I* Inès; *G* Gaspard

1910 Lapeyrette *L*; Lassalle *F*; Albers
A; Malvini *B*; Gantéri *I*; De
Poumayrac *G* / chorus and orch. /
Ruhlmann
Pathé 1551–71; Bourg BG 4001–3

1955 (in Italian)
Simionato *L*; Poggi *F*; Bastianini
A; Hines *B*; Magnani *I*; De Palma
G / Florence Festival Chorus and
Orch. / Erede
Decca GOS 525–7
Richmond SRS 63510

1956 (in Italian)
Barbieri *L*; Raimondi *F*;
Tagliabue *A*; Neri *B*; L. di Lelio
I; M. Caruso *G* / Italian Radio
Chorus and Orch., Turin / Questa
Cetra ℗ LPS3256
Everest ℗ 405(3)

1973 (in Italian) (live performance)
Nave *L*; Pavarotti *F*; Buison *A*;
Giaiotti *B*; Bybee *I*; Atherton *G* /
San Francisco Opera Chorus and
Orch. / Cillario
UORC 294

1977 (in Italian)
Cossotto *L*; Pavarotti *F*; Bacquier
A; Ghiaurov *B*; Cotrubas *I*; De
Palma *G* / Teatro Comunale
Chorus and Orch., Bologna /
Bonynge
Decca D96D3 ④ K96K33
London OSA 13113 ④ OSA
5–13113

1930 (excerpts – in Italian)
Zinetti *L*; Solari *L*; Maugeri *A*;
Zambelli *B*; Mannarini *I*; Nessi *G*
/ La Scala Chorus and Orch. /
Molajoli
Columbia (Italy) GQX 10064–8*

1953 (excerpts) –
Couderc *L*; Fouché *F*; Cambon *A*
/ Pasdeloup Orch. / Allain
Vega ⓜ 80020

1953 (excerpts – in Italian)
Garofalo *L*; Formichini *F*;
Borgonovo *A*; Washington *B*;
Zanolli *I*; Mercuriali *G* / chorus
and orch. / Curiel
Columbia (Italy) ⓜ 33QSX12006
Angel ⓜ 35322

Nabucco

HAROLD ROSENTHAL

'With this opera it is fair to say my artistic career began. And in spite of the difficulties I had to contend with, *Nabucco* was born under a lucky star.' So Verdi summed up his first great triumph nearly forty years after the opera's première in a famous conversation with Giulio Ricordi in 1879 which was embodied in Pougin's *Giuseppe Verdi; Histoire Anecdotique* (1881). Of course, Verdi was right, *Nabucco* was the work which introduced the composer's music to the rest of Europe; it was the work in which his future wife, Giuseppina Strepponi, created the role of Abigail, and as a result of the artistic collaboration between composer and soprano in *Nabucco*, a friendship, which was to turn into love, sprang up between them; and it was the work which marked Verdi as the composer who was to become most closely identified with the Risorgimento.

Between 1842, the year of the opera's première, and 1861, *Nabucco* clocked up 121 performances at La Scala, and then inexplicably vanished from the repertory until 1912, when it was revived with Carlo Galeffi in the title role and Nazzareno de Angelis as Zachariah. There followed another twenty years of neglect at La Scala until Vittorio Gui conducted it on the opening night of the 1933–4 season with virtually the same cast as had opened the Florence Festival the previous May (Gina Cigna, Ebe Stignani, Giovanni Voyer, Galeffi and Tancredi Pasero – in Florence Gabriella Gatti and Alessandro Dolci had been the Fenena and Ishmael). It was also the opera chosen to reopen La Scala in 1946 with Maria Pedrini, Fedora Barbieri, Mario Binci, Gino Bechi and Cesare Siepi with Tullio Serafin conducting.

The first London performance of the opera was at the Royal Italian Opera in the Haymarket (not Covent Garden) in March 1846. Because of Victorian susceptibilities over the staging of works with biblical subjects, it was given under the title of *Nino, Re d'Assyria* with Luciano Fornasari as Nino, alias Nebuchadnezzar, Giulia Sanchioli as Abigail, Amalia Corbari as Fenena and Botelli as Zachariah, renamed Orotapse in this version; the conductor was none other than Balfe. The first Covent Garden performance was on 30 May 1850, when it appeared under yet another title: *Anato* with Ronconi in the title role (he had been the creator of Nabucco at La Scala), and a cast that included Jeanne Castellan, Enrico Tamberlik, and Joseph Tagliafico. In addition to Anato, Ismael was renamed Dario and Zachariah was called Rodiano! The Covent Garden management evidently thinking that Verdi's score was too short for a full evening's entertainment filled out the bill with Act 3 of Rossini's *Mosè* (given under the name of *Zora*) and Act 2 of *Lucrezia Borgia*. The work was very coolly received, and except for performing the middle two acts as an appendage to a performance of *Il Barbiere di Siviglia* later that season it was not heard again at Covent Garden until 1972, when Elena Suliotis sang Abigail. It was revived on a few occasions at Her Majesty's Theatre in the 1850s, always under the title of *Nino*. In 1857 a leading London critic could write, 'Strength of voice is the one thing needed in Verdi's music; and the consequence is that the singers of the present Italian school strain their voices till they very soon wear them out.'

Nabucco was not heard again in Britain until 1952 when the Glasgow Grand Opera Society revived it with Tom Williams in the title role, and it was conducted by Walter Susskind. In October the same year, the Welsh National Opera Company mounted the work with Ruth Packer as a most impressive Abigail, and it was for long a favourite with the company; this is hardly surprising as Verdi's magnificent choruses are just what the Welsh choristers love to sing.

As in Italy, *Nabucco* suffered long neglect in Germany until its revival in Mannheim in 1928. Its subject matter, however, was highly unlikely to appeal to the Nazis, and from 1933 it was rarely given, though there was a production in Berlin in 1935 by the Jüdischer Kulturbund, and then in 1939, Julius Kapp, the dramaturg of the Berlin State Opera, produced a new 'version' in which the characters were again changed – this was produced in Cassel in 1939. After the war, however, it returned to popularity in Germany, beginning with the famous Carl Ebert production in Berlin with Christel Goltz as Abigail and Marko Rothmüller in the title role. In the United States it has had a few revivals in recent years: at the Metropolitan in the 1960–1 season with Leonie Rysanek, Cornell MacNeil and Cesare Siepi; in Chicago in 1963 with Danica Mastilović, Tito Gobbi and Boris Christoff; and in San Francisco in 1964 with Gladys Kuchta, Gobbi and Giorgio Tozzi. It can hardly be called a popular Verdi opera in that country.

Possibly because of the two long periods of neglect mentioned above, *Nabucco* featured little in record catalogues in pre-LP days. There were, of course, the odd discs by Stracciari, Titta Ruffo, José Mardones and De Angelis; a handful of overtures and the 'Va pensiero' chorus. Of the great Verdi sopranos, only Giannina Russ recorded some of Abigail's music; and except for Nabucco's prayer, 'Dio di Giuda', in the last act, there is not really any 'detachable' music in the title role. Even that great Verdi bass Pinza did not record a note of Zachariah's music until almost the end of his career. And so *Nabucco* did not really come into its own on record until the LP era.

There are five complete recordings, beginning with the once-pirated but now 'legal' Cetra live set which is the first complete performance on disc of

Callas in opera. It was broadcast and recorded on the opening night of the 1949–50 season at the Teatro San Carlo in Naples and conducted by Vittorio Gui. There were three performances, the last of which was on 27 December; I was in Milan that night, in Rome a few days later and in Naples for *Wozzeck* on New Year's Eve. Had I known then that the 27 December performance would be the last time that Callas was ever to sing Abigail, I would have rearranged the whole of my Italian schedule!

Callas was twenty-six years old at the time of that performance, and she was utterly fearless in her attack, hurling herself into the dramatic recitatives in an almost reckless but always exciting manner, and showing, even at that early stage in her career, an uncanny way of getting right inside the character and singing the music as if it was being heard for the first time. The voice sounds young, there is little or no sign of the wobble or squally top notes that were to become unfortunate hallmarks of later Callas performances; and one can only regret that she never again could be persuaded to sing the role in the theatre or for a complete recording in studio conditions, though I doubt whether, without the challenge of a live audience, she would ever have proved quite so exciting in the studio. Listen to the ease and the purity with which those top Cs are taken, whether *forte* or *pianissimo*, at the end of the cavatina 'Anch'io dischiuso'; in the cabaletta, with its trills she is breath-taking and at the end of the second verse, she throws in an additional top C for good measure.

Gino Bechi in the title role is no match for Callas. Why his brilliant career was so short remains something of a mystery; he was, after all, the leading Verdi baritone of the 1940s and was compared by many to Ruffo. But already by 1949 he had lost much of the dramatic drive and thrust that marked his performances of Amonasro and Renato during the war years; however, he does respond to Callas in the great Act 3 duet. Luciano Neroni is a routine Zachariah, Gino Sinimberghi an unimaginative Ishmael and Amalia Pini makes little of Fenena.

The second complete recording, also on the Cetra label, originated in the Radio Italiana's performance on 16 January 1951 which inaugurated the Verdi year. It has some cuts, mostly of repeats, and the actual sound varies from the coarse, with blasting in many of the *tutti* passages, to the tolerable in the quieter passages. Paolo Silveri's Nabucco is uneven; at his best, as in the 'Dio di Giuda', he sings with expression and feeling. Caterina Mancini as Abigail is apt to sound wild and undisciplined, and there are a few moments when the eardrums are shattered; but she certainly has no inhibitions about the role. Antonio Cassinelli's Zachariah lacks nobility and he often sings in a pedestrian manner. Mario Binci, remembered from the 1946 San Carlo season at Covent Garden, is a good Ishmael. Gabriella Gatti, a correct soprano Fenena (the role is more often sung, at least in Italy, by mezzos), is sweet-voiced and lyrical. The conductor is Fernando Previtali who offers a fiery and unpolished reading of the score. The Radio Italiana's chorus is heard to good effect.

The Decca set, released in 1966, was made in Vienna; but under Lamberto Gardelli's inspired conducting and with the Scala's chorus master, Roberto Benaglio, in charge of the Vienna State Opera chorus, we have first-rate orchestral and choral performances. So do we of the title role with Gobbi in his very best voice, giving one of his most inspired performances as the demented king. The Abigail is Elena Suliotis, who at that period of her career sounded like a young Callas. Even at that time the various registers of her voice were not closely knitted together, and the middle lacked support; but her performance, as a whole, leaves the listener breathless. Although Carlo Cava sings 'nicely' as Zachariah he does not possess the vocal and dramatic stature to dominate the scenes in which he appears. Bruno Prevedi is an excellent Ishmael, but Dora Carral is inadequate as Fenena.

Twelve years elapsed before the next complete *Nabucco*. The HMV recording is notable for the conducting of Riccardo Muti and the assumption of the role of Abigail by Renata Scotto. Matteo Manuguerra (Nabucco) is a fine Verdi baritone and his singing gives constant pleasure, but I was rarely moved by him as I was by Gobbi. Scotto's Abigail was one of her first *lirico spinto* roles and proves a most interesting performance. More than once I was reminded of Callas by the way Scotto treats the text – also by ugly and shaky top notes. None the less hers is an exciting portrayal and there is much to praise in it. The beefy Russian mezzo soprano, Elena Obraztsova, as Fenena seems a misguided piece of casting; a more youthful-sounding and lighter voice is surely needed for this role. Nicolai Ghiaurov should have been an imposing Zachariah, but he was not in his best voice when he made this recording and there are passages when the voice does not sound as it did. Veriano Luchetti is a first-rate Ishmael and makes what is, after all, a minor role, into something rather more.

In the spring of 1982, the Deutsche Oper in West Berlin revived Gustav Rudolf Sellner's 1979 production of *Nabucco*, which had originally been conducted by Jesus Lopez-Cobos, and had Ingvar Wixell in the title role, Angeles Gulin as Abigail and Bengt Rundgren as Zachariah. The 1982 revival, which Deutsche Gramophon planned to record, was conducted by Giuseppe Sinopoli, with Piero Cappuccilli in the title role, Ghena Dimitrova as Abigail, and Evgeny Nesterenko as Zachariah. The DG recording, which naturally employed the orchestra and chorus of the Deutsche Oper, is very strongly cast indeed. In addition to Cappuccilli, Dimitrova and Nesterenko, there are Lucia Valentini Terrani as Fenena, Lucia Popp in the tiny role of Anna, Placido Domingo as Ishmael and Kurt Rydl as the High Priest of Baal.

The performance is, however, most disappointing. For this the controversial Sinopoli must take the blame. Although he generates a certain excitement, the result is a hard-driven performance marked by extremes of tempo. Sinopoli has, I would suggest, been 'over-sold' by the publicists who consider him the new Messiah among conductors; I see him as a prime example of gramophone-industry promotion.

Cappuccilli may be a seasoned Verdian, but one Verdi role sounds very much like another as far as his performances are concerned. He is rarely inside his part although he does manage to catch the pathos of 'Dio di Giuda'. Dimitrova has made a speciality of Abigail, the role in which she made her debut in Sofia in 1965 when she was twenty-five years of age. She has sung it with success in South America, the Verona Arena and elsewhere. She is a true dramatic soprano in the Arangi-Lombardi, Eva Turner, Gina Cigna mould. Unfortunately, at the time of the Berlin performances in 1982 she had not fully recovered from a three-month's illness that had left her virtually voiceless. Under the scrutiny of the microphone her vocal method sounds less than perfect, and there are a few unpleasant sounds at the top; none the less hers is an exciting performance. Nesterenko is a rich-voiced Zachariah though his characterization remains rather muted.

Domingo succeeds in turning the thankless role of Ishmael into something rather more than that; Valentini Terrani is specially impressive as Fenena and displays her *bel canto* technique in her aria. Popp unfortunately has little to do as Anna.

The orchestra and chorus of the Deutsche Oper are good but certainly not outstanding, and cannot approach the richness of sound achieved by the excellent Vienna forces in the Decca recording.

Muti and the Philharmonia Orchestra give an invigorating and exciting account of Verdi's youthful score, and the orchestral playing has a Mediterranean warmth which the Ambrosian Singers do not equal. In any case, only an Italian (or perhaps Welsh) chorus can sweep into 'Va pensiero' as to the manner born.

A Saga disc of excerpts was recorded in Hamburg under Georg Singer with Lawrence Winters displaying too much vibrato in the title role, and a lady called Norma Giusti over-parted as Abigail. Giuseppe Savio makes little of Ishmael, but Erika Wien is an attractive Fenena. The Hamburg chorus sounds out of its element; this is unfortunate as Nicola Rossi-Lemeni as Zachariah summons them to the cause with great authority.

The DG excerpts disc includes the three Zachariah arias, the Abigail-Fenena-Ishmael trio, Fenena's aria, the Abigail-Nabucco scene and the 'Va pensiero' chorus all sung in German, by a mixed nationality cast: the American baritone Thomas Stewart as Nabucco and his wife Evelyn Lear as Fenena; the German Wagner soprano Liane Synek as an unwieldy Abigail; the Hungarian tenor Sándor Kónya as an Italianate Ishmael; and the Finnish bass, Martti Talvela, as a sonorous and Sarastro-like Zachariah. Horst Stein conducts the orchestra and chorus of the Deutsche Oper in West Berlin.

There is a 'private' issue of parts of a concert performance of the opera at the Concertgebouw in Amsterdam in 1960 (not 1957 as the label says). This performance marked the reappearance after her semi-retirement of Anita Cerquetti; but her Abigail is only a shadow of what one had hoped it might have developed into after her earlier appearances in that role. Dino Dondi's Nebuchadnezzar is a clumsy, unsubtle performance, but Ugo

Trama's Zachariah has moments of distinction. The orchestra and chorus of
Radio Hilversum are conducted adequately by Fulvio Vernizzi.

Nabucco is divided in four parts, not acts, and each part is given a title
(as in *Il trovatore*): Part I is 'Jerusalem'; Part 2, 'The Unbeliever' or 'The
Wicked Man'; Part 3 'The Prophecy' and Part 4, 'The Shattered Idol'. In
addition to these titles, there is a subtitle to each section, either a direct
quotation or a paraphrase of a quotation from the Book of Jeremiah. The
overture, supposedly composed by Verdi in a café during the rehearsal
period, is based on themes from the opera, including the famous 'Va
pensiero' chorus, which is far less effective in three-eight time than in the
lovely flowing four-in-a-bar, in the second scene of Part 3. It is not one of
Verdi's best overtures, but makes a rousing beginning to the opera. There
are some twenty different recorded versions, including nine on 78s, of which
those of the Milan Symphony Orchestra under Antonio Guarnieri (Od.
176879) and of the EIAR (Radio Italiana) Orchestra under Sergio Failoni
(Parlo. BB 25011) give a fair idea of the gifts of these two conductors. Of
the various LP versions that by the Philharmonia under Tullio Serafin (MFP
2059) shows the great Italian conductor shaping the sweeping phrases in the
true Verdi tradition, while that by the Philharmonic Promenade Orchestra
[*sic*] under Charles Mackerras (SXLP 30019) demonstrates similar virtues;
so do Chailly and the National Philharmonic (SXDC 7595). Karajan and the
Berlin Philharmonic (DG 2531 145) are exaggerated and self-conscious, and
Abbado and the LSO (RL 31378) surprisingly lacklustre.

The opening chorus, 'Gli arredi festivi giù cadano infranti', in which the
Hebrews, Levites, and Hebrew Virgins lament their defeat by Nebuchadnezzar leads straight into the first of several magnificent scenes for Zachariah.
He is the first of Verdi's great 'ecclesiastical' basses, and encourages his
people, reminding them that hope is still left to them – 'Sperate, o figli!'. In
the ensuing cabaletta, 'Come notte', which could almost be a Salvation Army
tune, but which is, none the less, very difficult to sing, Zachariah and the
people exhort Jehovah to disperse the invading Assyrian hordes. This whole
scene right from the rise of the curtain is sung by the younger Ghiaurov and
the Ambrosian Singers, with the LSO, magisterially conducted by Claudio
Abbado (GRV 6). Ghiaurov's lovely bass voice and beautifully controlled
singing are immediately apparent, but what one misses, at least on record,
is the singer's ability to create a strong and identifiable character. Far more
dramatic is Nicola Rossi-Lemeni's performance (ALP 1099) with the Royal
Opera House chorus and the Philharmonia Orchestra under Anatole Fistou-
lari, which begins at 'Sperate, o figli!' Rossi-Lemeni makes an honest attempt
really to sing the music – though there is a bit of 'ho, ho-ing' in the cabaletta
– and displays a big line and ample tone. Towering above both his rivals
vocally and dramatically is Boris Christoff (SLS 5090), with the chorus and
orchestra of the Rome Opera under Gui, who knows just exactly how to
pace this kind of music. To hear Christoff telling the Israelites to curb their
fears, 'Freno al timor!', creates a vivid picture in sound of the High Priest.

Unfortunately the cabaletta is not included. Nazzareno de Angelis, with his rich Italianate bass and splendid phrasing, sings 'Sperate, o figli!', recorded in the 1930s (CQX 10196; LV 85).

The only other extract from Part 1 available on disc is the short confrontation between Zachariah and Nebuchadnezzar as the latter tries to enter the Temple on horseback. Titta Ruffo first sings the lines of the High Priest, beginning with the words, 'Che tenti? O trema, insano!' and then, as the King threatens to drown the Hebrews in a sea of blood – 'Tremin gl'insani'. Ruffo successfully darkens and deepens his voice for the first part of the scene, and then becomes his recognizable vocal self as Nebuchadnezzar. Ruffo recorded this vocal duet with himself about 1914–15 (DA 358; Rococo R16).

Part 2 opens with Abigail's recitative and aria 'Ben io t'invenni . . . Anch'io dischiuso un giorno', in which she discovers that she is not the daughter of Nebuchadnezzar after all, but a slave. She expresses her horror at this discovery and then thinks of her love for Ishmael. In the cabaletta, 'Salgo già del trono', she resolves to seize the throne for herself. By far the most exciting version available is that made by Callas in 1958 (ASD 3817), even though that final high C is not what it should be vocally – nor indeed is it what Verdi originally wrote. This is not the only recording by Callas of this *scena;* she sang it in a Radio Italiana concert in Rome in February 1952, and this performance has been officially reissued by RCA. Her Paris Radio performance in June 1963 conducted by Georges Prêtre was issued 'privately'. This last version is to be avoided, as the voice seems to be out of control in the recitative and she is clearly in difficulties in the cadenza, opting for the lower A rather than the high C.

Renata Scotto's performance on her Verdi recital (CBS 76426) was made a year or so before her complete recording. When I first reviewed it I wrote that she had developed into a first-class Verdi soprano and on the strength of the recital prophesied that 'she should also make a formidable Abigail'.

Anita Cerquetti only sings the recitative and aria (GRV 13), but her performance fills one with regret that her career was so shortlived. Birgit Nilsson's steely, Wagnerian tones (SXL 6033) are certainly exciting, but she does not sound quite authentic. A 'Golden Age of Opera' disc (EJS 421), devoted to Donizetti and Verdi arias sung by Leyla Gencer, includes the recitative and aria, but not the cabaletta. The Turkish soprano was in particularly good voice on this occasion. There are also recordings by the Rumanian soprano, Arta Florescu (Electrecord ECE 0164) and the Russian soprano, Nelly Tkachenko (Melodiya S 01 234/4).

The second scene of Part 2 opens with Zachariah's Prayer, 'Tu sul labbro', the most frequently recorded aria from *Nabucco*. It is preceded by a particularly beautiful orchestral passage, some 16 bars long, in which the solo cello is very prominent. Zachariah bids a Levite, carrying the Tablets of the Law, to come and stand by him 'Vieni O Levita', and then praises Jehovah in the aria 'Tu sul labbro', which Verdi instructs should be sung 'tutto sotto voce'.

De Angelis (GQX 10196; GV 95) and José Mardones (Victor 6434–A; LV 268) represent the earlier generation of recording artists. I found Mardones, in particular, most moving and noble, and could well imagine why his Father Guardian in *La forza del destino* was so highly regarded.

The most frequent Italian interpreter of the role before Cesare Siepi was Tancredi Pasero; but I find his somewhat gruff way with this music not at all to my liking (DB 5440; LV 261). Pinza, as I have already pointed out, never sang the role on the stage and only recorded the aria towards the end of his career in 1951 (RCA RB 16040) – nor is it one of the singer's better efforts. The early Siepi (Parlo. R. 30024) reveals a most beautiful sound, but not quite enough backbone; while his later version (Decca 411 659) displays increased authority and a maturity not previously shown. Rossi-Lemeni (ALP 1099) is a bit woolly; Ghiaurov (GRV 6) spoils the vocal line by being over-sentimental; the Polish bass Bernard Ladysz (33CX 1678) is unidiomatic and his Italian sounds very odd; an Hungarian bass, Béla Venczell (1881–1945), who retired in 1930, sings the aria in Hungarian, accompanied on the piano (Qualiton LPX 11311) – a curiosity this; and Giorgio Tozzi sings most beautifully and impressively (RCA RB 16089) – far more so indeed than when I heard him in the role with the San Francisco Opera in 1964. A version by Jerome Hines (Epic BC 1334) I have not heard.

In the scene immediately following, the priests round on Ishmael and accuse him of treachery 'Il maledetto non ha fratelli'. This has been recorded by the tenor Giovanni Voyer and chorus (Col. GQ 7188); Voyer sang the role at La Scala in the 1933–4 season, and elsewhere in Italy both before and after the war. Part 2 ends with the spectacular moment when Nebuchad-nezzar is struck down by lightning. 'Who has snatched my royal sceptre?' asks the King ('Chi mi toglie il regio scettro?') in various unsatisfactory versions by Enrico Nani (Fono. 69171), Umberto Urbano (Poly. 72973), Riccardo Stracciari (Col. 4032; Club 99.29) and Galeffi (Col. 74798; LV 220) – unsatisfactory because one really wants the whole enormous ensemble which leads up to this extract to appreciate Verdi's mastery here.

The first scene of Part 3 includes one of Verdi's father-daughter duets which has rarely been recorded, as far as I have been able to trace, except for a performance by Enrico Nani and Giannina Russ (Fono. 69172/3/4) which begins with Nabucco's words 'Donna chi sei?' and continues through to the end of the scene – a considerable extract for those early days of recording. Russ was an underrated singer in Anglo-Saxon countries, possibly because the slight vibrato she displayed was not to the liking of audiences in England and America; but her voice was a beautiful one, perhaps too beautiful for Abigail, and her musicianship and phrasing are of the highest order. Nani too was an underrated singer, but in an age that boasted such outstanding Verdi baritones as Ruffo, De Luca, Stracciari and Galeffi, to mention but four, that is hardly surprising.

Scene ii, on the banks of the Euphrates, opens with the most famous chorus in all Verdi, 'Va, pensiero'; this is the chorus that became synonymous to the Italians with their own suffering under the Austrian occupation, and the chorus that the huge crowds sang spontaneously at both Verdi's and Toscanini's funerals. Obviously I have not heard even half of the forty or more recordings of this chorus in the catalogues. Possibly the most moving account of this scene is that conducted by Toscanini in one of his wartime broadcasts (31 January 1943) with the NBC Symphony Orchestra and Westminster Choir (RCA RB 16139 or LM 6041–1). Also highly recommended is Serafin's performance with the Scala orchestra and chorus (33CX 1376) which has a real theatrical tang about it. As has also a performance by the Welsh National Opera Chorus and Orchestra on a disc devoted entirely to Verdi opera choruses (ASD 3811); their wonderfully uninhibited singing shows that the Welsh choristers can challenge the Italians on their own ground.

'Va, pensiero' is immediately followed by Zachariah's 'Prophecy'. He arrives on the scene, chiding the children of Israel for weeping, 'Oh, chi piange?' and then prophesies that Jehovah, here referred to as the Lion of Judah, will triumph and that Babylon will be destroyed – 'Del futuro nel buio discerno'. Once again it is Christoff who is supreme in this scene (SLS 5090); there are the same reservations about Rossi-Lemeni (ALP 1099) and Ghiaurov (GRV 6) as expressed above when commenting on Zachariah's first scene. The Ghiaurov version incidentally begins with 'Va, pensiero', most genteelly sung by the Ambrosian Singers. There are also versions by Mardones (Am. Col. 5061 M; LV 269, RLS 743) and Georg Hann and the Stuttgart Opera's forces (Poly. 64851) which I have not heard.

The final Part of the opera includes Nebuchadnezzar's 'Mad scene', ending with his prayer to Jehovah, who restores his sanity – 'Dio di Giuda'. The only modern single versions of this are by Giampiero Malaspina (Parlo. RO 30006; OASI 529) which is blistering, Giuseppe Valdengo, at the end of his career (Supraphon SUA 50617), finding him in poor voice, and Tito Gobbi on side five of 'The Art of Tito Gobbi' (RLS 738). Gobbi recorded ten items in Rome under Olivero de Fabriitis in October 1955 for an unpublished disc. It eventually appeared in the album at the same time as the baritone's autobiography was published in 1979. From an earlier generation, Riccardo Stracciari (HRS 1103; Club 99.29) and Carlo Galeffi (Regal 16388; LV 220) are to be heard as fine Verdi stylists. I have not heard versions by Enrico Nani and Umberto Urbano.

The last extract is Fenena's Prayer 'Oh, dischiuso è il firmamento!', which she sings as she is being led with the Hebrews to the altar to be sacrificed to Baal (of course she and everyone else are saved in the nick of time, and Abigail meets her deserved fate). As already noted Fenena is very often sung in Italy by mezzos, such as Stignani, Barbieri and Fiorenza Cossotto, who has recorded this Bellini-like cavatina most beautifully on Philips AL 3443.

NABUCCO

N Nabucco; *I* Ishmael; *Z* Zachariah; *A* Abigail; *F* Fenena; *HP* High Priest

1949 (live performance – Teatro San
     Carlo, Naples)
     Bechi *N*; Sinimberghi *I*; Neroni *Z*;
     Callas *A*; Pini *F*; Riccò *HP* / San
     Carlo Opera Chorus and Orch. /
     Gui
     Cetra ⓜ LO16 (3)
     Turnabout ⓜ THS 65137–9
1951 Silveri *N*; Binci *I*; Cassinelli *Z*;
     Mancini *A*; Gatti *F*; Gaggi *HP* /
     Italian Radio Chorus and Orch.,
     Rome / Previtali
     Cetra ⓔ LPS 3216
     Everest ⓔ S455 (3)
1965 Gobbi *N*; Prevedi *I*; Cava *Z*;
     Suliotis *A*; Carral *F*; Foiani *HP* /
     Vienna State Opera Chorus and
     Orch. / Gardelli
     Decca SET 298–300 ④ K126K32
     London OSA 1382 ④ OSA5–1382
1977 Manuguerra *N*; Luchetti *I*;
     Ghiaurov *Z*; Scotto *A*;
     Obraztsova *F*; Lloyd *HP* /

Ambrosian Opera Chorus,
Philharmonia / Muti
EMI SLS 5132 ④ TC-SLS 5132
Angel SCLX 3850Q ④ 4X3X-3850
1982 Cappuccilli *N*; Domingo *I*;
     Nesterenko *Z*; Dimitrova *A*;
     Valentini Terrani *F*; Rydl *HP* /
     German Opera Chorus & Orch.,
     Berlin/Sinopoli
     DG 2741 021 ④ 3382 021
     ⓒⓓ 410 512–2
1960 (excerpts)
     Winters *N*; Savio *I*; Rossi-Lemeni
     Z; Giusti *A*; Wien *F* / Hamburg
     Radio Chorus and SO / Singer
     Saga XID 5173
     ASCO A106
1964 (excerpts – in German)
     Stewart *N*; Kónya *I*; Talvela *Z*;
     Synek *A*; Lear *F* / German Opera
     Chorus and Orch., Berlin / Stein
     DG 2537 008 ④ 3306 008

Les Vêpres Siciliennes

LORD HAREWOOD

In 1853, while he contemplated tackling the vast subject of *King Lear,* Verdi received Scribe's libretto for *Les Vêpres Siciliennes,* his second commission for the Paris Opéra (*Jérusalem*, a drastic revision of I Lombardi was the first). Before long, he was writing to the Director of that institution to protest against the libretto's contents and the apparent reluctance of Scribe to make alterations. Scribe agreed to change virtually nothing and Verdi's final Italian version of the score, unlike that of *Don Carlos,* is effectively a literal (and not very good) translation of the French, with none of the music recomposed.

The libretto's main disadvantage lies in the patent and odious treachery of the Sicilian patriots, who are its ostensible heroes but to whom the end apparently justifies any means. Procida for instance, music apart, is an unsympathetic, even two-dimensional figure. But there, of course, lies the point; with Verdi, the music is *never* 'apart', and if one can accept the motivation, looking at it from the point of view – say – of the citizen of an occupied country in 1942, there is not so much to cavil at. Verdi may have disliked the plot, but he accepted it and knew that the situations he and Scribe hammered out were of a kind to inspire dramatic music, full of the clash of personality and motive which he looked for, and of pathos, which brought out one of the best sides of his compositional nature, and recent major revivals in Hamburg, Paris, at the Metropolitan and the London Coliseum, always in one or other manifestation of a splendid production by John Dexter, have had consistent success.

The one truly complete recording seems superficially to be based on the Metropolitan performance, but in point of fact it antedates it by a year (1973; the Met première was in 1974), and was made in London. All the small parts are excellently done with prominent British and American singers, and the leads are finely taken by Martina Arroyo, singing beautifully if with none too personal a quality; Sherrill Milnes, a younger-sounding baritone than a role of Montfort's seniority suggests, but at his best in the *dolcissimo* section of the aria; and Ruggero Raimondi, the voice already rather 'brown' in colour for what is one of Verdi's grandest and noblest bass roles. Placido Domingo brings excitement from his first vocal entry, and brilliance and intensity throughout, but I began to wonder whether now, with performances of the difficult, high-lying role to his credit, he would not give a maturer performance than he could then. All the same, he sings even the awkward *melodia* of the last act stunningly – he cut it altogether when I heard him at the Met in 1975.

James Levine conducts an absolutely uncut performance, as is now *de rigueur* on record, though it is a long work and some trimming is perhaps advisable in the theatre. It goes with a swing but some of the excitement is a little hectic, and, as with Domingo, one could wish he had had more experience of the work in the theatre before he came to conduct the complete set. The ballet music, enjoyable but long, sounds well; it is perhaps Verdi's best essay for dance, with one or two really beautiful tunes, and it is ironical that it was cut in each of the Dexter productions including that for Paris, where its 1855 première took place. Much cut, but in spite of frequently muddy sound, particularly in the orchestra, of high musical and historical value is the Cetra set made at a performance in Florence in May 1951. As always with the great Erich Kleiber, clarity is the watchword and he keeps things moving without exaggeration. As I remember from the performance, he provides time and space for his singers, who are never hustled into anti-vocal tempi, and, in the case of Maria Callas and Boris Christoff, he allows them, for purely musico-dramatic ends, more than a little latitude. Enzo Mascherini's baritone is dark and beautiful but much of his singing less than ideally smooth, and the tenor, Giorgio Kokolios, gifted with a good solid ring to his voice, shows more fire than subtlety. From the start Boris Christoff establishes the high-minded purpose of Procida, but in the studio he might have allowed himself a wider dynamic range than he was apparently prepared to risk in the theatre.

Far the most valuable part of the set, however, comes with Callas's unsurpassed Elena, and there is not a bar which remains unilluminated by her imagination, from the veiled and mysterious quality of her entry, through the magical poise at the start of her opening cavatina (much helped by Kleiber's buoyant accompaniment) to the launching of the cabaletta, one of the major recorded illustrations of her theatrical supremacy. The full sound of her *pianissimo* singing never fails to astonish, and here it is deployed in a huge theatre rather than in a studio; but then one reminds oneself that public performance always brought out her best.

With virtually the same cuts as Kleiber imposed on the score (presumably they were standard in Germany, as Kleiber conducted a famous revival in Berlin in the early 1930s) is an enjoyable performance in German dating from 1951 as I believe rather than 1941 as the record sleeve states – the life of Schlusnus co-authored by his widow refers to it as one of his last operatic performances, the other *Traviata* in Coblenz and gives the date as 28 January 1951. Moreover, Schlusnus lived after the war in Frankfurt, whose radio station was referred to as Frankfurter Funk until after the war, when it became Hessischer Rundfunk. Schröder's conducting is rather old fashioned and the acoustic is characteristic of radio at the time, but at least two of the singers are outstanding. Heinrich Schlusnus one of the finest Verdi baritones Germany produced (Kleiber's Montfort in Berlin), was in his early sixties at the time of the recording. His authority is total and both he and the tenor Helge Rosvaenge show welcome confidence in their singing. Rosvaenge was already showing the tendency to over-emphasis which, for me, spoils most of his later singing, but the brilliance of the top is rare and invigorating and to hear in Act 3 the big tune of the overture sung first by Schlusnus and then by him is an invigorating experience. Neither Maud Cunitz nor Otto von Rohr is on this level, he rather cavernous of tone, she with a tendency to the tremulous. But one easily sees why Deutsche Grammophon decided to issue the recording.

The work has been revived from time to time in Italy, and Tullio Serafin, as one would expect, was associated with some of the performances of the 1950s. An arbitrary selection from the performance he conducted in Palermo in 1957 is available on a 'private' issue and shows the brilliant upper register and humdrum musical quality of the tenor Mario Filippeschi, the reliability of Antonietta Stella and Giuseppe Taddei, and the unusually strong voice of Bernard Ladysz, the Procida. Emphasis is on solos and duets; the performance is on a decidedly provincial level.

The overture is one of Verdi's most famous, and leading Italian (or Italianate) conductors have tended to record it. Toscanini played it with the NBC in 1942 and the listener starts by thinking this no-nonsense approach to the music is classical in feeling but ends by suspecting that to take the later part at this speed is to ask the impossible of an orchestra. De Sabata recorded it a few years later in Rome and, while achieving Toscanini's intensity though with less hectic tempi, suggests more than his great predecessor the gloomy events to which this overture is a prelude. Better still is Giulini's with the Philharmonia (SXLP 30094) – very clear and full of energy and expression. The overture lasts over eight and a half minutes and yet Giulini's, so much clearer than Toscanini's, is only fifteen seconds longer! There is a grand sweep as well as dynamic contrast and superb playing from Karajan and the Berlin Philharmonic (DG 2531 145) but they cannot prevent an element of the sentimental from creeping into their treatment of the famous cello tune. So uncharacteristically tame are Abbado and the LSO (RL 31378) that I must suppose the recording was taken on an off-day. Muti and the New Philharmonia (ASD 3366) make a very different impression with a reading that pulsates with Italianate drama from the outset and finishes with a *prestissimo* last section which seems about to defy the laws of gravity and take off. It would be hard to imagine a more brilliant performance.

The beautiful entrance aria of Elena has never been commercially recorded but a live performance by Antonietta Stella is available on a 'private' disc, with the cavatina floated imaginatively and the bravura of the cabaletta holding no terrors for her. From a 1974 Met. performance comes the duet for tenor and baritone that finishes the first act, done by Nicolai Gedda and

Cornell MacNeil on another 'private' record; it shows the tenor ideally impetuous, MacNeil properly forthright.

I traced twenty-four performances of the great bass aria, 'O tu Palermo', and heard twenty-one of them. Neither of those by Mark Reizen, one in Russian (Melodiya D 1316–7) and the other in Italian (D 8483–4) shows him at his best; this laboured, heavy-breathing singing is unrepresentative. Wilhelm Strienz (EH 960 – in German; 1C 047–28557) is lightweight, uninvolved, and neither of the versions by Norman Allin (L 1553; BNOC 1 – in English) and Malcolm McEachern (Voc K 05130 in Italian; SYO 1) makes much dramatic impact, though each sings with considerable vocal weight.

An early performance in the original French, which sounds well and is well sung, is by Pierre d'Assy (032104) and it is something of a curiosity as, even played as slowly as 72rpm, it still 'sounds' up a semitone. Joseph Rouleau some seventy years later also sang it in French (SXL 6637) fluently but without ideal authority or indeed firmness at the top of the voice. Ludwig Weber in Italian (LX 1310; 1C 177–00933–4) is an example of a Germanic inability to combine the legato which Italian music requires with the fire which this aria absolutely needs. More committed and powerful is Paul Schöffler (AVRS 6022), recorded I suspect in the 1960s. His Italian is faulty, but the singing meticulous and generous. Kim Borg (EPL 30236) is no Verdian bass, but the aria was recorded at the top of the career of an always interesting singer, which cannot be said of Cesare Siepi's performance (R 30007; LPC 55038) made in 1947 when he was still in his early twenties and as a result sounded lightweight and lacking in purpose. José Mardones (Vic. 6434; LV 269) produces massive sounds but demonstrates a rather cavalier attitude to rhythmical niceties.

Bernard Ladysz (33CX 1678) displays much vocal splendour, and the tone, but unfortunately not the pronunciation, is thoroughly Italianate. Christoff (RLS 735) recorded the aria in 1952 but it was unissued until recently; in spite of the purposeful singing, it is not amongst his finest efforts. Nor, one could argue, is the performance in Italian by Alexander Kipnis (Poly. 65724; LV 37) one of his, but it is sung cleanly and with clarity though in peculiar Italian. The great Ezio Pinza never to my knowledge sang the role on stage but recorded it for a second time (RB 16040) in 1951 when he was fifty-nine with Leinsdorf conducting. There is some tendency to sing slightly below the note and one cannot help feeling that by then it had become for him nothing but a concert aria. No such reservations need be made about his famous 1927 version (DB 1087; LV 27), which shows ardent phrasing, a voice of black velvet, and such fire and drama as to banish any notion of it as no more than a concert piece. A word of warning; the original must be played at around 76rpm if you are to hear it at the correct pitch.

Nicola Rossi-Lemeni recorded the aria with formidable intensity (ALP 1099) and makes a noble, brooding patriot. Only some explosiveness in the singing slightly detracts from a splendid performance, which, however, lacks the control displayed by Nicolai Ghiaurov in his 1970 recording (GRV 6) which has the advantage of being accompanied by the LSO conducted by Claudio Abbado. The natural opulence of Ghiaurov's great voice is very much in evidence, but I think if I had to choose a single version it would be that of Tancredi Pasero (E 11373; LV 34), for many years a dominant figure in Italian operatic life and the leading bass in Italy (Pinza was in America) in the years before and during the war. The voice is even throughout the range, the approach full of drama, and Pasero commands a fine legato style. Truly noble singing!

The opera's third act starts with Montfort's fine soliloquy and there are three different performances by Schlusnus, all in German. That of 1933 (Poly. 35003; LV 110) was made a year after Kleiber's Berlin revival and shows a glorious voice in its prime; there is one small cut. By the time he recorded it again in 1942 in the studio with Arthur Rother conducting, the voice was showing little decline, though there were problems of intonation. The recitative is included but there is a big cut in the aria (Poly. 68119). Schlusnus sings it in full on Acanta DE 21487, also in 1942 and accompanied by Rother, and this is better than the studio performance, although it is transferred a semitone down and must be played at 34rpm to sound in the proper key.

The first revival at La Scala this century was in 1907 with Nazzareno de Angelis as Procida (who did not record the famous aria), Esther Mazzoleni and Riccardo Stracciari, who both made *Vespri* records. Stracciari's (Fono. 92623: CO 375) gives us only half the aria but demonstrates the great voice and direct, powerful vocalism which always characterized this singer. Fischer-Dieskau recorded the aria in 1959 (1C 137–01 063) and relies on vocal and musical subtlety to compensate for what he gives away in weight to his two competitors. This is a heavy Verdian role, but the well-tuned *dolcissimo* section is so delicately sung as to compensate for any shortages elsewhere.

This scene is followed by the confrontation between tenor and baritone during which the former discovers he is the son of the latter, whom he had hitherto considered his greatest enemy. Rosvaenge and Schlusnus sang it with Kleiber in Berlin in 1932 and recorded it the following year (Poly. 90204; DG 2535 802); the singing is exemplary but there is a cut before the baritone's *adagio*, unlike a 1943 broadcast performance (Acanta DE 21487), which is complete. It is also full of drama and demonstrates the strong singing of both.

The ballet of the Four Seasons has been recorded with great panache by the Cleveland orchestra under Lorin Maazel (SXL 6726) and hardly less so by the Monte Carlo orchestra under Almeida (Philips 6599 601).

The first and fourth acts are perhaps the most wholly successful in the opera, and Act 4 begins with a splendid aria for Arrigo (Henri in French), whose agonizing and indecisiveness – can he help his condemned friends? Will they accept him now that he has apparently defected to the enemy? – are perfectly conveyed in the vacillation between major and minor in the aria itself and then in the *allegro* which tries to accommodate the orchestra's determination to play in C major what Arrigo insists on singing in E. The strength of the upper fifth of his voice apart, Filippeschi demonstrates a provincial level of singing, though some theatricality, a quality which is noticeably absent from the controlled, serious performance by Richard Tucker (CBS SBRG 72336), which is nevertheless powerfully sung. Nicolai Gedda is heard from a live performance in 1974 on a 'private' disc and reveals some subtleties of phrasing and dynamics in a recording which is unfortunately of rather murky technical quality.

There are three outstanding versions. Two benefit from inclusion of the impressive orchestral prelude and the recitative. The first is by José Carreras (Philips 9500 977), whose beautifully rounded quality of voice is underpinned by an athletic, almost spontaneous approach to the music, and whose long-breathed phrasing makes for an exciting performance. Even shorn of orchestral prelude and recitative and with a small cut before the end, I marginally preferred the recording by Rosvaenge in German and dating from 1932 (Telef. E 2553; 6.42084 AJ). Here is singing such as one might hope to find in a great theatrical performance, controlled, clear, powerful, full of contrast and energy. The voice rings out with rare splendour, and this disc is for me, with that from *Fidelio,* his finest recording. Best of all is Carlo Bergonzi (Philips 6599 925), who shows his usual meticulous attention to musical detail and ability to convey drama without distorting the musical line. The singing is totally honest, and nothing is shirked – but this would be to make a negative appraisal of a performance of a very high quality indeed. It is hard to imagine better vocalism at the service of a composer in one of his most ambitious and completely achieved scenes.

An interesting curiosity is the recording of the aria Verdi wrote for the 1863 revival in Paris for the tenor Villaret: 'O toi que j'ai chérie'. He had apparently been disappointed by Gueymard's performance of the original 'O jour de peine', but it seems odd to the listener 120 years later that he replaced the powerfully dramatic original with a weaker and much less positive aria, agreeable enough in all conscience though one can't, even without knowing the quality of Villaret (a notable Arnold *Guillaume Tell*) conceive it as having been more likely to be effective in context. Pavarotti, with the help of the orchestra of La Scala and Abbado's conducting (CBS 740377), sings it with beautiful tone, impeccable line and in fair French (also tiny departures from the text provided as appendix in my French score).

The tenor's aria is followed by an extended duet with the soprano, from which four famous singers have extracted a beautiful solo passage (a fifth has had her public performance 'pirated'). Ester Mazzoleni was only twenty-four when she sang Elena at La Scala in 1907 and curiously enough her version has less *rubato* than modern accounts. It is none the less an impressive performance (Fono. 92544; Tima 8). Katia Ricciarelli included it on her first disc (SB 6863) made in 1972, and enjoyable as it is, it was cut long before she became the sensitive artist of the last few years. Renata Scotto's was taken from a live performance in 1976, probably at the Met. The singing is expressive and to my mind one of her best performances.

There are, however, two versions to which the adjective 'great' might legitimately be applied. Callas recorded it in the studio (2C 165 541 78–88) thirteen years after her memorable appearance in Florence. The sound is beautiful and the phrasing meticulous, and only in the second of three slow descending chromatic scales (which constitute the aria's cadenza) does she falter for a brief moment. No such fault can be laid at the door of Montserrat Caballé (SXLR 6690), who demonstrates exquisite sensibility throughout and a *pianissimo* top C just before the end of the aria which is one of the loveliest I ever heard on record. This 1974 performance is nothing less than perfection.

There remains the ubiquitous *Bolero* 'Mercè dilette amiche' of which I have traced twenty-seven versions and heard all but three. Of no more than souvenir value are performances by Rina Gigli (DB 6459), agreeable of voice but clumsy of style; Rita Streich (DGM 19137), at a slow tempo making rather heavy weather of the aria's brilliance; Stella (ALP 1366), a mixture of good and bad and far from her best; Maria Chiara (SXL 6605) spirited but rather lacking in definition; Lilian Blauvelt (Am. Col. 30091; Cantilena 6228), more at home in concert than opera; even the lovely Sigrid Arnoldson (53466: Rococo 5205), who demonstrates a beautiful lyrical sound but sings only half the aria; Miliza Korjus (EH 914; 1C 147–30819–20) who makes with her light voice a dazzling coloratura display piece that includes a top F sharp in an interpolated flourish at the end.

One would expect singers of the old school to make much of this war horse and they do not disappoint. Boninsegna (her 1904 version is on GV 518; I could not find her 1907 version) sings fluently and powerfully with a strong trill, but considerably cut. Mazzoleni (1908–Fono 74133; ORX 508) is rerecorded a semitone sharp but adopts a measured tempo that has the confidence of Scala performances behind it. The voice, like Boninsegna's, is a flexible dramatic soprano. Marcella Sembrich (Victor 88143; Rococo R 23) recorded in 1907–8 with some distinction and in the most powerful of all the 'light' voices of the period. Like many others at that time, she pulls the tempi about, by no means to total disadvantage. Selma Kurz (053276: CO 324) eschews *rubato* but ends the aria with a succession of those trills for which she was specially famous. Even better perhaps is Tetrazzini, who recorded the aria twice (2–053033 made in London; 2–053118 made in America). She was the Horowitz of vocalists and there is an exemplary clarity and firmness about all her singing. The London version (1910), unlike the American (1914), ends with a top E, and each contains some extraordinary singing. Both are reissued on GEMM 220–7. Claudia Muzio recorded the *Bolero* for Pathé in 1917–18 (OASI 564), with great fluency and perhaps more brilliantly than in her 1924 Edison (Rubini RS 310). There is no trill but the voice has an unusual beauty of its own, though hardly as much as had that of Rosa Ponselle (Am. Col. 49686; Odyssey Y 31150). The voice sounds right when played at 80rpm when the aria emerges transposed down a semitone. The performance is youthful and spirited, and the glorious, dark sound has its usual brilliant overtones. There is a marvellously articulated trill. Rosa Raisa (Vocalion 30115; Club 99.92) adopts a spanking pace considering that she had a voice of considerable weight but gives an unusually brilliant performance.

Felicia Weathers (Telef. AG.641947) sang the opera in Hamburg and her performance is very confident, as is that of Anna Moffo (SB 6664). Moffo essays only one verse but that with scrupulous observation of the printed markings. Leyla Gencer, on a 'private' disc, is individual and appealing in a bold and perhaps less than perfect version (from a public performance), and Anita Cerquetti (GRV 13) admits of no difficulties in a performance more notable for clarity and power than charm.

Three versions seem to me the most enjoyable of those made in recent times. Callas recorded it with Serafin and the Philharmonia early in her career, adopting a deliberate tempo and singing with delicacy and tenderness, and yet somehow contriving to combine these qualities with the grand manner (ALP 3824). Joan Sutherland (SDD 146) takes a much faster tempo, but her very 'straight' performance is sung with clarity and an almost unparalleled confidence which makes it very attractive. Caballé (SXLR 6690) was the first Elena at the Metropolitan and her performance is full of colour and contrast, though one cannot pretend that hardness does not occasionally creep in.

LES VÊPRES SICILIENNES

E Elena; *P* Procida; *M* Montfort; *A* Arrigo

1951 (broadcast performance – in German)
Cunitz *E*; Von Rohr *P*; Schlusnus *M*; Rosvaenge *A* / Hessian Radio Chorus and Orch. / Schröder
DG ⓜ LPEM 19244–6

1951 (live performance – Teatro Comunale, Florence)
Callas *E*; Christoff *P*; Mascherini *M*; Kokolios *A* / Florence Festival Chorus and Orch. / E. Kleiber
Cetra ⓜ LO5 (3)

1955 (broadcast performance)
Cerquetti *E*; Christoff *P*; Tagliabue *M*; Ortica *A* / Italian Radio Chorus and Orch., Turin / Rossi
Replica ⓜ RPL 2433–5

1973 Arroyo *E*; Raimondi *P*; Milnes *M*; Domingo *A* / Alldis Choir, New Philharmonia / Levine
RCA ARL 4 0370

Verdi's Requiem Mass

ALAN BLYTH

Toscanini's interpretation of the Verdi *Requiem* was once described, by Alec Robertson, as the Old Testament reading, Giulini's as the New Testament, an apt and illustrative distinction that sums up, if too simplistically, the impression left by these two classic performances of the work. 'Dramatic' as compared with 'devotional' might be another description of their differences. Yet, for all this contrast in approach, there is a greater similarity between the two Italians than there is between their performances and those by many other conductors who have challenged their ascendancy. Indeed with three notable and unexpected exceptions, it is the Italians who come closest to understanding the spirit of the work and to conveying it in a truthful and unexaggerated manner. I use those two epithets advisedly, for it is on a fidelity to Verdi's text, particularly to his dynamic and tempi markings, that the success of so many of the most cogent interpretations rests, whether those interpretations be dramatic or devotional.

To show just how much licence some conductors have taken, compare the time taken in two sets from the start of the work to the entry of the tenor soloist. Sir John Barbirolli, one of the most dilatory of all interpreters, begins at crotchet=50 (instead of Verdi's 80) and allows himself 6 minutes 13 seconds over the passage. Toscanini, conforming to the composer's tempo in his 1951 version, goes through the same music in 4 minutes 33 seconds, an amazing difference, when you consider the section is only of 77 bars length. Nobody expects, or wants, a conductor to obey Verdi to the letter, but there should be an attempt to match his intentions if the music is to retain its proper character. Too many conductors ignore that fact.

Timing was of the essence, in another sense, in Toscanini's reading, as Spike Hughes pointed out in his detailed study of the 1951 performance.* Not something easily analysed, it permitted him to include *ritardandi* and *accelerandi*, even unmarked ones, while maintaining a basic pulse; and those subtle variations feel natural and unforced. In all three of Toscanini's extant performances, one also notes his attention to pertinent orchestral detail, and

---

* *The Toscanini Legacy* (Dover Books, 1969).

an incandescence of manner and spirit that imbues them with a single-minded, unfettered view of the *Requiem*.

Toscanini I derives from a 1938 Queen's Hall performance, part of a London Music Festival. All who remember hearing or taking part in it agree that it was a very special occasion, and that sense of being present at the experience of a lifetime can be felt through the somewhat dim recording. I do not think it is fanciful to hear just how much the famed Queen's Hall acoustics contributed to the aura of the evening. Toscanini's speeds are close to the asked-for ones, and time and again one remarks on the beauty of the detail and the way it is played by the BBC SO. In the Kyrie the staccato semiquavers (bar 96) are *leggerissimo* in delivery as required. The bassoon and cello precision near the movement's close (129ff) are as precise as you will hear them. In the *Dies Irae*, taken at absolutely the right tempo, the amount of detail to be heard, in particular the piccolos (32ff), is common to all three Toscanini readings; as is the tremendous incandescence – the word must be used again – of the interpretation, though here the superb singing of the BBC Choral Society remains unrivalled. Later in this movement one observes Toscanini's secure pacing of the 'Salva me' ensemble, his sympathetic attention to the needs of the soloists, the timpani at bars 504 and 506 in 'Oro supplex', here slower than in 1951, but at the same pace as 1940; in the *Offertorio*, the ethereal wind over the cantabile passage for soprano, in *Sanctus* the diaphanous orchestral sound, again unique to Toscanini, and once more the vivid quality of the chorus, in *Lux Aeterna*, the way Toscanini (bar 20) insists on articulation of the triplets by the soloists. In the finale, apart from the terror of the hell-fire implicit in the conductor's approach, there is yet again so much detail clarified that it is usually left to fend for itself.

1938's soloists are an impressive team. Kersten Thorborg's 'Nils' in 'Liber scriptus' have a shivering, frightened effect all their own. Throughout she sings in grave, steady if hardly Italianate tones which, in 'Recordare' and *Agnus Dei,* finely set off Zinka Milanov's clear, fresh soprano. 'Huic ergo', with its rise *pp* to a high A, is predictably radiant, ethereal, while the 'Sed' dropping from E to E flat *pianissimo*, always a supreme test of the soprano's mettle, is here done as well as anywhere and the final solo phrase of the movement is *legato* and *dolcissimo* as marked. Against that has to be set a placid *Libera me* (1940 far superior in that respect), some sliding in 'et timeo' (41ff) and a break (also present unfortunately in 1940) before the change of key in the *andante* section, which at the right pace (crotchet=80) is finely phrased. It might be as well to state here just how important it is that this section should be taken *andante*, not *adagio*, in order that it should be a reflective moment in the otherwise dramatic finale, not something separated from it. Helge Rosvaenge sings stoutly, but in too Germanic a way. The 'Ingemisco' (same speed as 1940, slower than 1949) is sensitively phrased and ends with a ringing B flat, but is a trifle lachrymose in expression. The important 'Hostias', which Toscanini, again rightly, does not dawdle over, is adequate, no more. The wholly non-Italian team is completed by the reliable, uninteresting Greek-born Nicola Moscona.

He is transformed by the time we reach Toscanini II, taken from a performance at Carnegie Hall on 23 November 1940. Authority, and a neo-Pinza timbre, have now been added. 'Oro supplex' is properly sombre and imploring and the support at the bottom of the ensembles is exemplary. Milanov has also grown in stature as an artist in every respect, steadier and more ethereal where needed, finely urgent in *Libera me*, providing a soaring high C at the movement's climax. Her voice is clearly contrasted with Bruno Castagna's in *Agnus Dei*, where both catch the chantlike, monastic quality of the writing. Elsewhere Castagna is rather dull, breathing too often for the good of her legato, failing to dig deep into her phrases or to grasp their full import. But, apart from hearing yet again Toscanini's masterly interpretation, the reason for listening to this performance is to catch Jussi Björling, at his very best, in a classic account of the tenor part. 'Qui Mariam' is nowhere so plaintive or *dolce*, or the 'Hostias' so poised and inward (no trill, however) and throughout his perfect pitching in the unaccompanied passages for the four soloists is a source of strength. The American choir sounds small in size, confident in execution, but not comparable to the BBC chorus. Björling apart, this is I suppose the most dispensable of the Toscanini sets.

For a detailed description of Toscanini III the reader is referred to Hughes. 'A great spiritual and emotional experience,' is his general description of this 'near-ideal performance'. Toscanini has undoubtedly grown more severe with the years, but at the same time no less spontaneous and loving in his attitude towards a work that so obviously moved him deeply. The recording is the most tolerable of the three, though far from being good even for its day. One notices the even tauter control of form, the terrifying intensity now of *Dies Irae*, the still more overwhelming 'Tuba mirum', the turmoil so vividly depicted at 'Confutatis', the expressive cellos introducing the *Offertorio*, the *leggiero* strings at 'Pleni sunt coeli' in *Sanctus*, the lightness of the *Falstaff*-like orchestral support to *Lux aeterna*, the clipped tension of the resumed *Libera me* fugue (312).

A notable indication of the conductor's late, more impatient style is the quicker tempo adopted for both 'Ingemisco' and 'Oro supplex': Hughes states that the former is thus given lyrical warmth without sentimentality, but I would suggest that the 1940 'Ingemisco' with Björling at Verdi's crotchet= 72 is in fact even more restrained and lyrical than the 1951 with its suggestion of hurry. On the whole, Toscanini here boasted his best integrated quartet of soloists. Herva Nelli does not scale Milanov's heights but nor does she commit her colleague's occasional solecism: her tone, in her most important recorded performance, is fresh and full, her singing unfussy, to the point, the very antithesis of, say, Schwarzkopf in this music. Fedora Barbieri, bumpy to start with, gains in steadiness and feeling as the work progresses and laments with the best mezzos in any set at the start of 'Lacrymosa'. Giuseppe di Stefano, not (seemingly) in his best voice is none the less fervent and appealing in timbre and expression. Completing this happily Italian quartet is the solid, malleable bass of Cesare Siepi, inspired by Toscanini to surpass his usual rather placid form. The disciplined choir gives its all in the Toscanini cause to help create one of the gramophone's true classics.

His disciple Guido Cantelli, had he lived, might have presented us with another. As it is, we have to be content with his flawed 1954 'live' performance. Without quite the master's authority, Cantelli achieves much of the same impact, but some of the detail, so inevitable in Toscanini's accounts, here becomes exaggerated. Where the older conductor gives us *animando* just where Verdi asks for it, Cantelli anticipates it. The American-sounding choir has not been, as had Toscanini's, infused with the meaning of the text. In brief, the performance was probably not as well rehearsed as Toscanini's and it shows, but the beseeching cellos in 'Recordare' (437ff) indicate Toscanini's influence. The soloists are unidiomatic in utterance, unsatisfactory in voice. Herva Nelli, now less confident than under her mentor, goes completely awry near the start of *Libera me*, turning the passage between bars 24 and 40 into some kind of atonal parody of Verdi. She only just regains her confidence for the *andante* section. Claramae Turner, unsettled and edgy, at least suggests good intentions until she loses her voice towards the end of *Lux aeterna*. Eugene Conley's monochrome, hard tenor is not up to the task in hand. Moscona, rusty to start with, begins to show his experience in this work by his contribution to 'Hostias', showing Conley how to phrase its solemn, sweet melody. As a memento of Cantelli's often compelling direction, this is interesting – but not for much else.

Cantelli is, as it were, only a parenthesis to Toscanini, whose close contemporary and fellow-Italian Tullio Serafin comes closest in his two remarkably similar versions to matching Toscanini's faithfulness to Verdi. To take Serafin II, his LP version, first. For those who think he may have laid a more yielding, indulgent hand on the work I would recommend a hearing of the *Dies Irae* or *Libera me* in this version. Both are released with tremendous energy and with the same conviction that marks out Toscanini from his inferiors, and the opening movement, with tempi properly managed, unfolds naturally, inevitably. Detail is clear if not given the same point as by Toscanini. The chorus is heard as typically Italian – the Rome singers are obviously of mature years, vibrating uncomfortably and sounding, for better or worse, Italian. When the soloists enter, they immediately announce themselves as a most interesting and individual group. That they confirm in their succeeding solos and ensembles. The Lebanese Shakeh Vartenissian, who has a real Verdian soprano, is matter-of-fact in expression, too phlegmatic one might surmise not knowing any of her other work, but the steadiness is welcome; so is the soaring over the orchestra in 'Salva me'. The young Fiorenza Cossotto immediately suggests the right manner and voice in 'Liber scriptus' conveying awe before the seat of judgement, and deeply expressive at the start of 'Recordare' without the hardness that later afflicted her tone. Eugenio Fernandi, a tenor rightly appreciated by Walter Legge, is plangent and literally appealing (as he should be) in 'Ingemisco' – 'qui mariam' taken in one phrase and ended with a *morendo*. Nor is an extra breath needed in the final (and very difficult phrase), which here rises immaculately to the high B flat. Just before that, Serafin and tenor reserve the *animando* until bar 488 as Verdi enjoins. Boris Christoff, who has earlier shown his authority in keen consonants and impressive delivery, is a little over-emphatic in 'Oro supplex' with Serafin yielding too much to him in the matter of tempo (too slow). Then Christoff cleverly changes vocal colour for his 'Lacrymosa' entry, which is now warmer, more pliant. The three lower soloists make the most of *Lux aeterna*. There is much more to admire (but no space to describe) in this well-recorded, perceptive and unhackneyed performance.

Serafin I, recorded in Rome with similar forces twenty years earlier (no change of chorus-master in all that time, I note), is the set by which I learnt the work. Returning to it after a long absence, I found it no less admirable than in the past. Just like the later version, it flows along with a natural inevitability, and conveys a tradition passed on without growing stale. As in 1959, Serafin's tempi are right, and in the 'Oro supplex', with Pinza as the unsurpassed bass soloist, the speed is here up to Verdi's metronome mark. The choral singing is fresher in sound. As *The Record Guide** commented, 'Serafin achieves a high degree of precision without any loss of intensity or fire.' That book also described Pinza's account of the bass part, quite rightly, as 'flawless'. Listen to the second verse of 'Oro supplex' if you want to hear the epitome of Verdian style. Listen also to his contribution to the start of *Lux aeterna:* he is like a high priest answering the supplications of mezzo and tenor. Earlier, 'Mors stupebit' suggests horror without exaggeration. Ebe Stignani is almost as exemplary in her richly etched account of the mezzo music: how grateful to the voice it sounds, how easy to deliver, when sung so satisfyingly as here, the tone grand yet heart-easing. Gigli is Gigli in his third period, soulful, impassioned, inimitable, indeed definitely not to be imitated, all the nudges to the line forgiven in pleasure at the sweet, warm voicing of emotions. Maria Caniglia deviates from pitch in the earlier part of the work, but matches up to most of the challenges of the finale in her own, somewhat melodramatic way. The blend with Stignani is fine, but here as in other ensembles Verdi's dynamics are too often ignored; that is forgotten in enjoying the sheer opulence of all four singers.

The last wholly admirable Italian is Giulini. Here, for those who find Toscanini's blinding vision and dramatic impulse almost too terrifying to contemplate or Serafin a little too predictable, is the eloquent approach personified. This is a Requiem for a human and lovable person, not the final rites for the whole world as encompassed by Toscanini. Ever since its first appearance in the catalogues in 1964, it has been accepted as more or less the *fons et origo* where the Requiem is concerned, in stereo at least, and on reappraising it for this study I found little reason to quarrel with the verdict

---

* Collins, London, 1955.

of the years – or indeed with much of what Alec Robertson said in his original review. He wrote that 'There is no lack of vitality [in Giulini's reading] but always he is remembering that the *Requiem* mourns the man, Alessandro Manzoni, whom Verdi worshipped "as the purest and holiest of our glories". This gives a special depth and pathos and warmth to his interpretation.'

Contrary to what is often said about Giulini's conducting here, it is not by any means slow, rather yielding within basically correct speeds, and the marvellous responses he obtains from chorus and orchestra are the result, surely, of long preparation, long familiarity each with the other. As with Toscanini, nothing is left to chance, yet spontaneity can be felt in every bar. From the start we are aware of the detailed care over dynamics taken by the Wilhelm Pitz-rehearsed Philharmonia Chorus. To quote AR again, 'Many choruses can sing *Dies Irae*: but how many can sing the unaccompanied "Te decet hymnus", ranging from *f*, through *diminuendo* to *ppp*, the men observing the staccato marks at "votum in Je(rusalem)", *crescendo* to *f*, *p* to *f*, with *diminuendo* to the exquisitely modulated close (24 bars) with the perfection here shown.' On the larger canvas of *Sanctus*, the singing is no less acute, no less pleasurable to the ear, nor has the unaccompanied support to the soprano in the *Libera me* ever been sung with such hushed beauty as here. The orchestral performance is as imaginative matching the subtlety and appropriateness of Verdi's writing. The offstage perspective of the trumpets in 'Tuba mirum' is perfectly adumbrated, as is the pining wind in 'Quid sum miser'.

The soloists are as well balanced a team as in any set, and highly accomplished, at times inspired as individuals. Schwarzkopf is the most controversial among them. No other soprano has lavished so much intelligence on her phrasing or (perhaps) caught so precisely the passages of meditative loveliness – the poised high G flat in 'Salva me', 'huic ergo' in the 'Lacrymosa', that difficult 'sed' in the *Offertorio*, practically all of the *andante* of the *Libera me*: in all of these the technical control is beyond praise. Yet when that is said, it has to be admitted that hers is not the ideal voice for Verdi, and here, more than in her earlier set, the strain of the *spinto* sections of the work is self-evident. Her voice blends with and sets off Christa Ludwig's to perfection in 'Recordare' – 'quaerens me' is inexpressibly beautiful and *Agnus Dei*, the lower voice a pure shadow of the high one. On her own, Ludwig is rewardingly opulent whether she is using her dark lower register to depict terror or her free upper one to proclaim hours of judgement, and her contribution to *Lux aeterna*, in particular her long-breathed phrasing at the start, is impeccable: Nicolai Gedda is not in her class. For all his musicality, exemplified in fidelity to the score in so many respects, his is a dullish account of the solos, the 'Hostias', where his trill is neat, apart. Nicolai Ghiaurov also lacks individuality, but one is thankful for his strong voice and often stirring accents: only inner feeling seems wanting. In the many unaccompanied passages, however, both men surpass almost all their rivals in sensitivity by which I mean dynamic control (Walter Legge's influence?) and careful modulation of their voices to those of the ladies. The recording, at least in its most recent pressings, provides a fine balance between soloists, chorus and orchestra, all caught in a warm acoustic. For this and the time spent in perfecting the performance, we must thank Legge.

From here onwards we cannot but observe a decline in standards whether we look backwards or forwards. Continuing with the Italians, we come to the somewhat problematic Riccardo Muti set. Without a doubt this is the most realistically recorded version with the choral sound hardly imagined in the Toscanini or even the Giulini eras. We hear a conductor who has, in many respects, followed in the Toscanini tradition in tempi (two major ones excepted), care for detail, and indeed incandescence. What may be found missing is the spiritual element, admittedly difficult to define and, almost as hard to explain, a comparative failure to encompass that imperceptible mastery of timing already referred to. In brief, there is occasionally a slightly contrived, and self-regarding character about the interpretation. It is most to the fore in the two sections where Muti strays furthest away from Toscanini – and Verdi – namely the *Dies Irae* chorus, raced through and hard-driven at each appearance, and the brisk *Sanctus,* which only a professional choir such as Muti employed could manage at this pace. The advantage of having these professionals is to be heard in the manner by which the singers respond to his demanding beat with flair and virtuosity, itself caught by the engineers in a truthful, full-blooded acoustic (Kingsway Hall). Every fast semiquaver is in its place and can be heard as such. Yet there is no want of feeling when that is the overriding need. The appeals of 'Salva me' are as pliant and beseeching as the sound of the Last Trump is arresting. The Philharmonia players, though marginally less precise than their predecessors in the same band in the early sixties, provide the singing tone (strings) so essential in Verdi.

Muti's solo quartet is a felicitious ensemble, obeying most but not all Verdi's myriad instructions. Renata Scotto, as is the case in her later career, sounds strained at the top of her voice under pressure. A few other notes discolour, but from her ethereal entry in the *Offertorio* right through her marvellously vibrant use of the text in *Libera me*, with an imaginatively phrased account of the *andante* section, she is direct in expression, spontaneous in reaction to the text. Agnes Baltsa's mellifluous, even mezzo lacks some weight for 'Liber scriptus' and could be said to avoid temperament, but she uses it with consistent intelligence and feeling. Veriano Luchetti's plaintively urgent 'Ingemisco' and prayerful, finely accented 'Hostias' are the work of a dedicated artist. Yevgeny Nesterenko is the firm, unaffected bass, secure in his musicianship though not tonally quite idiomatic. The start of the *Offertorio* shows the team at its best. The piece is up to tempo from the start, the cellos phrase eloquently, the three lower soloists demonstrate their blend, then Scotto floats in tenderly on 'sed', makes her *crescendo* and draws back to a *pianissimo* for the semitone drop. All in all, a version that is consistently thought-provoking, never dull (as are so many of its near contemporaries) and always alive – perhaps it can be characterized as a young man's long-distance look at death.

Claudio Abbado gives a curiously blank interpretation. There are few of Muti's idiosyncrasies, also few of his perceptions. Abbado conducts the work as though he disliked it; or at least as if he is overawed by it. He is not helped by the recording, which emphasizes the extreme ends of the dynamic range and varies in its acoustic properties. The Scala Chorus is assuredly authentic in its operatic approach – the men sound, not inappropriately, like the priests in *Aida* at 'Rex tremendae' – but often one is conscious of doubtful intonation, imprecise ensemble and ill-adjusted vibratos. Tempi often accord with the metronome, or thereabouts (a slow 'Oro supplex' being an exception), but they tend to plod because of Abbado's slack pulse – 'Lacrymosa' is a case in point. The total effect is anonymous and enervating.

The work of the soloists, an ill-assorted quartet, does little to redeem this version. Katia Ricciarelli is the most satisfying of the four. Cloudy and poorly focused notes are forgiven for the generally easy and fresh character of her singing. 'Huic ergo' is ethereally done and the difficult phrase, a few moments later in this section, from bar 651, rising to a high B flat, one of the most rewarding but difficult to bring off in the entire work, here receives its due; so does the final phrase of the *Offertorio*, starting 'fac eas'. The *andante* of the *Libera me* has true inwardness but is spoilt by an unsteady B flat at its close: as ever with this singer the most laudable intentions are often vitiated by incomplete technique. Ricciarelli's verbal definition also leaves something to be desired. Shirley Verrett's husky timbre is a poor match for Ricciarelli's voice in *Agnus Dei*, but on her own, as at the start of *Lux aeterna,* she offers a customary commitment and largeness of heart, aware of the text's import. Domingo is in staid, uncommunicative form, as if completing just another recording assignment: he is heard to greater advantage under Mehta (see below). Ghiaurov, in his third recording of his part, is less convincing than of old and now reaches for high notes previously attacked without fear.

The last (the early 78rpm version apart) and least admirable of 'official' versions conducted by an Italian is surprisingly, given his reputation in the work in his own country and in Britain just after the war, that conducted by Victor de Sabata. The supplement to *The Record Guide* described his speeds as 'positively grotesque', a verdict I wholeheartedly endorse. All are far below Verdi's metronome marks with disastrous results on the work's structure. The opening is almost as ponderous as Barbirolli's, 'Oro supplex' static, *Agnus Dei* soporific. The chorus is operatic in the worst sense with over-tremulous women, superannuated men. Some consolation is to be found in the work of the soloists, Oralia Dominguez, the mezzo (who created Madame Sosostris in Tippett's *A Midsummer Marriage*) is the most telling of the four. The great weight of the seat of judgement is felt in 'Liber scriptus', and her voice blends ideally with Schwarzkopf's in 'Recordare' and *Agnus Dei* as if a penitent and her alter ego were being heard. Schwarzkopf, in youthfully fresh voice, sings 'huic ergo' with perfect poise, but takes a huge breath just before the B flat a few minutes later, a point she had corrected by 1964 with Giulini. Throughout she uses all her artistry and pure, technically assured singing to make us forget that hers is not a Verdian soprano, at least until the *Libera me*, where her exaggerated chest register gives the game away. Giuseppe di Stefano is too overt with his emotional responses and refuses to sing *pianissimo* until 'Hostias', where he spoils the calm of his intoning by carelessness over note values. Cesare Siepi sings with less inspiration and variety than for Toscanini. This set is perhaps best sampled in the 'Lacrymosa'. Schwarzkopf and Dominguez begin by pouring out the lamenting phrases with feeling and the whole section is built to an overwhelming climax by de Sabata.

De Sabata's 'off-the-air' performance, given on 27 January 1951, the fiftieth anniversary of Verdi's death, and recently issued on Fonit-Cetra's 'Documents' series, is a much more inspired performance than the studio effort of three years later. Speeds are still on the slow side, but this is a warmer, more vibrant interpretation. A total view of the work can be felt, also a keen ear for relevant detail. Nell Rankin is a secure but uninteresting mezzo, Nicola Rossi-Lemeni an idiomatic but wobbly bass. In contrast Giacinto Prandelli's liquid, sensitive tenor (of a kind apparently extinct today in Italy) is among the best, and here – at last – is a representation of Renata Tebaldi's fervent, soaring soprano in this music that ideally suited her, a poised 'huic ergo', finely floated 'sed signifer', electrifying, as is De Sabata, in the 'Libera me', its *andante* section up to speed and quite beautifully and spontaneously sung. All in all, this late arrival takes a very high place in the discography of this work.

A number of non-Italians have recorded the *Requiem*, none with complete success. One of the best is the most recent, that directed by Zubin Mehta, an unexaggerated, devout reading that nicely relates tempi one to another. It is true that he starts slowly (5 minutes 33 seconds) to the tenor's entry, but there he is more or less at one with most recent interpreters, but elsewhere he is reasonably faithful to Verdi. His choir and orchestra are precise and involved. The choir, larger than Muti's or Abbado's (among recent competitors) is more spiritual than the Ambrosians, more accurate than the La Scala Chorus. The New York Philharmonic provides strong strings and some affecting wind solos.

The soloists make a well-blended team – two Spanish stars, two American stalwarts. Montserrat Caballé surpasses even her lovely singing for Barbirolli (see below) some twelve years earlier, floating the A flat at 'huic ergo' ideally and carrying up to the B flat a little earlier, a difficult moment, with consummate ease. Similarly, the phrase marked *cantabile dolce* in the third movement at bar 69 is as ethereal as one could wish, ditto the *andante* of the *Libera me*. Only descents to a weak chest register and a few moments of self-indulgence give cause for complaint. Bianca Berini, whom I once much admired in this work at the Festival Hall, is a generous-voiced, impassioned mezzo, not often bettered elsewhere – try her at 'et lux perpetua' in the sixth movement. She matches Caballé's timbre in the *Agnus Dei*.

Domingo, in the best of his recorded *Requiems*, equals Björling in plangent sound and pure phrasing in the 'Ingemisco', but is inclined to overlook *piano* marks, except in the 'Hostias', which he delivers in a rapt *mezza voce*. Paul Plishka is sound vocally and involved emotionally without calling on histrionics; 'Oro supplex', taken at Verdi's tempo, proves just as supplicatory that way. The first digital recording of the work is none too happy, less natural in sound than the analogue Muti.

If Mehta's version sounds like a well-mannered studio effort, and in consequence a bit bloodless, the second of Solti's performances catches the sense of a real occasion, having been recorded after live performances in Chicago. A vivid recording allows us to hear more orchestral detail than on almost any other set, indeed sometimes it seems unrealistically highlighted. Much of the fire and sensitivity in the conducting suggests a close study of Toscanini's recordings, and there is more sense of an occasion than in Solti's lifeless Decca set. The well-trained choir has an American flavour to it, an innate eagerness and quick response, a fresh, though not particularly Italianate sound. Sometimes, as happens in *Sanctus*, the voices are almost overwhelmed by the large orchestra. Tempi are well maintained; consolation tempers the drama of the earlier reading, even if there is still a lack of shape to the piece as a whole.

Janet Baker is, in every sense, the exceptional mezzo soloist. Hers is not a voice intended by nature for this music, but her singular intelligence gives new, or at least renewed, meaning to the text. 'Liber scriptus' indicates the occasional strain put upon her resources, but we are soon made aware of her distinction of phrase, her involvement in her work, even when this leads to the occasional overemphasis as at the start of 'Lacrymosa'. The dark sorrow of 'Judex ergo' earlier and the radiance of *Lux aeterna*, shining through darkness, are just two instances of a wonderfully individual approach. It is crowned by the real benediction of 'quia pius es'. She pairs well with Leontyne Price in *Agnus Dei*. Price herself offers a lovely piece of singing in the *andante* of *Libera me* to make up for an uneven performance earlier in the work, where glorious phrases alternate with many disturbed by unequal tone or uneven phrasing. There is too much here that was better done at the start of the great Verdian soprano's career for Reiner some seventeen years before (see below). José van Dam is steady, even noble at times, a tower of strength in ensemble but finally a little too phlegmatic for this work. Luchetti is much as for Muti, special thanks being due for his simple, restrained 'Hostias'. All in all a puzzling version, off-centre in some ways as an interpretation but never uninteresting.

And 'uninteresting' is, I fear, just the epithet for Solti's 1968 set. Its rhythmic stodginess, bland orchestra (the Vienna Philharmonic having a poor session) and blown-up sound are relieved only by a diaphanous *Lux aeterna* in which the Vienna violins recover their laurels; tempo and dynamics are finely controlled by Solti, and the unaccompanied passages go particularly well. Elsewhere, the Vienna State Opera Chorus is wobbly without being Italianate and not well disciplined. Joan Sutherland is yet another singer out of her element in this work, groping at a 'role' she does not seem to understand and worrying the music to the extent of destroying line: her final contribution to the *Offertorio* is obvious evidence of this point. Her opening of the *Libera me*, melodramatically intoned, has become a classic of mistaken interpretation. Yet the sound remains as lovely as ever, most obviously in the *andante* of the finale. Marilyn Horne is the formidable mezzo, but the firm impressive singing is seldom illuminated by interior feeling. Luciano Pavarotti excels at 'qui Mariam' in the 'Ingemisco', but is hampered in this solo by four-square support; the 'Hostias' is too heart-on-sleeve – but the sheer beauty of the tenor's tone cannot be resisted for long. Martti Talvela sings sonorously, with feeling, but lacks some element of graceful legato. In many ways, Sutherland excepted, this is a safe, 'gramophonic' performance, but not one to take anyone to the inspired heights on which Verdi's genius is working.

Eugene Ormandy's set comes into a similar category. This is a typically big-scale American performance, a massive, extroverted reading of the work. Ormandy is in some respects more faithful to Verdi's intentions than, say, Giulini; Ormandy does not anticipate *rallentandi* as did the Italian in his roughly contemporaneous version, but obeying the letter of the score in this case does not mean catching its spirit. He is also attentive to detail as at 'quantus tremor' in *Dies Irae*, but the playing of the Philadelphia is respectful rather than persuasive. None of the soloists offer a specific insight into his or her part. Lucine Amara has the power to dominate ensembles, but her voice, often fluttery and uncertain, cannot mould the quieter sections with any degree of security. Maureen Forrester's closed vowels and gusty, unsubtle approach leaves a 'plummy' impression on all the important alto solos. A *pianissimo* seems to mean nothing to Richard Tucker, who sings most of his part *mezzo-forte* and betrays not a sign of sensitivity even in 'Hostias'. George London's voice does not carry the weight needed for the bass's contribution, but his 'Mors stupebit', full of foreboding, is still among the best.

The version conducted by Erich Leinsdorf has much more to offer, including a Boston chorus and orchestra technically accomplished and imaginatively inclined. Tempi are well adjusted, and those averse to Giulini's free way with the score ought to respond to Leinsdorf's stricter approach which, like Solti's, owes something to Toscanini (they both worked with him before the war at Salzburg). The music flows, there is a give-and-take among everyone, preparation has been careful. Ezio Flagello is a reliable rather than inspired bass. Carlo Bergonzi is musical and suitably reverential, obedient to Verdi's dynamics, taking the final phrase of 'Ingemisco' in a single breath, and giving us a refined, unaffected 'Hostias'. Offering a full tone throughout a wide range, the mezzo Lili Chookasian is firm in attack, never dull in her

inflections. All three make much of *Lux aeterna*. There they are spared the
company of Birgit Nilsson; her pitch is too frequently suspect, she slides
uncomfortably between notes, and in general does her reputation much
harm, in spite of her thrilling top, most in evidence in the finale.

Bernstein, Barbirolli and Karajan are the next three 'international' conductors to have given us their variously flawed readings. Bernstein's 1970 set,
recorded in the Albert Hall after a performance there, is nothing if not
involving, but throughout one has the sense that everything is being manipu-
lated for emotional effect. The start is exaggeratedly hushed and slow, even
turgid, *Dies Irae*'s vigour and drama is lessened by ear-splitting timpani, the
double-dotting and *sotto voce* at 'Quantus tremor' are overdone, the *andante*
in *Libera me* is a dragging *adagio*. Against that, and the all-too-familiar and
unwanted *accelerandi* and *rallentandi*, has to be set very many points left
unobserved by other conductors, such as the *frizzante* horns in 'Tuba mirum',
the real *cupo* in Josephine Veasey's voicing of the end of 'Liber scriptus' and
the *dolce pp* Domingo manages at 'inter oves'. The *Sanctus*, at the correct
speed, is marvellously alert and, at 'Pleni sunt coeli', light. The fugue in
Libera me has bite and real precision. In both these movements the LSO
and the Arthur Oldham-trained LSO Chorus are commendable. The results
of having a dark-toned soprano and a light mezzo are not always felicitous,
but Veasey is at all points deeply eloquent, not least at the start of 'Lacrymosa', which is really mournful. Martina Arroyo, by contrast, is no more
than correct, and her vibrato becomes intrusive after a time; nor can she
float the relevant passages. Domingo sings 'inter oves' prayerfully as already
noted, does the same for 'Hostias', and is in general stylistically admirable,
if not individually communicative. Ruggero Raimondi, with a tone like a
light, dry Burgundy, sings with beauty when he can avoid sliding up to notes,
but is not a perceptive interpreter.

Barbirolli's must be the most perverse version ever recorded. I have
already noted the ludicrously slack start, but that is only the beginning of an
interpretation that plods its way wearily through even the most dramatic
passages. Indeed Barbirolli conducts the piece as though he was in charge
of his own Requiem. As if to match the reading, the sound is curiously
muffled and soft at the edges, obscuring what seems to be good performances
by New Philharmonia forces. What merit resides in this interpretation comes
from the solo quartet. Together they make a refined, well-balanced team:
the unaccompanied 'Jesu pie' has not been surpassed elsewhere for sensitivity
and good vocal manners. Montserrat Caballé and Fiorenza Cossotto catch
the hieratical character of *Agnus Dei*: the effect is 'as if one voice had
acquired a halo of overtones' (John Warrack in *Gramophone*). Caballé
answers a prayer in her accomplishing of 'huic ergo' and in the *Offertorio*,
her held E natural at 'sed' moves down to the E flat with imperceptible grace
while the following phrase 'signifer sanctus Michael' is filled with the 'holy
light'. Then in *Libera me*, one senses not the customary melodrama but the
terror of a youthfully trembling soul. The control of the *andante* section is

exemplary, with the most lovely singing reserved for 'et lux perpetua': the section might have been written with Caballé in mind. Cossotto, though not as pleasing as with Serafin, still responds with much warmth and passion to the mezzo's grateful music, her attack as secure as ever. Vickers, as ever working intelligently on his music, sentimentalizes much of it by sliding up to notes or almost crooning; 'Hostias' is the worst example of this. Ruggero Raimondi is generally not as impressive as he is for Bernstein, but never less than involved: one just wishes that his technique was more secure.

Karajan's DG set is also most notable for its soloists. Christa Ludwig repeats her rich, personal account of the mezzo solos, Mirella Freni is a straightforward, wholly committed soprano, Carlo Cossutta, despite some fur on his tone and a slight excess of vibrato, is a purposeful tenor, Ghiaurov gives perhaps the best of his four performances, secure and impassioned. What rules this set out of consideration is the inconsistency of the recorded quality and Karajan's slack conducting, often at slow tempi (the *Sanctus* is the worst example). Accents are too often smoothed away, legato overdone, 'quantus tremor' almost inaudible. Tapes of Karajan's interpretations at the 1979 and 1980 Salzburg festivals reveal a transformed conductor, alive to the drama and vision of the piece, exact in his observation of tempo and dynamics, instinct with the sense of an occasion. He ought to record the work again.

Karajan's earlier performance, taken off-the-air from a 1949 Salzburg Festival performance, is itself a much more vivid affair, the *Sanctus* here taken at its proper tempo, and the Vienna forces energetic and enthusiastic. Even then, Karajan was supportive of his singers, and allows Helge Rosvaenge, now effortful as compared with his prewar form but still an important singer, too much leeway to make a meal of his 'Ingemisco'. Margarete Klose's glorious mezzo is still in good trim, though whether it was ever a suitable vehicle for this kind of music is another matter (the Germanic 'Kvee' is much in evidence). The youthful Christoff is already imposing his own terms on the music, somewhat to its detriment. Much the most appealing of the soloists is Hilde Zadek, whose soft-grained yet strong soprano (she sang Aida at Covent Garden) is used expressively throughout, culminating in a totally unaffected, natural, unmannered account of the *andante* section of *Libera me,* taken up to tempo.

Two other faulty readings need not detain us long. Fritz Reiner's is debilitated by drawn-out tempi and too many *rallentandi*, indifferent chorus and orchestra, but to some extent redeemed by its soloists, a notable team, headed by Leontyne Price, here at the peak of her career, not only in wonderful voice but intensely personal in her utterance. Rosalind Elias is scarcely less admirable, offering an even mezzo intelligently used: only the last ounce of passion and inwardness is missing. Björling, in his last recording of any work, cannot match his performance in the unofficial 1938 Toscanini set, but by any other standards sings with impeccable style and great feeling.

Giorgio Tozzi, lacking a true Verdian bass, compensates for that with the sincerity of his approach.

If it is possible, Alain Lombard is even more lethargic than Reiner, and there is no redemption here from the soloists, of whom only Paul Plishka's bass is in any way up to his duties. Joyce Barker has the right voice, but is dull in phrasing. Mignon Dunn is tentative and uneven, Ermanno Mauro pseudo-Italian in the very worst way. Carlos Paita's version is more orthodox but betrays many signs of hasty preparation. The choral singing and orchestral playing are often slack and poorly coordinated. As in the concert hall, the impression this conductor makes is of being overheated to the point of intemperance. As one would expect, Heather Harper gives a well-considered account of the soprano role. Josephine Veasey is much as for Bernstein but in less equal voice. The ladies react intelligently to each other in their duets. Carlo Bini is a run-of-the-mill tenor, Hans Sotin an impassive bass.

Now we begin to travel back in the LP era, meeting first on the way the most considerable of non-Italian performances, that conducted by Igor Markevitch, recorded in Russia with superb Bolshoi forces. Here indeed is a thrilling, immediate view of the work that, as John Warrack has pointed out, should show 'how an element of drama plays a crucial part in so sincerely felt a work' or what Luigi Barzini refers to as the 'element of spectacle' in Italian consciousness. It can be heard in the elan of the brass in 'Tuba mirum', the direct passion of the 'Salva me' ensemble. After a slow start, tempi tend to be on the fast side, *Dies Irae* particularly so. The whiny tenor apart, the soloists are all of interest. Galina Vishnevskaya sometimes phrases awkwardly or sings sharp, but everything she does is inspiriting, alive with meaning and, in the finale, spine-tingling. Nina Isakova, the mezzo, is still better. The way she cuts off her 'Nils' almost in terror, starts 'Lacrymosa' *piangente* as asked, or blends with her soprano in *Agnus Dei* adds to the impression she at once makes of a strong and serious singer. Ivan Petrov starts a little roughly but comes into his own with a sympathetic, eloquent 'Oro supplex', and follows Vladimir Ivanovsky's bland 'Hostias' with a more inward account of the gratifying music. The helter-skelter of the *Dies Irae* apart, this is a set to be reckoned with.

So is the one conducted by Paul van Kempen, whose records were much admired in the fifties. Speeds, dynamics, and detail are all given due respect. The Santa Cecilia Choir is excellent as is its orchestra. Oscar Czerwenka makes an uncouth bass soloist, Petre Munteanu a reedy, ineffective tenor. But the ladies are admirable. Maria von Ilosvay, taking time off from duties on Valhalla, proves herself throughout an appreciable Verdian. Something like a Baltsa of her day, she was hardly recognized as such. Everything, from her double-dotting in 'Liber scriptus' to her glorious launching of *Lux aeterna,* bespeaks an innate musician and a heartfelt one. Gré Brouwenstijn, though not Italian, was acknowledged as an eminent Verdian and confirms that repute here, even if we might ideally ask for warmer tone, a more immaculate attack. The slightly uncomfortable tonal quality mars an otherwise fine *Libera me*, in which one feels the world trembling about this supplicant.

More widely distributed in its time was the Ferenc Fricsay set. Indeed the authors of the *The Record Guide*, in one their few questionable judgements, dared to prefer it to Toscanini III. However, one can agree that it is 'scrupulous in its adherence to Verdi's demands' and that Fricsay's tempi are 'thoroughly convincing', also with the praise for the St Hedwig's Cathedral Choir. The marvelling at the sound, superb for its day, no longer applies. The four non-Italian soloists continue the good work with their rapt singing of unaccompanied passages and generally, as a team, eschew untoward histrionics or excessive *rubato*. Maria Stader, a Mozartian soprano, might seem light for this music, but she achieves much through perfect intonation, clean movement from note to note, and thoroughgoing musicality, although her *Libera me* lacks dramatic thrust. Marianna Radev is a sympathetically expressive mezzo, Helmut Krebs a mellifluous but restrained tenor, Kim Borg a firm bass. The Italian language is subjected to Germanic perversion. The 1938 Stuttgart Radio performance is notable for Joseph Keilberth's lyrical, unafraid conducting and for some rich, old-fashioned singing from the Munich-based mezzo Luise Willer. Rosvaenge is his accustomed self, emotive and full-blooded, Teschemacher too Germanic in expression.

We are left with odds and ends, among them an ancient Nixa set conducted by one J. H. Ossewaarde, using an organ instead of an orchestra and third-rate soloists, the Concert Hall version conducted by Gianfranco Rivoli of no more than provincial standard if we except brief moments of distinction from Gloria Davy (soprano) and Heinz Rehfuss (bass-baritone – a prayerful, tenderly phrased start to 'Salva me' for instance), the Remington performance conducted by Gustav Koslik with Austrian forces that boasts one or two notable phrases from Ilona Steingruber (soprano), one or two imposing ones from the veteran but passé Rosette Anday, and the uninteresting unidiomatic Patané set. I have not heard the listed sets conducted by Ricci, Walter Goehr, Balzer or, in more recent times, by Marinov and Buchei.

Of complete versions, that leaves me with the earliest recording of all, the 1929 La Scala set, which held the platform alone for eleven years until the first Serafin version was sent from Rome to rival it. Carlo Sabajno, who was then HMV's Italian chief, is the unremarkable conductor. His tempi are much as Serafin's were to be, except when he has to hurry to cope with the length of 78rpm sides. As far as one can tell from the ancient recording and the heavy surface noise always inherent with the HMV 'D' series, the chorus and orchestra are distinctly superior to their successors who were to record the work twenty-five years later with de Sabata. The chorus, in particular, sing with brio and lightness in 'Sanctus'.

Two of the soloists are at the very highest level of achievement. Irene Minghini-Cattaneo, a much underrated artist (or so it would seem), sings throughout with full tone, complete steadiness and opulent phrasing, while not forgetting to consider the meaning of what she is interpreting. She may not be a subtle artist, but in every other respect she is to be admired. Pinza is even better than for Serafin, seemingly more involved in the sense of the text and providing a secure resonant lowest line to all the ensembles. Maria Fanelli, the soprano, is a no more than average Italian soprano, an honest worker but uninspired, and she sings with a too consistent loudness. Franco Lo Giudice has a fiery, strong tenor, but tends to use it too tearfully, particularly in his 'Ingemisco'. There is a small cut towards the end of 'Salva me'.

The 78rpm discography of individual items is not extensive. The most frequently recorded extract is the tenor's 'Ingemisco', starting with Francesco Marconi, then already retired from active service, in 1904 (052057; RLS 7705). We hear the remnants of a fine, free voice and a respectable style, but the primitive recording and the failure to modulate at 'Qui mariam' make this version little more than a curiosity. Giovanni Zenatello (Edison 82214; Club 99.49) sings strongly, but the phrasing is rough and ready. Caruso's famous 1914 record (DB 138; GV 536) is invested with his customary full and golden, third-period sound, but the tempo is treated in rather a cavalier fashion. Evan Williams's 1910 disc (DB 458) is secure enough, but unvaried in tone and expression and curiously pronounced. Moving into the electric era, we find Alfred Piccaver in his most opulent voice and more involved than usual in a version well worth seeking out (Poly. 95354; Discophilia P2): the ease of delivery indicates that Piccaver had one of the most glorious tenor voices of the century. But even he is surpassed by Björling, whose 1938 version (DB 3665; 1C 147–00947–8) trumps even that on Toscanini II. This performance has everything: ideal tone, right tempo, no hurrying, prayerful interpretation but no lachrymose intrusions.

Two late 78s, by John McHugh (DX 1469) and Luigi Infantino (LX 1080), are both strongly sung but without any special qualities. In the LP era the performances by Franco Corelli (ASD 599), weepy and coarse, Mario del Monaco (SXL 6234), simply coarse, and Kenneth McKellar (SKL 6118), over-parted, are best forgotten. I have not heard the recordings by Louis van Tulder, Rudolph Schock and Robert von Ilosfalvy.

Records of 'Confutatis' begin with Oreste Luppi in 1906 – except that he doesn't start until 'Oro supplex': the voice is strong, but the phrasing awkward and wooden. José Mardones (Victor 6420; LV 268), recorded in the early twenties, colours his magnificent tone most sympathetically but articulates the text in lazy fashion. Not so Heinrich Rehkemper in 1924 (Poly. 66005; LV 107), who gives proper weight to the words with his lighter but not inconsiderable voice. Pinza, in a disc (AGSB 103; GEMM 162) made at almost the same time as his first set, is as resplendent as ever in this music. Has it ever been better done? Tone, attack, feeling are all in perfect accord. Pinza's earliest, 1924 version (DB 956; HLM 1435561) is a little lighter in tone, but still magnificent. Mark Reshetin (Melodiya 33CM 02091/2), in his slow, woolly version, sounds tame beside Pinza. I have not heard versions by Gitowski, Denijs and Arimondi.

I end this survey with two fine discs of the *andante* section of 'Libera me'. That by Margherita Perras from the 1930s (C 2794; LV 73) is pure and poised. That by Elise Elizza, Viennese in spite of her name, made in 1903 (43445; CO 318), comes nearer to the ideal than any soprano on the complete sets. The voice sounds full yet it is perfectly placed and pure. At the same time the music seems deeply felt and it is phrased with great plasticity rising to poised, floated B flat – a disc recalling a golden age indeed.

My ideal 'cast' for the *Requiem* would be Tebaldi or Milanov, Minghini-Cattaneo, Björling and Pinza with the BBC forces of 1938 under Toscanini.

REQUIEM MASS

1929 Fanelli, Minghini-Cattaneo, Lo Giudice, Pinza / La Scala Chorus and Orch. / Sabajno
HMV D1751–60*
Victor set M96*

1938 (live performance – Queen's Hall, London)
Milanov, Thorborg, Rosvaenge, Moscona / BBC Choral Society, BBC SO / Toscanini
Olympic ⓜ ATS 1108–9

1938 (broadcast performance)
Teschemacher, Willer, Rosvaenge, Hann / Stuttgart Radio Chorus and Orch. / Keilberth
Preiser ⓜ LV 151–2
Discophilia ⓜ KS 18–9

1939 Caniglia, Stignani, Gigli, Pinza / Rome Opera Chorus and Orch. / Serafin
World Records ⓜ SH 103–4
Seraphim ⓜ IB 6050

1940 (live performance – Carnegie Hall, New York)
Milanov, Castagna, Björling, Moscona / Westminster Choir, NBC SO / Toscanini
Arturo Toscanini Society ⓜ ATS 1005–6

1949 (live performance – Salzburg Festival)
Zadek, Klose, Rosvaenge, Christoff / Vienna State Opera Chorus, Vienna PO / Karajan
Cetra ⓜ LO 524 (2)

*c.*1950 Anonymous soloists, Berlin Cathedral Choir and SO / Balzer
Royale ⓜ 1377–8

1951 (live performance – La Scala)
Tebaldi, Rankin, Prandelli, Rossi-Lemeni, La Scala Chorus and Orch. / De Sabata
Documents DOC Discorp 202 32

1951 (live performance – Carnegie Hall, New York)
Nelli, Barbieri, Di Stefano, Siepi / Shaw Chorale, NBC SO / Toscanini
RCA (UK) ⓜ VL 46010
(US) ⓜ LM 6018

1951 Hunt, Moudry, Knowles, Smith / Calvary Church Choir, Ossewaarde (organ)
Concert Hall ⓜ CHS 1311

1951 Kaye, Pirazzini, Sinimberghi, Beuf / Rome Opera Chorus and Orch. / Ricci
Urania ⓜ URLP 213

1952 Steingruber, Anday, Delorko, Czerwenka / Austrian SO and Chorus / Koslik
Remington ⓜ 199–105

1954 (live performance – Academy of Music, Boston)
Nelli, Turner, Conley, Moscona / chorus, Boston SO / Cantelli
Cetra ⓜ LO 503 (2)

1954 Stader, Radev, Krebs, Borg / Berlin RIAS Chamber Choir, St Hedwig's Cathedral Choir, Berlin Radio SO / Fricsay
DG ⓜ 2721 171

1954 Schwarzkopf, Dominguez, di Stefano, Siepi / La Scala Chorus and Orch, / de Sabata
Columbia ⓜ 33CX 1195–6

Angel ⓜ 3649 BL
1955 Brouwenstijn, Von Ilosvay,
Munteanu, Czerwenka / Santa
Cecilia Academy Chorus and
Orch. / Van Kempen
Philips A 00284–5 L
1956 Bijster, E. Pritchard, Garen,
Wolovsky / Netherlands
Philharmonic Choir and Orch. /
Goehr
Concert Hall SMS 2038
1959 Vartenissian, Cossotto, Fernandi,
Christoff / Rome Opera Chorus
and Orch. / Serafin
EMI SXDW 3055
TC-SXDW 3055
Capitol (US) SGBR 7227
1960 Vishnevskaya, Arkhipova,
Ivanovsky, Petrov / Leningrad
Glinka Academy Choir,
Leningrad PO / Melik-Pashayev
Melodiya ⓜ D 035389 / 92
1960 Vishnevskaya, Isakova,
Ivanovsky, Petrov / RSFSR
Academy Choir, Moscow PO /
Markevitch
Philips ⓜ 6768 215
Turnabout (US) TV 34210–1
1960 L. Price, Elias, Björling, Tozzi /
Vienna Singverein, Vienna PO /
Reiner
Decca DJB 2003 ④ KDJBC 2003
London JB 42004
1963–4 Schwarzkopf, Ludwig, Gedda,
Ghiaurov / Philharmonia
Chorus and Orch. / Giulini
EMI SLS 909 ④ TC-SLS909
Angel SBL 3649
1964 Amara, Forrester, Tucker,
London / Westminster Choir,
Philadelphia Orch. / Ormandy
CBS (UK) 72297–8
(US) Y2–35230 ④ YT-35230
1965 Nilsson, Chookasian, Bergonzi,
Flagello / Boston Pro Musica
Boston SO / Leinsdorf
RCA (UK) SER 5537–8
(US) LSC 7040
1967 Sutherland, Horne, Pavarotti,
Talvela / Vienna State Opera
Chorus, Vienna PO / Solti
Decca SET 374–5 ④ K85K22
London OSA 1275 ④ OSA5–1275
1967 Davy, Leal, Peterson, Rehfuss /

Vienna State Opera Chorus and
Orch. / Rivoli
Concert Hall SM 2312
1969 Caballé, Cossotto, Vickers,
Raimondi / New Philharmonia
Chorus and Orch. / Barbirolli
EMI CFPD 4144283 ④
TC-CFDD 4144285
Angel RL 3201
1970 Arroyo, Veasey, Domingo,
Raimondi / LSO Chorus, London
SO / Bernstein
CBS (UK) 77321
(US) M2–30060
1972 Freni, Ludwig, Cossutta,
Ghiaurov / Vienna Singverein
Berlin PO / Karajan
DG 2707 065 ④ 3370 002
1973 Wiener-Chenisheva, Milcheva-
Nonova, Bodurov, Ghiuselev /
Obretenov Chorus, Sofia PO /
Marinov
Harmonia Mundi HM140 ④
HM4140
Monitor 90108–9
1976 Harper, Veasey, Bini, Sotin /
London Philharmonic Choir,
RPO / Paita
Lodia LOD772–3 ④ LOC 772–3
London OS21140–1 ④
OS5–21140–1
1976 Barker, Dunn, Mauro, Plishka /
Slovak Philharmonic Choir,
Strasbourg PO / Lombard
Erato STU 70965–6
Musical Heritage Society MHS
3672
c.1976 Eichner, Schubert, Johns,
Ridderbusch / Gütersloh
Society Choir, Herford PO /
Buchei
Ricordi SHRE 1202–3
Ariola-Eurodisc 80926XR
1976 L. Price, Baker, Luchetti, Van
Dam / Chicago Symphony
Chorus and Orch. / Solti
RCA (UK) RL 02476
(US) ARL2–2476 ④ ARK2–2476
1978 Scotto, Baltsa, Luchetti,
Nesterenko / Ambrosian Chorus,
Philharmonia / Muti
EMI SLS 5185 ④ TC-SLS5185
Angel SBZ 3858 ④ 4Z2Z-3858
1970s Molnar-Talajic, Lilova, Ottolini,

Giaiotti / Leipzig Radio Chorus and Orch. / Patané
Eterna 826694–5

1980 Ricciarelli, Verrett, Domingo, Ghiaurov / La Scala Chorus and Orch. / Abbado

DG 2707 120 ④ 3370 032

1983 Caballé, Berini, Domingo, Plishka / Musica Sacra Chorus, New York Philharmonic Orchestra / Keilberth
CBS 36927

Mignon

JOHN T. HUGHES

It is not mere coincidence that so many singers in the past found arias from *Mignon* worth recording: Thomas knew how to write for the voice, an art which seems to be lost. Indeed, in the last century, *Mignon* was the fifth opera to be presented at the new Metropolitan Opera House, New York, when on 31 October, 1883, Christine Nilsson sang the title role, Victor Capoul was Wilhelm, and the opera was sung in Italian. In Paris, the 1000th performance of the work at the Opéra-Comique was given only twenty-eight years after the première. London audiences first witnessed it in 1870, at the Theatre Royal, Drury Lane. It was for that performance that the gavotte, 'Me voici dans son boudoir', was inserted for the mezzo-soprano Zelia Trebelli-Bettini, the Frédéric.

Among those arias that were so frequently recorded in those early days of the gramophone were 'Adieu, Mignon' and 'Elle ne croyait pas', both well suited to the light, somewhat plangent tones of so many French tenors; 'Connais-tu le pays', that most gentle expression of longing, evoking a memory of a childhood gone and long gone; the contrasting Styrienne; the gavotte that Thomas formed from the entr'acte to make what must be one of the most sheerly charming of arias in all opera; Philine's dazzling 'Je suis Titania': all these arias, plus some fine ensemble pieces, do not deserve the neglect that fashion has bestowed on them.

Mignon exists in various editions. Not only does the part of Frédéric differ, the one version being for tenor and the other for mezzo-soprano, but there are several different endings in existence. There is not space here to discuss these, but readers are recommended to read the notes with the complete CBS set.

Of the complete sets, the earlier is on Decca (never issued in Britain), which has a tenor Frédéric, includes cuts (one in the middle of 'Adieu, Mignon'), and has some simplified coloratura passages. Although the chorus and orchestra are Belgian, one supposes that this is more or less the version given at the time at the Opéra-Comique. It dates from 1952, takes three discs, and is in mono. On my Richmond pressing, the sound fluctuates, but the voices come through clearly, as they usually did on mono records. The conductor is Georges Sebastian, and the leading singers are Geneviève

Moizan, Libero de Luca, Janine Micheau and René Bianco. In no way does it measure up to the CBS issue as far as they are concerned.

Moizan, as Mignon, sounds elderly. Although she sings, 'Connais-tu le pays' with feeling, there is little light and shade, and p and f markings are ignored. In the first verse, on the word 'bleu' the note collapses. She is better in the duet 'Légères hirondelles' (the Swallow Duet), though there is no *ad lib* coloratura at the end. In 'Elle est là', she sings the higher alternative. The Swiss tenor Libero de Luca has a strong voice, rather hard. He sings mainly on one level, though in 'Adieu, Mignon' he scales down his voice but finds the tessitura something of a strain when he is not singing at full power. Only the second verse of 'Elle ne croyait pas' is sung, with a different ending from the usual one. This is an interpretation that lacks charm and subtlety. Janine Micheau, as Philine, was more a lyric soprano than a *leggiera*. In the runs she sounds matronly, although she was not quite forty. Occasionally the voice seems worn and shrill, and there is a touch of yelping in the Polonaise. Lothario, a role usually sung by a bass, is here the baritone Bianco, whose voice, a second-rate one, lacks beauty and is not always well focused. Better in the Swallow Duet than in the verse of 'Fugitif et tremblant', he is best of all in the Berceuse, which he sings intelligently and affectingly.

As Frédéric is given to a tenor, the gavotte is omitted and the role is negligible. There is a good Jarno in Noël Pierotte, with a better voice than many *comprimarii* have.

The CBS set, in splendid sound on four discs, is conducted thoughtfully and feelingly by Antonio de Almeida. The tempi seem just right: he catches both the pathos of Mignon and the scintillating fun of Philine, and the overture is sprightly. This recording, generally well cast and boasting two world-class mezzo-sopranos, legitimately deserves the word 'complete'. It eclipses the earlier in every department except that of two minor roles.

Marilyn Horne takes the part of the eponymous girl. The role has few of the roulades and ornaments at which Horne is expert, and it may be thought that her voice is too overpowering for the young 'orphan'. 'Connais-tu', sung very slowly (actually 6 minutes 5 seconds as against the 4 minutes 55 seconds of Moizan), reflectively, elegantly and eloquently phrased, with the voice reduced in power in the second verse, is sung with a touch more vibrato than her earlier, Decca version or the later one on Bongiovanni; but the vibrato just occasionally turns into a beat, and the voice is not as young as perhaps Mignon's should be. The Styrienne, 'Je connais un pauvre enfant', is sung in a much more extended version than that which Moizan chooses, especially in the coda. Mignon's next aria, 'Elle est là, près de lui' (the Air du Feu), finds Horne switching from one alternative line to the other (as printed in the Heugel vocal-score) and adding a third variation, the whole being delivered with panache and great technical accomplishment. (Moizan sings the higher line every time.) Despite the few strictures that I list above, I find Horne's a most enjoyable performance.

As Wilhelm Meister, the young man who comes to Mignon's aid and then falls in love with her, Alain Vanzo, the finest of today's French tenors, whose neglect by the large record companies has parallelled their neglect of French opera, has a voice whose tone is well suited to the role. In the rondeau ('Si l'amour sur la route'), it is ringing and free, the slow middle section sung with honeyed tone. 'Adieu, Mignon' is too emphatic, more so than in the HMV record of excerpts, as though Vanzo is concerned with stressing the drama at the expense of the tone. On 'Ne pleure pas' there is a sob, which disturbs the line. There is no need for it, as the voice has the inherent sweetness and sadness that are necessary for this aria. Similar comments can be made with regard to 'Elle ne croyait pas', though the 'faults' are not so pronounced. The final verdict must be: 'Very good but could have been better.'

The fun-loving Philine, the kind-hearted actress, must be sung with a deft coloratura technique, but not one that makes one think of Hoffmann's doll. Ruth Welting gives here what is probably her finest display on record, her agile voice having enough edge to avoid tweetiness. She has the personality to make Philine a living creature, not just a cardboard character with a myriad of notes to sing. In the Polonaise the slight *ritardandi* that Welting introduces overcome the mechanical approach that can afflict such an aria – and which does so in some of the separate versions that I shall be considering later. The runs are sparklingly sung.

The first character whom one hears is old Lothario, sung here by the Greek bass Nicola Zaccaria, whose contribution proves to be something of an enigma. In the first piece, 'Fugitif et tremblant', the voice is worn, the top notes effortful, but Zaccaria sings with great feeling. In the Swallow Duet, when he has to jump to high notes, the voice is pushed and sounds rough, nor does it blend well with Horne's. The phrasing and the command of legato, despite the beat in the voice, are the finest features in the Berceuse. How good Zaccaria would have been in the role fifteen to twenty years earlier.

Another fine artist, and one whose voice is in its prime, is the second of those two mezzo-sopranos to whom I referred earlier: Frederica von Stade, who is a nonpareil Frédéric. She sings beautifully, the words lightly touched, the tone forward and on the breath, equal from top to bottom. The line is not broken, but she still suggests the young man's urgency and fluttering of the heart. One relishes the legato and the exquisite phrasing. The set is worth having in one's collection for this alone.

Is everything near perfection then? Well, no, for in the role of Laërte is André Battedou, who employs overemphasized diction in place of full line and unimpaired tone. One cannot create tone on a consonant, and though consonants are important, they should not obtrude.

On the final side are two appendices. The first is an aria for Philine in Act 2, accompanied by flute and harpsichord (not orchestrated by Thomas). It is an empty piece. The second is the Paris finale, with Philine singing a *forlane* (quoted in the overture), thus forming a far livelier ending than the one in general use. Welting performs as well as she has done throughout the recording, and it is good to have these two pendants.

I have been unable to find a copy of one of two German-language issues on Deutsche Grammophon, the one with Schlemm, Fehenberger and Streich. Of the five that I have heard, two are sung in French, two in German and one in Russian.

On the DG excerpts disc in French comes a disappointing effort from Jane Berbié as Mignon. Her voice is not well supported here, the intonation doubtful, the tone tapering off at the top. Described as a soprano-Dugazon rather than a mezzo-soprano, she brings firmer voice to the Styrienne, but there is no coloratura, not even at the end. She replaces the running notes by a leap. She is represented best in 'Elle est là', in which, with one exception, she takes the higher alternative line. Philine is Mady Mesplé. Hers is a very French-sounding voice, but here it is not as acidulous as it later became, and she sings the Polonaise quite well though the frills are rather bumpy. She clearly differentiates between the staccato and legato runs.

Gérard Dunan takes the part of Wilhelm. He has a pleasant voice, hardening at the top, but he is recorded too far back. He sings the shortened version of 'Adieu', in which the voice sounds small and pushed. There is some feeling in his second aria. That is more than one can say for Xavier Depraz's interpretation of Lothario's Berceuse, in which the voice is kept at a constant level and which is taken very quickly. He is no more than acceptable in the Swallow Duet.

HMV provides the other record of excerpts in French which makes a far superior impression. Not only are the selections more interesting than those on the DG disc (two trios are included), but the singing is finer too. Jean-Claude Hartemann conducts what I wish had been a complete recording.

Jane Rhodes's large, expansive voice is really too unwieldy and heavy for the role, but the quality is good without being among the best. It is doubtful if this Mignon would have accepted the treatment meted out to her by Jarno, and it may be felt that Rhodes is not really in character. The record is worthy of acquisition for Vanzo's Wilhelm (the actual singing better than in the CBS set) and, to a lesser extent, for Andrée Esposito's Philine. Vanzo is in splendid vocal estate, the plangent quality well to the fore, but I should like him more caressing in 'Elle ne croyait pas'. Esposito produces a full-toned Philine, far more so than most singers of the part. Some downward scales are not as rippling as they should be, but this is an accomplished performance from a neglected artist. Michel Roux's throaty voice, very Gallic, is not too well supported, the tone wobbling at times, though his is a thoughtful performance.

From Electrola comes a record (in German) that wins respect for Fritz Wunderlich's Wilhelm, a thinking, caring soul, who sings in wonderfully liquid tones but occasionally as though he has slipped in to a Lehár operetta. 'Adieu' (thankfully sung complete) begins quite differently from the marked p. The first repetition of the phrase is quieter, the second repeat best of all.

Mignon here is sung by an unequivocal soprano: Pilar Lorengar, who at this time was in good vocal condition; the vibrato, which in later years was to become a flutter, was under control, except during the prayer in the final trio. There is a hardening at the top of the register. As Philine, Ruth-Margaret Pütz presents a voice even throughout its range, with no changing of gears and no tweetiness. Once again it is the Lothario who is the weak link: Gottlob Frick in rusty voice. He gives Lothario unsympathetic treatment: no light and shade.

The DG set of excerpts in German has a Mignon from Irmgard Seefried that finds the soprano in tones that have lost their freshness. She sings 'Kennst du das Land' slowly, contemplatively, but she pushes the voice on higher notes, causing some shrillness, which is apparent again in the Swallow Duet, in which she is joined by an ordinary Kieth Engen. The Styrienne lacks sparkle, and, in 'Elle est aimée', the voice sounds worn. Catherine Gayer gives a dull account of the Polonaise: the voice does not 'speak' quickly enough, and so the necessary effect of effortlessness is not achieved. Tone is lost in some of the runs. Ernst Häfliger finds the tessitura of 'Adieu, Mignon' uncomfortable. There is no caressing of the line; the voice is constricted and produces a wobble under pressure. Lack of smoothness spoils the other aria too. Engen gives a thoughtful account of the Berceuse in a voice not quite steady enough in production of tone or line. The fine conducting of Jean Fournet deserved better support. Seefried's solos have been reissued recently on 'Irmgard Seefried: a Portrait' (DG 410 847–1).

The fifth of these records of excerpts, in Russian, emanating from a broadcast (Melodiya 33M10–36031/2), offers a strange selection of items, which have a number of internal cuts. There is a good Jarno from Vsevolod Tyutyunnik. The Lothario is Georgi Abramov, who was not one of Russia's leading basses. The timbre, dark grey rather than black, is suited to this serious role. There is nothing special about Mignon, N. Aleksandriyskaya, but her attractive, rather elderly-sounding voice is more than adequate. The Philine is Nadezhda Kazantseva, whose Polonaise is not included here. (It can be found on a two-record set devoted to her – Melodiya D 031759/62.) Her slightly shrill and acid voice is heard in two trios. Though it is not included here, I found in her Polonaise that the notes were negotiated cleanly and accurately, the voice agile but lacking a trill. She obeys the *ritenuto* markings.

The Wilhelm is Georgi Vinogradov; and if one is searching for the finest Wilhelm that search stops here. If you can find this record, buy it, if only for Vinogradov, a neglected tenor who rivals the best that Russia has produced: not quite so plangent as Kozlovsky, not quite so warm as Lemeshev, but with a sad, wistful quality that is a joy to hear and which suits the character perfectly. He makes his first appearance in the trio in Act 1 for Philine, Wilhelm and Laërte ('Eh! quoi! . . . mon cher Laërte'), taking the ornamented variation on the word 'disent', singing fifteen notes instead of the alternative two. A couple of bands later we hear him in 'Adieu', and how can one resist? Indeed, one wonders how Mignon did. The voice is almost erotic in its sensuality, heartbreaking in its sadness. Beautifully phrased, with a finely controlled *diminuendo* on 'douleur' at the end of the first verse, then a gentle lift into the repetition of the words 'Adieu, Mignon', this is the finest version of the aria, leaving one to regret greatly the omission of the second stanza. Vinogradov appears also in the two excerpts from Act 3: 'Je suis heureuse' and the finale.

We come now to the extracts. I have commented on every record I have heard. I start with 'Fugitif et tremblant', which comes in the middle of a choral section. It is not very effective out of context, mainly because of its brevity. I have heard only two separate recordings of it, one by a famous singer and the other by someone unknown to me. Vanni-Marcoux (DA 4867; FJLP 5035), who was said to be renowned for his histrionic ability, has a clear voice of no intrinsic beauty. His phrasing is jerky, his light rather flat tone lacks smoothness. Silvio Queirolo (Favorite 1–39027), of whom I know nothing, has a tremolo-ridden voice not well supported, though his performance is thoughtful. But there is nothing to suggest that his neglect is unjustified.

Wilhelm's rondeau I have heard in versions by Karl Erb and by Arthur Preuss. Unfortunately, I have been unable to trace Helge Rosvaenge's Polydor. Erb (Od. 98002; 1C 147–30772) sings (in German) both the rondeau and 'Ah! Que ton âme enfin', a section from the duet 'Je suis heureuse' in Act 3. Neither of them afforded me any pleasure. The voice is squeezed out for the top notes, and in the second piece there is some questionable intonation at the beginning, with the whole aria sung at a uniform level. The difficult middle section of the rondeau is omitted, which is just as well considering how careless Erb is over note values, particularly dotted notes. Preuss (3–42392) throws off the shortened version that he sings quite well and better than Erb, though his last phrase is not tidy: a sort of hiccup intrudes.

In Mignon's 'Connais-tu le pays', she recalls the far-off land in which she spent her childhood. It has been committed to disc by a varied assortment of suitable and ill-advised singers from the earliest years of the gramophone to those of LP. From a vanished time comes Gemma Bellincioni (Pathé 4394; GV 83) in only one verse, a common foreshortening in the days of the 78. Known for her interpretations of *verismo* heroines, Bellincioni proves to be far too intense and melodramatic, the voice displaying a hoarseness and a pronounced tremolo: 'Mignon' out of Mascagni. Far better (but then she *was* a better singer) is Marcella Sembrich (Victor 88098), who phrases well. Her top notes gleam, though occasionally pressure on the voice causes it to lose resonance. It is a generally enjoyable version, with smooth descents of the scale. On a Pathé disc (4373), Emma Carelli treats the listener to a decidedly *un*enjoyable account, in which she shows how thin the voice is at the upper extremes and how flat-toned at the lower, all contained in an exercise in gear-changing that would guarantee her failing her test even with the most indulgent of examiners. Three recordings of this aria by Emmy Destinn come next. Destinn seems to excite in many collectors a great love, while others vilify her with an equal amount of ardour. She is in fine voice on her Fonotipia record (39420), but her phrasing is rather four-square and there is some noisy breathing (and not just the intake of breath). Tempi are pulled about and the attempted *diminuendo* on 'toujours bleu' is only a thinly produced quiet note. But despite all that she brings a great deal of sympathetic if idiosyncratic treatment to the piece. She is much the same on the second record (GC 3754), though here the phrasing is perhaps more eloquent. The worst of the three versions (Od. 50023) reveals a more heavy-handed account, and the aforementioned *diminuendo* is ignored.

Claudine Armeliny, a 'soprano/mezzo' has a voice that we think of as very 'French': it is metallic in tone in the middle and pure at the top. Here is a pleasing version (33676). Armida Parsi-Pettinella's two recordings (Fono. 39394, with piano, and Fono. 92036) are similar to each other, in tone, in phrasing, even in timing. Beautiful unforced tone in cantilena, evenly produced, the voice moving forward steadily, closely holding the line so as not to disturb it, show that overdone vocal histrionics, whether applied for the sake of dramatic emphasis or for diction, are completely unnecessary if one's technique is right. The diction here is good. The one 'black mark' is for a breath taken before the last word in the phrase 'aimer et mourir'. These fine performances gave me much pleasure. Less was provided by Zélie de Lussan (Victor 81003; Belcantodisc EB 6), who takes her one verse, cut, at so slow a pace that it falls apart: very self-conscious. The voice itself is a well-produced mezzo.

From a later generation comes another slow account, that of Anna Case (Col. DOX 55; GV 41). She too sings only one verse, this time the second! She seemed to have a voice more suited to oratorio than to opera: pure, silvery tone, which is produced here on quite a good line (apart from one explosive start). For some reason (presumably for display purposes only), she hangs on to the top note at 'aimer' as though she is afraid of finishing the aria. A one-verse rendering by Lucrezia Bori (DA 1017; LV 298) finds her drawing out the line, sweetly if a little self-consciously. Ninon Vallin is here at the other extreme from Case and de Lussan as regards tempo (Od. 171032; GV 509). She would have benefited from dwelling more lovingly and longingly over the piece, for her voice is effortless in production, equal, warm; the phrasing just right. This is a very creditable version. That it does not quite touch the heart as some others do is partly because there is not enough variety in that glorious tone. A contemporary of Vallin was Lotte Lehmann, who takes almost as long over one verse as Vallin does over two. This is sensitive, creating exactly the right mood. She shows that the German language *can* be sung smoothly, and there are some lovely floated tones with exquisite *morbidezza* (Parlo. R 20137; 1C 137 30704/5). Also in the correct mood – and in German – is Emmy Bettendorf, whose two recordings (Parlo. P 1360; LV 136; and Homokord B 8180) are practically the same, both dreamily sung in a firmly focused voice produced on a smooth jet of silvery tone. Again only one verse is given, admirably presenting the girl reflecting wistfully on her youth.

Born in the same year as Lehmann was the Russian soprano Elena Katulskaya, who recorded 'Connais-tu' at the age of sixty about forty years after her début. She too offers a slow performance (in Russian), well sustained (Melodiya D 118853/4). The voice shows a few, a very few signs of age: the occasional held note is not as steady as probably it once was; but her attractive, slightly reedy tone is without the shrillness that has affected many Russian sopranos. Hers is a fine piece of singing that earns a place among the best in this aria. A later Russian, this one a mezzo, Irina Arkhipova (Melodiya D 011811/2), is in rich, sumptuous voice, with a fair amount of characterization. Her tone is not plush, but vibrant, at times sounding not quite under perfect control. The composer's p and f markings are frequently ignored, as they are by so many singers, both past and present, but this is a more than adequate account. Between Katulskaya and Arkhipova was the Kiev-born Xenia Belmas, who was an Aida at the Paris Opéra. The voice, though attractive, is not right for Mignon, and she does nothing to compensate (Poly. 66746; LV 79). A fourth Russian, Maria Kurenko, she of the silvery tone, sings sweetly, indeed delightfully, allowing us to enjoy the lovely sound, but more characterization is really needed (Am. Col. 214M). The Rumanian mezzo Zenaida Pally (Supraphon SUF 20053), singing in French, as did Belmas, adheres to Thomas's markings, taking the first part of each verse quietly and then opening out in full voice, as required, on 'c'est là que je voudrais vivre'. Quality is lost when she is singing softly, with the beat becoming pronounced, the tone losing evenness.

The Italian field is well enough represented on record in this piece. Three of them are dealt with here. Ebe Stignani, the oldest of the three, sings in light and bright voice (Parlo. R 30030; OASI 543), but unsteadiness mars the effect. A 1949 recording by Giulietta Simionato (Col. GQ 7235; 3C 065–18031) shows off a splendid voice which was so admirable in Verdi, but is too heavy, too dramatic for the simple Mignon: Azucena in the wrong tribe of gipsies. Her later version (LXT 5458) is sung thoughtfully, in French, but the voice spreads and the vibrato is pronounced. I find that the best of this trio is Pia Tassinari (Cetra LPC 50033). Singing both verses, in French, she puts more feeling into the piece than either of her compatriots, though the voice itself is less thrilling than Simionato's. One or two Italianate mannerisms, such as leaning on initial notes, intrude, but this is a worthy account. And to continue this Latin section, I come to Spain and to Conchita Supervia, who recorded the aria in Italian in 1929 (Parlo. R 20105; RLS 1436143) and in French in 1931 (R 20192; HLM 7039). The Italian version, of only one verse, is sung with a great deal of feeling, gently, sweetly. There is the occasional overstressed start to a phrase, and a little sob mars the last line. In the French performance, in which both verses are given, Supervia sings more smoothly, which is more in keeping, but at a quicker tempo, the first verse taking only about two-thirds of the time taken over the earlier version. I presume the quicker speed was adopted in order to accommodate both verses in the very restricted space of the 78 disc. In both recordings, Supervia treats us, as was her wont, to good singing and legato.

Lucy Perelli (Disque P 612) exhibits a pleasing tone, slightly vibrant, and is well in character, more so than the Dutch contralto Maartje Offers (DB 913; LV 263), who sings in a manner more fitting to oratorio. Similarly, Essie Ackland (C 2535) has neither the right voice nor style. Her version is really too 'English', but it is undeniably a lovely piece of singing, despite the top notes lacking the warmth that invests the middle and lower regions of the voice. Karin Branzell (Bruns. 15180; Rococo 5214) recorded one verse, in French, with haunting tone, effortlessly produced and rock-steady. It has the virtues of Ackland plus the right approach.

Although *Mignon* is a French opera, the source was Goethe, and German sopranos have been very much to the fore in the number of artists who have recorded some of the heroine's arias. A 1944 recording by Irma Beilke (Historia H683), probably from radio, sung in German as 'Kennst du das Land', opens with the words 'das Land' repeated. Beilke's voice, more soubrette than lyric, is unsteady and not particularly appealing. The fresh-voiced Margot Guilleaume (Telef. TM 68025) sings prettily but does not convey a sense of longing. Elisabeth Grümmer was for me the greatest German soprano of the postwar era. The adjective most suiting the voice is 'radiant'. She recorded 'Connais-tu' in 1953 (EH 1440; 1C 047–28553). It may lack some of the interpretative qualities of others, but good singing is more than *just* interpretation: it is beautiful sounds, fine technique, eloquent phrasing and unbroken legato, all of which Grümmer has in abundance. She was more than a mere actress: she was a great singer.

The French mezzos Solange Michel and Isabelle Andréani provide a startling contrast. The distinguished Michel (Pathé PDT 227; DTX 137) brings lush, easily produced tone, a lovely sound, but with little light and shade, and the tempo is too quick for my taste. Andréani (Véga 30LT 13012) lacks the ability to sing legato, and every word is a headline. The soprano Déva Dassy (DA 4859) offers an account that is neatly sung and adequately interpreted but has no special merit to place it among the finest.

The last four singers whom I have heard in this aria are Americans. The oldest is Gladys Swarthout, who sang the part of Mignon at the Metropolitan. On her recording (Victor 11–8281; VIC 1490), made in 1942, she sings well enough in that somewhat reedy mezzo but treats the piece superficially. Among the first recordings of Risë Stevens (Am. Col. 71192D; Y31738), in 1941, is a 'Connais-tu', taken as quickly as was Vallin's and sung attractively in a voice of soft silkiness, aptly expressing Mignon's nostalgia. The earlier of Marilyn Horne's two recordings (SXL 6345) is one of the best of all versions, dreamily but firmly sung. Sounding younger (which she was) than in the complete set, Horne imparts a fervent hope that one day she will see those orange trees again. The cantilena is to be admired. In 1980, from a 'live' recital at Parma, she is again in first-class vocal estate, as though indeed youth has returned, and she shows what a truly great singer she is. This is a beautifully controlled performance, a shade quicker than the Decca and sung more softly. She draws out the final 'oui, c'est là', as on the CBS set (Bongiovanni GB 11).

There are two ways of longing for one's early years. One, as portrayed by Horne and Katulskaya, is to resign oneself to the idea that there is no returning; the other, depicted by Von Stade (CBS 76522), is one of pleasure and determination to return one day to the place where happiness seemed all powerful. Von Stade sings the first half of each verse reflectively, and then the tone (always beautiful, whether sad or smiling) becomes less plaintive as Mignon states that it is there, in that country, that she wishes to live, to love and to die. One can sense the young girl's spirits rising as she dreams of going back one day. This is a delightful record.

In the Swallow Duet, Mignon and Lothario sing to the swallows to open their wings and fly away. From the early years of recording I have heard six couples. In the first, Anna Hellström's Scandinavian-type soprano, with no vibrato, is cleanly produced. Hellström, who died at the age of forty, gives an adroit performance which pleases, even if it is really too cold in temperament for Mignon. Her partner, Oscar Bergström, sounds more like a concert singer than an operatic one, thus he too is not ideal for the part (G&T 84012). A second Swedish performance (84086) finds Davida Hesse and John Forsell giving a slightly better version all-round. Hesse has a lighter voice than Hellström, sweeter but not quite so smooth. Forsell improves on Bergström, though his strong, rather hard-sounding baritone lacks, perhaps, the necessary sympathetic tones. A fine reading comes from Gertrud Runge (Gramm. 944245), the tone full and cleanly emitted, but once again the male partner is inferior. This time it is Robert Leonhardt, who has a dark, steely, rather throaty bass and nothing special to offer by way of interpretation. Another German pair, the ill-fated Ottilie Metzger and her husband, Theodor Lattermann (Parlo. P14444; LV 242), leave an impression of heavy-handedness, because of the lugubrious bass and plodding tempo. The fifth of these versions found its way in to Volume 1 of 'The Record of Singing': that of Minnie Nast and Leon Rains (Od. 99565; RLS 7706). In the book accompanying that set, Michael Scott describes Rains as having 'a firm voice and limpid legato style'. To my ears, he is throaty, his tone dull. Nast sings cleanly but with the squeezed tone that was not uncommon in German sopranos of those days. There is no *ad lib* passage at the end. Far superior to those five records is that by Geraldine Farrar and Marcel Journet (Vic. 89038; GV 530), with the bass giving a most sympathetic portrayal in warm, mellifluous sound. Farrar's voice is pure and strong. She gives the impression of launching herself at some of the higher notes, with uncovered tone, which is somewhat disconcerting, but she hits them all cleanly. The *ad lib* passage is included here, thus rounding off the duet effectively.

Vincenzo Bettoni does better than I had expected, for he does use his voice more varyingly than one imagines some other buffo-basses would have done. This record, however, is notable for the Mignon of Supervia, who is charming, if a shade too quick. She sings sparkingly, and her downward *portamenti* are done lightly, without the 'boots first' effect of many of the older singers (Parlo. R 20105; HLM 7039). Another good performance in the wrong language is the 1939 German version of Friedl Beckmann and Arno Schellenberg (DA 4474; LV 140). Beckmann begins softly and gently, her warm voice well under control, though it tends to lose some of its roundness on top notes. She lacks Supervia's sparkle: hers is more the wistful approach. Schellenberg produces some fine legato singing and is well within the character. This is a lovely record, despite the fact that there is no cadenza. Just as good is a German performance from ten years earlier (Poly. 66862; LV 41) by Felicie Hüni-Mihacsek and Willi Domgraf-Fassbaender. The soprano caresses the vocal line with a soft tone, effortlessly created, with just the right weight and timbre for Mignon: really delectable. Domgraf-Fassbaender was not, to judge from his records, one of the greatest of interpreters, but in this case that is a minor matter in view of the beautiful singing, the voices blending harmoniously.

From the abridged recording that Columbia issued on six 78 discs (RFX 33–38; Am. Col. RL 3093), the Swallow Duet (Cernay and Demoulin) finds the mezzo singing with bright but not brittle tone, the voice well suited, the vibrato attractive, the interpretation sympathetic. Demoulin is strongly voiced but over-dramatic. Cernay made the duet separately with Pierre Dupré, who has a plummy tone, forward, quick-speaking, very French. It is a light voice which moves smoothly, even though the tone itself has a noticeable tremolo. There are some elegant *diminuendi* from him. This is a good example of artistry overcoming second-rate vocal equipment (Od. 188758).

Mignon was last given at the Metropolitan in 1945. Its first performance that season had Risë Stevens and Ezio Pinza (the last had Jennie Tourel and Virgilio Lazzari). In their recording (Am. Col. 72371D; Philips SBF 290), which begins before the duet proper, Stevens and Pinza, despite the absence of the variations at the end, create the right atmosphere. Pinza is firm of voice and, of course, phrases well (but he omits the triplets). Although the voice has lost the plushness that once it had, it is still in good shape. Stevens is here as fresh-sounding as on her record of 'Connais-tu'; she suits the character admirably. Back to German for the last two examples: both from the LP era From the DG disc of excerpts that has escaped my attention, I have heard the Swallow Duet, which was issued on an EP (EPL 30276). Anny Schlemm, gives a straightforward, capable performance. Her partner, Toni Blankenheim, ignores the triplets but otherwise gives, like Schlemm, an adequate account. The voice is on the rough side. Two decades later, an over-resonant recording issued by Eurodisc (27306 XBR) presented Rohangiz Yachmi and Hermann Prey. Prey is in his most sensuous voice but also over-emphatic. The glorious sound is still there, but the line is not smooth enough. Yachmi has a creamy mezzo that is freely produced.

If 'Connais-tu' showed the sad, yearning side of Mignon, the Styrienne, 'Je ne connais un pauvre enfant', presents the lighter, more flirtatious side of her nature. A Zonophone record of Jeanne Marié de l'Isle (X 83109) could be called a variation on an original theme, with more of her than of Thomas, which is unfortunate considering that he was better at the game. The clean, clear, rather metallic sounds of Geraldine Farrar ring out in the upper reaches of this song, but the lower notes do not have much tone (Vic. 88152; GV 530). On the sleeve of the Rubini reissue, John Steane speaks of 'the fine scale-work, a striking cadenza and a neat trill'. The trill I find a little disappointing. For a *very* fine trill, one turns to Selma Kurz (Edison 35016; LV 253). Her recording is more an appendix than a comparative version. She begins slowly, lethargically, then sends Thomas packing and installs Kurz. If Kurz supplies fireworks that are superficial, Zélie de Lussan (Beka 8314; Belcantodisc EB 6), at the other end of the vocal scale, provides none at all, the rich voice sounding too doleful for this aria. Emmy Destinn (Fono. 39422) fails to produce the necessary sparkle. If the last two ladies are not well suited, they are paragons compared with Karin Rydkvist (X 1046; 7C 153–35354), whose voice is weak, thin-toned and badly supported.

Lucy Perelli (Disque P 857) is less effective here than in her 'Connais-tu', the singing of the repeated 'la la' is a shade careless, and she omits the run on the final 'Mignon'. Xenia Belmas (Poly. 66746; LV 79) is much as in the earlier aria. Of two Italians, I expected Ebe Stignani (Parlo. E 11344; LV 237) to sing the Styrienne in a Verdian manner, grand and imposing. I was wrong. The voice moves easily, the tone lighter that it was to become in postwar days. The coda happily does not have the Kurz pyrotechnics but it does require Stignani to skip around a bit, which she does most creditably. Immediately after the Stignani I played Simionato's 1949 recording (Col. GQX 11503; 3C065–18031) for Simionato was the successor to the older singer in many roles. Her performance compares well with Stignani's, and I find it impossible to prefer one to the other. A later recording (Fonit-Cetra LMR 5006, one of a splendid series of Martini and Rossi broadcasts that Fonit-Cetra has issued) finds Simionato in powerful voice. Again sung in Italian, this presents a Mignon who could look after herself with no trouble at all: good Simionato but less good Thomas.

A number of singers give a better account of this aria than of 'Connais-tu'. One is Gladys Swarthout (Vic. 11–8281; VIC 1490), who sings with some sparkle. Solange Michel is also better here, the voice again in wonderful condition, but there are no *ad lib* passages, and the ascending run on the final 'Mignon' becomes simply a 'lift' from lower note to upper.

Only five recordings have come my way of Frédéric's Gavotte. The earliest, by Parsi-Pettinella (in Italian, Fono, 9205; CO 372) equals the calibre of her versions of Mignon's solos; it is wonderfully eager and buoyant. That by Lucrezia Bori (DA 1017) has a freshness to the sound and a youthful approach, though she doesn't tease out the words as others do. Bruna

Casagna's performance (DA 1951; OASI 605) is super-charged. There is no trill, but the voice moves easily. Mildred Miller, one of many fine American mezzos, sings an eager, urgent account, velvety of voice, varied in approach. The tone is well projected (maybe an occasional low note lacks body) and is even throughout its range. There is no trill, but despite that it is a first-rate performance (JH 100). A predictably praiseworthy performance comes from Horne (SXL 6345), changing from Mignon to Frédéric, whose immediately recognizable voice provides all that we have come to expect: rich tone, agility, flexibility, a good trill. Perhaps, though, this version ultimately lacks the feeling of 'mon coeur battre d'espoir' that Von Stade and Miller provide.

Listening to more than fifty recordings of the tenor aria 'Adieu, Mignon' has given me a great deal of pleasure. What a delightful piece it is, with Wilhelm tugging at one's heartstrings as he bids farewell to Mignon. Alessandro Bonci (Fono. 39079; RDA 002), splendid stylist, sings appealingly, the vibrato adding to the charm of the song. This is a highly recommendable version which suffers ever so slightly from the voice tending to spread on high notes. From Fernando de Lucia (052111; RS 305) comes a very slow, self-indulgent contribution. It has many virtues (good legato; beautiful *diminuendo*) and some faults (a couple of sobs; a long pause, which though *for* effect somehow *spoils* the effect). It provides more pleasure than a recording by Giuseppe Anselmi (Fono. 62279; GEMM 252/6), a mixture of some charming vocal effects and much out-of-tune singing, one of Anselmi's poorest efforts. Léon Beyle (Zono. 82505), baritonally tinged, smoothly vocalized, needs more variety and caressing of the tone. The good recording allows us to hear how well he phrases, as does Léon Campagnola (032228), who is also lacking light and shade. He is more outgoing than resigned. Another French tenor, one Cloerec-Maupas (Aérophone 943) has a slightly nasal voice lacking colour. There is not much notice taken of the composer's markings. Better is Albert Vaguet (Pathé 4543; GEMM 252/6). There is a dull effect on the high notes, the voice not ringing, but the tone is spun out on a gentle flow of sound. One exquisite piece of singing is the lift in to the head voice on the reprise of the words 'Adieu, Mignon'. Edmond Tirmant (Od. 111369) takes the aria at a leisurely pace, which displays his firm voice, thoughtful phrasing and intelligent singing. I found him more acceptable than the better known David Devriès (Pathé 4593; GV 543), whose tremolo I consider intrusive and whose tone lacks the necessary sweetness. Of a later vintage, the Belgian Marcel Claudel (Poly. 524065) is a man in a hurry, with no time to stop and caress. Also missing the ultimate expression of longing is Gaston Micheletti (Od. 188506), but he does sing affectingly, and there is a well-controlled descent on 'mes voeux suivront tes pas'. One of the best is André d'Arkor from the abridged Columbia issue (RFX 33–38). Sung strongly, in a well-focused tone, this is a very commendable offering, the forward vocal production well served by the excellent recording.

Of Italian tenors singing in Italian Angelo Bendinelli (Col. D 5503) disturbs the line with an occasional splurge of tone. He sings expressively, partly compensating for the hard quality and lack of warmth in the voice. Giuseppe Lenghi-Cellini made two versions of the aria in question. On one (Vocalion L 5034), some effective touches (a couple of *diminuendi*) are spoilt by an ugly sob or gulp immediately following. He is better on his earlier disc (Beka 9008; GV 572), where the long-breathed phrases are stylish and correct. Top notes are covered, whereas in the Vocalion they take on a harshness. Roberto D'Alessio (Col. DQ 1088; Club 99–116) provides subtle and elegant phrasing. The voice is not inherently beautiful, but its owner certainly knows how to use what he has. I shall comment on him more fully when we come to the companion-piece: 'Elle ne croyait pas'.

There are not many versions in Italian that equal that of D'Alessio, and that by the Portuguese Tommaso Alcaide (Col. CQ 350; OASI 640) is not one of them. He has a lachrymose voice and gives a 'heart-on-sleeve' performance, whereas with Nino Ederle (Parlo. E 10781) one feels that a Neapolitan song may be ready to pop out at any moment. Ederle's light voice, with tone that tends to sag, because of imperfect support, is basically right for the part, but he pulls the tempo about considerably and takes too many liberties. The tone of Luigi Fort (Col. DB 1664; OASI 567) is too open, the line too jerky.

None of those singers could be reckoned among the most well known of the Italian school but of those who could, not all are successful in this piece. For instance, Giacomo Lauri-Volpi (Fono. 152019) uses a glottal-stop as a launching-pad. His tone is squeezed out. Of course, it is difficult for the more dramatic tenors to sound as elegant as their lyric counterparts, but Lauri-Volpi is simply in the wrong class. Taking the remaining six in order of age, I come first to Tito Schipa (DB 843; LV 185). The tone is somewhat hard on upper notes, and the aria is rather squarely sung, though there are pleasant touches, such as skilful *diminuendi*, but also an occasional slide up to an initial note. Honeyed tone is what one would expect from Beniamino Gigli (DB 1270; GEMM 165), plus that wonderfully forward vocal production. Against that must be weighed the lack of correct style and characterization. He cannot be considered among the best. Compared with that version, the one by Dino Borgioli (Col. D 5034; GV 538) commands more respect. He is slightly white of tone, maybe even thin, but he has the style and grace that Gigli lacks. An excellent legato provides a clean line, which at times takes him through the rests that the composer inserted. What a pity it is that this is an abridged version. And should you think that none of the other Italians will match Borgioli, try to hear Giovanni Malipiero (DB 5356; TIMA 14), for there you will find much elegance of phrasing. Listen as he sings the Italian equivalent of 'et mon âme attendrie partage la douleur . . . Adieu, Mignon', all taken in one breath, creating an effect that is utterly charming, and he is well in character: a piece of great singing.

Beautiful forward tone and a sweet *mezza voce* (in parts) come too from Ferruccio Tagliavini (Cetra BB 25119), with a lift to 'addio' that carries on to the next phrase. Unfortunately his account is spoiled by a surfeit of sobs.

The youngest of these six singers is Giuseppe di Stefano, who recorded two versions (DB 6618; RLS 756 and DB 11311; QALP 10394). The first presents him in glorious voice. He offers a Wilhelm who is distraught at the idea of losing Mignon. Without a flood of hysterical sobbing the sadness and dejection are yet more openly displayed than by Borgioli or Malipiero. The version on DB 11311, although earlier, is less good, for the tone is darker and does not have the freshness of the other.

Having already considered some 'French' tenors from earlier years, I must now turn to five from the postwar era, among them Charles Richard (DB 11119), whose vocal equipment is good, the notes are sweet, and there is an amount of feeling, but there is not a great deal by way of interpretation. Basically the right voice for this aria is that of Henri Legay, but it hardens when a high note is sung loudly and there is a whiteness in the tone. The aria is taken too quickly and is abridged (Col. FCX 607). Also abridged is Nicolai Gedda's recording (SLS 5105), in which he sings intelligently, effortlessly, and varies his tone. But again, there is something that causes it to fall short of the select. Of two Canadian tenors, Richard Verreau (RCA LM 2458) is not gentle enough. He has a free upper register, easily produced, and though more shading would have been beneficial this is certainly a performance to be reckoned with. Léopold Simoneau gives a lovely interpretation of what, regrettably, is an abridged version (DGM 19101). He abides by the composer's markings, slowing the tempo, diminishing the voice, offering a sweetly sung rendering that is definitely among the finest I have encountered.

Of recordings in German, Alexander Kirchner (Anka 5336) sounds like a refugee from Wagner, and the tone sags in places. Artur Preuss (3–42200) brings an attractive voice with quick vibrato. He sings intelligently but takes the final phrase up an octave, as does Herman Jadlowker (432311), who phrases eloquently in that squeezed tone of his. Much to be admired is Richard Tauber (Od. 0-8229; GEMM 153–4). This is a thoughtful, grammatically correct performance, with good control and fine legato; the voice is generally free and smooth, though the line becomes bumpy as pressure is applied soon after a note has been started. Similar virtues distinguish Alfred Piccaver's stylish singing (Od. 76961; LV 26): one of the best accounts. In the same class is a lovely record by Herbert Ernst Groh (Parl. R 1166). As heard on disc the voice, a typical one for operettas and much in the Tauber category, is beautifully produced, with no Teutonic tightness. Similar qualities inform Julius Patzak's plaintive, typically smooth and intimate version (Poly. 30014). A darker voice is that of John Gläser (Parlo. P 9084). It tends to drag downwards in the lower reaches, but, as with Groh, there is none of the strangulated effect that afflicted some of the German tenors of the interwar years. He has the right intentions, though they are a trifle studied. From a lesser name, Bernhard Bötel, comes a record that gives much pleasure, with neat phrasing and a nicely controlled *diminuendo* on 'Partage ta douleur'. If all his singing is on this level, Bötel deserves to be better known

(Polyphon 23771). Of other German artists, August Seider, a heavier tenor in tone, sings in a restrained manner, the darkish voice coping well (Historia H 706–7), but sweeter and smoother sound comes from Marcel Wittrisch (EG 2412; TC 9044), though there is not enough grace. An ordinary performance comes from Walther Ludwig (EH 810; LV 232), whose voice has no great beauty. Ordinary too is Rudolf Schock (EH 1452; E 80791), who sings without much imagination or variety, except that towards the end he shifts gear in to a head-voice (not a very good one) for a while, rather as though it was time for his public to hear that part of his vocal equipment.

'Adieu, Mignon' should be sung gently, with the sadness of Wilhelm's thoughts conveyed in sweet tones. Portraying Wilhelm's feelings convincingly, in attractive tone (and, as usual, everything that needs to be said is in the music), is George Meader (Gram. 942573), who is another lesser-known singer to give a better account than some of the so-called 'stars'. Imparting much ardour, sometimes with a light sob that does not detract from a good performance, is Mario Chamlee (Bruns. 50141; RLS 743), taking note of Thomas's markings and singing pleasantly apart from some harshness on high notes when he presses. A third American, Richard van Vrooman (Harmonia Mundi HMS 30804), sounds a little overparted, his light voice losing quality the higher it goes. The Swedish tenor Carl-Martin Öhmann (Nordisk Polyphon S 42242; GV 31) has more than a tendency to attack notes from below and then lean on them to bring them to pitch, so that the whole thing sounds slurred.

The disc by Anatoly Orfenov (Melodiya M10–37067/70), from the 1950s, finds the tenor's voice no longer in full bloom, but the phrasing is unimpaired, and this is an enjoyable version, if lacking the poignant treatment of his compatriot Vinogradov.

From Wilhelm, we turn again to Mignon and to her aria 'Elle est là', the Air du Feu, of which five separate accounts have come my way. Jeanne Marié de l'Isle (Zono. 83111) presents little characterization and a voice which is acescent at the top. Not wholly suited to the role is the fresh, sweet voice of Claire Dux (HMV Z 128; RLS 743). She takes the higher alternatives in most cases, but the low notes (with *no* alternatives) are weak and toneless. She has a good line and is generally pleasant to listen to, but there are better records of Dux and better of Mignon. One of the latter is Ninon Vallin's (Od. 171032; GV 509), again with the higher alternatives in all but one place. This has more feeling than Dux's, more pathos, with only one slightly sour top note to mar the vocalism. Déva Dassy's recording (DA 4859) is well sung and pleasant enough, but is on a lower plane than Vallin's or that of Marilyn Horne (SXL 6345), who gives just what one would expect of her: a thoughtful performance, but with Mignon angry at seeing Wilhelm with Philine (rather than her being sad, as in Vallin's account). Horne presents a mixture of what we may think of as the soprano and mezzo versions, with a few variations of her own. She is in splendid voice.

The second duet of Mignon and Lothario, 'As-tu souffert?', has been less

frequently recorded than the Swallow Duet and only three versions have
come my way. One, by Davida Hesse and Thor Mandahl (Lyrophon 1822;
7C 153–35350), she then twenty-eight and he thirty, is reissued in the box
devoted to singers from the Royal Opera, Stockholm, a fascinating collection
on nine discs. Unfortunately, this is one of the least desirable items therein.
Hesse sings reasonably well, but her partner has a third-rate voice, with a
pronounced tremolo, though they blend well when that tremolo does not
interfere. The Cernay/Dupré recording is just as good as their Swallow Duet,
with which it is coupled. And let me recommend, as before, Beckmann and
Schellenberg, who are even better than in the earlier duet: attractive in tone,
smooth in production, persuasive in interpretation. This should be in every
collection.

The vocal showpiece of the opera, and not a mad scene, is 'Je suis Titania',
the Polonaise, sung by the actress Philine. Of the many versions that I have
heard it would be hard to find any two alike. Complete with coloratura runs,
trills and variations, it is a marvellous vehicle for any soprano leggiera worth
her salt. Many of the ladies whom I have heard fail the test, but others give
a dazzling display of agility and technique, and that is what it is all about.
Micheau, the Philine of the complete Decca set, recorded the Polonaise
separately (Decca K 2126; LXT 2528). This earlier performance finds her in
fresher voice. There is one passage in the score which is treated in almost
every combination in the thirty-odd versions that I have heard. It comes on
Page 213 of the Heugel vocal score. The composer asks the singer to vocalize
legato on 'ah' in a group of notes, then repeat staccato, and finally legato
again. Micheau sings staccato, legato, staccato: the exact opposite of what
is written. I shall make reference to some other variants as they come.
Another French soprano who recorded in those early days of LP is Mado
Robin, a high-note specialist. If any singer would bestow on the Polonaise
an abundance of interpolated high notes it must be Robin, or so one would
have thought. In fact, she refrains from any additions to the score, of which
the middle section is delightfully on the breath, with the word 'fuit' sung as
only the French can sing it (Pathé DTX 276; 2C 053–11691).

Much in the Robin mould is Mady Mesplé, who gives on a recital-disc (2C
069–10411) a better account than in the DG record of excerpts. A touch
shrill and reedy of tone, she sings neatly and cleanly, can produce a sweet,
soft head-note and interpolates a high note at the end. Odette Turba-Rabier
(DA 5029) also possesses a very French-type voice, this of acidulous quality
in which there is little beauty. A neat performance is that of Pierrette Alarie
(Philips S 06094 R). She does not follow Robin in leaning slightly on the
initial note of the triplets in the twenty-third bar, though Thomas has marked
it. (Robin is a model here.) The interpolated high note is here too, as it is
in another competent performance without anything special to commend it,
that of the small-voiced Gwen Catley (C 3696; HLM 7066), who provides
some neat staccato singing but lacks brilliance in coloratura passages. The
adjective 'genteel' comes to mind. Her interpolation is thin. No better is

Margherita Perras, who is no Philine. There is a lack of sparkle, sketchy scalework, and no trill (DB 4438; LV 73). A shrill-sounding Margherita Carosio is no improvement (Parlo. E 11024; Rococo 5309). The coloratura is bumpy: without a good technique in singing divisions no soprano should essay this aria. One of Carosio's contemporaries, Lina Pagliughi (Parlo. E 11324), also skates over the divisions, but her sweeter, fuller tone provides some pleasure, more so than Toti dal Monte (DB 1318; LV 184), who is adequate, although the trill is nothing special. She switches round those legato/staccato bars.

Italy is more worthily represented by two older singers, the first of whom is Luisa Tetrazzini (DB 540; GEMM 220–7). This is one of the best versions. She sounds full of extrovert sparkle that suits the character of Philine. One or two trills are not as well formed as they should be, and she sings that third 'ah' staccato, thus spoiling the desired effect. That, however, is a relatively minor detail in view of the fine performance, with some shimmering descents in semitones. Highly recommended. The second of these front-rank Italian versions is by Amelita Galli-Curci (Vic. 75653; GEMM 189), who is in fresh voice, with sprightly execution, the tone equally bright throughout its range. She has a fondness for staccato singing and gives short measure on the trills. In spite of this, it is in the top category.

'Variations on an original tempo' is how one might describe the recording by Maria Barrientos (Fono. 39461; CO. 403). Light, airy, sweetly vocalized, it is sung with the right feeling. The middle section is omitted. Of Irene Abendroth, Vivian Liff wrote in the sleeve-note to the Rubini LP: 'Listening to her recordings, it is not too difficult to detect, especially in the middle register, the vocal problems which doubtless led to her early retirement.' He commends her agility but regrets her poor sense of rhythm. Those comments are most apt. I would add that the top notes are thin, squeezed, vibrato-less and (the final one) painful (43245; GV 32). In case anyone should think that the Abendroth record is the worst of those to which I have listened, let me introduce Hedwig Francillo-Kauffmann (Parlo. P 1331; CO 356). The first note suggests that we are listening to Philine practising Brünnhilde's war-whoops. Slack coloratura, no trill, thin tone nullify the more favourable impression created in the slow section. By the way, those three bars are sung staccato/staccato/staccato!

The enigmatic Margarete Siems (043024; Rococo R 20) provides some neat coloratura and some high notes that are lacking in bloom but she treats the piece to a spirited interpretation. Lillian Nordica (Col. 30661; SYO 6) pulls the rhythm about but offers lovely tone. She is less good than a fellow American: Mabel Garrison (RCA VIC 1394). One wonders again and again how some singers make a great career while others, who sound on record to be in the same league, are virtually forgotten. Garrison gives a very fine performance, flexible of voice, attractive of timbre, and mellifluous of tone: top class. So too is Evelyn Scotney (Vocalion 52040). Suffice it to say that hers is a rendering to 'trip it light and airy', as the voice cascades in a glitter of silvery notes, with a sparkling cadenza and a fine trill. I expected something of the same from Lotte Schöne (Vox 339B; GV 16), but it was not to be, for there is only a good trill to it. The coloratura is laboured, the tone thin. Did she make a worse record? Hélène Cals (Parlo. E 10990) is pleasing rather than outstanding. The runs are a bit approximate, and there is a patch of unsure intonation.

Eight singers from Eastern Europe include five Russians. I commented on Nadezhda Kazantseva when writing about the Melodiya disc of excerpts. Galina Oleinichenko (Melodiya D 5398/9) takes the aria slowly (conducted by Boris Khaikin) but not dully. She has no trill, a somewhat sour quality, but sings with intelligence. A superior voice to either of those is that of Galina Kovaleva (Melodiya S10–09063/6), but she is ultimately the least satisfying, for she lacks fluency, taking short breaks on occasions, as if to marshal her resources. The best two of the Russians are from the past. Evgenia Bronskaya (Col. 5210) offers clean attack, pure tone and a good, firm trill. The other is probably the best Philine of them all: Antonina Nezhdanova, she of the heavenly voice, the equalized register and the accomplished technique (023122; GV 587). This is simply a magnificent performance, for Nezhdanova, apart from regularizing a couple of dotted notes (I mention them for any budding Beckmesser), sings with respect for Thomas's markings, produces with ease her full, flowing tones, and catches Philine's gaiety without giving the impression that this is just a vocal exercise. The other three eastern Europeans are Halina Lukomska from Poland (Muza XL 0310), Rumanian Yolanda Marculescu (Orion 79351) and Sylvia Geszty from Hungary (Telef. 641945 AG and Eurodisc 27306 XBR). Of Geszty's two recordings, the first is in French, the other in German. The treatment is similar, although the interpolated high note appears in the Eurodisc only. She sings with some sparkle, managing the divisions easily, with an occasional little yelp as she hits a note. Lukomska has a warm lyric voice and presents a good account that has no outstanding feature. The Orion LP of Marculescu is composed of recordings from some twenty years ago, made in Rumania before she left to settle in America. The silvery voice has the necessary agility to make the piece glitter, the scale passages in place, the tone even throughout. This is among the best.

On a DG LP called 'Curtain Up' (DGM 18169) comes a delicious performance of the Polonaise by Rita Streich. This is one of the slowest versions that I have encountered, yet Streich's fresh tone, beautifully placed, is utter joy. She does not dazzle as some do but treats the piece more reflectively. Listen to the perfectly poised note at the top of the descending scale eight bars from the end of the voice-part. It helps to lift this performance above so many and place it alongside so few.

What does one say about Maria Callas at this stage? She has been lauded almost to a state of deification and condemned as if she had done her critics an irreparable harm; the truth lies somewhere between, of course. In the Polonaise we experience clean passage-work and raw tone, neither of which we can or should ignore. She cannot bring to this aria the great dramatic gifts that she possessed, though she could never sing anything dully (1C 053–00 540). Many of the roles that Callas rediscovered were later taken by Beverly Sills (ASD 2513), despite the drawbacks of recording, Sills is worth hearing. She was a fine artist, although not wholly at home as Philine.

Lothario's Berceuse, 'De son coeur, j'ai calme la fievre', is really rather a dull aria and needs above all an ability to sing a seamless line and to shade the voice, neither of which it receives from Louis Morturier (Disque P 797), who simply sings through monotonously. More authoritative but short-breathed in a very abbreviated version is Paul Payan (Od. 188661). Nor does Jean Claverie (Parlo. 29543) caress the line with his lightish voice. Oscar Bergström's firm, throaty voice lacks variety of colour. He sings without much feeling and phrases woodenly (G&T 82828; 7C 153–35350–8). With regard to another Scandinavian, Ivar Andresen (HMV Z93; GV 95), the husky catch on three initial notes are not enough to detract from a well sung, intelligent performance. Two versions that contribute little are those by Francesco Navarrini (Fono. 62034; Rococo 5302) and Vanni-Marcoux (DA 4867; FJLP 5035). Navarrini maintains the same level of volume throughout, mixing smooth tone with an occasional jerky delivery. Lack of variety, both in volume and tone, is also a fault in Vanni-Marcoux's record, which is surprising when one reads how good an actor he was (or was said to be). How much better is Adam Didur (Pathé 60074; GV 45), offering an interpretation that has feeling, steadiness of line, firm tone and well-controlled soft singing. It seems strange, however, that someone with such fine legato should insert an aspirate to enable him to move up just one note. Effortless, charming, beautifully phrased, with soft tones reflecting Lothario's paternal love for Mignon, that is the version by Gerhard Hüsch (EG 6136; LV 285). On the same high level is Pol Plançon (Vic. 85126; GV 76), whose unforced vocal production, elegant phrasing and musical line show him to be the great singer that he was. I feel that there is a touch of dolefulness about his performance, however, and is it not odd that a Frenchman should sing this aria in Italian? If I had to pick just one version (rarely a sensible or worth-while exercise) it would probably be that of Ezio Pinza (DB 1086; LV 27). The glorious richness of tone is subjugated by Pinza's decision to sing *mezza voce* (it *is* a lullaby), perfectly under control, splendidly phrased, spun out on a thread of legato singing that is in itself a joy to hear. In the phrase 'Dors pauvre enfant! pauvre enfant!', he lifts the voice up to meet the second 'pauvre', a far more satisfying effect than simply stopping and then singing the higher note. But then, it is what the composer wanted.

Many of the tenors who recorded 'Elle ne croyait pas' on 78s coupled it with 'Adieu, Mignon', therefore I shall make no extended comment on these unless it is necessary. When no number is given, it is the same as for the earlier aria. Charles Richard gives another good performance, though needing a little more breadth of treatment. Less good is Nicolai Gedda, with tight and backward tone, an overstressed 'r' causing explosions in the line.

But Henri Legay is better here than in his coupling with less pressure on the voice, though still too much. He ignores the *forte* marking on the second appearance of 'O mon coeur', but there is a fine *morendo* on 'vermeil'. Richard Verreau is much as in 'Adieu', but more so, and George Meader is equally consistent. Tito Schipa too has the same virtues and faults, plus some altering of note values to their detriment. Here I find a rolled 'r' overintrusive, and some of the finer touches seem fabricated rather than being the product of a first-class technique. Giuseppe di Stefano repeats the merits of his respective versions of 'Adieu'. It is a pity that he should attack so many notes from below, but one feels that the interpretation is straight from the heart; spontaneity was one of Di Stefano's virtues. The version by Edmond Tirmant, less effective than its coupling, is taken quickly with little individuality of voice, the top of which sounds precarious. Once again, the Beka version of Lenghi-Cellini is better than his Vocalion, with some grammatically effective long-phrasing. Tauber is even finer here than in the Farewell, the virtues yet more noticeable now in Volume 3 of 'The Record of Singing' (Ex 290 1693). Also similar here to their records of 'Adieu' are those of Léon Beyle (Zono. 82500); Bernhard Bötel, a pleasant performance; and Tommaso Alcaide, dry of voice, top notes tight, but with a delightful *diminuendo* on the A on 'O mon coeur'.

Giovanni Malipiero not only coupled 'Elle' to his 'Adieu' on HMV but recorded it separately (Parlo. DPX 25; OASI 607). There is very little to choose between the two, neither of them done as well as the other aria. On the Parlophone he begins in soft voice, rises sweetly on 'O printemps', but when the voice produces more volume it acquires a rather harsh edge. The HMV is also intelligently sung, though with too much contrast between soft and loud; not volume, but tone. Just as enigmatic here as in his recording of 'Adieu' is Beniamino Gigli, with gulps, sobs, aspirates and a tone that is frequently lachrymose. He also projects glorious tone in his wonderfully forward vocal production. Piccaver displays the same virtues as in his coupling, but there is a feeling of monotony here.

I turn to others who recorded both arias, though not necessarily coupled together. Fernando de Lucia (2–52518) is better remembered by other records. While examining the unrecommendable, let us hurry, as the singer hurries, through the graceless, four-square version by David Devriès (Pathé 4596; GV 543), who gives the impression that he wants to go home as soon as possible. One verse only, in which the voice sounds hard, a little grating, lacking charm, with no coloratura to bewitch his listeners, is sung by Jadlowker (Od. 99083; GV 62).

Those are just three examples of how the 'big names' do not always produce the finest performances. So let us pass to Giuseppe Anselmi (Fono. 62161; Cantilena 6225), who vastly improves on his singing in the Farewell. A husky edge on the voice is apparent at times, but once the note has been formed it rings freely. He adds *gruppetti* liberally. He is even better on Edison 83015, where the voice seems to 'speak' more smoothly and quickly, and the melody is delicately vocalized. From Dino Borgioli (Col. D 5034; GV 538) comes another admirable performance. The opening is sung dreamily, perhaps sentimentally, the voice almost crooning at one point. The singer opens out for the second part of the verse but maintains the control of line that distinguishes the whole record. From the abridged Columbia set, André d'Arkor's recording has been transferred to LP by Belgian HMV, the composer's requests for *p* and *pp* are honoured, and the legato is first rate. The warm voice loses quality a shade on the top A and he prolongs the held note (on 'de') in the penultimate bar too long for my liking, but this is still one of the best versions that I have heard (RFX 33–38; 2C 051–12032). Coupled with the Farewell, Albert Vaguet's account has the same good points, and the high notes ring out more. On the other hand, he tends to break the phrasing in order to elongate notes. Léon Campagnola (032216) produces a glorious piece of controlled singing: the A on 'O mon coeur' is taken *forte* as in the score and is then fined down to a thread of tone as he links with the following note. He does not copy this in the second verse but sings the A full out and continues thus for the rest of the phrase: intelligent and effective. Finally in this section on singers in both arias are two who are among the best. Roberto d'Alessio (Col. DQ 1088; Club 99–116), voice forward and with a slight vibrato, phrases in wonderfully long-breathed spans and colours the voice considerably. Listen to the section beginning 'Sa fraîcheur' (he actually sings in Italian). His breath control and phrasing are such that he spins out a fine legato for some twenty seconds without pausing for breath. The second of these two splendid accounts is that by Léopold Simoneau (DGM 19101), the honeyed tone caressing the line, with gentle *portamenti*. In both arias, Simoneau produces the great singing that we expect from a great singer.

Of the singers whom I have heard only in 'Elle ne croyait pas', I shall consider first some of the less well-known names, of whom Jean Anzani (Col. LFX 130) gives pleasure with his strong voice, full from top to bottom. Unfortunately he spoils a beautiful *diminuendo* as he comes from 'O' down to 'printemps' by putting pressure on that second word instead of retaining the soft tone. Also generally pleasing are the version by Léon David (Od. 97175) who sings tastefully, in a voice a shade throaty, and that of Georges Régis (3–32840), which has no major fault but is rather perfunctory. Smoothly but monochromatically sung is Paul Dufault's record (Col. 600). Cristy Solari is preferable and gives a deal of pleasure without being among the best (Col. D 5697; OASI 612). He is certainly superior to Franz Kaisin (Poly. 561025), who sings with little feeling in a flaccid voice that is rather flat of tone, but Kaisin is a paragon of virtue compared with Léon Cordier (Zono. X 1232), who has badly phrased, laboured singing, breaths taken in the wrong place at times, and who plods through with a faulty sense of rhythm. Indifferent versions come from Roberto Vanni (Col. 1232), and from Marcello Govoni, who has a tearful approach but sweetish voice (Col. D 5063; Bongiovanni GB 1009). Reasonable, but not more so, is José de Trevi (Disque P 738), taking the piece quickly. Sweetness is a commodity that has graced the voices of many Swedish tenors, from Björling downwards. David Stockman (2–82481) has it, apart from when he produces an odd exposed note. He is rather unvarying as regards tempo. An interesting version that deserves a hearing or two is that by Giuseppe Paganelli (Col. D 4460; GV 549). He has a strange voice of a throaty quality but no tightness, not particularly attractive in itself; he is able, nevertheless, to spin out a note with the best of them, refining it to a wisp of tone, but then he mars the whole effect with a number of aspirates. A further second-rank voice, this one rather dry, belongs to Dimitri Onofrei (Electrecord ECE 01607), who is also addicted to popping aitches in, though he treats the piece intelligently. In our own time, Michel Cadiou (Versailles STDX 8025) brings a very forward, rather husky light voice, probably smaller than a close-up recording would suggest.

A trio of Americans comes next, one of whom is even freer with his aspirates than Paganelli and Onofrei. This is Charles Hackett (Col. 9032M; OASI 515), whose hard, brilliant voice, with its metallic timbre, is not suited to Wilhelm. It is an emphatic piece of singing with no charm. Hughes Macklin (Col. 830) brings an oratorio-type voice – from the time when 'her' was sung as 'har'. There are one or two intonation faults, and top notes are ugly, losing tone, but there are some carefully shaded *diminuendi*. The third, Thomas Hayward, was for many years a comprimario, and a very good one, at the Metropolitan. His 'private' recording (UORC 363) is probably from the radio, dating from 1949. The voice is not a great one, in any sense, though it is certainly not unpleasant, until he applies force at the end of each stanza, when the line is then disturbed by a push or a glottal attack.

Gianni Raimondi, singing the aria in a Martini and Rossi recital from Italian Radio (LMR 5007), presents a warm, thoughtful performance that lacks the elegance of some and the crudeness of others. In one of Heddle Nash's earliest records (Col. 830R; GEMM 210), there is perhaps too much urgency; one would like him to linger a little and savour the mood more, but the technique is good and the phrasing eloquent. Nash sings in English, as does John McCormack, who presents a charming demonstration of how to produce a smooth singing line. The tone is fresh, there is a variety of shading, and the feel of the piece is conveyed affectingly (Od. 57581; RLS 743). All of this leaves us with two Russians: not, sadly, Vinogradov, whose 78rpm record I have been unable to trace, but Leonid Sobinov and Anatoly Orfenov. Sobinov proffers a sweet voice, lacking the delicacy that one finds in Vinogradov or Simoneau, for example, nor does he have the variety of tone, and at the end of most lines (and sometimes in the middle) there is an unmusical gulp as the singer inhales, but it is still a very pleasant piece of singing (2–22660; GV 585). In fresher voice than in 'Adieu', Orfenov (Melodiya D 2948/9) is a little wiry of tone under pressure. There is a fine *morendo* on the second-verse 'O mon coeur'.

Of only three records that I have heard of the Mignon-Wilhelm duet 'Je suis heureuse', two have Suzanne Brohly, who sings sweetly, sounding light-voiced for a mezzo in her partnership with Léon Beyle (034079; GV 556–7), but he is far less ingratiating than in his solo numbers and does little for the music. Why aspirate a triplet? Fortunately, Brohly finds a more worthy partner in a later recording: Louis Cazette, whose style, technique and dulcet tones are all superior to Beyle's. There is some fine shading on the tenor's part (Disque P 437; GV 556–7). The third version of the duet is a provincial one from Lina Tomezzoli and Vittorio Salbego (Favorite 1–39024): pleasant voices unable to sing triplets.

Sometimes on 78 discs a section was extracted from this duet and sung as a tenor solo. It is too short to be really effective, and on some records half the side is occupied by an orchestral passage. The piece begins at the words 'Ah! Que ton âme enfin'. Karl Erb (Od. 98001; 1C 147–30772) starts off with suspect intonation and sings on one level throughout; Fernando de Lucia (2–52475; RS 305) sings as in his recordings of the other arias, unfortunately; Isadoro Agnoletto (Favorite 35285) has a thin timbre; René Lapelletrie (HMV U 27; GV 60) does not sing badly in his ordinary, dry voice, though the top B is ill supported and rattles. Fernando Carpi (Fono. 69166) has a pleasant lyric tone that lacks the ultimate in melodiousness, plus a vibrato that may seem obtrusive. Three superior accounts are those of the dulcet-toned Alessandro Bonci (Col. D 8087; Rubini RDA 002); by Georges Régis (332959), cleanly produced, well focused, with a spot-on attack on high notes; and by Louis Cazette (Disque 437; GV 556–7), which is possibly even better than Régis's, with the same mellifluence that the short-lived Cazette brought to his other records. Only the approach to the top note in the final line causes some displeasure. Why do the good die young?

Last in this survey is the prayer 'O vierge Marie', taken from the final trio, which both Marié de l'Isle (33830) and Destinn (Od. 50232) sing tenderly.

And which of these singers would I choose for my preferred cast? The leading quartet would have to be something like this: Mignon – Von Stade; Wilhelm – Vinogradov; Philine – Nezhdanova; Lothario – Schellenberg or Pinza (depending on whether a baritone or bass is required). Waiting in the wings to take over would be such as Horne, Lehmann, Simoneau, Streich, Hüsch.

MIGNON

M Mignon; *P* Philine; *WM* Wilhelm Meister; *L* Lothario; *F* Frédéric

1952 Moizan *M*; Micheau *P*; De Luca *WM*; Bianco *L*; Deschamps *F* / Brussels Monnaie Theatre Chorus, Belgian National Orch. / Sebastien
Decca ⓜ LXT 2783–5
Richmond ⓜ RS 63014

1977 Horne *M*; Welting *P*; Vanzo *WM*; Zaccaria *L*; Von Stade *F* /
Ambrosian Opera Chorus, New Philharmonia / Almeida
CBS (UK) 79401
(US) M4–34590

1933 (excerpts)
Cernay *M*; Tragin *P*; D'Arkor *WM*; Demoulin *L* / Brussels Monnaie Theatre Chorus and Orch. / Bastin

Columbia RFX 33–8*
CBS (US) ⑩ RL 3093
1947 (excerpts – in Russian)
Aleksandriyskaya M; Kazantseva
P; Vinogradov WM; Abramov L; /
USSR Radio Chorus and Orch. /
Orlov
Melodiya 33MIO-36031/2
1954 (excerpts – in German)
Schlemm M; Streich P;
Fehenberger WM; Blankenheim L
/ chorus and orchs.
DG ⑩ LPEM 19004
1961 (excerpts – in German)
Lorengar M; Pütz P; Wunderlich
WM; Frick L / Berlin Komische
Chorus, Berlin SO / Klobučar

EMI STE 80639
1963 (excerpts)
Berbié M; Mesplé P; Dunan WM;
Depraz L / Raymond St-Paul
Chorus, Lamoureux Orch. /
Fournet
DG 136279
1963 (excerpts – in German)
Seefried M; Gayer P; Haefliger
WM; Engen L / chorus,
Lamoureux Orch. / Fournet
DG 136418
1964 (excerpts)
Rhodes M; Esposito P; Vanzo
WM: Roux L / Paris Opéra-
Comique Orch. / Hartemann
EMI 2C 061 11687 ④ 2C 263 11687

The Operettas of Offenbach

RONALD CRICHTON

Offenbach was a genius of a special order. He was tied to the boulevard theatre, he wrote for his own world and his own audience. He wrote in a hurry, because his world expected quick production, because he loved success, and because he was brimming with ideas. The haste, though it shows from time to time, hardly matters. The ability to sum up a mood or a situation in a few bars of swift music is invaluable for a theatre composer on any level. Offenbach had an enormous melodic gift. He could write long tunes that rarely do quite what you expect and short phrases that stick in the mind and seem to have been born with the words they set. There is in his pre-1870 music an undercurrent of frenzy that with hindsight we may consider exceedingly well suited to the situation in France (or at least in Paris) in the years before the Franco-Prussian war. This aspect of Offenbach can be exaggerated, but the feeling of dancing on a volcano is there. After the war, in the few years left to him, it disappeared, but we are beginning to understand that his later music has been underrated: it is here that his command of his métier becomes fully apparent. The break between the two styles was not so sudden as has been believed.

Most of the works treated in this chapter are described as *opéras bouffes*. However, the term 'operetta', more general, more international, seems better suited to the varieties of designation into which Offenbach and his librettists were tempted by the French love of categorization. In fact, work lists such as the one in *Jacques Offenbach** by Alexander Faris reveal that operettas or *opérettes* were in the majority. The term was first used for a work by Offenbach in 1856. If you include the subdivisions *opérette bouffe* and *opérette féerie* there are thirty-one. The term *opéra bouffe* first appeared in 1861. Including subdivisions (*opéra bouffon, fantastique, féerie*) there are twenty-nine. It may come as a surprise to learn that Offenbach wrote as many as sixteen works described as *opéras comiques* – another indication that the ascent to the degree of seriousness represented by *Les Contes d'Hoffmann* was gradual rather than abrupt.

Fortunately for the harassed discographer, though unhappily for the

* Faber & Faber, London 1980.

collector, many of the operettas have not been recorded at all, so far as can be ascertained, others only in part. The one-acters have been as scurvily treated by record companies as they have been by opera houses. Even so, there is no lack of material. The following lists are not complete. Most regrettably, for reasons of time and space, the 'private' recordings mentioned in Andrew Lamb's *Offenbach's Recordings on LP Discs* (published in the centenary tribute issued by the [London] Offenbach 1980 Committee) had to be excluded. Too few German recordings are included. Some German opera-doctors have no doubt done terrible things to Offenbach's operettas, but German-speaking lands have amply honoured and, what is more, performed him. In Vienna, where he was introduced by the actor and dramatist Johann Nestroy and later translated by the satirist Karl Kraus, he was a founding-father of the local school of operetta. But German recordings of Offenbach are not easy to come by in Britain or the US.

Even more, perhaps, than in the outwardly more respectable spheres of French grand opera and *opéra comique*, this is a world where vocal scores, when available, by no means always match up with librettos, where works are altered, sometimes drastically, by the composer for revivals, where texts may be rewritten and music reorchestrated by other hands (the question of Offenbach orchestrations sorely needs investigation), where consistency is no more to be looked for on record labels than on title pages. The forms in which singers' names appear vary between the extreme formality of an invitation list ('Monsieur Musy de l'Opéra Comique et Madame Musy') to a degree of illegibility not entirely due to wear and tear. Some first names remain untraceable. Consistency in the titling of arias is equally elusive.

The contents of the various LP reissues of Offenbach 78s, for instance the valuable Rubini record of Simon-Girard and Tariol-Baugé, discussed item by item under the appropriate heading, are listed in full on pages 181–2. For convenience, works represented on record are discussed not chronologically but alphabetically. Unless otherwise stated, all French theatres referred to are in Paris.

BARBE-BLEUE

Opéra bouffe in three acts, libretto by Meilhac and Halévy. Variétés, 1866. One of the collaborators' major works (to their names should be added that of Hortense Schneider, who had one of her great successes as Boulotte, the heroine), under-represented in the catalogues until the appearance of the Bourg set from the INA (Institut National de l'Audiovisuel) archives. This was a radio performance of 1967, with many cuts, some commentary and a great deal of dialogue very well spoken by the singers. There is no libretto – only a sketchy synopsis; the sound is acceptable.

Meilhac and Halévy adapted their libretto from Perrault's *Mother Goose* tales. Their Bluebeard is thus descended from the notorious Gilles de Rais or Retz, subject of a recent opera by the Belgian composer, Philippe Boesmans.

Because these librettists had their finger on the pulse of their own time, they reach through the climate of irreverence and fantasy and touch the nerve of our own. Listening to Henri Legay's blithe and unconcerned recitation of Bluebeard's marital adventures, one can't help raising an eyebrow – though we know what Bluebeard doesn't, that his alchemist Popolani had not poisoned but drugged the five wives and immured them in luxury for his own pleasure. Legay judges just how far to go when he sends up the Peter Quint melisma at the end of Bluebeard's mock-Romantic recitative introducing the couplets only after he has shown that he can sing it. Note his subtle shading of the last-act lament for Boulotte into indecently hysterical joy at the idea of renewed freedom to murder more wives.

Possibly because one hears it less often, Boulotte's music gives more immediate idea of Schneider's art than the familiar *La Belle Hélène* and *La Grande Duchesse*. Lina Dachary's voice has sap and zest, her dialogue tingles. Even if her high spirits seem more urban than rustic, they are infectious. The duet 'Vous avez vu ce monument', sung when Boulotte, after only eight days of marriage, is about to be despatched to make way for wife number seven, is a jewel (though there is a cut). René Terrasson as Count Oscar has the once-famous number 'Qu'un bon courtisan s'incline'. Though military life is barely touched on, court life is satirized as freely as in *La Grande Duchesse*. Against this intrigue-ridden, obsequious background, the figure of Boulotte, buxom, irrepressibly frank, equally full of native wisdom and good nature, stands out sharply.

Two ancient 78s survive on mixed LPs: in Vol. 1 of the Club 99 'Tales of Offenbach' (2–42283; Club 99–110) the German tenor Carl Meister gives Bluebeard's lively account of himself as a merry multiple widower. On the Rubini 'Offenbach Centenary' record (GV 600) shared by Juliette Simon-Girard and Anna Tariol-Baugé, the latter sings the 'Couplets de la rosière' with any amount of rustic gusto and a most attractively full-bodied voice which brought her from the Bordeaux Opéra via Russia, North Africa and Marseilles to Paris, where she sang operetta and ended her career as a star of the music hall.

The recent recital by Jane Rhodes (2C 069–16386) ('Offenbach – airs célèbres') has the same number, plus Boulotte's other first-act solo. Plenty of gusto here, too – but the voice only just escapes being too heavy. As an encore to her live, mixed Desto recital (DC 7118–9) Jennie Tourel sings, rather breathlessly, an excerpt which I could not identify.

BA-TA-CLAN

Chinoiserie musicale in one act, with a libretto by Halévy. Bouffes-Parisiens, 1855. This was the success of the opening programme of Offenbach's new venture in the Passage Choiseul. His invention at this period was as raw as cut garlic, full of vitality. Mock-orientalism is diversified by a *duo italien* for tenor and bass with a swinging Bellinian march-tune and, in the finale, by two effectively placed quotations of the Lutheran chorale 'Ein' feste Burg' used in Meyerbeer's *Les Huguenots*. There is a prominent part for a kazoo. The Erato (also Musical Heritage) recording has, especially from the tenors Raymond Amade and Rémy Corazza, the required zest and brio; but it introduces, admittedly in a mild form, a recurrent problem with complete operetta recordings – what to do with the spoken dialogue? The solution here is a short commentary, written by Emile Noël and spoken by Jean Desailly. For a first run-through commentaries may be preferable – but for repetitions? Even Desailly, an impeccably stylish actor, may pall.

LES BAVARDS

Opéra bouffe in two acts, libretto by Nuitter (based on the Spanish comedy *Los habladores* formerly attributed to Cervantes). Bouffes-Parisiens 1863, revision of *Bavard et bavarde*, Bad Ems 1862 (the English title was 'Beatrix the Chatterbox Wife'). The story is more or less *The Silent Woman* in reverse, in a Spanish setting. Saint-Saëns, not a great operetta man but a shrewd judge, called *Les Bavards* 'a little masterpiece'. No doubt Bizet felt this too; the more one hears Offenbach in Spanish vein the more apparent becomes the debt owed to him by *Carmen*. The patter-numbers, one of which foreshadows that of the Lord Chancellor in *Iolanthe* (nineteen years in the future), have a characteristic lightness and vivacity. There is a ravishing duet for the wife and her lover over a descending bass figure and a slow waltz for the hero's creditors, languishing in the midday sun – 'La chaleur est accablante'. The Erato recording has dialogue and quite a lot of it. There are too many sound effects – footsteps advancing or retreating, etc. – but the performance, with Lina Dachary as Béatrix the chatterbox and Aimé Doniat as Roland, the amorous young man brought in by the husband to out-chatter her, is enjoyable. The part of Roland was originally written not for a tenor but for a soprano, and, in fact, the *buffo* duet between Roland and Sarmiento the husband (bass) would go better with the higher voice.

The desirable Rubini two-disc album 'Rarities from the French repertoires' (033163: RS 302) contains one excerpt from *Les Bavards* – unfortunately the only Offenbach number in the collection – 'C'est l'Espagne'. The singer is the Bordeaux soprano Marie Lafargue, who appeared at the Paris Opéra and Opéra-Comique about the turn of the century. Excellent, clean, spot-on singing, yet she hasn't the spark of potential lunacy that marks the true operetta star.

LA BELLE HÉLÈNE

Opéra bouffe in three acts, libretto by Meilhac and Halévy; Variétés, 1864. 'Age cannot wither her, nor custom stale . . .' Offenbach's Helen of Troy, after more than a century of wreaking havoc and scattering intense pleasure, sails blithely on. This legend survives the decay in classical education. Indeed the only thing the operetta has probably lost beyond recall is the power to shock through irreverence. Not even the topicality behind the Greek façade, the fact that Sparta and Nauplia are really Napoleon III's Paris and Trouville, has proved much of a disadvantage. Contemporary equivalents to the Second Empire pastimes, charades and games of chance, can be devised – in the London Coliseum production the competition, so easily won by Paris in the first act, was staged as a TV contest. Whatever one may think about the way this was done, the transformation was logical. One of the work's strengths is the third act. In spite of their many talents Meilhac and Halévy were casual constructors (and in any case operettas, like comic operas, tend to crumble away towards the end) but in this case librettists and composer excelled themselves.

The old Nixa recording is, to a large extent, a yardstick with which to judge others. The restraint of the conductor René Leibowitz (Schoenberg pupil and author of an introduction to the twelve-note system) and the dryness of the recording may surprise those accustomed to Offenbach in big theatres and to the swimming-bath acoustics favoured by some French recording engineers. The shock may be salutary. Offenbach is expressive and vital enough to do without the coating of *Schmalz* appropriate to Johann Strauss and his Viennese followers. Janine Linda's Helen is cool, but she makes her points in the Invocation to Venus more clearly than some of her larger and warmer successors.

The recent Barclay complete recording, made at Strasbourg under the precise and stylish direction of Alain Lombard, is efficiently recorded (though with some stridency towards the beginning), with a generous allowance of French dialogue and a strong performance of the title role by Jane Rhodes – too strong, perhaps. She avoids the slack rhythms that mar some of her other Offenbach recordings, she fines down well for the Dream duet and blends well with the smaller voice of her Paris, Rémy Corazza, but though like most 'big' Helens she is splendid in the last-act Couplets, Rhodes weighs into the dialogue with the lip-smacking avidity of a Hermione Gingold. Rémy Corazza's Paris is good in spite of dry vocal patches. Renée Auphan's Orestes really sounds like a debauched boy prince. Michel Trempont as Calchas (a role often under-cast in French recordings), Jules Bastin as Agamemnon and Jacques Martin as Menelaus give one of the best available accounts of the splendid 'patriotic trio'.

Perhaps this is the moment for a word on musical parody in the operettas. Probably there are few people alive who can spot all the allusions in the works of Meilhac, Halévy and Offenbach. They are even more enjoyable when the targets are identifiable, but surely nobody ever failed to enjoy the patriotic trio, for instance, simply through missing allusions in words and music to a greater (and more solemn) patriotic trio for male voices in Rossini's *Guillaume Tell (qv)*. In Offenbach's parodies, the atmosphere of absurdity and comic exaggeration, aided by a caricaturist's feline touch, works of its own accord. And what he was chiefly parodying was not the original music or the conventions but stale and routined performances of them.

Not much need be said about the EMI Pathé complete version, with its mixture of commentary and dialogue arranged by the composer's great-grandson, Pierre Comte-Offenbach. Sound and balance are horrid (the Marche des Rois comes out like *Rienzi*) and some of the scoring sounds tarted up. Danièle Millet, the Helen, is another full-voiced mezzo, without much character, at her best when she rounds on Menelaus in the last act. The conductor Jean-Pierre Marty leans on the music till it goes soggy.

The EMI/Electrola recording from Munich, issued during the centenary year, has excellent surface and sound quality, except for a brief admixture of echo after Paris reveals his identity – was this supposed to underline the dramatic significance of the moment? The orchestra sounds unnecessarily large but the effect is not vulgar, merely dull. The indomitable Anneliese Rothenberger and Nicolai Gedda are Helen and Paris, she calm, collected, not unwitty but definitely unsensual; he untiring, bright and a little hard. This version (German translation by Ernst Dohm) is unfamiliar, with a two-part introduction to the ensemble following the exposure of Calchas's cheating, which is a gain, and a long, elaborate coloratura solo for Helen in Act 3 which does not compensate for the absence of her usual couplets and, still worse, of the patriotic trio, depriving the promising contributions of Benno Kusche (Calchas), Ferry Gruber (Menelaus) and Klaus Hirte (Agamemnon) of their rightful climax. German translation by and large suits Offenbach but produces some difficulties: Helen's arpeggios on 'l'homme à la pomme' in the first act don't sound nearly so fluent on 'es ist der Apfel-mann'. Brigitte Fassbaender's Orestes is high-powered. The whole perform-ance is assured but definitely mature.

There are two interesting French sets of excerpts. On Philips, Manuel Rosenthal conducts with authority, characterizing the music to the utmost. The Helen is again Jane Rhodes, a little less heavy here and matched with one of the best Parises on record – Bernard Plantey. Good patriotic trio from Jacques Doucet, Jean Giraudeau and Bernard Demigny. The recording is satisfactory except for an abuse of sound-effects. The EMI/Pathé disc (recorded in the Théâtre des Champs-Elysées for the series 'L'Opérette') is bright and brash in sound with plonking basses, but the performance under Jules Gressier is lively. Déva Dassy is a delicious Helen, suggesting downy youth as well as experience – listen to 'Un mari sage' in the Act 2 finale. That number, in Geoffrey Dunn's translation, is also well done by Joyce Blackham in the Sadler's Wells highlights, though her voice did not record particularly well. Kevin Miller is a Puckish Paris. The rest are fair, but the work does not suit the company so well as *Orpheus* (see page 170).

On singles, as one might expect, the most often recorded numbers are Paris's song in Act 1, 'Au Mont Ida trois déesses' and the Dream duet 'Oui, c'est un rêve' for Helen and Paris in Act 2. As for the former, Jussi Björling's Swedish version (HMV X 6090, included in 'Tales of Offenbach' Vol. 1, also on RLS 715) must take the prize, for vocal splendour, gusto and what seems to be a keen appreciation of the words. Louis Arnoult (Ultraphone AP 224) couples 'Mont Ida' with the Tyrolienne from the last scene of the opera. The latter, which recurs in 'Tales of Offenbach', suits him the better of the two. A 'Shepherd's song' (Col. DB 815, also on 'Tales of Offenbach') admirably sung in English by Heddle Nash to amusing words by A. P. Herbert, presumably from the Cochran-Messel *Helen!*, is apparently an interpolation by Korngold. Whether or not it comes from another Offenbach work I do not know. The song turns up again sung in German by Gerd Niemar (as 'Lied des Paris') on Electrola EG 2326, backed by the same tenor singing the Helen-Paris duet with the luscious Jarmila Novotna. Niemar is dim compared to Nash, and the soupy orchestration is mercifully obscured. Both Simon-Girard (33309) and Tariol-Baugé (33810) do Helen's first solo, 'Amours divins!' Both articulate the refrain 'Il-nous-faut-de-l'amour' as if they had absolutely no doubt what they meant. Tariol-Baugé had the more beautiful voice, but in spite of the date (1903) and the poor condition of Simon-Girard's records one can admire the compactness of her tone and a sort of wholehearted single-mindness – a lesson to modern singers who don't take operetta wholly seriously. Other *Belle Hélène* excerpts on 'Tales of Offen-bach' include 'Amours divins!' and the Invocation 'Dis-moi, Vénus' (Disque W 973) sung by Mireille Berthon, a soprano familiar to record collectors, always efficient and stylish but lacking, it seems to me, a definite vocal personality; also an ancient but rather good 'Dream' duet from the couple Léo Demoulin (tenor) and Berthaud (soprano). On LP recitals Régine Crespin (with 'Dis-moi, Vénus') on SET 520–1 and Rhodes (the same, plus 'Amours divins!') on 2C 069–16386 run true to form: Crespin takes the Invocation at a speed which avoids heaviness, giving the *cascader* phrase full value without overdoing it. Rhodes is a little ponderous and in these excerpts her words go dull.

LA BOULANGÈRE A DES ÉCUS

Opéra bouffe in three acts, libretto by Meilhac and Halévy; Variétés, 1875. This was Offenbach's last collaboration with Meilhac and Halévy. The principal role was designed for Schneider, but she flounced out of rehearsals once too often and, to her surprise, found herself replaced. Halévy wrote disparagingly about the piece, but if the two short numbers recorded by Reynaldo Hahn are typical, he was being unduly self-deprecating. 'Les farin-iers, les charbonniers' describes the predicament of the coal merchant's wife with a lover who is a flour merchant and who spends his spare time brushing the black or white dust (as the case might be) off her clothes. 'Que voulez-vous faire?' is a cynical view of woman's virtue as capital – 'I know quite a few who have not only spent capital and income but who are also absolutely riddled with debt.'

Hahn, as well as being a distinguished composer, conductor and critic, knew, cared and wrote much about singing. He did not sing in public, but his private performances, for preference accompanying himself on the piano, a cigarette dangling from his lips, were cherished. Fortunately he made a handful of records. The two *Boulangère* excerpts (Col. D 2022; Rococo 5322) are treasure: intimate Offenbach on a level that explains the attraction his music had for composers like Bizet, Fauré, Debussy and Messager. Such complete stylistic identification is likely to become rarer and rarer. Hahn's voice was a small, light baritone (several of Offenbach's stars, Schneider included, had small voices), beautifully placed, capable of infinite inflection, word and tone melting into one another. The timing of the piano accompaniment is a joy in itself. It would be surprising to learn that Cathy Berberian (in her Edinburgh Festival recital, RCA LRL1 5007, recorded live in 1973) did not know Hahn's record of the second number. She captures the style unerringly, but these words, falling from a woman's lips, sound disloyal.

LES BRIGANDS

Opéra bouffe in three acts, libretto by Meilhac and Halévy; Variétés, 1869. 'I want to put situations to music,' Offenbach wrote to Halévy, 'not to pile songs on songs . . . the public is tired of little tunes and so am I.' Kracauer (*Offenbach and the Paris of his Time*) describes *Les Brigands* as 'at once comic opera and operetta, the two living side by side'. A band of robbers operating in a Salvator Rosa landscape plan to intercept the party of the Princess of Granada on her way to wed the Duke of Mantua. The robbers do not know that the Duke's cashier has embezzled three million francs due to be paid to the visitors – 'one must steal according to one's position in society'. Somewhere in among the visiting Spaniards, the Mantuans and the robbers are the *carabinieri,* whose usefulness is compromised by their habit of arriving on the scene too late.

The extended ensembles (foretastes of *Carmen* again and, in subject, at least, echoes of *Fra Diavolo*) do not in any way quench Offenbach's high spirits. There is hilarious mock-Spanish music and a once-celebrated scene in which, during an orgy, the brigands become aware of the approach of the *carabinieri* ('J'entends un bruit de bottes, de bottes. . . .'). The effect is at once funny and slightly sinister. Commentators have noted that within a short time the tramp of by no means unpunctual Prussian boots was heard in the land, but that did not prevent a revival of *Les Brigands* in Paris soon after the troubles (and the Second Empire) were over. The flatfoot echoes were duly heard again (in Anglo-Saxon lands this time) in *The Pirates of Penzance*. Of the major neglected works of Offenbach this is possibly the most urgent candidate for revival.

A group of 78s gives an idea of past popularity and past interpreters, some of them – Emma Luart, Louis Musy, Marcel Carpentier, Paul Payan, the conductor Georges Lauweryns – connected with the work's first appearance at the Opéra-Comique in 1931. On HMV K-6341, Musy's high baritone is wonderfully vivacious and precise in the 'Couplets de Falsacappa' and the 'Choeur des bottes'. His diction, consonants especially, is a marvel of clarity and expressiveness. There is a pleasantly informal touch when Musy and Mme Musy skip down an octave to sketch in the chorus parts. Luart from the Monnaie in Brussels was a notable Manon (see *Opera on Record*). On Odéon 238.814, in Fiorella's Rondeau 'Après avoir pris à droite' and the more sentimental Couplets 'Vraiment je n'en sais rien', she is forward and bright without glassiness (and with a soft top) – the tiny catches in the rhythm have something of Yvonne Printemps. On Odéon 238.816 Luart temporarily annexes the breeches part of Fragoletto (originally played by Offenbach's favourite, Zulma Bouffar) for the Saltarelle and 'Trio des marmitons' (scullions), with Carpentier (brilliant falsetto) and Payan. On Pathé X 92011 Luart is heard in the 'Choeur des bottes' and once again in the 'Trio des marmitons', this time with Léon Ponzio, another high baritone who can be mistaken for a tenor, and André Balbon. The mad Spanish number for the Princess of Granada's chamberlain Gloria-Cassis, 'Jadis vous n'aviez qu'un' patrie' with the refrain 'Y'a des gens qui se dis'nt espagnols', is heard from the comedian Duvaleix, complete with thick Southern accent, on Odéon 238.815. On the reverse is the Mantuan cashier's apologetic confession, 'O, mes amours! O, mes maîtresses!' about where the money has gone. The Couplets for Gloria-Cassis are also sung by Frédéric le Prin on Poly. 521993.

In the absence of a complete recording one must give some sort of a welcome to the French Decca disc of excerpts from a soundtrack. The sound quality is sometimes nasty, the score is slashed about, but one gets an idea of the riches it contains, while the Fiorella of Eliane Manchet displays a grace, charm and warmth not unworthy of Luart. Fragoletto is given to a tenor, the dapper Michaël Pieri. Dominique Tirmont is Falsacappa, the brigand chief, his voice disagreeably over-amplified.

From the sleevenote for the Milan label recording one might suppose this was a complete version. Not at all – two sides of excerpts performed according to producer Jaromir Knittl (or Knittel) and conductor Daniel Mourruau's idea of 'today's aesthetic standards', which apparently exclude repeats or any 'monumental' quality. Small, scrawny orchestra, large cast under-employed but doing incompetent duty also for chorus. Danièle Perriers, a one-time Glyndebourne artist, would be a charming Fiorella if the conductor let her fill out the music. Robert Manuel voicelessly grinds out what we hear of Falsacappa. Since on stage this actor is an adroit comedian, his treatment might get by in a short one-act burlesque. Not here. Fragoletto is given to a thin-voiced tenor. The downward transposition is especially woeful in the 'begging' canon. The low point is reached in another performer's assault on the Treasurer's song. Sleeve and labels are misleading about excerpts given: two vocal numbers listed are played by orchestra alone, without singers: an awful warning of what happens when the operetta pendulum swings too far from dull convention towards irresponsibility.

LA CHANSON DE FORTUNIO

Opéra comique in one act; Bouffes-Parisiens 1861. Libretto by Crémieux and Halévy. When Offenbach was director of music for the Comédie-Française he made a simple, memorable setting of Fortunio's verses in Musset's comedy *Le Chandelier*. Unfortunately Delaunay, the actor concerned, could not manage the song – his singing voice was too deep. Offenbach, who was pleased with it, put it by. A decade or so later Crémieux and Halévy wrote him a short sequel to the Musset play in which the tune was used as a kind of theme song. This time, taking no chances, Offenbach gave the role of the clerk who is the successor to Fortunio (now a grown-up lawyer) to a female voice. Though the libretto is not on Musset's level, the score, said to have been one of the composer's favourites, deserves a complete recording.

The attempt of the firm Bourg to fill the gap is a disappointment. In this recording of a French Radio version of 1973 (from the INA archives) the dialogue is omitted. Presumably it was included in the broadcast. Here, as the single act progresses and music and text should be more closely bound together, the effect is increasingly unfortunate. The provision of a libretto hardly makes amends, since there is not time to read the dialogue between numbers.

The role of Valentin, written for a travesti, is given to a tenor. If you have a male Valentin you must use men for his four fellow-clerks, all travestis in the original. The result, in spite of lively conducting by Alain Pâris (in an over-resonant studio) is boisterous where it should be light as a feather. André Vallabrera sings Valentin's (formerly Maître Fortunio's) song plainly and nicely but without the adolescent absorption or the tonal beauty of the best interpreters on the singles mentioned below. Some consolation comes from Lina Dachary in the boléro surprisingly given to Maître Fortunio's wife (Faris rightly notes an anticipation of *Carmen*) and in the merry couplets of Fricquet, the only clerk correctly sung by a man – in this case Joseph Peyron. For the coupling, see *Lischen et Fritzchen*.

There are surprisingly few singles of the song itself. On Parlophone 29.522 Leila Ben Sedira, an Opéra-Comique soprano with a rapid but not unpleasing vibrato (she sings Yniold in the Désormière *Pelléas*) brings to it plenty of feeling but is outclassed by Tariol-Baugé (33811; GV 600) – what verbal and vocal relish!

There is a masculine version, under the title 'Serenade' by Emilio de Gogorza (DA 177) sung without comparable relish but with incomparable refinement – damson-coloured tone and faultless emission. If Delaunay had sung like this, there would have been no need for Offenbach to write another work. But a baritone voice would not be right in the theatre; neither, to judge from George Foix's recording of the song in French on (English) Decca F 1717, would a tenor voice – even such a cultivated light tenor as this one, though it is used with a charm a little too conscious for the music. Except for a tendency to emphasize the strong beats, the style might be modelled on Printemps. There is a tantalizing snippet from the song in the 'Potpourri d'Alain Gerbault' recorded by Yvonne Printemps and reissued on her mixed LP EMI/Pathé Marconi FALP 30.320.

CHRISTOPHER COLUMBUS

Opéra bouffe in four acts (pastiche); Ulster Hall, Belfast (concert performance) 1976. Libretto by Don White, dialogue by Don White and Lorraine Thomas. In view of the number of works by Offenbach rarely or never performed, the making of pastiche operettas may be considered a superfluous exercise. For *Christopher Columbus*, however, there was an excuse. Opera Rara (London) were invited by the Ulster Orchestra (Belfast) for something to celebrate the bicentenary of American Independence. Remembering that Offenbach visited the States for the first centenary in 1876 and that, though he wrote some numbers for *La Boite au lait* on the Atlantic crossings, he did not find time to write a new operetta for his hosts, they concocted *Christopher Columbus*. The score was expertly put together out of numbers well worth salvaging from little-known or forgotten Offenbach works, with the addition of a few bars of 'The Star-Spangled Banner' – enticing morsels from (among others) *Le Docteur Ox*, *Le Pont des soupirs*, *Dragonette*, *Maître Peronilla*, *Vert-vert* and, to mention operettas briefly treated in this chapter, *Madame L'Archiduc* and *La Boulangère*. The libretto is an outrageous fantasy in which Columbus, having refused the advances of Isabella of Spain (in this version of history as fond of the gentlemen as she is of the bottle), is packed off on a voyage of discovery. What is more, the Queen sends all the company with him as crew, excluding the timid King Ferdinand but including the hero's three ex-wives and present fiancée. They end up in 'a forest, somewhere in downtown Manhattan'. Columbus, one step ahead, marries Princess Minnehaha and discovers a way of enriching them all by means of liquid gold extracted from the cola nut.

The complete recording is enjoyable; the London Mozart Players perform crisply under Alun Francis. Except for one or two passages for which the scoring could not be traced the orchestrations are Offenbach's. The title role is taken by Maurice Arthur, an agreeable light tenor without a strong 'presence' but with good, easy diction in song and dialogue. Christian du Plessis sings Luis the Round Earth expert who consoles Beatriz, the neglected fiancée. Beatriz is Joy Roberts, who has her moment in one of Offenbach's sentimental, Sullivanesque pages but is otherwise out-sparkled by Johanna Peters, Lissa Gray and Marilyn Hill Smith as the three ex-wives. Anna Dawson's remarkable Isabella is the female equivalent of the seasoned French comedians who perform Offenbach's male character roles.

LA FILLE DU TAMBOUR MAJOR

Opéra comique in three acts, libretto by Duru and Chivot; Folies-Dramatiques, 1879. The last big success of Offenbach's lifetime. A patriotic sentimental piece celebrating the arrival of the French troops in Milan during the Napoleonic wars. For Offenbach's special public, at least, tone and subject would have been inconceivable in the years before 1870. There is nothing in the score to show that the composer was an exhausted, ailing man. Melodic invention and rhythmic vitality are still vigorous; episodes such as the scene of recognition between the Duchess and her former husband the Drum Major are most skilfully handled. Only the sensuality has gone, and this story hardly calls for it.

Neither of the LP versions has much to recommend it. The two-disc French Decca set is fairly complete, though cuts come thick and fast before the end. The veteran Musy is a valiant Drum Major. There is abundant dialogue, but Duru and Chivot write workaday stuff. The recording is indifferent, with nasty fadings in or out of music and dialogue. The single EMI Pathé disc of excerpts was presumably taken from a complete recording. Quality is poor and each track lurches out of a crackly haze, but Rémy Corazza sings the tailor's couplets with his usual finish, Suzanne Lafaye and Dominique Tirmont do the second duet for the Duchess and Drum Major well, while the big Act 3 finale, which culminates so stirringly in Méhul's 'Chant du départ', is better handled than in the Decca set.

The distant past is more rewarding. The original Stella (the Drum Major's Daughter of the title) was Juliette Simon-Girard, but alas there is nothing from the opera on the Rubini 'Offenbach Centenary' record. However, Tariol-Baugé on the other side of that disc and Edmée Favart on 'Tales of Hoffmann' Vol. 1, both give spanking accounts of the song in which Stella (recently reunited with her true father) proudly proclaims her identity. Even so, the rs in their 'ra-ra-ras' are out-rolled by Sim-Viva (Od. 165.709), coupling the Chanson with the insidious 'Petit français, gentil français' from the finale of the previous act. The amorous tailor's Couplets are sung (4–32242) by Régis, a well-schooled tenor from the Opéra. On Odéon 166.121, Victor Pujol from the Opéra-Comique is slighty less elegant in the same song. He also contributes the tailor Griolet's second solo, the 'Couplets de l'uniforme'. On 34284, Régis is joined by Edmond Tirmont, Louis Dupuoy and Paul Payan in the 'billeting quartet' which has a touch of *Die Fledermaus*.

GENEVIÈVE DE BRABANT

Opéra bouffe in three acts, libretto by Crémieux and Tréfeu; Menus-Plaisirs, 1867. This was a revision of the two-act *opéra bouffon* with libretto by Jaime and Tréfeu produced at the Bouffes-Parisiens in 1859. There was a third version, an *opéra féerie* in five acts, at the Gaîté in 1875. *Geneviève* has more or less disappeared from sight, with the exception of one number, the

'Couplets des deux hommes d'armes' added for the 1867 version. As 'The Gendarmes' duet', this has been virtually anglicized. I have found one French version, by Alexis Boyer and Dambrine (Zono X-84011), but the performers don't compare with the best British bobbies. It is true that Frank Mullings and Norman Allin (L 1735), with heavy piano accompaniment, are disappointing, but Walter Glynne and Stuart Robertson (HMV B 3030) are very good, while Malcolm McEachern ('Mr Jetsam') and Harold Williams (Col. DX 585) are splendid – McEachern sounds as oily as a phoney politician. Both pairs have orchestral accompaniment. Alas, the police are not what they were; in their recital 'The Dicky Bird and the Owl' (HMV EMD 5509), Robert Tear and Benjamin Luxon, with André Previn at the piano, prink the music up too much. In the (live) 'Darwin – Song for a city' recital (SXL 6719) Tom McDonnell and Clifford Grant (with orchestra) do much to restore confidence without matching the best of their predecessors.

DER GOLDSCHMIED VON TOLEDO

Pastiche in a prologue and two acts, libretto by Carl Georg Zwerenz partly based on E. T. A. Hoffmann's *Das Fräulein von Scuderi*; Mannheim, 1919; music arranged by Julius Stern and Alfred Zamara. Patzak's recording of Don Miguel de Favero's Serenade from Act 2, 'Lieblichste aller Frauen' is seductive but sounds totally Viennese (PO 5021; LV 1318). I've not heard a version by the British tenor, John McHugh (Col. DX 1224), singing in English.

LA GRANDE DUCHESSE DE GEROLSTEIN

Opéra bouffe in three acts, libretto by Meilhac and Halévy; Variétés, 1867. An outrageous but good-humoured lampoon directed against petty sovereignties whose bellicosity is intended to divert attention from domestic troubles. 'Gerolstein' was added to the title to placate the censor, who feared that offence might be caused to crowned heads visiting Paris for the Exhibition of 1867. The fact that the well informed, at least, were aware that real war was in the air added piquancy. Bismarck was among those who saw *La Grande Duchesse*.

In the CBS complete version (some cuts and abbreviated dialogue) Régine Crespin, Alain Vanzo and Robert Massard head the company from the Capitole, Toulouse, for the occasion. Michel Plasson conducts with brio and a little too much weight – possibly exaggerated by the acoustics – but takes great care over the 'Mélodrames' which add Mozartian grace to the score. Crespin's swagger and rhythm, with her ability to fine down for intimate moments such as 'Dites-lui', outweigh occasional unwieldiness. As Fritz, the humble soldier in love with the peasant girl Wanda, who catches the Grand Duchess's eye, is rapidly promoted to the rank of General and as rapidly demoted, Vanzo shows a gift for comedy rare in a leading tenor. His Marseillais accent adds to the general air of fantasy. Robert Massard is not really suited to the fire-eating General Boum, slighted by the Grand Duchess in spite of her avowed passion for the military. Massard's contribution to the ensembles is as good as one would expect, but 'Pif paf pouf' is spoilt by echo. To Charles Burles as the weary, patient Prince Paul fall the 'Couplets de la Gazette de Hollande' – these simple-seeming, subtly moulded strophic songs represent a quiet side of the composer and of his librettists too often overlooked.

Of the Leibowitz recording on Saga I have only heard the highlights. They show the same sure, light touch as this conductor's *La Belle Hélène,* but with the exception of John Riley's excellent Boum the singing is not distinguished enough to make up for poor sound and weak orchestral playing. Eugenia Zareska is miscast in the title role. She has little dash, and the quality of her voice is lamed by tight French vowels. André Dran as Fritz tends to shout.

Of single excerpts, the Wanda-Fritz duets were recorded (Pathé 2514) by Berthaud and Léo Demoulin (soprano and tenor, listed in that order) lively in spite of ancient sound – the disc is included in 'Tales of Offenbach' Vol. 1. André Noël from the Opéra-Comique offers a fine account (Pathé X. 90019) of the 'Gazette de Hollande' and the exemplary Louis Musy an equally fine one of 'Pif paf pouf' (Pathé PD 85). That will be found again in 'Tales of Offenbach' Vol. 1, where there is also an enjoyable but mature-sounding 'Voici le sabre' from Geneviève Vix (Pathé 0669). The rest are uninteresting – Lucienne Jourfier's 'Dites-lui' (Pathé PD 85), Mireille Berthon's 'Ah, que j'aime les militaires' and 'Voici le sabre' (HMV K-6312), Jane Morlet's 'Légende du verre' (Disque P 534) – or downright murky – Jourfier and Michel Dens on two sides, Pathé PD 86, from what seems to be an updated version with words by Willemetz. One exception, the 'Dites-lui' (HMV E 550) of Yvonne Printemps (also in 'Tales of Offenbach'), inimitable and self-indulgent, with impudently long-held notes.

Four LP mixed recitals have groups of excerpts from *La Grande Duchesse.* The most recent is the 'Offenbach – airs célèbres' of Jane Rhodes, who sings the usual three solos plus the 'Légende du verre'. Sensibly, since this number hardly seems to sit right in the last act, she puts it first. I find the opulence of the singer's tone needs buoying up with more dash and stronger rhythm than she here produces. The soupy orchestral accompaniments don't help. Crespin, in her two-disc album 'Prima Donna in Paris' (SET 520–1), shows exactly what is lacking. Her voice is really too big and there are dangerous moments at the top of the stave, but her 'Ah, que j'aime les militaires!', well supported by the conductor, Alain Lombard, has all the required snap. Frederica von Stade's 'Dites-lui', in her all-French recital (CBS 76522), is careful to the point of laboriousness. Sutherland, on the other hand, in her two disc 'Romantic French Arias' (SET 454–5) is carefree with rhythm and words – 'qui' for 'quoi' makes nonsense of one sentence – but the sound is gorgeous. No French scratchings here! Later in the recital Sutherland ripples through 'Ah! que j'aime les militaires!' as if it were the easiest thing in the world, but never suggests that the virtue of the military is in serious danger. The orchestrations (Suisse Romande Orchestra under Bonynge) convey 'luxury' in the estate-agents' sense of the word.

LA JOLIE PARFUMEUSE

Opéra comique in three acts, libretto by Crémieux and Blum; Renaissance, 1873. Written for one of Offenbach's postwar stars, Louis Théo. There was a student production at the Royal Academy of Music, London, in honour of the work's centenary in 1973. Simon-Girard's 'La famille Bruscambille' (33327, not included on the Rubini record), would hardly be worth hearing if it were not for the identity of the singer. The same number turns up as a duet sung in Italian (as 'Canzone Bruscanville' from *La bella profumiera*) by an anonymous soprano and baritone surprisingly resurrected on 'Tales of Offenbach' Vol. 1 – there is almost more piano than voice. In this number the *parfumeuse* of the title, Rose Michon, lifts the curtain on her early family life in Toulouse.

LISCHEN ET FRITZCHEN

Conversation alsacienne in one act. Bad Ems 1863, Bouffes-Parisiens 1864. Libretto by Paul Boisselot. Written in eight days, for a wager. Faris points out that Offenbach cheated to the extent of including one number, a setting of an adaptation of the La Fontaine fable 'Le Rat de ville et le Rat des champs', written many years before. Zulma Bouffar played the girl, Lischen. Scarcely more than a sketch concerned with the Alsatian dialect with its confusions of 'b' and 'p' and 'v' and 'f' and sudden switches into German. Because of their accent and consequent verbal misunderstandings, young Lischen and Fritzchen lose their jobs. All comes right in the end.

As in the coupling, *La Chanson de Fortunio*, the dialogue in this French Radio performance of 1970 (INA archives) is omitted, though a libretto is provided. The fable is also omitted, without explanation. What remains is a tiny handful of delightful music including a duet, 'Je suis alsacienne', suggesting a trial run for Gabrielle and Frick's 'Je suis gantière' in *La Vie parisienne*. Lina Dachary and Joseph Peyron, two experienced artists, are a little mature for the young couple. One can well imagine, however, that their handling of the dialogue would have been racy. If *Lischen* and *Fortunio* had been given in full on two discs, they would have been a valuable addition to the catalogue. The single disc is a monument to editorial obtuseness.

MADAME FAVART

Opéra comique in three acts, libretto by Duru and Chivot. Folies-Dramatiques, 1878. Two historical characters, the eighteenth-century actress and singer Justine Duronceray and her husband Charles Favart, author of plays

and comic operas, are involved in a plot concerning Justine's efforts to evade
the attentions of the notorious Maréchal de Saxe. Virtue triumphs. The
intrigue provides plenty of opportunity for the pastiche Offenbach could
blend so well with his own style – for some mid-nineteenth-century composers, the eighteenth century had a fascination not unlike the attraction of
Romantic music for certain composers today. Shaw (quoted by James
Harding in *Jacques Offenbach: a biography**) praised the 'grace, gaiety and
intelligence' of *Madame Favart.*

The Discoréale-INA set, described as 'premier enregistrement mondial',
is a recording of a French Radio broadcast of 1960, the first, it appears, of
a series to come from the archives of the INA. The first two acts are slightly
cut, the third savagely. The sound is elderly, but the performance is lively
and idiomatic enough for one soon not to notice. The title role is a gift for
an actress-singer with a turn for mimicry. The first Madame Favart was the
young Juliette Simon-Girard. Her successor here is Suzanne Lafaye, a
versatile singer who also deals admirably and at dazzling speed with dialogue
not in itself too sparkling – one suspects Offenbach chose Duru and Chivot's
libretto because, having been reviled during the recent war for his German
origin, he wanted to prove his mastery of French as opposed to Parisian
style. He certainly reveals himself as an heir of Auber, Adam and other
composers of *opéras comiques*. The smooth, elegant singing of Camille
Maurane as Charles Favart is a delight (why did we hear so little of this fine
baritone in London?). Lina Dachary and Joseph Peyron are the young couple
Suzanne (who has some good numbers) and Hector de Boispréau. Though
the ensemble is not always crisp, the conductor Marcel Cariven judges the
style to a nicety. Otherwise, admirers of *Madame Favart* must rely on a few
good singles.

The Ronde 'Ma mère aux vignes m'envoyit' is one of several character-
pieces sung by the heroine, this time in the disguise of a country lass serving
at an inn – the tune could easily be mistaken for a traditional one. There
are three distinguished versions, including one by the role's creator, Simon-
Girard. Of the three, Mme Simon-Girard (33310) takes the greatest licence
with the rhythm ('Pulling the time about', it would now be called), but there
is no doubt, in spite of hiss and crackle, of the vividness with which the
simple episode of a girl being tumbled on her way to the vineyard comes
across.

Between Germaine Corney (Poly. 522581) and Fanély Revoil (HMV K-
7635) it is difficult to choose. Both are examples of the best types of French
light soprano with bloom on voice and style. Revoil adds the 'Rondeau de
la vieille', in which Madame Favart pretends to be an elderly marquise
passing her sentimental life in review. A charming performance, though the
label promises the Menuet that precedes the Rondeau in the score and it
isn't there. There are two versions of husband Favart's deeply felt Romance

---

* John Calder, London.

'C'est la lumière, c'est la flamme', sung when events have temporarily separated him from his wife. Alexis Boyer on Pathé 2008 is preferable to René Gerbert on Pathé X 0713. Boyer's reverse, the 'Couplets de l'échaudé' in praise of puff-pastry, is an added attraction.

MADAME L'ARCHIDUC

Opéra bouffe in three acts, libretto by Millaud and Halévy; Bouffes-Parisiens, 1874. Edmée Favart on Pathé 2026 is so good (the first number graceful and touching, the second a lively waltz with chorus), the singer so appealing in both, that one is curious to hear the rest of the work.

MONSIEUR CHOUFLEURI RESTERA CHEZ LUI LE . . .

Opéra bouffe in one act, libretto by St Rémy, Halévy, Crémieux and Lépine; Bouffes-Parisiens, 1861. St Rémy was a pen-name for the Duc de Morny, illegitimate half-brother of the Emperor, statesman, friend of Halévy and admirer of Offenbach. Choufleuri is a *bourgeois gentilhomme* of the time of Louis Philippe, a successful tradesman out for social success. Although he detests music, he invites the singers Sontag, Rubini and Tamburini to perform at a soirée in his house. At the last moment they cancel. Choufleuri is obliged to substitute his daughter, her lover (a penniless composer) and himself. The result is a hilarious parody of Meyerbeer and the Italians.

Considering that the work is fairly often revived, it is surprising to find no French recording available (but see page 178). In Germany *Choufleuri* is known as *Salon Pitzelberger,* in which form it has been recorded in East Germany for Eterna, not quite complete, with a mixture of dialogue and commentary. Some of the singers have speaking-doubles, carefully matched (as a matter of interest, Pitzelberger is pronounced in the French way). The recording is good (with a very small orchestra) but the effect is coy and the parodies merely sound like average German opera singers struggling with Italianate music.

ORPHÉE AUX ENFERS

Opéra bouffon in two acts, libretto by Crémieux and (anonymously) Halévy; Bouffes-Parisiens, 1858 (new version as *opéra féerie* in four acts, Gaîté, 1874). The first of Offenbach's assaults on classical mythology still continues to draw the wider public. It has a hundred good things apart from the 'galop infernal' usually known and often danced as the can-can. The story works in the theatre even for those with the barest acquaintance with the Orpheus myth or with Gluck's opera. The vitality and variety of the music invite and frequently receive large-scale treatment of varying degrees of vulgarity. That is inevitable whether one likes it or not. Offenbach himself set the example, in size if not in vulgarity but quite possibly in both, with his postwar version mounted in 1874 at the Gaité – Faris mentions '120 choristers, 60 orchestral musicians, a military band of 40 . . . a corps de ballet of 60'.

There are recordings of both versions. Those seriously interested in Offenbach should hear the Leibowitz set of the first version on Nixa. The sound is dry, the casting less even than in his *Belle Hélène*, and towards the end of the first act Leibowitz is too reticent, almost sleepy. Yet his (in the musical sense) classical approach to the score is revealing – one realizes how well Offenbach knew his job. One number in particular that can easily get out of hand in the theatre, the 'Fly duet', is scrupulously done by Bernard Demigny (Jupiter) and Claudine Collart (Eurydice). Jean Mollien is a pleasant Orpheus. The final scene, which one would hardly expect to answer to a restraining hand, works well.

Plasson's recording of the later version, with his forces from the Capitole at Toulouse together with a large number of the best comedian-singers in France today, is not vulgar. In fact it is as much an improvement on his *La Grande Duchesse* as that was on *La Vie parisienne* (see below). There is no feeling that the sound has been fattened up. The balance between too much energy and too little is finely judged. The Eurydice, Mady Mesplé, has the kind of French timbre not always popular in this country, but listen through the thinness and you find a stylish, assured performer. Jane Rhodes is an authoritative Public Opinion, Michèle Command a luscious Venus, Jane Berbié a burly Orestes. Among the men Michel Sénéchal is the distinguished Orpheus, André Mallabrera makes much of Mercury's solo; for the genially simple, haunting 'King of Boeotia' song Bruce Brewer lends to John Styx a strange, presumably Boeotian, accent. Messrs Burles, Trempont and Lafont make their mark.

Offenbach in English seems to undergo a double translation, of attitude as well as language, but the Sadler's Wells highlights, memento of a production (in Geoffrey Dunn's English version) that remained in the repertory for a considerable time, show the company more at home than in *La Belle Hélène* or *La Vie parisienne*. The conductor is Alexander Faris, who has since published the book on Offenbach mentioned above. June Bronhill's Eurydice is brisk in a British way and extremely well sung. Orpheus suits Kevin Miller better than Paris, Eric Shilling is a strong Jupiter, Alan Crofoot one of the best John Styxes on record. On the whole the sound has worn well.

The complete *Orpheus in der Unterwelt* has a recording standard of a quality one could hardly hope to find in France, easily accommodating what sounds an unnecessarily large contingent of the Philharmonia Hungarica, but the results are staid – the seasoning has been left out. Adolf Dallapozza's Orpheus has little of the expected honey, Anneliese Rothenberger's Eurydice is trim but pallid. Benno Kusche is an experienced Jupiter, but the most interesting performance comes from the Styx, croaked rather than sung by the comedian Theo Lingen, who adds to his song one or two fairly topical verses (one about football). This practice, which may seem strange to English listeners, is usual in German-speaking countries, where for certain songs, not only in Offenbach operettas, extra verses are improvised on local topics. When you hear an experienced Viennese comic extending a song in, say, one of Raimund's comedies to cover recent municipal scandals and holding the audience in his hand, you begin to understand the kind of rapport that existed between Offenbach's artists and their public in the early, intimate days.

Singles from *Orphée* are not numerous. Luart (Pathé X 91027) in Eurydice's 'Couplets du berger joli' and the 'Couplets du baiser' – Cupid's kissing song from the 1874 version – is less winning than usual. Maryse Beaujon in the 'Hymne à Bacchus' and with Adrien Lamy (the two of them supplying their own chorus) in the 'Duo de la mouche' (Col. RF 57), is more rewarding. On Pathé X 91029 the distinguished tenor (and one-time director of the Opéra-Comique) Lucien Muratore in Pluto's songs, the first sung in disguise as Aristaeus, the second the remarkable 'air en prose', displays a fine voice, good diction but uncertain intonation. There are as many ways of doing Styx's song as there are singers. Albert Vaguet (Pathé 118) takes it fast, with steady, penetrating tone.

LA PÉRICHOLE

Opéra bouffe in two acts, libretto by Meilhac and Halévy; Variétés, 1868 (new version in three acts, Variétés, 1874).

The real Périchole (*perra chola,* native bitch) was an eighteenth-century Peruvian actress. Mérimée wrote a one-act comedy, *Le Carrosse du Saint-Sacrement*, about her which has very little in common with Meilhac and Halévy's libretto. Hortense Schneider had one of her greatest successes in Offenbach's title role, and was persuaded to reappear in the postwar version with an extra act containing some important new numbers (in his note for the booklet issued with the EMI/Pathé-Markevitch recording, Maurice Tassart suggests that 'Tu n'es pas beau' had already been added during the earlier run, evidently after the printing of the first vocal score).

La Périchole is one of Offenbach's richest scores. As P. Walter Jacob points out in his *Offenbach* (Rowohlt Bild-Monographien, Hamburg), one of the most informative general introductions to the composer, it forms a bridge between prewar and postwar manners. On the one side, parody of court protocol, Donizettian conspirators and an absurd absolute ruler (the Viceroy of Peru), on the other the real-life, genuine devotion of the Périchole to her Piquillo. Offenbach's style was developing and would have changed even if the Second Empire hadn't gone up in smoke. So, one suspects, would his librettists' outlook.

La Périchole is a longish work with copious dialogue, a problem for complete recordings. The Erato version with the Strasbourg forces under Lombard has a commentary written and spoken by Alain Decaux, author of a standard French book on Offenbach. On the whole, and in spite of an initial whiff of worldly cynicism, the commentary is economically and discreetly done (but why the French have so little confidence in the idiomatic, racy dialogue of Meilhac and Halévy, goodness knows). In any case the musical performance, well conducted by Lombard and strongly led by Crespin, Vanzo and Jules Bastin, would carry a greater handicap than this. Crespin's rhythm, her marvellous sense of words, her dignity and wholehearted integrity once again disguise the sheer size of the voice. Vanzo, light and sinewy, is as good a Piquillo as one could find today, Bastin proves the wisdom of casting the Viceroy from strength, the supporting cast is good.

On the French EMI set, the sound is good – the resonance of the early Plasson/Toulouse recordings has disappeared. The conductor's touch is sure and springy. Berganza and Carreras are Périchole and Piquillo. She is lighter than Crespin, he heavier than Vanzo, but the teaming works. The corking Spanish accents hardly matter except when the need for rapid articulation impedes Berganza and threatens to disturb her line. Carreras is more adroit with words. Her approach is classical, for all the Iberian ochre in the tone. Conventional blandishments are scorned. She is aloof, a little intimidating, not unconcerned. In the prison scene, perhaps inevitably, this couple suggest Carmen and José. Bacquier's Viceroy is first-rate. Smaller roles are well taken by (among others) Michel Sénéchal and Michel Trempont. A fair amount of dialogue is allowed, without admixture of commentary.

Nevertheless, Strasbourg and Toulouse still have competition from the old (1956) EMI complete version, conducted by Igor Markevitch with an elegance and style rivalling if not surpassing Leibowitz in his Offenbach recordings. This one has a not very satisfactory mixture of dialogue and commentary arranged by Pierre Comte-Offenbach, but once again the disadvantages are outweighed by musical merit. The conductor's stylishness spreads to the singers, especially to the Périchole of Suzanne Lafaye, who sings the role not as a series of numbers but consistently in character. The letter song 'O mon cher amant' is done, movingly, with the voice of a hungry young girl. 'Tu n'es pas beau' (without the hungriness, after a period in the Viceroy's palace) is equally persuasive.

The RCA excerpts in the English version of Maurice Valency show a quite different approach. Cyril Ritchard comperes and plays (one can hardly say he sings) the Viceroy. With all his throwaway charm he does not convince one that this role can be left to a comedian, however accomplished (turn back to Bastin and Bacquier). The Périchole is Patrice Munsel – good voice, hearty manner, sometimes soppy. She interpolates an aria. Theodor Uppman's Piquillo is hearty too, but his singing is good enough for one to accept his conventional approach.

Singles abound. Both Simon-Girard and Tariol-Baugé are represented (on Rubini), the former demonstrating her powers of expression in the Letter Song (33373 – what a good pianist she has!), the latter her superior vocal quality in the duet (Disque P 291, with Alfred W. Dambrine) 'L'espagnol et la jeune indienne', a much-recorded number combining a touch of exoticism (the insistent tritone) with the blatantly diatonic refrain 'Il grandira car il est espagnol', which has almost acquired the status of a proverb. The same duet is coupled by Berthaud and Demoulin (see *La Grande Duchesse*) with the Séguedille from the last act. He is a lively performer; she does not time her 'hop-las' too well. Emma Calvé is the somewhat unlikely interpreter of the Letter Song on a 1919 Pathé (0289; GV 57). The style may be a shade heavy. The verbal accents, the careful rubato and tonal shadings are subtly judged, amazing from a singer of sixty-one. In the Letter Song and 'Tu n'es pas beau' Fanély Revoil (HMV K 7556) combines a degree of modern strictness (or lack of confidence and imagination, as you prefer it) with much of the old charm and expressiveness. On returning to Jennie Tourel's celebrated records (CBS 61353) after a considerable time I felt some disappointment. The timbre is still lovely, but the up-scored orchestrations would disqualify anyone. Tourel does the drunk song ('Ah! quel dîner!') and 'Ah! que les hommes sont bêtes' with the skill of an experienced, versatile artist but into the Letter Song she pours a drop or two of *Schmalz*, and that little is too much. Corney gives a first-rate Letter Song. Maggie Teyte's 'Tu n'es pas beau' (Decca K 993; ECM 830) was for many of us an introduction to the more serious side of Offenbach's operettas. It remains as exquisite and finely spun as ever, yet it is a concert reading, barely related to character or context. As a curiosity there is a Russian version on 'Tales of Offenbach' of 'Ah, quel dîner!' from C. Novikova who (I am assured and can readily believe it) was a specialist in laughing songs.

In the LP mixed recitals Crespin (SET 520–1) is again admirable, particularly in the Letter Song. Rhodes (2C 069–16386) is opulent but flaccid, at her best in 'Ah! que les hommes sont bêtes' but still over-emphatic. Berberian's 'Tu n'es pas beau' (RCA LRL 1 5007) has the advantage of a voice dark in colour but light in weight, Von Stade's 'Mon Dieu! quel dîner' (CBS 76522) is a trifle serious. Sutherland (two-disc album 'Love Lives Forever', SET 349–50) pulls and tweaks the Letter Song about until it goes coy, and there is a verbal slip which no one has bothered to correct. In 'Ah! que les hommes sont bêtes' the speed forces the words forward, to their advantage. 'Ah! quel dîner!' is girlishly giggly on the grand scale. The group is likable and the vocal equipment superb, but the singer does not seem to have considered the Périchole as a character.

LE PONT DES SOUPIRS

Opéra bouffe in two acts (four scenes), libretto by Crémieux and Halévy; Bouffes-Parisiens, 1861 (new version in four acts, Variétés, 1868). The scene is fourteenth-century Venice. The ineffectual Doge Cornarino Cornarini, recently disgraced as Admiral of the Fleet, skulks in disguise with his equerry Baptiste observing the behaviour of his wife, Catarina. The lady, who favours her young page Amoroso, is pursued by the redoubtable *gonfaloniere* Fabiano Fabiani Malatromba. Cornarini spreads the false news of his own demise but is unmasked and condemned to death by the Council of Ten. Sentence is not, however, carried out until he and Malatromba (who plans to succeed him as Doge) have provided a carnival diversion by publicly climbing the greasy pole. Malatromba wins. Cornarini and Catarina are in compensation given the Madrid Embassy, with Amoroso as Secretary.

Such are the bones of a generously complicated plot. In the score, barcarolles, serenades, boleros turning into yodelling songs, jostle a burlesque mad scene for the heroine and filigree ensembles which pepper *bel canto* opera of the previous decades much as the librettists pepper corrupt city-state government. Though big tunes of Offenbach's world-conquering type are absent, there is abundant fresh melody and a crop of admirable solo numbers in couplet form, with words and music closely married – Malatromba has three. Faris in his *Jacques Offenbach* notes the influence of *Le Pont des soupirs* (staged in 1872 in London as *The Bridge of Sighs*) on *The Gondoliers* (1889). The considerable time-lag may explain why the waters of Sullivan's (and Gilbert's) lagoon are so placid by comparison.

The Bourg recording (of the 1868 version) derives, like the same firm's *Barbe-Bleue* from a radio performance (date 1968) in the INA archives, some commentary, much fluently spoken dialogue. Non-French speakers may find the absence of a libretto a greater disadvantage here than in the case of the familiar Bluebeard story. Some of the orchestral part, in the early scenes especially, is dimly recorded, but on the whole the musical style under Jean Doussard is good. Michel Hamel's Malatromba, one or two hard notes excepted, is a notable bravura performance. Aimé Doniat as the true Doge and Joseph Peyron as his henchman are scarcely less good. Claudine Collard (Catarina) is a French light soprano of some charm. René Lenoty as Cascadetto the town-crier has a lusty street-ballad about the defeat in battle of the Doge-Admiral, who is compelled, albeit in disguise, to listen.

ROBINSON CRUSOÉ

Opéra comique in three acts, libretto by Cormon and Crémieux; Opéra-Comique, 1867. *Crusoé* (in the French version of the English name) was the second of Offenbach's five assaults on the Paris Opéra-Comique (the fifth, *Les Contes d'Hoffmann*, was posthumous). It was neither a failure nor enough of a success to establish him there – the question of his repeated storming of that citadel is too complicated to go into here. It was not, of course, a case of insufficient talent, but of the nature of Offenbach's talent and of the way he used it. *Robinson Crusoé* is a rich but inconsistent score. The impression given by recent British revivals was that the main inconsistency lay in the difference between the domestic first act set – in an eighteenth-century Bristol interior – and the two remaining acts on the tropical island, but it goes deeper than this. The blend of almost *durchkomponiert* romantic opera with operetta style is spread over the three acts, and the mixture won't settle down – one example is the Act 2 finale culminating in Edwige's waltz song at the moment when she is about to be sacrificed by the cannibals. It doesn't make quite the right kind of nonsense.

The Opera Rara complete recording uses the autograph score, tracked down to the collection of one of the composer's numerous great-grandsons. Some music omitted in the Camden Festival and London Opera Studio revivals (also in the 1980 Prom performance on which the recording is based) has been restored. The practice of making opera recordings as full as possible is an admirable one, but I am not so sure about operetta, where a strong theatrical effect is desirable under any circumstances. I can't help feeling that Offenbach, with his passion for *bedides goupures*, would have been aghast. The pleasure given by the performance, in Don White's bright-as-a-button and often extremely ingenious translation, is, however, only slightly diminished. John Brecknock's easy, candid singing disguises the difficulty of much of the title role, but he suggests the do-it-yourself castaway more convincingly than the eager dreamer of the first act. Yvonne Kenny's voice records beautifully, and she manages Edwige's coloratura with disarming ease. Marilyn Hill Smith and Alexander Oliver as the second couple, Suzanne and Toby, have the style absolutely right. Sandra Browne with her full-bodied mezzo is there as Man Friday to remind us of her Camden Festival debut. Alan Opie – a good singer – unfortunately deprives Jim Cocks, the Bristol boy turned cannibal cook, of his West Country accent. The RPO under Alun Francis reflects Offenbach's heady enjoyment of a larger orchestra than he normally wrote for.

Sutherland starts the first side of her 'Romantic French Arias' (SET 454–5) with Edwige's waltz song 'Conduisez-moi à celui que j'adore', luxuriously sung but missing the glint of burlesque.

LA VIE PARISIENNE

Pièce mêlée de chants in four acts, libretto by Meilhac and Halévy; Palais-Royal, 1866. The description 'play mixed with songs' reflects the origin of *La Vie parisienne*. Plunkett, director of the Palais-Royal, a small theatre specializing in light comedy and farce, asked Offenbach for an operetta for his company – beauties and drolls of great talent and expertise without a decent singing voice among them. Offenbach made a counter-stipulation, that he should be allowed to import one singer – his favourite Zulma Bouffar – for Gabrielle the glove-seller, who has more music than the other female leads. The libretto of this unusual and remarkable work deals not with the imaginary past but the actual here and now – Paris in 1866 on the eve of the Exposition Universelle, the new capital of the town-planner Haussmann, regarded by over-excited visitors as one vast paradise of pleasure. This was the beginning of the creaking but still not quite extinct legend of 'Gay Paree' which reached a climax at the turn of the century.

For the imbroglio (the libretto is more than the ramshackle piece of work it can be made out to appear) Offenbach wrote a nervous, crackling, airborne score that hardly seems to touch the ground. Even memorable tunes like the Baron's 'Votre habit a craqué dans le dos' and Métella's waltz-rondeau are the kind which can be touched on by actors' voices with the aid of discreet orchestral doubling. The light-footedness perfectly suits the atmosphere of masquerade: the impecunious men-about-town, Gardefeu and Bobinet, pass themselves off as guides, Gardefeu passes off his quarters as an annexe of the Grand Hotel, Bobinet passes off his absent aunt's mansion as his own, tradespeople and servants dress up as Second Empire notables with absurd names. The Swedish Baron, for whose benefit most of the deception is practised, is not taken in. If the illusion is so enjoyable, why complain? In the end he is restored to his wife, who has amused herself in her quiet way, by the courtesan Métella who wants her ex-lover Gardefeu back.

Plasson's French EMI recording with the company of the Capitole, Toulouse, is less good than his *Grande Duchesse* and still less good than his *Orphée aux enfers*. The fault lies not so much with the performance (though the energetic, snappy Plasson is not the most light-handed of conductors, and there is a major error of casting) as in the swimming-bath acoustics, coarsening the sound, leading to bad balance with plonking basses. Behind the boom and wish-wash one can detect some excellent shaping, in the third act finale, for example. As Gabrielle, Mady Mesplé is once again thin, but also agile and stylish. Crespin on the other hand is too much for Métella. Here, as in her other Offenbach recordings, she shows complete understanding of the role and her spoken dialogue is a treat to hear – but her way with the vocal lines suggests something like a double-decker bus in a country lane.

Excerpts include a memento of the Barrault-Renaud centenary production mounted in 1966 at the Palais-Royal (and revived at the Odéon with some cast changes). Not so much excerpts as a 'potted' version, with the essentials of the plot and a great deal of style and atmosphere. Here was a drama company with as little experience of singing as Plunkett's (but with rather a different repertory) performing on the intimate scale originally envisaged. The result, at the Odéon at least (I did not see the other), was a revelation: high spirits, absurdity, mockery, mounting hilarity – far more intoxicating than the efforts of opera companies in this piece. The record captures some of this in spite of its age. Madeleine Renaud's frail-toned Baroness is unmistakable, the Gardefeu and Bobinet of Jean Desailly and Jean-Pierre Granval entirely remove those characters from the taint (which they invite) of musical comedy *jeunes premiers*. By the time he reaches 'Il est gris' in the third act finale, Pierre Bertin's Baron begins to give some idea of his extraordinary performance on the stage: this versatile actor was also a gifted musician, formerly associated with Satie and Les Six. The Gabrielle, Simone Valère, belonged to the company; the import in this case was Suzy Delair, who gives Métella's songs with a delicious hint of gurgle.

The Vox excerpts (definitely excerpts, with only one of Métella's songs) are well cast and well conducted, with the peculiarity that all the women tend to sound alike. The Brazilian and bootmaker Frick of Willy Clément have gorgeously extravagant accents. The Sadler's Wells record is sound but decorous, with so little sense of frenzy that they might be singing the praises of Bournemouth. The best things are the duet for the Baron (Eric Shilling) and the disguised lady's maid Pauline (Cynthia Morey), smooth as Sullivan, suited to the English style, and the solo for the Baroness (Anna Pollak) rescued from the original fourth act jettisoned soon after the first performance, when the original five acts were reduced to four – it was also included in the revival at the Théâtre Musical de Paris (Chatelet) in 1980.

Among the miscellaneous singles there are interesting relics of a spectacular production at the Théâtre Mogador in 1931, which by chance I saw as a schoolboy on the first evening of my first visit to Paris. Félix Oudart (Col. DF 483) gives the Brazilian's solo 'Je suis Brésilien, j'ai de l'or' with a great charge of energy and backs it with the Couplets 'Pour découper adroitment' sung by the bogus major-domo. The gem, however, is Col. DF 482, containing Métella's two rondeaux sung by Danielle Brégis. The voice, though the soft top Gs slip out like pearls, is not especially attractive, and the first impression may be of extreme rhythmic licence. But listen again and you find that the singer (ably supported by the conductor, Diot) knows very well what she is about. Métella is not the star part, but her two solos can steal the show if they are done as well as this. Brégis builds them up with detailed care, using occasional discreet drops into *parlando*. They emerge as miniature dramas about two important aspects of Paris in those days: in the Letter Song, the nostalgia of the returned traveller; in the waltz, with strange, hollow instrumental doublings above and below the voice, the fun of being there, hangovers and all, with ambiguous greetings from the early streetworkers to returning revellers. I wish I could truthfully say that I remember Brégis after fifty years, but the only detail that stands out distinctly among the general whirl is a memory of Max Dearly (the Baron, also the producer of the show) crawling under a crinoline.

Gabrielle's 'Glove rondo' from Act 2 and an excerpt from the Act 3 finale are well done on Odéon 238.381 by H. Régelly, Henry-Laverne and Oudart again with the same Mogador orchestra and conductor. Gabrielle's 'Je suis veuve d'un colonel' (disguised in black veils for the bogus table d'hôte) comes from Tariol-Baugé on the Rubini Offenbach Centenary disc, also from Mireille Berthon, with an air of engaging dottiness (HMV K-6126). On the reverse, the same singer's 'Frou-frou' song from Act 3 is too acid for comfort. On HMV K-6127 Emile Rousseau's cynical head-waiter's couplets 'Avant toute chose' and the Baron's Act 2 couplets are spoiled by poor recording. One of the less frequently recorded numbers, Bobinet's 'Elles sont tristes les marquises', is well done by the comedian Dréan on Pathé X. 91008. The reverse, with Bernadette Delprat (a visitor to Covent Garden during the Beecham régime) singing Métella's Letter Song, is uninteresting. *La Vie parisienne* is scantily represented in modern recitals: Rhodes's account in her

EMI Offenbach disc of Métella's songs supports the view that big singers are wise to leave this role alone.

TRIPLE BILL

POMME D'API
Opérette in one act, libretto by Halévy and Busnacht; Renaissance, 1873.

MONSIEUR CHOUFLEURI RESTERA CHEZ LUI LE . . .
Opéra bouffe in one act, libretto by St Rémy, Halévy, Crémieux and Lépine; Bouffes Parisiens, 1861. (see also p.169).

MESDAMES DE LA HALLE
Opérette bouffe in one act, libretto by Lapointe; Bouffes Parisiens, 1858.

These three one-acters were performed together, under the general title 'Vive Offenbach!', at the Opéra-Comique in December 1979. They were revived the following season and again in 1983. The entertainment, produced by Robert Dhéry, designed by Bernard Daydé and conducted by Manuel Rosenthal (an experienced Offenbachian, responsible many years ago for arranging the Massine ballet *Gaîté parisienne*) was one of the foremost successes of the Offenbach centenary year, 1980. There is no connection between the three works, but since the three French EMI records are sold together in an album, it may be less confusing to treat them together. An apparent, but unreal, unity of time and place was contrived by setting all three operettas in or near Les Halles markets and by implying that the date was 1873 – the year of the first performance of *Pomme d'api*. *Monsieur Choufleuri*, however, is a satire on the *bourgeois gentilhommes* not of the Third Republic but of the time of Louis-Philippe – the full title continues *restera chez lui le 24 janvier 1833*. The inference that Sontag, Rubini and Tamburini were still active in 1873 adds a new and unhelpful twist of fantasy – Tamburini was over seventy, the others were dead. In the theatre, with the fun fast and furious, there was little time or inclination to worry.

   Mesdames de la Halle, a romp about three brawny market women past their best but still game for love, a drum-major, a pretty young fruit-seller and a kitchen-boy, richly deserves revival (it has not been altogether neglected – Rouché, the future director of the Opéra, presented it as part of another triple bill, at the Théâtre des Arts in 1913, with Rameau's *Pygmalion* and the first performance of Roussel's *Le Festin de l'araignée*). Freed from restrictions on numbers, with a large cast and a chorus at his disposal, Offenbach is flexing his muscles. *Orphée aux enfers* is only months away, but *Mesdames de la Halle* has a rougher vitality with streaks of melancholy possibly recalling the Jewish strains of the composer's childhood. The recorded version of the final scene is, I think, different from the one performed at the 1980 revival.

   The slight but charming *Pomme d'api* has recently had more success than any other of Offenbach's post-1870 works except *Hoffmann*. This domestic trifle deserves a recording; it concerns a Pasquale-type bachelor, Rabastens, who likes his servant-girls young and changes them often, unwittingly engages Catherine, the mistress of his own nephew, gives the couple his blessing and a dowry. (Pomme d'api, or 'lady-apple', is the girl's nickname.)

Once again the conductor is Manuel Rosenthal, this time with the Orchestre Philharmonique de Monte-Carlo (where the recording was made). Many of the cast are the same as in Paris. One important change brings Mady Mesplé to the three soprano roles. Very good she is, limpid and agile, with little of the glassiness that marred some of her previous records and has dogged French high sopranos throughout recording history. The lyric tenor Léonard Pezzino is so accomplished that one may overlook the fact that nephew Gustave in *Pomme d'api* and kitchen-boy Croûte-au-pot in *Mesdames de la Halle* are really *travesti* roles. Charles Burles gives excellent *buffo* tenor performances as the aspiring composer (and pseudo-Rubini) Babylas in *Choufleuri* and as drum-major Raflafla in *Mesdames de la Halle*. The market ladies, Mesdames Poiretapée, Madou and Beurrefondu, are taken respectively by Michel Hamel, Michel Trempont and Jean-Philippe Lafont with pantomime-dame broadness but real singing. Hamel and Trempont (hilarious in *Choufleuri* as Petermann, a Belgian servant masquerading as English butler) have been mentioned several times in these notes. Lafont, a vigorous and resourceful baritone, heard here in all three operas, is less well known on records.

These able artists, under Rosenthal's firm and purposeful direction, know how to give the operatic burlesques their point – the sudden swerve in *Choufleuri* into *Robert le diable* melodramatics before the guests arrive and the riotous *trio italien* at the party, wicked ensembles in *Mesdames de la Halle* flicked with screaming Meyerbeerian piccolos. The edge cuts sharp but the tone stays light. Clear recording, not too many sound effects. The cast speak their own dialogue. Librettos provided, with English translation.

A handful of short works recorded with varying degrees of success under the Bourg label demand brief mention on the grounds of unfamiliarity. The least unfamiliar is *Les Deux Aveugles* (*bouffonnerie musicale* in one act, libretto by Moinaux; Bouffes-Parisiens, 1855). This sardonic sketch about two bogus 'blind' beggars, one with a trombone, the other with guitar or mandoline, who accidentally choose the same pitch on one of the bridges over the Seine in Paris, was the success of the opening night of the original, tiny Bouffes in the Champs-Elysées. In spite of its brevity, the piece has a rough vitality which has kept it in the repertory. The 'arrangement' by the conductor of the recording, Louis-Vincent Bruère, dispenses with a trombone. The singers, Régis Ducrocq and Gilles Butin, are willing but too youthful-sounding to capture the grotesque, slightly sinister undertones. The coupling indicates Offenbach's already wide range – *Le Violoneux* (*opérette* in one act, libretto by Mestépès and Chevalet; Bouffes-Parisiens, 1855), which came later during the same season, is a sentimental anecdote about a village fiddler. Schneider made her Parisian début as Reinette. Christophe Mortagne as the Fiddler, Mathieu, sounds younger than his prospective son-in-law, Pierre (Gilles Butin). Marie Modeste sings Reinette, the conductor and arranger is Louis-Vincent Bruère. Librettos are provided for both works, but, with no dialogue recorded, the effect is meagre.

Croquefer ou le dernier des Paladins (*opérette bouffe* in one act, libretto by Jaime fils and Tréfeu; Bouffes-Parisiens, 1857) was written for the new, more central Bouffes by the Passage Choiseul. Offenbach was chafing under official restrictions confining him to one-acters with four characters. To the cast of this mad burlesque about Crusader Ironcrunch ('without Faith or Decency') he added a fifth role for a dumb Knight who shrieked or groaned and held out placards but did not speak or sing. There is some wild grand opera parody, with raids on Rossini and Meyerbeer among others. As done here, with libretto provided but only scraps of dialogue recorded and a minimal orchestra (conductor and arranger Louis-Vincent Bruère), *Croquefer* hardly stands a chance. The singers are Jean Kriff (Croquefer), Jean de Beer (Boutefer, his equerry), Régis Wilem (Ramass'-ta-tête, his nephew), Chantal Reyjal (Princesse Fleur-de-soufre).

At least in the early days, Offenbach's one-acters were produced under ramshackle circumstances quite likely to endanger the survival of the original material. But details of the original scoring, where known, and of publication, would be welcome. A serious study of Offenbach, as composer, not merely as symbol of the Second Empire, is overdue. This does not mean that these engaging and diverse short works need be treated as sacrosanct – the most enjoyable of this bunch of recordings is the one which presumably departs furthest from the original, an 'arrangement and orchestration' for synthesizers by Stéphane Gasparini of *La Leçon de chant électro-magnétique* (*bouffonnerie musicale* in one act, libretto by E. Bourget, Kursaal, Bad Ems, 1867; Folies-Marigny 1873). The subject – an Italian singing teacher turning a thick-eared Normandy peasant into an operatic tenor by electromagnetic means – lends itself to the disembodied chortlings and swishings of synthesizers. Many may find them preferable to the unimpressive live accompaniments for the three works discussed above. Jacomo Zanetti and Jean Kriff sing the teacher, Pacifico Toccato, and pupil, Jean Matois. On the reverse the accompaniments are repeated without voices, to encourage listeners to have a go themselves. Since Offenbach poured some of his most beguiling Italianate and French-pastoral inventions into the four numbers, one can only suppose that there are more good amateur singers among record buffs than one had imagined.

All-Offenbach reissues on LP and modern all-Offenbach recitals:

'OFFENBACH CENTENARY', RUBINI LIMITED EDITION, GV 600

Side One – Anna Tariol-Baugé

1	*La Chanson de Fortunio* – Si vous croyez		G.C. 33811
2	*Les Brigands* – Couplets de Fiorella		33814
3	*La Vie Parisienne* – Je suis veuve		33815
4	*La Grande Duchesse* – Ah! Que j'aime les militaires!		33817
5	*La Grande Duchesse* – Dites-lui		33808
6	*La Périchole* – Duo de l'espagnol et la jeune indienne (with Dambrine)		34253
7	*La Périchole* – Tu n'es pas beau		33837
8	*La Fille du Tambour Major* – Chanson de la fille	Zono	X-83090
9	*La Belle Hélène* – Amours divins		X-83231

Side Two – Juliette Simon-Girard

1	*Barbe-bleue* – Couplets de la rosière	G.C. 33809
2	*La Belle Hélène* – Amours divins	33309
3	*Madame Favart* – Ronde des vignes (CR)	33310
4	*La Jolie Parfumeuse* – La Famille Bruscambrille	33327
5	*La Périchole* – Air de la lettre	33372
6	*La Périchole* – Couplets de l'aveu	33373
7	*La Grande Duchesse* – Légende du verre	33374
8	*La Grande Duchesse* – Dites-lui	33375

'TALES OF OFFENBACH' – VOL. 1, CLUB 99–110

Side A

1	*La Boulangère a des écus* – Charbonniers et fariniers. Que voulez-vous faire? (Reynaldo Hahn)	Col. D 2022
2	*La Belle Hélène* – Au Mont Ida (Swedish) (Jussi Björling)	HMV X 6090
3	*La Belle Hélène* – Amours divins (Mireille Berthon)	Disque W 973
4	*La Belle Hélène* – Dis-moi Vénus (Mireille Berthon)	Disque W 973
5	*La Belle Hélène* – Shepherd's song (English) (Heddle Nash)	Col. DB 815
*6	*La Belle Hélène* – Ce n'est qu'un rêve (Demoulin and Berthaud)	14" Pathe 2334 (1909–11)
7	*La Belle Hélène* – Tyrolienne (Louis Arnoult)	Ultra AP 224
8	*La Grande Duchesse de Gerolstein* – Pif! Paf! Pouf! (Louis Musy)	Pathé PD 85
9	*La Grande Duchesse de Gerolstein* – Voici le sabre (Geneviève Vix)	Pathé X 0669
10	*La Grande Duchesse de Gerolstein* – Dites-lui (Yvonne Printemps)	HMV E 550

Side B

*1	*Barbe-bleue* – Legende (German) (Carl Meister)	G&T 042100 (1906)
2	*Madame Favart* – Ma mère aux vignes m'envoyit (Germaine Corney)	Poly. 522581
*3	*La Fille du Tambour Major* – Tout en tirant (Albert Vaguet)	Pathé 0231
*4	*La Fille du Tambour Major* – Chanson de la fille (Edmée Favart)	Pathé 0984

5	*La Périchole* – Air de la lettre (Germaine Corney)	Poly. 52281
6	*La Périchole* – Ah! Quel dîner (Russian) (C. Novikova)	USSR 6300
7	*La Périchole* – Tu n'es pas beau (Maggie Teyte)	Decca K 993
*8	*La Périchole* – Séguedille (Demoulin and Berthaud)	Pathé 2341
*9	*La bella profumiera* (La Jolie Parfumeuse) – Canzone Bruscanville (anonymous soprano and baritone)	Pathé 82212
10	*Rheinnixen* – Barcarolle (Jarmila Novotna)	Vic. 11–9263

* Acoustic, pre 1925.

'JACQUES OFFENBACH – AIRS CÉLÈBRES', EMI PATHÉ MARCONI, 2C 069–16386

Jane Rhodes/Orchestre de Bordeaux Aquitaine, Ensemble vocal Eliane Lavail/Benzi

Side One

1 *La Périchole* –
   a. Ah! Quel dîner
   b. O mon cher amant
   c. Ah! que les hommes sont bêtes
   d. Tu n'es pas beau
2 *Barbe-bleue* –
   a. Couplets de Boulotte (Y'a des bergers)
   b. Couplets de la rosière (V'la z'encor)
3 *La Vie Parisienne* –
   a. Rondeau de la lettre
   b. Rondeau de Métella

Side Two

1 *La Grande Duchesse* –
   a. Légende du verre
   b. Ah! Que j'aime les militaires
   c. Voici le sabre de mon père
   d. Dites-lui
2 *La Belle Hélène* –
   a. Choeur des jeunes filles
   b. Amours divins
   c. Dis-moi Vénus

Mefistofele

JOHN HIGGINS

It is an open question whether Arrigo Boito, some sixty years after his death, is now better remembered as Verdi's librettist for *Otello* and *Falstaff* or as the composer of *Mefistofele,* for which of course he also provided his own words. Or put it in a different way: was Boito's contribution to opera greater as a supplier of poetry or of music?

Cambridge University supplied its answer in 1893 when it awarded Boito an honorary doctorate of music. But posterity might well disagree. His posthumous opera *Nerone,* staged at La Scala in 1924 with Pertile in the title role, is now all but forgotten, although it has recently been recorded. *Mefistofele,* his masterpiece, is rarely given a hearing outside Italy nowadays. It is one of those operas which comes up regularly when the future repertory is being discussed, but when the final plans are made and the contracts are being drawn up then it is dropped by the wayside in favour of something safer. Its well-chronicled weaknesses are brought up once more: the sprawl of the action from heaven to Frankfurt on to Ancient Greece and back to heaven again; the lack of dramatic cohesion; the mighty choral demands; the pallid characterization of Margherita. And so *Mefistofele* goes back on the shelf again and with it the chance of hearing Faust's farewell to life, 'Giunto sul passo estremo', and Boito's majestic depiction of the struggle between good and evil. The last major performances in London were at the Royal Festival Hall. One was in May 1972, a visually unsatisfactory affair where a number of red spotlights were used to suggest the powers of Old Nick but only succeeded in giving the evening the atmosphere of a pantomime at the village hall. Vocally matters were much better. José Carreras at the beginning of his international career was Faust and he managed to suggest why Gigli chose this role to make his Met debut in 1920; another fifteen years passed before Gigli decided to tackle Gounod's version. Carol Neblett made her British debut as Margherita. And Cesare Siepi, who had claimed the part of Boito's Devil for his own in Italy, sang the title role. The second was in March 1974 when Norman Treigle sang Satan.

The Welsh National Opera had *Mefistofele* in its repertory in the late fifties and brought it to Sadler's Wells in 1957, but otherwise the best chance of catching the opera outside Italy was to go to the City Opera in New York, where in 1969 it was mounted in a flashy production chiefly for the benefit of Treigle with Julius Rudel conducting; New York had its first sight of the work in 40 years. Treigle went on to sing Mefistofele all over America, frequently with Rudel conducting, and the two men recorded it for EMI in 1974.

The record companies have been almost as wary as the opera houses of backing *Mefistofele*. Fifteen years separated this EMI issue, which was clearly aimed at the American market in general and the Treigle supporters' club in particular, from the first complete recording made by Decca. The problem with *Mefistofele* is that it promises far more than it achieves. The Prologue in heaven is truly cosmic music, a kind of operatic *Star Wars,* with Evil, in the shape of Mefistofele, throwing down the gauntlet to God and Good. It shows Boito as the arch-Romantic, not only in the literary sense, but as a composer demanding almost Mahlerian forces, cherubim and seraphim, to say nothing of the hosts in heaven and the Tannhäuser-style penitents on earth. It comes as no surprise that this was one of Toscanini's favourite pieces, which he used in his one postwar appearance at La Scala. He also recorded the Prologue for RCA with the NBC Symphony Orchestra, the Robert Shaw Chorale, the Columbus Boychoir [sic] and Nicola Moscona as Mefistofele. The sound quality is dismal and the Robert Shaw Chorale's command of Italian distinctly shaky. It scarcely gives much impression of the Toscanini approach to Boito and indeed seems to be little more than a fill-up to Act 3 of *Rigoletto* on side one, one of the gramophone catalogue's more bizarre couplings.

It was this Prologue which got such applause as was going at the première of *Mefistofele* at La Scala in March 1868. Thereafter the performance degenerated into a battle of noise between the new and the old guard, with the latter, led by the professors of the Milan Conservatoire, having considerably the better of things. The whistles in the theatre were certainly not all coming from Mephistopheles himself, and the comments in the press afterwards did not exactly apply salve to the wounds. 'Not poetry, but dirt.' 'Why attempt to create a giant of an opera with the resources of a pygmy?' The *Gazzeta Musicale* rather more politely advised Boito to go back to being a poet and to stop writing works for the stage. Boito declined the invitation, rewrote and shortened *Mefistofele* and when it was performed in Bologna in 1875 in the version we know today it was a great success.

At the time of the Scala première Boito was known principally as a poet. He was only twenty-six, 'a thin, blond, distinguished looking youth', according to his biographer Corrado Ricci*. And it was almost certainly his literary involvement which made him tackle both parts of Goethe's *Faust* instead of taking only the first section, as Gounod's librettists, Barbier and Carré, had done nine years earlier. Boito generally gets credit for his wide vision, for doing greater justice to Goethe, for devoting himself far more to

* *Arrigo Boito,* Corrado Ricci, Fratelli Treves, 1919.

the eternal struggle between good and evil while Gounod contents himself basically with the love story of Faust and Marguérite, but his ambition, the young man's zeal to conquer mountains, is at the same time his undoing.

When *Mefistofele* wanders off into *Faust II* in its fourth act it loses direction. The Devil takes Faust to the Vale of Tempe for a sight of Helen of Troy much in the same way that another Mephistopheles, Nick Shadow, in *The Rake's Progress,* condemns poor Tom Rakewell to madness and his vision of Venus in Bedlam. But where Stravinsky's writing is taut and ironic that of Boito is soft and repetitive: the listener longs to get on to the Epilogue, which is as effective as the mighty Prologue. The Vale of Tempe Act also poses the problem of whether to cast a second soprano as Elena (Helen) or whether to treat her as another facet of Margherita. All three complete recordings use different sopranos, although in that Royal Festival Hall concert performance Carol Neblett took both roles with ease after the indisposition of the scheduled Elena. The music of the fourth act is never included in selections of highlights from the opera, and it could possibly be considered optional in a stage performance, in much the same way as the Walpurgisnacht Ballet in Gounod's *Faust.* George Bernard Shaw did not much like Boito's version of the earlier Brocken Scene either, dubbing much of it as 'ingenious tiddy-fol-lol'. But then he dismissed Boito himself as 'an accomplished literary man without original musical gifts' – so much for that Cambridge doctorate – and went on to say that 'Gounod has set music to *Faust,* Boito has set *Faust* to music'.

Corno di Bassetto was always one for a flip sentence, an attention-grabbing paradox, but there is somewhat less to this epigram than meets the eye. Boito did try to compose a mighty romantic opera, which reflected as truly as possible Goethe's play. He did not always succeed, but he was totally serious in his aims. Anyone performing *Mefistofele* on record or on stage has to be equally serious. It is for this reason that I prefer Decca's set of the two earlier complete recordings. It has the twin advantages of Cesare Siepi, still close to his prime, in the title role and Tullio Serafin, vigorous and commanding despite his years, in charge of the Santa Cecilia.

Siepi is the most powerful of Devil's advocates because of his suavity, his total relish for the part. He may end a loser, but he certainly starts off a winner, sure that he will gain his wager with the Almighty. He is the very spirit of negation, confident of being a superman like that other Mephistophelean character Siepi also played so well, Don Giovanni. There is the vigour there, total security of voice, plus the refusal ever to consider being a pantomime devil.

Serafin's conducting is never flashy. It is possible to accuse him of being a little too restrained in the Prologue: this may be in part attributable to the age of the recording (1959), but I suspect that it is more a matter of the conductor's own temperament. There is consistent evidence of his enjoyment of the lyric moments of the score, Faust's 'Dai campi', a Victorian drawing room favourite, or the almost Donizettian lightness of the Garden Scene.

He understands the architecture of the opera, so that the climax, with Faust's 'Giunto sul passo estremo', is at the same time a farewell to life and a hymn to the future of humanity. Serafin receives only modest support from the Santa Cecilia Chorus, but the Orchestra gives him everything.

For Faust and Margherita, Decca employed for their first set their regular tenor/soprano team of the time, Mario del Monaco and Renata Tebaldi, although they began with Giuseppe di Stefano, on whose own Faust some comment later. It has been suggested that Boito drew on his own *Mefistofele* when he was creating the character of Iago for Verdi. Del Monaco's performance implies that he might also have had Faust in mind when he was sketching Otello. Del Monaco is at his best in the second half of the opera, whether dreaming of a future far, far away with Margherita, 'Lontano, lontano', much as Cavaradossi and Tosca look forward to their unfettered future in the last act of Puccini's opera, or in 'Giunto sul passo', which here Del Monaco turns into Faust's finest hour in the way that Otello aspires to the heights in 'Niun mi tema'. Earlier he is much more warrior than philosopher and 'Dai campi' is unfeeling and too loud.

Margherita really only comes into her own at the point of death. Here Renata Tebaldi confounds those critics who claimed that she made each role sound the same in her phrasing of Margherita's eerie dream of the murder of her unborn child, 'L'altra notte'. Tebaldi's principal rival, Maria Callas, made the definitive recording of this aria, again under Serafin's expert guidance (ALP 3824), but Tebaldi is by no means disgraced by the comparison. It is also worth noting the contribution of Floriana Cavalli, who only had a brief recording career, as Elena.

The sound of the 1959 set is somewhat tinny by contemporary standards: it has plenty of brightness but not much depth. There is a bad fade towards the end of Mefistofele's 'Ecco il mondo', which was tidied up when Decca reissued the recording on the Ace of Diamonds label, which all in all is a good deal more pleasing to the ears than the original mono discs.

The other great quality of this *Mefistofele* set is that it employs a one hundred per cent Italian cast. Boito's opera is as Italian as Gounod's version is French, possibly another reason why it travels so rarely outside its native land. EMI's set has only one Italian, Josella Ligi in the small part of Elena, and looks instead to America for its Mefistofele (Norman Treigle) and to Spain for the Faust and Margherita (Placido Domingo and Montserrat Caballé). Domingo and Caballé have never had any trouble with their Italian, but Treigle often sounds unidiomatic and it is very much on personal reaction to him that approval or disapproval of the EMI issue depends. I confess to never having been a Treigle admirer and a return to this set makes neither the heart nor the mind grow fonder. Treigle's Devil is a capering, self-centered fellow, up to all sorts of tricks, but also lacking the authority to make him a worthwhile adversary. In an interview Treigle once said that he made the most of the beginning of the opera because Mefistofele ends by losing. He does indeed make the most of the first three sides – and most is much too much. Here is the pantomime demon rather than Beelzebub, crafty in manner and red in claw. The whole performance sounds crude beside the refinement of the rest of the cast and in particular the Faust of Domingo, a model of lyricism in 'Dai campi' which forces one's mind back to the way that Gigli used to handle this aria. Caballé turns 'L'altra notte' into a concert aria, beautiful but chill although she combines admirably with Domingo in the subsequent duet. Among the rest of the cast it is worth noting Thomas Allen's contribution as Wagner, a role normally assigned to a tenor.

EMI's main plus over the first Decca comes in the matter of sound. It is superbly recorded so that the music of the spheres, to say nothing of cherubim and seraphim (Wandsworth School Choir) can have their full effect. Rudel, who often comes across cold and authoritarian on record, here gives one of his very best performances with the LSO.

With the advent of the set issued in 1984, there was at last a chance to hear Ghiaurov take the title role in an official recording of *Mefistofele*. Once again it was Decca championing Boito's opera in a version which was started back in 1981, but which for reasons the record industry prefers to describe as 'technical' had been long held up. There was absolutely no need for Decca to be bashful, for the latest of their attempts at Boito also happens to be the most satisfying of the complete *Mefistofeles*. Ghiaurov himself, alas, is not the prime reason for this judgement. His qualities and faults remain those of the earlier highlights issue (see below). The command is there, especially towards the end as Mefistofele sucks Faust into his power. But the interpretation remains ponderous and Ghiaurov lacks the sophistication which has to be part of any respectable Devil's make-up. In the duet with Faust, 'Fin da stanotte', which should go with a gallop as both men whiff the pleasures ahead, Mephistopheles sounds a bit like a willing cart-horse.

Such strictures cannot be made about the other principals. Luciano Pavarotti's Faust is among the most winning of his recent characterizations on disc. The voice is resonant and lyrical, with 'Dai campi, dai prati' sung with a reflective grace that defeated Del Monaco. There are one or two notes that should have been corrected in the last act as Faust contemplates Elena (Montserrat Caballé switches from Margherita on EMI to take this minor role for Decca) in 'Forma ideal'. But throughout Pavarotti responds to the wistfulness of the part and the pure Italian quality of Boito's vocal writing could scarcely suit him better.

Decca have also chosen their Margherita wisely. Mirella Freni is at the point in her career where she can still shade her voice to be the shy village girl of the Garden Scene ('la fanciulla del vilaggio') and yet carry the weight and darkness of timbre for 'L'altra notte'. Boito's Margherita has vocally something in common with Puccini's Manon Lescaut in its range of requirements, and Miss Freni is one of the few international sopranos around who can answer them.

There are one or two weaknesses in the supporting roles (the Wagner is one of them), but none at all in the orchestra and the spaciousness of Decca's recording. Indeed, one of the most powerful reasons for acquiring this set is the authority the veteran conductor Oliviero de Fabritiis extends over each and every moment with the National Philharmonic. De Fabritiis exaggerates nothing, but he always responds to the lyricism of the writing. It is a very Italian reaction of a very Italian conductor, who was insufficiently recognized outside his own country. It was the last opera he recorded before his death and Decca very properly dedicated this *Mefistofele* to his memory. It is a most proper monument.

The only other *Mefistofele* set I have found is from a 'private', live performance on 6 October 1965. No mention is made of the orchestra, the chorus or the opera house in question. However, the presence of Nino Sanzogno would suggest that a rummage through the archives of the major Italian opera theatres to see who was playing what on that date would soon solve the mystery. The recording has all the usual defects of live performance records: indifferent sound, a lot of thumping on stage and audience applause for non-musical events. The cast is strong: Tebaldi and Elena Suliotis as Margherita and Elena respectively, Ghiaurov as a gruff-sounding and not particularly winning Devil. The quality of the set rests mainly on the splendid Faust of Alfredo Kraus. His account of the first-act aria is a model of its kind, despite the very slow tempi chosen. Sanzogno's school orchestra also shows up reasonably well. The great pity is that no record company thought of enticing Kraus into the studio for a proper recording. I have not heard the oddly cast Cetra live set of 1958 nor the 1952 briefly available Nixa version.

Mefistofele, with its mixture of melodic peaks and uninspired deserts, should be a natural work for extracts. Decca, who seem to have more partiality for this opera than any other company, have produced two records of highlights, one featuring the Faust (Di Stefano) and the other the Mefistofele (Ghiaurov); poor Margherita is cast to one side. The Di Stefano disc is clearly a spin-off from what was recorded by Decca before he was replaced by Del Monaco. The forces are identical: Siepi, Tebaldi, Serafin and the Santa Cecilia Orchestra. The only surprises are that Di Stefano was removed, because his Faust reflects the change from the sweet lyricism of the opening to the sombre pathos of the close, and that the record was not issued in Britain until 1973. Six years earlier Ghiaurov was the Devil in a record which was never intended to be part of a complete set: a heavyweight, commanding interpretation, weak on Italian and low on charm. Franco Tagliavini sings such of Faust's music as is left and Margherita is cut out altogether. Silvio Varviso and the Rome Opera do not make much of a mark and it is no surprise that the sleeve features a close-up of Ghiaurov in devilish make-up.

Ghiaurov is heard again in the exciting Prologue recorded by DG with Bernstein as conductor. The Prologue conducted by Robert Shaw, also for DG can be safely ignored.

Individual arias from the opera have been recorded since the invention of the gramophone, particularly by tenors. Among the best of those are 'Dai campi' and 'Giunto' made by Giuseppe Anselmi (Fono. 62282–3; CO 359) and Caruso. Anselmi allows himself to stretch Boito's vocal line to its utmost, but all is forgiven when he produces such eloquent sounds and ones which are so faithful to the spirit of the text, in particular the close of the final aria, which suggests Otello near the end of his life just as Del Monaco was to do fifty years later. Caruso makes a false start on the earlier of his 1902 discs of 'Dai campi' (52348; HLM 7030) but quickly atones for it – another marvellous record. The November 1902 version (DA 550) has no mistake, but is less ardent. The 'Giunto' of the earlier session (DA 550; HLM 7030) catches the weariness of Faust's meditation.

John McCormack recorded both these tenor arias in 1912 (DA 498; GEMM 156). His interpretations, if that is the right word, are exactly as expected: exquisite tones, especially in 'Giunto sul passo estremo', coupled with touches of laziness and exhibitionism. McCormack is more interested in McCormack than in Faust. Gigli made several recordings, reflecting his love of the role. There is not much to choose between the sensuous quality of the 1918 (7–52110, 7–52112; RLS 7710) and 1921 (DA 222; GEMM 202) performances. Lauri-Volpi on Fonotipia shows how a heavier tenor deals with 'Giunto sul passo estremo'. The voice is admirably weighted and always secure, but the lack of colour drains all the emotion from this most touching of arias. Giovanni Zenatello (Fono. 92204–5; GV 27) has similar qualities.

Dimitri Smirnov (DB 582; CO 379) in the same piece is predictably suave, Aureliano Pertile (Col. GQ 7183; OASI 634) typically impulsive, but his early Italian Columbias of both arias, plus 'Lontano' with Rinaldi Pavoni (all reissued on LV 1319) reveal a tenor of much greater delicacy than his reputation leads one to suspect. Pavarotti included the two tenor arias in recital discs, of which the latest is similar to his versions in his complete set.

Among older accounts of 'L'altra notte' the following are worth seeking out: Frances Alda's for its wholehearted quality (DB 635; CO 383), Claudia Muzio's for its heart-rending passion, albeit short-breathed (LCX 25; 3C 053–00932), Geraldine Farrar's for its purity and style (DB 654; CO 315), Magda Olivero's for its desperation and despite aspirated runs (Cetra BB 25049; LPC 55015). The only contemporary soprano to come close to rivalling these is Régine Crespin, a most aristocratic piece of singing, with light, almost weightless phrases, which seem to hover in the air (SDD 313), although Maria Chiara is worth hearing (SXL 6548). Even so, Maria Callas (ALP 3824), as already stated, eclipses all competition. She sang Margherita only three times on stage, but 'L'altra notte' was regularly in her concerts, particularly towards the end of her career, a reflection perhaps of her own unhappiness. In her appreciable version, Scotto (ASD 4022) is a fair facsimile of Callas.

Many famous basses have had a high old time in Mephistopheles's pieces. Most renowned among them was Chaliapin, perhaps caught at his most devilish on the stage at Covent Garden in 1926 under Bellezza's direction (DB 940; DB 942; RLS 710). Some may prefer the more disciplined, equally Satanic Marcel Journet (DA 482; DB 615; GV 562), the voluminous Tancredi

Pasero (Col. DQ 1087, 1085; LV 34), the fiery Adam Didur (Fono. 39537; CO 360), the massive-voiced José Mardones (A5216) or the impressive Nazzareno de Angelis (L 2071; EX 290 1693), also the bass in the old 78rpm set conducted by Lorenzo Molajoli, which the *Record Guide* rightly described as 'acceptable though not distinguished'. Mafalda Favero's Margherita was possibly its most satisfying component. Of more recent basses we need note only Boris Christoff (DB 21047; RLS 725) and, above all, Pinza, supreme as ever (DA 829, 567; GEMM 163).

Gigli was concerned with a couple of duets in the acoustic era, both worth seeking out for his refined 1918 self. They are 'Se tu mi doni un'ora' with Scattola and 'Lontano, lontano' with the feeble-voiced Gemma Bosini (DA 223; DB 271; RLS 729). Ferruccio Tagliavini and his wife Pia Tassinari were well suited to the latter piece (Cetra AT 0185; Everest 3275), but the sweetest, most lyrical version of this lovely page is that by Farrar and Edmond Clément (DB 172; Rococo R40), recorded in 1913. Margherita's third-act solo, 'Spunta l'aurora pallida' has been left by, among others, Burzio (Fono. 62415; Club 99–87/8), Giannina Russ (Fono. 92236; GV 58) – as involving as on all her discs – Bianca Scacciati (Col. DQ 1077; LV 243), Maria Zamboni (Col. DQ 114), and Mafalda Favero (Col. D 6016; Tima – 38), most eloquently.

All these recital discs have one common factor: the arias in every case are sung in the original language, indication, if any more were needed, of how Italian an opera *Mefistofele* is – although it might be as well to note that Agustarello Affre recorded the tenor arias in French on Pathé and Wilhelm Rode 'Ave Signor' in German on Polydor.

MEFISTOFELE

Mef Mefistofele; *F* Faust; *M* Margherita; *Mar* Martha; *W* Wagner; *E* Elena; *P* Pantalis; *N* Nereo

1930 De Angelis *Mef*; Melandri *F*; Favero *M*; Mannarini *Mar*; Nessi *W*; Arangi-Lombardi *E*; Monticone *P*; Venturini *N* / La Scala Chorus and Orch. / Molajoli
EMI ⓜ 3C 153 18413–5M
CBS (US) ⓜ EL9

1952 Neri *Mef*; Poggi *F*; Noli *M*; Ticozzi *Mar*; *P*; Del Signore *W*; *N*; Dall' Argine *E* / Milan Opera Chorus and Orch. / Capuana
Nixa ⓜ ULP 9230
Vox (US) ⓜ OPBX 156

1954 Neri *Mef*; Tagliavini *F*; Pobbe *M*; Ticozzi *Mar*; Benzi *W*; *N*; De Cecco *E*; Gandolfo *P* / Teatro Regio Chorus, Turin; Italian Radio

Orch., Turin / Questa
Cetra ⓜ LPO 2054
Everest ⓔ 409 (3)

1956 (omits Act 4)
Christoff *Mef*; Prandelli *F*; Moscucci *M*; Pini *Mar*; De Palma *W* / Rome Opera Chorus and Orch. / Gui
EMI ⓜ 3C 153 03150–1
RCA (US) ⓜ LM 6049

1958 Siepi *Mef*; Del Monaco *F*; Tebaldi *M*; Danieli *Mar*; *P*; De Palma *W*; *N*; Cavalli *E* / Santa Cecilia Academy Chorus and Orch /
Serafin
Decca GOS 591–3
London OSA 1307

1958 (Live performance – Teatro alla
　　　Scala, Milan)
　　　Siepi *Mef*; Poggi *F*; Broggini *M*;
　　　Cavallari *Mar*; Ricciardi *W*;
　　　Cossotto *P*; Mercuriali *N*; De
　　　Cavalieri *E* / La Scala Chorus and
　　　Orch. / Votto
　　　Cetra ⓜ LO 81 (3)

1974 Treigle *Mef*; Domingo *F*; Caballé
　　　M; Begg *Mar*; Allen *W*; Ligi *E*;
　　　Wallis *P*; Fyson *N* / Ambrosian
　　　Opera Chorus, LSO / Rudel
　　　EMI SLS 973
　　　Angel SCLX 3806

1984 Ghiaurov *Mef*; Pavarotti *F*; Freni
　　　M; Condò *Mar*; De Palma *W*;
　　　Caballé *E*; D. Jones *P*; Leggate *N*
　　　/ Trinity Boys' Choir / National
　　　PO / De Fabritiis
　　　Decca D 270 D3 ④ K 270 K33
　　　London LDR 73010

1948 (Prologue and Act 3)
　　　Siepi *Mef*; Prandelli *F*; Nelli *M* /
　　　La Scala Chorus and Orch. /
　　　Toscanini
　　　Cetra ⓜ LO532 (2)

1954 (Prologue – broadcast
　　　performance)
　　　Moscona *Mef* / Shaw Chorale,

NBC SO / Toscanini
RCA (UK) ⓜ AT 131
(US) ⓜ VIC 1398

1958 (excerpts)
　　　Siepi *Mef*; Di Stefano *F*; Tebaldi
　　　M; Danieli *Mar*; De Palma *W* /
　　　Santa Cecilia Academy Chorus
　　　and Orch. / Serafin
　　　Decca SET 558
　　　London OS 26274

1966 (excerpts)
　　　Ghiaurov *Mef*; Fr. Tagliavini *F* /
　　　Rome Opera Chorus and Orch. /
　　　Varviso
　　　Decca SXL 6305
　　　London OS 26021

1977 (Prologue)
　　　Ghiaurov *Mef* /
　　　Gumpoldskirchner Spatzen,
　　　Vienna State Opera Chorus,
　　　Vienna PO / Bernstein
　　　DG 2707 100 ④ 3370 022

1977 (Prologue)
　　　Cheek *Mef* / Morehouse-Spelman
　　　Chorus, Young Singers of
　　　Callanwolde, Atlanta SO Chorus,
　　　Atlanta SO / Shaw
　　　Telarc DG 10045

La Gioconda

ALAN BLYTH

In the United States and Italy *La Gioconda* is part of the staple repertory; in Britain it still awaits a professional production in the postwar era. Apparently British taste is too fastidious or too modest for the overt melodrama of Ponchielli's opera to a libretto by 'Tobia Gorria' (Arrigo Boito in anagram disguise), based on a Victor Hugo play. It seems that Shaw's sour dictum that it is a work with Verdi's manner without any of his substance has remained with the opera ever since. That is a pity, for as the old *Record Guide* more sympathetically had it: 'It is a powerful piece, a succession of "strong" situations which the practised hands of Boito and Ponchielli have made exceedingly effective. If you enjoy "Cielo e mar", "Voce di donna", "O monumento" and "Suicidio", you will enjoy them all the more when they are set in their rip-roaring Venetian context.'

I would plead an even stronger case for the piece. It seems to me, on repeated hearings, to present a telling picture of private grief and tragedy, that of Gioconda and her mother, against the public rejoicing around the Lido. The title role itself, in the hands of a great soprano, presents a truthful, rounded portrait of a woman hopelessly wronged. While it is fair to say that Ponchielli learnt much from Verdi, he very surely fashioned an individual style, the Verdian traits incorporated into his own, and let it be said that Verdi, or at any rate Boito, took something of *Gioconda* over into *Otello* – the plotting, even some of the wording of Act 1, where Barnaba is a very obvious predecessor of Iago, Enzo's entrance 'Assassini' foretells Otello's 'Esultate', and Alvise's sardonic greeting to his guilty wife that of Otello to his in Act 3 of Verdi's opera, and above all Barnaba's 'O monumento', Iago's Credo. Ponchielli's sole success depends on the composer's lyrical impulse, which is considerable. 'He's one of the few composers of his time who could bring something personal to bear on a style that was on the point of being outworn. He even has his own melodic fingerprint – sinuous lines which generally move the interval of a third' (Julian Budden). The vocal line has another characteristic – a tendency to swoop down from top to bottom of a singer's register.

What cannot be disputed is that the work is a magnificent vehicle for full-blooded singing, and demands a quintet of the absolute front rank if it is to succeed. In that it has been comparatively lucky on record, even if no set can boast five outright winners. Of course, none can survive without a complete diva as protagonist, which immediately rules out the 1952 Urania/Nixa version, not that the supporting cast has much to offer. Giuseppe Campora, always a reliable tenor, is an adequate Enzo, Anselmo Colzani a slightly more than routine Barnaba. Fernando Corena, in one of his few non-*buffo* appearances on disc, is a suitably implacable Alvise. But, by and large, this is not a version to convince a single disbeliever in the rightness of the opera's cause.

The 1957 Gavazzeni set suffers from a crucial weakness at its centre. Anita Cerquetti undoubtedly had the vocal equipment for the taxing title role, but her matter-of-fact interpretation leaves all too much to be desired. There are imposing moments – the arching phrases towards the end of Act 1 for instance – but too much else that has not been thought out sufficiently in terms of the text, not least 'Suicidio', which is bumpily sung as well as being unimaginatively inflected.

The role of Enzo requires an Otello-like power to cope with the character's tempestuous outbursts, 'Assassini' and 'Vituperio', in Act 1, the imprecations against Gioconda's supposedly foul behaviour towards Laura's 'body' in Act 4, but he must also have the sensitivity to find the poetic impulse behind 'Cielo e mar', much of the duet with Laura, not to forget the poignancy of the lament at his beloved's alleged poisoning 'Già ti veggo' in the big third-act ensemble. Mario del Monaco in this, the earliest of the four Decca versions is of course type-cast in the passages calling for metallic declamation yet he is surprisingly sensitive elsewhere, managing an effective *diminuendo* at 'Buona notte' just before 'Cielo e mar', itself a bit steely but not without some delicacies. In the 'Laggiù' passage with Laura his *piano* singing lacks body but is at least a sign of an artistry he was not often reputed to have during his estimable career.

Barnaba – Iago and Scarpia rolled into one devilish character – is as taxing a part as any in the Italian baritone's repertory. Ettore Bastianini finds no difficulty in conveying, Stracciari-like, the man's vaunting ambition; his voice and delivery have presence allied to power, 'O monumento' delivered with malign energy. Laura has to establish her rather passive character with little material – 'Stella del marinar' is not one of Ponchielli's most successful inspirations. Giuletta Simionato, as ever in the studio as compared with the theatre, is not as urgently dramatic as one might wish, but the manner is authentic. 'L'amo come il fulgor', the great confrontation of Enzo's two ladies, is launched with true *spinto* force to which Cerquetti answers in kind but neither singer bites into her phrases with ideal pertinacity.

Alvise, unthinking and heartless as he may seem, must exude authority. Cesare Siepi spoils a goodish performance by some lack of steadiness; his tone is also too soft-grained. The Cieca of Franca Sacchi (an erstwhile Tosca) is tolerable, no more.

As it happens this is one of the strongest points about the second Decca version. Oralia Dominguez manages to sound venerable without wobbling and she has the sweet expressiveness Ponchielli asks for in 'Voce di donna' while maintaining a flexible line. Carlo Bergonzi gives a thoroughly characteristic performance; that is to say he has all his accustomed merits of tone, line and well-mannered style without suggesting he is wholly involved in his portrayal. Robert Merrill does well in portraying the leering evil of Barnaba. The famous 'Enzo Grimaldo' duet with Bergonzi's effortless Enzo represents mid-1960s singing at its most reliable. That vicious confrontation between Gioconda and Laura gives us something more in the superbly weighty singing of Renata Tebaldi and Marilyn Horne, the singers' chest registers quivering with jealous taunts. Altogether Horne is about the most vivid Laura in any complete set, splendidly supported by the Roman orchestra under Gardelli, who is much more appreciative of the score's finer and more dramatic points (one of the most delicate ballets) as compared with Gavazzeni's slacker conduct. Indeed, apart from Panizza in the 'off-the-air' set referred to below, Gardelli is the most persuasive advocate of the piece. Incidentally, his is the only version to present the score absolutely complete and include the sections usually snipped out of the Act 2 finale and out of the trio in Act 4. These cuts are always made in the theatre. No wonder when this set first appeared Andrew Porter averred in *Gramophone* that the opera is 'not just enjoyable; it is a *good* opera, imaginatively conceived and excellently constructed . . . with so many admirable, eloquent melodies, such skilful scoring, so sure and unconventional sense of form'.

Tebaldi is its most difficult quantity to assess. Porter commented that she 'gives an excellent account of the passionate, varied role', but he, like me, obviously felt some dissatisfaction with the state of the voice itself. Callas-influenced, she had obviously added histrionic colours to it, but where Callas (see below) seems to be working from inside out, one sometimes feels that Tebaldi, for all her gifts, is working the other way round.

Milanov, Tebaldi's near rival (from the point of view of recording the part), was reigning Gioconda at the Metropolitan for twenty-five years; a pity that she had to wait almost until the last of them before recording the complete part on discs, or at least regularly available ones, with Fernando Previtali as a vivid, no-nonsense conductor. The beauty and feeling of her quiet singing remained unmarked by time – 'Ah! come t'amo' with the rise to a pianissimo B flat perfectly managed is just what Milanov was famous for; it is here more easily accomplished than by any of her rivals. Many of her verbal accents are just as memorable: the pathos of 'Son la Gioconda' when she saves Laura for the first time, the sense of total sacrifice at 'O madre mia' after she has rescued Laura for the second time – the final phrases 'Io la salvo per lui' given an eloquence only Callas can match. 'Suicidio' is as fatalistic as it should be, but there is a feeling here that the voice, under pressure, is past its best while the *fioriture* at the end of the work, when Gioconda pretends to beautify herself for Barnaba, always a tricky matter for a *lirica-spinta*, are none too happy.

Giuseppe di Stefano, also not in his youthful prime (high notes are often hard and effortful), is a vital, involved Enzo, singing the part with his accustomed wholehearted responses and immediately accessible verbal attack. Leonard Warren is a plausibly sinister Barnaba, neither the least nor greatest of the despicable breed, rather effective in the way he works up the Venetian seamen against La Cieca, a close cousin to what we have of the same baritone's Iago. Rosalind Elias, the Laura, sings with the proper fire and flexibility but not always with the requisite incisiveness.

Now we can also hear Milanov's Gioconda in quite other circumstances, indeed twenty years earlier when, as the announcer at a Metropolitan matinée tells us on this 'off-the-air' set, the work was returning to the house's repertory for the first time in twenty years. In sound that is only fair to murky (although it never distorts vocal tone), we can hear the Milanov voice in its prime and as in no other recording. Here her Gioconda sounds like a young girl, helpless and distraught in unsympathetic surroundings and so at the end of her tether. Her tone soars shining to the heights with consummate ease, as at the end of Act 1 in 'Ah! o cuor! dono funesto!'. Most of the verbal accents to be heard in the later-recorded version are present here, and in the context of a live show, Milanov rises to great heights in Act 4. All the demands of 'Suicidio' are fulfilled as are those of the following recitative, its desperation almost palpable, as in the cry 'Amor, ah Enzo!'

But then Milanov is in the company of Martinelli, who almost turns Enzo into a noble character. Throughout he demonstrates the classic virtues of line and diction. They can be heard in his opening outburst; again at 'O grido quest'anima' in the confrontation with Barnaba leading to the Otello-like cries of 'Infamia'. A similarly virile attack informs the phrase 'il dalmato segnal' in the recit. before 'Cielo e mar', itself sung with great aristocracy of phrase – musingly begun, it continues with growing intensity of passion without the singer ever indulging in breaks of line: it resembles a fine chalk drawing. Later the lament over Laura's supposed corpse brings out all Martinelli's gift for plangent expression. Indeed I find Kolodin's comment in *The Metropolitan Opera*** that his Enzo was 'a dim likeness of its best' impossible to comprehend, even if there is an occasional flatness. Carlo Morelli, the Barnaba (and incidentally Renato Zanelli's brother) is a De Luca-like Barnaba, subtle and inveigling. Bruna Castagna's Laura is rather sedate ('Stella del marinar' is missing from the performance). As Alvise, Nicola Moscona gives his not inconsiderable imitation of Pinza. Over all presides Ettore Panizza, in Toscanini manner, making the very most of all the genre music and getting superb support from the Met. chorus and orchestra. Altogether a version to hear if you can, but beware, some transfers are made a semitone too high.

Still more important are the two Callas recordings. She is said to have stated about the final side of her second recording that 'It's all there for

* Alfred Knopf, New York, 1966

anyone who cares to understand or wishes to know what I was about.' Indeed
her reactions to the thought of killing Laura are just as immediate as those
when she contemplates killing her children as Norma, while the use of
coloratura in the final moments matches that in her Lucia. The whole of the
beginning of the act is a magnificent and tragic soliloquy in which soul, verbal
acting, tone are all bound together in a convincing whole. The part as a
whole is more confidently sung in the Cetra set. That phrase at the end of
Act 1, already quoted, is even more 'drenched with emotion' (as Ardoin has
it in *The Callas Legacy*,* where he describes her performance in this opera
in great detail) than is Milanov's, but she has to give best to her predecessor
at 'Ah! come t'amo', where Callas is wobbly in both her recordings. Of
course the viciousness of Gioconda's verbal battle with Laura is mighty in
Callas's rendering and Fedora Barbieri (Cetra) is a fit partner for her.
'Siccome il leone' is truly Callas-Gioconda's way of loving Enzo. The 'Oh,
madre mia' prayer in both versions, but particularly in the earlier one,
expresses unerringly what saving Laura for her mother's sake has cost
Gioconda. In the earlier set, 'Suicidio' is more earthy, more instinctive, but
not without the pathos required for the quieter sections. Barbieri apart, the
Cetra performance is weak in support of Callas; Silveri is ordinary, Neri
authoritative but wooden, Poggi appalling.

This version was made in 1952, when Callas was singing the role on stage
and her star was in the ascendant. Seven years later the greatest glories of
her career were almost past, but she had just fallen in love with Onassis,
and the new softness and womanliness in her personality are surely there in
her Gioconda. There is now less instinct, more subtlety and variety in her
portrayal. The voice is in as excellent a shape as in any of her stereo remakes,
the top B climax of 'Suicidio' actually more secure than in the first version,
and her legato singing throughout exemplary. I would not be without either
interpretation; they are both quintessential Callas. Fiorenza Cossotto, in
regal voice and phrasing with long breath, is no match for Callas in reading
expression into her role, but she finds the prayerful guilt of 'Stella del
marinar'. Her husband, Ivo Vinco, is an imposing Alvise, Piero Cappuccilli
a threatening rather than subtle Barnaba, Pier Miranda Ferraro a stentorian
Enzo. Votto conducts both versions, makes disfiguring cuts, but in the second
set he brings out much of the score's colour and variety of feeling, and always
allows Callas time to make her points, none more so than the tenderness of
'Quest'ultimo bacio' in the final scene.

In sum, whatever Callas set one listens to, one realizes that here a singer
and a role make a perfect match. Every piece of recitative, every vocal line
is imprinted with a wealth of feeling that is ideally suited to its utterance.
The searing force of her interpretation makes us believe wholly in Gioconda's
plight; what more can one ask of the interpreter of any part?

The most recent set, and the fourth from Decca, doesn't encompass the

* Duckworth, London, 1977

work as vividly as either Callas version, but is not to be despised on that count. Montserrat Caballé conveys the emotions and tragedy of Gioconda most persuasively, with the expected distinction of phrase. 'Enzo adorato! Ah! come t'amo' is just the kind of thing she can manage most successfully, with the high B flat as finely poised as it is in Milanov's reading. Similarly the 'domando al cielo' section of 'Suicidio' has all the tranquillity and sweetness Ponchielli asks for, as does Gioconda's reprise of La Cieca's 'A te questo rosario'. But the voice sounds under-powered in the confrontation with Laura. One sometimes feels that Caballé is too slight, vocally speaking, for a *spinta* role and at others, as with so much later Caballé, that she is fidgeting with the part self-indulgently, not singing it in a spontaneous way: 'Quest'ultimo bacio' is such a moment (*cf* Callas, so much more eloquent at a slightly quicker pace). She also wants a resonant chest register, so essential here.

On the other hand, I find Baltsa's lighter timbre, lighter than most Laura's that is, to the good, helping her suggest a young wife who easily complies with Enzo's impassioned advances and vulnerably moving when her jealous husband decrees her death. Her singing is firm, boldly phrased, 'Scenda per questa fervida orazione/Sul capo mio Madonna del perdono' taken easily in two breaths. Pavarotti's Enzo makes a forceful entrance at 'Assassini'. He proceeds to sing with his accustomed ardour and generous phrasing, 'Cielo e mar' may not be free from effort, the tone tightening uncomfortably under pressure, but 'Deh! non tremar' spins away attractively.

Sherrill Milnes's Barnaba is one of his best portrayals on record, with a sneer and a snarl in his tone, while observing the vocal proprieties, especially in 'O monumento'. Nicolai Ghiaurov exhibits the proper authority and nasty complacency as Alvise, but the voice by 1979 was already showing signs of wear. Alfreda Hodgson makes the most of La Cieca's grateful solo, treating it broadly but not sentimentally. Bruno Bartoletti, a sympathetic accompanist, keeps the work on the boil, relaxes nicely for the Dance of the Hours, but isn't always as sensitive as Gardelli.

Of the highlights discs, I have not heard the Cetra as such but its component parts turn up in discs of individual items discussed below. The Russian record, not deriving from any complete performance, should not be overlooked. Borisenko begins it with a sympathetic, rather fruity 'Voce di donna'. Zakharov possesses one of those gloriously forward, vibrant Russian baritones, and he gives great presence to 'O monumento', even if the vernacular text makes Barnaba sound more like Galitzky. Next we hear the Act 1 finale up to the end of the Forlana. Watery Russian horns introduce Alexandrovich's 'Cielo e mar', begun in a sweet, dreamy manner ideal for the music. The performance is slow, but the tenor uses the extra time to phrase with Lemeshev-like care, and he actually ends the piece with written G rather than the unwritten high B flat; it makes a much more satisfactory close. At the end of 'Stella del marinar' Postavnicheva opts for the low E, an authorized alternative to the usual high A. Although she unfortunately breaks the phrase beginning 'Scenda per questa', she more easily suggests youthfulness than many of her Italian colleagues. Petrov, as expected, makes a truly menacing Alvise in his aria, and 'Ombre di mia prosapia' is sung for once in a *voce cupo* as Ponchielli asks for.

The Gioconda of Arutyanova, rather matronly, is the least happy part of what is otherwise an excellent cast. We hear her sounding effortful in her vocal battle with Laura and laboured in 'Suicidio' too, but at least she is steadier than most Russian sopranos. Also included are the Dance of the Hours and the final duet with Zakharov sounding deliriously happy as he savours his coming conquest.

There exists another disc of highlights, 'off-the-air', taken from a concert performance at San Francisco in 1948. It has Stella Roman as a squally Gioconda, Margaret Harshaw, in her mezzo days, an appealing Laura, Kurt Baum a stentorian, not ineffective Enzo, Leonard Warren (as in his complete recording) a powerful Barnaba. Blanche Thebom's average 'Voce di donna' is sung without a chorus.

That takes us back to the era of 78rpm records, and the first-ever complete performance on disc. It makes out a strong case for the opera in, for its day, above-average sound. Giannina Arangi-Lombardi, the Gioconda, is the kind of *spinta* soprano we so keenly lack today, absolutely secure and full-toned in her upper reaches and with a powerful chest register in support, plenty of body in between. By all reports she was a conventional actress, but here she exhibits a sure understanding of the role's histrionic needs. The prayer at the end of Act 1 is affecting, 'O madre mia' eloquent, the gear-changes apart, and 'Suicidio' well above average. Unlike other sopranos on complete sets, Milanov apart, one does not feel she is going beyond the abilities of the voice; quite the contrary, as with a three-litre car, there always seems plenty of reserve in hand. The young Stignani, an appropriately youthful Laura, offers no distinctive insights, but she matches her soprano in vocal splendour in their forceful confrontation. The Peruvian tenor Alessandro Granda is like a second-line Pertile, a bit lachrymose but filling such passages as the lament over Laura's body with real feeling. Gaetano Viviani, on the evidence here (and I know of no other) a baritone of panache, and a vicious Barnaba, with snarling delivery proper for the part. Corrado Zambelli is an undistinguished Alvise. That ubiquitous comprimario tenor Giuseppe Nessi makes much of little as Isepo. Lorenzo Molajoli is the sure-footed conductor. The usual theatre cuts are made.

In the seemingly endless number of extracts recorded, one can reach back almost but not quite to the earliest of the work's interpreters. Certainly the plethora of artists who gave us something of their interpretations in the old Fonotipia catalogue (whose founder, the composer Frédéric D'Erlanger, if I may enter a personal note, happens to have been my godfather, though I never benefited by inheriting any of his collection!), suggest to us how the piece was performed around the turn-of-the-century. The readings are strongly influenced by the *verismo* style (though *Gioconda* is not truly a *verismo* opera), with the histrionic, almost melodramatic element evident. The trio 'Figlia, che reggi' for Gioconda, Cieca and Barnaba was made in 1905 by those Fonotipia stalwarts Giannina Russ, Armida Parsi-Pettinella and Antonio Magini-Coletti (Fono. 74004; Saga XIG 8016) with piano accompaniment. The thirds and semiquavers of the distinguished singers are accurate and well integrated. On a much-later HMV record (DB 448; LV 66) De Martis, Irene Minghini-Cattaneo and Apollo Granforte start a few bars earlier at 'Madre adorata'. This version is dominated by the burnished threatening tone of the baritone. The reverse finds Minghini-Cattaneo giving a central performance of 'Voce di donna': idiomatic, broadly taken and with a welcome legato. Before discussing other versions of the piece, I must mention an important record of Enzo's Otello-like entrance, 'Assassini!!' by Lauri-Volpi in his prime (DA 1081; LV 36) in which the great tenor gives an object-lesson in measured declamation, the cries of 'Vituperio!' stinging in their forcefulness.

'Voce di donna', one of Ponchielli's most graceful passages, for singer and audience, has been seized on by mezzos many of whom would on stage have sung the longer role of Laura rather than of La Cieca, the blind woman. Parsi-Pettinella recorded it with piano (Fono. 39395) in 1906 and with orchestra (Fono. 92118; CO 372) in 1908, both equally recommendable, sung with firm, rich but not too plummy tone, natural, unforced accents, and a true legato. Her near contemporary Ottilie Metzger, singing it in 1908 in German (Od. 52105; CO 318), suggests the old woman's weight of weariness in her deeply felt phrasing, using more *portamento* than would be allowable today. Margarete Matzenauer (Victor 6471; Collector's Guild 611) is almost too Erda-like, overdoing the chest register, impressive nevertheless. Gabriella Besanzoni finds the piece a wonderful vehicle for her gorgeous voice (Victor 64876), reissued in 'The Record of Singing', Vol. 2 (RLS 743) where Michael Scott rightly comments on the 'beautifully graded mezza voce' in 'A te questo rosario'; she then follows precisely the *espandendosi* injunction for the climax at the final two 'Sulla tua testa'; there is true feeling here to add to the great singing. However, even she is surpassed by, in this case, the incomparable Sigrid Onegin (Brunswick 50039) singing with that warm, plush tone of hers, a loving, lovely account of the piece full of tenderness while still managing to impart frailty to the characterization. By the side of these great contraltos, their contemporary Kirkby Lunn (2–053074; Club 99. 506) sounds dull and uninvolved. Anna Meitschik, in one of the only two Fonotipia titles (92469), sings with generous line and feeling, quite one of the best.

In the next generation Ebe Stignani is vocally ample, interpretatively dull (Cetra BB 25055; LPC 55074), Karin Branzell (Parlo. 9804; LV 47), in 1927, more involving with her real *dolcissimo* at 'A te questo rosario' and her generally sympathetic approach to notes and musical values. By comparison Blanche Thebom (Victor 11–9795) reveals a smooth, well-schooled mezzo but offers no special insights. Her contemporary Fedora Barbieri (DB 11319; 3C 061–17014) has a warmer heart but a more bumpy delivery. More recent

versions by Nadia Afean (Balkanton), Marianna Radev (Jugoton) and Fiorenza Cossotto (Philips) are little more than souvenirs of the singers, but
Ruža Baldani (*née* Pospiš) on Jugoton (LPY–V–647) is very good indeed,
evincing sympathy and gratefulness for the blind woman being saved by
Laura's intervention, upon which so much of the story turns. Rita Gorr
(ASDF 857) sings with too much authority, lacking the nuances of the best
versions but impressing by her care over phrasing the passage. I have not
heard versions by Pederzini and Castagna that may be worthy of
investigation.

The tenor-baritone duet beginning with Barnaba's 'Enzo Grimaldo, Prin-
cipe di Santafior, che pensi?', revealing that he knows the hero's true name,
has been recorded by many imposing pairs, although Caruso, a notable Enzo,
never committed it to disc. Pasquale Amato, often Caruso's duet partner,
made a magnificent (and complete) version with Giovanni Zenatello in 1907
(Fono. 62012–3; GV 544) with piano accompaniment. Amato's incisive
accents and quick vibrato could hardly be bettered, nor his sneer near the
end at 'Buona fortuna': here is the real spy and subtle plotter. Zenatello's
clarion tones and ardour are precisely right for respectively the cries of
'Infamia' and the thoughts of his beloved Laura. Amato recorded the piece
again a year or two later, now with orchestra but with the much less impressive Rinaldo Grassi as Enzo (Fono. 92565–6; CO 389). Gigli recorded it
three times, the two best versions dating from the mid-1920s. That with Titta
Ruffo (AGSB 49; RLS 7710), although not very well recorded (Gigli's voice
too backward), is full of character and verbal presence: the veteran baritone
exudes authority and malignancy, even if the vibrato has loosened with the
years. Gigli is exuberant. Unfortunately this, like the other versions with
Gigli, is cut. De Luca is subtler, less vocally resplendent than Ruffo, Gigli
much as before (DB 1150; GEMM 146). Gigli's 1918 disc was made with
Dario Zani (DB 267; RLS 729), who has an appropriate bite in his tone.
Gigli is at his most fresh and youthful. John McCormack and Mario
Sammarco (DB 608; SH 399), who start only at 'Badoer questa notte' sing
in their usual fluent manner but without ever convincing one that they are
Enzo and Barnaba. Nino Piccaluga and Ricci (reissue Club 99.33) are simply
provincial. I have not traced the versions by Ciniselli and Inghilleri and by
Marini and Vanelli. The duet seems to have been curiously neglected on LP,
possibly because duet recitals are such rare occurrences. The coming-together
of Richard Tucker and Robert Merrill in a 'live' Carnegie Hall programme
with piano in 1973 was all too late in the singers' careers to make their
encounter memorable. Placido Domingo and Sherrill Milnes (SER 5593),
recorded in 1971, early in their careers, are well matched, sing powerfully
and accurately, but their expression is strangely externalized and studio-
bound.

The baritone's malicious outpouring of spleen, 'O monumento', has also
been neglected in modern times, and it was not recorded all that often in 78
rpm days. Viglione Borghese (Fono. 92650; LV 283 – in 1910) has the

requisite presence but sings in a rough manner. Fourteen years later (Poly. 72939) the voice is weaker, the performance even less remarkable. Giuseppe de Luca (Fono. 39950; CO 391) would not have been natural casting for the part even in these, his palmiest days, but what he lacks in vocal weight he makes up for in his expressive diction: he makes much of rolled 'rs', keeps strictly to note values, suggests something darkly sinister at 'la spia'. Antonio Magini-Coletti (Fono. 92042; Rococo 5221), woolly in tone, declaims with menace. From the next generation, Benvenuto Franci, vocally ample and vibrant (DB 1117), portrays a conventional villain, as does his contemporary Giovanni Inghilleri (D 1698; LV 169): but like De Luca, Inghilleri benefits from the clarity of his words and sings off them. Cesare Formichi (LX 236; OASI 512) pours scorn on the world round him in his big-scale yet mellifluous interpretation, full of character particularly at 'un vecchio sceletro', the verbal picture of a skeleton very present. Apollo Granforte (DB 835; LV 90) recalls his Iago; looking at the photo of a kindly man on the Preiser reissue, one wonders how he could exude so much evil in his singing, with a menacing high G at the close. Umberto Urbano (Parlo. P 8536; LV 278) has presence, obeys the double-dotting at 'Spalanca la tua fauce', but strains at the top of his register. Paolo Silveri (LX 1359) is much as in his complete recording, Antenore Reali (Cetra BB 25150; LPC 50029) no more than respectable.

From the end of Act 1, Russ and Parsi-Pettinella, sporting a chorus and organ even in the first decade of the century, sing the passage starting 'Angele Dei' in full, steady voice. That is something of a parenthesis before we return to Barnaba in his second solo, the lively 'Pescator', where the spy dressed up as a fisherman sings his Barcarolle. We now meet notable baritones who do not appear to have recorded 'O Monumento'. Most important among them is Pasquale Amato, whose insinuating, flexible singing suggests the seemingly bonhomous Barnaba to the life in both his Fonotipia (92513; GV 544) and HMV (DA 126; GV 561) versions of the piece. Riccardo Stracciari also recorded it twice; his incisive tones and customary brio do not project the passage as subtly as does Amato but are admirable on their own account (Col. D 1625; Rococo 5355 and Fono. 92426; CO 375). Mario Sammarco catches a lighter vein in his very Edwardian-style version (Fono, 39295; Belcantodisc BC 218) with an evil chuckle in his voice. Borghese (Poly. 72929; LV 283) is poor. George Baklanov (reissued on LV 108) bites eagerly into the rewarding solo. Franci (DB 1117; QALP 10145) lightens his tone amazingly to suggest Barnaba's more jovial side, simulated as it may be: this is a splendid version. So is Formichi's (Col. D 5534); what a vivid singer he must have been on stage. In this piece De Luca (DB 1436), for all his attributes, is too good-natured but one cannot help but yield to the nice lilt and subtle *rubato*, or to the light-headed version by Ramón Blanchart (Col. A 5176). By comparison, Sherrill Milnes (SXL 6609), recalling the role in which he made his London debut, albeit in concert, is ordinary beside his account on his Decca set.

And so we arrive at the marathon of 'Cielo e mar', of which I have heard some fifty versions and then, no doubt, only skimmed the cream. Here one must begin at the fount with Caruso, who recorded the Romance three times. Unfortunately on each version he made a damaging cut from the first verse right on to the *poco più mosso* conclusion, excusable in 1902, perhaps in 1905 but surely not in 1910 when the primitive years of the gramophone were past. But on each occasion Caruso takes his time, singing with the utmost voluptuousness appropriate to the piece. The G&T of 1902 (DA 547; HLM 7030) is as good example as any of the beauty and freshness of the youthful tenor's voice, and the opulence of the phrasing is shown in the way, like few other tenors, he sings the G and A flat of 'Vi conquide, o sogni' in one breath. By 1905 he makes a break and adds a curious turn on 'sogni' between the G and F. Still I think this in-character version is the best of the three, the feeling properly pensive, the tone luscious (DB 113; ORL 303). The 1910 disc (DB 696; RCA RL 11749) is more laboured and deliberate, less poetic.

Practically all Caruso's important contemporaries recorded their version, and most of them sang it complete, making Caruso's foreshortening all the more inexplicable. As you would expect, Alessandro Bonci (Fono. 69017; Rococo R42) is poetically inclined, makes free with the music, delights us with his refinements of phrase. Giovanni Zenatello's burnished tones make for a persuasively ardent version (Fono. 92208; CO 359), excellently articulated but also free with note values. Giuseppe Anselmi (Edison 83004; GV 64) sings with appropriately liquid tone and vital ardour but flattens on certain notes as was his wont. Tito Schipa, in one of his earlier discs, made in 1913/14 (252130; GV 29), makes Caruso's cut and adds the grace note (as did Anselmi) at 'dell'amor' near the end; his is, predictably, a lighter, airier way of performing the piece than that of his peers. Martinelli's version (DA 331; LV 271) has those peculiar, particular accents of his but the excision weakens the performance; his Enzo is heard to greater advantage twenty-five years later in the Met. recording or, in between, in the broad arches of the 1929 Edison (83002; GV 70), a glorious performance.

Gigli is in his element in this music. He begins in appropriately dreamy, romantic vein as if in a languorous reverie at the approach of his Laura, and his tone is golden. Then at 'Vieni, o donna' he adds erotic passion as his expectation of her arrival grows. His 1921 version (2–052142; RLS 7710) is slightly to be preferred to the more self-indulgent electric disc (DB 1499; GEMM 204) but both are superb. He is just as recommendable in the 'Deh non tremar' section of Enzo's duet with Laura (DB 267; RLS 729), where the homogeneous sound of his tenor and its open quality are again to the fore. Aureliano Pertile, Gigli's more forthright contemporary, also recorded 'Cielo e mar' twice. There is not too much light or shade, but his spontaneous approach and easy high notes are undeniably attractive. The earlier version (Fono. F 5546; GV 505) is, contrary to received opinion, less restrained than the later, HMV (DB 1208; LV 46), which has a more poetic start. I feel this to be the central, unaffected way to sing the piece, with a proper forward movement. Fernando de Lucia (Phonotype M 1771; GV 503), though in his late fifties, shows no vocal decline. As was his wont in most music, he spins out the piece at a leisurely pace, and offers all sorts of unauthorized turns and graces. Giuseppe Taccani (Col. D 14455; GV 550), recorded at about the same time as De Lucia, is rather ordinary. Francesco Merli, Taccani's Italian contemporary, is more attractive in timbre, but tends to hurry (L 2208; LV 162). Nino Piccaluga's version (Parlo. PX 56506; Club 99.33) is too rough to suggest anything better than the Italian provinces. Similarly Costa Milona (Parlo E 10081; SYO 2), in his cut version, lacks elegance in his tight-throated singing. Giacomo Lauri-Volpi (DB 6352; 3C 065–00738) was recorded too late in his career (he was fifty-four when this was made in 1946); his former vibrancy has degenerated into something more emphatic and bumpy.

Among non-Italians Hermann Jadlowker (Gram. 72577; CO 406), long-breathed and poetic, includes the turn in the penultimate phrase. Leo Slezek (Col. A 5396), if you ignore his effortful upper notes, presents a very romantic vision of Enzo; whatever you feel about his vocal production, the man suggests a presence in spite of the primitive recording. Alfred Piccaver (Poly. 66769; LV 106) is honeyed and bland. Mario Chamlee – cut version (Brunswick 15056; LV 220) – is inclined to force his clear, natural tenor. Tino Pattiera (Bruns. 15019; Rococo 5256) is more notable, in another truncated version, for warmth of tone than for his style. The Greek Ulysses Lappas (L 1762) has Mediterranean glamour and effusion. The Russian reading of David Yuzhin (Amour 22889; GV 63) wants polish. The French one by Léon Campagnola (032233) is typically straightforward and unaffected. John Coates (02092), in a 1907 cut version, sings with elan and ends with the G.

Coming to more recent times one can dismiss a good number of versions as no better than representations of the tenors concerned. Among them are Gianni Poggi (LX 1398); Rudolf Schock (Véga); Nikola Nikolov (Balkanton); Barry Morell (Westminster WST-17148); Pedro Lavirgen (Westminster WST-17159); Sándor Kónya (DG LPEM 19214) – too lachrymose but a finely poetic start; Róbert Ilosfalvy (Qualiton); Antonio Gallié (Fontana); Donald Smith (OASD 7584); Mario Binci (C 3606).

However, the postwar generation has its candidates for immortality. Kenneth Neate, recorded in 1945 just before he appeared at Covent Garden (Rococo 5387), has something of Martinelli in his clean, attractive timbre. Giacinto Prandelli (LXT 2688) builds carefully and stylishly towards the first climax but fails to sustain his singing through the second verse. Nicolai Gedda made two recordings of the aria. The first (33CX 1130) is intelligently phrased, with a nicely floated *mezza voce* at the start of verse two and a *messa di voce* on the final B flat. The later version (SLS 5250), made some fifteen years later, in 1968, is much less persuasive, the tenor having declined in artistry. His Swedish compatriot, Jussi Björling shows a similar falling-off between his classic version of 1937 (DB 3302; ALP 1620), with its outpouring of golden, finely proportioned tone, and his later, more effortful disc (DB 21563): he and Gedda both offer a grace note in the penultimate phrase. Luciano Pavarotti's 1971 recording (D236D2) has many of the attributes of Björling's first version: youthful ardour and broad phrasing. Placido Domingo (SXL 6451), recorded at the start of his career, sings with style but, at a slow speed, lacks the requisite forward pulse. Alfredo Kraus (Carillon CAL-7) is also slow but he makes better use of the extra time with his finely spun tone and specific vocal character, similar to Schipa's. Like Gedda, Kraus manages a delicate *messa di voce* at the close. Jon Vickers (LSB 4106), also in the early part of his career, is interesting and predictably intelligent without quite striking the right idiom. Alain Vanzo (Orphée) offers good, clean Gedda-like tone, singing in French. José Carreras (Philips 9500 771) is mellow in tune and predictably ardent, but showing signs of wear at the top of his range. Finally Josef Traxel (1C 147–30775): despite the German text, he sounds an ideally musing, lyrical note and completes this survey of 'Cielo e mar' with a finely poised G, again proving the written note to be superior to a stentorian B flat.

Minghini-Cattaneo and Lionello Cecil recorded the Laura-Enzo duet from 'Deh non tremar' (DB 1432): the mezzo once more exhibits her warm, firm voice as Laura but her partner, despite some delicacies, is inclined to bleat. In 1973, Renata Tebaldi and Franco Corelli, neither any longer in their prime, teamed up for the piece (SXL 6585). Her voice sounds sadly worn and her reading is matter-of-fact. She cannot manage a *dolcissimo* reply to her partner's ardent 'Deh! non turbare' nor a real *piano* for the concluding 'laggiù' section. For that you need to go to Gigli and Elvira Casazza (2–054085; RLS 739).

When Enzo has left her, Laura sings her Romance 'Stella del marinar'. Alive with passion she prays – oddly – to the Virgin Mary to assist her in her love and give Her blessing. Of the six versions encountered, Margarete Arndt-Ober (Victor 64442) sounds uninvolved in Laura's plight. Louise Homer (Victor 81055; LM 6171) with piano, recorded in 1905, is as steady as ever but hardly evokes the agitation of this solo. Stignani (LX 1253; 3C 069 17659) is more confident than on the set she recorded fifteen years or so earlier and manages the arching phrase starting 'Scenda per questa fervida' in a single breath. Cloë Elmo (Cetra BB 25009; LPC 55069) gives an even firmer impression of a woman in love but is stretched by the final high A. Fedora Barbieri (DA 11304; 3C 061–17014) is perhaps the best of all; she evinces the urgency and uncertainty of Laura's feelings besides singing with a plush tone. Rita Gorr (ASDF 857) spoils an appreciable performance by a slow speed. Elmo turns up in the fiery confrontation 'E un anatema' between Laura and Gioconda. As in the aria, she suggests overwhelmingly the description and passion of her love, here in her verbal battle with the formidable Gioconda of Gina Cigna: this is a justly famous version of the duet (R 30013; LPC 55074). Minghini-Cattaneo is just as impressive in partnership, however, with a tiresome soprano (DB 1432; LV 66). Destinn and

Kirkby Lunn (DB 517) are too stolid. In more recent times Montserrat Caballé and Shirley Verrett made their points with an admirable attention to the score's markings (SER 5590).

The passage for Gioconda and Enzo after Gioconda has facilitated Laura's escape – 'Laura! Laura! ove sei?' – was recorded in 1910 by Mazzoleni and Zenatello (Fono. 92879; XIG 8016), a record notable for its vivid declamation: here, one senses, through the ancient recording, that these are precisely appropriate voices for this music.

Act 3 starts with Alvise's aria 'Sì, morir ella de!' A rare G&T made in Milan in 1902 (52343) by Giovanni Gravina is disappointing: tempo and rhythm are all over the place and the voice is not remarkable. Amleto Galli (052299) from the same generation is little better. Tancredo Pasero (L 2301; LV 34) has a fast vibrato that will not be to everyone's taste, but he exhibits a firm legato at 'Là del patrizio veneto' and is superbly vital throughout. Siepi (Cetra BB 25249) is steadier than in his complete recording. What a pity that Pinza never recorded this aria, for his version of the succeeding duet with Risë Stevens (Am. Col 72371D; Odyssey Y 31148) is one of the most telling records in this whole survey. He portrays the implacable, wronged husband superbly in his rounded, firm singing and biting, consonantal attack. Stevens is adequate, no more, as the disturbed Laura. Pasero is almost as fine as Pinza in his version with the young Stignani (Col. D 1654; LV 261). He suggests the Otello-like irony of Alvise's opening phrases, she real eloquence in the plea for her life in the latter part of the duet.

Three versions have been found of the big ensemble at the end of this act including the tenor's 'Già ti veggo'. An ancient record led by De Gregario (054303) is ordinary. The only thing to commend the 1927 La Scala version is the soaring top line of Eva Turner (L 1817; HQM 1209). Minghini-Cattaneo, Tina Poli-Randaccio and Inghilleri help make an Odéon version more interesting but once more the tenor is a cipher.

Act 4 brings us to Gioconda's famous 'Suicidio!' of which there are a vast number of recordings. I shall deal with them in ascending order of merit. As the standard is high, even some quite distinguished versions have to be eliminated early, among them Giannina Russ (Fono. 74112; Saga XIG 8016) who sings strongly but has little finish to her concept of the part. Karin Branzell, a mezzo attempting soprano repertory (Homochord 8447; LV 47), has the range but makes an impassive impression. Emmy Destinn is to be admired for attacking the B natural at 'al cielo' cleanly (many sopranos scoop up to it), deplored for her yowly tone (DB 223; CSLP 501). Helen Traubel (Am. Col. 71960D; Odyssey Y 31735) also hits the B cleanly, but she has nothing to say about the character, having not (I presume) sung the part on stage. Joan Hammond (C 3901; HQM 1186) is accurate with the music, as was her wont, but her Italian is peculiar, and she lacks a chest register. Maria Luisa Fanelli (Disco S10297) is too light in tone. Versions that are no more than souvenirs of the artist concerned are those by Orianna Santunione ('off-the-air'), Antonietta Stella (LPEM 19290), Gràce Bumbry (1C 062–02055) and Sylvia Sass (SXL 6921), who, in trying to imitate Callas, succeeds in pulling about the music unmercifully and is unsteady. Astrid Varnay (Acanta DE 22645) is clumsy, also edgy.

Maria Caniglia (GQX 10043; OASI 538) suggests Gioconda's overwrought state, but tends to bumpy vocalization, as does her famous predecessor in the part Eugenia Burzio (IRCC 3136), who draws out her phrases in a melodramatic way, giving a very personal, almost aggressive idea of the lady's unhappy situation. She also sings the later passage 'Ecco la barca', enunciating like some Sarah Bernhardt of the lyric stage – a little 'over the top' we may think it today but doubtless effective on stage. By contrast, Maria Jeritza (DB 355; LV 122) offers some wonderful singing as such but little character. Celestina Boninsegna slows up unconscionably for 'Domando al ciel', but has a splendidly vivid, secure delivery both in her 1904 G&T (53373) and her 1909 (Am Col. 30358; GV 512) discs. She manages the lift off to the high B quite successfully even if it is not what the composer intended. Eva Turner (L 1976; HQM 1209) shows just how to do it, but then unaccountably leaves out the final few bars of the solo. I like the spontaneity of Dame Eva's version and its fierce passion too. Gina Cigna (CQX 10593) has the temperament, and a vibrant, perhaps too vibrant delivery has much to commend it: hers is the verismo style personified. Caballé (SXL-R 6825), four years before her complete set, sounds too studied and specific but, of course, the *tranquillo dolcissimo* of 'domando al ciel', the appeal to heaven, has a delicate, consolatory face to it.

Next, we come to Eileen Farrell (33CX 1596) whose spacious phrasing and sovereign tone manage also to be dramatically quite appropriate. Lillian Nordica had some of this splendour in an earlier generation and supplemented it with a dramatic pulse that bespeaks the stage. I also like her firm but unexaggerated lower register – so important in this piece. Her unpublished version (IRCC 232) yields place to the published one (Col. 74021) both reissued on Sunday Opera SYO 6. Amalia Pinto, made her debut in 1899 in the part of Gioconda. In her extremely rare 1902 G&T (53240; IRCL 7012), she attacks the high B as written and her generally accurate, unflinching approach allied to a strong histrionic sense are considerable assets. Helene Wildbrunn (Poly. 72835; LV 70), beginning at 'in questi fieri momenti', sounds a more womanly note than many others, gives us a view of Gioconda as the gentle singer of songs she may have been. After the *verismo* approach of many Italians, this soft-grained German came as a solace. To Wildbrunn's tenderness, Meta Seinemeyer (Parlo. P 9015; LV 111) adds a sense of greater urgency and also vulnerability, helped by an attractive, fast vibrato and the warm colours in the tone. 'E un di leggiadro' is meltingly lovely here, yet there is power in reserve for an utterly secure 'vinsi l'infausta'. In a brighter, more vital way, the Russian, Natalya Yuzhina (2–23314; GV 63) is almost as imposing; here is a trenchant voice that demands attention, even when singing in Russian rather than Italian. Rosa Raisa (DB 2122; Club 99.52), with a well-paced, securely felt reading, comes near the highest category, but her voice is not quite distinctive enough in character to enter it.

Four sopranos are almost ideal. Giuseppina Cobelli (Toscanini's Eboli and a notable Italian Isolde), in an extremely rare record (7–253147 – a very early electric of 1925), catches almost better than anyone Gioconda's exhaustion, with the 'con disperazione' at 'vinsi l'infausta' fully obeyed, and a marvellous climax carried up from the C to the high B. The voice itself has a raw intensity all its own. Milanov, recorded six years before her complete set, gives a thoroughly commendable performance (VICS 1336): here is grandeur and authority personified in tone and phrasing, the voice, as Max de Schauensee put it 'carried proudly, darkly in the lower and middle ranges, touched with a silvery brilliance in its powerful upper flights' (he heard her in the part at the Met.). To her qualities Rosa Ponselle, like Cobelli, added something more – a sense of Gioconda's impending fate, harrowingly expressed – at least in her later, 1925 version (DB 854; OASI 621), where the youthful good looks, as it were, of the voice in the earlier, Columbia version have given way to the age of experience. In this performance words and tone seem in perfect accord, complementing not hindering each other. The chest register is used sparingly but it is securely there. The *rubato* at 'domando al ciel' is not exaggerated, and the forward pulse of the whole is commendable. In recent times only Régine Crespin, unexpectedly, has reached the Ponselle class. Her version (GRV 12), with all the benefits of modern recording, and helped by Edward Downes's even pacing, is careful yet wholly spontaneous in a way Caballé, say, is not. Allowed the slightly slower speed given to her by the LP form, she uses it not for self-indulgence but to show us her eloquence of expression that elevates Ponchielli's marvellously persuasive music. Crespin, captured at a live performance on Discoreale in the Gioconda/Laura confrontation with a wobbly Michèle Vilma, and in part of the last act from 'Ecco il velen di Laura', with Vilma and Carlo Cossutta, shows that she carried all the necessities for the part in her prime, a more girlish, less fatalistic Gioconda than Callas or Milanov, but one to be set in the highest class her seniors inhabited, particularly in terms of tonal ease and intense utterance; 'Quest'ultimo bacio' is sensual and pathetic, all at once, but without the overtones of Callas.

Three versions of the finale, 'Così mantieni' all come from the early years of recording. The best-known of them feature Battistini as Barnaba (DB 216; GEMM 166). By 1921 when the recording was made, his tone had become dry but his art with the words had grown. The relishing of 'Ebrezza! Delirio!', as he anticipates his seduction of Gioconda, is suggestive of Barnaba's lecherous thoughts. The unknown soprano, De Witt, adds little to the performance. Burzio and De Luca recorded with piano (Fono. 740437; Club 99.87/8) some years earlier are more evenly matched; indeed it is the melodramatic soprano who is here more to the fore, indicating Gioconda's overwrought state. De Luca again sounds light for Barnaba but is well inside the role. Mazzoleni and Amato (Fono. 74144; CO 347) are even better. Her *fioriture* may be a bit wild but she gets the hectic quality of the scene almost to a fault, while Amato is exemplary in vocal manners and dramatic presence, bringing the survey to an exciting end.

An ideal cast? Callas, undoubtedly, for the title part with Ponselle, Crespin or Milanov waiting in the wings in case Callas might be out of sorts; Gigli as Enzo; Amato as Barnaba; Barbieri as Laura; Onegin as La Cieca; Pinza as Alvise, all conducted by Panizza. What a performance that would be!

LA GIOCONDA

G La Gioconda; *C* La Cieca; *B* Barnaba; *A* Alvise; *L* Laura; *EG* Enzo Grimaldo

1930 Arangi-Lombardi *G*; Rota *C*; Viviani *B*; Zambelli *A*; Stignani *L*; Granda *EG* / La Scala Chorus and Orch. / Molajoli
EMI ⓜ 3C 01643–5M
OASI (US) ⓜ 581

1952 Callas *G*; Amadini *C*; Silveri *B*; Neri *A*; Barbieri *L*; Poggi *EG* / Italian Radio Chorus and Orch. / Votto
Cetra ⓜ LPO 2012
Turnabout ⓜ THS 65051–3

1952 Corridori *G*; Cavallari *C*; Colzani *B*; Corena *A*; Pirazzini *L*; Campora *EG* / La Scala Chorus and Orch. / La Rosa Parodi
Nixa ⓜ ULP 9229
Urania ⓜ URLP 229

1957 Cerquetti *G*; Sacchi *C*; Bastianini *B*; Siepi *A*; Simionato *L*; Del Monaco *EG* / Florence Festival Chorus and Orch. / Gavazzeni
Decca GOS 609–11
Richmond SRS 63518

1958 Milanov *G*; Amparan *C*; Warren *B*; Clabassi *A*; Elias *L*; Di Stefano *EG* / Santa Cecilia Academy Chorus and Orch. / Previtali
Decca D63D3
London OSA 13123

1959 Callas *G*; Compañez *C*; Cappuccilli *B*; Vinco *A*; Cossotto *L*; Ferraro *EG* / La Scala Chorus and Orch. / Votto
EMI SLS 5176
Seraphim SIC 6031

1967 Tebaldi *G*; Dominguez *C*; Merrill *B*; Ghiuselev *A*; Horne *L*; Bergonzi *EG* / Santa Cecilia Academy Chorus and Orch. / Gardelli
Decca SET 364–6
London OSA 1388

1980 Caballé *G*; Hodgson *C*; Milnes *B*; Ghiaurov *A*; Baltsa *L*; Pavarotti *EG* / London Opera Chorus / Nat. PO / Bartoletti
Decca D232D3 ④ K232K3
London LDR 73005

1948–9 (Excerpts)
Cigna *G*; Stignani *C*; Reali *B*; Siepi *A*; Elmo *L*; Prandelli, Masini *EG* / Italian Radio, SO, Turin / Baroni, Basile
Cetra ⓜ LPC 50020

1950s (excerpts – in Russian)
Arutyanova *G*; Borisenko *C*; Zakharov *B*; Petrov *A*; Postavnicheva *L*; Alexandrovich *EG* / Moscow Radio Chorus and SO / Samosud and Bron
Melodiya ⓜ D 015041–2

Manon Lescaut

EDWARD GREENFIELD

'Manon is a heroine I believe in' Puccini wrote to his publisher and mentor, Giulio Ricordi, in 1889. 'She cannot fail to win the hearts of the public.' He had just made his choice of subject for an opera which, as both of them well appreciated, would make him or break him. As always it was the attraction of the heroine which above all decided him, and in this instance he had doubly to justify himself, for only five years earlier Massenet's *Manon* had appeared, another operatic adaptation of the Abbé Prevost's novel. The young Italian had obviously to show why the same subject could and should be used again, but the very challenge of rivalry – as so often later in the composer's career – was part of the attraction.

In the event Puccini's heroine hardly matches her French counterpart in subtlety or charm, but against the odds the whole opera triumphantly justifies itself, the first example of fully mature Puccini riotously full of great melodies, the piece that gave him his first runaway success and established him firmly as the successor to Verdi, a title he quickly came to loathe.

Challenging Massenet had one curious and paradoxical result. Though it is the heroine who was Puccini's first love, who gives her name to the opera and who has the most popular aria, 'In quelle trine morbide', the hero takes first place to a degree not matched by any other Puccini opera. One clear reason is that in trying to avoid the scenes and situations used by Massenet, Puccini developed the role of the hero at the expense of the heroine, so much so that in compensation he had to tack on a last act which is little more than an epilogue, giving Manon in her death throes the dramatic vocal opportunities missing till then.

Though on record there have been countless versions of 'In quelle trine morbide' and at least one supremely compelling account of the heroine's role in a complete set, Maria Callas's, the items for the tenor have produced a richer store of recorded repertory, at least in the days of 78rpm records. Enrico Caruso recorded only one item from *Manon Lescaut*, the aria 'Donna non vidi mai' (DA 106; GV 558), but that is a splendid characterful example of his art as it had developed just before the First World War. The tempo is slowish, majestic even, and every word is carefully weighed, so that each phrase brings a touch of individuality, and every area of the voice is superbly exploited. There is no question of inconsistency between the baritonal lower register and the ringing, forward upper register.

At exactly the same period in 1913 Dimitri Smirnov in Russia made another memorable version (5–52851; GV 74), one with exceptionally wide dynamic contrasts and one dramatically extreme *diminuendo*. As recorded the voice displays a hint of flutter but it remains a clean, specific sound. With Francesco Merli (Col. D 1642; LV 162) – who also recorded the role entire in the only complete set made in the days of 78rpm discs – one notes some similarities of approach in this same aria, the light and shade, the *diminuendi* at the ends of phrases, not to mention a hint of flutter.

Not all the versions of the period are as admirable. Giuseppe Anselmi (Fono. 62396; GV 88) pushes his tone so hard he tends to go sharp, and when he allows himself so many *tenuti* the result is sluggish, but the *dolcissimo* phrase just before the high B flat is most elegantly done. Giovanni Martinelli recorded the aria even earlier than Caruso, in 1912 at the beginning of his career (Edison 82507; Celebrity CEL 500). Like Caruso's version Martinelli's is unusually slow, but in its noble stateliness it lacks the detail of the older tenor, and on balance the later better-known HMV version (DA 331; LV 271) is preferable. Nearly forty years later, in 1950, Martinelli recorded more from *Manon Lescaut* (with piano accompaniment) and though the earlier, glorious resonance has gone, and 'No, no, pazzo son' has plentiful glottals, 'Ah Manon' is amazing for a man nearing seventy, steady and true in the lower register, if rather rough at the climax (Continental CLP 103).

Beniamino Gigli's recordings from this opera are worth hearing, an upstanding, heroic account of 'Donna non vidi mai' beautifully phrased (DA 856; GEMM 146) and an account of 'Ah! Manon' with gorgeous tone, open vowels and clean words leading to a long-held B flat (DA 5411; RLS 729).

The tenor who in 78 days made more recordings from this opera than anyone else was Aureliano Pertile. He recorded Pathé and Columbia versions (the latter, possibly the best, most restrained, have recently been collected on LV 1319) of the big arias before doing them again for HMV – the two Act 1 arias on DA 1105 ('Tra voi belle' as well as 'Donna non vidi mai') reissued on LV 46, 'Ah! Manon' (DA 1162; LV 279) and 'No, no, pazzo son' (DB 1111; LV 245). He also did the Act 2 duet with Margaret Sheridan (DB 1281; LV 279), taken very fast to get it on a single side, leading on to 'O tentatrice' on side two. These were strong and individual performances (the voice among the most distinctive ever recorded) marred by sudden excesses of passion which in 'No, no, pazzo son' verged on the hysterical with sobbing laughter after 'imploro'. By contrast in this aria Francesco Merli has no hint of sobbing at all (Col. D 14642; LV 162), a version recorded at much the same period as the complete set, in which not surprisingly he completely outshone his Manon, the twittery Maria Zamboni. Among earlier singers who made multiple recordings of items from *Manon Lescaut* was Giovanni Zenatello, who recorded 'Donna non vidi mai' no fewer than three times, as well as 'Ah! Manon' and 'No, no, pazzo son'. That last is marred by sobbing, but the legato line is wonderfully pure. By contrast Anselmi in 'Ah! Manon' (Fono. 62397; CO 359) is disappointingly lachrymose at a slow tempo, tremulous, with poor legato.

Alfred Piccaver, the darling of Vienna, recorded 'Donna non vidi mai' in 1919 (Od. 76807; LV 26), and – in odd Italian – produced a pure stream of lovely lyrical sound. Piccaver's British background and training come out hardly at all, but the period Englishness of Browning Mummery in that same aria, quaintly translated, 'Never did I behold a fairer maiden' (HMV B 3160) is its dominant characteristic. His is a light clean voice nicely shaded (as in 'Manon Lescaut they call me') with beautiful diction and no coarsening on top.

Generally the Italian tenors from 78 days (Lauri-Volpi provides another example in his 'No, no, pazzo son' on DA 1385; LV 260) represented a lyrical tradition that was interrupted in the early years of LP. For all the ringing resonance of tone, Mario del Monaco's portrayal in the complete Decca set opposite Renata Tebaldi is depressingly coarse in its insistent *fortissimo*. That is so even in the delicate first aria, 'Tra voi belle', which comes out in an unvaried throaty roar. More disappointing still – because he has since established himself as one of the most sensitive and intelligent of tenors – is the complete recording of 1972 from HMV featuring as Des Grieux Placido Domingo, singing opposite the Manon of Montserrat Caballé. Domingo gives a performance lacking in detail, delivered for the most part – like Del Monaco's – at *forte* or above, varied only by the fact that the balance engineers seem unable to settle the scale of the voice. In most of his duets with Caballé his placing is noticeably less prominent than that of the soprano, but fascinatingly the recording which Caballé made of the Act 2 duet 'Tu, tu amore tu' a year earlier than the complete recording brought quite a different balance between soprano and tenor (ASD 2723). In that instance Des Grieux is sung by Bernabé Martí, Caballé's husband, and close placing brings the voice into sharp focus, a creditable performance but one which pales before the drive of Caballé herself, in even finer voice than on the complete set. She thrusts ahead of her conductor, Sir Charles Mackerras, in the opening section, but later relaxes ravishingly in the linking unaccompanied phrases marked *a piacere* before Des Grieux's 'O tentatrice'.

Separate recordings of that second-act duet are relatively rare. One which commemorates success at the Met. in New York is from Dorothy Kirsten and Richard Tucker contained in a series of excerpts from this opera with Fausto Cleva conducting (Am. Col. ML 4981, Odyssey Y 31737). In that as well as Kirsten's 'L'ora o Tirsi' and 'Sola perduta abbandonata' Cleva insists on a brisk metrical beat. Tucker compensates with some lachrymose attack, but Kirsten sounds disappointingly matter-of-fact despite her lovely bright voice.

Another series of excerpts connected with live performance was recorded in Stockholm in 1929 when the first Swedish performance of this opera was given with Joseph Hislop as Des Grieux and Greta Söderman as Manon.

Never circulated outside Scandinavia, the original recordings – in Swedish – (DA 1083–4; DB 1394) have been splendidly transferred by Rubini (RS 308) with Hislop at the age of forty-five singing vividly and with great passion. Because of a strike, the recording had to be made in a Stockholm hotel, but the sound is clear and in 'Tra voi, belle' they even manage to include a chorus. Other items are 'Tu, tu amore tu' as well as the later second-act duet, 'Ah Manon', and 'Guardate, no, no, pazzo son' from Act 3.

Later, towards the end of the 78 era, came a version of 'Donna non vidi mai' that set new standards of refinement, a noble reading, naturally commanding, with clean, ringing tone (DA 1908; RLS 715), and the singer may well have been influenced by those Stockholm performances. It was the great Swedish tenor Jussi Björling, who in the mid-fifties went on to record the role complete for RCA opposite Licia Albanese with Jonel Perlea conducting, a performance that established lyrical standards for a new generation. This version of *Manon Lescaut*, limited as its circulation has been in Europe, is arguably Björling's most characteristic performance in a recorded opera. Certainly he shines above every rival in the complete recordings.

'L'amor? L'amor? Questa tragedia, ovver commedia, io non conosco!' That line of interruption makes an off-beat first entry for the hero, but Björling gives it just the right point – the youthful boastfulness, the hint of irony. As in 'Tra voi, belle', which follows almost at once, he shows a striking ability to convey forward movement, a sense of urgency, while paying close attention to detail. Here and all through his part he uses a free *rubato*, a fluctuation of tempo that has little in common with the ungainly push and pull of Del Monaco. 'Con grazia', wrote Puccini over the first notes of 'Tra voi, belle', and Björling is one of the few modern tenors to observe that instruction, matching the staccato accompaniment with a light, heady tone. Giuseppe di Stefano on the Columbia set from La Scala, with Tullio Serafin conducting and Maria Callas as Manon, like Björling, conveys the humour, and he sings *con slancio*, but by comparison he is heavy-handed.

The beginning of the love duet, 'Cortese damigella', emphasizes these contrasts, and into my comparison comes Flaviano Labò, who sings Des Grieux opposite Anna Moffo in the Puccini half of RCA's 'Portrait of Manon'. Labò sounds fresh and young, but plainly he is never inside the part. When it comes to the aria, 'Donna non vidi mai', his legato is reasonable enough, but the phrasing throughout is completely unimaginative, so that it rarely leads the ear onward. Björling by contrast utters the words 'Cortese damigella' almost to himself, in the tones of one who has just seen a miracle, and again at the opening of 'Donna non vidi mai' he conveys a similar inward quality without ever losing command. If there is a particular moment in this sequence which illustrates Björling's mastery more vividly than any other, it is on the words: 'E in voi l'aprile nel volto si palesa e fiorisce' ('In your face, April appears and flowers'). 'Con calore', writes Puccini over the first phrase, and qualifies that with a sequence of tempo indications – *a tempo* for two notes, then *animando* until the final note of the second phrase, which brings *poco rit*, extended for the tenor into the first two notes of the third phrase 'E fiorisce', after which *a tempo* is indicated for the last four notes. The point about Björling's interpretation is that he observes these markings minutely, and in doing so (with the help of his conductor, Jonel Perlea) transforms the whole passage. 'E fiorisce', allowed to relax after the preceding phrase, brings a moment of *frisson* that the others completely miss. Here and elsewhere Di Stefano gets nearest to Björling, but even he does a clumsy triplet on 'fiorisce', and when it comes to Del Monaco, there is no attempt at any variation of tone colour over the three phrases. The only point in favour of the Del Monaco approach at this point is that Tebaldi's Manon is made to sound the more tender, with her phrases 'Manon Lescaut mi chiamo' uttered genuinely 'con semplicità'.

Björling's contrasts of tone colour are of course extremes – in between 'susurro gentil' and 'Deh! non cessar!' for example at the end of 'Donna non vidi mai' – and, as ever, the top notes tend to sharpen a fraction under pressure (parallel with Pertile) but the refinement is what stands out. This is the Chevalier Des Grieux, a passionate student perhaps but a nobleman too. That comes out most strikingly at the climax of 'no, no, pazzo son' at the end of Act 3, where Björling uses the colouring of the voice (notably on the superb top B and following phrases 'Ah, pietà') to convey tears. Del Monaco, Di Stefano and Domingo all indulge by contrast in forced sobbing in the bar's gap after 'imploro'.

Earlier in the same aria, Björling's shading of tone on his sad thoughtful cries of 'No, no, pazzo son' has one visualizing the man thinking for a moment to himself, before launching into his passionate appeal to the ship's captain: 'Guardate'. Di Stefano may also begin this aria compellingly, but even in 1957 when this set was made, he would fall from time to time into the raw, throaty production which spoilt so much of his later singing.

As to the portrayals of the heroine in the complete sets there is no doubt that Maria Callas's is by far the most vivid, but in breathing life into Puccini's relatively conventionalized heroine she departs even farther than usual from the figure presented in the Abbé Prevost's novel. In Act 2, Manon is made to sound not so much bored with the riches around her as just plain bad-tempered, ready to snap the head off of even the most protective millionaire. Callas takes 'In quelle trine morbide' at a very measured pace, sustaining the line superbly, but she cannot completely disguise the vocal difficulties for her. She does not attempt a real half-tone at the beginning, finding it hard to place the voice gently on the exposed notes, first E flat, later G flat with which the big sequential phrases begin. The two top B flats later in the aria bring hints of spreading, but they are minimal, and what matters is the detailed imagination, each phrase newly illuminated, both musically and in word meaning. Apart from the beat on the final D flat the last phrase of the aria is magical, literally 'come un sogno gentile', though some might complain that she ignores the instruction not to slow down. Her interpretation on her celebrated Puccini recital record (ALP 3799) is very similar, but the recording acoustic is kinder and the B flats are firmer.

'In quelle trine morbide' marks the high point of Tebaldi's interpretation of the role of Manon. Her care over phrasing, her poise which makes a fairly fast tempo sound relaxed and easy, give her account a formal perfection that put it at an opposite from Callas's. Not that the singing is in any way stiff. The opening done on a half-tone is wonderfully light, and again the half-tone returns for the change to 2/4 in the second half. She observes Puccini's characteristically detailed indications (including the 'senza rallentare') but still manages to phrase with an easy, spontaneous-sounding *rubato*. The tone is not always quite so golden at the top – better in stereo than mono – but it is the evenness, the sheer reliability that makes this so satisfying an account of the aria.

In terms of characterization, one could well argue that Licia Albanese, who sings Manon opposite Björling, gets closest to the composer's own conception. There is no doubt that she conveys a petted and pampered character in this Act 2, but throughout her performance it is very hard indeed to ignore the uneven production. In fact it was Albanese's misfortune at an age when many sopranos retain their full youthful freshness to sound older than she was. It has something to do with the plaintiveness of tone colour coupled with a fairly pronounced vibrato. So, though 'In quelle trine morbide' is done lightly with nice pointing, the image of Manon is not very convincing. It is the same at almost every point. 'L'ora, o Tirsi', later in the act, brings a most unstylish account of the difficult semiquaver phrases, clumsy and insecure, but then in the second half she sounds more confident and produces a fine top C out of the hat. Tebaldi too has to tread carefully in 'L'ora, o Tirsi', at least in the first half which has far too many intrusive 'hs' helping to define the semiquavers and the merest apology of a trill. Only in the second half does the phrasing regain its confidence. In this brief passage, of course, Callas points more delicately than anyone else, with semiquavers, turns and trills all stylishly defined, and a warm expansiveness in the second half.

Curiously Moffo's selection misses out 'L'ora, o Tirsi'. Generally this is a disappointing account of the role. Having presented the Massenet so charmingly on the companion disc, Miss Moffo seems over-anxious to inject meaning into every phrase. 'In quelle trine morbide' is marred by a continual suspicion of under-the-note attack, of a kind that if pressed harder would provide a soprano equivalent of Gigli's pouting manner. The codetta is done with beautiful simplicity, but that is the exception. Similarly in the final aria of Act 4, 'Sola, perduta, abbandonata', Moffo rather curiously chooses a fastish, flowing tempo that makes it easier to phrase, but then seems to regret the inevitable (and inappropriate) lightness of manner by pointing the words exaggeratedly.

Albanese also points individual words with great care in the final aria, but the result is genuinely expressive, and the build-up before the *allegro* is strongly sustained. But then the fast tempos seem to undermine her confidence, and she sounds flustered. Here as elsewhere the actual voice quality is distractingly inappropriate. Tebaldi takes something of the same approach as in 'In quelle trine morbide' with a fastish tempo disguised, this time, with dark, heavy tone colour. The variation of tone from phrase to phrase is finely controlled with a superb climax in the D-flat section.

On the 1972 HMV set, Caballé gives what is arguably the most beautiful rendering of the role of Manon in the complete recordings. In the early seventies her voice was at its peak with the wide range of tone consistently even and firm at every level of dynamic. 'In quelle trine morbide' is light and flowing, marred only by some excessive underlining. At no point is she much helped by the perfunctory manner of the conductor, Bruno Bartoletti, and one has to wait for the last act for a degree of coolness in the manner to disappear. But there her account of 'Sola, perduta, abbandonata' is commanding, not at all uninvolved, with consistently firm tone and clean attack.

But even Caballé in this curious epilogue of a fourth act has to yield before Maria Callas. She more than anyone justifies it as a necessary and satisfying conclusion to the opera. The weight and darkness of voice at the opening might in principle seem wrong for the character of Manon, but Callas immediately makes one feel that such a weight is implicit in the music. To hear her sing such a line as 'Ahimè, son sola!' in her unique chest register is unforgettable. Her intensity carries her with gathering momentum, until the D-flat section brings just the lightening and contrast most sopranos fail to find. Unless a clear contrast is made, as is done by Callas, the passage sounds simply as though the composer has strayed into a major key by accident, forgetting his purpose for a moment.

As for the final outburst on 'Non voglio morir', Callas conveys a depth of conviction that makes most other interpretations sound trivial and false. Curiously she adds an extra, unscripted 'No!' after the final 'aita!' ('Help!') – not with any authority I imagine but simply the overwhelming compulsion of the moment.

Though in her recital record version (ALP 3799) the chest register may not be quite so resonant, the performance gains in other ways – as does 'In quelle trine morbide' – from the less boxy acoustic. Accompanying her, Tullio Serafin is if anything even more understanding in his expansiveness. Certainly the recital disc is a necessary supplement to the complete recording.

Dorothy Kirsten's version of that last aria with Met forces has already been referred to, and it includes the closing duet, again with Richard Tucker. Kirsten, though still not relaxing, gives a deeply felt performance, lightening well for 'Mio dolce amor, tu piangi' in the final duet. Other notable separate versions of 'Sola, perduta, abbandonata' include one by Galina Vishnevskaya (Artia ALP 157) the voice pure and concentrated, betraying little of the unevenness that has sometimes afflicted it. The singing is clear and intense, and builds up to a superb, powerful climax but detail and characterization are limited with changes of face not well established. Dame Joan Hammond recorded 'Sola, perduta, abbandonata' twice, on 78 in the late forties (C 3720) and ten years later on LP (RLS 2900 143). The contrasts between the two are fascinating. The 78 version – which supplemented Dame Joan's recording of 'In quelle trine morbide', very slow, rather plain but deeply felt (B 9705; RLS 2900 143) – has an idiosyncratic text. This aria, just too long to contain conveniently on a 78 side, is here truncated at the end (at Fig. 14 in the score) before the final climax with its top B flat. It is replaced by a monotone on low F. But earlier, more surprisingly, some eight bars are added, presumably from an early Puccini edition, immediately before 'Terra di pace' six bars before Fig. 12. That prepares the way for the modulation to D flat and the *dolce* marking, but Puccini was plainly right to omit those bars when the sudden emergence of sunlight in the major key is magical and needs no such preparation.

Dame Joan's LP version is textually unexceptionable, the performance more relaxed and measured, suggesting that indeed the 78 side-length had brought a degree of inhibition. The LP brings a slow, darkly expressive performance with words underlined in reflection of the detached *marcato* passages. There is fine tonal contrast with a superb top A on 'Ah tutto e finito' if a touch of rawness on the final B flat. Few versions can match this in the range of volume suggested.

Just before Dame Joan recorded her 78 version of that final aria, EMI had recorded another in Italy, with Adriana Guerrini (DX 1431; OASI 618), and that too had a cut text, with the whole section between Fig. 11 and Fig. 12 omitted so that the contrast of 'Terra di pace' disappears. It is a rich Italianate voice of no special distinction with a ripe chest register. There is good scaling down for 'asil di pace' and a splendid top B flat. Much more distinguished is the account of 'Sola, perduta, abbandonata' which Magda Olivero recorded for Cetra (BB 25277; LPO 2008), where the contrasts of mood are unforgettably established, the opening grave and concentrated with Olivero's rapid flutter very characterful, 'Terra di pace' almost soubrettish in its lightening of mood followed by a big *stringendo* for the final climax, which has the singer snorting fire in her vehemence.

One of the earliest recordings of 'In quelle trine morbide' came – along with an account of 'L'ora, o Tirsi', the other *arioso* from Act 2 – from the soprano who had created the role in 1893, and who was also the first Mimì, Cesira Ferrani (G&T 53283; MCK 50). They are straightforward readings, the opening phrase of 'In quelle trine morbide' attacked hard, unfloated. Another very early version (undated) was included in the first album of HMV's 'Record of Singing'. Lina Cavalieri was the first Manon in the United States, singing opposite Caruso at the Met. She was dubbed 'the most beautiful woman in the world' and many years later her life story was portrayed on film by Gina Lollobrigida. After that her singing seems nothing special, at least as caught on record (Col. A 5178; RLS 7706). 'In quelle trine morbide' is sung with fresh tone but the downward scoops are ugly and rhythmic control non-existent, until in the second half Cavalieri steps ahead briskly in march rhythm.

Frances Alda made an acoustic version of 'In quelle trine morbide' (Victor 87106; CO 383), and then in 1928 only a year before her retirement, well into the age of electrical recording, went back to the same aria, adding 'L'ora o Tirsi (DA 1156; Club 99.45). In the first aria there is not a sign of wear in the voice with consistently clean attack and beautifully spun out top B flat at the end of the first half. 'L'ora o Tirsi' is similarly clean and sparkling, with big *tenuti* and a pure top B flat. As one admirer put it, the performances have 'the touch of a Marchesi pupil'. It was in 1929 that Alda sang this role opposite Gigli and De Luca in her farewell performance at the Met.

The twenties brought a spate of recordings of 'In quelle trine morbide'. Claudia Muzio anticipated the trend in one of her first recordings, made in New York in 1917 (Pathé 5608; GV 576). After a lightweight start she plunges into tragic darkness, and at the very end on the last phrase her half-tone *tenuto* has wonderful poise. At that time too Carmen Melis (later to become the teacher of Tebaldi) recorded a fresh and bright version, sympathetic but without much shading (Fono. 69272; Rococo 5259). Another singer who very early in her career recorded the aria was Rosa Ponselle, who did an acoustic version in 1923 (Col. 2014 M; GVC 9) which already brings out her characteristically creamy tone with finely shaded dynamics and a superbly sustained top B flat at the end of the first half. The last phrase of all is very slow and thoughtful, the turn on C flat sung in slow motion.

Another thoughtful performance came from Hina Spani later in the twenties in electric days (DA 879; LV 147) accompanied by the orchestra of La Scala. The first half is light and flexible, expanding into a slow and reflective second half with the final phrase sung as though in self-communion. In 1924 before the end of the acoustic era Lotte Lehmann recorded the aria in German (Od. Lxx 80936; 1C 137–30704–5), the first half urgent and forthright with word meaning brought out in each phrase, the second slow and sustained with little shading except at the very end. Her compatriot, Meta Seinemeyer, recorded the aria in 1927 in rather German-sounding Italian (Parlo. P 9819; LV 112), and unusually for the period she observed the marking *lo stesso movimento* at the beginning of the second half (maybe the influence of her conductor and husband-to-be, Frieder Weissmann), keeping the tempo the same, where the custom (as Puccini must have anticipated) was to slow down markedly.

In Dusolina Giannini's recording, made in 1929 with the Berlin State Opera Orchestra under Clemens Schmalstich (DB 1264; LV 8) the hard attack at the start contrasts sharply with fine shading later on, notably on the very last phrase where the turn is most gracefully executed. Those who heard her often said that the microphones used for electrical recording hardened her voice, and from this one can believe it. From the same year comes the first of Mafalda Favero's versions (Col. D 6016; Tima-38), also a trifle hard in tone, but touching in expression. By 1937 when she recorded it again (DB 3200; Tima-38), the shading and inflections were deeper.

Quite the most extraordinary version of the aria from 78 days came from a British soprano not usually associated with opera, Lillian Stiles Allen. For Edison Bell on a twelve-inch disc (X 566) she managed to sing the aria twice over, linking the two performances. The first is urgent and bright-eyed with the final phrases beautifully moulded, but then to one's surprise the final D flat of 'd'amor' rises to D and up to E flat to start the aria a second time. On the repeat the modulation in the middle from E flat major to G flat major is completely ignored with the phrase 'O mia dimora' returning on B flat instead of D flat.

From the age of LP two unusually interesting versions stem from live concerts in 1964. Bidu Sayão (Club 99 : 40) with her distinctive timbre makes the first half heavier than the second, while the legendary Magda Olivero – who was in her early fifties at the time of the concert in Amsterdam – gives a performance rather like Spani's, fast and characterful, full of contrasts, with the final phrases of each half drawn out lovingly.

Generally the age of LP has brought greater concern for details of the score, and that is so, whether at one extreme Tebaldi has concentrated above all on vocal beauty (her recital version of 'In quelle trine morbide' is characteristically firm and reliable (LXT 2507) like that in the complete recording) or at the other Callas has found a whole new unsuspected stratum of emotion. Raina Kabaivanska, an appreciable Puccini soprano of recent years, supports her reputation in her version (RL 31476). Sylvia Sass (SXL 6841) is, predictably, more mannered.

There is little need to pause over the other roles. The part of Lescaut is almost incidental: even his most memorable arioso at the beginning of Act 2 is little more than a preparation for 'In quelle trine morbide' a few pages later, anticipating the second half of that aria in its own second half, albeit at a slightly faster tempo, *andantino mosso*. In the Björling/Albanese set Robert Merrill sings with fine tone and characteristically clean attack, far more impressive than Mario Borriello the weak Lescaut in the Decca set. Vicente Sardinero takes the role in the Domingo/Caballé set, giving a stylish, youthful-sounding performance, well contrasted with the distinctive Geronte of Noel Mangin. Otherwise the Geronte to note is Fernando Corena on the Decca set. For the comprimario role of Edmondo HMV in the Domingo/Caballé set chose Robert Tear, acknowledging the prominence of the part in Act 1. He is much more of a foil for the principal tenor than the ubiquitous Piero de Palma on the Tebaldi/Del Monaco set or even Mario Carlin in the Björling/Albanese.

Of other LP sets the Cetra version of 1953 was very quickly overtaken by the Tebaldi/Del Monaco, but recorded a few years earlier still, in 1946, was a Russian version which has had little circulation in the West, like the Qualiton disc of excerpts recorded by the Budapest State Opera Company in 1966. The surprising thing is that after the burst of activity in the mid-fifties the record companies have so neglected the piece.

The HMV set of 1972 was a stopgap merely, and when DG recorded the opera again in January 1984 with the conductor who had been in charge of the Covent Garden performances the previous year, Giuseppe Sinopoli, the tenor who was again chosen was Placido Domingo, benefiting from stage experience. Opposite him was Mirella Freni, who at the end of 1983 had sung her first Manon in San Francisco, also benefiting from having sung the role on stage. Ten years earlier she had recorded the Act 2 duet, 'Tu, tu amore, tu' with Franco Bonisolli (Acanta DC 22007), giving a tender, vulnerable, very feminine performance, beautifully shaded, one which promises well for the complete recording. With Renato Bruson as Lescaut, Kurt Rydl as Geronte and John Tomlinson as the Sea Captain, that set, unissued at the time of writing, is the hope of the future in a work which, considering its special effectiveness on record, remains under-represented.

MANON LESCAUT

M Manon Lescaut; *L* Lescaut; *G* Grieux; *Ger* Geronte; *Ed* Edmondo

1930 Zamboni *M*; Conati *L*; Merli *G*;
 Bordonali *Ger*; Nessi *Ed* / La
 Scala Chorus, Milan SO / Molajoli
 EMI ⓜ 3C 153 18411–2M
 CBS (US) ⓜ SL 111

1946 (in Russian)
 Rozhdestvenskaya *M*; Zakharov
 L; Tarkhov *G*; Polyaev *Ger*;
 Shadilor *Ed* / Moscow Radio
 Chorus and Orch. / Orlov
 Melodiya ⓜ D 09245–50

1953 Petrella *M*; Meletti *L*;
 Campagnano *G*; Latinucci *Ger*;
 Pane *Ed* / Italian Radio Chorus
 and Orch., Turin / Del Cupolo
 Cetra ⓜ LP0 2053
 Everest © 461 (3)

1954 Tebaldi *M*; Borriello *L*; Del
 Monaco *G*; Corena *Ger*; De
 Palma *Ed* / Santa Cecilia Academy
 Chorus and Orch. / Molinari-
 Pradelli
 Decca GOS 607–8
 London OSA 1317

1954 Albanese *M*; Merrill *L*; Björling
 G; Calabrese *Ger*; Carlin *Ed* /
 Rome Opera Chorus and Orch. /
 Perlea
 RCA (US) ⓜ VIC 6027
 RCA (Italy) ⓜ VL 43544

1957 Callas *M*; Fioravanti *L*; Di Stefano
 G; Calabrese *Ger*; Formichini *Ed*
 / La Scala Chorus and Orch. /
 Serafin
 EMI ⓜ RLS 737 ④ TC-RLS737
 Seraphim ⓜ IC 6089 ④
 4X3G-6089

1972 Caballé *M*; Sardinero *L*; Domingo
 G; Mangin *Ger*; Tear *Ed* /
 Ambrosian Opera Chorus, New
 Philharmonia / Bartoletti
 EMI SLS 962
 Angel SBLX 3782 ④ 4X2S-3782

1984 Freni *M*; Bruson *L*; Domingo *G*;
 Rydl *Ger*; Leggate *Ed* / Royal
 Op. Chorus, Philharmonia /
 Sinopoli
 DG (awaiting release)

1963 (excerpts)
 Moffo *M*; Kerns *L*; Labò *G*;
 Rocchi *Ed* / RCA Italiana Opera
 Chorus and Orch. / Leibowitz
 RCA (US) LSC 7028
 RCA (Italy) GL42558 ④
 GK42558

1966 (excerpts – in Hungarian)
 Házy *M*; Melis *L*; Ilosfalvy *G*;
 Maleczky *Ger* / Budapest State
 Opera Chorus and Orch. /
 Erdélyi
 Qualiton SLPX 1254

La fanciulla del West

EDWARD GREENFIELD

In gramophone circles, the story is told of two British recording teams meeting in Italy. Curious, an EMI executive asked his Decca opposite number what the rival group was up to. 'Oh, *Fanciulla del West*,' came the answer. 'That's funny,' said the first. 'so are we!'

At that point in the mid-fifties, only Italian Cetra had come out with a complete recording of this Wild West opera, and that was an indifferent set. A 1954 recording of a live performance in Florence, conducted by Mitropoulos, has also been listed by Cetra but has had virtually no currency. The field was, therefore, wide open, and it was not much of a coincidence that both EMI and Decca spotted the gap simultaneously. Their work was so successful – or at least, they satisfied that market so completely – that it was only after a gap of twenty years that another recording appeared: from DG, directly based on the Covent Garden production of the opera conducted by Zubin Mehta.

As in the opera house – where wild enthusiasm following the Metropolitan première, under Toscanini, evaporated all too quickly – *La fanciulla del West* has been the most neglected of the major Puccini operas on record. Unfairly so, when technically it is the most advanced Puccini opera before *Turandot*, with Debussy's device of the whole-tone scale turned into something totally Puccinian and with exotic sources used unexpectedly and imaginatively. It also boasts a closing scene – when the reformed bandit, Dick Johnson, rides happily off into the sunset along with Minnie, the Girl of the Golden West – which is arguably the most tear-laden of all Puccini's final curtains, outstripping all his tragic endings.

It was by calculation that Puccini sought, after *Madama Butterfly*, to exploit in this American subject the same areas of popularity as the then rapidly developing world of the silent cinema. The ending is clearly cinematic, but so is the whole subject, when the Wild West – admittedly with cowboys rather than goldminers – was that medium's prime subject. Like *Butterfly*, *La fanciulla* (or *The Girl* as Puccini himself habitually called it in his correspondence) was based on a play by David Belasco, but where *Butterfly* had immediately captured the composer's imagination the moment he saw the play, *The Girl of The Golden West*, first seen by Puccini early in 1907 when

in New York for the first American performance of *Butterfly*, took longer to
fire him. In April he asked for a copy of the play, and by June he was
seriously considering it, but it was not until August 1909, after a distressing
episode in his private life, when his wife's accusations against their servant
girl Doria pushed her to suicide, that he got down to work seriously.

Puccini always found it hard to settle on the subject of an opera, knowing
that he needed to be totally involved in the story if he was to write an
inspired score, but the gap between *Butterfly* in February 1904 and *La
fanciulla* in December 1910 – nearly seven years – was the longest between
operas in his whole career. For long it was felt that the circumstances behind
the choice of subject and the composition of the opera had indeed left their
mark on the finished result, and certainly with several obvious exceptions,
above all the tenor aria 'Ch'ella mi creda', it is not so readily tuneful as its
predecessors. Puccini, from the start, was anxious to break away from the
'old carcases – *Bohème*, *Butterfly* and Co.' and to write an opera 'modern
in construction, and moving', yet during composition he sometimes referred
to *La fanciulla* as another *Bohème*, meaning that the crowd scenes of the
goldminers were aiming at a comparable admixture of comedy. However,
the striking Puccinian precedent for *La fanciulla* is *Tosca*. As Mosco Carner
has said in his formidable study of the composer*: 'In a sense it was *Tosca*
translated from Rome to the Cloudy Mountains of California . . . As in
Tosca the plot of *The Girl* centres on a triangular contest among two men
and a woman in which the stakes are the woman's honour and her lover's life,
and in which the villain of the piece is the Scarpia-like character occupying a
position similar to that of the Roman Chief of Police – the Sheriff Rance.'

In the opera house, the Wild West subject – unlike the colourful Japanese
setting of *Butterfly* – has generally worked against *La fanciulla's* acceptance,
but although it too often evokes the wrong overtones for Grand Opera, it is
easier to accept the idea of tough miners with names like Sid and Harry
weeping tears of homesickness when one hears the piece on record. On
record one is also readier to accept the slow dramatic pace of the long first
act. Though there is plenty of incident in the first scene, nothing is directly
related to the main plot until the belated arrival of the heroine, when, after
her bible class, Rance makes his first advance. The arrival of the hero is
even more belated, but musically the structure is satisfying, and in this act
Puccini effectively exploits his new style of aria or arioso, less immediately
tuneful than those of previous operas. The set piece of Rance's 'Minnie dalla
mia casa' immediately followed by Minnie's 'Laggiù nel Soledad', similarly
autobiographical, has fine economy and sharpness of focus. In his music
Puccini, as in *Tosca* and *Butterfly*, succeeded in heightening cheap original
sources, and if in *La fanciulla del West* he failed to create characters as
strongly three-dimensional, this lay in their intrinsic inconsistencies rather
than in any shortcomings in the score.

* Duckworth, 2nd ed. 1974

If the opera is to carry conviction, much depends on the conductor, and the four recordings, Cetra, Decca, HMV and DG, illustrate sharp differences of approach. The 1950 Cetra set under Arturo Basile brings contributions from chorus and orchestra as rough as the solo singing, and though, like other opera recordings from this source, it seems to stem from a performance given for radio, it fails to convey much dramatic thrust. Franco Capuana on the Decca recording of 1958 with Renata Tebaldi, Mario del Monaco and Cornell MacNeil makes many of his dramatic points with a degree of reticence. Influenced perhaps by the Debussian source of much of the inspiration, and helped by stereo recording which at the time set new standards and can be made to sound refined even today, Capuana presents consistently fresh, clean textures. He may sometimes underplay big emotional climaxes and the very opening of the opera is not as immediately exciting as in rival versions, but the cool beauty of the Jack Wallace minstrel song, 'Che faranno i vecchi miei', irresistibly haunting, is superbly captured, and the very end of the opera, taken evenly and steadily, is the more touching for that relative avoidance of overt expressiveness.

The views of both Lovro von Matačić on the HMV set with Birgit Nilsson as the heroine and Zubin Mehta on the DG performance based on Covent Garden's production are more highly coloured. As Mosco Carner has pointed out, 'No other source of Puccini's, not even that of *Turandot*, is studded with so many markings for excessive dynamics and a "barbaric" manner of playing.' Mehta in particular, with contrasts of tempo as well as of dynamic sharper than usual, consistently intensifies the drama. It is not just the wider-ranging, more aggressive 1977 recording that reinforces that impact of the performance, but the actual approach. Plainly it helped to have the recording made in conjunction with stage performances, with all contributions – orchestra as well as soloists and chorus – knowing the music thoroughly and conveying that with total commitment. That concluding scene of the opera is more luscious than with Capuana, more overtly emotional with the impact of climaxes superbly timed. Matačić, often effective in his comparably expressive style, is at this point less convincing than either, when the underlining carries less conviction, sounds more contrived.

If the pattern of each of these performances is quickly established by the conductors first in the prelude, then in the minstrel song – Giorgio Tozzi on the Capuana set the most darkly resonant, closely matched by Gwynne Howell for Mehta – their character also depends fundamentally on the sopranos taking the title role. Renata Tebaldi's performance on the Capuana set is among the finest of her many interpretations on record, even though at the time of the recording she had not sung the role on stage, and was not to do so for many years. In 1958 the open strength of her singing conveyed the forthright quality of Minnie's character with the characteristic timbre firm and forward, marred only by rawness on exposed notes above the stave. The most striking example of that – almost endearing in context – is the *fortissimo* top C in the climactic phrase of the Act 1 aria 'Laggiù nel Soledad' on the words 'S'amavan tanto. Ah!' Less well suited to the Tebaldi voice and technique is the aria in Act 2, 'Oh, se sapeste', with its quick dotted rhythms and what Carner calls 'its un-Puccinian heartiness in gambolling coloratura', with intrusive aitches punctuating the semiquavers. It is a precise account, but cautious not warm.

In that aria it is very evident how much more comfortable both Nilsson and Carol Neblett (on DG) sound, both of them sopranos who, in notable performances, have coped with Mozartian coloratura, Nilsson as Donna Anna in *Don Giovanni* and Neblett as Vitellia in *La clemenza di Tito* (in the Salzburg Festival production). Nilsson is the more agile and her top B is firm and clean, but the tone is not beautiful. Neblett swallows her words, but musically she is more imaginative with the voice adroitly lightened for the 'gambolling coloratura' but with warm, rounded tone elsewhere, except on the top B which is a little raw.

Nilsson in 1958 was not the first choice for the EMI recording. That would seem to have been Maria Callas, but at two weeks' notice Nilsson was asked to step in and, as it was her first major recording offer, she promptly accepted. Even today she remembers the extreme problems of learning the role, when, as she says, there are so many uneven bar lengths, and when the exposed top notes put just as extreme a strain on the voice as the role of Turandot, with which she was later to be associated and which in fact she finds less sympathetic. Unusually for Nilsson there are many passages, particularly in lower registers at less than full volume, where vibrato intrudes, and the relatively backward recording balance does not help her to make her full impact, but she nevertheless establishes clearly the place of Minnie as a sort of Puccinian Brünnhilde, one who, in the final scene, comes galloping up on her steed to save her hero.

The inconsistencies in the character of Minnie – the tough, gun-toting gal, able to stand up to a whole regiment of men, who yet has never been kissed – are hardly sorted out in Nilsson's performance. The subtle, offbeat ending to Act 1 is a disappointment where, over offstage humming from six tenors of the chorus, Minnie muses to her own theme and Puccini refuses to allow a final tonic chord, ending the act on an unresolved discord, B and D added to a C major triad. That moment, as Carner says, seems to pose a question 'to which the answer is to be given in the next act', and Neblett more than both her principal rivals conveys not only the strength and warmth of Minnie as a character but the vital element of vulnerability which that close so clearly indicates. Tebaldi to a degree conveys it too, but Neblett, with her intensive experience of playing the part on stage (not just at Covent Garden), gives the most complete performance. Hers is a Minnie completely attuned to her background, where even the warm-hearted Tebaldi might have arrived in the Polka bar the previous week.

In 'Laggiù del Soledad' the sharpness of pointing by Mehta in the accompanying cakewalk rhythms heightens the tenderness and warmth of Neblett's singing, vulnerability already evident. Then for the climax of the passage on

'S'amavan tanto' Neblett is the more moving for starting *pianissimo*, taking her cue for that dynamic from the marking for the orchestra. The vocal line as such has an immediately preceding *crescendo* which can be taken to justify the more extrovert *fortissimo* start from Tebaldi and Nilsson, but there is no doubt how much deeper emotionally Neblett is in the controlled shading of her expressiveness from *piano* to full *fortissimo* within five bars.

The superiority of Neblett as Minnie – and for that matter the superiority of other points in the DG set – is confirmed in the difficult close of Act 2, where Minnie, in her poker game with Rance, triumphantly puts down three aces and a pair, 'Tre assi e un paio!' Tebaldi does it rather comically with an implication of a schoolgirlish 'So there!', and Nilsson does as well as anyone can while trying to sing the notes actually notated, which is virtually impossible to do convincingly. Neblett by contrast makes it a superb and confident pay-off, and Sherrill Milnes as Rance comes back most effectively with a muttered 'Buona notte!' far more telling than either the overtly melodramatic manner of Andrea Mongelli opposite Nilsson for HMV or the straight matter-of-fact manner of Cornell MacNeil for Decca.

If Neblett as Minnie outshines her direct rivals on the DG set, Milnes as Rance (though not in the Covent Garden cast) even more strikingly surpasses them in giving a fully rounded portrait, making the sheriff both sinister and noble at the same time. As Belasco's original makes clear, Rance is far from being so double-died a villain as Scarpia, brutal as he may be. MacNeil on the Decca set sings with fine firm tone, but there are few sparks of imagination, and the result is that nobility in Rance is emphasized too strongly, though that is convincing enough in the Act 1 aria 'Minnie dalla mia casa', where his tone of understatement – the good guy put in the role of baddie – is touching. Mongelli, on HMV, also produces rich tone, but the style is less pure with some intrusive sliding between notes. After both of them, Milnes provides a revelation for, while the unexpected element of nobility is clear, the malice in the character comes out vividly, when the words are presented in such detail, and the sly caddish side of Rance is brought out. One can imagine that this Rance might genuinely be in love with Minnie, but he is none the less a villain for that.

The Minnie on the Cetra set, Carla Gavazzi, and the Rance, Ugo Savarese, are no match for their rivals on the three subsequently recorded sets and neither is the Dick Johnson of Vasco Campagnano. Curiously their voices as recorded all suffer from a similar fault, for each has a distracting flutter, and it is possible that the recording is partly responsible. But in any case there is little imagination shown in any of their performances, and Campagnano's culminates in an account of the big Act 3 aria, 'Ch'ella mi creda', which as well as being crudely lachrymose makes a slow tempo sound even more sluggish than it might do, with expressiveness exaggerated.

Mario del Monaco is very different, not just in that aria. To a surprising degree he follows the straight, forthright manner of the conductor, Capuana. As usual with the singer in his heyday there is crudity in the performance, not just in the blaring *fortissimo* which he consistently prefers to any subtler shading but in ugly rising *portamenti* and unwanted glottal attack on exposed notes. But the tone is thrilling and heroic, and 'Ch'ella mi creda' at a fastish, flowing, tempo has a straightforwardness and lack of mannerism that makes it freshly compelling, even though there are ugly slides up to top B flat twice over.

João Gibin, the unexpected choice of hero for the HMV set, has a voice of very distinctive timbre, with its rapid, controlled flutter reminding one of such singers as Francesco Merli or Aureliano Pertile. From recording alone it is hard to judge the size of the voice, but his vocal acting is often most effective. At a generally faster tempo, the Act 1 duet between Johnson and Minnie, the approach in the Matačić performance is lighter, and Gibin's touches of humour add to that lightness. 'Ch'ella mi creda' is marred by some lachrymose attack and Matačić is strangely sluggish in the second half with mannered phrasing, but Gibin, unlike his rivals on the other sets, does start with an attempt at *pianissimo* and the shading of tone and dynamic is beautiful, as it is in his account of the other Johnson aria, 'Or son sei mesi' in Act 2, the hero's defiant response to Minnie when she learns that he is a bandit – an exact autobiographical equivalent to Rance's 'Minnie dalla mia casa' and Minnie's 'Laggiù nel Soledad' in Act 1.

In that 'new style' aria, unlike 'Ch'ella mi creda' (the one old-style aria in *La fanciulla*), Del Monaco's straight, forthright style is relatively ineffective. There is a proud Otello-snarl on 'di banditi da strada', but no magic whatever when, for the passage where Johnson talks of his dream of going off to 'a life of love and honest work', Puccini modulates into a warm E flat major. This is a moment which, by contrast, Placido Domingo (DG) interprets with moving tenderness and intensity. With Mehta characteristically favouring bigger contrasts of tempo than usual, fast and sharp at the start, relaxed later, Domingo gives the whole passage the emotional resolution Puccini intended, expanding gloriously at the end. Domingo's concern for detail throughout his performance, helped by his stage experience of the part, gives it an added dimension. It is a performance on a naturally heroic scale, and the pity is that Domingo is reluctant to sing quietly. That becomes a serious shortcoming, in what, surprisingly, is a disappointment in his performance, his singing of 'Ch'ella mi creda', which starts loud and rather coarse in tone, slightly forced until the first top B flat brings a fine opening out. Mehta's expressive style then allows for subtler expression in the second half, but for once there is too little contrast.

When it comes to items from *La fanciulla* separately recorded, 'Ch'ella mi creda' is by far the most popular passage, not surprisingly when it contains the most clear-cut tune, one which is said to have been adopted by the Italian troops on the Macedonian front in the First World War as their equivalent to *Tipperary*. As I have already implied, it needs more than a loud voice, yet can fall apart in its simple outlines if injected with too much expressiveness. Perhaps the most successful of all separate versions is that of Jussi

Björling recorded in the days of 78rpm (DA 1584; RLS 715), taking a near-ideal course between those extremes. Harold Rosenthal, surveying the recordings of this opera in the early sixties, was able to track down some fifty-four separate versions and it is a comment on changing taste that the December 1980 *Gramophone* catalogue listed only one – Jussi Björling's LP version, also superb, of the 1950s (GOS 634–5). Indeed, apart from one 'highlights' disc from the DG set, only one other item at all from *La fanciulla* was listed, Sherrill Milnes's separate version of Rance's 'Minnie dalla mia casa', also strong and resonant.

Among the fifty-four and more versions from the days of 78s and early LPs, there are quite a number in languages other than Italian – an early one in Swedish by Björling (Swedish HMV X 4436; Rococo R 31), one in English by Frank Titterton (Decca M 48), two elegant ones in French from Enrico di Mazzei (Od. 188562) and José Luccioni (Col. RF 70; 2C 053–10643) and a whole collection in German from such tenors as Peter Anders (Telef. A 1478; 6. 43012 AJ), Julius Patzak (Poly. 90182), Torsten Ralf (DB 5620; Rococo 5233) and Waldemar Kmentt (S 06076 R). Recorded live at a concert in 1959 when he was in his early sixties is a version by Helge Rosvaenge, still impressive in its big, fat *Heldentenor* tones (Preiser PR 3058).

Among the Italian versions there are such oddities as two accounts recorded live, with piano accompaniment, by Beniamino Gigli right at the end of his career, one at his New York farewell (ALP 1329), the other in Rio de Janeiro in 1951 (HRE 213) when he was just over sixty, the tone throttled and no longer steady and with a big glottal on the final phrase. Even so, one can appreciate what it once might have been and it is sad that Gigli never made a regular commercial recording. Giacomo Lauri-Volpi also recorded 'Ch'ella mi creda' at the end of his career, in 1957 when he was sixty-five, and the result is coarse and disappointing, no reminder at all of the fine version recorded in 1942 on 78 (DA 5427; LV 260) with the voice at its most ringing and bright.

Notable among later versions is Giuseppe di Stefano's, one of the finest discs of his maturity (RLS 756), and perhaps surprisingly some of the earliest versions are also among the least stylish. Alfred Piccaver for example made a very early version in German in 1914, the year after he and Maria Jeritza had appeared in the first Vienna performance of the opera (Od. 99939; LV 26). The start is sluggish, heavy with no flow at all, though it works up to a fine climax with an added turn on the final phrase. That added ornamentation is a feature too of Piccaver's better known and more stylish version of 1928 with Julius Prüwer conducting (Poly 66768; LV 2003). There the ringing tone leads on to a passionately urgent close, hectic but certainly committed.

Another early version has Dick Johnson sung by Edward Johnson (Eduardo di Giovanni) recorded about 1918 (DA 166; Cantilena 6216). There is a hint of nasal tone (more than is implied by the acoustic recording) but the voice still rings superbly clean with pure, poised legato.

Bernardo de Muro was a tenor who never sang the role on stage, for though he had a voice of stentorian size, he was physically diminutive. He recorded the Act 2 aria, 'Or son sei mesi', twice over, the electrical version (DA 997; Bongiovanni GB 1028/31) clean focused and bright but consistently loud and not so detailed as the acoustic (DB 551; GV 527).

'Or son sei mesi' in the days of the 78 attracted a score or so different versions, not just De Muro's but a celebrated one from the Spanish tenor Antonio Cortis (Parlo. 6469; Rococo 5212) a singer who recorded the passage from *La fanciulla* in Berlin in 1923, a very slow account, finely shaded. Another version from that period is Hipolito Lazaro's (L 2056; GV 510), even finer in its way, ringing and noble with evenly produced tone leading to a superb expansion at the climax.

But perhaps the most remarkable, if not exactly the finest, version of this aria came from Giovanni Martinelli, recorded not during his active career but as late as 1962 when he came to England to celebrate the fiftieth aniversary of his first appearance at Covent Garden (CDN 5105). He was then seventy-seven (or maybe eighty-two if the suspected earlier date of birth is correct) and the result is amazing for the precise ringing tones, the voice clearly identifiable with some of the old bloom still remaining.

By comparison with the tenor's arias, those of the heroine have been relatively neglected. For the singer they present more problems and fewer rewards, though as I have indicated in my discussion of the complete sets, they provide acute and detailed vignettes of the character. One of the most attractive versions from 78 days of 'Laggiù nel Soledad' comes from Tina Poli-Randaccio, beautifully detailed, the depth of passion kept under fine control (DA 713). An Italian singer later in the 78 period, Gina Cigna, is ham-fisted by comparison (GX 7186; OASI 588), chesty and coarse, while from LP days Antonietta Stella (ALP 1428) is faceless.

In the early days another solo for Minnie was also recorded separately. 'Io non so che una povera fanciulla', taken from the long love duet at the end of Act 1, including a very wobbly account from Maria Farneti, then past her prime (GQ 7171; LV 264), but the other principal recording item for Minnie is 'Oh, se sapeste' from Act 2 with the 'gambolling coloratura' already mentioned. No doubt because of its difficulty this has been relatively neglected though versions are listed by Linda Cannetti and Eugenia Magliulo, who also recorded 'Laggiù nel Soledad'.

Most memorable, if hardly good examples of her art, are three versions in English by Joan Hammond, devastatingly gusty but unforgettable in their bluff characterization – first on 78 (B 974), then on LP (BLP 1086), and also on a previously unpublished 1946 record (HLM 7042).

Jack Rance's only significant solo passage is his Act 1 aria of self-explanation 'Minnie dalla mia casa', but until relatively recently it had attracted surprisingly few recordings. One exception was the acoustic account of Cesare Formichi, massively resonant (D 5533; LV 229), and there are versions by Taurino Parvis, Antenore Reali, Giampiero Malaspina and Carmelo Maugeri.

It was not until singers of our own time began their careers that any really memorable versions were made: Giuseppe Taddei rich in tone (LPC 55006) and, above all, Tito Gobbi in two different and equally vivid versions, both of them included on the fine HMV three-disc collection 'The Art of Tito Gobbi' (RLS 738). In 1942 near the beginning of his career he gave a superb dark-toned rendering, brilliant at the top (DA 5430), but even finer was the, previously unpublished, account of 1955 with Gobbi's control of legato and tonal shading displayed at its most seductive, leading up to a top F sharp of ringing power. One's only regret is that Gobbi never found time later in his career to record the role complete, but then, once those rival accounts of 1958 were made, we had to wait a whole generation for a successor. One hopes the gap will not be so long this time.

LA FANCIULLA DEL WEST

M Minnie; *DJ* Dick Johnson; *JR* Jack Rance; *JW* Jake Wallace

1950 Gavazzi *M*; Campagnano *DJ*; Savarese *JR*; Caselli *JW* / Italian Radio Chorus and Orch; Turin / Basile
Cetra © LPS 3215
Everest © 453 (2)

1954 (live performance – Teatro Comunale, Florence) Steber *M*; Del Monaco *DJ*; Guelfi *JR*; Tozzi *JW* / Teatro Comunale Chorus and Orch. / Mitropoulos
Cetra ⓜ LO 64 (3)

1958 Nilsson *M*; Gibin *DJ*; Mongelli *JR*; Zaccaria *JW* / La Scala Chorus and Orch./ Matačić
EMI SLS 5079 ④ TC-SLS 5079
Seraphim SIC 6074

1958 Tebaldi *M*; Del Monaco *DJ*; MacNeil *JR*; Tozzi *JW* / Santa Cecilia Academy Chorus and Orch./ Capuana
Decca GOS 594–6
London OSA 1306

1977 Neblett *M*; Domingo *DJ*; Milnes *JR*; Howell *JW* / Royal Opera House Chorus and Orch./ Mehta
DG 2709 078 ④ 3371 031

Andrea Chénier

WILLIAM MANN

On the stage *Andrea Chénier* can be a tremendously exciting experience: with strong characterization even in many small roles; a vigorous, diversified plot full of atmosphere and incident; and a storehouse of purple patches. If you remember, as you look and listen, that it had its première in the same year as *La Bohème*, its musical strength seems all the more remarkable – how much of the music looks forward to *Tosca*! – and you wonder why Giordano did not become as distinguished an opera composer as Puccini.

But he didn't, and listening to *Chénier* on the gramophone one can hear why. The best moments of *Chénier* are superb, and quite individual – Giordano's style is fundamentally more direct and diatonic than Puccini's – but his invention was spasmodic. When the stage is taken away and you are left alone in a room with the music, the note-spinning passages, in which the orchestra runs on without saying anything in particular, stick out a mile; and you are made aware, too, that the pseudo-pastiche of eighteenth-century music, though charming as a background to a lively and colourful stage performance, is not in itself quite up to standard.

Even so, it is an enjoyable opera to listen to, and the *longueurs* are, as the Irishman said, pretty short; there's always a succulent passage waiting round the corner. Even before the arrival of LPs, the gramophone found room for *Andrea Chénier*. The first supposedly complete set came from HMV in 1921. I have not located a copy.

In 1931 came another set from La Scala, issued on Italian Columbia, and later dubbed on to microgroove. Its best features were the Gérard of Carlo Galeffi, and Salvatore Baccaloni's spiritedly characterized Roucher, a minor but important role. The rest is not much, and now sounds decidedly feeble. More enjoyable was the wartime HMV set of 78s with Gigli in the title role later transferred to LP.

There was a good deal of pleasure to be had from it if you could put up with Maria Caniglia's unsteady moments, and the dullness of Gino Bechi's Gérard. Chénier was Gigli's favourite part, and though his earlier excerpts are more endearing he gives other complete-set Chéniers copious lessons in variety of expression and generosity of phrasing – and he could stand and deliver with the best of the barnstormers. The courtroom scene is particularly spirited, the whole far and away superior to the Nixa-Urania set (Sacchi/Sarri/Serra) which was brash but also vocally less enjoyable and conductorially much less vivid – and was poorly recorded as well. The Cetra LP set of 1953 with Renata Tebaldi, José Soler and Ugo Savarese has not come my way except in excerpted form. It, and the Urania, took six sides; more recent sets have shown (especially on reissue) that the opera can fit on to four sides without undue haste. The Cetra-Live performance from La Scala in 1955 is notable only for Callas's Madeleine, and even in her case this was less then her most telling role, though the aria is sung with even greater potency than in the 'single' version noticed below.

A much more exhilarating standard was set in 1957 with the appearance of the Decca set conducted by Gavazzeni, not only because it is cast from strength, but because the performance as a whole is full of vitality and atmosphere. Tebaldi, Mario del Monaco, and Ettore Bastianini are the three principals, a trio of rumbustious voices, each at his or her best in the impassioned vocal rhetoric, *fortissimo con somma passione*, that abounds in *Chénier.* For me Tebaldi's voice always carries an undertone of fish-wife's rasp that mars the illusion of a high-born *demoiselle*, but she gives some affecting singing in the love duet 'Ora soave' and elsewhere; there is plenty of heart, and plenty of voice, if not much subtlety. The same goes for Del Monaco who gives a thrilling performance, if you don't let your mind dwell on other interpreters of the famous solos. Bastianini's portrayal of Gérard is no less robust and no less spontaneous, but rather more impressive because there is more variety of nuance and colouring: what mingled emotions he contrives to suggest, perfectly clearly, in the outburst (from his famous monologue) 'Un servo obbediente di violenta passione! Ah, peggio! Uccido e tremo, e mentre uccido io piango!' Gérard is not a proletarian Scarpia, as many singers of 'Nemico della patria' suggest. The interest of the character is that he has finer feelings, and a social conscience, as he admits ruefully in the last section of the same monologue. That is what makes his later duet with Madeleine significant.

The smaller parts are at least alive, and Gavazzeni's conducting, though not distinguished (there is some ragged playing, and the chorus is a letdown), sustains tension to keep you interested in what comes next. There is some unrhythmical or pitchless vocalization; in the excerpts discussed below, many interpreters do the same now and then. This Decca set has held its place in the catalogue, variously reissued. It was not challenged until 1964 when EMI produced a version recorded in Rome under Gabriele Santini, whose principal attraction was the popularity of Franco Corelli's loud and excitable tenor voice in the name part. Even more than the Decca, this is a set that stands or falls by its principals: the choral and orchestral work are but passable, though the crowd effects contribute atmosphere in this drama of popular revolution, and Santini conducts expertly, without special pertinence.

Corelli's Chénier was full of faults, vague intonation, slovenly *portamento* (a vocal refinement of maximum potency when the singer controls it exactly), intrusive aspirates, addiction to lachrymosity, even microphone-hogging (the exact antonym of lily-gilding, alas!). And yet the hero contrives to emerge, Houdini-like, from the fetters with which this singer's unmusical personal conceit constrains it. Chénier's *Credo* and his courtroom *Apologia*, 'Sì, fui soldato', find his art at its most winning, though not ideal. The two famous monologues are too careless to be taken seriously, if you have heard them sung with real mastery and sensibility. The same goes for Antonietta Stella's Madeleine, bright, fluttery, coarse like Tebaldi but lacking her natural eloquence: she never wins a circumspect listener to her portrayal. The great attraction of this set is Mario Sereni's Gérard, an impersonation sung and verbally articulated with exceptional artistry and intelligence, as well as a glorious light baritone voice, captivating on stage, weighted more strongly on record, but not to distortion. Each of his solos is a real event, his duet with Madeleine a moment of high drama. In *Chénier* recordings it is usual to double some subsidiary roles, but here it sounds wrong to have Roucher and Fouquier-Tinville obviously sung by the same baritone.

The 1977 recording of *Andrea Chénier* on RCA is conducted by James Levine. It is much the most satisfactory version, (though the announced Decca may rival it), the recording rich in atmosphere, particularized and contrasted to the full in the second and third acts especially, the choral and orchestral contributions gloriously exhilarating, witness the gavotte at the end of Act 1 as ironical background for the entrance of the downtrodden crowd. Renata Scotto's Madeleine has ample passion (the climax of her first duet with Chénier, 'Non temo la morte', could hardly be sung and played more fervently yet still musically), and an uncommon nobility, poise, charm, vulnerability; her newly acquired dramatic soprano is admirably controlled. So much does she care, in performance, for verbal overtones as well as musical detail, that I was disappointed when, in 'Soffocco, moro', she does nothing with the arcane and piquant references to Basilio and Montgolfier as fashion-designers.

Placido Domingo's Andrea is heroic, and marvellously sung; his monologues are surpassed in point-making by others listed below, but the call to romance in Act 2, 'Credi all' amor, Chénier' could not be more thrillingly voiced, and the duet with Madeleine (mentioned above) leaves his superiority beyond question, in the context of other recorded performances. He also excels in the fizzing duet with Roucher (Allan Monk, a fine voice and character), done with likable vivacity. Gérard customarily brings out the best in a dramatic high baritone, and Sherrill Milnes is no exception; rather, he contrives to put more into each of his numerous solos and ensembles than his rivals on other sets, so that the character appears more interesting and individual than usual. Maria Ewing's vibrant, charming Bersi, Gwendolyn Killebrew's credible Madelon (she lifts her short appearance far above the embarrassment it habitually occasions), and the keenly focused Informer of Michel Sénéchal, all contribute strongly to the effect of the piece as a whole.

Because, as I have suggested, *Chénier* moves from purple patch to purple patch, it is an opera from which excerpts have often been recorded, four of them, in particular, being standard selections for the appropriate voices.

The curtain has not long been raised before Gérard the butler is inveighing against the *ancien régime* in the monologue 'Son sessant' anni'. This has been excerpted a few times on records, sometimes beginning earlier, at 'Compiacente a' colloquii', where Gérard fancifully addresses the sofa upon which so many dandies have wooed ladies of maturer charms. Of the earlier, shorter versions, that of Pasquale Amato (Fono. 92498; CO 389) displays his easy, attractive top register in 1909, and his vivid declamation, short on legato and musical inwardness at this stage in his hardworking career. Riccardo Stracciari's darker, yet gleaming baritone is authoritatively deployed, the words strongly savoured too (Col. D 12512; LV 136). Of two by Benvenuto Franci, the Columbia (DQ 1130; LV 171) is the less unsteady vocally, though hardly more winning than the HMV (DA 1093). The longer excerpt is splendidly sung by Piero Cappuccilli in a series recorded live at the Verona Arena (SDD 571): there is plenty of vocal acting, from caricature to compassion and indignation, and the orchestral contribution is likewise lively. Ivan Popov, for Balkanton (BOA 415), makes more of denunciation than of the sarcasm in the opening passage, and though we may relish his upper register, the middle of the voice is not quite steady.

Decca highlights, and an old Odéon disc by the chorus of La Scala, select the masque chorus 'O pastorelle, addio', which has a very pretty, fragile tune in A major (Giordano despised key signatures, but not keys); I wonder why sopranos, in the days of ten-inch 78s, didn't try Maddelena's 'Soffoco, moro' which would make a charming short solo.

Then comes Chénier's first monologue, the 'Improvviso,' 'Un dì all' azzuro spazio', sometimes starting earlier at 'Colpito qui m'avete'. Here you can have Tamagno (HMV DR 102; GEMM 208–9), slow and spacious and finely expressive, or Amedeo Bassi, whose charming tenor is just audible, the piano seldom so, on an early Pathé (4239; Rococo 5323), or Edward Johnson, beautifully liquid of tone and urgent in manner on Columbia (D 17537; Rococo 5254); but for me the finest is the 1907 Caruso (DB 700; RL 12766), which is perfectly controlled and aristocratic yet full of feeling. The 1922 Gigli (DB 670; GEMM 202–6) is youthful and legato but seems careless and sentimental after Caruso, though the voice is more beautiful than in later versions. There are some fine, noble notes in Bernardo de Muro's 1912 HMV (DB 553; LV 135), and also some ugly ones, when he bleats or broadens his vowels unpleasantly. Despite its tendency to go clean off the rails, I like the version of Ulysses Lappas (L1514, orchestra conducted by Ketelbey!); his cry of 'T'amo, tu che me baci', is as thrilling as any. There are at least four versions by Zenatello of which I know two, beginning at 'Colpito', the earlier with piano (52702; GV 77), then one with primitive orchestral support (Edison 83052; GV 593), both remarkable for urgency and animal vigour. Zanelli's (DB 1339; LV 148) is bright and full of attractive feeling; Georges Thill (Col. D 41012; LV 224), exceptionally vital and rich in timbre with a strong ringing top; Lauri-Volpi (DB 2263), which is so honeyed as to sound soppy, and disappoints by ignoring the legato up to 'T'amo'; Martinelli with exciting climaxes, notably at 'Ecco la bellezza', but with bleats and shouts, and rolled 'rs' like machine-gun bursts; Pertile's account (DB 1118; LV 245) is for those who like his style of pushing. Nor can I warm to the constricted Germanic style of Tino Pattiera (Rococo 5256). Merli's blend of enthusiasm and tenderness, given wings by the fizzing honey of his unmistakable voice, marks his version out among early electrics (Col. D 14705; QCX 7378), but all his records are thrilling.

Among postwar Chéniers, there is a nicely turned account by the Welsh tenor Brychan Powell (Delysé EC 3136), a dull one by Mario Lanza (DB 21486; DPS 2012) and a vigorous one, notably well recorded, by Giuseppe di Stefano (GRV 14), more successful than other things on this recital disc. Del Monaco made several versions on the lines of that in the Decca set. The early one for HMV (DA 11350; 1C 147–18 227), easily the best; the reissue includes Chénier's other solos splendidly sung. One by Corelli in a recital record (ASD 529) sounds similarly patchy. By, conversely, the same token, Domingo's version with the Berlin Phil and Santi (SXL 6451) is exquisitely polished, even more spontaneously poetic than on the set under Levine. There is a strong, noble performance from Carreras (Philips 9500 771), slightly marred by a hint of judder under pressure. In his Tchaikovsky Prize record of 1966 (Mel. S 01431–32) Vladimir Atlantov gives a decent imitation of an Italianate sound, but the style is choppy and explosive, adjectives that could also describe James McCracken's account (SET 404), though his idiosyncratic method of singing produces thrills and vexations of a quite different nature. I respect and admire Bruno Prevedi's representation of Chénier's solos (SXL 6114), more heroic than amorous, and again too explosive for satisfaction. Luciano Pavarotti (SXDL 7504) brings to the music possibly the most wonderful voice, objectively considered, of any Chénier on record. He abuses it, with intrusive vowels that break the line (e.g. after 'Non'), by tirading when the context is no more than conversational, and by heaping Pelion on to Ossa at every top note, regardless of the composer's dynamic structural planning. There is much to deplore, but also a sense of excitement and lyrical amplitude that are central to Italian opera of the *verismo* heyday. Pavarotti's record also includes 'Sì, fui soldato', and 'Come un bel dì', the former verbally committed to strong purpose, the latter slow to find form, the acoustic worth commendation. Jon Vickers (LSB 4106) can be faulted for want of vocal ring, or on his Italian pronunciation twenty years or so ago, but his versions of 'Un dì' and the 'Improvviso' are delivered with a superior legato technique, a voice perfectly even in scale, and an involvement in the precise moment, that postulate another degree of superiority, halfway between Caruso and Pavarotti, in some moods best of all (the whole record is a superb memento of a great singer).

Chénier's solo at the beginning of Act 2, 'Credo a una possanza', takes some time to arrive at a good tune and ends with the stirring cadence, 'Credi all' amor, Chénier, tu sei amato', that accompanies the lovers to the guillotine – this was worth more people's attention. Antonio Cortis made an exciting record of it (DA 1154; LV 289) with dark compact tones and plenty of fizz in the closing pages; at one point, in order to disguise the absence of Roucher, Cortis sings the orchestra's tune. Zenatello also recorded this solo, the voice raw but instinct with spiritual elation (Fono. 92757; GV 77).

Then the love duet, variously entitled according to where it is started. Decca highlights begin at the entry of Madeleine and Bersi, 'Ecco l'altare'. Seinemeyer and Pattiera (Parlo E 10976; LV 111) begin a bit later, in the middle of Madeleine's solo, at 'Al mondo Bersi', which gives a bonus portion of Seinemeyer's rich creamy voice and beautiful phrasing. As a matter of fact, despite the information on the label, what she sings is 'Die Berse hat sich meiner angenommen', and Pattiera interrupts with 'Heil dir, o Süsse', complete with a *coup de glotte* on almost every note (the one on the second note of 'Ora' seems to be traditional, though) because this is a rather heavy performance in German. Giordano into German doesn't go well, as we shall see later: and, even if it did, I could wish that beautiful Seinemeyer had been granted a partner who was not what Germans call a *Kravattentenor*, apparently being strangled by his neckwear. The records commemorating the old Metropolitan in New York include (MRF 13) this duet sung by Caballé and Corelli, beginning at 'Eravate possente, the start of Madeleine's solo. The recorded balance must have happened extempore, but both singers are in fine voice, and rise appropriately to the occasion. Some duettists begin a few bars after 'Al mondo Bersi' at 'Udite son sola'. Among these are Tebaldi and José Soler on a Cetra disc (LPC 50178) evidently taken from the complete set (the rest of the disc consists of other love duets). Soler is a decent tenor, and Tebaldi sounds more radiant and winsome of voice than in the Decca set – I like this Cetra performance a lot, and it is very sympathetically recorded. Among HMV's Archive reissue (VA 52; Tima CDB 11501) was a comic performance of the love duet, starting at 'Ora soave', by Oltrabella, who sounds much too jolly and heartless, and De Muro, who bleats at the slightest provocation. In the end they both scream their way to top B flat, avoiding Giordano's more tasteful conclusion. There is a version by Käthe Heidersbach and Helge Rosvaenge (unpublished; Rococo 5269).

Each act of *Andrea Chénier* has progressively more juicy moments. In Act 3 there are three, one for each of the principals. Gérard's great monologue, 'Nemico della patria' – was recorded by its creator Sammarco (Fono. 92170; CO 348). His voice sounds noble and fluent, expressive to a fault – most modern singers pace these monologues more shrewdly – but rather too passionate than dull. In the earlier days of the gramophone, this monologue was either shorn of a page, or else (as with Sammarco) the record started later, at 'Un dì m'era di gioia'. Mario Ancona did this on an old Victor disc (Victor 88170; Rococo 5213). I found it slow and uninteresting, rather lumpy in line. Eugenio Giraldoni, chosen for the first Scarpia by Puccini on the strength of his Gérard, was thought lacking refinement, but in this record (Fono. 92422; RLS 7705) one must nowadays praise the dignity and expressive restraint of his singing. Titta Ruffo, wonderful singer, made two versions of 'Nemico', both abbreviated in the middle. The earlier one (DB 242; OASI 558) is decidedly the better, richer of voice, full of feeling, and with a perfectly spontaneous laugh at the start. The later (1929) version (DB 1397) is dramatically poor and lacking in vocal subtlety; at Gérard's climax of self-reproach, Ruffo sounds as if he were having trouble with his false teeth. Apollo Granforte (DB 1453; LV 90) starts at 'Un dì m'era' and sings with superb feeling and dignity – perhaps too much dignity for 'Uccido e tremo', but his voice is a little backward in production. Amato also starts there, and in the words just quoted he is thrilling, though subtlety was not much up his street in 1909 (Fono. 92497; CO 389) – and yet, in his later records, for all the intelligent singing, do we not miss that effortless, exquisite top register? There is more refinement and depth in Stracciari's version of the same (Col D 14673; LV 136), and it is forthright as well, worth acquiring. Carlo Galeffi recorded it (D 12490; GQ 7036) in 1926, but the version on LV 220 is taken from the set and does not escape sentimental excess. I did expect much from Gerhard Hüsch (DB 4510; Rococo 5248) and he sings with marvellous technical and interpretative control, delightful except that the German language so distorts Giordano's musical style: it sounds like D'Albert's *Tiefland*, as well it might. But that is not Giordano. His compatriot Schlusnus sang it in Italian (Poly. 66851; LV 110), a monotonous reading, I think, with heavy accompaniment. Willi Domgraf-Fassbaender (Acanta DE 22695) is much more fiery, with lively cynicism, a good laugh, a bright ringing, faintly wobbly top, and thrilling verbal declamation; but again, we are listening to quite another opera.

Coming nearer to our own time, there was a characteristically moving version by Marko Rothmüller (C 4019), and a rather too restrained but still impressive one by Paolo Silveri (DX 1521), a dramatic, rather saturnine one by Rolando Panerai (33C 1052), and one by Robert Merrill (RB 16029) who sings in a virile but uninteresting manner. Fischer-Dieskau, singing in Italian (DG.LPM 18 700), is characteristically fascinating, though the thick timbre does not belong to the music, which needs a translucent sound, whether dark or bright. Tom Krause's version has good qualities, but the tone lacks real focus, and the aria is chopped up into disparate sections, as with some early singers (SXL 6327). Cappuccilli's Verona record again includes a superior account of the music (SDD 571).

The version from which I hoped most, that of Mariano Stabile (Fono. 74923; Rococo 5277) proves unexpectedly bland, beautiful singing but little musicianly detail. Lawrence Tibbett's version (Rococo) has more of the character that one expects, yet it is restrained in emotion, just when the aria should be most confessional: at least the top of the voice is a treat to hear.

Enter to Gérard the defenceless Madeleine, who is persuaded to yield to him in return for Chénier's freedom. The earlier part of this scene, from her entrance, was recorded by Käthe Heidersbach and Domgraf-Fassbaender (Acanta DE 22695): again he compels attention, and she sounds lovely, but the music seems out of style, too many words and too little legato. She tells her story to him in her solo 'La mamma morta', another highlight. There was a beautiful G&T recording of this (1904) by Emma Carelli (053034), exquisitely phrased, and marred only by a suspicion of excessive nasal resonance. Rosetta Pampanini (LX 239; LV 221) brings plenty of verve and some affecting expressive moments, with a voice like heavy velvet, to her version. Rosa Raisa (who created the title role in *Turandot*) recorded a squally interpretation (DB 2123; Club 99.52), replete with tearful yodels but saved by the singer's enthusiasm and by one beautiful *crescendo* on a sustained F sharp. Claudia Muzio's performance (LX 655; 3C 053–00932) was justly renowned. The lower reaches of the tessitura find her voice rather hard, and she sins by altering the vocal line so as to finish an octave higher, but many other sopranos do this too. Phrase after phrase is lit up by Muzio's artistry – a *subito piano* on the minim Cs at 'con Bersi errave' at once projects the fearful midnight escape, for instance, and there is a world of remorse in her delivery of the phrase about bringing bad luck to all who wish her well. This is an unforgettable interpretation that surpasses at every point her acoustic version (Edison 82224; RS 310). Gina Cigna (CQX 10593) comes close to Muzio in expression, but tends to be a little too explosive; still this is undoubtedly the voice for the music. Lotte Lehmann's performance – 'Von Blut gerötet' (Parlo R 20025; 1C 137–30704/5) – is of special interest. The delivery is urgent, the legato typical and moving, eloquently phrased and nuanced as it is. The German text will not readily be accepted, but true eloquence is there.

German sopranos were fond of this solo: Meta Seinemeyer (Parlo P 2089; LV 276) overdoes the bosomy chest tone at the beginning, like others, then warms to her task with warm timbre and lovely legato. Maria Reining (DB 7648; E 60632) is her radiant self. Leonie Rysanek (RB 16148) is recorded more kindly than usual, singing exquisitely, and in Italian, though still with an unspontaneous and undramatic sense of effort. Hammond, also in Italian (SXLP 30205), falls below the standard we expect of her. A version by Amy Shuard (MFP 2057) includes some poetic soft singing and legato line, as well as an incisive delivery. Top notes lack the required vibrancy: the intonations are heroic, the results alas plebeian. Zinka Milanov (VICS 1198) begins well, then hurries her recollection of the burning house, loses spirit in Madeleine's self-pity, and reveals a thread of dullness in her middle register that needs the pushed-up ending to restore confidence in her voice. Much the same happens in Caniglia's independent HMV version (DB 5361; OASI 538), and her stiff vocal delivery compounds the dullness. Callas (ALP 3824) bids fair to surpass all contenders by verbal potency, mastery of vocal colour and inflection, and ultimately what we expect from arias, though the maidenly ardour is no longer in her voice. It is a great performance. The vividness of Grace Bumbry (1C 063–02055) recalls her teacher Lotte Lehmann, but the top of the voice seems overtaxed. There are two versions by Caballé: in the MRF set she sounds squally and capricious; on a Decca recital (SXLR 6825) some touching passages are vitiated by a vehemence that suggests the fishwife. Leontyne Price lacks clarity (SB 6742) though the smokily attractive nature of the voice gives a special charm to her singing. So it is with Maria Chiara (SXL 6864), breath catching at 'Porto sventura', but careless about the continuity of the piece. Raina Kabaivanska (BOA 1155) sounds hard and squally.

Then comes the trial scene. Chénier defends himself in 'Sì, fui soldato'. Bassi's version (Pathé 4243; Rococo 5323) needs the ear of faith. Gigli (DA 1312; HLM 7004) scores in this heroic declamatory solo, but Zenatello (DA 1079; Club 99.25) catches you off guard by starting with Chénier's previous words – 'Tu menti!' and thence lets go superbly in the vein of his celebrated *Otello* records. Renato Zanelli declaims the solo almost but not quite as well (DB 13339; LV 148). De Muro's pre-electric HMV version (2–052122; LV 135) is sterling stuff, with touching gentleness at 'passa la vita mia', and a grand climax worthy of his reputation in the role. Pavarotti's version is mentioned above. Eduardo Garbin (Fono. 92298) is weighty, more stevedore than poet. Paoli (EB 75) makes more of the text but the voice sounds edgy. Merli's version (CQX 10245), less involved than his 'Improvviso', still coerces attention. Prevedi (see above) is at his best here.

The last act consists of two purple patches and not much more. The curtain has hardly risen when Chénier recites his verses of farewell, 'Come un bel dì di maggio'. This should start as if lost in a dream, infinitely tender and caressing. This is the way Tagliavini sings it (Cetra BB 25217; LPC 50155) in a glorious performance; so does Jussi Björling (DA 1836; RLS 7105) who seems just less interesting and vital. You would expect Schipa (DA 5352) to shine too, but with all his neatness and grace he doesn't bring the music to life, and he funks the B flat at the end. Martinelli's account (DB 1143; LV 230) is chesty and far from tender. Piccaver's (Poly. 95354; LV 500) sounds somewhat hurried, as if afraid Mme La Guillotine might call before he'd got to the end. The 1922 Gigli (DA 556; GEMM 202) begins heavily but gathers spirit and reaches a rousing climax, granted a quantity of sobs. These are the least of the flaws in Pertile's version of 1929 (DA 1185; LV 46), a disgraceful exhibition of slovenly singing. There are tasteful modern versions by Bergonzi, Brychan Powell, and Campora, a less convincing one by Di Stefano. Those by Corelli, Pavarotti and Vickers are mentioned above. The 1916 Caruso (RB 6572), dark and profoundly reflective, exquisitely controlled, again belongs in a special class.

The rousing final duet, in which Madeleine comes to share death with Chénier on the scaffold, and the two go off to the tumbril shouting 'Long live death together' on a top B, has had some eminent gramophone interpreters. Margaret Sheridan and Pertile (DB 1289; LV 279), Seinemeyer and Pattiera (Parlo. E 10619; LV 111), Scacciati and Merli (LX 12; LV 243), Augusta Oltrabella and De Muro (7–54026/7). Joan Hammond here offers more excitement than her partner Rudolf Schock (DB 21260; 1C 147 28963–4); Tebaldi and Soler give much pleasure; so too does the HMV Archive by Boninsegna and Bolis (VB 4), a finely stylish and expressive version. For the real thing, go to Scotto and Domingo, or Tebaldi and Del Monaco, in the relevant sets. But Caballé and her husband, Bernabé Martí, have recorded it most appreciably twice. The early version (Vergara 748 STL) is the more elegant, the later full of atmosphere.

ANDREA CHÉNIER

AC Andrea Chénier; *M* Maddalena; *G* Gérard

1921 Lupato *AC*; Bartolomasi *M*; A. Pacini *G* / La Scala Chorus and Orch. / Sabajno
HMV S 5220–52

1931 Marini *AC*; Bruna Rasa *M*; Galeffi *G* / La Scala Chorus and Orch. / Molajoli
Columbia (Italy) GQX 10106–18*
CBS (US) ⓜ EL 10

1941 Gigli *AC*; Caniglia *M*; Bechi *G* / La Scala Chorus and Orch. / De Fabritiis
World Records ⓜ SH 105–6
Seraphim ⓜ IB 6019

1951 Sarri *AC*; Sacchi *M*; Manca-Serra *G* / Rome Opera Chorus and Orch. / Paoletti
Urania ⓜ URLP 218
Nixa ⓜ ULP 9218

1953 Soler *AC*; Tebaldi *M*; Savarese *G* / Italian Radio Chorus and Orch., Turin / Basile
Cetra ⓜ LPO 2047
Everest ⓒ 412 (2)

1955 (live performance – Teatro alla Scala, Milan) Del Monaco *AC*; Callas *M*; Protti *G* / La Scala Chorus and Orch. / Votto
Cetra ⓜ LO38 (2)

1957 Del Monaco *AC*; Tebaldi *M*; Bastianini *G* / Santa Cecilia Chorus and Orch. / Gavazzeni
Decca GOS 600–1
London OSA 1303

1964 Corelli *AC*; Stella *M*; Sereni *G* / Rome Opera Chorus and Orch. / Santini
EMI SLS 1436533 ④ TC-SLS 1436539
Angel SCL 3645

1977 Domingo *AC*; Scotto *M*; Milnes *G* / Alldis Choir, National PO / Levine
RCA (UK) RL 12046
(US) ARL 3–2046 (4) ARK 3–2046

1984 Pavarotti *AC*; Caballé *M*; Nucci *G* / London Opera Chorus / National PO / Chailly
Decca / London 410 117–1 ④ 410 117–4

1942 (excerpts – in German)
Rosvaenge *AC*; Heidersbach *M*; Domgraf-Fassbaender *G* / Berlin State Opera Chorus and Orch. / Heger
Acanta ⓜ BB 21361

Prince Igor

DAVID HAMILTON

At the conclusion of his important essay on Borodin's opera,* after quoting Glazunov's account of how he and Rimsky-Korsakov completed *Prince Igor,* Gerald Abraham made the following observation: 'In view of this statement and considering what we know of Rimsky-Korsakov's treatment of *Boris, Khovanshchina,* and *The Stone Guest*, it would be interesting to know whether he also made melodic and harmonic "improvements" in *Igor.* It is highly improbable that he refrained from doing so.'

To the best of my knowledge, Abraham's suspicions about the fidelity of the standard – indeed, the only – edition of *Prince Igor* have not so far been pursued by anyone with access to the source material. Nobody has published a critical edition of the *Igor* material as Borodin left it at his sudden death: the completely orchestrated passages (about eight numbers, including the Polovtsian Dances, which were jointly orchestrated in haste by Borodin, Rimsky, and Liadov on the eve of an 1879 concert), those that were only carried as far as piano score, the sketches, and the documentary evidence (letters, memos, scenarios, and the like) that bears upon the opera, (though David Lloyd-Jones did provide a performing edition, based on his study of primary sources in Russia and on an unpublished edition by Pavel Lamm, for his Opera North production at Leeds in 1982).

Glazunov was quite frank about the broad outlines of his participation, and some of what he did will probably have to be accepted on faith; for example, there is apparently no written evidence for the chorus of Russian prisoners in Act 2, which he wrote down from memory ('but I do not vouch for its complete accuracy'). Contrary to the popularly accepted story, he did not write down the overture from memory, but 'composed' (his word) it 'roughly according to Borodin's plan'. A proper critical edition would allow us to measure precisely the extent of Rimsky's and Glazunov's intervention, and would furnish the raw materials for any possible improvements in the opera's present form.

That some improvement might be desirable may be inferred from one aspect of standard performance practice: many productions, and the majority

* 'The History of Prince Igor', *On Russian Music* (London, William Reeves, n.d.), p. 147ff.

of 'complete' recordings, omit the third act, the one which owes the most to the posthumous ministrations of Borodin's colleagues. This is a pretty drastic omission; if *Igor* is a drama as well as a splendid musical pageant of medieval Russia, its principal events are the capture and the escape of the protagonist. The first of these events already takes place offstage; when Act 3 is omitted, the second becomes a matter of inference. The relative proportions of action and music, of character and colour, are not satisfactory as the third act stands, no doubt – but to excise it entirely bespeaks extreme misgivings about the possibility of performing it convincingly. The more so because its omission reduces the fairly juicy role of Khan Konchak to little more than a single aria, plus whatever stage presence the singer can bring to the role (obviously considerable in the case of a Chaliapin). Various intermediate remedies have been tried in the past, without winning approval: the 1937 Covent Garden version, in French, rearranged Acts 2 and 3, with the overture as an interlude between the two scenes, and the Dances at the end, after Igor has escaped.

Even if Act 3 is included, *Igor* trails loose ends, many of which can only be clarified by reference to the scenario by Stassov on which Borodin initially based his opera: we never find out, for example, what happens to Galitzky when Igor returns. Whether this disregard of narrative propriety was Borodin's specific design, or simply the result of his unsystematic working habits and their untimely interruption, we can only surmise; he addressed himself to writing words and music for whatever episodes in the scenario took his fancy, and never got around to fitting his jigsaw puzzle together and filling in the missing pieces. As it stands, *Igor* appears to have a structural kinship with *Boris* – tableaux from an historical epic, rather than a continuous narrative – but it lacks the strong central thread of the protagonist's psychological development that gives Mussorgsky's opera great dramatic tension. Especially without Act 3 and the tensions that come to the surface there (and even with it, for the music does not succeed in realizing those tensions forcefully), *Igor* consists primarily of character sketches and genre scenes.

Perhaps this explains its sporadic survival in the Western repertory. At home, audiences bring to it a lively cultural and historical awareness, for the events of the story – and especially the European-Oriental polarity that it embodies – can still be related to the living texture of Russian society. To induce a comparable awareness in a Western audience, a production would have to be imaginative indeed – an effort surely worth making, for the music at its best is irresistible.

Not surprisingly, all the 'complete' recordings come from Eastern Europe: three from Moscow's Bolshoi, one each from Belgrade and Sofia. Less expectably, they all manifest serious deficiencies, of performance, textual integrity, or both – and none is recorded in a way to make the most of the brilliant instrumentation. From a hearing of all five, one begins to appreciate the potential of the opera, and can imagine what a carefully restudied, brilliantly played and recorded performance, with particular attention to the music's expressive and dynamic variety, might sound like.

The first set reaches back before the Second World War, and appears to have been something of a compilation. Two conductors are involved, and the Dances were apparently recorded on an occasion when no Konchak was present, for his lines therein are not sung; the presence of two Igors in the cast list apparently betokens the later substitution of Ivanov sides for Baturin sides. I have only been able to hear a small part of this set; selections, but never the entire set, were published on various Western labels. What I have heard – the Yaroslavna-Galitzky duet (No. 5), the opening chorus of Act 2 (7), Konchak's aria (15), the Polovtsian Dances (17), and the reunion of Igor and Yaroslavna (27) – is enough to suggest that this is an important performance, though far from a complete one; from the side numbers and other information in WERM, I surmise that the Prologue (1), the Act 1 finale (6), and all of Act 3 except the Polovtsi March (18) were omitted, and other incidental cuts were taken along the way.

The Yaroslavna is Xenia Derzhinskaya (1889–1951), whose career began under the Tsars but who still sounds in fine voice, true and well rounded, singing with authority and rhythmic vitality; no subsequent singer of this part offers a comparably ductile and secure voice and method. Pirogov, his tone well focused, is an insinuatingly oily Galitzky, who caves in at the end of the duet with a vividly depicted shrug of the shoulders. Andrei Ivanov is a firm, light-toned Igor; and Mikhailov a strong Konchak. Best of all, despite the antediluvian sound, is Melik-Pashayev's exciting traversal of the Act 2 Dances, with full-throated choral singing and hotly virtuosic wind playing; though not much detail can be distinguished, what one hears is surpassingly barbaric and theatrical. It would be wonderful to have a good LP transfer of this set; the Vladimir (Ivan Kozlovsky) was also an important Soviet singer.

Ivanov, Pirogov, and Melik-Pashayev are still on hand for the early postwar Bolshoi set. This time, Act 3 is omitted entirely, and passing cuts are taken in 2, 3, 10, and 28. Ivanov's voice is fuller, his phrasing grander than before, his loudness perhaps too unremitting. Pirogov has gone downhill vocally; the character is still there in the fast-moving music, but it evaporates in the tenuous pitching and frayed legato of sustained lines. The prize vocal performance is Mark Reizen's big, confident, easy-ranging Konchak – wonderful not only for the sheer vocal splendour, but also for the interpretative control: Reizen maintains a firm rhythmic stride even in the slower parts of his aria, laying a foundation on which music and character both build steadily. Sergei Lemeshev's appeal is compromised by a poor patch in the middle of his reedy voice, but he makes an earnest effort to sing softly. Borisenko, by contrast, has so much plummy, over-vibrant tone that it threatens to get out of control – but it never does, and she carves a firm and vigorous line. (Would that the unnamed Polovtsi Maiden at the start of Act 2 could do as well!) Evgenia Smolenskaya's hot, 'white' tone is rarely varied, and her solos become tiring, but she reacts effectively in the scene with Galitzky. The meaty Bolshoi choral sound counts for more than in the first set, but the orchestra doesn't play nearly as well, and the sound, though improved, still puts a damper on the climaxes. At its best this is an absorbing performance, though not often a subtle one.

Decca/London's Belgrade series of the mid-fifties filled a gap at a time when high-quality recordings from the Soviet Union were still unobtainable. The *Prince Igor* still boasts two assets: the energetic conducting of Oscar Danon, and an uncut score. There is also one wonderful if brief piece of singing: Biserka Cvejic, before the start of her international career, sings the best of all recorded Polovtsian Maidens. Melanie Bugarinović's rich tones already seem too maternal for Konchakovna, but the effect becomes absurd when she confronts the whiney, immature Vladimir of Noni Žunec, who is musically sloppy to boot. Quavery, edgy and scoopy, Valeria Heybalova's arias are not alluring, but she musters some declamatory authority in the finale to Act 1. Dušan Popović (Igor) is an expansive singer with occasional uncertainties of pitch, but these pale beside the sounds emitted by Žarko Cvejic (doubling Galitzky and Konchak, in the Chaliapin tradition); like the ageing Pirogov, Cvejic is a disaster in sustained music, though some skills at characterization can be inferred. Here and there, the listener familiar with Russian recordings of this music may be troubled by the unfamiliar Western Slav accents. Despite palpable imperfections of detail in the choral and orchestral work, Danon projects more of a sense of the opera as a continuity – not just a sequence of cameos and landscapes – than any conductor since on records. One of the early stereo recordings, this set shows its age primarily in the big choral numbers, when the shallowness of the sound becomes constricting. At budget prices, and with the earlier sets hard to come by, this one remains worth consideration.

Not until 1967 was *Igor* again recorded, in a set clearly conceived as a vehicle for Boris Christoff, as both Galitzky and Konchak. Lacking Act 3, it adds little to our knowledge of Christoff's Konchak, and the really brutal abridgement of many numbers rules this set out of serious consideration as a representation of the opera (2, 6, 10, 12, 14, 25, 27, 28, and 29 are variously abridged). Christoff does a capital job on both parts, as far as they go, though he is clearly no longer in his vocal prime; also deserving of a better context are the steady and musical Yaroslavna of Julia Wiener, the fine Konchakovna of Reni Penkova, and the respectable Vladimir of Todor Todorov. Constantin Chekerlisky's thick-toned and monotonous Igor is no asset, nor Jerzy Semkov's ponderous and clumsy direction.

Which brings us to what should have been the solution to the *Prince Igor* problem on records – but is not. The 1969 Bolshoi version of the complete score, with some of the biggest names among recent Soviet singers, sounds like a performance not for the Bolshoi Theatre, but for that six-thousand-seat Kremlin Palace of Congresses in which the company also plays. Everybody is working at *forte* or above nearly all the time, and they seem to have been recorded with microphones in their throats. Worse, Mark Ermler conducts without much sensitivity to the score's weaknesses – or to its strengths either;

the tempi are often ill chosen, the transitions are clumsy, and there is little sense of line or harmonic motion. The orchestra scrambles at the notes, and even the Bolshoi chorus disappoints: that haunting peasants' chorus in Act 4 comes out stiff and boring.

A shame, for the cast surely has potential. Though ageing, Ivan Petrov's Igor remains a considerable performance. Vladimir Atlantov conceives Vladimir's aria on an heroic canvas, but sings it monotonously and scoopily, negating his considerable vocal assets. Elena Obraztsova is a similarly stentorian Konchakovna. More tolerable, because more in character, is Artur Eizen's coarse Galitzky, and Alexander Vedernikov's light-voiced Konchak is genuinely attractive, especially in the recitative after his aria. Tatyana Tugarinova's Yaroslavna is simply squally. All in all, alas, this is a boring and unstylish affair.

The excerpt recordings cluster around a relatively small number of selections, primarily the arias for the male singers. I have come across but one version of Yaroslavna's first aria, that of Nina Koshetz, recorded in 1928 (DB 1204; HMV CSLP-502, Club 99.36), whose distinctively Slavic voice is well managed, with much more shading than in modern recordings of the piece. Koshetz makes some cuts, but none so drastic as those taken by Natalia Stepanovna Yuzhina in her 1911 version of Yaroslavna's fourth-act lament: this includes only the beginning and end of the long and beautiful piece (2–23486; GV 63), and the singing is neither neat nor expressive. One wants to hear Derzhinskaya's recordings of these two arias.

What is almost certainly the oldest recording from *Prince Igor* dates from 1898, just eight years after the first performance; it is a dim-sounding private cylinder, taken at a party, of Galitzky's aria sung by Feodor Chaliapin, with no discernible accompaniment (reissued on OASI 630). In accordance with the spirit of the occasion, or perhaps to make a stronger impression on the wax, Chaliapin belts out even the *dolce* central part of the aria. His later studio versions are more temperate, and no doubt more indicative of his public performances. In 1911 (022224; Rococo 5337), he was granted the services of a chorus to sing a lone introductory line, but Victor was not so lavish in 1927 (DA 891; GEMM 152). Chaliapin's approach is more vernacular, more Varlaamesque than that of Lev Sibiriakov (3–22821; GV 1), who is also free with the metre but is more interested in making a strong line than Chaliapin. Later recordings incline toward Chaliapin's approach: Alexander Kipnis in 1946 (Vic. 11–9285; VIC 1221) is steadier, and less of a grotesque; Boris Christoff sticks close to the notes yet suggests a more vulgar figure of a prince (DB 21127; RLS 735), and so does Nicolai Ghiaurov (SXL 6147). All of these singers are in good vocal state (though Chaliapin, even in 1911, is not always truly in pitch), which cannot be said of Nicola Rossi-Lemeni's hollow and unfocused version (DB 21559; 3C-053–03249). Of other versions early and late, I would like most to hear that of Boris Gmyria.

Most single recordings of Vladimir's cavatina are abridged: they include the recitative, but skip the first half of the aria, picking up at the recapitulation, drastically reducing the amount of harmonic contrast and often leaving the singer at a loss to adjust his interpretation to the changed circumstances. Two famous early recordings cope well with the problem. Andrei Labinsky (3–22830; GV 84) brings to the fore the piece's metrical tension (the melodic stresses generated by the higher pitches are usually on the offbeats) and, except for a lunge to the high B flat, sings firmly and securely. Dimitri Smirnov (022271; CO 379, GV 75) retails his gorgeously heady high notes, but doesn't moon unnecessarily. In a 1923 remake (2–022025; LV 1306), Smirnoff sings the recitative and aria complete, at a very fast tempo and not without some technical problems and choppy phrasing. Recorded in 1904 with piano accompaniment (2–22662; USSR 33D–25209/12), Leonid Sobinov skips the recitative, but still must hurry the aria; despite the speed, he achieves both an apt mood and a remarkable amount of dynamic shading. An abridged electrical version, in Russian, by Joseph Rogatchewsky (Col. D 15012; LV 239) is effortful, except for a lovely final head note.

Vladimir Rosing twice recorded the aria complete: acoustically with orchestra (Vocalion K 52022; TAP 320), electrically with Ivor Newton at the piano (Parl. E 11251). To fit on one side, the piece is taken at an absurd tempo and achieves all the expressive ambience of a foxtrot; even in the earlier version, the voice is worn and quavery, and cannot articulate all the notes. Charles Friant, one of the heroes of *Opera on Record*, does manage to make it work without cuts on a single side (032422; RLS 743, GV 524); sung in French and piano-accompanied, this is well phrased and accented, with an apt sense of direction. Friant's electrical version with orchestra (Od. 123543; dubbed sharp on Rubini GV 524), was allotted two sides, and is consequently expansive – almost to a fault, for it droops noticeably before the recapitulation. André d'Arkor, also in French, is abridged, stiff, and moodless (Col. RF 27; Rococo 5234); Charles Kullman, the Vladimir of Beecham's 1935 Covent Garden production in German, offers vague words and liquid sound (LX 396; LV 255). In English we encounter Walter Widdop, his excellent diction at the service of a translation full of awkward stresses, his tone squeezed and bleating in the upper register (D 1353; GEMM 218). Jussi Björling made three recordings, all in Swedish and all cut, even the LPs! The first dates from 1933 (X 4108; RLS 715): musically secure, radiantly youthful in sound, it is also somewhat passive in character. The 1957 RCA version (RB 16149; SER 5706, RCA Victor LM 2269) is more of a proclamation, the tone steelier and more brilliant – how wonderful it would have been to have had this potential expanded to cover the full aria! Finally, a 1960 concert performance with piano (VICS-1659) shows the tenor still in masterful vocal command. I haven't heard Nicolai Gedda's early recording in Swedish (MOAK-1001); his 1962 Russian version (BEOS 5; C 137–78233/6) is, like Björling's, cut and less lyrical than one might wish.

In 1924, Chaliapin poached on baritonal territory with a recording of Igor's aria (DB 799; USSR D 018015/6, dubbed flat on Scala 869); this, too, is cut slightly. An effective lightening of the voice is expectable; the restless subsidence of the final page is individual and striking. Four years later, Georges Baklanov (Parlo E 11014; LV 118) sings with weight and power, though there's not much plush left on his voice for the big tune. Kim Borg (DG 135090) sings strenuously, to little avail, and Tom Krause also fails to vary dynamics or tempo sufficiently (SXL 6327). The best modern version is certainly George London's vividly contrasted 1951 studio recording (Columbia ML 4489; Preiser PR 135027); his later concert performances (MEL 097 and MEL 228) are less steadily sung. Fascinating evidence of the extent of the revolutionary diaspora, though without musical interest, is an early electric (Victor 4118) by one K. L. Knijnikoff, accompanied by the 'Russian Opera Orchestra, Harbin, Manchuria'.

Heinrich Schlusnus made a famous recording of Igor's aria in German (DG 67057; LV 110), touching up the standard translation to improve the prosody; vocally polished, Schlusnus also seems rather hard-boiled in his projection of the love theme. From the fifties, also in German, Ferdinand Frantz is sometimes vague of pitch and infirm of tone (1C 047–29127), Josef Metternich (EPL 30030; PR 135013) expressive despite the strain of the high tessitura and the rapid tempo. Paul Schöffler (Acanta DE 22694, recorded in 1951) sings, surprisingly, in French – and very clumsy French it is – with monotonously proclamatory vigour. The Italian contingent is represented by Paolo Silveri (LX 1530; 3C 053–03769), monotonously fast and foggy of tone. There are versions by George London, Bernard Ladysz, and (in translation) by John Hargreaves and Roger Bourdin among others.

The problem of cutting to fit on a 78 side recurs in Konchak's aria – almost tragically, for it spoils both of Chaliapin's recordings. The cut removes an essential contrast of tempo and of character; even so, according to Desmond Shawe-Taylor, the basic tempo is faster than Chaliapin used in the theatre. The result is not without vivid traces of a great portrayal, but its true scale can only be grasped by inference, at least by those who have not memory to draw upon. There isn't much to choose between the 1924 version (DB 799; USSR D 018011/2, dubbed flat on Scala 869) and that from 1927 (DB 1104; COLH 100, Jap. Angel GR 2015) except better sound in the latter and, I think, an even more vivid contrast between Konchak's music and the single line of Igor's recitative that Chaliapin ventriloquizes.

From the standpoint of musical form, tempo and scale, Boris Christoff's may have been the first satisfactory recording (DB 21262; RLS 735), and masterful it is, though a certain crafty lightness of touch in Chaliapin's Konchak is not matched. A later Christoff version (ASD 574) is also very good, though the tone is raspier. Ivan Petrov's voice isn't flexible enough for the faster material, but it is rich and solid all the way down to the low F, and he is a forceful presence if not as volatile as Chaliapin or Christoff (ASD 2408, from a Melodiya original). Kim Borg (DG 135090) just isn't in the same league vocally, and he has intonation problems. Ghiaurov (SXL 6147) sings with splendid tone, but little of the personal charm that should accompany the Khan's authority. In Hungarian, Mihaly Székely (Hungaroton SLPX 11444) sounds edgy and breathy, but the voice is still intact and makes an effect of power and presence.

Among the countless recordings of the overture and the Act 2 Dances, which I have not surveyed in detail, memory retains a vivid image of Beecham's 1934 Leeds performance of the Dances (remarkably transferred by Anthony Griffith for World Records' Beecham centennial set, SH 100). Somewhere between the uninhibited if not always precise vigour of this performance and the chilly instrumental perfection of Karajan's Philharmonia versions, there must be a happy middle path in the performance of *Prince Igor,* for this music has more elegance than emerges in most recordings, which concentrate too single-mindedly on the 'barbaric' Orientalisms. *Igor* needs two things at this point: a new critical edition of the score, and an intensively restudied recorded performance – preferably in that order.

PRINCE IGOR

I Igor; *Y* Yaroslavna; *V* Vladimir; *G* Galitsky; *K* Konchak; *Kon* Konchakovna

1930s Baturin and Ivanov *I*;
Derzhinskaya *Y*; Kozlovsky *V*;
Pirogov *G*; Mikhailov *K*;
Antonova *Kon* / Bolshoi Theatre
Chorus and Orch. / L. P.
Steinberg and Melik-Pashayev
USSR set
Excerpts issued on Colosseum
(US) ⓜ CRLP 122

1950s Ivanov *I*; Smolenskaya *Y*;
Lemeshev *V*; Pirogov *G*; Reizen
K; Borisenko *Kon* / Bolshoi
Theatre Chorus and Orch. /
Melik-Pashayev
Chant du Monde ⓜ LDX 8034–6
Artia (US) ⓜ MK 215–D

1955 Popović *I*; Heybalova *Y*;
Žunec *V*; Z. Cvejic *G*; *K*;
Bugarinović *Kon* / Belgrade
National Opera and Orch. /
Danon
Decca GOS 562–5
Richmond SRS 64506

1967 Chekerlisky *I*; Wiener *Y*;
Todorov *V*; Christoff *G*; *K*;
Penkova *Kon* / Sofia National
Opera Chorus and Orch. /
Semkov
Angel SCL 3714
EMI CAN 176–8

1969 Petrov *I*; Tugarinova *Y*; Atlantov
V; Eizen *G*; Vedernikov *K*;
Obraztsova *Kon* / Bolshoi
Theatre Chorus and Orch. /
Ermler
Chant du Monde LDX 78475–8
Angel/Melodiya SDL 4116

A Night in Venice
and *The Gipsy Baron*

ANDREW LAMB

A NIGHT IN VENICE

Johann Strauss's *A Night in Venice* contains some of his loveliest music, and there are few (if any) more sublime passages in all operetta than that glorious first-act finale that ends with night falling on Venice as Caramello's beautiful Gondola Song fades into the distance. For Strauss, however, the composition of the operetta proved less than a sublime experience. At an early stage in composition his young second wife ran off with the manager of the Theater an der Wien where his works were customarily launched. Thus it was that *A Night in Venice* received its première not in Vienna but in Berlin – though by that time his friendship with the woman who was to become his third wife had soothed matters sufficiently for a Theater an der Wien production to be arranged for just six days later. Yet that in itself proved a dubious blessing when the piece was badly received in Berlin. Strauss and his collaborators had to do some hasty rewriting before the work received a rapturous reception from his faithful Viennese public.

With a few further changes, the score reached its definitive, published form. However, the work never became an unqualified success. While the beauties of the music and setting have encouraged frequent revivals, the complexities and shortcomings of the book have led to a succession of revisions that at times have taken us a long way from that 1883 score. The most celebrated of these revisions is that of the text by Ernst Marischka and the music by Erich Wolfgang Korngold for a production at the Theater an der Wien in 1923. Their most obvious alterations concerned the part of Guido, Duke of Urbino. At the Berlin première the Duke's Lagoon Waltz had been roundly hissed, and for Vienna it had been reconstructed – the tempo slowed down and new words provided – and transferred to the character of Caramello, played by the idol of the Viennese public, Alexander Girardi. This left the Duke without a formal solo, and, to provide a worthwhile part for Richard Tauber, Marischka and Korngold added two new solos. The first, 'Sei mir gegrüsst, du holdes Venetia', used music from Strauss's operetta *Simplicius*, while the second, 'Treu sein, das liegt mir nicht', was a setting of new words to the music of Annina's solo 'Was mir der Zufall gab'.

Altogether Marischka and Korngold did their job with style and restraint. Some themes were taken from other operettas, a few numbers moved around, and the orchestration slightly touched up. Perhaps the most damaging aspect of their version is the substantial number of cuts, ranging from single bars to whole sections, that stunt Strauss's expansive 1880s lyricism in favour of a 1920s tautness. Yet the popularity of the extra tenor arias and the availability of performing material have meant that the Marischka/Korngold version has been the one most frequently used for gramophone purposes.

A. *Original 1883 Published Version* (lyrics Richard Genée)

Overture

Act 1

1   Introduction (Chorus): 'Wenn vom Lido sacht' Song (Pappacoda, Chorus): 'Ihr Venezianer, hört'
2   Song (Annina, Chorus): 'Seht, o seht!'/'Frutti di mare!'
3   Duet (Ciboletta, Pappacoda): a. 'Heiraten, ja'*
 b.   ''s ist wahr, ich bin nicht allzu klug'
4   Song and Tarantella (Caramello, Chorus): 'Evviva, Caramello!'
5   Duet (Annina, Caramello): 'Annina! Caramello!'/'Pellegrina rondinella'
6   Quartet (Annina, Ciboletta, Caramello, Pappacoda): 'Alle maskiert'
7   Finale: a. 'Hier ward es still'
 b.   Gondola Song (Caramello): 'Komm in die Gondel'
 c.   'Komm nur, liebes Kind'

Act 2

8a.   Orchestral Introduction (Gondola Song)
 b.   Female Chorus: 'Nur ungeniert hereinspaziert'*
 c.   Song (Agricola): 'Venedigs Frauen herzuführen'
9   Song (Annina): 'Was mir der Zufall gab'
10   Duet (Annina, Duke): a. 'So sind wir endlich denn allein'*
 b.   'Sie sagten, meinem Liebesfleh'n'
 c.   'Ach, was ist dass? Im Saale tanzen meine Gäste'
11   Ensemble (Caramello, Pappacoda, Chorus): 'Solch ein Wirtshaus lob' ich mir'/'Noch sah Ciboletta ich nicht'
12   Quartet (Duke, with Annina, Ciboletta, Delacqua): 'Ninana, Ninana'
13   Finale: a. 'Lasset die ander'n nur tanzen da'
 b.   Song (Pappacoda): 'Takke, takke, tak, erst hack' ich fein'
 c.   'Nur ungeniert hereinspaziert'*
 d.   'Jetzt ist's Zeit zur Lustbarkeit'

Act 3

14   March and Chorus: 'Karneval ruft uns zum Ball'
15   Lagoon Waltz (Caramello): 'Ach, wie so herrlich zu schau'n' (lyric Franz von Gerneth)
16   Mocking Song (Annina, Female Chorus): 'Ein Herzog, reich und mächtig'*

* Sections entirely omitted by Marischka/Korngold.

17a. Processional March
  b. Dove Chorus: 'Die Tauben von San Marco'
  c. Melodrama
  d. 'Wie sich's gebürt'

B. *1923 Marischka/Korngold Version* (additional lyrics by Ernst Marischka)

Overture – original, with cuts

Act 1

1 - original, with cuts
2 - original
3 - original 3b only, with new refrain from *Prinz Methusalem*
4 - original, with cuts
5 - original, with cuts
6 - original, with 2 bars cut
6a. Song (Duke): 'Sei mir gegrüsst, du holdes Venetia' – music from *Simplicius*
7 - original

Act 2

8 - original 8a and c only
9 Song (Duke): 'Treu sein, das liegt mir nicht' – music from original 9
10a. Duet (Annina, Caramello): 'Hör mich, Annina' – from original 10c
  b. Duet (Annina, Duke):– original 10b only
11 - original, with cut
12 - original
13 - original 13a and d only, with cuts

Act 3

14a. - original 14
  b. Dove Trio (Annina, Ciboletta, Duke, Female Chorus) – from original 17b
15 - original
16 Duet (Ciboletta, Pappacoda) – from original 13b
17 Finale – original 17a (part), c and d

The earliest 'complete' LP version was in the marvellous EMI series produced by Walter Legge. The text is basically Marischka/Korngold; but the inability of Erich Kunz to encompass the tenor role of Caramello means that, as well as his Lagoon Waltz being transposed down a third, the Gondola Song in the first-act finale is transferred to Nicolai Gedda – a musicianly solution, but one that makes nonsense of the action. To balance out Gedda's gain here, Schwarzkopf sings the original 'Was mir der Zufall gab' in place of its Marischka/Korngold *alter ego*. But all textual considerations are dwarfed by the sheer joy of the music-making. Schwarzkopf's whipped-cream tone makes the heart beat faster, whether she is selling fish in Act 1 or tempting the Duke in Act 2. From the characterization aspect Kunz is admirable, and the young Gedda is a beautifully lyrical Duke, while Emmy Loose is as ever charming and Peter Klein, Karl Dönch and Hanna Ludwig all worthy members of the cast. Otto Ackermann makes the score unfold beautifully, with supreme lilt and phrasing.

For their stereo remake EMI again used Marischka/Korngold, but padded the piece out with five extra songs (all Strauss arrangements) to provide parts for Anneliese Rothenberger and Hermann Prey. The result is an unstylish patchwork textually, though otherwise it again has much to commend it. Gedda is less lyrical than before, but rather more the lecherous Duke. Cesare Curzi is variable, inclined to some ill-advised high notes, yet generally agreeably free-toned and often sounding curiously like Gedda. (And surely it *is* Gedda who sings the Lagoon Waltz?) Hans-Günther Grimm is Pappacoda – rightly a baritone this time, and offering an excellent comic performance. Well though Streich sings as Annina, one is immediately struck by the pallor and lack of excitement of her interpretation; and the use of a nonsinging Delacqua seems a mistake. The performance is directed less liltingly, more vigorously, but always intelligently by Franz Allers.

The third 'complete' version appeared from BASF in 1976. It sets itself resolutely against Marischka and Korngold and makes use of the critical full score of the operetta published in 1970. However, not content with restoring Strauss's definitive score as contained therein, the adapter dips into the appendices for passages dropped after the Berlin première and even raids the editorial notes for variants rejected during the compositional process. In itself all this would have been reasonable enough, had not the adapter gone on to provide an altered story, move musical numbers around, reallocate some to different characters, and then import further numbers from other operettas. The claim that this is 'the first recording of the original version' is thus a monumental piece of effrontery. Yet one does have individual numbers intact and one is at last able to get a better idea of the scale of Strauss's conception. The recording was made in conjunction with a television production and thus contains more dialogue than is usual on record, but this is clearly spoken, and the interpretation as a whole steers an agreeable middle course between the relaxed lilt of Ackermann and the more consciously lively approach of Allers. Carlo Bini is a coarse-grained Duke, Frieder Stricker a lightweight Pappacoda, but Wolfgang Brendel is quite superb as Caramello, giving a youthful, lively performance with his rich baritone dominating his scenes and taking the high-ranging Gondola Song with ease. His seems to be an ideal Caramello. Jeannette Scovotti, too, produces a really glorious 'Was mir der Zufall gab' that bears comparison with Schwarzkopf's. The Budapest chorus and orchestra are occasionally a little ragged but always full-blooded.

It would have been sadly true to say that no LP performance gave a true impression of the overall structures, scale and balance of Strauss's score had it not been for the recent near-miraculous appearance of an LP transfer of a Berlin radio performance transmitted on 22 January 1938. True Annina's 'Was mir der Zufall gab' is fitted with yet another set of words and handed this time to Caramello, and there are also a few cuts. Yet in all essentials the performance follows the original published score. The sound, of course, leaves a lot to be desired, with Pappacoda's frying pan seemingly audible throughout and Venice having apparently acquired the odd express train. Moreover, the performance nearly comes to grief in the first-act finale when Delacqua enters a bar early. Yet it really is a winning performance, revolving as it does around Marcel Wittrisch's superb ringing tenor supported by a distinguished cast that includes Karl Schmitt-Walter, Margarethe Arndt-Ober and Rosl Seegers.

There are also at least two LP excerpt recordings that use the original published score. The first was made in 1951 by Bregenz Festival forces assembled (curiously enough) for a production of *Der Zigeunerbaron* on the lake. The recording has appeared on various labels, the most complete version apparently being that on Saga 5423. This runs for an hour, and the master tape apparently includes a further eight minutes of music which would make it effectively a complete version – albeit with significant cuts within numbers. The performance lacks polish – perhaps from lack of rehearsal – but it remains a sound, idiomatic version with honoured Viennese operetta performers. Karl Friedrich as the Duke appropriates the Gondola Song from the baritone Kurt Preger in the role of Caramello. Philips S 04026 includes fewer numbers but often in more complete versions, incorporating, for instance, the calls of market traders in the opening chorus, the chorus of senators' wives in Act 2 and Annina's Mocking Song that were all cut by Korngold. Alas, Rudolf Moralt tends to rush the score; but the cast is a winning one, engagingly led by the creamy-voiced Caramello of Rudolf Christ and Waldemar Kmentt as the Duke. Also, on Pye MAL 856, are to be found Donald Grobe in the Gondola Song and Sonja Schöner with 'Was mir der Zufall gab' from what would appear to be a third version using the original score – though I have failed to track down any issue in fuller form.

With the 1960 EMI excerpt version we revert to Korngold, here with even bigger cuts. This is of interest primarily for the two tenors – a classic combination of Fritz Wunderlich and Rudolf Schock, the former ringing out with glorious youthful exuberance and the latter, if occasionally showing signs of strain, his usual involved, characterful self. The permutations of tenors are continued in the 1962 Eurodisc version, with Schock as Caramello somewhat tested in the Gondola Song and Curzi more suited as the Duke than he later was as Caramello, albeit a little over-ambitious at the end of 'Treu sein'. This is a sound, rather than exciting, version, with Erika Köth a shrill Annina and the other characters given relatively little to do.

Two further German excerpt records are of relatively little interest. The 1968–9 East German recording uses the version prepared for the German Opera, Berlin by Walter Felsenstein, who solved the problem of the anti-climactic third act by dropping it altogether. The original score is followed reasonably faithfully until the Act 2 finale, where it departs quite markedly. The performance is competent rather than inspired, with the tempi adopted by Heinz Rögner frequently unfamiliar and too often lacklustre. Finally,

Telefunken 6.22916AF presents an obviously low-budget single side of excerpts, with scaled down and modernized orchestration, a total lack of Viennese lilt and singing that is at times distinctly unpleasant.

In English there are two offerings. Everest SDBR 3028 is a souvenir of a production by Mike Todd at the Jones Beach Marine Theatre in New York, with Korngold banished but some extraneous music added and the story rewritten. It is Ciboletta, not Annina, who takes Barbara's place in the gondola and has the big Act 2 numbers, while Annina's Mocking Song in Act 3 is rewritten as a solo for Delacqua. The performance comes to life with the appearance of Norwood Smith as Caramello; but American accents are strong and the spaghetti overdone in the English version by Ruth and Thomas Martin, though the latter's conducting is agreeably idiomatic. The single-side selection on Reader's Digest RDS 9332 is a faithful enough rendering of the Korngold version with William Lewis an ardent Duke and Anna Moffo in sweet voice as Annina.

Among the usual offering of potpourris is an agreeable one by Frederick Engels, emphasizing the scope of the tenor material in the Marischka/Korngold version (Telef. E 2322), while on LP there is a brief run-through by Anders and Streich (Polydor 46509), another by Heinz Hoppe and Sonja Schöner (originally GMA 25 and subsequently re-used in various formats) and one with Hoppe as the Duke, Peter Alexander as Caramello and Ingeborg Hallstein as Annina (Polydor 2430 263).

Individual excerpts are virtually confined to the tenor arias. However, there is also a somewhat plain version of Annina's 'Frutti di mare' by Ingeborg Hallstein (RCA VL 30409), and Sona Ghazarian presents an attractively fresh and lively version of 'Was mir der Zufall gab' on Amadeo AVRS 14075. There is also a swinging 'Alle maskiert' sung by Emmy Loose, Lotte Rysanek, Murray Dickie and Karl Terkal, accompanying Dickie's soft-toned and heartfelt 'Komm' in die Gondel' (CFP 40091). Elsewhere, a passionate Marcel Wittrisch is joined (EG 2166; Rococo 5223) by Lotte Schoene, who sings with tenderness and bell-like clarity in two Korngold arrangements, the duets 'Annina! Caramello!' and 'Hör' mich, Annina'. The former is given a curious Oscar Strausian-style coda and the latter filled out with a Strauss waltz. These duets complement Wittrisch's marvellous recordings of the four major tenor arias – the Gondola Song with ravishing high notes and well-judged *rubato* (EG 2545; Roc. 5223), the Lagoon Waltz more in disgust than reflectively (EG 3385) and the two arrangements ('Treu sein' in its original soprano key) with grace and feeling (EG 2167; Roc. 5223).

Of the tenor songs, by far the most often recorded is Caramello's beautiful Gondola Song, which is always made more effective as a separate number with the inclusion of the introductory 'Ho-a-ho' and a link to the second verse sung at the very close of the act. On 78s there is Julius Patzak in 1930, seductive and with clear top notes (PO 5021; LV 1318), Charles Kullman in 1933, singing with freely ringing tones but with an unnecessary high note at the end (Columbia DW 3046; LV 144), Herbert Ernst Groh, open, free-voiced, with passionate swelling of voice and a lovely falsetto top note (Parlo. R 1257 – a later version on Telef. GMA 45, more popular in approach, is less effective), Peter Anders with charm and elegance (Telef. A 1834; TS 3141), Max Lichtegg, reliable enough (Decca K 1564 and LXT 5563) and Erich Kunz in 1949 with a downward transposed but effective version that doubtless helped to secure his place in the Legge LP series (LX 1544; World Records SH 284). On LP, Heinz Hoppe is inclined to anticipate the beat (GMA 55), Rudolf Schock is hard and forced (CLP 1681) and Fritz Wunderlich, though exciting as ever, is surprisingly strained at the top and hindered by an inauthentic choral entry (Eurodisc 70 347 IE). In English there is a very free 1939 version with an unrelated text 'Love Can Be Dreamed' by John Charles Thomas (Victor 16184: RCA LPV 515) and a worthy and full-blooded one by David Hughes (Col. TWO 319). Of all the versions I have heard, perhaps none has impressed so much as that by Sándor Kónya (Polydor 46 522 LPHM), with thrilling top notes and ravishingly beautiful lyricism tinged with the right note of tension.

Of Caramello's other number, 'Ach, wie so herrlich zu schau'n' (the Lagoon Waltz), there are versions by several of the same singers. Patzak's 1931 version is rushed and has a curious orchestral prelude (Poly. 10251; LV 1318), while Max Lichtegg's has a crude ending (Decca K 1880 and LXT 5563). Erich Kunz's 1949 version, as ever a third down, is most affecting (Col. LB 86; World Records SH 284), and other versions come from Groh (Od. 0 26303), Hoppe (SLE 14244–P), Schock (Eurodisc S 70221 KE). Additionally there is Werner Krenn in 1971, suitably crestfallen and reflective – altogether beautifully done (Decca DPA 595–6).

Neither of the two Korngold songs for the Duke offers quite the same opportunities for singers as Caramello's. In 'Sei mir gegrüsst' there are admirable versions by Franz Völker in 1928 (Poly. 21043; Heliodor 88015) and Max Lichtegg (Decca K 2368), a less winning one from Walter Anton Dotzer (Philips SBR 6203) and a most wayward one from Koloman von Pataky, marked by curious accent, poor regard for note lengths and a vocal line that the singer appears at one stage to be making up as he goes along (Parlo. R 2205). In 'Treu sein' Karl Friedrich never really seems to get going (Decca LX 3068), but Erich Kunz swells beautifully at the words 'Ja, morgen an' (Col. LB 117; World Records SH 284). There is also Peter Anders, typically elegant (Telef. TS 3141), Ernst Schütz, a light tenor with a faster version (Telef. GMA 105), Kurt Wehofschitz producing a good swing (Volksplatte SMVP 6018) and Werner Krenn with his usual poise (Decca DPA 595–6) – though perhaps all cede precedence to Fritz Wunderlich, superbly involved and with an exciting climax (Eurodisc 70346/7 IE). Yet no singer makes more of these two arranged numbers than Tauber in his 1924 creator's recordings with Korngold and the Theater an der Wien Orchestra, singing with feeling and superb control of dynamics and beautifully spinning out the held high notes (Od. O 83391; 1C 147–30 226/7).

THE GIPSY BARON

After the problems he suffered with *A Night in Venice,* Strauss was persuaded by his new wife-to-be to set his sights higher. Herself of Hungarian extraction, she introduced him to the Hungarian novelist Mór Jókai, and it was one of his stories that provided the source for *The Gipsy Baron.* This was the start of Strauss's flirtation with the higher realms of music that culminated in the opera *Ritter Pázmán*, and indeed *The Gipsy Baron* itself was at one time announced for the Vienna Court Opera. Although eventually produced at the Theater an der Wien, it remains more ambitious, more serious, musically more extended than anything of Strauss's that had gone before.

Several of the singers in the original Berlin and Vienna *Night in Venice* also created roles in *The Gipsy Baron.* It is no surprise to find that Ottilie Collin, the Berlin Annina, was also the first Saffi or that Therese Schäfer, the Vienna Agricola, was the original Mirabella. Equally, it is consistent with our ideas of the voices required for *The Gipsy Baron* that the role of Carnero was created by Carl Adolf Friese, the original Frank in *Die Fleder-maus.* But who could guess that the parts created in *The Gipsy Baron* by Alexander Girardi and Josef Joseffy, respectively Caramello and the Duke in the Vienna *Night in Venice,* were actually Zsupán and Homonay, two roles often sung by baritones and even basses? Both Girardi and Joseffy were later significant recording artists, and the former recorded not only his own 'Ja, das Schreiben und das Lesen' and 'Von des Tajos Strand' on ten-inch G&Ts (2–42589/90) but also Carnero's 'Nur keusch und rein' on a seven-inch (2–42122). In addition Carl Streitmann, the original Barinkay, recorded 'Als flotter Geist' on a ten-inch Berliner (42377).

The Gipsy Baron was one of the best books Strauss ever enjoyed, so that there has been none of the wholesale chopping and changing of text that has so dogged *A Night in Venice.* The sole textual option comes in the finale of Act 2 where, shortly after the première, Strauss replaced the original waltz conclusion ('So voll Fröhlichkeit') with a much improved ending incorporating the Rákóczi March. To find a home for the displaced waltz theme Strauss then tagged it on as a duet at the start of the Act 2 finale, where it is to be found in the Vanguard recording under Anton Paulik and the three EMI sets under Ackermann, Hollreiser and Allers. However, following Viennese tradition, the Decca version under Clemens Krauss and the Eurodisc under Robert Stolz omit it even there. Following another (non-Viennese) tradition, however, Stolz uses the theme in its original choral form as an introduction to Act 3, while the 1949 recording under Marszalek includes the duet alternative as a separate item. The original waltz conclusion to Act 2 is also to be found on the 1955 Moralt excerpts disc and the 1965 Sadler's Wells English version.

One result of *The Gipsy Baron* being such an extended operetta score is that a truly complete recording would require five LP sides, so that all existing versions make various omissions. These commonly include the orchestral preludes to the acts as well as some stretches of melodrama and certain specific vocal numbers. Carnero's 'Nur keusch und rein' (12), which has one of the most lilting tunes in the score, is to be found only in the Vanguard set under Paulik and the 1955 Moralt excerpts record, while Arsena's 'Ein Mädchen hat es gar nicht gut' (15) is included only in the Electrola version under Allers. There appears to be no commercial recording at all of Mirabella's 'Just sind es vierundzwanzig Jahre' (4) or the Act 3 opening chorus 'Freuet Euch' (14).

The first LP recording, under Krauss, has to cut more than most to keep to four sides, inspite of excluding dialogue. Vocally there is much pleasure to be derived from the likes of Alfred Poell and Rosette Anday, the leisurely charm of Patzak's Barinkay and Emmy Loose's delightful Arsena. But Krauss's conducting is extraordinarily slow and lacklustre, almost as though this was a practice run-through. Krauss's way with Johann Strauss was to let the music flow, and that is unsuitable to a score that needs more positive handling. That certainly was achieved in the Vanguard recording under Paulik, where the spotlighting of percussion gives an almost bandmasterish impression. Yet the result is altogether more successful, most obviously where the singer is the same as under Krauss (Kurt Preger as Zsupán, as well as Emmy Loose as Arsena). Waldemar Kmentt is a tight-throated yet utterly compelling Barinkay, Scheyrer a thin-toned yet perfectly adequate Saffi, and there is an admirable depth to the cast with minor roles taken by Erich Kunz and Eberhard Wächter. Altogether the presence of a Viennese team of operetta specialists under a Viennese conductor makes this the most specifically Viennese sounding of all the 'complete' versions.

Walter Legge and his EMI operetta team got round to *The Gipsy Baron* relatively late in the day. Although the recording was made in mono only, the wait was well worth while, especially as Gedda had by then grown in stature to the point where he was able to devote the full glory of voice and characterization to the role of Barinkay. 'Als flotter Geist' is really splendid, with a glorious high C at the end. Also, Kunz was vocally far better suited to the role of Zsupán than the tenor roles he had been thrust into earlier. He is far more faithful to the written note, as well as bringing a marvellously broad Hungarian accent and a rich vein of character to the role of the earthy pig farmer. Schwarzkopf is an aristocratic gipsy girl, perhaps; but nobody else can match the glory of her Gipsy Song with its superbly held 'Tsching-rahs'. In the love duet, 'Wer uns getraut?', the sense of hesitation and the infatuation of the couple ooze out from her and Gedda. Erika Köth is a sweet Arsena, Gertrud Burgsthaler-Schuster a particularly fine Czipra and the young Hermann Prey an exciting Homonay. Otto Ackermann is surprisingly slow and pensive at the start of the overture; but the subsequent dramatic build-up is all the more impressive. Altogether this is one of those recordings where everything seems to go right.

As though to make up for their tardiness first time round, EMI were first with a stereo remake. Heinrich Hollreiser conducts, the overture proclaiming more conventional speeds if ultimately less excitement. The cast is always sound, often more so, without achieving the outstanding standard of its predecessor. Kunz is much as before, but Gueden tends to slide over her notes and force her words in the Gipsy Song. Generally her romantic charms are not heard to advantage in this more dramatic role. In 'Als flotter Geist' Karl Terkal endearingly portrays a sense of wonderment at his lot; but he is a musically accurate rather than engaging performer. Anneliese Rothenberger is a sweet enough Arsena, though the final note of her solo is unpleasant, and Walter Berry is a sombre Homonay (his solo down a semitone). The version is slightly fuller than its EMI predecessor.

The 1965 Eurodisc version proves remarkably good. Schock sings with his usual brio and expressiveness (a suitable note of mystery at the mention of 'Hexenmeister' in his solo), if showing strain on the high notes. Ferry Gruber is an eager Ottokar, Lotte Schädle an expressive Arsena, the veteran Karl Schmitt-Walter a suitably officious Carnero, Wächter an excellent Homonay (his 'Werberlied' a tone down). The outstanding contribution is from Benno Kusche as Zsupán, the Hungarian accent played down but achieving comic, earthy effect. The problem is the Saffi, Erzsébet Házy, who produces a most wild performance – appropriately so, perhaps, from a dramatic standpoint, but less endearingly from a musical one as her notes sometimes hit target beautifully but at other times fall cruelly off pitch. Stolz proves an admirable conductor – a little leaden in the waltzes, but altogether more responsible and imaginative than in others of his recordings. There are some prominent sound effects, including water flowing at the opening of Act 1 and a virtuoso performance on the coconut shells as Homonay arrives in Act 2.

The final EMI version under Franz Allers proves ultimately disappointing. Right at the start of the overture there is a curious alteration to the rhythm, and subsequently the waltzes prove somewhat heavy-handed, the ensemble at times less than perfect. Gedda now distinctly overplays Barinkay, the notes more constricted and forced, the final high C of his solo much less clean. Grace Bumbry (Saffi), too, is less than happy with the highest notes, and her big solo is lacking in gipsy fire. Kurt Böhme is an exaggeratedly pompous, slow Zsupán; his second solo taken a tone down. Prey again sings Homonay's solo with fine aplomb. Rita Streich fully justifies the inclusion of the extra number for Arsena.

The earliest collection of excerpts on LP is a substantial one (over an hour) recently retrieved from the archives of Cologne Radio. It comes from a 1949 broadcast and well displays the more sharp-edged, less indulgent German style in the work. Peter Anders and Sena Jurinac fully justify the retrieval, though each is less effective in his or her solo than in the ensemble numbers. The Act 1 finale in particular is as well done as anywhere. Again there is a strong supporting cast. Another early LP collection with German, rather than Viennese, forces is a much shorter one with Walther Ludwig and Hans Hopf doing Barinkay's, Homonay's and Zsupán's solos with style and Maud Cunitz no less impressive as Saffi.

From Vienna comes the 1951 Remington record, offering an extended collection of excerpts sensitively conducted and authentically performed by a proficient team of operetta singers with a good Barinkay. SBR 6217 is a much shorter sample, but offers a particularly good team of Viennese operetta singers of the time, led by Rudolf Christ as a stylish Barinkay and Sári Bárabás as Saffi, with Rudolf Moralt conducting idiomatically. Otto Edelmann seems a surprising choice as Zsupán, under-characterized and over-operatic in approach, his Act 3 number sung a third down.

The 1957 Vox recording may be speedily despatched. It is a quite amazing collection of snippets stitched together from all over the score. The 1959 EMI record follows their usual pattern of the time, with relatively short excerpts making up a single LP side and always proficiently done – here with Schock, Köth and Kusche making up an excellent team of principals. The 1964 Hamburg version (Pye MAL 560) is another straightforward and respectable German provincial opera house version, with Donald Grobe shining as Barinkay. The 1965 Telefunken record is also good in its way – with Reinhold Bartel a ringing Barinkay and Böhme a fruity Zsupán, but with the excerpts linked by a German narrative marred by execrable pronunciation of the Hungarian names.

Two excerpt records in English are sadly disappointing. The Reader's Digest recording has Jeannette Scovotti an expressive and attractive Saffi and John Hauxvell a welcome Homonay; but William Lewis is stretched as Barinkay, and there is too much tentative singing and playing under Lehman Engel. The Sadler's Wells recording of 1965 presents the least successful of their operetta productions of the time. Vilem Tausky promises well enough in the overture, and there are worthy contributions from, among others, Ann Howard as Czipra; but Nigel Douglas sounds too refined a Barinkay, and June Bronhill has neither the control needed for the Gipsy Song nor the refinement of tone for the love duet. I have not heard the promising 1960 French version under Alain Lombard with Guy Chauvet, Janine Micheau and Jean-Christophe Benoit; but only collectors of curiosities need try another French EMI issue with Georges Guétary turning various numbers from the score indiscriminately into between-the-wars French chansons.

There is again the usual bunch of potpourris, including a 78 with Wittrisch, Willi Domgraf-Fassbaender, Leo Schützendorf, Irene Eisinger and Else Ruzicka incorporating a curious fusion of Zsupán's 'Ja, das Schreiben und das Lesen' and Arsena's 'Ein Falter schwirrt ums Licht' (EH 725), another with Patzak and Maria Reiner (Poly. 15212) and a fine one from April 1934 with Peter Anders and Anita Gura (Telef. E 1673; HTP 517). LP selections include Anders again, with Trötschel and Benno Kusche (Poly. 46 509) Melitta Muszely (Saffi), Heinz Hoppe (Barinkay) and Heinrich Pflanzl (Zsupán) on Telef. GMA 25, and a longer one with Sándor Kónya as Barinkay, Ingeborg Hallstein as Saffi and Willy Schneider as Zsupán (Poly. 237 160).

Turning to individual excerpts, one starts conveniently with Barinkay's entrance song 'Als flotter Geist', with its lilting waltz refrain. There are exciting versions by Charles Kullman with lovely *rubato* at 'is nit schwer' (Columbia DW 3067; LV 144) and by Rupert Glawitsch, singing with real involvement and verbal clarity (Telef. HTP 502). Tauber, too, is characterful and uses *rubato* to good effect (Parlo. RO 20252; 1C 147 29137–8). Joseph Schmidt is serious and uninteresting (Parlo. R 1330; 1C 147 29140–1), while Koloman von Pataky is leisurely and produces an excellent top note (Poly. 23471). Wittrisch is admirable as ever, singing with neat inflections and attractive lilt and always maintaining the interest of the words (HMV EG 1278), as is Franz Völker, bringing out his compellingly controlled musicality in 1928 (Poly. 19791; Heliodor 88015). Anders is to be heard with typical stylishness and ringing tones, though too hasty a tempo, in a 1951 Baden-Baden radio performance (1C 147 29142–3), while Wunderlich is likewise as exciting as ever on Eurodisc 70 347 IE. In English there is Walter Glynne with a 'pretty', light-voiced version (HMV B 4271), John Charles Thomas with a ballad-style version (Victor 16184; ARL 2.0553) and Max Lichtegg with poorly accented German and totally unrelated words (Decca K 1563).

Of Saffi's entrance song ('O habet Acht') there are two versions by Elisabeth Rethberg – a 1922 acoustic (Od. 8010; LV 29) and a later electrical (Parlo. RO 20115) – the latter freer, but both instilling an appropriate sense of mystery and tellingly spinning out key notes. Also on 78 there is Anni Frind, sweetly reflective (EG 3640; IC 137 46347/8), Vera Schwarz, whom I have not heard (Od. O 11530 – coupled with 'So voll Fröhlichkeit'), Else Kochhann revealing expression and feeling but ending weakly (Poly. 27182), Jarmila Novotna building up well and with beautiful 'Tsching-rahs' (VIC 1383) and Maria Cebotari expansive and powerfully dramatic in 1949 (DB 6947; 1C 147 29119). By comparison LP versions are generally disappointing: Irmtraud Kruchten weak, even scrappy (Telef. GMA 55), Ljuba Welitsch dully accompanied (CBS 61088; Odyssey 32 16 0078), Anna Moffo tending to croon in the lower reaches (Telef. SLE 14545–P), Cristina Deutekom unsteady and again inadequately accompanied (CFP 190). Rather better are Sylvia Sass in Hungarian (Hungaroton SLPX 16607) and Pilar Lorengar – an unlikely recruit to the ranks, but spirited and involved and with admirable use of light and shade (SXL 6525).

Some of the same singers are also to be heard in the Act 2 Treasure Trio, for example an excellent version by Kochhann and Völker with Emma Bassth (Decca-Poly. PO 5002) and a sound enough one by Rudolf Schock with Anny Schlemm and Gertrud Stilo (CLP 1681). The main combinations of Barinkay and Saffi are, however, for the lovely duet 'Wer uns getraut?'. From interwar years there are Else Kochhann and Helge Rosvaenge (Poly. 25105; LV 514), Vanconti and Tauber (Od. 8355), Erna Berger singing sweetly with Charles Kullman in 1933 (Col. DW 3067; LV 144), Aulikka Rautawaara with the right touch of anxiety opposite the stylish Peter Anders (Telef. E 2572; HTP 515), Emmy Bettendorf and Herbert Ernst Groh rather less inspiring (Parlo. R 1257), Walter Glynne and Gerda Hall with a dainty version in English (HMV B 4271), and a truly uplifting version in Swedish by Jussi Björling and Hjördis Schymberg (HMV X 6146; RLS 715). Novotna does it as a solo (VIC 1383), and there are late 78 rpm versions from Lisa Della Casa and Helge Roswaenge in 1949 (Decca K 2181; LM 4520) and Leni Funk and Max Lichtegg (Elite Special 7012). LP recordings include a radio version by Nata Tüscher and Peter Anders (RCA VL 30319–2), one with modernized accompaniment by Sonja Schöner and H. E. Groh (Telef. GMA 45), one by Ruth-Margaret Pütz and Heinz Hoppe (Telef. 6.22 226 AF), another by Schock with a husky Anny Schlemm (CLP 1681), an authentic and charming one (in German) by Adele Leigh and Nigel Douglas (Philips SGL 5842) and another warm and winning one by Renate Holm and Werner Krenn (Decca DPA 595–6). I have not sought out versions of the duet's reincarnation as 'One day when we were young'.

Of Zsupán's two solos there are also several versions. I have not heard couplings of the two by Schützendorf (Telef. A 684; HT 19) or August Griebel (Col. DW 3064); but Gustav Neidlinger's rich bass may be heard in a swinging 'Von des Tajos Strand' and a heavy 'Ja, das Schreiben und das Lesen' on Volksplatte SMVP 6018. Nor have I heard 'Ja, das Schreiben und das Lesen' sung by Willy Schneider (DG 2416 175) or Georg Hann (DG EPL 30 199); but there is an early and formative version of it by Erich Kunz from 1949 (Col. LB 86; World Records SH 284), one in English by Eric Shilling with underpowered accompaniment (Pye NSPH 6) and a 'pop' version by Peter Alexander with Schrammel accompaniment (Ariola 27 931 XE). For the rest there is a tantalizingly brief gathering of Lotte Lehmann and Richard Tauber with other singers in abridged versions of the finales to Acts 2 and 3 (Parlo. R 20104) and a few versions of Homonay's recruiting song – Willi Domgraf-Fassbaender dignified but ponderous (HMV EG 2336), Arno Schellenberg (EG 7006) and Völker, his superb control and easy high notes making a perfect case for the more brilliant effect of the original tenor casting (Poly. 27072; Heliodor 88115).

Notwithstanding marvellous individual interpretations, perhaps neither *A Night in Venice* nor *The Gipsy Baron* has yet benefited fully from what the LP medium has to offer. The former has been dogged by the preference for arrangements which, whatever their merits on stage, are totally unnecessary on record, while the latter really needs that fifth LP side. From the prewar era there are many happy reminders of distinguished artists in individual numbers, and it is a marvellous bonus that radio archives should have yielded up such substantial and admirable souvenirs of Wittrisch's *Night in Venice* and Anders's *Gipsy Baron*. One can only wish that by some miracle the same might have happened for the likes of Völker, Tauber, Rethberg, Lehmann and others whose voices ring out all too briefly from their 78rpm recordings.

A NIGHT IN VENICE

C Ciboletta; *A* Annina; *Car* Caramello; *P* Pappacoda; *D* Duke; *Del* Delacqua; *Agr* Agricola

1938 (original)
Seegers *C*; Spletter *A*; Wittrisch *Car*; Zimmermann *P*; Schmitt-Walter *D*; Sauter-Sarto *Del*; Arndt-Ober *Agr* / Chorus and Orch. of Reichssender, Berlin / Steiner
Anna ⓜ ANNA 1048

1951 (original; excerpts)
Boesch *C*; Rethy *A*; Preger *Car*; Meyer-Gamsbacher *P*; Friedrich *D*; Jerger *Del* / Bregenz Festival Chorus, Vienna SO/Paulik
CBS (US) ⓜ SL119
Saga ⓔ 5423 (virtually complete)

1954 (Marischka/Korngold)
Loose *C*; Schwarzkopf *A*; Kunz *Car*; Klein *P*; Gedda *D*; Dönch *Del*; H. Ludwig *Agr* / Philharmonia Chorus and Orch. / Ackermann
EMI ⓔ SXDWS 4043 ④
TC2–SXDWS 4043
Angel ⓜ 3530 BL

1968 (Marischka/Korngold, with interpolations) Görner *C*; Streich *A*; Curzi *Car*; Grimm *P*; Gedda *D*; Oppelberg *Del*; Litz *Agr* / Bavarian Radio Chorus, Graunke SO / Allers
EMI 1C 157 29095–6

1976 (Barth)
Schary *C*; Scovotti *A*; Brendel *Car*; Stricker *P*; Bini *D*; Dönch *Del*; Steiner *Agr* / Hungarian Radio Chorus, Hungarian State Orch./Märzendorfer
Acanta EB 225275
CBS (US) M2-35908

1953 (original; excerpts)
Boesch *C*; Siebert *A*; Christ *Car*; Preger *P*; Kmentt *D*; Henčl *Del;* Zörner *Agr* / Vienna Chamber Choir, Vienna SO / Moralt
Philips ⓜ S 04026 L
Epic ⓜ LC 3324

1959 (Martin; excerpts – in English)
Fairbanks *C*; Hurley *A*; N. Smith *Car*; Stuarti *P*; Russell *D*;

Hayward *Del* / chorus and orch. / Martin
Everest SDBR 3028

1960 (Marischka/Korngold; excerpts)
Schirrmacher *C*; Otto *A*; Wunderlich *Car*; Mercker *P*; Schock *D*; G. Völker *Del* / Günther-Arndt Chorus, Berlin SO / F. Walter
EMI 1C 037 28127

1961 (Marischka/Korngold; excerpts – in English)
Scovotti *C*; Moffo *A*; Grover *Car*; Palmer *P*; W. Lewis *D*; Gaynes *Del* / chorus and orch. / Engel
RCA / Reader's Digest RDS 9332

1962 (Marischka/Korngold; excerpts)
Schirrmacher *C*; Köth *A*; Schock *Car*; Pauly *P*; Curzi *D*; Stoll *Del* / Berlin RIAS Chorus, Berlin SO / Schmidt-Boelcke
World Records SOH 130
Ariola I 89894 E ④ D 55896 E

1964 (original?; excerpts)
Schöner *A*; Grobe *Car*; Wohlfahrt *P* / Hamburg State Opera Chorus and Orch. / Müller-Lampertz
Europa 564

1968 (Marischka/Korngold; medley)
Bartos *C*; Hallstein *A*; Bartel *Car*; Alexander *P*; Hoppe *D* / orch. / Marszalek
Polydor 2430 264 ④ 3260 263

1968–9 (Felsenstein; excerpts)
Rönisch *C*; Ebert *A*; Neukirch *Car*; Süss *P*; Ritzmann *D*; Vogel *Del* / Leipzig Radio Chorus, Dresden PO / Rögner
Philips 6530 047

1976 (Küster; excerpts)
Perry *A*; Wohlers *Car*; *D* Graunke SO / Falk
Telefunken AF6. 22916

1977 (excerpts)
Schmidt *C*; Geszty *A*; Curzi *Car*; Piso *P*; Ridder *D*; Kunz *Del*; Migenes *Agr* / Bavarian Radio Chorus and Orch. / Eichhorn
Philips 6623 116 ④ 7585 352

THE GIPSY BARON

H Homonay; *C* Carnero; *B* Barinkay; *Z* Zsupán; *A* Arsena; *O* Ottokar; *Cz* Czipra; *S* Saffi; *P* Pali; *M* Mirabella

1951 Poell *H*; Dönch *C*; Patzak *B*;
Preger *Z*; Loose *A*; Jaresch *O*;
Anday *Cz*; Zadek *S*; Bierbach *P*;
Leverenz *M* / Vienna State Opera
Chorus, Vienna PO / C. Krauss
Decca ⓜ ECM 2148–9
London ⓜ A 4208

1955 Kunz *H*; Wächter *C*; Kmentt *B*;
Preger *Z*; Loose *A*; Späni *O*;
Rössl-Majdan *Cz*; Scheyrer *S*; Fez
M / Vienna State Opera Chorus
and Orch. / Paulik
Philips ⓜ G O4200–1 L
Vanguard (US) ⓜ VRS 486–7

1955 Prey *H*; Ferenz *C*; Gedda *B*;
Schmidinger *O*; Kunz *Z*; Köth *A*;
Burgsthaler-Schuster *Cz*;
Schwarzkopf *S*; E. Paulik *P*; M.
Sinclair *M* / Philharmonia Chorus
and Orch. / Ackermann
EMI ©️ SXDW 3046 ④ TC-SXDW
3046
Angel ⓜ 3566 BL

1960 Berry *H*; Heater *C*; Terkal *B*;
Kunz *Z*; Rothenberger *A*; Equiluz
O; *P*; Rössl-Majdan *Cz*; Gueden
S; Sjöstedt *M* / Vienna
Singverein, Vienna PO /
Hollreiser
EMI ASD 394–5
Angel SBL 3612

1960s (in Russian)
Soloists / Moscow Radio Chorus
and Orch. / Silantyev
Melodiya SM 03129–34

1965 Wächter *H;* Schmitt-Walter *C;*
Schock *B*; Kusche *Z*; Schädle *A*;
Gruber *O*; Schärtel *Cz*; Házy *S*;
Röhrl *P*; Konetzni *M* / German
Opera Chorus and Orch. / Stolz
Ariola-Eurodisc XF 71455 E; XD
88613 E ④
SG 56698 E
Everest S 469
World Records OC 173–4

1970s 'Grosses Operetten-Ensemble'
(artists include Ebert, Geiler,
Katterfield; Ritzmann, Hellmich;
Krämer), Leipzig Radio Chorus

and SO / Rögner
Fontana 701 522–3

1971 Prey *H*; Anheisser *C*; Gedda *B*;
Böhme *Z*; Streich *A*; Brokmeier
O; Cvejic *Cz*; Bumbry *S*; Litz *M* /
Bavarian State Opera Chorus and
Orch. / Allers
EMI 1C 163 28354–5

1949 (excerpts – broadcast
performance)
Schmitt-Walter *H*; Schneider *C*;
Anders *B*; Hann *Z*; Hollweg *A*;
Schröder *Cz*; Jurinac *S*; Lasser *M*
/ Cologne Radio Chorus and SO
/ Marszalek
RCA ⓜ VL 30310 AF

c.1950 (excerpts)
W. Ludwig *B*; *H*; Hopf *Z*;
Cunitz *S* / Rudolf Lamy Chorus,
Bavarian Radio Orch. /
Schmidt-Boelcke
Mercury ⓜ MG 15005

1951 Telasko *H*; Meyer-Welfing *B*; F.
Krenn *Z*; Funk *A*; Rózsa *Cz*;
Seidl *S* / Vienna Choral Union,
Vienna SO / Schönherr
Remington ⓜ 199–47
Acanta ⓜ BI 1863
Saga ©️ EROS 8004

1953 (excerpts)
Witte *B*; Frei *Z*; Stilo *Cz*; Janz *S*
/ Leipzig Radio Chorus and Orch.
/ Dobrindt
Eterna ⓜ 340047–8

1954 (abridged)
A. Kunz *B*; Miller *Z*; Tüscher *Cz*;
Heusser *A*; Graf *S* / Radio Zurich
Chorus and Orch. / Goehr
Musical Masterpiece Society ⓜ
MMS 130
Concert Hall ©️ SMS 2025

1955 (excerpts)
Brand *H*; Preger *C*; Christ *B*;
Edelmann *Z*; Siebert *A*; Kmentt
O; Milinkovic *Cz*; Bárábas *S*;
Riegler *M* / Vienna Chamber
Chorus, Vienna SO / Moralt
Philips ⓜ SBR 6217
Epic ⓜ LC 3041 (with narration)

c.1956 (excerpts – in Hungarian)
Orosz; Szilvássy; Rösler;
Nagypál; Raskó; Maleczky;
Udvardy *B*
Qualiton ⑩ HLP 6509

1957 (medley)
Agrelli *H*; Wolinsky *B*; Horn *Z*;
Krämer *A*; Zapf *Cz*; E. Kertész *S*
/ Frankfurt Radio Chorus and
Orch. / Szöke
Vox ⑩ VX 1600

1959 (excerpts)
Cordes *H*; Strienz *C*; Schock *B*;
Kusche *Z*; Hildebrand *A*; Wagner
Cz; Köth *S*; Willenberg *M* /
Berlin Municipal Opera Chorus,
Berlin SO / Schmidt-Boelcke
EMI 1C 037 28185

1960s (excerpts – in Hungarian)
Udvardy *B*; Radnai *Z*; Ágay *A*;
Barlay *Cz*; Házy *S*; Szabo *M* /
Hungarian State Orch. /
Breitner
Hungaroton SLPX 16557

1960 (excerpts – in French)
Chauvet *B*; Benoit *Z*; Micheau *S*
/ Duclos chorus, Pasdeloup Orch.
/ Lombard
Véga 130.516

1961 (excerpts – in English)
W. Lewis *B*; Hauxvell *Z*; Elias *A*;
Cz; Scovotti *S* / chorus and orch.
/ Engel
Reader's Digest RDS 5041

1964 (excerpts)
Grobe *B*; Ferenz *Z*; Muszely *S* /
Hamburg State Opera Chorus and
Orch. / Müller-Lampertz
Somerset 598
Pye ⑩ MAL 560

1965 (excerpts)
Schneider *H*; Toman *C*; Bartel *B*;
Böhme *Z*; Bartos *A*; Schütz *O*;
Bence *Cz*; Köth *S* / Rudolf Lamy
Chorus, Bavarian Radio Orch. /
Michalski
Telefunken AF 6 21286

1965 (excerpts – in English)
Hawthorne *H*; Folley *C*; Douglas
B; Hammond-Stroud *Z*; Eddy *A*;
K. Miller *O*; Howard *Cz*; Bronhill
S / Sadler's Wells Opera Chorus
and Orch. / Tausky
EMI CSD 1629

1965 (medley)
Ostenburg *H*; Kónya *B*; Schneider
Z; Hollweg *A*; H. Walther *Cz*;
Hallstein *S* / Cologne Radio
Chorus and Orch. / Marszalek
Polydor 237 160

Ariadne auf Naxos and *Arabella*

MICHAEL KENNEDY

Of all Richard Strauss's operas, *Ariadne auf Naxos* has the most complex history. It was his third collaboration with Hugo von Hofmannsthal as librettist and the second in which they began from scratch (*Elektra* was an adaptation of Hofmannsthal's version of the Sophocles play). After the phenomenal success of *Der Rosenkavalier* in 1911, their next venture was of crucial importance to them. It was with the pre-eminent theatrical director of the day, Max Reinhardt, in mind that Hofmannsthal devised a curious juxtaposition of play and opera; he had seen Molière's *Le bourgeois gentilhomme* while on a visit to Paris and realized that he could combine his own adaptation of this famous play about the *nouveau riche* M. Jourdain (surely the 'original' for Faninal in *Der Rosenkavalier*) with an earlier idea of his own about a castle to which an *opera seria* company and a troupe from the *commedia dell' arte* are invited simultaneously. He wrote a linking scene, *without music*, in which Jourdain's Music Master is identified with the interests of the opera company, and his Dancing Master with the harlequinade. A bombshell lands on the preparations for the evening's entertainment when Jourdain rules that, in order to leave time for a fireworks display, the opera and the *commedia dell' arte* must be performed concurrently.

The composer of the opera, horror-stricken by this act of philistine vandalism, is contrasted with the lively and flirtatious Zerbinetta of the harlequinade. Their conversation epitomizes Hofmannsthal's philosophical concept in *Ariadne*: 'fidelity in woman'. He was concerned to show on the one hand Ariadne, capable of being only one man's wife or lover, and on the other Zerbinetta, happily flitting from man to man. Deserted on the isle of Naxos by Theseus after helping him to kill the Minotaur in her royal father's labyrinth on Crete, Ariadne hopes only for death. But a miracle awaits her, the arrival of a god, Bacchus, who carries her off. She gives herself to him because, Hofmannsthal said, 'she believes him to be Death; he is both Death and Life at once'. But to Zerbinetta, god or man, it makes no difference, it's the same old story, off with the old, on with the new. The first (1912) version of *Ariadne auf Naxos* comprised the Molière play with Strauss's incidental music, the linking scene, and the opera *Ariadne auf Naxos*.

Strauss's initial reaction to the idea was discouraging and patronizing, but as rehearsals under Reinhardt in Stuttgart progressed, he became enthusiastic and rightly referred to his score, composed for an orchestra of thirty-seven players, as 'a real masterpiece'. Not unexpectedly, the work was a failure, since it was aimed at two different publics, straight theatre and opera, and, even in 1912, the economic difficulties of combining rehearsals etc. for actors and singers were formidable. Yet, in an ideal situation and as Beecham (who much preferred the first version) showed at the Edinburgh Festival in 1950, *Ariadne I* is a magical experimental idea. Perhaps this Beecham performance may yet be issued in full for the delight of collectors. That an 'off-the-air' tape exists is proved by the extract of very acceptable quality, issued on Acanta DE23 316/17 as part of an album of duets and arias featuring the tenor Peter Anders, whose death in a car crash in 1954 at the age of forty-six was a loss comparable with that of Fritz Wunderlich a decade later. The extract is the Bacchus-Ariadne duet, from 'Circe, Circe' to its conclusion in the first version, where it is faded out before the return of Zerbinetta and the comedians and Jourdain's final speech. There is additional interest in being able to hear the short orchestral passage which Strauss later cut. Anders sings Bacchus with the unforced lyrical ease and power which are all too rarely encountered where this role is concerned, and Hilde Zadek is an appealing, accurate and very feminine Ariadne. But the star of the recording is undoubtedly Beecham. In the excitement and atmosphere of a live performance, his zest for this music, his affection for its detail and his driving passion in the broad melodic lines of the duet come across with undiminished fervour. There are some roughnesses in the playing of the Royal Philharmonic Orchestra but many more felicities; and for music-making as electric as this, one is ready to forgive the flaws which merely prove that human beings, not automatons, were involved on that summer evening in the King's Theatre, Edinburgh.

In 1916 the collaborators decided on a revision. They dropped the Molière play (the incidental music is preserved as a suite) and in its place Strauss composed a prologue, the text of which Hofmannsthal had written in 1913. This was an adaptation of the linking scene from the first version, which showed the consternation caused to the Composer by M. Jourdain's instruction. But now Jourdain and France are jettisoned: the action – moved forward half a century – takes place in the house of the 'richest man in Vienna' who is never seen but is represented by his Major Domo (a speaking role). The Composer, a part which Strauss inexplicably at first found 'downright distasteful', is assigned to a *travesti* soprano (or mezzo soprano). It ranks among Strauss's finest offerings to the female voice. Not surprisingly, and although the prologue lasts barely forty minutes and the Composer does not appear again, leaving the singer free to return to her hotel for dinner or whatever else she fancies, the role has never ceased to attract the most distinguished artists of the day. Indeed, this first great chamber-opera of the twentieth century combines, like *Der Rosenkavalier*, three rewarding soprano parts, the others being Ariadne herself, who has the bonus of appearing in the prologue as the Prima Donna, and Zerbinetta, a coloratura role but one that must be sung with feminine warmth and not interpreted merely as a capricious coquette.

Ariadne II has fared well on disc. The first complete set to be considered, although not specifically made for the gramophone, is in many respects unsurpassable. It is a recording of the performance given in the Vienna State Opera House on the evening of 11 June 1944 – Strauss's eightieth birthday – in the presence of the composer. Sound quality and balance are remarkably good and only a dullard could miss the sense of occasion (and what an occasion!) which informs and excites the whole performance. The set is additionally historic because it preserves one of the earliest successes by one of the great post-Second-World-War stars of opera, Irmgard Seefried. She had joined the Vienna company in 1943 from Aachen and was twenty-four at the time of this performance. What a birthday treat for the octogenarian composer to hear his Composer – he imagined him 'like the young Mozart' – sung in this way.

Of all the Composers on record, none approaches the young Seefried for youthful petulance, when the voice becomes purposely shrill and callow, for the radiant idealism needed for 'Musik ist eine heilige Kunst', and for conveying a sense of spontaneous inspiration at 'Du Venus sohn'. So vivid is this interpretation that one can easily visualize the Composer veering from rage at the philistine treatment of his opera to surrender to a romantic rapture as his music is fuelled by his unexpected attraction to Zerbinetta. The Ariadne is Maria Reining, then not halfway through her long reign in Vienna from 1937 to 1955. She has not had the recognition in Britain that she deserves, mainly because her recorded Marschallin with Kleiber for Decca came when her career was almost over (hear the Cetra Live set of Szell's 1949 Salzburg *Rosenkavalier* to discover how good she was in the role). Her Ariadne has the tragic dignity the part requires and her voice, here in its prime, easily covers the wide range Strauss demands. That regal authority combined with melting femininity which is the *clou* of so many Strauss soprano roles comes effortlessly to her, and it stems partly, of course, from superb technique and breath control, so that the long lines and broad phrases form a vocal parabola, and partly from that thorough absorption in and understanding of the text without which there can be no really great singing, only accomplished vocalizing. Reining's 'Es gibt ein Reich' takes the listener to the core of Ariadne's despair, and she marvellously sustains the lyricism of the long final duet with Bacchus.

Strauss's opinion of tenors was low, and he asked a lot from the breed here, for Bacchus must not only sing as a *Heldentenor* but must look 'young, magical, dreamy'. Few do both, alas, but only the vocal aspect need concern the listener at home. Max Lorenz is the Bacchus here, tending at his climactic moments to revert to a Bayreuth bark but pleasing in quieter passages, and there is no mistaking his wholehearted response to the emotion of the occasion. Alda Noni is the lively Zerbinetta, singing the formidable display piece 'Grossmächtiger Prinzessin' with sparkle and poise. (This aria was considerably shortened by Strauss in revision after 1912 and lowered by a whole tone for most of its course.) Zerbinettas come in two models: those who are brilliant and inclined to be shrill and those who, both vocally and dramatically, reach out to the part's deeper implications. Noni belongs to the former category, where she ranks high. Other peaks in this performance are provided by the avuncular and steady Music Master of Paul Schöffler, the Harlequin of Erich Kunz and the Naiad of Emmy Loose. Alfred Muzzarelli's Major Domo is under-characterized. The conductor is Karl Böhm, relishing the amazing colour and richness of the score and obtaining impassioned as well as delicate playing from the Vienna orchestra. Solo passages, notably the cello, are lovingly played and Strauss's inspired use of the harmonium to provide extra 'body' for his small orchestra comes over well.

Böhm is the conductor of a live Salzburg Festival performance recorded on 7 August 1954 and issued in Melodram's Richard Strauss Edition (MEL S 104). The sound quality is good and the cast includes some great names, not all of them, alas, in great form that night. Seefried is the Composer, and her performance, ten years after the Viennese salute to Strauss himself, has lost none of its impetuosity and rare sense of elation. I have heard no other interpreter of this role who captures its quixotic mood so exactly. Paul Schöffler is again the Music Master, still rock-like in his steadiness of tone and suitably exasperated in his exchange with the excellent Major Domo of Alfred Neugebauer. The lesser roles are filled out by singers of a calibre upon which Salzburg has built its reputation – Walter Berry as the Wigmaker, Alfred Poell as Harlequin (less characterful than some others discussed here), August Jaresch, Oskar Czerwenka and Murray Dickie as the other comedians, Rita Streich, Hilde Rössl-Majdan and Lisa Otto as Naiad, Dryad and Echo respectively.

Hilde Gueden is Zerbinetta, a performance which, while being skilful and accurate, never fully convinces me that this was her role. Nor, on this evidence, was Ariadne the best of Lisa Della Casa's Strauss. There are some beautiful passages, but many more which are strained and, at one point in the final duet, ugly, as she struggles with phrases which lie too low for her. The Bacchus, Rudolf Schock, can cope with the part's demands but he does not produce that flood of lyrical sound which is the only means by which this part can fully succeed. To add to the disappointments of this set, the Vienna Philharmonic brass were having a most unhappy evening, coming to grief entirely at the climax of the passage before Ariadne greets Bacchus as a god, and 'fluffing' elsewhere much too often. These flaws are the inevitable concomitant of live recording; in some great performances they hardly seem to matter. Here they come into the foreground.

The first studio recording was made in London in the summer of 1954 under the guidance of Walter Legge, with Herbert von Karajan a most sympathetic and percipient conductor, lavishing his art on the chamber-music textures but not stinting the passion. The Philharmonia Orchestra plays superbly for him. What is missing from the prologue is the atmosphere of delightful muddle and backstage banter – in *Ariadne*, as in others of his operas, Strauss is at his best in depicting the theatrical milieu in which he spent most of his life. The device of recording the Major Domo separately and in a different acoustic, and inserting his speeches into the tape, kills the opening exchanges with the Music Master; here, Alfred Neugebauer sounds a pensionable Major Domo, nowhere near as good as he was with Böhm. Compared with Schöffler, Karl Dönch is a lightweight and petty Music Master. These apart, there is a strong and admirable cast. Seefried is again the Composer, still youthfully ardent and singing marvellously if rather more self-consciously in the 'Du Venus sohn' passage. Elisabeth Schwarzkopf, a Lady Bracknellish Prima Donna in the prologue, is a vulnerable Ariadne, if a trifle mannered, less regal than Reining and less confident throughout the whole vocal compass, but savouring the text. Rita Streich's Zerbinetta is my own favourite – sung with such easeful authority – and she has a particularly distinguished and well-blended quartet of comedians in Hermann Prey (Harlequin), Fritz Ollendorff (Truffaldino), Helmut Krebs (Brighella) and Gerhard Unger (Scaramuccio). Rudolf Schock is an ardent Bacchus, though his voice becomes constricted in his final outpouring. A delight of the set is Hugues Cuenod's Dancing Master, unique in my experience in its stylish artificiality, and the small but important role of the Lackey is finely sung by Otakar Kraus.

Those who heard Sena Jurinac as the Composer at Glyndebourne and elsewhere reserve a special place in their hearts for the memory of her performance. I have to admit to disappointment with her singing of the part in Decca's 1959 set – the first stereo *Ariadne* – which is conducted with a rather heavy hand by Erich Leinsdorf. There are splendid moments and subtle touches, but the interpretation is consistently serious in mood with none of Seefried's volatility, and the excessive vibrato under pressure becomes worrying. But then almost everyone in this performance seems either to be below par or not quite first rate – too many allowances have to be made, for Walter Berry's pompous Music Master, for Leonie Rysanek's Ariadne (tremulous at times, rarely producing the lustrous tone of which one knows her capable) and most of all for Jan Peerce's disagreeable Bacchus. The Zerbinetta of Roberta Peters is an appealing characterization but, compared with others, she does not sound wholly in command. Even the Vienna Philharmonic, well as they play, sound as if they are performing by rote.

As near to an ideal performance of the opera as one is likely to find on records is the 1968 Rudolf Kempe issue. What a marvellous Strauss conductor was lost to us with his death. With the Dresden Staatskapelle playing superlatively – listen to the solo cellist, violist, oboist and first horn, to name no more – and with a recording acoustic which is resonant but still preserves the work's intimacy, this has few rivals among any Strauss opera recordings. If one still needed to refute Ernest Newman's outdated verdict that *Ariadne* was only an 'interesting failure', this is the recording with which to do it, for the sheer conviction of Kempe's interpretation sweeps aside all doubts and, more even than Böhm and Karajan, he reveals the beauty, wit, delicacy and sonority of the score (and the technicians let him do so without contrivance).

Gundula Janowitz's Ariadne approaches Reining's in its tragic depths (literally so in the Stygian A flat of '(Toten)-reich'. This performance is Straussian singing at its best. In the final duet her top register becomes slightly strained but this is a small price to pay for such a majestic impersonation. She, Kempe and the orchestral soloists make the passage from 'Ein Schönes war' into magic. On this level, too, are Teresa Zylis-Gara's Composer and Sylvia Gestzy's radiant Zerbinetta. The comedians, led again by Hermann Prey, and the nymphs' trio are well blended. When it comes to Bacchus, James King is no worse than several of his rivals and better than most. There is no disguising that he finds the high notes a strain, nor is his voice particularly beguiling in tone at full stretch in the middle register. But, as in many of his recorded performances, it is his wooden phrasing that lets him down rather than specific vocal shortcomings.

Böhm did not record the work in the studio until 1969. The bustling, vigorous accents of the orchestral opening to the prologue tell us at once how differently from Kempe and Karajan he sees the work. Throughout there is a liveliness and thrust which never – as is the case with Leinsdorf – threaten to become heavy and oppressive. Not that poetic expansiveness is lacking where required; Böhm loves the score and he has his own key to unlock its secrets. If only the Bavarian Radio Symphony Orchestra consistently had the bloom and virtuosity of Dresden! Unfortunately, too, some of his cast are not worthy of such distinguished conducting. The pervasive vibrato of Tatyana Troyanos's singing of the Composer becomes wearisome. She sings with much diligence, but there is little light and shade or variation of pace, and her deep mezzo – almost contralto – does not suit the youthful impetuosity of the part. Dietrich Fischer-Dieskau is an overbearing Music Master, but Franz Stoss is easily the best Major Domo on record. Hildegard Hillebrecht's Ariadne is a pale performance set beside Janowitz's, for one example. The voice sounds under strain, the tone rarely having that lustrous sheen so necessary in Strauss and the interpretation, not to put too fine a point on it, is matronly. Of Reri Grist's Zerbinetta, it can at least be said that it is a consistent performance, concentrating wholly and, within these guidelines, efficiently, on the superficial side of the character and giving little insight into its more interesting aspects. Much to her credit, though, is that she sings the words to the notes as Strauss set them, whereas most Zerbinettas resort to (literally) breath-taking liberties. But if the three principal women are in some measure unsatisfactory, the nymphs' trio of Arleen Augér, Unni Rugtvedt and Sigrid Schmidt is the best on record, perfectly blended. Their 'Ach, wir sind es eingewöhnet' is exemplary. Barry McDaniel is a resonant Harlequin and Gerhard Unger a stylish Dancing Master. As Bacchus, Jess

Thomas gives a very fine performance; how I wish he had been Janowitz's partner in the Kempe set.

Sir Georg Solti recorded *Ariadne* in London in November 1977. The London Philharmonic Orchestra play for him with the Straussian style and panache they have acquired in the pit at Glyndebourne. Solti's interpretation is both pungent and affectionate: it is typical of his care that he should have engaged a first-rank accompanist, Geoffrey Parsons, to play the important piano part. Orchestrally this is a highly distinguished and distinctive recording. It also has the best Zerbinetta since Streich. Edita Gruberova brings to the role insight beyond the confines of coloratura. Walter Berry is a better Music Master for Solti than he was for Leinsdorf, and it is delightful to have the veteran Erich Kunz as a Major Domo who exudes glee at the thought of the havoc his pronouncements are causing. Troyanos is again the Composer, singing with more feeling than she did eight years earlier but still not for me an ideal exponent. René Kollo is a young and ardent but not really very compelling Bacchus and Leontyne Price's Ariadne is a disappointment to her admirers. Her interpretation remains earthbound and, though there are a few exciting and moving passages, there are far more where squally and wobbly singing obscure the marriage of text and music.

Of recordings made before 1939, the fullest is a 1935 Stuttgart broadcast performance (Acanta DE 21 806) which omits the prologue. Its exceptional interest lies in its being conducted by one of the great Strauss specialists, Clemens Krauss. The spontaneous-sounding tempi, accurate playing and noble phrasing easily persuade the present-day listener into a realization of why Strauss himself so much admired Krauss's performances of his music. From the evidence of some of her records it is sometimes less easy to understand why the composer held Krauss's wife, the soprano Viorica Ursuleac, in such esteem – 'Everything I ever wrote for this type of voice seems to be made to measure for her,' he wrote. But no such qualms arise where her Ariadne is concerned. Although her voice is occasionally hard-pressed in the upper reaches, it has that mixture of warmth, regality and sensuousness which are indispensable for really great Strauss singing (a mixture in which, for instance, I find Schwarzkopf lacking, much as I admire her). Moreover, she is matched here with easily the finest Bacchus on disc, Helge Rosvaenge, who has a ringing tone which never loses quality under pressure and who sings with rare intelligence and subtlety. As for beauty of tone, listen to his 'Weh! Bist du auch solch' eine Zauberin?' where only Lorenz approaches him. Erna Berger's renowned Zerbinetta I find shallow and, on this occasion, not too well sung. The Harlequin, Karl Hammes, is the best on disc and as Naiad there is Miliza Korjus to remind us of what a good singer Hollywood robbed opera. But there is no doubt that this set derives all its authority from Krauss.

Among recorded extracts, two involving the soprano Maria Cebotari are well worth possessing. The creator of Aminta in *Die schweigsame Frau* perhaps lacks some of the tonal richness required for Ariadne, but she gives a lovely account of 'Es gibt ein Reich' with the Vienna Philharmonic under Karajan (DB 6914; SH 286). This was recorded in November 1948, seven months before she died at the early age of thirty-nine. Thirteen months earlier, on 13–15 October, 1947, she recorded the final duet with the Royal Philharmonic Orchestra conducted by Beecham, having performed it on 12 October at Drury Lane at one of the concerts of the Strauss Festival. Her singing of the passage 'Gibt es kein Hinüber' is wonderful. Unfortunately Karl Friedrich is another addition to the army of also-rans as Bacchus and was probably the reason why Beecham refused to release these records. (He may also have felt that the RPO were not at their best in the overture and that the English trio of nymphs were disconcertingly amateur-operatic.) Nevertheless in Beecham's centenary year (1979) RCA issued these by then historic records on RL 42821 (Legacy series) and they were right to do so for the sake of Beecham's lovingly stylish conducting and Cebotari's singing.

Lotte Lehmann created the role of the Composer in Vienna in 1916 (a famous photograph shows how splendidly convincing she looked). She did not record any of the part, but after she had graduated to Ariadne she recorded 'Es gibt ein Reich' in 1928 (Parlo. R 20147; 1C 147 29116–7). She makes no attempt to go down to the low A flat on '(Toten)-reich', and her performance is mainly notable for its tender exposition of Ariadne's feelings. Christa Ludwig's remarkable range, combined with her warmth and musicianship, makes it regrettable that all she has recorded is Ariadne's 'Ein Schönes war' followed by 'Es gibt ein Reich' (Eurodisc 27 991 XCR and World Records SCM 84). Another fine performance of the same section is that by Hilde Zadek, with the Vienna Symphony Orchestra under Rudolf Moralt (Philips ABR 4004). She sang Ariadne when Beecham revived the 1912 version at Edinburgh in 1950. Della Casa's separate 'Es gibt ein Reich' (Decca 411 660–1) is more indicative of her gifts than her complete 'live' records of the role. Though low-lying passages cause her problems, she soars gloriously near the close. But probably the most treasurable 'Es gibt ein Reich' is that by Maria Jeritza, the creator of Ariadne in both versions (Stuttgart 1912 and Vienna 1916). This first appeared on Od. 790001–2, reissued on RLS 743. The accuracy, diction and sheer artistry of this performance put it in a class of its own. Another impressive performance, notable above all for its sustained intensity as the climax is reached, is that made by Frida Leider in 1925 (Poly. 72976; LV 172).

Several other interesting recordings, not all of which he had been able to hear, were listed by Alan Jefferson in his *Ariadne auf Naxos* survey ('Opera on the Gramophone': 20) in the September 1968 issue of *Opera* (pp 703–13). Among them are Ariadne's Aria and Lament sung in about 1913 by Elisabeth van Endert on German HMV ('Ein Schönes war' and 'Den Namen nicht' on a ten-inch, 2–43416/7 or 923414/5 and 'Es gibt ein Reich' on twelve-inch, 043223–4 or 0943041–2). Annelies Kupper (Polydor DGG 30119), also recorded 'Es gibt ein Reich'.

The other aria which has been popular with recording companies is Zerbinetta's display piece. Alas that Margarethe Siems who amazingly, as it still seems, was both the first Zerbinetta and the first Marschallin, did not record the original version. But it was recorded in full (Discophilia KG-B-1B) by Hermine Bosetti, the Berlin Opera soprano who was Hofmannsthal's first suggestion for the role when he and Strauss were working on the opera in 1911. She first sang it in Berlin in 1913, when Leo Blech conducted, and it must have been a dazzling performance. Even with the limitations of acoustic recording it is clear that the fearsome first version of the aria held no terrors for her. She is accurate (a few shrill notes may I think be debited to the primitive recording rather than to the singer), and there is a perceptible warmth which clears her of any charge that her Zerbinetta was the 'singing automaton' so disliked by Hofmannsthal.

Hedwig Francillo-Kaufmann, who alternated as Zerbinetta with Hermine Bosetti in the first (1913) London performances, recorded some of it in London that year (Beka-Meister M113; CO 356). She begins at 'Noch glaub' ich dem einen ganz mich gehörend'. Mr Jefferson described it as 'perfectly terrible . . . a hacked-about fragment . . . embellished with frightful squawks and gargling'. I think that is rather harsh; she conveys a good deal of the brilliance of the music when it was newly minted. A complete recording of the 1912 version was made by Bosetti (Od. 76942–3; Discophilia KG-B-1). Elizabeth Harwood has broadcast the 1912 version; tapes exist of her performance. Of recordings of the 1916 version, there is a cut, free-ranging and exciting performance by Maria Ivogün (DB 44051 and VB 67; Electrola 0 83395). Lea Piltti's version with the Berlin State Opera Orchestra under Fritz Zaun cuts the final cadenza (DB 7606). A fetching, accurate performance was recorded in 1933 by Adele Kern (Poly. 95490; LV 57). What an enchanting Zerbinetta she must have made on stage – the merriment in her voice is infectious. Mr Jefferson also lists rare acoustic recordings of the 1912 version by Adelaide Andrejewa von Skilondz, Margarete Heyne-Franke and Maria Gerhart. There is also Ilse Hollweg's mixture of both versions recorded on Decca LX 3054. So the way is open for some brave lady to record both versions in the interests of musicology if nothing else.

As a footnote, it is worth mentioning that Polyna Stoska, a soprano briefly active at the Met in the late 1940s, gave a rousing account of The Composer's part from 'Sein wir wieder gut' (Am. Col. 72514D).

ARABELLA

This was the last collaboration between Strauss and Hofmannsthal. The libretto was completed in 1928 but Strauss wanted Act 1 to be redone and its revision was finished in July 1929. Strauss was thrilled by it but still wanted an extra aria for Arabella at the end of the act. Eight days later he received the text of 'Mein Elemer' and three days after that Hofmannsthal died. Strauss composed the music between July 1929 and October 1932. The first performance was in Dresden on 1 July 1933. Krauss conducted, Ursuleac sang Arabella, Alfred Jerger was Mandryka and the Zdenka was Margit Bokor. In the Vienna première on 21 October, Lehmann sang the title role. Like *Ariadne*, the opera was not at first a success (it did not reach New York, for instance, until 1955) and has only achieved real popularity since about 1965. Inevitably it was regarded as a second, but inferior, *Rosenkavalier*.

To compare it with the earlier work is a superficial procedure. There are resemblances, but they are immaterial. Both are set in Vienna, *Arabella* a century later (1860); both have waltzes in the score, but whereas in *Der Rosenkavalier* the waltzes are almost principals in the plot, in *Arabella* they are merely what one would hear at a ball and are background music. The importance of *Arabella*, apart from its intrinsic charm, is that it is a further stage in Strauss's development of the melodic-recitative conversational style, punctuated by lyrical arias, which reached its apogee in *Capriccio* ten years later. Harmonically it is more complex than *Rosenkavalier*, orchestrally it is much more restrained and simple. Just as the *Rosenkavalier*'s Vienna of 1760 was evoked in the musical idiom of 1910, so the Vienna of 1860 was realized in the harmonies of 1930 Vienna. The staircase music which opens Act 3 was subconsciously – or perhaps consciously – remembered by the European émigré composers who invaded Hollywood in 1933. It is the music of a contemporary of Gershwin, and the irony is compounded when one recalls that the words of a famous Gershwin song, 'Some day he'll come along, the man I love', are an epitome of the plot of *Arabella*: 'Der Richtige, wenn's einen gibt für mich, der wird auf einmal dastehn.' 'The right man, if there is one for me, will appear all of a sudden.'

EMI's Munich-based *Arabella*, issued in 1981, is the first digital recording of a Strauss opera. He is well served by the clarity of this process; it is doubtful if so much of the score's subtle and often beautiful detail has been heard before, lovingly presented to us in the playing of the Bavarian State Opera Orchestra and by Wolfgang Sawallisch, whose interpretation is full of passion and humour. He brings out the romantic ardour at the core of the work, but does not dawdle in the livelier episodes. Moreover, he gives us the work almost complete (some of Matteo's music is cut). Julia Varady sings Arabella, not without the occasional bit of insecure intonation, but always with the requisite richness and variety of tone. Hers is a strong Arabella – rightly so – but her adoration for Mandryka, her impulsive, naive lover from the Croatian hinterland, is beautifully projected and makes her anguished bewilderment in Act 3 all the more convincing.

Varady's husband, Dietrich Fischer-Dieskau, sings Mandryka, which for many years has been one of his favourite and finest roles. Idle to pretend that the voice does not show a few signs of wear under pressure, and there are also signs of the old tendency to bark a phrase, breaking up the melodic line, but no other Mandryka of our time is such a fully realized characterization, big in vocal as well as physical stature. Other parts are well sung, notably Walter Berry's Count Waldner (Arabella's father) and Adolf Dallapozza's Matteo, Arabella's tenor suitor, others less remarkably. Helen Donath is an outstandingly good Zdenka. Although not ideal in every respect, this *Arabella* leads the field.

The only other studio recording is the 1957 Decca set conducted by Georg Solti, one of the first Strauss operas to be made in stereo. It has Lisa Della Casa as Arabella, the Strauss role which above all others she made her own and which she sang best. Her Ariadne and her Countess in *Capriccio* suffer slightly from lack of warmth, but, more than any of her recorded rivals, she presents a believable Arabella – young, wilful and haughty, but loving and lovable. When she sings 'Aber der Richtige' we can imagine her eyes lighting up, so touchingly radiant is the vocal characterization. Unfortunately the Solti of 1957 seemed to have little patience with the underlying sentiment of the score, or he was terrified of making it too sugary, for he scarcely gives his singers time to float their phrases. The second-act love duet between Arabella and Mandryka becomes almost perfunctory, her 'Du wirst mein Gebieter sein', one of the most moving moments in the work, going for comparatively little. George London is a good Mandryka, with the mixture of naiveté and old-world courtesy which seems so out of place at the Vienna cabbies' ball. The rest of the cast is strong, too – Hilde Gueden a charming Zdenka, Anton Dermota excellent as Matteo – and the Vienna State Opera Orchestra do all that Solti asks of them. I would be surprised, though, if this conductor did not present a more expansive and relaxed view of the work, without sacrificing its sparkle, if he were to record it again. After reading John Culshaw's account in his autobiography* of what went on when this recording was made, it is surprising that it is as good as it is.

A point in favour of the Sawallisch and Solti sets is that they are of the work's original version. The other two complete sets, both live performances, are of the 1939 Munich version which runs together Acts 2 and 3 and cuts some of the music given to the coloratura-soprano part of the cabbies' mascot, the Fiakermilli, a poor man's Zerbinetta. The later of these sets is a recording of a 1963 Munich Festival performance. Della Casa is again Arabella and although Joseph Keilberth's conducting is not consistently inspired he does at least give the music a chance to breathe so that we can relish the soprano's cantilena and her entirely winning conception of the part. Dietrich Fischer-Dieskau is a strong and expressive Mandryka as a suitor, but there is a displeasing trace of caricature in the latter part of Act 2. Anneliese Rothenberger is a sweet Zdenka and Karl Christian Kohn a believable Count Waldner – this comic part may seem foolproof but, like that of Ochs, it gains most from understatement. Although the recording has the imperfections inseparable from public performance, there is the compensation which comes with the sense of immediacy, and Della Casa is wonderful.

If only Karl Böhm had conducted Della Casa on record; what might have

---

* Secker and Warburg London 1981

been achieved is measurable from the Salzburg Festival performance of 12
August 1947 (issued complete on Melodram S 101), where she sings Zdenka
with high-spirited urgency. For the connoisseur this is an indispensable set.
It has Maria Reining as Arabella, singing gloriously. Even Della Casa did
not later match the thrill of her high register at 'Die Sonne blitzt' and it is
clear throughout how much the Zdenka learned from the Arabella at this
festival. Reining's voice was perhaps too mature for the role by then, but
she contrives to sound like a young girl during the Act 2 duet, where her
Mandryka is Hans Hotter, unsurpassed for the nobility of his interpretation
not only in this passage but later in the act where, half-drunk, hurt and
angry, he retains dignity whereas Fischer-Dieskau becomes raucously petu-
lant. There are some vivid character-sketches of the lesser roles. A veteran
of Krauss's famous pre-1939 Strauss company, the bass Georg Hann, is in
ripest voice as Waldner, while Horst Taubmann's Matteo lends credibility
and even some heroic ardour to that thankless tenor role. And perhaps only
Salzburg could have lined up Julius Patzak, Josef Witt and Alfred Poell as
Arabella's three previous suitors. Böhm's pacing of the opera proves that
Solti's fears, if fears they were, were unfounded – he draws out the orchestral
postlude after the love duet to its fullest, but so beautiful is the Vienna
Philharmonic's playing and so aristocratic his phrasing that there is no danger
of the music cloying. After Reining's lovely final aria in Act 3 (although she
shows signs of tiring at this point), the horns have a lapse from grace but
nothing to spoil one's delight in this classic performance.

A generous record of highlights was first issued by Columbia in 1955 (RLS
751). It contains Arabella's first-act entry and duet with Zdenka; part of the
Waldner-Mandryka scene in Act 1 from 'Welko, das Bild!'; Arabella's 'Mein
Elemer' to the end of Act 1; the second-act love duet starting at 'Sie woll'n
mich heiraten'; Arabella's farewells to her three suitors in the ballroom in
Act 2 and the subsequent Matteo-Zdenka exchanges, overheard by Mandryka; and the Act 3 finale from 'Das war sehr gut'. Schwarzkopf sings
Arabella, not without mannerisms but with a lustrous tone. She is too sophisticated – this Arabella, one feels, would have packed her bags and gone back
to Vienna after a week in Mandryka's Croatian estate. Josef Metternich is
an appealing Mandryka, with smooth tone and broad legato, Nicolai Gedda,
Walter Berry and Murray Dickie are Matteo, Lamoral and Elemer, and
there is stunning playing by the Philharmonia Orchestra conducted by Lovro
von Matačić. Perhaps we tend to underestimate Matačić's work as a Straussian until we remember he was the conductor who provided Ljuba Welitsch's
incomparable 1944 singing of Salome's final aria with an orchestral accompaniment of equally sensational splendour. Della Casa recorded 'Aber der
Richtige' (with Gueden) and the closing duet (with Alfred Poell) for Decca
(LW 5029) a while before her first complete recording. Her voice is pleasingly
fresh, her interpretation less mannered than Schwarzkopf's.

All that remains of the original cast's interpretation is brief extracts
recorded by Ursuleac, Bokor and Jerger, with Krauss conducting (Decca-

Poly. DE 7024–5). They comprised 'Aber der Richtige', the Act 2 duet from 'So wie Sie sind' and the final scene of Act 3 from 'Das war sehr gut'. It is difficult to form a reliable estimate of Ursuleac's performance from these discs, but she sounds preferable to Lotte Lehmann, the first Vienna exponent of the part, whose 'Aber der Richtige' and 'Mein Elemer' (Parlo. PO 171; 1C 147 29116–7) are warmly enunciated but support the view she expressed in her book *Singing with Richard Strauss** that 'Arabella has never been very dear to my heart'. She nowhere approaches the excited rapture which Margarete Teschemacher (the creator of the title role in *Daphne*) and Christel Goltz (Zdenka) bring to the sisters' first-act duet, one of three extracts recorded in 1943 with the Dresden Staatskapelle conducted by Böhm (Acanta DE 23 280/81, with extracts from five other Strauss operas). Teschemacher is superb, too, in the second-act duet and Act 3 finale with the Mandryka of Mathieu Ahlersmeyer, an ardent, black-voiced baritone whose interpretation resembles Hotter's. The Act 3 excerpt sounds to have been recorded in a different acoustic from the first two and is of less good quality, but the intensity of Böhm's approach is undimmed.

Two pre-1939 Dresden Opera principals, Marta Fuchs and Paul Schöffler, recorded the Act 2 duet beginning at 'Und du wirst', and Fuchs and Elsa Wieber the Arabella-Zdenka duet beginning at 'Aber der Richtige' (Telef. E 1477; Acanta KB 22179). These are mellow performances, Fuchs warmly appealing, Schöffler somewhat retiring, and their voices blend well. The Berlin Philharmonic is conducted by Wilhelm Franz Reuss. A Berlin Arabella, the adorable Tiana Lemnitz, gives by far the most entrancing and most thrilling recorded interpretation of the role and one dearly wishes it was preserved in full. Her 'Ich möcht meinem Freuden Mann' from Act 1 is a subtle penetration into the contradictions of Arabella's character. With Gerhard Hüsch as a Mandryka of the Lieder-platform, she sings the Act 2 duet from 'So wie Sie sind'. These extracts were recorded in 1940 (DB 5606; SHB 47). In 1942, again with Hüsch, she recorded the final scene beginning at 'Das war sehr gut' (Acanta MA 22110). The Straussophile who can listen to this glorious singing with dry eyes does not deserve the name. Perhaps some of the soft high notes are tentative, but Lemnitz at forty-five still sounds the most girlish of Arabellas. Incidentally, Strauss enables us to date the action of the opera a little more precisely than just 1860. It must have happened after 15 May 1861, which was the date of the first Vienna performance of Wagner's *Lohengrin* – for, as the orchestra tells us in Act 1, that is the opera Arabella has been to hear that evening. A typical Strauss touch!

* Hamish Hamilton, London, 1964.

ARIADNE AUF NAXOS

C Composer; *Z* Zerbinetta; *A* Ariadne; *B* Bacchus; *MM* Music Master; *N* Naiad; *D* Dryad; *E* Echo

1935 (broadcast performance – prologue omitted) Berger *Z*; Ursuleac *A*; Rosvaenge *B*; Korjus   *N*; Rünger *D*; Holndonner *E* / Stuttgart Radio Orch. / Krauss Acanta Ⓜ DE 21806

1944 (live performance – Vienna State
Opera House) Seefried *C*; Noni
Z; Reining *A*; Lorenz *B*; Schöffler
MM; Loose *N*; Frutschnigg *D*;
Rutgers *E* / Vienna State Opera
Orch. / Böhm
Acanta Ⓜ DE 23309–10

1954 Seefried *C*; Streich *Z*;
Schwarzkopf *A*; Schock *B*; Dönch
MM; Otto *N*; Hoffman *D*;
Felbermayer *E* / Philharmonia /
Karajan
EMI Ⓜ RLS 760
Angel Ⓜ 3532CL

1959 Jurinac *C*; Peters *Z*; Rysanek *A*;
Peerce *B*; Berry *MM*; Coertse *N*;
Rössl-Majdan *D*; Maikl *E* /
Vienna PO / Leinsdorf
Decca 2BB112–4
London OSA 13100

1968 Zylis-Gara *C*; Geszty *Z*; Janowitz
A; King *B*; Adam *MM*; Wustman
N; Burmeister *D*; Stolte *E* /
Dresden State Orch. / Kempe

EMI SLS 936
Angel SCL 3733

1969 Troyanos *C*; Grist *Z*; Hillebrecht
A; Thomas *B*; Fischer-Dieskau
MM; Augér *N*; Rugtvedt *D*;
Schmidt *E* / Bavarian Radio SO
/ Böhm
DG 2721 189

1977 Troyanos *C*; Gruberova *Z*; L.
Price *A*; Kollo *B*; Berry *MM*;
Cook *N*; Hartle *D*; Burrowes *E* /
London PO / Solti
Decca D103D3 ④ K103K32
London OSAD 13131

1947 (excerpts)
Field-Hyde *Z* and *N*; Cebotari *A*;
Friedrich *B*; Garside *D*; Furmedge
E / RPO / Beecham
RCA (UK) Ⓜ RL 42821

1959 (excerpts)
Della Casa *C* and *A*; Schock *B*;
Otto *N*; Puttar *D*; Kirschstein *E* /
Berlin PO / Erede
EMI 1C 063 00824

ARABELLA

A Arabella; *M* Mandryka; *Mat* Matteo; *Z* Zdenka; *L* Lamoral; *D* Dominik; *E*
Elemer; *W* Waldner

1947 (live performance – Salzburg
Festival)
Reining *A*; Hotter *M*; Taubmann
Mat; Della Casa *Z*; Poell *L*; Witt
D; Patzak *E*; Hann *W* / Vienna
State Opera Chorus, Vienna PO
/ Böhm
Melodram Ⓜ MEL-S101

1957 Della Casa *A*; London *M*;
Dermota *Mat*; Gueden *Z*;
Pröglhöf *L*; Wächter *D*; Kmentt
E; Edelmann *W* / Vienna State
Opera Chorus, Vienna PO / Solti
Decca GOS 571–3
London SRS 63522

1963 (live performances – National
Theatre, Munich)
Della Casa *A*; Fischer-Dieskau *M*;
Paskuda *Mat*; Rothenberger *Z*;

Günter *L*; Hoppe *D*; Uhl *E*; Kohn
W / Bavarian State Opera Chorus
and Orch. / Keilberth
DG 2721 163

1981 Varady *A*; Fischer-Dieskau *M*;
Dallapozza *Mat*; Donath *Z*; Becht
L; Kuper *D*; Winkler *E*; Berry *W*
/ Bavarian State Opera Chorus
and Orch. / Sawallisch
EMI SLS 5220
Angel SCX 3917

1954 (excerpts)
Schwarzkopf *A*; Metternich *M*;
Gedda *Mat*; Felbermayer *Z*; Berry
L; Pröglhöf *D*; Dickie *E*; Schlott
W / Philharmonia / Matačić
EMI Ⓜ RLS 751
Angel Ⓜ 35194

L'Heure espagnole
and L'Enfant et les sortilèges

FELIX APRAHAMIAN

Whatever Ravel chose to compose, he composed exceptionally well and with finished artistry. Each musical medium he essayed he endowed with a prime example. Full-length ballet, piano sonatina, string quartet, song cycle with orchestra or chamber ensemble, piano trio, virtuoso violin piece, virtuoso piano piece, orchestral show-piece – the list could be extended: in every instance, naming Ravel's contribution is to name a masterpiece of twentieth-century music. And on the occasions when he returned to a form – only two instantly spring to mind – he provided totally contrasted examples, each a masterpiece. Ravel's two piano concertos (of which one is for left-hand alone) share this distinction with his two one-act operas, each of which shows a different but equally typical aspect of this most fastidious of composers.

L'Heure espagnole reflects both his paternal and maternal background in its subject and setting. From his inventive engineer father, Ravel must have inherited his love of mechanical toys and clockwork, like the musical humming-bird still to be seen in his house at Monfort-l'Amaury; while the Spanish setting, reflecting Ravel's consistent involvement with Spanish musical idioms, particularly around the time that the opera was written (1907), is a colourful reminder that his mother was a Basque, and that he himself was a native of Ciboure, not far from the Spanish border. It was a neighbourhood to which he often returned, on holiday or to work, during his adult life.

Similarly, the later *L'Enfant et les sortilèges* (1925) crystallizes in music Ravel's intense love for and real understanding of children. He was one of those who much preferred their uncomplicated company to that of sophisticated adults. His own dandy-like sophistication was but an aspect of the childlike simplicity he never lost.

Reverting to *L'Heure espagnole*, one can readily understand Ravel's delight in setting Franc-Nohain's play, which unfolds in a watchmaker's shop in eighteenth-century Toledo: as a libretto, it is, in the words of Ernest Newman, 'one of the most perfect things of its type ever written'. It was Jean Le Grand, the son of Franc-Nohain (a pseudonym for Maurice Le Grand), himself better-known as Jaboune, author of the texts of some children's songs by Poulenc, who, on a visit to London in the forties, told me of

Ravel's piano play-through of *L'Heure espagnole* to his father. Franc-Nohain had no ear for music: his sole comment after hearing it was, glancing at his watch, a bald statement of the time it had taken. He must be numbered among the Maeterlincks, Yeatses and Housmans, among those who were deaf to the perfect translation of their words into the language of music. For this is what Ravel achieved: nothing less.

Ravel's 'Spanish Time', 'An Hour of Spain', or, as Newman mischievously suggested, 'The Immoral Hour', requires a cast of five: the watchmaker Torquemada, his amorous wife, Concepción, her two would-be lovers – the one a young poet, Gonzalve, the other an elderly banker, Don Inigo Gomez – and a muscular muleteer, Ramiro. To a symphony of ticking and chiming clocks with automata, Torquemada sits at his work. Ramiro brings in his watch for repair. While Torquemada is inspecting it, Concepción enters to remind her husband that he should be out attending to the municipal clocks. The seemingly scatter-brained watchmaker hurries out, asking Ramiro to await his return. Concepción has not counted on the presence of a tiresome witness on the one day of the week when she can be sure of her husband's absence for an hour. For his part, the muleteer deplores the fact that he is quite inexperienced in polite conversation with ladies.

Concepción seizes on a plan which will keep him out of the way for a while. Pointing to one of two large grandfather clocks standing against the wall, she asks whether moving it upstairs would need one or two men. Delighted at having something to do, Ramiro hoists the clock on his shoulders and carries it upstairs to her bedroom single-handed, just as Gonzalve makes his entry. Time does not exist for the poet, who greets Concepción's passionate impatience with a series of lyrical effusions. By the time Ramiro has returned, she has decided how to enjoy Gonzalve's company undisturbed. She has changed her mind as to which of the two clocks she prefers in her room. While Ramiro goes to fetch the first clock down again, Concepción secretes her poet-lover in the second clock, which, in due course, is transported upstairs on the back of the willing and unsuspecting muleteer. As the comedy proceeds, the two clocks go up and down in turn, the ineffectual poet being replaced by the elderly and equally ineffectual Don Inigo Gomez, who, like Gonzalve, has also taken advantage of Torquemada's absence to pay court to Concepción. While Ramiro is fetching down the second offending timepiece, Concepción's frustration reaches its climax and, in her one extended *scena,* 'Oh! la pitoyable aventure!', her hot Spanish blood boils at the deficiency of her two lovers. When Ramiro, on his return with the clock containing Don Inigo, naively offers to go on with the furniture moving, Concepción, smitten with admiration for his stamina, orders him upstairs once more – this time, clockless.

The two inmates of the clocks have hardly realized each other's presence, when Torquemada returns and promptly sells them the clocks in which they appear to be so interested. Ramiro and Concepción come downstairs. The portly Don Inigo is extracted from his narrow prison and, together, all five point a doubtful moral in a brilliant quintet, the only ensemble in the piece.

Now, Newman, in his detailed account of the opera*, considers it 'difficult for anyone who has not seen a theatrical performance of it to realize just how much of the fun depends on the neat stage-carpentry of the piece'. The real fun, nevertheless, depends more on the absolutely clear enunciation of every syllable of the text with its sometimes untranslatable puns and *double-entendres*. Complete subservience to a chosen text and its clear projection had been established by Debussy's *Pelléas et Mélisande*. The lessons of that revolutionary masterpiece were not lost on Ravel who, within a year of its première (1902), had shown the same exquisite sensibility in his *Shéhérazade* song cycle (1903) and further refined this word-setting aspect of his art in the *Histoires naturelles* (1906). To achieve similar success in *L'Heure espagnole,* the ever-precise Ravel took the precaution of specifying the *genres* of the singers required. Concepción (*Soprano*) and Gonzalve (*Tenor*) are plain sailing; so is Don Inigo Gomez (*Basse-bouffe*) but Torquemada calls for a *Trial* and Ramiro for a *Baryton-Martin*. The former implies a high, even nasal tenor. (Antoine Trial flourished in French eighteenth-century opera, but, as one of Robespierre's active agents, had to renounce the stage on his master's fall, and eventually poisoned himself.) The second implies a baritone with a higher range than usual (Jean-Blaise Martin, a junior contemporary of Trial's, an actor-singer with such a voice gave his name to the type), exemplified by the tessitura of Debussy's Pelléas. It is interesting to note that the first Pelléas, Jean Périer, was also the first Ramiro, when Ravel's *L'Heure espagnole* reached the stage of the Paris Opéra-Comique on 19 May 1911.

None of the five Western European recordings of *L'Heure espagnole* is inadmissible for lack of clear enunciation, a prerequisite in this work. Even the earliest, a seven-record Columbia set, made in the early thirties, provides a model projection of the text. The cast is led by the Concepción of Madame J. Krieger, a spirited account of the part, perky and splendidly exasperated in 'Oh! la pitoyable aventure!' Then, for a recording half a century old, the orchestral sound ('Symphony Orchestra' – conductor: Georges Truc) is vivid and colourful: Ravel's score is partly responsible, for it is as jewelled as the finest Swiss chronometers, defying mushiness in recorded reproduction. The quartet of males, alas, is nothing like as satisfactory on disc, for all of them – Louis Arnould (Gonzalve), Raoul Gilles (Torquemada), I. Aubert (Ramiro) and even Hector Dufranne (the original Golaud) – have been vocally emasculated in the recording process, as if all four voices were being filtered through the same megaphone, causing them to bleat in the high register and depriving even the redoubtable Monsieur Dufranne of a sonorous bass register in which his Don Inigo would provide a more solid contrast to the nervous and jerky Torquemada of Monsieur Gilles.

* *Opera Nights,* Putnam, 1943

Three versions of *L'Heure espagnole* appeared in 1953. The first was a Vox record, still in some ways the most authentic, for not a word is lost and the voices are sharply characterized. The jokes, verbal and orchestral (French Radio Orchestra, conductor: René Leibowitz) are all there and their impact is immediate. Janine Linda's youthful Concepción is full of seductive guile, and her *portamenti* are delicious but she is sorrowful rather than furious in the declamation of her big *scena*. André Dran paints an effete Gonzalve with distinction, while Lucien Mans well conveys the seniority of Don Inigo. Jean Hoffman hardly suggests *force musculaire* by his well-mannered singing, nor does Jean Mollien's voice suggest that he is any older than the muleteer. Nevertheless, this is a disc with which one would not part.

Within a few months, the other two versions appeared simultaneously, one from Decca the other from Columbia. For its French repertory, Decca relied at the time largely on Ernest Ansermet and his Suisse Romande Orchestra: the orchestral playing in *L'Heure espagnole* maintains their usual standard. Ansermet brings his Gallic wit and sparkle – this is not eliminated in Protestant French Switzerland – to a scintillating score unfolded with elegance. And that is how Suzanne Danco sings the part of Concepción. Her vocal line is faultless as usual, though it remains prim rather than suggestive of a smouldering passion kept in check. The four men are splendidly portrayed by an accomplished quartet – Paul Derenne (Gonzalve), Michel Hamel (Torquemada), Heinz Rehfuss (Ramiro) and André Vessières (Don Inigo). Vessières has a noble sonority and is ideally cast here as the most affluent of the characters. Beautifully sung, beautifully played, this is the most refined and finely balanced of the three 1953 versions.

Those who came under the spell of Denise Duval's stage appearances in the three Poulenc operas in which she starred will, understandably, have a weakness for the third (Columbia) version, even if her Concepción is neither vocally nor texturally flawless. It is, on the other hand, perhaps truer to the amorous character of the lady than the others. Not for nothing was Madame Duval an accomplished performer at the Folies Bergères before her translation to the stage of the Opéra-Comique. Her Concepción is at the opposite pole to Danco's, as impetuous and highly charged as the other is calculating. And in appropriate contrast, René Hérent's Torquemada offers her a husband of credible age, forgetfulness and a touch of decrepitude. Jean Giraudeau, accomplished as ever in driving Concepción impatiently distracted by his poetic musings, Jean Vieuille as an equally credible muleteer, well endowed by nature with physical stamina, and Charles Clavensy, as a suave, elderly Don Inigo, complete a cast well in the foreground throughout the recording. But the Paris Opéra-Comique Orchestra under André Cluytens, while offering close support, does not enjoy so clear a recorded sound: Ravel's crisp, bright orchestral colours seem to acquire opacity in ensemble, though individual instrumental strands fare better.

The most recent version of *L'Heure espagnole*, dating from 1965 was reissued in 1981 in double harness with *L'Enfant et les sortilèges* (DG: Privilege 2726 076). A Paris recording, with the Paris Opéra Orchestra conducted by Lorin Maazel, who, as a protégé of the one and only Pierre Monteux, has as close a kinship to French music of this kind as any other living conductor; it has several points to commend it. The orchestral timbres and ensemble are beyond reproach, though a generally brighter *and* louder sound would have been welcome, for in sheer volume the actual recording is at a lower level than any of the other versions. When the controls are turned up, one can better enjoy the characterizations of a splendid cast, led by the spirited singing of Jane Berbié as Concepción, vocally as secure and expressive as any. An interesting feature is the exchange of roles by Jean Giraudeau: Gonzalve in the Columbia version, he reappears here as Torquemada – a *Trial* for a *Ténor* – and is equally at home in the still higher tessitura. The new poet is Michel Sénéchal, perhaps more lively a Gonzalve than some of the others, suggesting that he had given Concepción more satisfaction on earlier occasions.

At this point, it is worth considering in parenthesis how consistently well the two tenor parts are supplied from a small, select group of French singers whose names recurred in performances of earlier French music in the two decades following the liberation of Paris. Without Derenne, Hamel, Giraudeau, Sénéchal, and others (like the ever-regretted Raymond Amade – whose name once found its way into an Opéra-Comique performance of *L'Heure espagnole* when, instead of 'Impressions d'Hamadryade . . .', the acute-eared might have heard 'Impressions d'Raymond Amade. . . .'), the much missed Roger Désormière would have had difficulty in casting the Rameau operas he revived, in France and for the BBC. The precision and refinement they brought to the vocal lines of Rameau, Grétry and their like, served them equally well in the no less demanding *boutique* of Ravel's eighteenth-century Toledo watchmaker. Among the basses, Vessières belonged to that same happy family. Alas, that Amade's charming high tenor voice was never perpetuated in a recording of *L'Heure espagnole* or, for that matter, a performance conducted by Désormière. They flourished just too soon for the record boom of the sixties.

Returning to the Maazel version, it will be noticed that the two deeper voices, those of Gabriel Bacquier's virile Ramiro and José van Dam's far from decrepit Don Inigo, when heard in proximity, as in scenes vii and viii, are insufficiently contrasted in timbre to render obvious the seniority of the banker. And, even if this confusion could only exist when the opera is heard and not seen, and then only at first hearing, it is desirable whenever possible that both the lower and higher pair of male voices should comprise two contrasted timbres as well as tessituras.

To sum up, the four LP versions discussed present no easy choice. Interpretatively, all are unexceptionable, for the basic requirement that the opera should be sung clearly and comprehensibly in the original French is fully met. With its technical advantage of twelve years and stereo, this latest version should be an easier choice than it is, but not even the recorded panache, vocal and orchestral, of the concluding bars eclipses individual felicities in the older versions. No one in his musical senses would part with any of them.

With *L'Enfant et les sortilèges*, which makes more extravagant demands on personnel – vocal and instrumental – to achieve a masterpiece of musical refinement in Ravel's later manner, the choice of recorded version is less complex. Not only a sentiment of gratitude towards old loves will inspire retention of the three earlier of the four versions, even if the most recent may win on points. Let us approach it chronologically, considering first the score itself.

It began with Colette's submission of her text to Jacques Rouché, the director of the Paris Opéra, some time during the First World War. He proposed to her the names of several composers who might be able to set it, but only Ravel's aroused any enthusiasm in her: she remembered him from the *salon* of Madame de Saint-Marceaux where, regularly on Fridays ten years previously, a brilliant company – which included Debussy as well as Ravel's own one-time professors, Fauré and Messager – would gather informally. A copy of the text sent to Ravel in 1916, when he was on war service, failed to reach him. A second copy, sent in 1917, fared better, and Ravel agreed to set *L'Enfant et les sortilèges*, a subject utterly appropriate to him. In 1919, the score was still unwritten, but a letter from Ravel to his librettist showed that it was taking shape in his mind. By 1921, some of it was actually written down, but other work intervened, and only a contract which obliged Ravel to complete the work within a few months caused him to concentrate on the opera during 1924. The score was finally ready in time for the scheduled first performance at Monte Carlo, on 24 March of that year. The conductor was Victor de Sabata.

L'Enfant et les sortilèges is the tale of a naughty child. There are two linked scenes. In the first, he misbehaves out of sheer boredom. With whoops of joy he smashes the teapot and cup, tears up his books, pokes the caged squirrel with his pen, pulls the cat's tail, upsets the kettle on the fire, slashes the wall-coverings and swings on the pendulum of the grandfather clock. Gazing with satisfaction on the devastation he has wrought, he sinks exhausted into the armchair. This is where the magic starts. The furniture comes to life. The Armchair walks away to dance a sarabande with another chair. The Clock comes forward, unable to stop chiming and thoroughly indisposed. The Wedgwood Teapot and China Cup dance a foxtrot to suitable nonsense in English and what may pass for Chinese. The Child shivers with fear and loneliness, but even the Fire will have none of him, expressing her anger in a florid aria. 'Get back,' she sings, 'I warm the good, but I burn the bad.' The rebukes of Fire and Ashes are succeeded by the modal laments of the pastoral figures of the *toile de Jouilly* he has slashed. These are followed by the Princess of the fairy tales he has torn up, but she must now leave him for ever. In his desolation, the Child sings to her ('Toi le coeur de la rose'), but she disappears, and her place is taken by a little old man,

Arithmetic, surrounded by his chorus of digits. Their *crescendo* is maddening and the Child drops down in a daze. The Cat jumps to the window-ledge to sing a duet with his lady love in cat language, during which the Child finds himself transported to the now moonlit garden, the second scene of the opera. But even there the trees and small creatures – dragonflies, moths, bats and squirrels – lament his cruelty, and conspire against the Child who has ill-treated them. They turn to attack him. He is scared and cries 'Maman'. In the general confusion, a small squirrel is hurt, and the Child's first reaction is to bandage its wound. There is a sudden silence. The creatures of the garden are at a loss to understand this change of heart. Then they notice that the Child, too, is hurt and is bleeding. They are powerless to help, but they try to utter the magic word. Soon the garden echoes to the call of 'Maman'. Gently, the Child is carried to the house, where, to the soothing strains of an *a cappella* chorus in praise of the good Child sung by the departing creatures, he sinks into the arms of her whose name they all called.

Who among European composers of the time could have hoped to give more sensitive musical expression to such a scenario? In the seven years it took him to complete the score, musical art had travelled far, and so had Ravel. His own already refined mode of musical expression had been further distilled, but it had also acquired new elements. He admitted to having treated Colette's tale in the manner of an American musical comedy, confessing to a mixture of styles which included Massenet, Puccini, Monteverdi, and one that he could not have absorbed earlier – jazz. He achieved the synthesis brilliantly in a score which, for all its surface sophistication, proves moving in its fundamentally childlike simplicity.

All this was revealed in the first complete recording by a Parisian team in 1948, with Ernest Bour, then at the outset of his career, conducting the French National Radio Chorus and Orchestra, on a set of 78s. They became available on LP in France and in America and still delight. The recording is close, bringing Colette's tale and its creatures right into the nursery, rather than unfolding it in a slightly distant, more spacious opera-house acoustic and in stereo. Eleven singers share twenty-one roles. Ravel specified that those of the Fire, Princess and Nightingale should be sung by the same soprano, but, in this first recording, the Fire and Nightingale are shared by Odette Turba-Rabier, and Martha Angelici is the Princess: both are adequate rather than ideal. Ravel's only other similar stipulation is that the same tenor should sing the roles of Arithmetic and the Tree Frog, although the cast list designates the former as *Le Petit Vieillard (Trial)*. Here, Joseph Peyron doubles the Tree Frog and Black Wedgwood Teapot, while the Little Old Man is Maurice Prigent. But these permutations and combinations of the roles, Ravel's stipulations and suggestions, and the actual recording casts, can be confusing: only the last (DG) version observes Ravel's stipulated tripling and doubling of roles.

André Vessières, doubling the Armchair and Tree, is splendid, with a bass timbre almost as ripe as that of the contrabassoon which precedes his entry in his slow dance with the anonymous Easychair. Solange Michel, memorable here as the Squirrel, is less happy as the Shepherdess. Yvon le Marc'Hadour, who specialized in recitals and the troubadour repertory, found scope for his characterizations here as the Clock and Tom-Cat: the cat duet dividing the two scenes is a classic performance. Nadine Sautereau's Child has the voice of a normally well-behaved chorister rather than that of a child potentially mischievous from the start. Denise Scharley has the right warmth as Mother and Dragonfly and happily partners Peyron's Teapot as the Porcelain China Cup.

There are lovely and touching things in this first version which, despite the technical improvements of its two successors, one would never be disposed to lose.

The second (Decca) version of *L'Enfant et les sortilèges* is more spacious and covers a wider sonic range, which makes its quieter end sound more distant and less intimate than the first version. Flore Wend is a perhaps more childlike Child; Suzanne Danco, a cool Princess, but even cooler Squirrel. Adrienne Migliette is a precise and vocally brilliant winner as Fire and Nightingale. Of the rest of the cast, Hugues Cuenod is outstanding, as always, fulfilling Ravel's required tripling of the roles of Teapot, Arithmetic and Tree-Frog. Ansermet's performance is as fastidious as ever, if less loving in effect than Bour's.

The third version (DG), conducted by Lorin Maazel, not only observes Ravel's soprano tripling and tenor doubling, but further reduces the cast to eight with no apparent loss of timbre, for the characterizations are all exceptionally accomplished. Françoise Ogéas has the right pure tone for the Child. Sylvaine Gilma brings the right purity, too, to the Princess, and also the right brilliance to Fire and Nightingale, throwing in the Owl as a bonus. With the versatile Michel Sénéchal as Teapot as well as doubling Arithmetic and Tree-Frog, Heinz Rehfuss doubling Armchair and Tree, Janine Collard, Jane Berbié, Colette Herzog, and Camille Maurane, all familiar performers, sharing the remaining roles, this is generally a most proficient version, always maintaining an ideal balance between voices and instruments and bestowing a kind of acoustic magic on the garden scene. As with both previous versions, one is left marvelling at the imaginative and moving beauty of Ravel's score, proof enough that its essential message has been communicated.

More than half a century after its creation, Ravel's *fantaisie lyrique* has, notwithstanding its obvious and unusual difficulties, established its place in the world's greatest opera houses, even if revivals of it are by no means annual. But long after its first English staging, its enchantments were familiar to lovers of Ravel's music through the earlier recordings considered above. Some of these, for one reason or another, will always be held in particular affection. To anyone coming fresh to the score, there is perhaps better reason to commend the latest recording.

André Previn represents a more recent generation of conductors, but his credentials could not be more appropriate. His recordings of French music have generally shown him to be closely sympathetic to the idiom, be it Debussy's, Ravel's or Messiaen's. Moreover, a strong case could be made for his especial affinity with Ravel's later music, the works in which the composer acknowledged his indebtedness to jazz. Not only does that form part of Previn's own musical background, but he has also shown himself to be a faultlessly idiomatic pianist – for instance as a soloist in Ravel's G major concerto. All this, together with his charismatic personality as a popularizer of music, equally persuasive with adults and adolescents, suggests that Ravel's *L'Enfant* will find in him an ideal interpreter. And this, the latest recording justifies.

It achieves a wonderful balance between voices and instruments, with Ravel's jewelled orchestration projected as clearly as his vocal lines. There have been more boyish-sounding Enfants than Susan Davenny Wyner, but his Mother (Jocelyne Taillon, also doubling three other roles (China Cup, Dragonfly and Little Owl)) and his victims are among the best: Jules Bastin (Armchair and Tree), Jane Berbié (Easychair, Bat and Squirrel), Philippe Huttenlocher (Grandfather Clock and Black Cat), Linda Finnie (Shepherd and White Cat), Linda Richardson (Shepherdess) with the compelling coloratura of Arleen Augér (Fire, Princess and Nightingale) and the ever-versatile Philip Langridge (Teapot, Arithmetic and Tree-Frog), not to forget the admirable Ambrosian Singers. Sentimental attachment to previous versions cannot reduce the absolute excellence of the latest.

For the sake of completeness, it should be added that both of the Ravel operas were recorded in Moscow in the sixties under Gennadi Rozhdestvensky, with Russian singers singing in Russian, which invalidates them from serious consideration, for, apart from Debussy's *Pelléas et Mélisande*, there can be few operas more dependent on the very vowels and consonants as well as the sense of the words set. In any other language but French, *L'Heure espagnole* and *L'Enfant et les sortilèges* might as well be rewritten and reorchestrated.

Two excerpts clamour for attention. A record of 'Airs d'Opéras Français' by Fanny Heldy (DB 1512; LV 223) ends with 'Oh! la pitoyable adventure' and, with the help of an unnamed Gonzalve and Ramiro (now identified as Pierre Fayreau and Louis Morturier), continues to the end of the following scene. The performance is the sexiest on record and leaves no doubt that her Concepción must have been one to reckon with. The other excerpt is by Bidú Sayão (Odyssey Y33130): 'Toi, le coeur de la rose' (with piano). The expression is perhaps more mature than called for by these few bars, heart-rending in their very simplicity,but the voice is adorable, a warm *bel canto* curiously reminiscent of Maggie Teyte, a vocal product of the same teacher – Jean de Reszke.

Among the ever-to-be-regretted might-have-beens of recorded opera was a version of *L'Enfant et les sortilèges* by its first conductor. The orchestral material furnished for the première was not impeccable, but, in Ravel's own words in a letter written on 16 March 1925, to his friend, the violinist Helène

Jourdan-Morhange: 'Malgré l'état désastreux du matériel – c'est ma faute, tsk . . . tsk . . . – on est arrivé à débrouiller la partition, grâce à un orchestre supérieur et à un chef vraiment extraordinaire.' A quarter of a century later, the 'chef vraiment extraordinaire' conducted a concert performance of *L'Enfant* at the Royal Festival Hall in London. Not long after the Second World War, Victor de Sabata, who, attached to La Scala since 1930, succeeded Toscanini there, began a very fruitful association, now legendary, with the London Philharmonic Orchestra. So, as one of the British orchestras engaged to perform in the London season of the Festival of Britain in the summer of 1951, the LPO invited De Sabata to conduct a Ravel programme at one of these prestigious events in the newly opened Royal Festival Hall, for which, with official help from the French Government, they were also able to secure a Parisian cast for *L'Enfant*. It proved an unforgettable experience for all who were there, performers as well as audience, but it was neither broadcast nor recorded, and so an interpretation of *L'Enfant* that had won Ravel's seal of approval at the first performance was lost for ever. I was curious at the time to know the reaction of the French participants. But knowing De Sabata's prodigious, infallible musical memory, and having witnessed an improvised coaching session by him in my own music room, I had a clear idea of how his piano rehearsal with the French visitors would go: they were, of course, dumbfounded. Immediately after it, one of them, Solange Michel, visibly moved, came to tell me how the already legendary conductor had rehearsed them without a score at the piano, completely master of every note and every syllable. Even more curious than the fact that the creator of *L'Enfant* was never enticed into the recording studio to record it was that he never conducted anything in Paris.

L'HEURE ESPAGNOLE

C Concepción; *G* Gonzalve; *T* Torquemada; *R* Ramiro; *DI* Don Inigo

c.1932   Krieger *C*; Arnould *G*; Gilles *T*; Aubert *R*; Dufranne *DI* / Truc
Columbia (France) D15149–5S
CBS (US) set OP 14

1953   Danco *C*; Derenne *G*; Hamel *T*; Rehfuss *R*; Vessières *DI* / Suisse Romande Orch. / Ansermet
Decca ECS 786
London ⓜ CM 23249

1953   Linda *C*; Dran *G*; Mollien *T*; Hoffman *R*; Mans *DI* / French Radio SO / Leibowitz
Vox (UK) ⓜ PL 7880
(US) ⓜ OPL 150

1953   Duval *C*; Giraudeau *G*; Hérent *T*;
Vieuille *R*; Clavensy *DI* / Paris Opéra-Comique Orch. / Cluytens
EMI ⓜ 33CX1076
Angel ⓜ 35018

1965   Berbié *C*; Sénéchal *G*; Giraudeau *T*; Bacquier *R*; Van Dam *DI* / Paris National Orch. / Maazel
DG 2720 076

c.1965   (in Russian)
Sakharova *C*; Yelnikov *G*; Usmanov *T*; Budrin *R*; Dobrin *DI* / Moscow Radio SO / Rozhdestvensky
Melodiya S 0999–1000

L'ENFANT ET LES SORTILÈGES

C The Child; *M* Mother; *AC* Armchair; *EC* Easychair; *Cl* Clock; *T* Teapot; *Cup* Cup; *F* Fire; *S* Shepherd; *Sh* Shepherdess; *P* Princess; *A* Arithmetic; *TC* Tom-Cat; *SC* She-Cat; *Tr* Tree; *D* Dragonfly; *N* Nightingale; *B* Bat; *Sq* Squirrel; *Fr* Tree-Frog

1948 Sautereau *C*; Scharley *M*; *Cup*; *D*; Vessières *Ac*; *Tr*; Michel *EC*; *Sq*; Le Marc' Hadour *Cl*; *TC*; *N*; Peyron *T*; *Fr*; Turba-Rabier *F*; Angelici *P*; Prigent *A*; Legouhy *SC*; Verneuil *B* / French National Radio Chorus and Orch. / Bour
EMI (France) ⓜ FCX 30030
CBS (US) ⓜ ML 4153

1955 Wend *C*; Montmollin *M*; *Cup*; *D*; Lovano *Ac*; *Tr*; Touraine *EC*; *SC*; *B*; Mollet *Cl*; *TC*; Cuenod *T*; *A*; *Fr*; Migliette *F*; *N*; Bise *S*; Bobillier *Sh*; Danco *P*; *Sq* / Geneva Motet Choir, Suisse Romande Orch. / Ansermet
Decca SDD 168
Richmond SRS 33086

1960 Ogéas *C*; Collard *M*; *Cup*; *D*; Rehfuss *AC*; *Tr*; Berbié *EC*; *S*; *SC*; *Sq*; Maurane *Cl*; *TC*; Sénéchal *T*; *A*; *Fr*; Gilma *N*; *F*; *P*; Herzog *Sh*; *B* / Choirboys of ORTF, French National Orch. / Maazel
DG 2720 026

1963 (in Russian)
Postavnicheva *C* / Moscow Radio Chorus and SO / Rozhdestvensky
Melodiya S 0373–4

1981 Wyner *C*; Taillon *M*; *Cup*; Bastin *AC*; *Tr*; Berbié *EC*; *B*; *Sq*; Huttenlocher *Cl*; *TC*; Langridge *T*; *Fr*; Augér *F*; *P*; *N*; Finnie *S*; *SC*; Richardson *Sh* / Ambrosian Singers / LSO / Previn
HMV ASD 4167 ④ TCC-ASD 4167
Angel DS 37869

English Opera in the Twentieth Century:
The Operas of Delius, Holst, Vaughan Williams, Walton and Tippett

JOHN STEANE

An English gentleman of the nineteenth century compiling a list of 'things best left to the foreigners' would almost certainly have included grand opera. 'Grand' meant 'Italian' and though it might be reckoned that composers like Balfe and Wallace could invent as pretty a melody as the best of them, nevertheless when it came to the *sospiris* and *lagrimes* and 'the demned fal-lals', the Italians had the field to themselves. Towards the end of the century, *The Veiled Prophet* by Stanford was given the honour of a single performance at Covent Garden, and a few years later his *Much Ado about Nothing* was heard twice. Early in the twentieth, it seemed that our leading opera composer was Ethel Smyth. Beecham introduced *The Wreckers*, disturbing the peace of the royal box, in 1910; and when her fourth opera, *The Boat-swain's Mate*, enjoyed some success at the Shaftesbury Theatre in 1915 the gramophone also took notice. Nine single-sided records were issued, the singers including Rosina Buckman, Courtice Pounds and Frederick Ranalow, accompanied by 'the Symphony Orchestra'. That pioneering enterprise was followed by another in 1924 when excerpts from Vaughan Williams's *Hugh the Drover* were recorded, five double-sided records this time. But, with a very few exceptions (a passage from Eugene Goossens's *Judith*, for example), the rest was virtually silence as far as English opera on records was concerned, till after the Second World War. Then, with Benjamin Britten giving the lead, composers turned towards opera with more interest than ever before: there was something of a renaissance. The record industry supported it cautiously. The première of *Peter Grimes* in 1945 was one of the most exciting musical events of the century but fourteen years passed before a recording of the work appeared. (Britten's operas are discussed in *Opera on Record*.) Even now, in 1984, *Gloriana* remains unrecorded. All the same, British opera is known to exist, and at the time of writing the current *Gramophone* catalogue lists twenty-three works (not including Handel or Gilbert and Sullivan). Moreover, the revival of activity among present-day composers has contributed towards a renewed interest in the past. For some, the gramophone has by now done very well; much better indeed than they would have thought it realistic to hope for. And this is particularly true of the operas of Delius.

Five of them are now recorded, leaving only the first, *Irmelin* (1892), the prelude to which is of course well known as a concert piece (Beecham's recordings of 1938 and 1948 are included, respectively, in the invaluable Beecham-Delius albums issued by World Record Club, SHB 32 and SHB 54). The second opera, *The Magic Fountain* (1893), closely related in ideas to *Irmelin,* was given its première in a British broadcast in 1977. The recording of this performance on the BBC Artium label appeared three years later and found an enthusiastic welcome. Set in the early sixteenth century, the opera tells of a Spaniard's quest for the legendary fountain of eternal youth in the newfound land of Florida. The orchestral writing is both rich and delicate, the voice parts are eminently singable, and the chorus is most effectively used to create atmosphere in a way that is very much Delius's own. Norman del Mar conducts a performance sensitive to the languorous, lotus-eating mood of the opening and yet strong and full-blooded in the passionate love music of the last act. A greater test, perhaps, is set by several slow, even-paced and quite extensive passages in between, where much of the interest lies in subtly changing shades of orchestration that in less able hands might be soporific. The two principal soloists, Katherine Pring and John Mitchinson, are not ideally cast though the power of their voices and the intelligence of their reading earn gratitude. Katherine Pring's mezzo-soprano is appropriately rich and warm in tone but one sometimes wishes for greater firmness on sustained notes. Mitchinson's is not a romantic voice: the love music of Act 3 wants a more honeyed sound. Nor is he always convincing in his vocal acting: for instance, the libretto gives 'an awed whisper' as its direction at the line 'A breeze! then I am heard' in Act 1 but the performance here is relatively inexpressive. Yet it's a remarkable voice, coping extremely well with the low-lying tessitura, where many tenors would be toneless, and drawing on considerable reserves of power in the climaxes. The most impressive solo work comes with the entrance of the Indian seer, Talum Hadjo, in Act 2. This is sung by Richard Angas, a deep bass, distinctive in timbre, firm and colourful, and his monologue is the best of the opera's solos. The production includes surf noises, bird song, a realistic storm from the effects department, and of course plenty of gurgling from the fountain. Some (possibly all) of this may be dispensable, though it may help the sense of flow which the composer said was 'the main thing'. For most listeners 'the main thing' will be sheer gratitude to all concerned in bringing the long-silent score back to life.

Delius's next opera was *Koanga* (1897). If the merits of *The Magic Fountain* make it surprising that the work should have had to wait so long for a hearing, those of *Koanga* are great and obvious enough to prompt the question of why it has not become a genuinely popular opera. The colour is brighter, the melodic invention stronger, the handling of the drama more assured. To some extent this was recognized, for it achieved a production in 1904 and, thanks to Beecham, reached Covent Garden in 1935 (hard, though, to imagine the gentlemanly John Brownlee in the voodoo name part or the magnificent but inescapably Slavonic Slobodskaya as the mulatto girl Palmyra). Out of the American première in 1970 and performances at the British Camden Festival in 1972 came the two recordings of the opera, both of them having Eugene Holmes and Claudia Lindsey in the leading roles. The American version is 'live' from the Lisner Auditorium in Washington, a composite of tape recordings made during four performances. Technically, the quality is much inferior to the English recording under Sir Charles Groves, but it still has some features of interest and there are passages where as a performance it may be found preferable.

The Company is the Opera Society of Washington DC under Paul Callaway, organist at the Cathedral and responsible for many first performances in the States. His reading of *Koanga* sometimes brings out more vigour than Groves's, and there is sometimes sweeter lyricism as in the ensemble at the end of Act 1. The separate voice parts in the quintet are more clearly audible in the English recording, but the general effect (stage perspective no doubt helping) is lovelier in the American. The vigour is felt where most needed, in the relaxed passages which can simply go to sleep: for instance, the prelude to Act 3 is no more than a shade quicker than Groves takes it but has a greater feeling of concentration and cohesion. The stage performance also brings a few moments when the singers emphasize a dramatic effect such as Eugene Holmes's venomous declamation of the words 'when on my white companions Koanga's vengeance falls'. The chorus also sounds well in the Washington performance, less smooth in tone but more idiomatic than the Alldis Choir. As against this, the recorded sound is comparatively rough and opaque – though the coughing of the audience throughout all the quieter music (some of it apparently straight into the microphone) comes out loud and clear.

Turning to the excellent studio recording, one is impressed afresh by the richness of the score, and indeed by the exceptional quality of Holmes's performance in the title role. The vibrancy of his tone is often thrilling; the voice a dark bass-baritone in timbre with an exciting ring in the upper notes. Claudia Lindsey also sings well and gains notably from the better recording. Both of these main parts carry complete conviction. Among the secondary roles, Raimund Herincx makes a suitably heavy-handed plantation boss, but the wife, the Voodoo priest and the slimy Perez are less adequately cast, while the girls in the prologue and epilogue, protesting 'Oh no, oh no' with prissy English vowels, sound like little maids from the D'Oyly Carte. There is hardly time, however, to give such quibbles more than a passing thought while listening to a work which constantly delights and surprises, and to a recording which so largely does it justice.

Delius's fourth opera, *A Village Romeo and Juliet* (1901), can be heard in three recordings, the best-known and most accessible being Beecham's (made originally on 78s in 1948) and the 1973 studio recording under Meredith Davies. Beecham conducts the Royal Philharmonic Orchestra and it is their playing that provides the great pleasure of this recording. Lorely Dyer and

René Soames as the lovers are both very light of voice, suitable for perhaps three-quarters of the score, but then sounding thin in the louder and more strenuous passages. In the quieter, lyrical music Soames is sweeter-toned and more even in production than Robert Tear in the Davies recording. It is also good to hear Denis Dowling (again firmer voiced than Benjamin Luxon), Margaret Ritchie as the boy Sali, Dorothy Bond fresh and clear as young Vreli, and Gordon Clinton as the Dark Fiddler (though recording does not quite do justice to that fine singer's full-bodied tone). Diction throughout is admirably clear, though not always appropriate, as with the 'leedylike' reproach 'You're far too respectable' and the 'refeened' proclamation 'Vagabonds are we'. Beecham's tempi are generally faster than Davies's (1 minute 34 seconds, for instance, in the opening, up to the entrance of the voices, compared to 1 minute 50 seconds), and his outlines are clearer, more decisive. This is a strong performance, surviving well in the quality of recorded sound and for its period often remarkably successful, as at the end of the opera, in conveying a sense of atmosphere.

The more modern recording, of course, brings the details of orchestration into a clearer light. Contrasting with the simplicity of the story and characters, a large orchestra (6 horns, 3 trumpets, 3 trombones and so forth) is employed with rich, sophisticated scoring. Davies, though never overindulgent, is more tender and romantic than Beecham in his approach. As Vreli, Elizabeth Harwood sings with much feeling, particularly fine in the opening of the fourth scene. Tear has the power that Soames lacked in climaxes but not the right voice-character for the part. The third main role, that of the Dark Fiddler, poses a problem, for although he is a sinister figure his music is innocent enough, and the interpreter may well be in doubt as to how far he should darken his tone. In the Beecham recording, Clinton occasionally allows malice to show through ('It pleases me to see the havoc they have wrought'), but John Shirley-Quirk remains thoroughly amiable, and possibly achieves a more sinister effect thereby. No such mildness marks the two brief appearances of Felicity Palmer: in the Fair Scene the First Woman stands out among the crowd, and, as the Slim Girl in the final scene, her jibing tone is earthy enough to recall momentarily a vocal image of old Edith Coates, the high mistress of such character portraiture.

The remaining version of the opera comes 'live' from the Bradford Alhambra Theatre in 1962. The performance is given by the Sadler's Wells Company, and, as in the commercial recording, Meredith Davies is the conductor. As with the other Delius operas recorded on the IGS label, the sound is restricted in spaciousness and clarity; and here too the audience seems to pick on all the quietest, loveliest passages for their coughing spasms. But the stage performance also brings the opera to a more urgent kind of dramatic life than it had in the studios. And the other great thing about this recording is that its lovers are truly suited to their roles. Elsie Morison gives a heartfelt performance as Vreli, and John Wakefield has just the kind of simple lyrical romantic quality in his voice that Robert Tear lacks. Not all of the singing can be praised: Neil Easton's Dark Fiddler has some character but not really enough voice, and Donald McIntyre is an excessively coarse-sounding Manz. Chorus work is good; the Sadlers Wells Orchestra is not the Royal Philharmonic, but plays with conviction. The total impression left by this recording may well be on balance the most vivid of the three versions.

In his next opera, *Margot la Rouge* (1902), Delius left the country for the town and the innocence of his young lovers for a pair who, as we say, have 'been around'. It's a strange piece, something of a cross between *Louise* and *La Navarraise*, and, although this is no place to debate its merits, perhaps I should say that I find it much the least enjoyable of these operas. It opens promisingly, with a prelude in which one catches an impulse, a feeling for the drama that is to unfold. Some rich, romantic orchestral writing after a noisy women's quarrel seems to promise more, and from time to time one thinks that fulfilment is nigh. But no: lush and lyrical enough, the love music wanders too loosely, and the big dramatic moments are never as effective as they should be. The recognition of the sergeant and the girl whom he saw fifteen years ago picking violets comes and goes without its music touching the heart, and when, in the last episode, the melodrama reaches its climax as Margot gives herself up to the police with magnificent defiance ('La Rouge? Vous voyez bien que c'est moi') one knows that the effect should be harrowing and that it is not.

Eric Fenby is responsible for the realization of the orchestral score: in the sleeve note he comments 'It may be that my use of the brass in the storm scene and later excitements may be more dramatic than Delius's original, but my zeal might be heard as a pardonable liberty!' Norman del Mar conducts, and the orchestral work is certainly the most enjoyable part of it. In the name part Lois McDonall characterizes convincingly but her singing gives limited pleasure; less limited, however, than that of her lovers, Sergeant Tibault (Kenneth Woollam) and 'The Artist' (Malcolm Donnelly). An effort has been made to produce some sense of atmosphere (chat in the tavern, heavy rain and thunder in the distance). The recording originates in a BBC Radio 3 presentation of the opera in 1981, a world première; a gallant, devoted exercise by all concerned, but a questionable success.

As different again is *Fennimore and Gerda* on which Delius finished his work in 1910 though in another sense it was never completed. The opera is subtitled *Two episodes from the life of Niels Lynne in eleven pictures after the novel of Jens Peter Jacobsen.* Delius wrote his own libretto and ended shortly after the start of the second of these episodes. The central character, Niels, has two loves, the first, Fennimore, bringing him tragedy. He then marries a much younger girl, Gerda, and it is at this point (before the death of mother and child and the outbreak of war) that Delius stopped. Opinions differ on the success and significance of this ending, and the studio recording under Meredith Davies may be contributing to the debate when it casts the same singer, Elisabeth Söderström, in both roles. In Jacobsen's novel the characters contrast markedly, for Fennimore is a mature woman of deep feeling whereas Gerda is a superficial, pretty, giggling youngster. The other recording, from a BBC broadcast of 1962, underlines the contrast. Fennimore is sung there by a mezzo and Gerda by a high, light soprano. With Söderström taking both parts the suggestion is quite different. The music itself changes character at this point: after so much that has been sombre, neurotic and tragic, there is now in the pastoral music a suggestion of healing power, recognized by Niels himself when he sings 'I'm healed now'. The identity of the voice when it sings both of the women's parts suggests that he sees something of Fennimore in Gerda, and that with his newfound happiness he can in a sense relive the past, this time as comedy instead of tragedy. If some such suggestion was intended by the casting, then at least a case can be made out for the dual role; if not it was a mistake.

Not that Söderström is a singer of whom one can readily have too much. She gives a magnificent performance as Fennimore, singing with the utmost beauty of tone and in excellent English. The scene where Fennimore receives the news of her husband's death marks the climax of the role, and the vividness of the emotions as Söderström catches them places it among the most striking pieces of vocal acting on record. Brian Rayner Cook makes a convincing and sympathetic if somewhat pallid Niels. Tear contributes quite a strong characterization of the spoilt, sterile artist husband. And always the orchestral score, its grey beauty occasionally taking fire, finds a sensitive interpreter in Meredith Davies and good players in the Danish Radio Orchestra.

As with the other operas, the secondary recording, though inferior in clarity, still deserves some attention. In this the BBC Symphony Orchestra is conducted by Stanford Robinson, with Sybil Michelow, John Cameron and Max Worthley in the principal roles. Michelow is a deeper-voiced Fennimore than Söderström. Her style is attractive in the early part of the opera and she sings with dignity to the end, but it is all too gentle, too mild, in the tragic scene which Söderström does with such intensity. Not nearly enough desperation is caught in 'All is now at an end . . . we can never atone for it', and there is no bitterness in her voice as she confronts Niels. Cameron and Worthley, on the other hand, are at least as good as their counterparts (Cameron very moving, for instance, in the cry 'Fennimore! 'tis him you love', and Worthley rather subtle in the new hard edge added to the voice as dissatisfaction changes Erik's sunny character in the third picture). A distinct superiority is felt in the BBC chorus work, at the start of Act 2 for instance, where it is much more spry and better shaped. Then occasionally there comes a flash of insight in Robinson's conducting: as the strings rise in the interlude between pictures 8 and 9 they shiver with cold and one sees the frozen surface of the fjord.

We are a long way, in this opera, from Florida and Louisiana where *The Magic Fountain* and *Koanga* had their colourful setting. There is a greater range in Delius's work than is often recognized, though one also becomes increasingly aware of inter-relationships. The recordings of these five operas help greatly in the appreciation of both the unity and the variety; they also open up a largely neglected area in which considerable and distinctive pleasure can be found.

HOLST

Equally distinctive, though in a completely different way, are the two recorded one-act operas of Holst. Like Delius, Holst wrote more operas than are now remembered. Five, now totally forgotten, precede *Savitri* (1909), but this is a masterpiece and fortunately has been recorded in a way that does it justice. Where Delius is expansive in style as in the forces employed, Holst is economical and restrained. He writes here for a chamber orchestra (two string quartets, contra-bass, two flutes and cor anglais), three soloists and a chorus, orchestra and chorus to be unseen by the audience. He also suggested that the performance should be given in the open air or in a small building. He has in fact written the first English chamber opera since the late seventeenth century. As Imogen Holst (who conducts the first of the two recordings) remarks in her sleeve note, this suits recorded performance well, and indeed the essential stillness and concentration are helped. Holst suggested that if a prelude to the opera was required, his *Hymn of the Travellers* should be used. This is the fourth of the *Four Choral Hymns from the Rig Veda*, op.26 no.3, a work of great imagination and beauty and included in its entirety on the record before the start of the opera. The fourth hymn forms an apt introduction partly because of its more explicit oriental style and quicker tempo (so that *Savitri* gains a vigorous opening); also because the god invoked in it is the guide of travellers along the roads of this world and along that leading to the next.

The opera itself opens with the voice of Death, heard from offstage and unaccompanied. Thomas Hemsley is careful to follow Holst's instruction that there should be 'nothing frightening or grotesque in the characterization', and it is only in his later appearance in the opera that we wish his tone sweeter (when the score marks *dolce*) and firmer (in the climax, 'Savitri, glorious woman'). The other male role is that of Savitri's axeman husband, not entirely well suited to Tear though he handles it with his customary reliable musicianship. As Savitri herself Janet Baker is superb. As with many great singers, her voice now carries associations with so many moving interpretations that any one part of her repertory gains from an experience of the rest. Thus the voice of Savitri, so very human, gentle and warm at the start, carries overtones of Lucretia and the Angel in *Gerontius*, just as they in turn will be enriched by Savitri. Yet the portrayal stands perfectly complete in itself, with its darkened tone echoing Death's 'I come for thy husband', its hushed awe in 'The forest is to me a mirror', the intense, unsentimental tenderness of 'I am with thee' and its radiant affirmation, 'Then shall my song like a trumpet in battle resound in triumph'. For all its economy of length and resources, the opera is generous and full in its emotions. This comes out wonderfully well in the recording, where the quiet acceptance (*dolce* again the marking) of Death in Savitri's 'Welcome Lord . . . thou art called the just one' is as strong as any *coup de théâtre* in Italian opera. The effect of the offstage chorus is also fine, and the voice of Savitri heard from the distance completes, again with marked dramatic effect, a work which is perhaps as near perfection as any: 'When in sorrow I am near, making it a thing of joy beyond all other joys'.

Felicity Palmer, the Savitri of the second recording, also creates a strong impression in a performance that is in many ways akin to Janet Baker's. The voices themselves could at several places be mistaken for each other, and the two singers have in common certain characteristics of style. Palmer had at the time of this recording become a mezzo after singing as a soprano for more than fifteen years; her high notes have a raw edge to them, where Baker (always a mezzo) produces the A flats and B flats with easy full-bodied resonance. The edginess that Felicity Palmer's voice acquires in such passages limits the effectiveness of the rapturous 'Ah Death, the Just One', which opens with splendid conviction in the excitement of Savitri's foreseen triumph. In quieter moments, such as 'The forest is to me a mirror' and 'Without thee I am as the dead', Palmer sings beautifully, and she also reaches great depths of feeling. Yet finally, in the very last solo with Savitri's voice coming from the distance, I found myself left relatively unmoved; there was more affection and warmth in Janet Baker's singing here. It will, in fact, be to the older record that I expect to find myself returning for *Savitri*, though there is much to be said for the new.

Philip Langridge brings a rather fresher, more rhythmical touch to Satyavan's homecoming song; Stephen Varcoe's beautiful voice is better able to do justice to the *dolce* of Death's phrases. The Chorus becomes a more positive presence, recorded more forwardly. Neither version makes every detail of the orchestration clear, but the newer, digital recording has the sharper focus. Richard Hickox, conducting the City of London Sinfonia, insists on precision in all note values and clarifies pictorial figures such as the creeping menace of the low strings representing the reappearance and gradual advance of Death. The brighter light shed upon the score may indeed be in the philosophical spirit of the opera, where 'Maya' (or the sense that 'we are such things as dreams are made on') is the enemy of Life. At any rate, though my personal preferences lie with the mellower approach of the 1966 original, and with the warmer quality of Janet Baker's singing in it, the 1983 recording is a worthy successor.

No other stage work of Holst's has enjoyed the success of *Savitri*. In 1924 he came out with a Falstaff opera, or as he himself described it, 'a musical interlude in one act': *At the Boar's Head*. It met with little success then, and the 'world première recording', issued in 1983, seemed to many of the record critics to show why. Dramatic structure was felt to be deficient (Holst said that the libretto was Shakespeare's, but he was too modest), and there was also a complaint about a lack of strong lyrical invention in the music. Actually, the structure has at the very least the virtue of clarity. The post-mortem on Gadshill makes the first episode; the mock interview of King and Prince, with the arraignment of Falstaff, the second; and in between is Hal's 'I know you all' soliloquy. Then come Doll Tearsheet and the Hostess, and news of a stirring world, with soldiers in the streets and then Falstaff off to the wars taking leave of Doll.

As for the music, I can only say that for anyone who loves its very English idiom, as I do, it is hard to be objective: I would feel that the reader whose taste and interest lead him to concern himself much with this chapter is unlikely to be disappointed. The performance, under David Atherton, brings out the full, splendid range of humour, majesty, grossness, delicacy and even pathos. Humour, for instance, as after Pistol's 'We have seen the seven stars' (straight out of Puccini or Mascagni) Doll shows herself a true critic with the comment 'For God's sake thrust him down the stairs'. There is majesty as the Prince is called to Westminster, and mock majesty as Falstaff, enacting royalty, commands Doll Tearsheet: 'Weep not, sweet queen'. The interchange of grossness and delicacy runs throughout, and the pathos is there, perhaps thanks to Felicity Palmer's rich characterization, in the apparently sincere tenderness of Doll: 'I love thee better than I love e'er a scurvy young boy of them all'. Briefly, it seems to me a score that pays yet another worthy tribute to Falstaff, 'the cause that wit is in other men'; and the recording does it full justice. John Tomlinson dominates easily through the generous body of his voice, vocally a veritable tun of man, and he has some fine fun with his part as when producing 'posh' vowels to represent the Establishment voice of His Majesty. Philip Langridge admirably suggests the youth, energy and latent authority of Prince Hal. And, as I say, Felicity Palmer is both comical and touching as Doll. The role of the Hostess needs something of that kind of panache (a rather pale performance here by Elise Ross), and the production might have gained from some suggestion of the 'great noise as troops pass in the street' and 'renewed cheering'. Otherwise plump Jack and the world are well served.

Holst's other one-act opera on record, *The Wandering Scholar*, might make a good double-bill with *Savitri*, or with Vaughan Williams's *Riders to the Sea*, for which a suitable companion piece is reckoned hard to find. It presents a marked contrast to both: a comedy, with a sardonic flavour, an English *Heure espagnole* (albeit in a French setting). It was the composer's last opera, written in 1929–30, though the score remained unrevised and for many years unpublished. In 1968 Imogen Holst and Benjamin Britten published their edition which is used in this recording. The story from Helen Waddell's *Wandering Scholars* involves four characters. Norma Burrowes plays the wife Alison charmingly, and it is good to hear Michael Langdon's ripe bass and strong characterization as Father Philippe. Tear shows a well-pointed sense of humour as he tells the tale that eventually brings retribution, and Michael Rippon is the husband who administers it. The production is admirable, as is the work of the English Chamber Orchestra under Steuart

Bedford. The coupling is the Ballet Music from *The Perfect Fool*; and though this, Holst's most ambitious full-length opera, failed at Covent Garden in 1923, one might wonder whether a new look at it would bring a revaluation.

VAUGHAN WILLIAMS

Vaughan Williams worked so closely with Holst at one time that he said they sometimes could not remember exactly who had written what. Certainly Holst's *Wandering Scholar* has a musical kinship with Vaughan Williams's *Hugh the Drover*, though it is both a more sophisticated and more limited work. The connection lies in the folk idiom, a certain jauntiness of rhythms and an outdoor feeling about both operas. *Hugh* was first produced in 1924 and records of the new work appeared much more promptly than they do today. Dr Malcolm Sargent, as he then was, conducted (and reputedly saved from disaster) the performances at the Royal College of Music and then at Her Majesty's Theatre. The cast was reassembled for recording, and the results are interesting in several ways, not least because they preserve some passages that were later cut. The five double-sided records have been well transferred to LP on the Pearl label, though it is a somewhat breathless business following them, for the excerpts go as fast as possible so as to cram in something of everything, and they cut and dovetail very nimbly. The opening goes at a tremendous lick, and with short cuts they manage to give a good idea of the first act up to Hugh's 'Song of the Road'. This, the main solo in the opera, is given a full side and taken at a more moderate tempo. The love duet follows and then the cuts begin to bite: one from the end of the duet up to the entrance of the Showman, another in the ensemble and the fight. The first scene of Act 2 was added later for a production in 1933 so none of that is included. The first side from Act 2 cuts a verse of Hugh's song, and then comes the duet for Mary and Hugh which in the published score is now placed near the end of the opera. Cuts and changes to the words continue through the next excerpt, but it is the last side of the original records that contains music now omitted. The farewells are prolonged in some quite beautiful concerted passages (it makes one wonder whether Vaughan Williams actually heard *Fanciulla del West*). Anyway, he must have decided in favour of tightening up and exercising restraint; so to hear his first thoughts we have to go back to these crackly old records of 1924, and no bad thing either. They have some good singing, notably in the fervour and brilliant ring of Tudor Davies's Hugh. And they represent something of a triumph for their time in the recording of the orchestra, well forward and full-bodied, giving a well disciplined zestful account of the score under young Dr Sargent's energetic direction.

The standard complete recording is conducted by Sir Charles Groves and has Tear in the name part. This, I think, is a piece of miscasting, for Tear's voice and style are wrong in associations: it is not a romantic voice or the voice of a countryman. When he sings the 'Song of the Road' he brings plenty of imagination to it, but the simpler art and freer production of James Johnston is preferable: he sang the role splendidly at Sadler's Wells when it was produced there in the early 1950s, and his record on a late 78 (DX 1668; HQM 1228) is well worth hearing. Sheila Armstrong makes a charming heroine, and among the smaller parts Robert Lloyd is outstanding as the Constable. All the ensemble and chorus work goes well (the chorus being the Ambrosians, so expert at making crowd scenes come to life on record). The recording deserves gratitude (we certainly had to wait long enough for it), and yet it does not quite present the opera as the enchanting thing it can be. There is a tendency among critics still to underrate the work; it is a marvellously fresh, strong score, with probably the best love music ever written by an Englishman and a wealth of feeling for the village life it portrays.

The same love for English life informs *Sir John in Love*, Vaughan Williams's Falstaff opera, completed in 1928. An admirable recording under Meredith Davies presents a score which is so much more than merely genial. There is a toughness in the rhythms, and very occasionally a suggestion (among others of compositions that have a more obvious kinship) even of the Fourth and Sixth Symphonies, which were still to be written of course: the prevailing good humour is strengthened every now and then by a little menacing contrast. Possibly the lyricism, including the 'set-piece' songs, hinders the drama; perhaps the libretto (Vaughan Williams's own) lacks the constructional skill of a Boito. On records such considerations matter less than they do on the stage, and they certainly do not cloud the pleasure of the recording as far as this listener is concerned. Raimund Herincx fattens his voice effectively till it (almost) expands to the dimensions of that tun of man; the merry wives (Felicity Palmer and Elizabeth Bainbridge) make a spirited pair; Wendy Eathorne is a particularly charming Anne Page; and Helen Watts as Mistress Quickly casts her beneficent beam over all. The love music (subtler than in *Hugh the Drover*), the choruses (sometimes jovial sometimes rapturous), the delicate orchestration of many of the lyrics; the Act 3 interlude added for the Bristol production of 1933: all are a joy. A joy too is the composer's statement of his modest intentions: 'My chief object in *Sir John in Love* has been to fit this wonderful comedy with, I trust, not unpleasant music.'

In marked contrast to *Hugh the Drover* and *Sir John in Love* is the one-act opera, *Riders to the Sea* (1937). Synge's play of the Arran Islands presents bleak deprivation, a world haunted by loss and the dread of more loss, the keening of women and the wailing of the sea winds. Vaughan Williams's score captures all this, sometimes anticipating the *Antarctica* Symphony, in music that is intensely moving in its compassionate gauntness. Much of this feeling is embodied in the old woman, Maurya, nobly sung by Helen Watts. The two girls, Nora and Catherine, are clearly characterized in the contrasting timbres of Norma Burrowes and Margaret Price (the latter most beautifully warm in the quality of her voice). And Benjamin Luxon deepens and blackens his tone aptly in the one male role of the opera. Davies is again the conductor, sensitive to all that the composer himself has provided to ensure that the essential monotony shall not be merely monotonous. Much of the effect here is cumulative (not helped, incidentally, by the place chosen for turning the first to the second side of the record), but the great emotional climax comes with a simple modulation into E major, the moment not of loss but of reconciliation to loss ('But it's a great rest I'll have now'), a moment most touchingly caught in the recording. Like Holst's *Savitri*, Puccini's *Gianni Schicchi* and little else, *Riders to the Sea* achieves perfection within the limited form of the one-act opera. It is surely Vaughan Williams's operatic masterpiece.

His own favourite, however, appears to have been *The Pilgrim's Progress*. He became familiar with all the complaints from people who said that it was not their idea of an opera, and he simply retorted that it was his. He would no doubt have been delighted by the recording under Sir Adrian Boult, and, if he did rise up by any chance to complain that it included a passage (just before Act 2) which the score said should be omitted unless required by the stage, he would not be likely to find many who would agree, for it contains some most lovely orchestral writing. While none of the solo singing is out-standing, nearly all of it is good. There is John Noble, a sympathetic Pilgrim, with John Carol Case whose natural production and exemplary diction are great assets in his portrayal of Evangelist. Ian Partridge sings beautifully as Interpreter, and Shirley-Quirk is Watchful, the Porter, in that fine Nocturne, written (Michael Kennedy's note tells us) as an afterthought, much of it in the train between London and Dorking. On the sixth side of the original three-record set, we hear Sir Adrian in rehearsal. Sharp-tongued and sharp-eared, he cries 'The diminuendo is *rotten* from 3a . . .', '3m . . . was an unholy mess on our test yesterday', and 'You talk (this is to the orchestra who purr with contentment as he admonishes them) . . . you talk like market women'. That, evidently, is how to get results.

Pilgrim's Progress was Vaughan Williams's contribution to the operatic renaissance of postwar years. It was produced at Covent Garden in 1950, after Britten's *Peter Grimes*, *Rape of Lucretia* and *Albert Herring*, as well as Arthur Bliss's *Olympians*. To come were *Billy Budd* in 1951, *Gloriana* in 1952, and then the 1954–5 season which had the première of both Walton's *Troilus and Cressida* and Tippett's *Midsummer Marriage*.

WALTON

Tippett went on to write three more full-scale operas, but Walton, characteri-stically, followed his success with only one other opera and that was a one-act comedy. *The Bear*, first produced by the English Opera Group at Aldeburgh in 1967, was recorded shortly afterwards, conducted by James Lockhart, with Monica Sinclair and John Shaw in the main roles. Years previously, after the first performance of *Façade*, Ernest Newman had suggested that Walton should write a comic opera. Here it is, not quite what Newman had in mind but a treatment of a satirical 'vaudeville' by Chekhov, allowing scope for some musical parody that is probably rather more amusing than the story itself. The libretto occasionally irritates, but, for better or worse, the words are all clearly audible. Monica Sinclair as Madame Popova does not sound quite the *young* widow as specified (there is a suggestion of the Dowager Duchess or Lady Bracknell perhaps), and phrases marked *soavamente* or *scherzando* may not be notably sweet or playful. But the rich luxury of bosomy contralto grief ('Life has no meaning for me'), the baleful depths of 'It would seem as if I really must enter a convent', and the song 'I was a constant faithless wife' (which might almost be out of *Ruddigore*) – all of these she does with zest and opulence, appropriate to what the composer calls his 'extravaganza in one act'.

When the same composer was asked about his work in progress on *Troilus and Cressida* he paused for a moment and answered: 'Well, it's a bit like Ivor Novello.' And perhaps it is – 'a bit'. It remains probably the most successful attempt since Puccini to write a singer's opera (part of Walton's declared aim) and to restore the 'grand' in grand opera. Nor does that formulation do it justice, for its musical idiom and the strength of its feeling are of a tougher consistency altogether than that would suggest. This much emerges clearly enough in the recording. All the same, it is a recording that leaves one with dissatisfaction in several respects. For one thing, the acoustic is curiously dead: the performance comes 'live' from the stage of Covent Garden, but an average studio recording has more sense of the theatre about it. More seriously, the role of Troilus forfeits virtually all its attractiveness as taken by Richard Cassilly. The hard tone, the uneven emission, the unpleasing vowel sounds detract from the liking which it is so essential that Troilus should command. As Pandarus, Gerald English was more acceptable to that part of the audience that had not known Peter Pears in the role, but on records the lack of a refined style and subtlety is apparent. And, alas, the greatest weakness of all derives from what is also the greatest strength of the performance, and that is the casting of Janet Baker as Cressida. The part was originally written for soprano, but with Baker in mind Walton had quite a lot of it transposed, some passages cut and others altered. In nearly all cases it can be argued that these changes are for the worse, and that the very idea of making it a mezzo-soprano role alters the basic characterization, losing that vulnerable, frail element which was so essential to the point of the love scenes and to the development of the woman's unhappy fate. Baker sings splendidly, especially in the last act, but her art is too outward-going and her voice-character too self-sufficient to be the Cressida of Walton's original and truer conception.

Fortunately, part of the original score is preserved in recorded excerpts. In the première at Covent Garden in 1954 the principal roles were sung by Magda Laszlo and Richard Lewis. Elisabeth Schwarzkopf had been approached to play Cressida, and, although she never sang the part on stage, she recorded the four main solos and two of the duets with Lewis under Walton's own direction. Lewis is never more gratefully heard than here, where he sings with ardour and lyrical grace. Schwarzkopf's voice is at its radiant best, and she brings an ideally personal, affectionate and imaginative touch to the music. Walton, with the Philharmonia, produces a richer orchestral sound than Lawrence Foster at Covent Garden. But the greatest value of the recording lies in its demonstration of what has been lost in the rewriting (and hence the need to revert). Where some of Cressida's music has been transposed by a tone and even as much as a minor third, the climaxes are dulled, and the fragile charm (as in 'At the haunted end of the day') has gone. In the Love Duet some rapturous pages are cut entirely and other phrases have disappeared. The opera wanted tightening, certainly, and many of the cuts elsewhere are well judged; but hearing Schwarzkopf again one can only conclude that as far as Cressida's role was concerned first thoughts were best.

One other brief reminder of the original *Troilus and Cressida* is to be found on records. The first and incomparable Pandarus, Peter Pears, is heard in just a few phrases from Act 2. Marie Collier sings Cressida (thrilling on high but rather shallow on lower notes, and a wrong choice for the role); Walton conducts; and we hear the inimitable grace of Pears's 'guess again'. It comes in a Covent Garden Anniversary Album published in 1968; all too little but better than nothing (SET 392–3).

TIPPETT

That Covent Garden album contains another extract of interest to us in this chapter. Michael Tippett has been well favoured by the gramophone companies in most respects, and three of his four operas have been recorded complete. *The Ice Break* (1977) remains and, until the recording of *King Priam* was made in 1981, there was just one short passage from the opera (Achilles's song, 'O rich soiled land') included in this same Covent Garden album. Richard Lewis sings it with guitar accompaniment by John Williams, as in the original production, with feeling, good tone and thorough mastery of the difficult idiom. But of course it does point, even in this brevity, to one of the outstanding facts about modern opera: it is *hard*, both for performers and listeners. Achilles's song does not represent modern opera or Michael Tippett at their hardest. Yet the relationship between the voice and guitar, and the precise mood of either part, tends to elude definition. Both the performer and the listener have to work at it. They will not necessarily mind this, but they will need some assurance that eventually it will prove worthwhile. The lack of such assurance makes the future of 'modern' opera so uncertain; and it becomes essential, therefore, that records, which offer unrivalled opportunities, should be able to show that this difficult music can prove itself. If *The Knot Garden* (1970), one of Tippett's two other recorded operas, remains difficult and unproven in the experience of many listeners,

The Midsummer Marriage (1955) must by now have been accepted by many more as one of the most joyful and fascinating works of our time.

The recording of *Midsummer Marriage* is based on the Covent Garden production of 1968 revived in 1970 with some cuts in the score sanctioned by the composer*. The original production of 1955 had had a mixed reception (though its cast headed by Sutherland and Lewis, and its sets by Barbara Hepworth were generally much to the liking of the present writer). By 1968 the music itself had worked its way into the system and the time was ripe for a second attempt at Covent Garden (the Welsh National had given it in the meantime) and shortly after that for a recording. Thus we have Joan Carlyle in Sutherland's original role, less radiantly full in tone and less brilliant in *fioriture* but still able in coping with the technical difficulties, sometimes making quite lovely sounds and always at least giving an impression of understanding (one has to put it that way because the singers of the première said they had only the haziest notion of what it was all about and yet still managed to sing with apparent conviction). Alberto Remedios takes over from Richard Lewis, and in him we have one of the best English singers of postwar years. His mastery of this most difficult music prompts the question of why he was not cast as Troilus. His clean-cut tone and careful lyricism are great assets here. His love song in the first act ('The summer morning dances in my heart') is a particularly fine piece of singing as well as having within it so much of the essence of the opera and of its composer at this period in his career. The second soprano and tenor (Bella and Jack) are lightly, attractively sung by Elizabeth Harwood and Stuart Burrows; Raimund Herincx does not over-brutalize the role of King Fisher; and, greatest relief of all, the Ancients are well and truly *sung*, with good, firm voices, by Elizabeth Bainbridge and the excellent Stafford Dean. Helen Watts as Madame Sosostris has not the opulence of her predecessor, Oralia Dominguez, but at least her diction makes the gnomic utterances as intelligible as they are ever likely to be. The unacknowledged heroes and heroines are the chorus: the intricacies, particularly of rhythm, must surely have been daunting, yet again the mastery appears complete. Colin Davis conducts, and the precise, spirited playing is that of a crack orchestra on top form.

Brilliant orchestral playing also distinguishes the recording of *King Priam*, where David Atherton's conducting of the London Sinfonietta brings out fully the aggression so dominant in this score. The musical idiom has of course changed radically from that of *The Midsummer Marriage,* as has the writing for the voice. With little lyricism and much declamation the voice parts present the singers with a hard task – not the least hard of which

---

* The main cuts are as follows (references to vocal score, published by Schott's): Act 2 Dances, figures 163–167, 188–194, 213–221, Act 3, figs. 259–266, 329–338, 358–360, 407–419, 481–487. Some of these involve only repeated material, but some are of concerted passages which it is a pity to lose. Tippett writes: 'I am sure we have been right to record this stage version which has been worked on for some years . . . the whole recording from my point of view is quite splendid.'

(perhaps because unlikely to be so consciously recognized as other kinds of difficulty) is that of keeping the voice completely firm and produced scrupulously as a singing instrument. Two members of the cast – Thomas Allen as Hector and Yvonne Minton as Helen – do this as though by second nature, and they add greatly to the musical pleasure of listening. Most of the rest, fine as they may be in other respects, allow into their singing some element of that more loosely spun tone that seems to be generally regarded as the acceptable norm in this sort of music.

Norman Bailey suits the role of Priam admirably up to a point. His voice readily suggests the authority of age (and even in the first scene, at the time of Paris's birth, Priam and Hecuba should be seen as 'mature' parents). His timbre, seconded by its associations in our minds with Hans Sachs and Wotan, can carry a feeling of generous humanity and natural dignity. Thus he is at his best here in the later scenes of Act 3, where Priam comes to Achilles's tent to beg the body of Hector, and where in the final scene he turns so unexpectedly and movingly toward Helen and kisses her whilst Troy burns and his own death is at the door. In scene ii of that act, however, Priam learns from Paris the news of Hector's death, and this point in the drama calls, I would say, for more imaginative intensity. 'Am I no longer king?' is a rhetorical challenge requiring sharper tension; 'O, I could have spared you well for Hector, for Hector my son' needs more bitterness, the wordless moaning more agony. This is all central to the emotional force of the opera; so too is the cursing by Priam of parents, life and soul, where Bailey again fails to make the emotion, and the words, bite.

Robert Tear's Achilles makes much of the strange contrasts in the part, both in the man's character and between the softer and louder phrases he has to sing; the yearning nostalgia of his guitar song is particularly well caught. Philip Langridge's tenor provides sufficient of a vocal contrast in his lighter-sounding Paris, though surely wanting some more ardent, Italianate resonance at the cries of 'We love, we love'. As in several of these recordings, the feeling that the singers are such well brought-up, freshly scrubbed young Englishmen does not really help the dramatic illusion. Nor does it seem that Tippett's notation makes it easy for a boy to give a dramatically convincing performance in the scene where young Paris meets his brother Hector out hunting.

In the women's roles, Minton sings with beauty and some seductiveness as Helen, Felicity Palmer with much character-projection, penetrative and even slightly raw as Andromache, and Heather Harper is a passionately concerned Hecuba, sounding well once over the unfortunate effect of her first major phrase, the jagged outline of which sounds dangerously like a parody of the old-school prima donna.

As to the recording itself, its technical ingenuities impressed the composer, who gives it his grateful blessing in a short sleeve note. John Warrack (*Gramophone*, November 1981) found two deficiencies, however: one at the point where Achilles calls out to the dead Patroclus, where more differentiation is needed among the trumpets at their three distances, and the other where at the end of Act 2 the voice of Achilles does not sound out sufficiently clear and dominant among the war cries from the Greek camp. Clarity is otherwise a notable virtue of this digital recording, just as mastery of the extremely difficult music impresses so regularly as to be almost taken for granted.

In *The Knot Garden* one again has to admire the assurance with which all concerned present this most demanding score. Again the recording is based on the Covent Garden production and Colin Davis is the conductor. This extraordinary opera, where seven very modern characters dance the antic hay and the music engrosses the working-listener within its labyrinth of motifs, is far less lovable than *Midsummer Marriage*, and one may sometimes curse its jabbing sounds, its embarrassing words, and its implicit assumption that somehow, amid the apparent silliness, it embodies wisdom. In my own experience, it is never quite possible to leave it at that; one returns. In the meantime the performance commands nothing but admiration. Josephine Barstow's account of the long solo for Denise, the maimed freedom-fighter, is, I think, one of the great pieces of singing on records. In purely traditional ways of listening, it is glorious in tone quality, the trills and staccatos, the sheer vocal range and of course the great range of expressiveness – in all these things Barstow is quite superb. Yvonne Minton as Thea is a little less sensitive in her solo towards the end (wanting a *crescendo,* for instance, towards 'Now, ah now, I know'), but she is admirably firm, exact and evenly resonant. Jill Gomez sings 'Die liebe Farbe' well, so hauntingly, enigmatically interpolated in Act 2. Tear, Herincx and Hemsley all make very sufficient answers to the demands of their roles; only Thomas Carey, as Mel, strikes one as less than good. The recording is again exemplary as record production. Indeed, everything is done for the work and its listener – except possibly in as far as a copy of the score is an almost essential adjunct.

A triumph, in many ways a culmination, the recording of *The Knot Garden* still points with an unsure finger to the future. Surely, one must fear, 'the average listener' (that mythical, vitally important creature) is lost. We have come along an English road, a mere path at first, and one that seemed to be petering out. Instead it broadened; even for a while looked like becoming a highway. But now it seems to lead where few can follow with any assurance of pleasure. Recordings make us aware of an inheritance which our nine-teenth-century gentleman would never have thought would be a national possession. Perhaps it will be the recordings that will prompt a new school of British composers to see the way ahead.

DELIUS
KOANGA

UJ Uncle Joe; *P* Palmyra; *SP* Simon Peres; *DJM* Don José Martinez; *K* Koanga;
C Clotilda; *R* Rangwan

1970 (live performances – Washington
Opera, Washington DC)
Pierson *UJ*; *R*; Lindsey *P*; W.
McDonald *SP*; Roy *DJM*;
Holmes *K*; Gerber *C* / Washington
Opera Society Chorus and Orch.
/ Callaway

International Gram Soc IGS081–2
1973 Estes *UJ*; *R*; Lindsey *P*; Erwen
SP; Herincx *DJM*; Holmes *K*;
Allister *C* / Alldis Choir, LSO /
Groves
EMI SLS 974
Angel SBLX 3808

FENNIMORE AND GERDA

F Fennimore; *G* Gerda; *NL* Niels Lyhne; *ER* Erik Refstrup

1962 (broadcast performance – BBC
Studios, Maida Vale, London)
Michelow *F*; J. Sinclair *G*;
Cameron *NL*; Worthley *ER* /
Ambrosian Singers, BBC SO / S.
Robinson
International Gram Soc ⓜ

IGS 023–4
1976 Söderström *F*; *G*; Rayner Cook
NL; Tear *ER* / Danish Radio
Chorus and Orch. / M. Davies
EMI SLS 991
Angel SBLX 3835

MAGIC FOUNTAIN

1977 (broadcast recording –
Hippodrome Theatre, Golders
Green, London)
Mitchinson *Solano*; Pring *Watawa*;
Welsby *Wapanacki*; Angas *Talum*

Hadjo / BBC Singers, BBC
Concert Orch. / Del Mar
BBC Artium 2001
Arabesque (US) 8121 L
④ 9121 L

MARGOT LA ROUGE

(broadcast recording – Hippodrome Theatre, Golders Green, London)

1981 McDonall *Margot*; Woollam
Sergeant; Donnelly *Artist*; Andrew
Lili Beguin/BBC Concert

Orch. / Del Mar
BBC Artium REGL 458
Arabesque (US) 8134 ④ 9134

A VILLAGE ROMEO AND JULIET

M Manz: *Mar* Marti; *V* Vreli; *S* Sali; *DF* Dark Fiddler

1948 Dowling *M*; Sharp *Mar*; Dyer *V*;
Soames *S*; Clinton *DF* / chorus,
RPO / Beecham
World Records ⓜ SHB54
1962 (live performance – Alhambra
Theatre, Bradford)
Folley *M*; McIntyre *Mar*; Morison
V; Wakefield *S*; Easton *DF* /
Sadler's Wells Opera Chorus and

Orch. / M. Davies
International Gram Soc ⓜ IGS
079–80
1972 Luxon *M*; Mangin *Mar*; Harwood
V; Tear *S*; Shirley-Quirk *DF* /
Alldis Choir, RPO / M. Davies
EMI SLS 966
Angel SBLX 3784

HOLST
SAVITRI

Savitri *S*; Satyavan *Sat*; Death *D*

1965 Baker *S*; Tear *Sat*; Hemsley *D*/Purcell Singers / ECO/I. Holst Argo ZK 98

D/Hickox Singers / City of London Sinfonia /Hickox Hyperion A66099

1983 Palmer *S*; Langridge *Sat*; Varcoe

THE WANDERING SCHOLAR

1974 Burrowes *Alison:* Rippon *Louis*; Langdon *Father Philippe*; Tear *Pierre* / English Opera Group, ECO

/ Bedford EMI ASD 3097 Angel S 37152

AT THE BOAR'S HEAD

1981 Langridge *Prince Hal*; Tomlinson *Falstaff*; Ross *Mistress Quickly*; Palmer *Doll Tearsheet*; Wilson-Johnson *Pistol*; Hall *Peto*; Suart

Bardolph; George *Poins* / Women's Voices of the Liverpool Phil. Choir / RLPO / Atherton EMI ASD 4387 ④ TC-ASD 4387

TIPPETT
KING PRIAM

1980 Tear *Achilles*; Allen *Hector*; Palmer *Andromache*; Bailey *Priam*; Minton *Helen*; Langridge *Paris*; Roberts *Patroclus*; Harper *Hecuba*;

Murray *Nurse*; Bowen *Hermes*/ London Sinfonietta and Chor. / Atherton Decca D246D3 ④ K246K33 London LDR 73006

THE KNOT GARDEN

1973 Herincx *Faber*; Minton *Thea*; Gomez *Flora*; Barstow *Denise*; Carey *Mel*; Tear *Dov*; Hemsley

Mangus / Royal Opera House Orch. / C. Davis Philips 6700 063

THE MIDSUMMER MARRIAGE

1970 A. Remedios *Mark*; Carlyle *Jenifer*; Herincx *King Fisher*; Harwood *Bella*; Burrows *Jack*; Watts *Sosostris*; Dean *Priest of the Temple*;

Bainbridge *Priestess of the Temple* / Royal Opera House Chorus and Orch. / C. Davis Philips 6703 027

VAUGHAN WILLIAMS

HUGH THE DROVER

M Mary; *AJ* Aunt Jane; *H* Hugh; *J* John; *C* Constable; *S* Showman; *Ser* Sergeant

1978 Armstrong *M*; Watts *AJ*; Tear *H*; Rippon *J*; Lloyd *C*; Sharpe *S*; Newman *Ser* / Ambrosian Opera Chorus, St Paul's Cathedral Choristers, RPO / Groves EMI SLS 5162

Angel SZBX 3879
1924 (excerpts)
M. Lewis *M*; Willis *AJ*; T. Davies *H*; Collier *J*; Anderson *C*; Michael *S*; Dawson *Ser.* / orch. / Sargent Pearl ⑩ GEMM 128

THE PILGRIM'S PROGRESS

1971 Noble *The Pilgrim*; Herincx *John Bunyan*; Case *Evangelist* / London Philharmonic Choir

and Orch / Boult
HMV SLS 1435133 ④ TC-SLS 1435139

RIDERS TO THE SEA

1970 Burrowes *Nora*; M. Price *Cathleen*; Watts *Maurya*; Stevens *A Woman*; Luxon *Bartley* / Women's Voices of the Ambrosian Singers, Orch Nova

of London / M. Davies
HMV ESD 1782991 ④ TC-ESD 1782994
Angel S 36819

SIR JOHN IN LOVE

1974 Herincx *Falstaff*; Lloyd *Ford*; Watts *Mrs Quickly*; Tear *Fenton*; Eathorne *Anne Page*; Palmer *Mrs Page*;

Bainbridge *Mrs Ford*; Noble *Page* / Alldis Choir, New Philharmonia / M. Davies
EMI SLS980

WALTON

THE BEAR

Mme Popova *P*; Smirnov *S*; Luka *L*

1967 M. Sinclair *P*; Shaw *S*; Lumsden *L* / ECO / Lockhart EMI SAN 192 Angel S36477

1977 Harris *P*; Yurisich *S*; Mangin *L* / Melbourne SO / Cavdarski Chandos ABR 1052 ④ ABT 1052

TROILUS AND CRESSIDA

C Cressida; *T* Troilus; *Cal* Calkas; *P* Pandarus; *E* Evadne

1976 (live performance – Royal Opera House, London) Baker *C*; Cassilly *T*; Van Allan *Cal*; English *P*; Bainbridge *E* / Royal Opera House Chorus and Orch. / Foster

EMI SLS 997
1954 (excerpts)
Schwarzkopf *C*; R. Lewis *T*; M. Sinclair *E* / Philharmonia / Walton World Records ⑩ OH217
Angel ⑩ 35278

Duke Bluebeard's Castle

DAVID MURRAY

Bartók and Béla Balázs would have been surprised to hear that they had written 'an ideal gramophone opera', and Balázs at least would have been offended. It is regularly miscalled that, on trivial and doubtful grounds. By coincidence the optimum playing time of a modern stereo LP accommodates *Duke Bluebeard's Castle* to a nicety. (Walter Susskind's old performance for the Bartók Recording Society was stretched less temptingly over four sides; for the first stereo recording, Ferenc Fricsay's, the opera was considerably cut.) The problem of where to place the side-break still has no happy solution, nor any agreed one: the Fifth Door – sustained *fff* with added brass and organ – has to be given the outside of Side 2, not the inside of Side 1, but a break anywhere during the Third and Fourth Doors is damaging.

Certainly the gramophone has assisted *Bluebeard's* fortunes. Like other operas of inconvenient shapes and sizes, it has to wait a long time for its turns on stage. Nothing in the operatic repertory seems to sit well with it in an evening's programme (Bartók suggested that it should be given together with his ballets *The Wooden Prince* and *The Miraculous Mandarin*), and it requires a very large orchestra.

It also requires Hungarian – or at least a language that resembles Hungarian in the relevant musical respects, as no Western language does. The metre of Balázs's verse text becomes in English the metre of *Hiawatha*, unfortunately: 'Give me keys to all your doorways! – Can you guess what lies behind them? – Now behold my spacious kingdom, gaze ye down the dwindling vistas!', German, the language of Häfner's and Fricsay's recordings, is no better off. What gives bite and variety to the original diction is the Hungarian snap, which studs the orchestral music too: a short, sharply accented initial syllable followed by a weak longer one. Hungarian is rich in words of that shape, giving Balázs the means to vary the profile of his metre effectively. Western languages lack the resources, and in translation the declamation of *Bluebeard* is inevitably flattened out. Yet *Bluebeard* needs to be closely followed, being a true dramatic piece. For non-Hungarians the gramophone and a bilingual libretto provide a solution.

Still, a dramatic piece is what *Bluebeard* is, and calling it 'an ideal gramophone opera' obscures its remarkable virtues. Whether it seems 'entirely lacking in dramatic action', as Halsey Stevens put it, is entirely a matter of performance. *Bluebeard* is quite unlike, say, Schoenberg's *Gurrelieder* (completed in the same year, 1911) – a tone poem with singing characters and a story attached, for which any visual realization would be not only redundant but also ridiculous. The action of Bartók's opera is calculatedly bare and schematic, but magnificently fraught; the music ensures that, fulfilling just what Balázs's scenario expected of it. It is indissoluble from the action, which is so vividly realized in it that nothing essential is lost in a performance for the ear alone. Of course the 'real' action is psychological, but Balázs set it out in visual (albeit transparently symbolic) events, and the music is strictly shaped to them: if not seen, they have to be imagined. Freud has nothing to do with it.

Music lovers hear of Balázs as the librettist of *Bluebeard* and also *The Wooden Prince*, a young Symbolist poet who revered Maeterlinck, who was the author not only of *Pelléas et Mélisande* but also of the libretto of Paul Dukas's Bluebeard opera, *Ariane et Barbe-Bleue* (1907). That is an authentic Women's Liberation piece: Ariadne, Bluebeard's latest wife, uses the forbidden keys and discovers five other wives, alive and well and wretchedly in thrall to him. (Despite the example of a concomitant revolt by his peasants, they refuse fearfully to accept their freedom, and Ariadne strides away alone.) The Balázs libretto, adapted from his original verse play, owes much to the French opera: the literary twist of the unmurdered wives, the vision of great doors with orchestral setpieces to illustrate what lies behind them, the reading of the story as a psychological struggle between man and wife, and above all the sketch of the new wife as a Modern Woman – free, enlightened, dauntlessly inquisitive. Balázs's Bluebeard is a maturer Lohengrin.

Cinéastes know another Balázs, the distinguished film theorist (*Der sichtbare Mensch*, 'The Visible Man') and screenwriter of the 1920s and 1930s. That was his eventual career, after he left Hungary for Austria and Germany; he returned to his native country, as a doyen of the cinema, only in 1945, the year of Bartók's death in exile. It is pleasing to learn from the Leyda/Montagu appendix to Eisenstein's *The Film Sense* that another old castle featured in his film career. When an international film congress was held at the chateau of La Sarraz in Switzerland, an allegorical spoof was improvised and shot on the spot in a day (it remained unfinished, and was later lost). A female delegate, 'clad in a white robe with two empty filmreels for breastplates, was suspended with ropes from the topmost tower where, as "the spirit of the artistic film", she was the object for contention of two armies: that of Commerce, led by Béla Balázs in full armour, and that of Independence, led by Eisenstein, mounted on a projection table and tilting with both lance and projection apparatus'.

It is the cinematic Balázs who tips his hand in the *Bluebeard* scenario, to the positive advantage of the composer. (Remember how exactly Eisenstein himself appreciated the role of music in the cinema – he produced *Die*

Walküre for the Bolshoi). In Maeterlinck's didactic libretto, much has to be explained in the text, and the business with the doors merely makes room for Impressionist orchestral effusions. Balázs had the inspiration of making the doors, which were after all the principal props in the original Perrault tale, carry the whole visible story.

Duke Bluebeard's Castle begins and ends in darkness. A spoken prologue, included only in Susskind's and Solti's recordings, warns us that we shall watch a myth – 'Where is the stage: within? without?' Bluebeard brings Judith home to his Gothic fastness. Shivering in the gloom, she espies seven great locked doors. She will fill his castle with sunlight: every door must be opened, all his secrets revealed – because, as she says repeatedly, she loves him. By turns reluctant and excited, he surrenders the keys one by one. The opening of each door places the situation literally in a new light (we need not see what lies behind each, for the music displays it). The first two reveal Bluebeard's torture chamber and his bloody armoury; the castle brightens, and Judith rejoices. Emboldened by her courage, Bluebeard gives up three more keys which disclose his treasury, his secret garden and his splendid realm. Judith insists on more, for she has seen bloodstains everywhere. The castle darkens as the Sixth Door opens on a lake of tears. Judith's suspicions rise to hysteria. From the Seventh Door come Bluebeard's three earlier wives, all as alive for him as she is. Bluebeard hymns each of them, and lastly the protesting Judith, as she takes her place among them and fades away.

The libretto was intended first for the composer Kodály. It is hard to believe that his gentler muse could have charged the schematic action with the intensity of Bartók's score, which tingles with suppressed violence. Balázs imagined no mere pageant: though the Doors are the nodes of the opera, the linking dialogue – which supplies the close-ups that fix the perspective of the long shots – contains the immediate dramatic contest. Its ballad style and unvarying metre might have prompted schematic music; instead, Bartók set it as music-drama, alternately stretched, compressed and broken by impassioned orchestral comment. Yet the vocabulary of the singers never loses its folk-inflections – Mussorgsky's *Boris* comes nearer to conventional arias than does *Bluebeard*, which rises vocally only to strophic songs. In discourse its protagonists maintain a kind of distancing decorum, and what they cannot utter is shrieked aloud by the orchestra. One result of this is that literary 'interpretations' of the opera – assigning it a didactic point, or moral – can only be attempts to capture the extra-verbal force of the operatic action. Is Bluebeard's final eulogy of Judith a valediction, and if so why? What *happens* is that he sings a radiant apostrophe (the fourth verse of a song, with a new last line and an orchestral peroration that Bartók added in his second draft), and as Judith vanishes through the Seventh Door the orchestra howls a version of her suspicion-music over a shattering B-flat pedal. Why should this be so moving?

Since the power of virtually every passage of *Bluebeard* derives from its exact location in the dramatic trajectory, the opera does not lend itself to recording in excerpts. (Someone did exclaim excitedly after a Boulez concert performance, 'They ought to release the Fifth Door as a single!') The highlights of the principal roles cannot be detached from their contexts, and anyway they would seem monochrome – the histrionic range of the parts is parcelled out over the whole opera. The folk-based vocal writing is uniformly modal and rhythmic; at climactic moments it is simply higher and louder.

Bluebeard is not a true bass role, though the character, sealed and saturnine, invites a bass quality, and Bartók sanctioned numerous alterations to make the role accessible to the bass Mihály Székely. The basic range of the part is from a low A to a high E, stretching to a top E sharp at the Fourth Door (the tessitura of the writing rises steadily from the beginning to that point); there are a very few passing, unemphasized low A flats and Gs, and the printed score offers an optional low F sharp in Bluebeard's first phrase – which everybody takes. The effect of the Székely adaptation is better heard in his 1956 recording with Ferencsik, where the weight and dignity of his performance is sufficient justification. (Much historical interest attaches to that recording, with another seasoned artist, Klára Palánkay, offering a heroine who sounds much lighter, more lyrical and clear-voiced than most modern Judiths. Ferencsik's faithful account of the score, slightly cut, is frugal with dramatic pauses and rather dully recorded.) Székely's performance with Dorati and Olga Szönyi was much less happy: the orchestral music was rushed and casual, Székely was no longer equal to the Fifth Door declamation and a rising squall afflicted Szönyi. In general, the nearer the true centre of a Bluebeard's voice is to bass territory, the more likely he is to sound overwrought – too vulnerable too soon – in the higher reaches at the Fourth and Fifth Doors. In just that respect there is a striking difference between Fischer-Dieskau's first assumption of the role for Fricsay and his recording in Hungarian – twenty years later, when the voice has naturally darkened – with Wolfgang Sawallisch.

The role of Judith is in its own terms more taxing. She is a mezzo-soprano with a top A for her terrors before the Seventh Door, and more forceful lower-register singing than Bluebeard has to muster. As the Fifth Door opens she screams briefly on high C, which is just what Katalin Kasza does in Ferencsik's 1971 recording. Most other Judiths cannot resist showing off the note at length, and it sounds like a triumphant Brünnhilde-greeting. A grave misreading: Judith has just been in elevated raptures over the Fourth Door garden, and Bluebeard has pressed her urgently to open the next door – but she is dazzled and cowed by the worldly splendour of his kingdom, as her broken responses (*piano* and *senza espressione* in a new flat key) to his proud exultation (pages of blazing major triads) show immediately. The telling effect is unaccountably thrown away by Rosalind Elias, Ormandy's otherwise sensitive Judith, who replies to Bluebeard here in firm, confident tones. She is recorded very close up, which emphasizes the toll her over-careful diction takes of lyrical phrases throughout. She and her excellent Bluebeard –

Jerome Hines, the most imposing bass in the role – sing in American, with the usual foreign disadvantages, but Ormandy secures a swift, vital performance, notably well played by the Philadelphia Orchestra.

There is every reason why Judith should sound young, and she needs a sharply focused attack in sustained high passages – just where Slav sopranos tend to have a rasping edge (like Rozhdestvensky's Polyakova) and Western ones to blot their pitch (like Fricsay's Hertha Töpper, though in her better range she is acutely sympathetic). On the other hand, she needs controlled power for all the low-lying recitative; and Bartók increased the hazards of the part by writing some rising outbursts right across the 'break' that threatens in many a mezzo voice. The modal shapes of the vocal line generally imply their own harmony (often they are just broken chords), sometimes confirmed by the orchestra, often poignantly enriched – and occasionally contradicted: a minor third in the voice, for example, against a major third in the orchestra. Distinct accuracy in passages of the latter sort brings expressive rewards, but is rare. Even István Kertesz's Christa Ludwig, an unfailingly vivid Judith, lets her pitch spread enough to compromise with the orchestra at some such moments. It is an enthusiastic fault which she shares with her Bluebeard, her then husband Walter Berry – but they play to each other so brilliantly as to earn special esteem: many Judiths and Bluebeards sound like cautious strangers to each other, and that is not what the opera is about.

Sawallisch's Julia Varady begins by offering beautifully intelligent singing, plausibly youthful, but later she draws so often upon a hard chest-register that her Judith comes to seem a formidable harridan. That is not what the opera is about either. Paired with the later Fischer-Dieskau's slightly frantic Bluebeard – impassioned heart on sleeve from the start, and liable to go sharp under pressure – she adds fortuitous overtones to the story despite Sawallisch's strong, objective account of the score. Solti's Sylvia Sass brings so much sophisticated intensity and refined wilfulness to her Judith that the folk-inflections of the part begin to sound false, though her performance grips the attention. Solti's Bluebeard – scarcely in contact with her – is Kolos Kováts, sonorously moving at the grand moments, opaque of pitch elsewhere. For Boulez, Tatiana Troyanos is seductively lovely, and with Siegmund Nimsgern – too bland at first but soon stronger, ringing out arrestingly at the Fifth Door – she makes uniquely good musical sense of the anti-duet at the Seventh Door. That is one of several passages more often 'acted' than sung, with a sacrifice of real operatic effect.

In the long run – and what else are records for but long acquaintance? – musical accuracy in *Duke Bluebeard's Castle* reaps dividends. Not only did Bartók take enormous pains with the word-setting, but he flagged the whole score characteristically and obsessively with metronome marks. Though the circumstances of performance may justify departures from numerical fidelity, relative proportions are of the utmost importance. (That is why cuts – even of seeming repetitions – are a serious matter, liable to upset calculated dramatic weightings. Fricsay's finely idiomatic performance – in German though it is, with Dieskau's first powerful Bluebeard – suffers more than a dozen cuts; the recent Rozhdestvensky version in Russian copies most of those cuts, and makes several more.) The Sixth Door, for example – the vista of unassuageable grief – is marked deadly slow: the music must seem to stop for a long time. The effect of shock is much reduced by both Kertesz and Solti, who hurry through the music, though Bartók kept it sufficiently eventful by cunning foreshortenings of its repeated hopeless waves. Kertesz also allows Christa Ludwig to be vociferously emotional here despite the *sempre pp* direction. Myths should be enacted by the book, not on subjective impulses.

Since the score is frankly sectional, Bartók took care to specify each transition: sometimes there is a *poco ritardando*, sometimes a pause marked *breve*, rarely a big dramatic hiatus. In the old Susskind recording they are all too piously recognized, and with Judith Hellwig's tame, passive Judith the result lacks any theatrical impetus. (The orchestral music is sensitively shaped, but weak in ensemble.) Solti too seems to present a series of panels, though in far more sumptuous sound; a generalized majestic intensity obscures the sharp profile of the action. So far as the main sections go, Boulez observes the due proportions rigorously, as might have been expected; but he is indulgent to his singers in recitative, and the earlier proceedings are excessively stately. (Like Kertesz, he holds the First Door to the right macabre tempo where other conductors rush excitedly – and lose the brightening effect of the Second Door; but Boulez allows the music before and after the First Door to droop.) The pacing of Sawallisch's account is virtually unerring: if only Dieskau and Varady were less indecorously melodramatic!

Obviously the sheer aural impact of the score matters – the Fifth Door ought fairly to knock one down. (With inspired restraint, Bartók recalls his supernumerary organ only one more time, to reinforce the final climax and to add four bars of numbly drifting postlude: there, Rozhdestvensky's organ is ruinously loud.) Still, orchestral virtuosity is not a prerequisite. Certainly Bartók borrowed Impressionist devices for the Door setpieces (and beyond: he had just discovered Debussy, and the last *Bluebeard* climax invokes the final surge of *La Mer*), but otherwise his orchestration is pungently plain. As in Janáček's operas, the wordless commentary less often illustrates the feelings of the principals than it conveys the meaning of their situation: consider the long *ostinato* churning before Judith descries the seven doors, the pointed clarinet solo when she spots the blood on the walls, the hopeful but failing dance while Bluebeard tries to persuade her to rest content with five open doors. In such places degrees of orchestral conviction loom large. There is no Hungarian snap in Solti's first clarinet, for example, which makes it less telling; with Kertesz, the accented string flourishes do not have a unanimous panache.

For its scrupulous representation of the operatic action, I prefer Ferencsik's 1971 recording. Occasionally it moves faster than Bartók prescribed – but

Bartók's markings were for stage performance, where things take longer to speak. The broad operatic proportions are preserved. If György Melis makes an uncommonly youthful Bluebeard, he has the advantage that the role lies perfectly for his voice. And Katalin Kasza is Judith to the life: nervily eager, selflessly intense. She is as precise with her music as any Judith (more than most), and she commands an astringent lower register, without any throaty bark or adipose richness. By comparison Christa Ludwig's Judith sounds almost maternal, too sympathetic and cuddlesome: how could she prosecute such a dangerous inquiry? The immediate pathos of the Kertesz *Bluebeard* reduces the objective dimension; Solti and Boulez, in their different ways, are hieratic at the expense of dramatic urgency and contrast. Theirs are distinguished performances, but Ferencsik strikes a true balance.

So he does on the recent Hungaroton recording (1982), and in brilliant digital reproduction. There is a glorious blaze for the Fifth Door; the wind-playing, a keen musical pleasure in itself, is beautifully captured. Yevgeny Nesterenko's Bluebeard is just about as good as one had hoped: severely formal in the early stages, he is also a bit cavalier about exact pitch, but the character develops with magnificent authority and commitment. The debatable element is Obraztsova's Judith. Unmistakably – and, as I think, inappropriately – a stentorian virago from the start, she does project self-doubt and tragedy with subtlety as well as power. If you can accept a Judith of such daunting maturity, you will also find that she strikes hard dramatic truth at important places. In all other respects, the performance is uncontroversially excellent.

There remains the echo, prescribed in the score but vexatiously difficult to realize, like the distant snapping-string sound in Chekhov's *Cherry Orchard*. Various recordings omit one or another of its occurrences; it should be heard, 'a cavernous sighing, as when the night wind sighs down endless, gloomy labyrinths' when Judith hammers upon the First Door, and again as she turns the key, and lastly at the Sixth Door. Surely what is needed is a distant soughing that might just be a disconsolate moan (perhaps the souls of the jury who rejected *Bluebeard* in a national opera competition as 'unperformable'). Ormandy has a hurricane-blast, Rozhdestvensky a remote avalanche, Dorati eerie wind-chimes, Susskind something that might be a prowling cat. Other recording engineers settle for an obvious amalgam of stiff breezes and sighing ladies. If there is ever to be an ideal recorded *Bluebeard*, it will do better.

Meanwhile, to have *Bluebeard* on record is at least to be spared the whims of producers. Balázs plainly envisaged the Doors as striking visual events, and assumed a broad gestural style for his principals; so much is essential, and it is enough. Stage producers who contrive less than that, or much more, or something entirely different, turn this potently suggestive work back into an 'ideal gramophone opera'.

DUKE BLUEBEARD'S CASTLE

B Bluebeard; *J* Judith

1953 (in German)
Sönnerstedt *B*; Nilsson *J* /
Swedish RSO / Fricsay
SR ⓜ SRLP 1377
1953 (in German)
Wiener *B*; Steingruber *J* / Vienna
SO / Häfner
Vox ⓜ OPL 100
1955 (in Hungarian – with prologue)
Koréh *B*; Hellwig *J* / LSO /
Susskind
Bartok Recording Soc ⓜ BRS
310–1
1956 (in Hungarian)
Székély *B*; Palánkay *J* / Budapest
Opera Orch / Ferencsik
Hungaroton ⓜ LPX 11001
1959 (in German-abridged)
Fischer-Dieskau *B*; Töpper *J* /
Berlin Radio SO / Fricsay
DG 2535 703
1962 (in English)
Hines *B*; Elias *J* / Philadelphia
Orch / Ormandy
CBS (UK) 72121
CBS (US) MS 6425
1962 (in Hungarian)
Székély *B*; Szönyi *J* / LSO /
Dorati
Philips 6768 600
Mercury (US) SR13–77012
1965 (in Hungarian)
Berry *B*; Ludwig *J* / LSO /

Kertesz
Decca SET 311
London OSA 1158
1971 (in Hungarian)
Melis *B*; Kasza *J* / Budapest
PO / Ferencsik
Hungaroton SLPX 11486
c.1972 (in Russian – abridged)
Kibkalo *B*; Polyàkova *J* /
Moscow Radio SO /
Rozhdestvensky
Melodiya S 01139/40
Westminster (US) WGS 8219
1976 (in Hungarian)
Nimsgern *B*; Troyanos *J* / BBC
SO / Boulez
CBS (UK) 76518
(US) M-34217
1979 (in Hungarian – with prologue)
Kováts *B*; Sass *J* / LPO / Solti
Decca SET 620
London OSA 1174
1979 (in Hungarian)
Fischer-Dieskau *B*; Varady *J*
/Bavarian State Orch /
Sawallisch
DG 2531 172
1982 (in Hungarian)
Nesterenko *B*; Obraztsova *J* /
B / Hungarian State Opera
Orch. / Ferencsik
Hungaroton SLPD 12254
CD HCD12254

Porgy and Bess

JOHN STEANE

Not a show, not a musical, not any sort of hyphenated breed (light opera, jazz or folk), but plainly and emphatically opera, to be approached and performed like other operatic masterpieces. That was the avowed creed of Lorin Maazel, conductor of the recording which first did proper justice to Gershwin's score. 'How glorious it is to hear the entire opera, without the dozens of cuts which have mutilated form, flow and dramatic tension.' Maazel again – writing his own review, one might object; but of course what he says is no more than the truth. Such an approach does not unify disparate elements or minimize their effect; ultimately it probably exposes more clearly the extent to which the masterpiece is flawed. Yet it reveals in its application a wealth of musical detail commonly obliterated by the broad sweep of melody and the potency of rhythms; and with the respect for craftsmanship that this induces come also renewed and greatly strengthened emotions. *Porgy and Bess* can be moving, almost alarmingly so, in a way that is all its own, a way that is none the less in its essentials generically that of grand opera.

The Maazel recording appeared in 1976, and just over a year later came a second version, also complete and highly competent. This was based on a stage production by the Houston Grand Opera which toured the United States and made the recording during its run in New York. The conductor, John DeMain, was working with good musicians, but comparisons confirm the superiority of Maazel's Cleveland Orchestra, and on balance that of his soloists too, which is, perhaps, as one would expect. In compensation it might be thought that the background of a live production would give to the Houston Company's recording some additional quality of vividness and authenticity. Vivid it certainly is, vigorous too, yet, oddly, it does not emerge as the more moving performance; on the contrary, the Maazel recording, in my experience, makes a notably deeper emotional impression even though it is entirely a studio production. This is exceptional. One often finds that an operatic recording made not necessarily live from the stage but during the course of performances by a company carries most conviction and makes the strongest impact. Here it is as though the reverse has happened. The stage company goes into routine and records the excellent show that has won applause during a long run. In the studio, with Maazel, the singers and players assembled with the sole purpose of making the recording have been touched afresh.

It is as though the conductor had said to them: 'Forget that you have ever heard "Summertime" or "I got plenty o' nothin'". Pretend it's *Káťa Kabanová* or *Pelléas* or something by Monteverdi that you are learning from scratch. Start from nothing and work it into your bones from there. *Listen* to it!' Whatever the origins and processes, the upshot is a performance of genuine creativity, all the more moving to the listener because of its relative innocence of mere routine among the artists.

Both recordings are strongly cast. With Maazel, Willard White sings Porgy with quite exceptional beauty of tone. His is a richly resonant, free-throated baritone, and the part suits him ideally. The Houston production has a deeper and possibly more powerful voice in Donnie Ray Albert. The bass-baritone quality detracts somewhat from the appropriateness of the voice; this is a heavier character, the voice less that of a lover, less of a humorist too. His performance as recorded (that needs stressing, for the impression created by his stage presence may have been quite different) is most apt in serious passages like the 'Buzzard' song or phrases like 'Night time, day time he got to travel that lonesome road' where he sings with breadth and nobility. The high notes of the 'Buzzard' song seem none too easy for him to sing with freedom and resonance, but the main limitation is that the buoyancy of spirits and sense of fun, so keen in Willard White's performance (compare, for instance, their singing of 'I got plenty of nothin'), are dulled or rather heavily weighted in Donnie Ray Albert's. The balance is restored a little by the Houston company's Bess. This is Clamma Dale who sets up a bold characterization and has a firmer voice than Leona Mitchell's in the Maazel recording. She also dramatizes vividly in the scene with Crown, acting out the dilemma, sensitive (as is Mitchell too) to the way in which the traitor is within the gates (the tone of that long half-yielding 'Oh' before 'What you want wid Bess' betrays it).

In most of the supporting roles Maazel's cast is the stronger. The opera needs two other good singers among the women; of the two solos that need most singing, one ('Summertime') is sung by Clara, the other ('My man's gone now') by Serena. Maazel has the excellent Barbara Hendricks as Clara, her high, clear tones rising with all due poise, delicacy and tenderness in that inspired opening Lullaby. Her opposite number, Betty Lane, has a less pure, even line, though hers too is a tender, warmly felt performance. The Houston Serena, Wilma Shakesnider, brings plenty of intensity to her role, and, in kind, her voice is not unlike Maazel's singer, Florence Quivar, but again it is with the latter that the finer quality is found. Maazel also has a better singer as Jake (quite an important part, with 'A woman is a sometime thing' for solo). And his Crown, McHenry Boatwright, gives the part a formidable brutality only fitfully present with Andrew Smith of the Houston company. This leaves the crucial character of Sportin' Life, crucial because he comes nearest to belonging to the world of the musical rather that to that of opera.

Here again the Maazel recording scores. Where the Houston Sportin' Life, Larry Marshall, brazens everything out with a harsh voice and much under-lining (shouting 'Sermon' for instance in 'I'm preachin' this sermon to show'), Maazel's François Clemmons brings not only a subtler, insinuating humour and snakyness, but also a genuine singing voice, used in just about the right proportion along with the 'character' voice. It should be added that among the minor parts Maazel has a most sympathetic Robbins (Samuel Hagan) and DeMain's Houston company a truly magnificent Maria in Carol Brice.

Once inside the recording studios, DeMain's singers certainly gave a complete performance. Their stage producer, Sherwin Goldman, no doubt deserves a great share of the credit. Thomas Z. Shepard, who produced the recording, pays tribute to the stage performances as having turned his own 'idealized' conception of *Porgy* into 'amazing reality'. The recording, he says, was completed in 'three incredibly intense days'. The handling of the crowd scenes is particularly successful. Settling down to the crap game, climbing stairs, throwing money in for the saucer-burial, picnicking on Kattiwah Island – the crowd is always there, vivid to the ear as it would be to the eye on stage. As the storm breaks the wind batters and screams, and its howling affords a well-devised mode of continuity between scenes. The detective prowls truculently in Catfish Row, Crown kills Robbins, Porgy kills Crown, and the sound is always effectively produced to call the scene to mind as though in a film. Musically too there are imaginative strokes, such as the powerful *crescendo* of voices reiterating the primitive 'wa-do-wa' figure in the overture.

Why then should the Maazel recording, in this writer's experience, have been the more moving? As suggested, it is partly because of a better quality (on balance) of voice and solo performance. It might also have to do with the nature of the recorded sound, the RCA (DeMain) recording being brighter, the Decca (Maazel) more kindly, less strident. The fact that Maazel was working with one of the great orchestras of the world contributed too. Yet none of this completely accounts for it. From the start the Maazel performance has a greater tautness, a way too of exercising restraint that generates more electricity, more excitement. For instance, though the *crescendo* on the 'wa-do-wa's' is bigger, more extreme, in the other recording, it registers as effective only in a crude way. Excitement lies in expectancy; noise tends to be not expectant but climactic. In the interest of sustained excitement, noise has to be restrained. That, I think, is why there is a magical quality in the Maazel recording at the start of the last chorus in Act 1 ('O we're leavin' for the promised land'); the syncopations, the addition of the piano to the orchestral texture, all the real skills of Gershwin's writing are made audible rather than being subsumed in a more generalized mass of loud sound. Similarly 'Oh I can't sit down' (finale of Act 2) bursts out with a brassier, more exciting sound in the DeMain Houston recording, but the truer rhythmic vitality is with Maazel, subtler in his means and essentially more attentive and respectful to the details of the score. Ultimately the explanation lies here, and we return to the basic view of the work – 'as an opera, as one worthy of the same care and devotion we would have accorded any operatic masterpiece'.

Another 'complete' recording existed before these – that is, a version with the kind of cuts referred to by Maazel but still presenting the opera as a whole rather than in extracts. It omits, for example, the Jasbo Brown piano music at the beginning, going straight from the introduction into 'Summertime' – a procedure which Todd Duncan, the original Porgy, reports Gershwin as readily sanctioning. This 1951 recording cannot compete with the later ones in clarity, and its voices are too near the microphone for a satisfactory balance. Yet the production, by Goddard Lieberson, is lively; the performance, under Lehmann Engel, carries conviction; and there is some attractive solo work. Lawrence Winters's Porgy is human, unexaggerated, and warmly sung, making a strong effect in the last scene. Camilla Williams as Bess does well in the scene with Crown, who sings his 'Redheaded woman' with the right kind of raw energy. Sportin' Life is Avon Long, famous in the role over many years (his appearance in New York in 1965 was described in *Opera* as 'a model of voiceless resourcefulness'). 'It ain't necessarily so' has just a few too many falsettos, but in its variety and sense of fun is superb. For many years this recording represented Gershwin's work as a whole amid a mound of bits and pieces: by no means an unworthy representation either.

That mound of extracts has in it much that belongs to the scrapheap (certainly from the point of view, I daresay, of most readers of this book), but it is worth raking through, all the same. The soundtrack of the Sam Goldwyn film, for example, deserves to be salvaged. For one thing it has the voice of Cab Calloway as Sportin' Life, possibly the most famous of all stage portrayals of the role. On the screen Sammy Davis Jnr appeared in the part (while Calloway sang), and the two artists matched ideally. 'It ain't necessarily so', always a *tour de force* with Calloway, has a marvellous succession of tones and facial expressions, all innocence one minute, reptilian insinuation the next. Sometimes he went over the top. A recording from 1953, included in A Collector's 'Porgy and Bess' (RCA AVMI 1742), is meaner than ever, with a big macho Goliath voice and a ga-ga Methuselah, a wideeyed tell-it-to-the-kiddies act for Jonah and the whale, a babel of extra 'Zim bam boodle-oo's: brilliant indeed but possibly a 'diddly-bab' or 'scatty-wa' too many. In the filmtrack he has the balance right: still giving the feeling of inspired improvisation but a touch more disciplined. In his other main solo, 'There's a boat that's leavin' soon for New York', many are the unforgettable touches ('sistah' insultingly breathed out), and the timing is expert. That is typical of the whole soundtrack: an exactness of dramatic effect, a way of making the voices as visual as sound can ever be, it all contributes towards an unusually evocative recording. It is interesting that the vibrant, operatic type of female voice has been avoided and, instead, tones nearer to a taste in pop music have been used. The score has been much adapted but pleasingly so, as indeed might be expected with André Previn in charge.

Two other highlights records deserve a place on the shelves, partly on their own merits, partly because both have a close historical connection with the first performances of all, those of 1935. One of them features the original principals, Anne Brown and Todd Duncan, with their conductor Alexander Smallens and the Eve Jessye Choir. Anne Brown differs from most subsequent singers in the role of Bess: her tone is virginal and her style relatively unimpassioned though never unfeeling. Duncan's voice is not rich but it is true and free, and he has a personal way with everything that is highly attractive. Gershwin's enthusiasm about his discovery of the young Harvard professor needs no justification, but records suggest that he was not quite accurate in describing him as 'another Tibbett'. The 'Buzzard' Song, for instance, wants a darker, more powerful kind of resonance, the kind of tone that Tibbett's own recording does find for it. Yet a spontaneous smile accompanies 'I got plenty o' nothin' '; 'Bess, you is my woman now' is winningly affectionate but not sentimental; and throughout there is strength in his moderation. Another singer from the original production, Edward Matthews, also appears in this record: he sings Jake's solos ('A woman is a sometime thing' and 'It takes a long pull to get there'), impressing with his fine voice and sure style. The choir, too, the soloists in the street cries (Helen Dowdy and William Woolfolk), and Avon Long making a brief but strongly characterized appearance towards the end as Sportin' Life, all add to the pleasure of this historically most authentic of recordings.

The missing link with those first performances turns up in an unlikely place. The Sportin' Life was John W. Bubbles, and when RCA produced a highlights record with Leontyne Price and William Warfield, they sought out this old Vaudeville artist from the once-celebrated double act of Buck and Bubbles, and cast him in his original role, where he triumphs again as he had done in 1935. Price and Warfield of course were, themselves closely associated with the opera. With Cab Calloway they played the leading roles in the historic revival of 1962, the production that opened at the State Fair Auditorium in Dallas and went on to tour the United States, South America and Europe (including the Soviet Union) playing to enthusiastic houses for four years. Price was at the height of her powers at the time when this record was made, and she gives a magnificent performance. There is not only the thrill of a great voice, one of a quality quite beyond that of any other singer so far mentioned in the role, but also a complete involvement in the emotions of the drama and the idiom of the music. Excellent, for instance, is the uninhibited and powerfully acted scene with Crown (McHenry Boatwright again impressive as in the recording with Maazel), and splendid in the soaring vocal line of 'I loves you, Porgy' that can so often sound strained or strident. She also sings the solos of Clara and Serena, with marvellous placing of the high B at the end of 'Summertime' and a fine intensity of lamentation in 'My man's gone now'. Warfield presents a positive, virile Porgy, not exceptionally rich in tone but strong in personality. It is in fact an excellent record quite apart from its claim to historical interest. As for Bubbles, he is superb: a husky, leery voice, smoky and snaky, just sufficiently attractive to be all too credible, and exactly right in the balance of freedom and adherence to the score.

Several of the individual items recorded in earlier times and worth preserving are to be found on the RCA disc called 'A Collector's "Porgy and Bess" ' – original numbers after each item – mentioned earlier. A version of 'Summertime' made in 1946 (Vic. 11–9186) by Eleanor Steber presents the Lullaby as 'straight' as can be; lovely in tone and quite tender in feeling, it is completely devoid of any sort of Negro character. 'My man's gone now', sung by Risë Stevens (7EB 6015), is somewhat similar, the voice being fine, the emotion true enough within limits, but the style basically alien. Robert Merrill has a much more idiomatic approach, singing 'A woman is a sometime thing' and the last scene of the opera with glorious roundness and the voice in full bloom (7EB 6015). These and some other numbers were recorded in 1950 with the Robert Shaw Chorale, that highly expert choir that was always a joy to hear. In this same collection are no solos by Paul Robeson, as there might have been (his rich, tasteful, somewhat undercharacterized perform-ances can be sampled on EMI NTS181). But it does include three items from the famous set made by Lawrence Tibbett and Helen Jepson (DB 2735–8).

That set dates back to a recording session only four days after the first New York performance. On 10 October 1935, *Porgy and Bess* had its first night at the Alvin Theatre, and on the 14 October what we would now call 'highlights' were recorded, with the composer present and Alexander Smal-lens conducting. The singers, however, were not from the stage company but from the Metropolitan Opera. Tibbett was then near the peak of his career, and Jepson's future at that time probably gave promise of a distinction that never quite materialized. At any rate, their participation ensured that the records were issued on 'celebrity' labels, and this in turn no doubt did something for the status of the opera itself. The acoustic is somewhat dry and studio-bound and the recordings are loud. But what should guarantee their survival is the brilliance of Tibbett's singing. Jepson's voice is firm and fresh and she is always competent, but there is nothing special there. Tibbett, however, is astonishing. Of course he had the relevant experience of working in *Emperor Jones,* in which his achievement was reckoned by some to compare with the great roles of Chaliapin. His feeling for the idiom, for rhythm and colour, is marvellously sure; his presence and concentration are immensely commanding, and the voice itself is magnificent. His handling of the melody in 'Bess, you is my woman now', his intensity in the 'Buzzard' Song, and his resonant, full-bodied and fully characterized performance of 'It ain't necessarily so' remain among his best work for the gramophone, and they are probably still the best pieces of singing among the men in the whole of the opera's history on records.

That history would be incomplete without two further additions. One is a recording from before that New York première, with Gershwin himself conducting a number of passages, announcing them and giving the orchestra its score references as at a rehearsal. The date is 10 July 1935, and the recording was discovered and transferred to LP only recently (Mark 56 667). Gershwin also plays the piano and even fills in as vocalist with a few 'Da-doo-da's'. So, with all of this and the presence of Anne Brown, Todd Duncan, Edward Matthews and the original Serena, Ruby Elzie, expectation runs high. In fact, I found it a trifle disappointing. Gershwin does not really rehearse (a working rehearsal would have been fascinating); his tempi and style strike one as relaxed almost to the point of sounding lazy; and, apart from an attractive performance by Matthews, the singing has no special merit.

The other addition to this account must be a brief and selective survey of the many guises in which the music has appeared, for it has proved itself almost infinitely adaptable. One might expect that listening to arrangements of 'Summertime' and so forth, one after another, would rank in memory as among the torments of the damned. But it ain't necessarily so. Least pleasure, to my mind, is afforded by the kind of superficial modern gloss given the score by such arrangers as Lorenzo Fuller, who conducts highlights on MFP 1154. Some verbal interpolations struck me indeed as insufferable. Bobby Richards's arrangements in another highlights record with Kenneth Alwyn conducting (WRC ST61) are less objectionable; even so the conventional orchestrations suggestive of glossy 'showbiz' jazz bands in expensive holiday hotels go far to cancel the pleasure of Lawrence Winters's well-sung Porgy and Ray Ellington's gravelly Sportin' Life. Better, and sometimes attractive, are the arrangements by Lennie Hayton and Robert Corman for Lena Horne and Harry Belafonte (RCA SF 5039). 'A woman is a sometime thing' turns into slow jazz, with a big band brass sound flashing out while Belafonte plays characteristic tricks with his voice; and an independent off-key accompaniment sophisticates 'I got plenty o' nothin' ' not quite beyond recognition. In the street cries, with chorus and a Jamaican complexion for the Honeyman, the record becomes distinctly enjoyable.

Arrangements for famous popular singers abound. Best of those I have heard is a two-record album (on Verve) by Ella Fitzgerald and Louis Armstrong. 'Summertime' begins as a trumpet solo, then comes a supple, low-voiced verse by Ella, with Louis Armstrong taking it up, slow and lazy, at 'One of these mornin's'. Finally a decorated verse with a murmuring accompaniment of charming nonsense, all ending with lots of 'Don't you cry's. There's magic here. 'I loves you, Porgy' is velvet, 'Oh where's my Bess' weeps unaffectedly, 'I got plenty o' nothin' ' grins irresistibly. Everything has a new look and yet nothing seems false to the originals; in fact I would say the record tells with great sincerity of love for them. There is style, too, if perhaps less humanity, in a record by Cleo Laine and Ray Charles (London 31D2). Inventive arrangements by Frank DeVol keep one listening closely, and both of the artists have such apparently endless resources to draw on that at very least the record is bound to intrigue. So too with some of the arrangements by the André Previn Trio, with Diahann Carroll as the singer (London LTZ T15165), made in 1959. With this, it is altogether easier to stop listening after a while, though there is clever playing and accomplished singing of its kind. The Swingle Singers also perform all sorts of ingenuities, rhythmical, tonal and contrapuntal (Philips 6311 007). Yet after all these, with their manifold sophistications, I'd return much more willingly to Pearl Bailey (SEG 7913). She knows instinctively how to loosen up the written notes and shake them free. And if she wants to add a verbal interpolation ('Yes, but boys let me tell you . . . A woman is a sometime thing') she will get it right.

Among purely instrumental arrangements, one might perhaps turn first to the selections played by Heifetz, with Emmanuel Bey, on Brunswick LAT 8066. The technical miracles are nearly always expressive, even to the point of producing Cab Calloway tone for Sportin' Life's solos. I daresay one would not return to the record all that often, even so. The playing that really does strike me as being a long-term pleasure is that of Oscar Peterson and Joe Pass in a duet-record with an unusual history (Pablo Super 2310 779). On one of Peterson's British television shows, Edward Heath appeared with his clavichord. This fascinated Peterson so much that he acquired one himself and used it in this delightful combination with Joe Pass's unamplified guitar. Their treatment of the material from *Porgy and Bess* (occupying both sides of the record, about an hour's worth of music) impresses as sensitive and strong, creative and disciplined. It is surely a token of Gershwin's strength that his music stimulates so much inventiveness in adaptation.

We have ended up remote, it might seem, from the opera and from Maazel's statement, so single-minded and simple in formulation '*Porgy and Bess* is an opera', and one which he and his company approached 'as we would . . . any operatic masterpiece'. The essential rightness of this is manifest, yet the whole truth may not be quite so simple after all. *Porgy* represents a wonderfully successful working agreement between the expressive modes of one culture and the artistic forms of another. Part of its unique character also lies in its links with the world of popular music: that it brings into the index of this book, for instance, such names as Ella Fitzgerald and Louis Armstrong. Their dealings with it go far from the letter of the score. They may not be so remote from its spirit, however, and if a day should come when *Porgy* becomes *simply* 'an opera' and loses its links with the more popular culture then part of its unique character will be lost too.

PORGY AND BESS

P Porgy; *C* Crown; *B* Bess; *Cl* Clara; *SL* Sportin' Life; *SW* Strawberry Woman; *Ser* Serena; *J* Jake

1951 Winters *P*; Coleman *C*; Williams *B*; McMechen *Cl*; Long *SL*; Dowdy *SW*; I. Matthews *Ser*; E. Matthews *J* / J. Rosamond Johnson Chorus, orch. / Engel
CBS (UK) (e) 77319
(US) 32360018E

early Tormé *P*; Hartman *C*; Faye
1950s *B;* Roché *Cl*; Kirby *SL*; Norman *SW*; Blair *Ser*; Rosolino *J* / Bethlehem Chorus and Orch. / Garcia (arr. and cond.) + Duke Ellington and his Orch.; Australian Jazz Quintet; Pat Moran Quintet; Stan Levey Group
Bethlehem (e) EXLP1

Ember (e) CEI 900

1976 White *P*; Boatwright *C*; Mitchell *B*; Hendricks *Cl*; Clemmons *SL*; B. Conrad *SW*; Quivar *Ser*; Thompson *J* / Cleveland Orch., Chorus and Children's Chorus / Maazel
Decca SET 609–611 ④ K3Q28
London OSA 13116④ OSA 5-13116

1976 Albert *P*; A. Smith *C*; Dale *B*; Lane *Cl*; Marshall *SL*; Bash *SW*; Shakesnider *Ser*; Smalls *J* / Houston Grand Opera Orch. and Ens / DeMain
RCA (UK) RL 02109 ④ RK 02109
(US) ARL 3–2109④ ARK 3–2109

The Stage Works of Weill

RODNEY MILNES

'I have never acknowledged the difference between "serious" music and "light" music. There is only good music and bad music.'
    Kurt Weill, in an interview in the *New York Sun*, 3 February 1940

Despite that disarming quote, so oddly reminiscent of Oscar Wilde on trial, the case of Weill – against him as well as for him – remains not proven. Appreciation of his music was interrupted, as was his own creative life, by the Nazi tyranny and the worldwide upheaval that it caused; critical reassessment after his tragically early death from a heart attack in 1950 (he was only as old as the century) started in a Europe that had hardly heard his music for twenty years, and critics in the old world saw a prodigiously gifted composer who, driven from his native land, sold his talent to mammon much as Korngold did. 'He was very interested in money . . . he got too involved in American show business and all the terrible people in it,' remarked Otto Klemperer. To which one must say that Klemperer, whose rejection of *Mahagonny* at the Kroll Opera must have made Weill's precipitate flight from Berlin in 1933 less professionally disruptive than it might otherwise have been, can have had no idea of the sort of people Weill worked with in America: they were very similar to his German collaborators – for the most part radical and committed intellectuals. And it must be said that Korngold's talent, miniscule in comparison to Weill's, only really flowered once he was safely ensconced in the studios of Warner Bros.

In the last decade such received critical opinions have taken a beating; there are those who would say that Weill's talent flowered only when he reached America. Weill scholarship is now firmly based in the United States, in the Kurt Weill Foundation at Yale and the Weill/Lenya research centre in New York; the two major biographies to date are by Americans; and the British musicologist David Drew, whose own book is eagerly awaited, has always flown in the teeth of European opinion, refused to acknowledge the conflict between an American Weill and a German Weill, and insisted on judging his work as a whole. Whereas twenty years ago, available records were almost entirely of Weill's German music, reissues of contemporary versions of his American scores have now been joined by new recordings of hitherto unavailable material: it is much easier for interested amateurs to see for themselves whether or not there are two Weills, one superior, one inferior. Having listened far and wide in preparation for what follows, this particular interested amateur believes firmly that there is only one, and that his genius is beyond dispute.

Weill's early music was naturally influenced by his teachers – by the neoclassical Busoni more than the conservative Humperdinck, though the latter's gentle lyricism may be glimpsed later – and by the *Zeitgeist* of the 1920s, but once he started writing for the commercial as well as the subsidized theatre, with or without Brecht, he blended neoclassicism with the popular song and dance idioms of the day, using European folk music much as Haydn did. That has been considered respectable by Europeans. But his use of popular American idioms was considered less respectable, save by Americans themselves, who are in a better position to judge what use he made of those idioms.

'It seems to me,' wrote Weill to the American critic Olin Downes in 1949, 'that the American popular song, growing out of American folk music, is the basis of the American musical theatre (just as the Italian song was the basis of Italian opera), and that in this early stage of the development, and considering the audiences we are writing for, it is quite legitimate to use the form of the popular song and gradually fill it out with new musical content.' That opinion, which would make as much sense with 'German' substituted for 'American' throughout and with the date 1929, points to the bewildering range and steady development of Weill's US output, which was by no means simply a string of concocted Broadway musicals: there were indeed some such, like the Cole Porter-ish *One Touch of Venus,* but there were also radical protest theatre pieces (*Johnny Johnson*), political satires (*Knickerbocker Holiday*), urban folk operas (*Street Scene*) and knockabout Hollywood film scores (*Where Do We Go From Here?*), and the musical content varied depending on time and place.

Weill carefully considered the audiences he was writing for, both in Germany and America. In the *New York Sun* interview quoted at the beginning, he continued: 'Schoenberg has said he is writing for a time fifty years after his death. But the great classical composers wrote for their contemporary audiences. They wanted those who heard their music to understand it, and they did. For myself, I write for today. I don't give a damn about writing for posterity.'

Therein is the nub of the Weill case. Will a posterity that recognizes Schoenberg's genius nearly fifty years after his death, one that is also prepared to recognize Mahler's (which it wasn't all too recently), reject Weill because he didn't give a damn for it? Today the answer is emphatically 'no', especially among those music- and theatre-lovers who as well as listening patiently to the latest posterity-orientated opera are inclined to go to a Sondheim musical. The irony is that, while Weill judged how much musical content his audiences could take without any commercial cynicism (few of his American works were smash-hits), posterity thus far is beginning to appreciate his music more warmly than his contemporaries did. Just what the climate will be in a hundred years' time I hesitate to guess. What will the relative status of Schoenberg and Mahler be, of Stravinsky and Weill, of Strauss and Berg, of Britten and Tippett? Who knows, but a man who could write two such perfect tunes as the 'Morität' from *Dreigroschenoper* and September Song from *Knickerbocker Holiday* is assured of immortality at one level, and one of the joys of investigating the American Weill is to discover that these are not isolated examples.

What follows is by no means a complete Weill discography – geographical considerations (much material is available only in the USA), the capricious reissuing policy of commercial record companies, and the fact that we are concerned only with the stage works preclude that, but readers are referred to the admirably comprehensive appendices of Ronald Sanders's *The Days Grow Short: the Life and Music of Kurt Weill**. Except in the case of *Dreigroschenoper,* there is little in the way of detailed comparison to be made, and this must be a survey of what has been available on record over the last twenty years or so. In the belief that most people are familiar with the German works, I will emphasize the American music, much of it still unknown here, hoping that the voyage of discovery will be as fascinating and rewarding to readers as it has been to me. Much material is to be found on recital discs, and in order to prevent the text becoming clogged with endlessly repeated record numbers, a list of collections and recitals is added to the discography.

The most serious gap in the recorded legacy concerns the pre-*Dreigroschenoper* works: nothing of *Royal Palace* (1927), nothing of *Der Zar lässt sich photographieren* (1928), and only a brief extract from *Der Protagonist* (1926) on the excellent London Sinfonietta set. This study of reality and fantasy to a libretto by the expressionist dramatist Georg Kaiser – a sort of *Pagliacci* for grown-ups – was premièred under Fritz Busch at the Dresden State Opera and demands stage revival. It deals with a troupe of Elizabethan players who act to order the same mime drama, once as farce and once as tragedy: 'Pantomime I' is the farce, played by a wind band of eight on stage. Theme, nine variations and finale (tempo di cancan), this is Weill at his most Hindemithian, atonal, neoclassical and dry. It is punchily played by the Sinfonietta, with the soloists occasionally bursting out of mime with explosive consonants, vocalises and even the odd word.

Two songs from this period should be noted: 'Muschel von Margate', the only surviving number from the incidental music to *Der Konjunctur* by Leo Lania (1927), and 'Das Lied von dem braunen Insel' from Feuchtwanger's *Die Petroleuminsel* (1928). Both works are epic-theatre assaults on international capitalism, the former directed by Piscator, and the two songs are on Teresa Stratas's recital record, fervently, perhaps too fervently sung.

* Weidenfeld and Nicolson, London, 1980.

'Muschel' is a characteristically perky pop song with the refrain 'Shell, Shell, Shell' and deserves immortality; the other Weill could have written in his sleep, and doesn't. Stratas's aptly titled album, incidentally, is a treasure trove of lost songs.

DIE DREIGROSCHENOPER
The Threepenny Opera

There are two interconnected points about *The Threepenny Opera* (1928). First, it is meant to be funny, a fine example of subversion via comedy. Secondly, like its source, *The Beggar's Opera* it is a trenchant satire on middle-class (or in the case of Gay's original, ruling-class) values. Productions of both works are almost invariably played as slices of low life seen from a middle-class point of view, which destroys the whole point: audiences enjoy a merry outing to the theatre having their prejudices massaged. Hogarth's contemporary painting of *The Beggar's Opera* shows the characters dressed in the high fashion of the ruling classes and the satire cannot have failed to hit home. Similarly, if the cynical obscenities of *The Threepenny Opera* are mouthed by picturesque denizens of an imaginary Soho underworld, then they have no point, but if they issue from the pearly lips of identifiable members of the professional middle class, from a Betjeman tennis-player of a Polly, say, or a Mrs Peachum who is a pillar of the WI, then they and the opportunistically amoral action strike a poisoned dagger at the heart of the audience. This is not irrelevant to recorded performances. The norm is what I call the 'snarl and shout' style of delivery, which enables audiences to distance themselves from what is happening, dividing the work and the performance into 'them and us' and reducing it to the level of actors insulting respectable audiences, which the latter of course love. Brecht's and Weill's deadly satire should be far more insidious in its attack.

The most important recording is the one under Brückner-Rüggeberg, if only because it is the most complete. It includes two numbers cut on the first night: the Ballad of Sexual Dependency, which the first Frau Peachum, Rosa Valetti, declined to sing because she thought it was obscene (which it indeed is), and Lucy's Jealousy Aria, a hilarious operatic parody beyond the capabilities of the actress playing the role – this is its only appearance on record and it is sung by Inge Wolffberg with just the right undisciplined attack. Neither number is in the Universal Edition vocal score, nor are the three extra verses of the *Morität* tacked on to the final Chorale which appear on all modern recordings; they were written by Brecht for Pabst's film (1930) and mark one stage in the dramatist's steady adaptation of the *Dreigroschen*-material from anarchic satire to orthodox Marxist tract, culminating in the *Dreigroschenroman* of 1934.

The Brückner-Rüggeberg recording is also satisfying as a musical performance, clearly recorded in forward mono sound. Johanna von Koczian's Polly has just the right knowing innocence about her, and Trude Hesterberg (who played Begbick in *Mahagonny* in Berlin, 1931) wraps her formidable quasi-baritone round Frau Peachum's music with irresistible relish. The rest of the cast has slightly less 'face' – though Erich Schellow emphasizes Macheath's charm without turning him into a mere matinee idol – and the 'snarl and shout' syndrome is rather too much in evidence, especially from the Streetsinger, who also bellows the title of each musical number (there is no linking dialogue).

Which leaves us with Lotte Lenya's Jenny, the role she created. Lenya was a unique *chanteuse* whose career faltered as her husband's took off; she worked little in the USA while Weill was alive, but after his death was almost solely responsible for the re-emergence of his work both in Europe and America. One must beware of appearing ungrateful to her. Her squeaky prewar soprano was not universally liked (more than one American enthusiast for Weill's German music, not knowing who Mrs Weill was, dropped frightful bricks when discussing prewar records) and by the 1950s when her recording career took off she had turned into a throaty contralto – if not baritone. Her highly individual delivery of Weill's songs must be regarded as authentic, but it nevertheless defies imitation – to that degree she may have founded an unfortunate tradition not unconnected with the 'snarl and shout' school.

Lenya certainly exerted a baleful influence on the text of *The Threepenny Opera,* in that she appropriated Pirate Jenny, the number originally sung by Polly as a cabaret turn at her wedding; the character of the whore Jenny and the sentiments expressed by the song could be said to coincide just as the names do, and instead of being a detached and ironical, even alienated number, it takes on a sort of quasi-realism that has no place in the work. The tradition has proved impossible to break: in virtually all performances, live or recorded, Jenny gets Polly's song and the character assumes more significance than Brecht ever intended. (Lenya also pinched Frau Peachum's lines in the second finale, which is less problematical.)

The more or less complete recording under F. Charles Adler is, to put it mildly, a curiosity. The leaden conducting robs the score of all vigour and wit, and the interest is largely for those opera buffs who will want to hear what such stars of the Vienna State Opera as Helge Rosvaenge, Alfred Jerger and Rosette Anday make of this music. Rosvaenge's *Morität* is disappointingly bland, but a near-voiceless Jerger delivers Peachum's numbers with marvellous verbal point, and Anday's fruity tone as Frau Peachum, with a wobble as wide as the Danube, makes one long to hear what she might have done with Sexual Dependency (which is cut). Kurt Preger's sleazy Macheath, with a real Viennese 'whine' to it, hangs on to the cries of 'Gerettet' in the finale as if he were Siegmund singing 'Wälse' – hilarious. The Polly is Liane Augustin and according to the (unreliable) sleeve of the Italian pressing I have heard she sings Pirate Jenny, but her voice is so different from that of the Polly in the other numbers that one doubts the accuracy of the attributions. The Frankfurt recording, poorly cast and conducted, can safely be ignored.

Both complete American versions have points of interest. That under Matlowsky commemorates the production that ran for seven years at the Theater de Lys in Greenwich Village from 1954, an important milestone in the postwar rediscovery of Weill (the fact that his German works needed rediscovering stems from his own rejection of them in his eagerness to become an American: from 1935 onwards he never spoke a word of German). The translation by Marc Blitzstein, a pupil of Schoenberg, colleague of Weill, and composer in his own right, is neat but fails to reproduce the cheerful vulgarity of Brecht's original. The bite of Lenya's Jenny survives the change of language, and not only does she get Polly's Pirate Jenny, but Polly's Barbara Song is reassigned to Lucy Brown just to add to the confusion. Scott Merrill is a glamorous rather than a seedy Macheath, the rest of the cast is good, and there is a fine theatrical feel to the performance.

But the 1976 recording of Joseph Papp's Shakespeare Festival production is in another class altogether. The translation by Ralph Mannheim and John Willett is accurate – the obscenities are faithfully reproduced – and authentic in tone. The modern stereo sound is ideally vivid, doing greater justice to Weill than any other modern recording (the tinkerings with the score are minimal). The Jenny, Ellen Green, may make a bit of a meal of Pirate Jenny but at least it is a meal at a restaurant with three rosettes; otherwise the tone is light and sardonic. Most members of the cast – including Raul Julia's dangerous Macheath and C. K. Alexander's pompous Peachum – affect 'refined' English accents to indicate that we are dealing with 'nice' people, not an imaginary underworld, and the results are hilarious, making one regret that Elizabeth Wilson's highly respectable Mrs Peachum is deprived of two verses of Sexual Dependency (this, and the arrival of the King's Messenger, are the only cuts). After a ponderous start Stanley Silverman catches all the humour of the score, even under the angry accusations of the second finale (that is true alienation), and this is altogether the funniest recording of the piece and so, to my mind, one of the best.

The excerpts under Theo Mackeben were made in 1930 in conjunction with the film soundtrack, in which Weill's score was heavily cut and mildly adapted by the conductor. What remains is fascinating. Lenja, then a soprano and spelt thus, gives her most detached account of Pirate Jenny – throwing away 'Alle' and 'Hoppla' with ideal insouciance – and also sings the Barbara Song and the extra verses of the *Morität* which bring Pabst's film to so unforgettable a close. Willy Trenck-Trebitsch (who sings Peachum on the Brückner-Rüggeberg recording) makes Macheath an elegant, charming creature, and the tone is altogether lighter, more detached than in the postwar versions, the score being sung rather than shouted. At the same time recordings were made in connection with the French version of the film starring Albert Préjean as Macheath. He sings the 'Chant des Canons' (with Jacques Henley), the 'Ballade de la vie agréable', a solo version of Polly's Love Song and the Tango Ballad with Margo Lion, all with truly Gallic suaveness. These recordings are available on a French disc (2C 061–91447) together with one of the innumerable reissues of the German cast. Perhaps this is the best place to dispose of the 1964 West German film, a grotesque misrepresentation of Weill (and Brecht) in cheap reorchestrations: only Hildegard Knef's Pirate Jenny, crooned about two inches from the microphone in a deep bass-baritone, has a certain something.

A 12-inch 78 entitled 'Die Songs der Dreigroschenoper' dating from 1929 (EH 301) is a revelation even though it contains only snippets from seven numbers. The main attraction is Carola Neher, who created Polly and was to die in a Soviet labour camp in 1936. She sings two verses of Pirate Jenny absolutely in character as Polly, fast and funny, the ultimate in detachment. This surely is how the number ought to go. Her Barbara Song is equally sprightly, with a sense of parody that is even more pronounced in the Love Song. She also sings a snatch of Peachum's Human Endeavour. Kurt Gerron, the first Brown/Streetsinger, sings a verse of the *Morität* and, with A. Schroeder, part of the Cannon Song. The labelling is unclear (and the sound is no help) but one verse of the Ballad of the Good Life is presumably by Schroeder. For Neher alone, and for a glimpse of how the work sounded at the time of its première, this record is essential listening; I can find no trace of a reissue, which is extraordinary.

Recordings of individual numbers run into hundreds. I have listened only to those by artists connected with stage performances. Lenya's on the original pressing of Berlin Theatre Songs (much reissued, with the *Threepenny Opera* items omitted when boxed, as currently, with the Brückner-Rüggeberg complete recording) are of course essential: how many listeners must have been initially attracted to Weill's music by this urgent, husky voice in the 1950s. But Gisela May, a sometime member of the Berliner Ensemble who sings in the same vocal range as Lenya, is in many ways a more formidable artist. Her voice is smoother, her phrasing more musical – and musical values count for much in the work of the Mozart of Unter den Linden. On her recital record she sings Pirate Jenny very persuasively, as if in character as Polly, the Barbara Song with sly cheerfulness, and Sexual Dependency with great relish but without, alas, the obscene third verse (bourgeois *pudeur* lives on in East Germany). The Viennese *chanteuse* Martha Schlamme, who followed in Lenya's wake as a popularizer of Weill's music in the 1960s and usefully inserted some American numbers into the standard German repertory, is a notable recitalist; she brings a certain Viennese sweetness to her singing of the expected numbers (her Tango Ballad with Will Holt in the Blitzstein translation makes up with suggestiveness what it lacks in directness) and lapses into 'snarl and shout' only in Pirate Jenny.

Two English-speaking singers deserve mention. Georgia Brown's recital is near-fatally compromised by ghastly sixties orchestrations, but she is a natur-ally musical and inventive artist, by far and away the best Anna I in *The Seven Deadly Sins* that I have heard in the theatre (iron determination behind the sweetest of smiles) and her responsive delivery of Pirate Jenny (in Blitzstein's version) and the Barbara Song is idiomatic and imaginative. Robyn Archer's voice is in itself unremarkable but her 'refined' account of Sexual Dependency (Willett/Mannheim) is well worth hearing.

Curiosities include Heifetz's encore arrangement of the *Morität*, an amazing showpiece with flurries of pizzicato and sky-high harmonics, which is pure delight (LAT 8020), and an extra number that Weill wrote for the Paris production of 1937 called 'Pauv' Mme Peachum' to a text by Yvette Guilbert who sang the role; less than earth-shaking musically, it is sung by Paula Lawrence on Bagley I. (The Bagley recital records, to which we shall return frequently, are hampered by unidiomatic orchestrations, relentlessly facetious sleeve-notes, and the sort of cover illustrations that assume that only men buy records. But they contain music that can be found nowhere else.) Brecht's own tonelessly rasped *Morität* has often been reissued, most recently on 'Brecht on Brecht' (Col. 025 203). Préjean's postwar 'Complainte de Mackie', in a tatty nightclub arrangement, is a sad disappointment, but four songs from *L'Opéra de quat'sous* (there's inflation for you) sung by Colette Renard to scarcely less unidiomatic accompaniment have a nicely clipped Gallic charm.

Just as Mozart made arrangements of his scores for wind band, so did Weill: his 'Kleine Dreigroschenmusik' was prepared at Klemperer's behest and premièred by the Prussian State Band at the Opera Ball in February 1929 – a bizarre combination. Free of the text one can revel in the purely musical values and extra-verbal wit of Weill's writing, and the suite has frequently been recorded. I have been unable to hear Klemperer's 1931 version, but his postwar record, which at first sounds rather straight-faced, gradually reveals hidden depths of dry humour – a lovely performance. The recording by the Sinfonietta under Atherton is clearer in sound quality, more brilliant instrumentally and equally joyful. The sluggish Nonesuch version pales beside both.

AUFSTIEG UND FALL DER STADT MAHAGONNY
Rise and Fall of the City of Mahagonny

The complete recording of *Aufstieg und Fall der Stadt Mahagonny* (1930) made in Berlin in 1956 has recently been reissued with refurbished sound and wears its years on the whole lightly; the pungency of the scoring is well conveyed in forward sound, with string and wind tone cleverly balanced, and the only serious drawback is some overloading of Heinz Sauerbaum's Jimmy in the Boxing and Drinking episodes. The text used is for the most part that adapted by Weill for the commercial run on the Kurfürstendamm, i.e. tailored to Lenya's capabilities (she did not sing Jenny at the Leipzig première). Transpositions are made, vocal lines swopped, the end of No. 5 is cut ('Ich kenn' die Jimmys'), and we have the alternative version of the Havana Song – I know of no recording of the original as printed in the

Universal score. Lenya sings much of the role an octave down – in the Crane duet she is at the same pitch as the tenor. But one must not complain, since without Lenya's inspiration and marketability there would have been no recording at all of one of the twentieth-century's great operas, a *Zauberflöte* for our time in which the eternal truths are rather less palatable, and a score in which Weill's neoclassical idiom and use of popular forms are heard in perfect balance. The performance is first-rate, conducted with unstoppable forward impulse by Brückner-Rüggeberg (the trial scene is very thrilling at a gut level) and vividly projected by a cast of fine character singers. Gisela Litz's poisonously lyrical Begbick, Horst Günter's forceful Trinity-Moses and Sigmund Roth's solid Joe are especially convincing.

Brecht's dissatisfaction with the way Weill's music dominated *Mahagonny* is well known and resulted in endless essays on 'culinary opera'; the words, too, written before the dramatist fully embraced Marxism, were later seen to be ideologically impure. *Mahagonny* has seldom been performed in East Germany since the war. All the more interesting, then, is the *Kleine Mahagonny* devised for the Berliner Ensemble (VEB Litera 860035): this, presumably, is how Brecht would have liked the work to go. The ideological stumbling block was the notion of the 'simple lumberjack from Alaska' inventing consumer capitalism; here, the three criminals on the run make that discovery right at the beginning. Most of the severely reduced text (the running time is under an hour) is spoken, with the obvious Songs inserted in chamber-orchestra arrangements: the Kurfürstendamm Havana Song, the Alabama Song (very military in tempo), Jakob Schmidt's zither number, God in Mahagonny, and the opening only of the finale. The performance is live, with members of the Berliner Ensemble, and the audience laughs dutifully.

Lenya recorded excerpts from the complete *Mahagonny* in 1930 (EH 736). 'Wie man sich bettet', sung straight and sweet (so much more insidious than when snarled and shouted), and the Alabama Song with backing from 'The Three Admirals' have been reissued on 1C–061–91447 with the film excerpts from *The Threepenny Opera,* but I can trace no reissue of HMV Z224 (the Scandinavian prefix for some odd reason), the 'Mahagonny Querschnitt' with 'Grossen Ensemble und Orchester des Theaters am Kurfürstendamm' conducted by Hans Sommer on two 78 sides. This is another fascinating document made in conjunction with the commercial run (first performance 31 December 1931) of which Zemlinsky was appointed musical director though not, apparently, conductor. Weill needed a strong personality to balance Brecht, with whom relations were now at breaking point and who wanted to cut as much of the music as possible ('that phoney Richard Strauss' as he called it, which would have offended Strauss as deeply as it must have wounded Weill). Had Brecht had his way, the result might have resembled the postwar Berliner Ensemble version. As in the case of the *Threepenny Opera* 78, this is a brisk canter through the score: an anonymous and ill-tuned tenor sings a snatch of 'Auf nach Mahagonny' followed by the *Freis-*

chütz parody; Lenya speaks much of the Alabama Song while the chorus takes Jenny's line (another feature of the postwar recording), sings part of the Kurfürstendamm Havana Song, and the second verse of 'Wie man such bettet' though without risking the top A; there is a substantial section of 'Wunderbar ist das Heraufkommen des Abends . . . aber etwas fehlt'; and a severely compressed trial and finale.

Gisela May also sings the Kurfürstendamm Havana Song on her recital, phrasing it very seductively, takes the top A in 'Wie man sich bettet', but omits the second verse ('Pretty boy') of the Alabama Song – more *pudeur* perhaps. Robyn Archer delivers a fair account of that song, but the point of interest on her recital is Brecht's own setting of the Benares Song, a dizzy mixture of 'There is a tavern in the town' and *Madama Butterfly* orchestrated by Dominic Muldowney. Bettina Jonic, who gave many Brecht/Weill concerts in the sixties, sings the Mandalay Song effectively enough, male chorus lines and all (XTRA D 1157); her generally operatic approach suits this number better than others both here and on her other recital disc (D'ART 12-6), in which the songs are submerged beneath her unsteady tone, taste for extremely slow tempi, and self-conscious application of expression.

The *Mahagonny Songspiel* that caused such a sensation at Baden-Baden in 1927 was a 'work-in-progress' appetizer of the complete opera: the London Sinfonietta's version is less compromised than their other vocal offerings by non-German-speaking singers since most of the numbers are in dog-American. The playing is superb. I have been unable to track down the Vox *Songspiel*.

HAPPY END

As a follow-up to *The Threepenny Opera, Happy End* (1929), was a commercial flop, probably as much for political reasons as for any others: it scarcely deserved to be. The play is even more innocent on the surface than its model but aims to pack an under-the-belt a punch; I suspect that Brecht disowned it because owing to a minute miscalculation the joke tends to rebound off its target of gangster-capitalists and back on to socialism. Modern revivals have shown it to be a highly diverting piece, with its Salvation Army lasses and gangsters anticipating both *St Joan of the Stockyards* and *Guys and Dolls*.

Musically it represents a considerable advance on *The Threepenny Opera* save for those who demand a whiff of Busoni in their Weill; here the song-element predominates but the melodies are more sophisticated and longer-breathed, and the accompaniments, with each verse varied in colour, surpass anything in the earlier work. The two complete recordings are complementary, flawed, but eminently worth hearing. Lenya's of 1960 is the best of the Brückner-Rüggeberg series, recorded in good, warm stereo. Lenya sings every number, in the right order, a tour-de-force even with choral help but hardly giving a fair idea of the work itself (the original cast included Carola

Neher, Helene Weigel, Peter Lorre and Oskar Homolka). The references to Rockefeller, Henry Ford etc., in the finale are suppressed. They are there in the London Sinfonietta version, which is reordered into a concert suite but lacks the Bilbao Song for reasons I have never been able to fathom. The use of British singers is rather more disturbing than in the *Mahagonny Songspiel,* especially on the male side. While there is a nicely brassy blare to the playing on the German recording, the Sinfonietta's account is more contained and marginally clearer – a distinct advantage with instrumentation as subtle as this – and it is more distinguished musically; the singing is less dramatically involved than Lenya's, though Ian Partridge's Song of the Liquor Dealer is beautifully phrased.

The exception to this general rule is Surabaya Johnny, another of Weill's great tunes. In the play it is sung by the Salvation Army lass and thus, like Pirate Jenny, can take a degree of alienation. On the Sinfonietta set Meriel Dickinson sings it extremely slowly and turns it into a fully blown torch song dripping with tragedy – marvellous in its way but a bit too much. Lenya is comparatively restrained. Gisela May's version, sadly without Weill's orchestration, is at the other extreme, fast, unsentimental but extremely musical: this, you feel, is how Dietrich might have sung it. May also sings the Mandalay and Bilbao Songs, the Ballad of Hell-Lily and the Sailors' Tango, establishing with each her claim to be considered the best German-speaking interpreter of Weill's songs. Lenya's earlier version of Surabaya Johnny on Berlin Theatre Songs lacks the proper orchestration, and the telling change from 3/4 to 4/4 at 'Du gehst jetzt weg, Johnny' in the third verse is ignored. There are countless other versions of this number, including Robyn Archer's (smokey but fairly straight), Martha Schlamme's (as full of heartbreak as Meriel Dickinson's but lighter of tone), and Georgia Brown's, two verses only in very individual German and to an unspeakable accompaniment. Both of Martha Schlamme's versions of the Bilbao Song are full of sweet nostalgia and humour.

'God bless Rockefeller' is included on Bagley II in a blessedly straight arrangement in Michael Feingold's translation. Philip Chevron's pop arrangements of five numbers (MOSA MOEP 4–12) need not detain us, save as a demonstration of Weill's continuing appeal to today's young.

DER JASAGER

I find this *Lehrstück* to a text by Brecht based on the Nō play *Taniko* pretty hard to take, as sinister in its implications as *Die Massnahme* and another significant milestone on the playwright's journey to Marxist orthodoxy, though this parable of the praiseworthy sacrifice of a weak individual to the common good could have been written by a totalitarian of any colour. That 'he who says yes' should be a child and the man who decides on the terms of the common good should be his schoolteacher only adds to the creepiness. Weill here is at his most ice-cold and didactic: gone is the song style, back is the neoclassicism, for once unleavened by wit or affection. The music takes no notice whatsoever of the child's self-sacrifice, returning blithely to the severely contrapuntal 'It is important above all to learn to consent' of the opening. *Jasager* (1930) is the exact reverse of *Mahagonny* in that the music is totally subservient to the text, and it probably also marks a milestone on the road to Weill's split with Brecht. As Lenya tartly remarked later, her husband was not interested in setting the Communist Manifesto to music. The only recording of *Jasager* (1956) is perfectly acceptable – the boy soprano a great deal more than that – but it is not one to which many of us will return with pleasure.

At this stage the absence of any records of the Weill/Caspar Neher *Die Bürgschaft* (1932) should be noted with regret; the tape of a postwar Berlin broadcast is on deposit at the Lincoln Center Library of the Performing Arts.

DER SILBERSEE

This is one of Weill's most problematical works, and one born under the darkest of stars. During rehearsals in January 1933 Hitler was appointed chancellor, and shortly after the successful première in Leipzig on 18 February the Reichstag was burnt down and civil liberties suspended. The following month Weill fled from Germany, and the Nazis went to great lengths to destroy everything they could lay their hands on connected with *Silbersee*, including the orchestral parts and presumably some records of extracts made at the time – none seems to have survived. Weill's voice was effectively silenced in Germany for thirteen years.

The problems stem from *Silbersee*'s form. Like *Threepenny Opera* and *Happy End* it is a play with music, but unlike them the music is inextricably bound to Kaiser's text: save for the Ballad of Caesar's Death (which was directed straight at Hitler) the musical numbers make little sense out of context. Kaiser's play, which lasts over three hours of which only one is with music (thence the original plan to have it premièred at the Deutsches Theater rather than the Leipzig Opera), is an allegory of social upheaval unmistakably 'about' the Weimar Republic and, in the words of the original director Detlef Sierck, 'ten times tougher than any Brecht play'. That is to say, the relationships among the characters mean something (that between the policeman Olim and Severin, the unemployed looter he shoots, wounds and subsequently befriends, is unsettlingly homoerotic) and no easy solutions are proposed. Of all Kaiser's plays, this is the least portentous, the most hypnotically fascinating. But the problems of performance remain hair-raising: *Silbersee* demands first-rate actors who have not just to sing, but sing with operatically trained voices, and for this reason if for no other it seems doomed to be staged but rarely, like that other hybrid masterpiece *L'Arlésienne* (in which at least no one has to sing).

All this, however, is little excuse for the radical adaptation under the title of *Silverlake* staged by the New York City Opera in 1980. Kaiser's text was rewritten by Hugh Wheeler, whose remark apropos his work that he was 'so bored with that 1930-ish, pissy-assed socialism' boded ill. The score was adapted by Lys Symonette, a Broadway colleague of Weill's, with numbers reassigned (Caesar's Death was taken from the heroine Fennimore and given to the villainess Frau von Luber, which is alienation of the wrong sort) and the use of Weill's still unpublished incidental music to Strindberg's *Gustav III* (1927) as *melodram*, thus turning a play with music into something like a through-composed work. That sour little number 'Muschel von Margate' from *Der Konjunktur* is turned into a 'friendship' duet.

The virtually complete recording of the NYCO *Silverlake* doesn't even work on its own terms – it is tempting to write that one is 'bored by all that 1980-ish pissy-assed Broadway sentiment'. The casting of Joel Grey as Olim is inexplicable: he can't sing and even his dialogue has to be recorded in a different acoustic. He speaks the lines in a quavery monotone. William Neill (Severin) can and does sing in a powerfully felt performance, and Elaine Bonazzi attacks Caesar's Death with much spirit. Elizabeth Hynes has little to do as Fennimore. Despite all this, the set is essential simply because it contains nearly all the original *Silbersee* music (only one vocal item, No. 3 in the Universal score, is cut) and extremely fine most of it is, from the bitter little waltz for the Salesgirls to the striking choral instructions to Olim. The music is well conducted by Julius Rudel. At least *Silverlake* makes one want to hear *Silbersee*.

The earliest surviving recordings of *Silbersee* are Caesar's Death and 'Ich bin nur ein arme Verwandte', sung by Lenya on Berlin Theatre Songs: the former is grist to her mill; and Martha Schlamme also sings it with fierce attack. Weill arranged an orchestral suite from the score in collaboration with Karel Salomon, which has been recorded by the MIT Symphony Orchestra under David Epstein (TV 34760). The playing is not especially distinguished, but listening to the music on its own points to its close connections with the second symphony and reminds us that the neoclassical Weill was not dead.

DIE SIEBEN TODSÜNDEN DER KLEINBÜRGER
The Seven Deadly Sins

Circumstances brought Weill and Brecht together for their last collaboration in exile in Paris; *Die sieben Todsünden* (1933) is a dazzling *jeu d'esprit* that turns the whole of bourgeois morality on its head in forty minutes. It is now firmly established in the repertory and needs no further comment here. As far as recordings are concerned there is an *embarras de richesse*: all three are essential.

The exact circumstances surrounding Lenya's creation of the role of Anna I are still shrouded in mystery. It was not written for her; at that time Weill and Lenya were estranged if not actually divorced. Presumably commercial pressures demanded that she sing the role at the première (the money had been put up by Edward James, husband of Tilly Losch who danced Balanchine's choreography as Anna II), since her success in the film of *The Threepenny Opera* had made her something of a star in Paris. At a late stage, then, Weill transposed those numbers in which Anna I sings down by a fourth, save for Anger, in which the transposition comes just before Anna's entry and the subsequent choral contributions are rewritten. Lenya sings the role at this pitch on the Brückner-Rüggeberg recording (the first of his series) with characteristic bite. Gisela May also uses the transposed version; her interpretation is less forceful, more detached, more musical, more insidiously evil – a marvellous performance. There are riches too in the family quartet led by Peter Schreier, and Kegel's conducting of the Leipzig Radio Orchestra is infinitely superior to Brückner-Rüggeberg and his anonymous band. (Brückner-Rüggeberg, incidentally, whose contribution to the postwar Weill revival was almost as significant as Lenya's, is amongst other things a Handel specialist; he was invited by Furtwängler to conduct a Beethoven cycle with the Berlin Philharmonic Orchestra in 1937, and since than has worked mainly in Hamburg and South America.)

Universal have published the score at its original pitch and it has been superbly recorded by Simon Rattle. Predictably enough *Sins* sounds brighter, more glittery in the right keys, and the playing is ideally alert with the instrumental detail emerging through modern digital sound. Elise Ross cannot compete with her predecessors as far as 'face' is concerned, but she sings sweetly and is only occasionally let down by breathing problems. Purely orchestrally, though, this is one of the great Weill recordings.

MARIE GALANTE

In Paris in 1933 Weill also wrote seven songs for Jacques Deval's dramatization of his sentimental novel about a Bordeaux tart stranded in Panama and trying to work her passage home. Having become involved in espionage to that end, she gets shot, and the play ends with her coffin being put on board the ship she has longed for throughout the action. 'J'attends un navire' is one of Weill's most perfectly wrought tunes, full of arching longing; it was reputedly used as a signal by the French resistance. It has been worthily recorded by Martha Schlamme on 'The World of Kurt Weill in Song', and by Margery Cohen on *From Berlin to Broadway*, the cast-recording of a well-meaning but not very penetrating off-Broadway survey of Weill's work; Miss Cohen sings the first verse in an English translation by Alice Baker and Gene Lerner, the second in French. Ships were to recur in Weill's songs almost as often as the name Jenny (there is scope here for a Rosebud-style investigation).

Another number recorded twice by Schlamme is 'Le Roi d'Aquitaine', a wholly bewitching little song. Both numbers sound quintessentially French: Weill the chameleon was already emerging. I have been unable to hear versions of 'J'attends un navire' and 'La grand Lustucru' by Laura Betti

(Orrizonte ORL 8028), of 'Les filles de Bordeaux' and 'Le Roi d'Aquitaine' by Florelle, the original Marie (Poly. 524012), or Lenya's 'J'attends un navire' from US Decca 5017–9, which should obviously be reissued.

In 1935 Weill's operetta *Die Kuhhandel* ran briefly at the Savoy Theatre in London, with English words by Reginald Arkell and Desmond Carter, as *A Kingdom for a Cow*. It dealt with the international arms trade and – predictably enough – flopped; two numbers have been published and none recorded.

JOHNNY JOHNSON

Weill's passport to America – he arrived in New York on 10 September 1935 – was his incidental music for the Reinhardt spectacular *The Eternal Road*, a historical pageant of Jewish history that after repeated delays opened in the extensively (and expensively) altered Manhattan Opera House, was well received, and lost a great deal of money. None of the music has been recorded and little published. While waiting for *Eternal Road* to happen, the composer enthusiastically fell in with the left-wing theatrical intelligentsia, many of whom knew his European work (*The Threepenny Opera* had run for only two weeks in New York in 1933 but the film was well known). It is good to be reminded that there was such a thing as an American left in those pre-McCarthy days, and theatrically it was centred on Group Theatre, a breakaway from the Theatre Guild dominated by Lee Strasberg, Harold Clurman and Cheryl Crawford. This was a radical collective some of whose actors were communists, and Weill spent the summer of 1936 at the Group Theatre camp working on *Johnny Johnson*, his first, thoroughly European Broadway show conceived in the sort of collaborative atmosphere of the Berlin theatre pieces. This fierce pacifist tract opened on 19 November 1936, directed by Strasberg in far too big a theatre and with a cast including Lee J. Cobb, Elia Kazan and John Garfield. It received sympathetic but hardly selling press coverage and closed after sixty-eight performances.

Weill and Paul Green, a southern liberal writer who had served in Europe in the First World War, at first considered setting either *Woyzeck* or *The Captain of Köpenick*, and elements of both survive. The action opens on the eve of America's entry into the war at the unveiling ceremony of a monument to peace, for which Weill wrote the stirring Democracy March; declaration of war is announced and the march is repeated note for note but with 'War, war, war' substituted for 'Peace, peace, peace' – a chilling effect. Johnny is rejected at the recruiting station for being too intelligent but taken on when he knocks a man down. He sails to Europe, is horrified by what he finds in the trenches, makes friends with a German sniper, and is wounded in the backside. He steals laughing gas from the hospital and releases it at a High Command conference and then, *Köpenick*-like, disguises himself as a general and proclaims an armistice. He is arrested and shipped home to a mental hospital, where he sets up a League of Nations for the inmates. Ten years later he is released and becomes an itinerant toy-seller, refusing to stock military wares.

Virtually the whole of the score was recorded in 1957, and it is first-rate Weill, much of it Berlinish in style – the limping march for the wounded French soldiers, the sleazy tango for the recruiting officer, the sour parody of a romantic song for Minny Belle, Johnny's perfidious girlfriend (sung on the record by Evelyn Lear, no less), the haunting refrain for three cannons that rear out of no-man's-land to sing sadly over the sleeping GIs who will die on the morrow, the bitter *melodram* for German and American Chaplains praying to one god in identical words but two languages (anticipating *Oh What a Lovely War!* by thirty years), and the satirical Psychiatry Song, one verse of which is scored for celeste and trombone only. There are parodies too, a Wild West song and a tea number for English officers.

Also on the record are Lenya, singing a touching number for a French nurse, and Thomas Stewart in good form as the Mayor and the US Chaplain. Johnny is a speaking role – he has a fine *melodram* addressing the Statue of Liberty as he sails for Europe, and the Statue replies more or less in the words of Mme Roland: 'What crimes are committed in my name' – until the very end, when he sings Johnny's Song. This is way up towards the top ten of Weill's tunes (it was in fact written in Germany, just as the overture is lifted from *Happy End*), beautifully shaped and a fitting climax to an undeniably stirring score. The actor Burgess Meredith sings it on the record to grand effect and I have seen it reduce strong men to tears with its blindly expressed optimism of 'faith and trust in all mankind' as the lobotomized Johnny wanders off with his tray, calling 'toys, toys, toys' over Weill's indescribably poignant postlude. This record is a must.

Johnny's Song was given a new text – 'To love you and to lose you' – for hit-parade purposes, which can be heard sung by Blossom Dearie on Bagley II, immediately followed by the original too croonily sung by Arthur Siegel. The Democracy March, which must have passed through Bernstein's mind just before he wrote 'Tonight' in *West Side Story*, and Johnny's Song are nicely enough done on *From Berlin to Broadway*. But in the case of Johnny's Song there is no substitute for Burgess Meredith.

KNICKERBOCKER HOLIDAY

Weill's collaborator for *Knickerbocker Holiday* (1938) was Maxwell Anderson, a sympathizer with Group Theatre and a founder member with Elmer Rice, Robert E. Sherwood and others of the related Playwrights' Producing Company. The original idea for this satirical comedy, drawn from Washington Irving's *Knickerbocker History of New York*, was to use the character of Governor Peter Stuyvesant as the basis for an attack on Roosevelt and the New Deal: Anderson was an old-fashioned libertarian who saw danger in too much government. Other members of the Playwrights' Company, however, felt that Roosevelt was at least a step in the right direction, and as they held seminars during rehearsals reading drafts of each other's plays, the anti-Roosevelt satire was watered down in favour of identifying Stuyvesant with Hitler. But Stuyvesant had only one leg and Roosevelt was crippled with polio, which immediately set up the connection in audience's minds, and much of the New Deal parody survives in the script.

The action starts with Washington Irving as narrator introducing Stuyvesant as he sails towards New Amsterdam ('They've got two hours more of democracy and stupidity, and then I arrive'). The present government is by Council ('chosen for their weight and density and intolerance of any corruption in which they have no share'); originally Tienhoven, the president of the Council, was to have been an out-and-out villain but he was turned into a buffoon, albeit a menacing one; he plans to hang the tenor hero to celebrate Stuyvesant's arrival and when his daughter protests 'that's not justice' he replies 'nobody says it was justice – we said it was legal'. The hanging turns to farce and Stuyvesant arrives with a wicked parody of a New Deal speech and an ensemble chorus that runs 'All hail to the political honeymoon, sing news to hoi polloi, of each individual man his boon, in the name of strength through joy'. The implicit association of Roosevelt with Hitler seems even more shocking today than it must have been in 1938.

Anderson obviously identified with the libertarian tenor hero, whom Stuyvesant promptly sets about rehanging ('When a man's guilty, what the hell's the use of a trial?'); the Council turns against him ('our government had the immense advantage of being incompetent and clumsy in its corruption, but your tyranny is efficiently vicious and efficiently corrupt') and Stuyvesant orders his troops to get ready to fire on the crowd to allow the hanging to proceed. Instead of the King's Messenger as in *The Threepenny Opera*, Washington Irving steps from the wings and stops the action. The Happy End is wholly artificial.

I have outlined the plot in some detail to dent the Klemperer theory of Weill's selling out: this is a nasty, sour little political satire and very daring for its day. Roosevelt himself saw a performance during the out-of-town previews and may perhaps have missed some of the barbs, but he objected strongly to a reference to his letter to Hitler at the time of the Munich crisis. The show ran for seven months on Broadway and the film rights were sold to Hollywood.

Weill's score is part parody (American operetta and Gilbert and Sullivan), part Broadway slick. The most interesting number musically is the romantic 'It never was you', which is far freer in structure than the standard Broadway hit, and the two tenor solos ('How can you tell an American' and 'There's nowhere to go but up') have truly transatlantic energy. The Political Honeymoon chorus is etched in acid. But the best known item is the September Song, the sweetener that ensured Walter Huston's taking the role of Stuyvesant – he wanted a romantic ballad and he got one in the form of another of Weill's great melodies (note the importance of the interval of the seventh in all of them). If the idea of a chimerical combination of Roosevelt and

Hitler getting a romantic ballad seems odd, it should be remembered that it is about a dirty old man with one leg propositioning a young girl, a fact that the revised lyrics as we know them tends to disguise.

The nearest thing to a complete recording of *Knickerbocker Holiday* is on JOEY 7243, a shortened version taken from the Theatre Guild on the Air broadcast of 1939. The sleeve is blank save for the name of Walter Huston, but one may assume that the rest of the cast is as on Broadway. Three vocal numbers are missing but two of them can be found elsewhere. There is much dialogue, very energetically delivered, and the off-the-air sound is acceptably clear. The original lyrics of September Song are used ('And I have lost one tooth, and I walk a little lame, and I haven't got time for the waiting game') and Huston sings it with engaging wit.

The film version dropped all Weill's music save for three songs (the gaps were filled by Jule Styne) which can be found on 'Kurt Weill in Hollywood' (Ariel KWH 10). Charles Coburn sings the original September Song unremarkably; Nelson Eddy is dim in 'There's nowhere to go but up'; but most important, there is one verse of 'The one indispensable man', a point number about corruption cut from the broadcast version. Weill sets the mordant lyric ('In every government whatever its intent, there's one obscure official with a manner innocent, his job invisible is purchasing good will, with lots of public money taken from the public till') in a mock-innocent manner reminiscent of Sullivan. *The Mikado* was indeed one of Anderson's models.

September Song has been recorded hundreds of times, nearly always with references to missing teeth and wooden legs removed, as a romantic and as often as not over-romantic love song. Huston made two versions; the first (reissued on Fontana TFL 5037) of 1938 with the original text is in better sound than on the broadcast, and the interpretation is laid-back and stylish; his postwar 78 (Bruns. 04658) uses the revised lyrics and inevitably sounds more sentimental. Ezio Pinza sings the revised lyrics absolutely straight in his inimitable English, with a beautiful legato line, much feeling, and iron control of dynamic (Victor 10–3256; RDS 6503); Jan Peerce's version, equally musically sung, is killed by a ghastly sixties arrangement (ANL1–2976). Lenya's 1958 version on American Theatre Songs is given the full souped-up treatment – she should have known better – but it is nevertheless a model of restraint compared to Georgia Brown. Will Holt is a good deal too sentimental on the Schlamme cabaret disc; Jerry Lanning's interior singing on *Berlin to Broadway* is greatly to be preferred. Also on this set is a duly acid version of 'How can you tell an American' (the answer is by his distrust of authority). Lenya delivers a wistfully romantic 'It never was you' on her American recital.

Of all Weill's Broadway works, *Knickerbocker Holiday* is by far the most surprising.

LADY IN THE DARK

I should hate to have to defend *Lady in the Dark* (1941) from Klemperer, but have to confess that it is one of my favourite Weill scores. Moss Hart's play may be high hokum, but it is high on an Everest scale, and while the psychoanalytical content wouldn't hold water on the stage today it must have seemed pretty startling in 1941. Briefly, it is about the psychological problems of Liza Elliott, editor of a fashion magazine; they stem from her being unable to make up her mind about the three men in her life – her sugar daddy, who suddenly proposes marriage, a Hollywood film star (created on stage by Victor Mature), and the magazine's advertising manager, whom she thinks she hates but, surprise surprise, ends up marrying. The action is divided between her office and the psychiatrist's couch, and the music is confined to three through-composed dream sequences in which the office characters assume fantasy roles.

These three little one-act operas, as they have often been called, are set with smooth technical assurance, and Weill responds with rare musical wit to Ira Gershwin's urbane lyrics. Despite the surface sparkle, the dreams all have a musically nightmarish quality, and they solve nothing. The key to Liza's problems turns out to be a song associated with a childhood trauma, 'My Ship', which the psychiatrist eventually unlocks. To make a song the turning point of a play or opera can be asking for trouble, but Weill gets away with it as surely as Offenbach did in *Le Chanson de Fortunio*: 'My Ship' is another memorable tune, used in fragments throughout the dream sequences and finally sung in full in the last scene.

The stereo recording is virtually complete (one instrumental number is missing from the Circus Dream) and the sound is good. John Reardon is excellent in the Victor Mature role, and Adolph Green enjoys himself as Russell Paxton, the camp photographer created by Danny Kaye (he gets the tongue-twisting 'Tchaikovsky' in the Circus Dream). Risë Stevens, a former Met Carmen, brings a certain star quality to her Liza, and conveys the character's panic in the dreams vividly. But her tone is wobbly and opaque and she effects some peculiarly D'Oyly Carte-ish vowel sounds. Nevertheless, as one of the few stereo Weill records, this must be recommended.

Even more recommended – indeed essential – are the six numbers recorded in 1941 by the original Liza, Gertrude Lawrence (VIC 1225). Her voice may in itself be unremarkable – thin and a little gritty – but her way with the music is irresistible: she puts across 'Huxley' in the Glamour Dream and the Saga of Jenny (again) with great verve, gets the duet 'This is new' to herself since Mature couldn't sing it (the introduction takes us straight back to Berlin and the tune itself is endlessly haunting), and delivers 'My Ship' with bewitching simplicity and instinctive musical insight. This is great singing.

The Saga of Jenny has proved to be the most frequently recorded single number, although musically it is one of the less interesting, relying on lyrics and action to make its point. (It follows immediately after 'Tchaikovsky', with which Danny Kaye was threatening to steal the show, and Gertie apparently gave 'Jenny' plenty of action.) Lenya's version, in full with chorus on her American recital, has the requisite zing, but her middle-European accent sounds odd, and Schlamme's recording is too shortened to make much effect. Georgia Brown is well suited to this number. Julie Andrews is far too genteel on the soundtrack record of *Star,* a biopic of Lawrence (Stateside SL 10233). No one can touch Gertie in 'My Ship', certainly not Miss Andrews, who recklessly breaks up the musical line, certainly not Miss Brown (though her accompaniment, complete with a Korngold-style sea symphony, is a collector's item for those interested in a musical chamber of horrors), but Margery Cohen on *Berlin to Broadway* catches the number's essential simplicity and is quietly effective. Danny Kaye recorded 'Tchaikovsky' more than once (the most readily available reissue is on MCL 1704), but I find Adolph Green much more satisfying.

A number cut from the show has been exhumed on Bagley I, its title – 'You are unforgettable' – proving singularly inapt. It is eminently forgettable. Moss Hart reads the opening scene of what he says is his favourite amongst his plays on Westminster 725; it is not always easy to tell who is speaking – patient or psychiatrist – without a copy of the book, but this is good archive material. Of marginal interest is a release on cassette only (Audio Arts VH 10468) of a 1953 Californian broadcast version with Judy Garland as Liza. This is plainly tied up with the release of the very poor Hollywood movie (Ginger Rogers wholly at sea, but Mischa Auer going calculatedly too far as the photographer): thus there is very little music – only a snatch of 'This is new' and not even the whole of 'My Ship' – and what there is is used as *melodram* under Hart's play. For devoted Garland fans only, then; she could of course have been marvellous in the stage show. Therein lies the problem with *Lady*: it can only work with a great big old-fashioned star, and it is hard to think of anyone today who could get anywhere near it. It was Weill's greatest Broadway success.

ONE TOUCH OF VENUS

The success of *Lady* was almost matched by *One Touch of Venus* (1943) which, directed by Elia Kazan of all people, ran for 566 performances. This is again pure Broadway, but Ogden Nash's lyrics and S. J. Perelman's book make it a great deal saucier – not to say tasteless – than one's usual idea of a Broadway musical. The plot, taken from *The Tinted Venus* by the English novelist F. Anstey (he of *Vice-Versa*) and in turn presumably inspired by Mérimée's *La Vénus d'Ille,* tells of a humble barber with the unlikely name of Rodney who by mistake brings a statue of Venus to life. He then has to run for his life from a woman with only one thing on her mind – 'Love isn't the dying moan of a distant violin, it's the triumphant twang of a bedspring'.

Substantial extracts were recorded on 78s by the original cast, now available on AEI 1136. Dietrich turned the title role down on grounds of taste, and it was given to the young Mary Martin, a lovely singer who must have listened closely to Gertrude Lawrence (their use of *portamento* is very similar) and defuses the more blatant moments with an artless innocence. 'Foolish heart' is a shapely Broadway waltz, very warmly phrased, and 'Speak low', a sultry number similar in mood to 'Begin the beguine' sung when Venus corners Rodney in his barber's shop, is a masterpiece of subtle suggestion in Mary Martin's hands. 'That's him', sung as Venus contemplates the sleeping Rodney in the hotel room where she has finally had her way with him, is in direct descent from Kern's 'My man Bill', one of those smoky songs in which the fair sex muses upon the attractions of what in the circumstances must be called the weak one; although Miss Martin's *sotto voce* chuckle after the line 'He's like a plumber when you need a plumber' is anything but artless or innocent, she manages to be enormously sexy without ever descending to mere vulgarity. The comic numbers include 'The trouble with women', a barber-shop quartet whose melody is lifted from *Happy End*, and 'Wooden wedding', Rodney's vision of suburban bliss that fails to interest Venus ('Payday will be a magic casement opening on something peachy, maybe a trip to a bargain basement or a double feature with Don Ameche').

The numbers missing from the original cast selection can be found on Bagley I. The title song, sung by Paula Lawrence (she also performed it in the original Broadway cast), contains the memorable line 'Venus showed them that the pantie is mightier than the pant'. 'That's how much I love you' is a pastiche of Cole Porter's 'You're the tops'. 'Very, very, very', Paula Lawrence again, is a point number with some dazzling Nash couplets: 'Since Sally ran off with her obstetrician, her hair's turned red and she looks like a Titian; of course I'd hate to swear in court, what kind of Titian – beaut or mort'. The Ballad of Dr Crippen is a Berlin-flavour cautionary tale about the perils of unbridled passion, brilliantly sung here by Chita Rivera in an especially nasty arrangement. 'Love in a mist', sung by Jo Sullivan, was cut from the score at an early stage and shouldn't have been. 'Way out West in New Jersey', a cod Western number sung by Arthur Siegel on Bagley II, is musically inconsequential but fun. Lenya sings 'Speak low' very throatily and effectively on her American recital, but is less convincing with 'Love shouldn't be serious'.

Again, it would be hard to defend *One Touch of Venus* from Dr Klemperer, but it is sophisticated Broadway at its best. 'Speak low' is well up amongst the Weill greats, and the two ballet sequences (included on the original cast selections) are, like 'Dr Crippen', pure Berlin.

THE FIREBRAND OF FLORENCE

The Firebrand of Florence (1945) brought Weill's run of Broadway successes to an abrupt halt – it ran for only forty-three performances. A romantic operetta, half parody, half straight, it is about Benvenuto Cellini (Pinza turned the role down), his love for one Angela, the Duke of Florence's pursuit of her, and the activities of his man-hungry Duchess. Lenya's performance in the last-named role, the first she had sung in any of her husband's American works, was held to be largely responsible for the flop.

No records were made of the original cast but a fascinating document survives in the form of acetates made privately for promotional purposes by the librettist Ira Gershwin with Weill at the piano. Most of the musical numbers are on the reissue ('Ira Gershwin Loves to Rhyme', Mark 56 721), smoothly sung by the librettist with occasional interjections from the composer, who takes the role of first street vendor; in his 'Souvenirs, hurry, hurry get your souvenirs' his European 'rs' make him sound like a tenor Dietrich. (I have been unable to track down Weill's own acetates of *One Touch of Venus* on Heritage LP-H 0051.)

Even if the score doesn't add up to much, there are some good individual numbers, notably 'There'll be life, there'll be love, there'll be laughter' (a good self-generating melody), the Duchess's entry song 'Sing me not a ballad', 'When the Duchess is away', in which Weill's cross rhythms neatly complement the enjambements in Gershwin's lyrics, and a comic Spoonerism number ('sturgeon vile' and 'virgin style' amongst much else). Gershwin's rhymes for Medici and Da Vinci are for connoisseurs of such things.

There are modern recordings of a few individual numbers. Lenya's own 'Sing me not a ballad' is on her American recital, complete with the introductory recitative missing on the acetates. Bagley II offers the brash 'Come to Paris', 'The little naked boy' (a good smoochy number appropriately delivered by Arthur Siegel), the romantic waltz song 'You're far too near me' sung by John Reardon and Jo Sullivan, and a poor version of 'Sing me not a ballad' by Nell Carter. It would be nice to be able to say that *Firebrand*'s neglect is unjustified, but I fear it isn't.

Weill and Gershwin also collaborated on the Hollywood movie *Where do we go from here?* (1944) and made demonstration acetates included on the Mark 56 double album; they include passages cut from the film, the soundtrack of which is on KWH 10. This is a patriotic extravaganza about an eager recruit turned down by the draft board (shades of *Johnny Johnson*, but the naturalized Weill worked tirelessly for the war effort) who finds himself transported by magic back into American history. There are two substantial fantasy musical sequences after the manner of *Lady in the Dark*. The first is set in the War of Independence amongst George III's Hessian mercenaries and includes a parody of *The Student Prince* and a delightful 'wrong-note' *Ländler*; the second is on board the Santa Maria in 1492, in which the sailors' mutiny is turned into a joke Italian opera: they insist that the earth is flat and that they are about to fall off the edge. This is wickedly funny in the best Gershwin/Weill style ('It's round' – or rather '*wound*' – shouts Weill on the acetates). A pair of lines when the hero tries to douse the mutiny by detailing the joys of America, 'The girls are delightful, their sweaters are right full', were thought to be too strong meat for the movie and are amended on the soundtrack. This is no immortal masterpiece, but a must for Weill/Gershwin aficionados.

This is also the best place to dispose of one further item from Weill's work for Hollywood, two songs for Fritz Lang's *You and Me* (1938), all that remains of what was originally to have been a full-length score. Both 'You cannot get anything for nothing', sung by an anonymous tenor, and 'The right guy for me', sung by Carol Paige, are very Berlinish in flavour (KWH 10). None of Weill's Broadway shows survived their film versions musically intact.

STREET SCENE

'Not until *Street Scene* did I achieve a real blending of drama and music', wrote Weill at the time of the première (1947). Purely technically this may very well be true: the 'real blending' of aria, arioso, *melodram* and dialogue in this account of a crime passionnel in a tenement block is faultless. But as the composer also remarked at the time, 'I address myself to Americans, and I don't think they want "Do you want another cup of coffee" to be sung', and there are a number of lines in Langston Hughes's lyrics rather too close to that for comfort. Some of the children's music does not quite avoid a cuteness oddly out of place in so sombre a plot, but in the end the burning sincerity of the music and the technical skill conquer even the string of verbal clichés at the close – a close that at least avoids the cliché of a Happy End for the young lovers. *Street Scene* still stands as one of the best American operas and although the Playwrights' Company, who produced it, shunned the use of the fatal word 'opera' in their publicity, that is how Weill always thought of it.

He had had Elmer Rice's play of 1928 in mind for setting since his earliest days in New York, and felt that in the late forties the time was ripe. Rice himself made the adaptation, and worked with Hughes on the lyrics. The score demands real voices – Polyna Stoska (Anna Maurrant), Anne Jeffreys (Rose) and Brian Sullivan (Sam) were all operatically trained. The reviews were good and despite strong commercial competition from *Brigadoon* and *Finian's Rainbow*, *Street Scene* notched up 148 performances, not much compared to *One Touch of Venus* but very respectable for an opera. It has since been successfully revived by the New York City Opera.

The abridged recording made by the original cast, transferred from 78s to Col. OL 4139, gives a very fair idea of the work. The influence of George Gershwin is detectable, especially in the opening sequence with its offstage radio music and janitor's blues (Weill attended rehearsals of *Porgy and Bess* soon after he arrived in New York), and Harry Easter – 'Wouldn't you like to be on Broadway?' – is a first cousin of Sportin' Life. There are also little echoes of *Peter Grimes,* which Weill cannot possibly have heard, though *Porgy* is the common source here.

Polyna Stoska's account of Anna's big aria 'Somehow I never could believe' is on an appropriately grand scale, and she catches the character of the disillusioned middle-aged wife powerfully. Anne Jeffreys has a good top and firm control of it, and her account of 'What good would the moon be', a fairly traditional sentimental ballad saved from triteness by imaginative orchestration, is very stirring. Brian Sullivan sings 'Lonely house' superbly – it is not easy. The supporting characters, recorded in the middle of the run, give vividly theatrical performances; vocally, full justice is done to the score, and only occasionally does the 1948 sound muddy the instrumentation (American recording techniques were surely far ahead of those in Europe at that time). A complete modern recording is urgently needed, but even when it comes this one will remain important simply as a document.

The only serious gaps are the Ice Cream Sextet, the trio 'There'll be trouble', and 'Moon-faced, starry-eyed', the last of which is on Bagley I, wretchedly arranged and brashly sung by Ann Miller. Bagley I also contains 'Italy in technicolour', an agreeable rumba cut in Philadelphia before the Broadway opening and sung by Jo Sullivan. Lenya's close-to-mike 'Lonely house' and 'A boy like you' (in which the singer must work hard to avoid mawkishness) are not too well suited to an operatic context, but Hal Walters sings 'Lonely house' charmingly on *Berlin to Broadway*.

DOWN IN THE VALLEY

This, the most determinedly American of Weill's scores, is a 30–minute folk opera completed in 1948 for non-professional performance. Again, the mixture of choral narration, song, *melodram* and speech is impressively flexible at a technical level, but the musical material is wan, based on the soupily harmonized folksong of the title and two others. The piece is so wholesome as to make one look upon apple pie with the gravest suspicion. The plot describes how Brack Weaver breaks out of gaol on the eve of his execution for accidentally killing Thomas Bouché for a last-minute reunion with Jenny (again!), over whom he quarrelled with the victim. They reminisce over their first meeting (revivalist hymns and square dances) before Brack gives himself up.

There are two recordings, both dating from 1950, both with minor cuts. The one on US Decca was supervised by the composer shortly before his death. Alfred Drake is a sonorous Brack and Jane Wilson a sweet, unsophisticated Jenny. Daniel Slick's Leader/Narrator is first rate. The RCA cast (on the other side of Gertrude Lawrence's *Lady in the Dark* songs) had recently appeared in a television transmission and their performance is much more theatrical. William McGraw may have a less well-honed baritone than Drake but he fields much more in the way of character as Brack, and Ray Jacquemot is a wonderfully sinister Bouché. Marion Bell sang Jenny at the première at the University of Indiana, and works a little too hard for her effects – Decca's Jane Wilson is preferable. There are a few more cuts on RCA than on

Decca, about which I am not prepared to fuss: this vies with *Jasager* as my least favourite Weill score.

LOVE LIFE

Love Life's respectable run of 252 performances (in 1948) coincided with an ASCAP strike: no recordings were made and the score was not published. In many ways it is Weill's most forward-looking score for Broadway, and needs re-investigation. The book and lyrics are by the young Alan J. Lerner, then temporarily estranged from Loewe. The subject is marriage, about which Lerner, having been married almost as often as Elizabeth Taylor, is well qualified to write. But the marriage is seen over 150 years of American history. We first meet Susan and Sam on a Connecticut farm in 1791; by 1821 Sam has opened a factory; thirty years later he is a railway magnate neglecting his wife; in 1890 Susan becomes involved in the Women's Suffrage movement; in the 1920s they split up; in the finale in the 1940s they may, or may not, come together again. Each stage of the threatened marriage is commented upon by ensembles or solos from characters detached from the main action, and these production numbers take the form of various American folk entertainments – minstrel show, vaudeville, soft-shoe shuffle etc., culminating in a circus (*cf. Lady in the Dark*) in which Susan and Sam are tightrope walkers edging towards each other.

Although there was no original cast recording, it is possible to get a fair idea of the work's shape and quality (top-notch) by piecing together recently recorded extracts in more or less the right order. 'Here I'll stay', which oddly enough opens the show, is sung by Felicia Sanders as a smoochy night-club song, which must have sounded odd in old Connecticut. 'Progress', a soft-shoe shuffle, comments bleakly on the American industrial revolution and its effect on the institution of marriage (recession, inflation and crash, all constitute progress); it can be heard both on *Berlin to Broadway*, and on Bagley/Lerner sung by Nancy Walker and Roddy McDowell. It is a very good number. When Sam opens his factory Susan responds with the most optimistic, positive song in this or any other Weill score – 'Green-up time', a piece of *Oklahoma*-style Americana sung by Lenya on her New York recital. According to Robert Cushman, Lerner is said to have kept Weill up to the mark on this, insisting on a major key and bright orchestration, remarking that he didn't want to hear 2000 years of Jewish misery creeping into the setting. They didn't.

Thence to 'Economics', another vaudeville ensemble commenting on the action with the refrain 'That's good economics but awful bad for love' – a number that idiom apart would not be out of place in Berlin. 'Susan's Dream', written to be sung by a black soprano from the sidelines, was inexplicably cut from the original show: it is first-rate melodically and beautifully sung by Martha Schlamme on the World of Kurt Weill in Song. (Susan dreams of a perfect family life and wakes up to discover that the dream is what she already has.) 'Love song' is sung by a tramp, also on the sidelines (Jerry Orbach on Bagley/Lerner, a fair number only). After the 1920s split Sam sings 'This is the life' sitting in a hotel room rejoicing in his freedom, but with everything reminding him of his loneliness; this is an astutely written *scena* cunningly characterized at both musical and verbal levels and very well sung by Jerry Orbach on Bagley/Lerner. It is pure Sondheim. Susan responds with 'Is it him or is it me?', musing on accusations and counter-accusations and trying to apportion the blame for the split, another touching song well delivered on Bagley I by Ann Miller. Sam's 'Locker Room' continues the story of his new freedom in a classic example of defiant male-bonding, complete with a masseur singing some good bone rhymes as he pummels away (John Reardon and Arthur Siegel on Bagley I).

A ballet introduces the final circus scene, which includes Susan's 'Mr Right', a bitter version of 'That's him' from *One Touch of Venus* commenting sourly on male stereotypes (Dorothy Loudon, very acid on Bagley/Lerner). It is difficult to place 'My kind of night' (Arthur Siegel, Bagley II) precisely in the score: it is a relaxed pastiche of American folksong, very attractive in its simplicity. Bagley has also dug up two other numbers cut before the opening – 'You understand me so' and 'What do I want?', sung by Chita Rivera and Jo Sullivan respectively – neither of them great losses. A version of 'I remember it well' did appear with different words (Reardon and Sullivan, Bagley I) but it is more familiar in Loewe's setting in *Gigi*.

This extraordinary musical, years ahead of its time in both content and form and musically very fresh, must be resuscitated.

LOST IN THE STARS

In his last completed work Weill resumed collaboration with Maxwell Anderson on a faithful adaptation of Alan Paton's admired novel *Cry the Beloved Country*. If the problems of race relations in South Africa and the USA could be solved by Christian good will and old-fashioned liberalism alone, then *Lost in the Stars* might still be valid, but tragically it has been overtaken by events. Even in 1949 both novel and musical smacked of condescension and Uncle-Tommery, and Paul Robeson turned down the leading role for that reason. Recent revivals in New York and San Francisco have flopped embarrassingly. This is sad, as purely musically there is much to be said for Weill's score. The structure is reminiscent of *Down in the Valley* in that the chorus propels and comments upon the action, but the most remarkable thing about this 'Musical Tragedy' is the virtuoso scoring for only twelve players. Virgil Thomson thought that purely instrumentally this was Weill's masterpiece. (It should not be forgotten that Weill surprised his Broadway contemporaries by scoring his own music as a matter of course and when, as in recent recordings, his numbers are given in arrangements the difference is startling and the results depressing.)

The original cast recording, made on 78s but soon transferred, contains

enough of the music and linking dialogue to qualify as complete, and save
for the big concerted numbers the sound is perfectly adequate – indeed, the
voices are very well caught. In the principal role of the black clergyman
whose son Absolom kills a young white liberal in the course of robbery and
is executed, Todd Duncan is outstanding: he has a naturally beautiful, very
black and well-trained voice. The title song can sound horribly naive to
today's ears, but Mr Duncan carries it off triumphantly with sheer conviction.
He even makes the post-execution reconciliation of the two bereaved fathers,
one black, one white, seem credible. As Absolom's girlfriend, to support
whose unborn child he commits the robbery, Inez Matthews sings her two
big numbers 'Trouble man' and 'Stay well' with touching intensity (both are
blues-influenced). 'Big mole', the cute number for boy soprano, will surely
be cut in any future revival: as in *Street Scene*, songs for children are Weill's
only Klemperer-style concessions to Broadway taste, but in *Street Scene* he
just carries them off whereas here he doesn't. The choral work is impressive,
though stereo sound would obviously enhance the excitingly written anti-
phonal 'Fear' for a double chorus of blacks and whites: this is one number
that certainly stands the test of time. For the moment, though, *Lost in the
Stars* must be admired for its purely musical dexterity; perhaps in a better
world it will be accepted as a well-meaning period piece.

The individual numbers are even more difficult to bring off out of context.
Lenya sings the title song, 'Trouble man' and 'Stay well' in inappropriately
elaborate arrangements. Martha Schlamme is also too sentimental in the title
song – as are countless others – but Walter Huston's version (Bruns. 04658)
is gentle and straight, and the excerpts on *Berlin to Broadway* are worthily
done.

HUCKLEBERRY FINN

Weill had written only five numbers for this projected Maxwell Anderson
musical at the time of his early death in 1950. One, 'This time next year'
(Ann Miller, Bagley I), would surely have been rewritten or dropped, but
the folk-based 'Come in mornin' ' (Arthur Siegel, Bagley II) shows the
composer at his most artless in a melody of bewitching simplicity and charm.

* * *

Weill composed for the theatre for eight years in Germany and for fourteen
in America. He is as much an American composer as Handel is a British
one. He wrote for audiences: like all great theatre or opera composers he
was a communicator. Those who accuse him of selling out should ask themselves what the point would have been of writing a string of *Threepenny
Operas* or *Silbersees* for American audiences. As it is, his pure-entertainment
Broadway shows are far outnumbered by those that question and probe,
often trenchantly, and those that entertain do so at the highest level.
Remember that *The Threepenny Opera* was written to entertain as well as

to poison. He was probably the last great composer of tunes – last-ever, perhaps, and you can learn more about melody by studying the structure of a Weill tune than one by practically any other composer – and as such his niche amongst the immortals is secure.

AUFSTIEG UND FALL DER STADT MAHAGONNY

1956 Lenya *Jenny*; Litz *Mrs. Begbick*; Markwort *Fatty the Bookkeeper*; Sauerbaum *Jimmy Mahoney*; Günter *Trinity Moses*; Mund *Pennybank Bill*; Göllnitz *Jake* and *Toby*; Roth *Alaska-Wolf-Joe*; Munch *Speaker* / North-West German Radio Chorus and Orch. / Brückner-Rüggeberg
CBS (Europe) 77341
④ 40–77341
CBS (US) M3X 37874

DOWN IN THE VALLEY

Jenny *J*; Brack Weaver *W*; Bouche *B*; Father *F*; Leader *L*

1950 Wilson *J*; Drake *W*; Atkins *B*; Pettersson *F*; Slick *L* / Orch. / M. Levine
US Decca DL 4239

1950 Bell *J*; McGraw *W*; Jacquemot *B*; Barrows *F*; Smith *L* / RCA Victor Orch. / Adler
RCA VIC 1225

DIE DREIGROSCHENOPER

Streetsinger *S*; Peachum *P*; Mrs Peachum *Mrs P*; Macheath *M*; Polly *Py*; Tiger Brown *TB*; Jenny *J*; Lucy *L*

1950
  Rosvaenge *S*; Jerger *P*; Anday *Mrs P*; Preger *M*; Augustin *Py*; Guthrie *TB*; Fassler *J*; Felbermayer *L* / Chorus and Chamber Orch. of the Vienna State Opera / Adler
  Vanguard SRV 2735D
1958 Neuse *S*; Trenck-Trebitsch *P*; Hesterberg *Mrs P*; Schellow *M*; Von Koczian *Py*; Cruner *TB*; Lenya *J*; Wolffberg *L* / Gunther-Arndt Choir / Radio Free Berlin Dance Orch. / Brückner-Rüggeberg
  CBS (UK) 78279
  (US) Y2–32977
1965 Kutschera *P*; May *Mrs P*; Korte *M*; Hueber *Py*; Hoerrmann *TB*; Techmann *J*; Dirichs *L* / Frankfurt Opera Chor and Orch. / Rennert
  Philips 6747 042
1930 (excerpts)
  Gerron *S* / *TB*; Ponto *P*; Trenck-

Trebitsch *M*; Helmke *Mrs P*; Lenya *J*; *L* / chorus / Lewis-Ruth Band / Mackeben
Telefunken ⓜ AJ6.41911
1954 (excerpts – In English: adaptation by Marc Blitzstein)
  Price *S*; Wolfson *P*; Rae *Mrs P*; S. Merrill *M*; Sullivan *Py*; Tyne *TB*; Lenya *J*; Arthur *L* / Theatre de Lys Chor and Orch., New York / Matlowsky
  MGM-Metro ⓒ 2536 025
1976 Brocksmith *S*; Alexander *P*; E. Wilson *Mrs P*; Julia *M*; Kava *Py*; Sabin *TB*; Greene *J*; Brown *L* / 1976 New York Shakespeare Festival Production / Silvermann
  CBS (UK) 61138
  (US) PS 34326
1962 (excerpts – film soundtrack)
  Mülhardt *S*; Frobe *P*; Hildebrand *Mrs P*; Jürgens *M*; Corber & Ritchie *Py*; K. Wagner *TB*; Knef *J*; Warrlich *L* / chor and orch. /

Sandloff
Ger Decca ⓜ BLK 16242
London (US) 76004
1964 (excerpts – in English: film
version)
Davis *S*; Irving *M*; Wilder *Py*;
Schlamme *J* / chorus and orch. /
Matlowsky

RCA (US) LSO 1086
(FR) 530.614
c.1965 (excerpts – in English)
Moray, Sammes, Huw Davies,
Laver, Little, Preston / Sammes
Singers / New World Show
Orch. / Braden
WRC ST253

KLEINE DREIGROSCHENMUSIK

1931 Members of the Berlin
Staatskapelle / Klemperer
Polydor 24172–3
Past Masters (US) ⓜ PM31
1961 Philharmonia / Klemperer
HMV SXLP 30226 ④ TC-SXLP
30226
Angel S-35927
1965 Boston SO / Leinsdorf
RCA (UK) SB 6827

(US) LSC 3121
1975 London Sinfonietta / Atherton
DG (UK) 2740 153
(US) 2709 064
1975 Contemporary Chamber Orch. /
Weisberg
Nonesuch H71281 ④ ZCH71281
1976 Westchester SO / Landau Vox
(US) CE36049 ④ CT2154

HAPPY END

1960 Lenya / chorus and orch. /
Brückner-Rüggeberg
CBS (UK) 73463
1976 M. Thomas; Langridge; Partridge;

Luxon; Dickinson / London
Sinfonietta / Atherton
DG 2740 153

DER JASAGER

1956 Prohaska; Bert; Vohla /
Düsseldorf Children's Chorus /

Düsseldorf CO / Kohler
Heliodor (US) HS 25025

JOHNNY JOHNSON

1957 Meredith *Johnny*; Lear *Minnie
Belle*; Lenya *French Nurse*;
Merrill *Captain*; Stewart *Mayor*

and *US Chaplain*; Sherman
Psychiatrist / Orch. / Matlowsky
Heliodor H/HS 25024

LADY IN THE DARK

1961 Stevens *Liza*; Reardon *Randy*;
Green *Paxton*; Bridges *Johnson*;
White *Nesbitt*; Augustine *Sutton* /

Orch. / Engel
Columbia OS 2390

LOST IN THE STARS

1949 Duncan *Stephen*; Matthews *Irina*;
Roane *Leader* / Orch. / M.

Levine
US Decca DL 8028

DER PROTAGONIST

Pantomime I

1975 M. Thomas *Girl*; Partridge
Husband; Luxon *Wife*; Rippon
Monk / London Sinfonietta /

Atherton
DG (UK) 2740 153
(US) 2709 064

MAHAGONNY SONGSPIEL

1976 M. Thomas; Dickinson;
Langridge; Luxon; Rippon /
London Sinfonietta / Atherton
DG 2530 897

1977 Barak; Etzion-Zak; Demirkazik;
Kuhn; Greiner Haparnass /
Jerusalem SO / Foss
Vox (US) CE 34675

DIE SIEBEN TODSÜNDEN DER KLEINBÜRGER

1956 Lenya; Katona; Göllnitz;
Poettgen; Roth / orch. /
Brückner-Rüggeberg
CBS (UK) 73657
(US) ⑩ KL 5175

1965 May; Schreier; Rotzsch; Leib;
Polster / Leipzig RSO / Kegel

DG 139308
1982 Ross; Rolfe Johnson; Caley;
Rippon; Tomlinson / CBSO /
Rattle
EMI ASD 4022 ④ TCC-ASD 4022
Angel (US)

DER SILBERSEE

1980 (in English)
Grey *Officer Olim*; Neill *Severin*;
Hynes *Fennimore*; Bonazzi *Frau
von Luber*; Harrold *Lottery Agent*

and *Baron Laur* / New York City
Opera Chorus and Orch. / Rudel
Nonesuch DB 79003

Recitals and Collections (in alphabetical order)

ROBYN ARCHER SINGS BRECHT
London Sinfonietta / Muldowney
HMV ASD 4166

BEN BAGLEY'S KURT WEILL REVISITED I
arr. Dennis Deal
PAINTED SMILES PS 1375

BEN BAGLEY'S KURT WEILL REVISITED II
arr. Dennis Deal
PAINTED SMILES PS 1376

BEN BAGLEY'S ALAN JAY LERNER REVISITED
arr. Norman Paris
PAINTED SMILES PS 1337

FROM BERLIN TO BROADWAY
arr. Newton Wayland
Paramount PAS-4000

GEORGIA BROWN SINGS KURT WEILL
arr. Ian Fraser
Decca SKL 4509

LOTTE LENYA: BERLIN THEATRE SONGS
arr. Roger Bean
CBS 78279

LOTTE LENYA: AMERICAN THEATRE SONGS
CBS 73499

LONDON SINFONIETTA
cond. David Atherton
DG 2740 153

GISELA MAY SINGT BRECHT WEILL
cond. Heinz Rögner
Eterna 825427

MARTHA SCHLAMME: THE WORLD OF KURT WEILL IN SONG
arr. Samuel Matlowsky
MGM E 405 2P

MARTHA SCHLAMME / WILL HOLT: A KURT WEILL CABARET
arr. Samuel Matlowsky
MGM E/SE 4180 OC

TERESA STRATAS: THE UNKNOWN KURT WEILL
acc. Richard Woitach
Nonesuch D–79019

Notes on Contributors

Felix Aprahamian, critic on the *Sunday Times* since 1948, has made a special study of French music.

Peter Branscombe is professor of Austrian Studies at St Andrew's University. A specialist in eighteenth- and ninetenth-century German and Austrian music, he is co-author of *Schubert Studies: Problems of style and chronology* (CUP 1982).

Ronald Crichton, former music critic of the *Financial Times* and author of two studies of Manuel de Falla.

Richard Fairman studied at the London Opera Centre, has worked at the National Sound Archive and is a freelance music critic.

Edward Greenfield, chief music critic of *The Guardian* since 1964, regular contributor to *Gramophone* and the BBC's 'Record Review', wrote *Puccini, Keeper of the Seal* (Hutchinson, 1958).

David Hamilton is music critic of *The Nation* (US) and for many years contributing editor to *High Fidelity* (US).

Lord Harewood, managing director of English National Opera, editor of *Kobbé's Complete Opera Book* (Putnam, 1976).

John T. Hughes, deputy chairman of the Recorded Vocal Art Society, is an authority on singers and singing.

Michael Kennedy, Manchester music critic of the *Daily Telegraph* since 1950, has written critical biographies of, among others, Britten, Elgar, Richard Strauss and Vaughan Williams.

Andrew Lamb, authority on operetta, contributed articles on the subject to *The New Grove*, and writes regularly in *Gramophone*.

Max Loppert is chief music critic of the *Financial Times* and a board member of *Opera*.

William Mann, former chief music critic of *The Times*, is a board member of *Opera* and artistic director of the Bath Festival.

Rodney Milnes is deputy editor of *Opera*, opera critic of *The Spectator*, and a regular broadcaster.

David Murray, lecturer on philosophy at London University, music critic on the *Financial Times*, and a specialist in twentieth-century music.

Richard Osborne is head of English at Bradfield College and contributes regularly to *The Times Literary Supplement*, *Gramophone* and 'Record Review'. He is writing a critical study of Rossini.

Harold Rosenthal, editor of *Opera* since 1953, author of many books on opera including (with John Warrack) *The Concise Oxford Dictionary of Opera*.

Lionel Salter, formerly head of of opera on both BBC TV and Radio, subsequently assistant controller of music. He has made performing translations of ten operas, line-by-line translations of sixty. *Gramophone* critic since 1948.

John Steane, head of English at Merchant Taylor's School, has written *The Grand Tradition: Seventy Years of Singing on Record* (Duckworth, 1974). Writes quarterly review on vocal music for *Gramophone*, contributes regularly to 'Record Review' and *Opera*.

Index